International Political Economy

SECOND EDITION

INTERNATIONAL POLITICAL ECONOMY

State-Market Relations in a Changing Global Order

edited by

C. Roe Goddard
Patrick Cronin
Kishore C. Dash

LYNNE
RIENNER
PUBLISHERS

BOULDER
LONDON

Published in the United States of America in 2003 by
Lynne Rienner Publishers, Inc.
1800 30th Street, Boulder, Colorado 80301
www.rienner.com

Library of Congress Cataloging-in-Publication Data
International political economy :   state-market relations in a changing global order   /
edited by C. Roe Goddard, Patrick Cronin, and Kishore C. Dash.—2nd ed.
      Includes bibliographical references and index.
      ISBN 1-58826-097-6 (pbk. :   alk. paper)
      1. International finance.   2. International economic relations.   3. Economic assis-
tance.
   I. Goddard, C. Roe, 1956–   II. Cronin, Patrick.   III. Dash, Kishore C., 1956–

   HG3881 .I5769   2002
   332'.042—dc21

                                                                        2002075162

Printed and bound in the United States of America

The paper used in this publication meets the requirements
of the American National Standard for Permanence of
Paper for Printed Library Materials Z39.48-1984.

5   4

Contents

Acknowledgments   vii

Introduction   *Kishore C. Dash, Patrick Cronin, and C. Roe Goddard*   1

Part I   Contending Views of International Political Economy

 1 The Nature of Political Economy   *Robert Gilpin*   9
 2 International Politics and International Economics
    Jeffry A. Frieden and David A. Lake   25

Liberalism, Interdependence, and Globalization
 3 Excerpts from *The Wealth of Nations*   *Adam Smith*   33
 4 Realism and Complex Interdependence   *Robert O. Keohane*
    and Joseph S. Nye   49
 5 The Invisible Hand vs. the Dead Hand   *Brink Lindsey*   59
 6 The Rise of the Virtual State   *Richard Rosecrance*   71

Economic Nationalism and the State
 7 Excerpts from *Report on Manufactures*   *Alexander Hamilton*   85
 8 The Theory of Hegemonic Stability and Changes in International
    Economic Regimes, 1967–1977   *Robert O. Keohane*   99
 9 States and Industrial Transformation   *Peter Evans*   119
10 Sovereignty   *Stephen D. Krasner*   139

Challenges to the Capitalist System
11 Excerpts from *Capital* and *Communist Manifesto*
    Karl Marx and Friedrich Engels   151
12 The Structure of Dependence   *Theotonio dos Santos*   167
13 The Future of Global Polarization   *Samir Amin*   179
14 Globalization Under Fire   *Robert Went*   191

Part 2   International Monetary Relations

15 Monetary Governance in a Globalized World
       Benjamin J. Cohen   215
16 The International Monetary Fund   *C. Roe Goddard*   241
17 The Asian Economic Crisis and the Role of the IMF
       Kishore C. Dash   269
18 The Euro Debuts: European Money, Global Money, or Both?
       Olufemi A. Babarinde   291

Part 3   Development and the World Bank

19 The Rise and Fall of the Washington Consensus as a Paradigm
       for Developing Countries   *Charles Gore*   317
20 A New World Bank for a New Century   *Robert Picciotto*   341
21 Still Waiting: The Failure of Reform at the World Bank
       Bruce Rich   353

Part 4   International Trade Relations

22 The Doha Round: Prospects for the Rules-Based Trading System
       Patrick Cronin   369
23 Regionalism, Multilateralism, and Deeper Integration:
       Changing Paradigms for Developing Countries
       Robert Z. Lawrence   391

Part 5   Transnational Enterprises and International Production

24 Theoretical Perspectives on the Transnational Corporation
       Rhys Jenkins   415
25 Defining the Transnational Corporation in
       the Era of Globalization   *C. Roe Goddard*   435

Part 6   Conclusion

26 Coping with Ecological Globalization   *Hilary French*   459
27 The Westfailure System   *Susan Strange*   495

Index   509
About the Book   515

Acknowledgments

With the passage of time—some six years since the first edition of this book was published—substantial changes have taken place in the global economy. After some reflection on these many changes and their impact on the study of international political economy, we realized that a major overhaul of the book was in order. This was not to be a simple tweaking of the old edition; instead, it turned into a year-and-a-half search for works that represented the most current thinking on IPE. When all was said and the difficult decisions done, only nine of the original twenty-eight chapters remained. Obvious classics were retained, but complemented with new and up-to-date information and analyses—on the Asian economic crisis and the international monetary system, the problems facing the multilateral trading system, and challenges to the dominant liberal paradigm, to name just a few areas. Despite the many new additions, we believe that readers of the first edition will recognize substantial areas of continuity: a blending of the classical and contemporary, empiricism and advocacy, and a commitment to offering different methodologies and perspectives. We hope that the second edition will retain its appeal to our old audience while reaching out to new readers.

We would like to thank our friends and colleagues who offered advice and support along the way. We are particularly indebted to our colleagues at Thunderbird, especially John Conklin, a coeditor of the first edition, and Glenn Fong for their advice and comments.

We are especially grateful to those who took the time to contribute original chapters to this new edition: departmental colleague Femi Babarinde, Jerry Cohen, and Robert Picciotto.

Assembling an edited volume requires a great deal of administrative support. We would like to extend special thanks to Georgia Lessard from the Office of Instructional Design and Support at Thunderbird.

We offer particular thanks to Lynne Rienner for her encouragement to take this long journey a second time and to her staff for their help in dealing with issues large and small along the way.

As with the first edition, we want to thank our students here at Thunderbird. Despite changes to the curriculum in recent years, IPE remains an integral part of the first trimester core and over a thousand students continue to pass through this class each year. Coming from all over the world, they bring with them the range of perspectives found inside this volume.

Finally, we owe a special debt to our spouses for their unwavering support and good humor and to our children for allowing daddy to spend too many nights and weekends on this project.

Patrick Cronin
Kishore C. Dash
C. Roe Goddard

Introduction

Kishore C. Dash, Patrick Cronin, and C. Roe Goddard

Although a scant six years have passed since the first edition of this book was published, a myriad of significant events have underscored both the importance and the changing nature of the international political economy. In the trade and monetary systems, these include the financial crisis in Asia, the launch of the euro, and the emergence of regional and transregional economic arrangements and their perceived challenge to economic globalization. More generally, the trends of the past decade have generated considerable debate about the role of knowledge, transnational corporations (TNCs), and multilateral institutions as vehicles for promoting growth and development.

While the virtues of economic globalization and the liberal market-oriented ideology continue to reign, evidence abounds of an increasing unease with the effects of unbridled market forces. The tumultuous events surrounding the 1999 ministerial meeting of the World Trade Organization (WTO) in Seattle, Washington, propelled the globalization debate into the public consciousness. Demonstrating amidst the tear gas in the streets outside the meeting hall was a disparate mélange of protestors. Included among this group were unionized workers fearful of losing more jobs in the name of free trade, environmentalists condemning the WTO for putting trade ahead of nature, and activists calling for global labor standards. Some of the protesters demanded the WTO be abolished while others called for it to be strengthened. Despite contradictory views on what should be done, uniting these groups was a shared sense that "globalization"—the increasing integration of national societies and the economic, social, ecological, and political changes that result—was extremely damaging. Levels of unhappiness in the streets were matched by the frustration of delegates inside the meeting rooms. With trade ministers unable to agree on an agenda for negotiations, the meeting broke up with much finger pointing over who was to blame for its failure.

The debate over globalization is not new. Indeed, scholars of interna-

1

tional political economy have been studying the globalization process for many decades. What is new is an acceleration in the pace of change and the increasing number of people actively challenging the integration process. For each person marching in the streets there are many others who are slowly—but steadily—growing uncomfortable with its costs. In recent decades technological change combined with market oriented policy changes have exposed more and more of us to what Joseph Shumpeter called a process of "creative destruction." He used this term to describe a capitalist dynamic that brings both good and bad at the same time. As the world's peoples are drawn more tightly together through trade, capital flows, and information technologies, a growing sense of anxiety has broken out. As consumers, this integrative process gives us access to a larger quantity of new and better products. But as workers and producers, globalization brings greater competition and less job security. And as citizens, globalization challenges traditional values and ways of life while upsetting the ecological balance.

For the foreseeable future, IPE as a field of study will necessarily focus on the struggles playing themselves out in the meeting halls and streets of cities around the world. At no point in the post–World War II era has the liberal international economic order been under greater pressure. Defenders of the liberal order—academics and policymakers alike—will be forced to engage their opponents as they never have had to in the past. This will entail an ongoing debate involving all of the perspectives in this volume.

Making selections from the rich and varied contributions to the study of IPE was a difficult task. We set out to identify a core literature that would blend the theoretical and empirical explanations of IPE in such a way that readers—experts and uninitiated alike—would benefit. Looking at the finished product, we believe we have assembled an outstanding collection of essays, containing both theoretical and empirical depth, analyzing various aspects of international political economy.

The first part of the book presents representative works from the three major perspectives that provide the basic conceptual foundations of IPE: liberalism, economic nationalism, and structuralism. Chapters by Robert Gilpin and Jeffry Frieden and David Lake provide the student with an informed introduction to the study of IPE and to each of the perspectives. Adam Smith's classic work describes the basic precepts of liberalism with its emphasis on the rationality of the market and free trade. Reflecting the core tenets of nationalism, Alexander Hamilton's influential "Report on Manufacturers" justifies state intervention to promote economic development. Karl Marx's seminal *Capital* and *Communist Manifesto* offer a stimulating platform for a critical discourse on global capitalism.

In an effort to provoke debate, we made a conscious decision to seek out modern expressions of each perspective. Chapters by Robert O. Keohane and Joseph S. Nye, Brink Lindsey, and Richard Rosecrance provide contemporary perspectives of liberalism. The state-centric streams of nationalist thought are well represented in the chapters by Stephen Krasner and Peter Evans. Krasner's essay analyzes the relative significance and positioning of the state in the global political economy. Evans offers an illuminating examination of the relevance of states in facilitating industrial transformation. Works by Samir Amin and Robert Went represent the structural perspectives, critically evaluating the nature and consequences of global capitalism.

The second part of this volume examines the international monetary system. Arguably no other area of IPE has been as profoundly affected by integration than global capital markets. With the fall of the Bretton Woods fixed exchange rate monetary system in 1971 and subsequent liberalization of capital flows in the following decade, it is the free movement of large quantities of capital that best represents "globalization." Since the first edition of this book was published, the world has experienced, as former World Bank chief economist Joseph Stiglitz phrased it, a "boom in busts." Instability in the world's capital markets was a hallmark of this period, wreaking havoc in Asia and at one point threatening the global financial system. Beyond Asia, countries such as Russia, Brazil, Turkey, and Argentina all suffered currency instability, capital flight, and attendant economic suffering. These problems provoked a sharp and ongoing debate on a variety of topics including the merits of capital mobility and the best way of dealing with monetary crises. In his contribution, Benjamin Cohen examines how traditional state-market relationships are being altered by the increasing integration of global capital markets. Roe Goddard provides an inside look at the International Monetary Fund (IMF): origins, organization, and evolving lending facilities. Kishore Dash investigates the political and economic causes of the Asian economic crisis and the role of the IMF in managing the resulting problems.

Overshadowed by problems in the international financial system were preparations leading to the introduction of a single currency within the European Union. The creation of the euro is part of the most ambitious attempt at economic integration to date among the world's major economies. Olufemi Babarinde scrutinizes this process, highlighting a number of key issues, the resolution of which will determine the ultimate regional and international impact of the euro "experiment."

Development, the subject of the third section of this book, remains an important issue within academic and policymaking circles. As we move deeper into a new century, it is clear that development achievements have fallen woefully short of meeting global needs. It is also widely recognized that the failure to raise standards of living in much of the world is a major factor in intra-state and inter-state conflict. The key question today, as it did over fifty years ago, revolves around the most appropriate strategy for development. From the backlash against globalization comes an emerging challenge to the hegemonic "Washington Consensus" stressing free markets and a minimal state role. Within the debate over the appropriate role of states and markets in development is a more specific one over the part to be played by the World Bank. Just as the WTO is the focal point for popular anger with the liberal trading system, the World Bank is subject to fierce attacks for its promotion of a market-based approach to development. The essay by Charles Gore examines the larger debate on development while those of Bruce Rich and Robert Picciotto present contrasting opinions about the role of the Bank in the twenty-first century.

The fourth part of this volume focuses on important dynamics in the international trading system, particularly those underlying events in the past six years. The "Battle in Seattle" represented a "coming out" party for the anti-globalization movement, not because its constituent groups were protesting for the first time—they were not—but because the media latched on to them in a way that they never had before. As noted above, the level of discord in the streets equaled that experienced inside the meeting halls by governments arguing over the direction of the "rules of the game" for international trade. A fragile consensus following the September 11, 2001 terrorist attacks on the United States enabled the launch of the Doha Round negotiations in November 2001. But, as Patrick Cronin details, serious doubts remain over a successful outcome. Adding to the uncertainty are a growing series of trade disputes, particularly between the United States and the European Union, that threaten to undermine the postwar consensus in favor of free trade. Moreover, growing state preferences for regional integration arrangements are raising concerns that this too will lessen commitments to a multilateral rules-based system. In his essay, Robert Lawrence examines the forces behind regional integration and, from a developing country perspective, the merits of regional, multilateral, and "deeper" forms of integration.

Part five examines transnational corporations (TNC) as key agents in the globalization process. Flows of foreign direct investment increased from $12 billion in 1970 to $1.3 trillion in 2000. As a result, the United Nations recently estimated that there were 63,000 TNCs owning some 700,000 foreign affiliates. The spread of TNCs has led to a substantial increase in the amount of intra-firm trade. One estimate suggests that as much as one-third of global trade may now be conducted within companies instead of the arms-length variety in David Ricardo's models. Simple statistics such as these suggest that TNCs are exerting a profound influence on capital and trade flows. As such, it is no surprise that they remain the object of considerable controversy, even more so in the context of the current debate over globalization. The contribution by Rhys Jenkins explores the theoretical underpinnings to a variety of common—and conflicting—views on the TNC. Complementing Jenkins, Roe Goddard defines the modern-day TNC by examining its varied nature, takes the reader inside the firm and explores the determinants of foreign direct investment, and surveys changing geographical patterns of post–World War II investment flows.

As in the first edition, we reserved the concluding section for "big picture" issues sure to be at the center of IPE studies in the future. While the environment does not yet command the space that trade and monetary relations do, we believe that it will be a central topic of debate in decades to come. Our conviction is based on the arguments of our final two contributors, Hilary French and Susan Strange, and on a veritable explosion in the amount of work on this subject. Indeed, we found the study of IPE and the environment to be fragmenting into sub-disciplinary niches like more traditional issues relating to trade and finance. In that sense our challenge was to find pieces that took a comprehensive approach to the study of the environment and the state-market relationship. We decided to end this volume with what is perhaps the final published work by the eminent political economist Susan Strange. In this provocative—but tantalizingly underdeveloped work—she expresses our own concerns about the ability of state-based international system to deal effectively with the most pressing issues facing mankind.

PART I

CONTENDING VIEWS OF INTERNATIONAL POLITICAL ECONOMY

I

The Nature of Political Economy

Robert Gilpin

Robert Gilpin presents a definition of international political economy (IPE) and discusses the scope of this field of study. According to Gilpin, the tensions and interactions between politics and the economy constitute the stuff of political economy. Although the relative influence of politics and the market changes over time, the two forces are forever linked; neither exists independent of the other. In this initial chapter, Gilpin discusses the parameters of the study of IPE and traces the concurrent rise of the modern state system and the global expansion of capitalism. He poses three questions to guide thinking about the subject: What are the causes and effects of the world market economy? What is the relationship between economic and political change? And what is the significance of the world economy for states? He concludes with an exploration of the rise of the market as a force that revolutionizes both societal and political relations within and among communities.

The parallel existence and mutual interaction of "state" and "market" in the modern world create "political economy"; without both state and market there could be no political economy. In the absence of the state, the price mechanism and market forces would determine the outcome of economic activities; this would be the pure world of the economist. In the absence of the market, the state or its equivalent would allocate economic resources; this would be the pure world of the political scientist. Although neither world can ever exist in a pure form, the relative influence of the state or the market changes over time and in different circumstances. Therefore, the

Reprinted with permission of the publisher from *The Political Economy of International Relations* by Robert Gilpin (Princeton: Princeton University Press, 1987), pp. 8–14, 18–24.

conceptions of "state" and "market" in the following analysis are what Max Weber has called ideal types.

The very term "political economy" is fraught with ambiguity. Adam Smith and classical economists used it to mean what today is called the science of economics. More recently, a number of scholars, such as Gary Becker, Anthony Downs, and Bruno Frey, have defined political economy as the application of the *methodology* of formal economics, that is, the so-called rational actor model, to all types of human behavior. Others who use the term political economy mean employment of a specific economic *theory* to explain social behavior; game, collective action, and Marxist theories are three examples. The public choice approach to political economy draws upon both the methodology and theory of economics to explain behavior. Still other scholars use political economy to refer to a set of *questions* generated by the interaction of economic and political activities, questions that are to be explored with whatever theoretical and methodological means are readily available (Tooze, 1984).

Although the approaches to political economy based on the application of the method and theory of economic science are very helpful, they are as yet inadequate to provide a comprehensive and satisfactory framework for scholarly inquiry. Concepts, variables, and causal relations have not yet been systematically developed; political and other noneconomic factors are frequently slighted. In fact, a unified methodology or theory of political economy would require a general comprehension of the process of social change, including the ways in which the social, economic, and political aspects of society interact. Therefore, I use the term "political economy" simply to indicate a set of questions to be examined by means of an eclectic mixture of analytic methods and theoretical perspectives.

These questions are generated by the interaction of the state and the market as the embodiment of politics and economics in the modern world. They ask how the state and its associated political processes affect the production and distribution of wealth and, in particular, how political decisions and interests influence the location of economic activities and the distribution of the costs and benefits of these activities. Conversely, these questions also inquire about the effect of markets and economic forces on the distribution of power and welfare among states and other political actors, and particularly about how these economic forces alter the international distribution of political and military power. Neither state nor market is primary; the causal relationships are interactive and indeed cyclical. Thus, the questions to be explored here focus on the mutual interactions of very different means for ordering and organizing human activities: the state and the market. . . .

The relationship of state and market, and especially the differences between these two organizing principles of social life, is a recurrent theme in scholarly discourse. On the one hand, the state is based on the concepts of territoriality, loyalty, and exclusivity, and it possesses a monopoly of the legitimate use of force. Although no state can long survive unless it assures the interests and gains the consent of the most powerful groups in society, states enjoy varying degrees of autonomy with respect to the societies of which they are a part. On the other hand, the market is based on the concepts of functional integration, contractual relationships, and expanding interdependence of buyers and sellers. It is a universe composed mainly of prices and quantities; the autonomous economic agent responding to price signals provides the basis of decision. For the state, territorial boundaries are a necessary basis of national autonomy and political unity. For the market, the elimination of all political and other obstacles to the operation of the price mechanism is imperative. The tension between these two fundamentally different ways of ordering human relationships has profoundly shaped the course of modern history and constitutes the crucial problem in the study of political economy.[1] . . .

The Issues of Political Economy

The conflict between the evolving economic and technical interdependence of the globe and the continuing compartmentalization of the world political system composed of sovereign states is a dominant motif of contemporary writings on international political economy.[2] Whereas powerful market forces in the form of trade, money, and foreign investment tend to jump national boundaries, to escape political control, and to integrate societies, the tendency of government is to restrict, to channel, and to make economic activities serve the perceived interests of the state and of powerful groups within it. The logic of the market is to locate economic activities where they are most productive and profitable; the logic of the state is to capture and control the process of economic growth and capital accumulation (Heilbroner, 1985, pp. 94–95).

Debate has raged for several centuries over the nature and consequences of the clash of the fundamentally opposed logic of the market and that of the state. From early modern writers such as David Hume, Adam Smith, and Alexander Hamilton to nineteenth-century luminaries such as David Ricardo, John Stuart Mill, and Karl Marx to contemporary scholars, opinion has been deeply divided over the interaction of economics and politics. The conflicting interpretations represent three fundamentally different ideologies of political economy. . . .

The inevitable clash gives rise to three general and interrelated issues that pervade the historic controversies in the field of international political economy. Each is related to the impact of the rise of a world market economy on the nature and dynamics of international relations.[3] Each is found in the treatises of eighteenth-century mercantilists, in the theories of classical and neoclassical economists over the past two centuries, and in the tomes of nineteenth-century Marxists and contemporary radical critics of capitalism and the world market economy. This long tradition of theorizing and speculation is crucial to an understanding of contemporary problems in trade, finance, and monetary relations.

The first issue is concerned with the economic and political causes and effects of the rise of a market economy. Under what conditions does a highly interdependent world economy emerge? Does it promote harmony or cause conflict among nation-states? Is a hegemonic power required if cooperative relations among capitalist states are to be ensured, or can cooperation arise spontaneously from mutual interest? On this issue theorists of different schools of thought have profoundly conflicting views.

Economic liberals believe that the benefits of an international division of labor based on the principle of comparative advantage cause markets to arise spontaneously and foster harmony among states; they also believe that expanding webs of economic interdependence create a basis for peace and cooperation in the competitive and anarchical state system. Economic nationalists, on the other hand, stress the role of power in the rise of a market and the conflictual nature of international economic relations; they argue that economic interdependence must have a political foundation and that it creates yet another arena of interstate conflict, increases national vulnerability, and constitutes a mechanism that one society can employ to dominate another. Although all Marxists emphasize the role of capitalist imperialism in the creation of a world market economy, they divide between the followers of V. I. Lenin, who argue that relations among market economies are by nature conflictual, and those of Lenin's chief protagonist, Karl Kautsky, who believe that market economies (at least the dominant ones) cooperate in the joint exploitation of the weaker economies of the globe. The alleged responsibility of the market system for peace or war, order or disorder, imperialism or self-determination, is embedded in this important issue, as is the crucial question of whether the existence of a liberal international economy requires a hegemonic economy to govern the system. The challenge to the United States and Western Europe from Japan and other rising economic powers at the end of this century dramatically highlights the importance of these matters.

The second issue pervading the subject of international political economy is the relationship between economic change and political change. What are the effects on international political relations and what problems are associated with structural changes in the global locus of economic activities, leading economic sectors, and cyclical rates of economic growth? And, vice versa, how do political factors affect the nature and consequences of structural changes in economic affairs? For example, one may question whether or not major economic fluctuations (business cycles) and their political effects are endogenous (internal) to the operation of the market economy, or whether economic cycles are themselves due to the impact on the economic system of exogenous (external) factors such as major wars or other political developments. It is also necessary to ask whether or not economic instabilities are the cause of profound political upheavals such as imperialist expansion, political revolution, and the great wars of the past several centuries.

[International political economy] is thus concerned in part with the effects of economic changes on international political relations. These economic changes undermine the international status quo and raise profound political problems: What will be the new basis of economic order and political leadership? Can or will adjustment to the changed economic realities, for example, new trading and monetary relations, take place? How will the inevitable clash between the desire of states for domestic autonomy and the need for international rules to govern change be reconciled? These issues of transition between historical epochs have again arisen with the global diffusion of economic activities and the profound shifts in the leading economic sectors taking place in the late twentieth century. It is important to probe the relationship between these structural changes and the crisis of the international political economy.

The third issue with which [international political economy is concerned] is the significance of a world market economy for domestic economies. What are its consequences for the economic development, economic decline, and economic welfare of individual societies? How does the world market economy affect the economic development of the less developed countries and the economic decline of advanced economies? What is its effect on domestic welfare? How does it affect the distribution of wealth and power among national societies? Does the functioning of the world economy tend to concentrate wealth and power, or does it tend to diffuse it?

Liberals and traditional Marxists alike consider the integration of a society into the world economy to be a positive factor in economic development and domestic welfare. Trade, most liberals argue, constitutes an "engine of growth"; although the domestic sources of growth are more important, the growth process is greatly assisted by international flows of trade, capital, and productive technology. Traditional Marxists believe that these external forces promote economic development by breaking the bonds of conservative social structures. On the other hand, economic nationalists in both advanced and less developed countries believe that the world market economy operates to the disadvantage of the economy and domestic welfare. Trade, in their view, is an engine of exploitation, of underdevelopment, and, for more advanced economies, of economic decline. This controversy over the role of the world market in the global distribution of wealth, power, and welfare constitutes one of the most intensely debated and divisive questions in political economy.

These three issues, then—the causes and effects of the world market economy, the relationship between economic and political change, and the significance of the world economy for domestic economies—constitute the major theoretical interests of [international political economy]. . . .

The Importance of the Market

The study of political economy focuses on the market and its relationship to the state because the world market economy is critical to international relations in the modern era; even in socialist societies the key issue in economic debates is the appropriate role for internal and external market forces. As Karl Polanyi said in his classic study of the transformation of modern society:

> the fount and matrix of the [modern economic and political] system was the self-regulating market. It was this innovation which gave rise to a specific civilization. The gold standard was merely an attempt to extend the domestic market system to the international field; the balance-of-power system was a superstructure erected upon and, partly, worked through the gold standard; the liberal state was itself a creation of the self-regulating market. The key to the institutional system of the nineteenth century [as well as our own] lay in the laws governing market economy. (Polanyi, 1957, p. 3)

Karl Marx, on the other hand, stressed capitalism or the capitalist mode of production as the creator and unique feature of the modern world. The defining characteristics of capitalism, as defined by Marx and his collaborator, Friedrich Engels, and which I accept, are the private ownership of the means of production, the existence of free or wage labor, the profit motive, and the drive to amass capital. These features provide capitalism with its dynamism; the dynamic character of the capitalist system has in turn transformed all aspects of modern society. As Gordon Craig has pointed out, the revolutionary nature of capitalism lay in the fact that, for the first time, the instinct to accumulate wealth became incorporated in the productive process; it was this combination of the desire for wealth with the economic system that changed the face of the earth (Craig, 1982, pp. 105–106). . . .

The dynamism of the capitalist system is due precisely to the fact that the capitalist, driven by the profit motive, must compete and survive in a competitive market economy. Competition weeds out the inefficient while rewarding efficiency and innovation; it encourages rationality. In the absence of a market, capitalism loses its creativity and essential vigor (McNeill, 1982). The distinctive features of the capitalistic mode of production, as defined by Marxists, would not have led to economic progress without the spur of market competition. In the presence of a market, however, even socialist or nationalized firms must strive to become profitable and competitive. The advent of socialism may not necessarily alter the underlying dynamics, provided that market competition or its functional equivalent survives. There is, as John Rawls reminds us, "no essential tie between the use of free markets and private ownership of the instruments of production" (Rawls, 1971, p. 271). Capitalism and the market exchange system are not necessarily connected.

The concept of "market" is thus broader than that of "capitalism." The essence of a market, defined in greater detail below, is the central role of relative prices in allocative decisions. The essence of capitalism, as noted above, is the private ownership of the means of production and the existence of free labor. Theoretically, a market system could be composed of public actors and unfree labor as envisioned in the concept of market socialism. The increasing role of the state and public actors in the market has recently led to a mixed economy of public and private enterprise. In practice, however, the market system has tended to be associated with international capitalism.

In summary, although the connection between the market exchange system and the capitalist mode of production is close, these terms are not the same—even though they will sometimes be used interchangeably in this [chapter]. Capitalism is too ambiguous a label to be used as an analytical category. There are in fact many varieties of capitalism that function differently. Is France truly capitalist, with 90 percent of its financial sector and much of its heavy industry nationalized and in state hands? How is one to categorize Japanese capitalism, with the central role of its state in guiding the economy? The contemporary world is composed largely of mixed economies that at the international level are forced to compete with one another.

Other scholars have identified industrialism, industrial society, and/or the development of scientific technology as the defining characteristics of modern economic life.[4] The development of both industrial technology and modern science are obviously important for the prosperity and character of the modern world. One cannot account for the Industrial Revolution and the advent of modern science simply as a response to market forces; without science-based technology the modern market economy could not have progressed very far.

The scientific breakthroughs of the seventeenth and eighteenth centuries that laid the foundations for modern industry and technology are not reducible to the operation of economic motives. Science is an intellectual creation resulting from human curiosity and the search for understanding of the universe. Yet without market demand for greater efficiencies and new products, the incentive to exploit science and develop innovations in technology would be greatly reduced. Although the advance of science increases the potential supply of new industries and technology, the market creates the demand necessary to bring the technologies into existence. Thus the crucial role of the market in propelling and organizing economic life is the reason for our focus here on the market and the implications of economic interdependence for international relations.

The concept of market or economic interdependence is a highly ambiguous term, and many different definitions exist.[5] In this [chapter] the *Oxford English Dictionary* definition of economic interdependence favored by Richard Cooper [is] used; it defines interdependence as "the fact or condition of depending each upon the other; mutual dependence" (Cooper, 1985, p. 1196). In addition, as Robert Keohane and Joseph Nye (1977) have noted, economic interdependence can refer to a power relationship, that is, to what Albert Hirschman (1945) calls vulnerability interdependence. Economic interdependence can also mean sensitivity interdependence, that is, changes in prices and quantities in different national markets respond readily to one another. . . .

If by increasing economic interdependence one means the operation of the "law of one price," that is, that identical goods will tend to have the same price, then global interdependence has reached an unprecedented level. The conclusions to be drawn from this fact, however, are not readily obvious. Although the integration of national markets into an expanding interdependent global economy is occurring, the effects that this growing interdependence is alleged to have upon international relations are uncertain. Interdependence is a phenomenon to be studied, not a ready-made set of conclusions regarding the nature and dynamics of international relations.

The Economic Consequences of a Market

Although a market is an abstract concept, a market economy can be defined as one in which goods and services are exchanged on the basis of relative prices; it is where transactions are negotiated and prices are determined. Its essence, as one economist has put it, is "the making of a price by higgling between buyers and sellers" (Condliffe, 1950, p. 301). Phrased in more formal terms, a market is "the whole of any region in which buyers and sellers are in such free intercourse with one another that the prices of the same goods tend to equality easily and quickly" (Cournot, quoted in Cooper, 1985, p. 1199). Its specific characteristics are dependent upon its degree of openness and the intensity of the competition among producers and sellers. Markets differ with respect to the freedom of participants to enter the market and also the extent to which individual buyers or sellers can influence the terms of the exchange. Thus, a perfect or self-regulating market is one that is open to all potential buyers or sellers and one in which no buyer or seller can determine the terms of the exchange. Although such a perfect market has never existed, it is the model of the world implicit in the development of economic theory.

A market economy is a significant departure from the three more traditional types of economic exchange. Although none of these forms of exchange has ever existed to the exclusion of the others, one type or another has tended to predominate. The most prevalent economic system throughout history, one that is still characteristic of many less developed economies, is localized exchange, which is highly restricted in terms of available goods and geographic scope. The second type of exchange is that of command economies, such as those of the great historic empires of Assyria and, to much lesser extent, Rome, or of the socialist bloc today; in these planned economies, the production, distribution, and prices of commodities tend to be controlled by the state bureaucracy. Third, there is, or rather there was, long-distance trade in high-value goods. The caravan routes of Asia and Africa were the principal loci of this trade. Although this trade was geographically extensive, it involved only a narrow range of goods (spices, silks, slaves, precious metals, etc.). For a number of reasons, markets tend to displace more traditional forms of economic exchange.

One reason for the primacy of the market in shaping the modern world is that it forces a reorganization of society in order to make the market work properly. When a market comes into existence, as Marx fully appreciated, it becomes a potent force driving social change. As one authority has put it, "once economic power is redistributed to those who embrace the productive ideal, their leverage as buyers, investors, and employers is seen as moving the rest of society. The critical step in establishing a market momentum is the alienation of land and labor. When these fundamental components of social existence come under the influence of the price mechanism, social direction itself passes to economic determinants" (Appleby, 1978, pp. 14–15).

In the absence of social, physical, and other constraints, a market economy has an expansive and dynamic quality. It tends to cause economic growth, to expand territorially, and to bring all segments of society into its embrace. Groups and states seek to restrain the operation of a market because it has the potential to exert a considerable force on society; efforts to control markets give rise to the political economy of international relations.

Three characteristics of a market economy are responsible for its dynamic nature: (1) the critical role of relative prices in the exchange of goods and services, (2) the centrality of competition as a determinant of individual and institutional behavior, and (3) the importance of efficiency in determining the survivability of economic actors. From these flow the profound consequences of a market for economic, social, and political life.

A market economy encourages growth for both static and dynamic reasons. A market increases the efficient allocation of existing resources. Economic growth occurs because the market fosters a reallocation of land, labor, and capital to those activities in which they are most productive.

Also, since market competition forces the producer (if it is to prosper or even merely survive) to innovate and move the economy to higher levels of productive efficiency and technology, the market dynamically promotes technological and other types of innovation, thus increasing the power and capabilities of an economy. Although both the static and dynamic aspects of markets have encouraged economic growth throughout history, the dynamic factor has become of decisive importance since the advent of modern science as the basis of productive technology.

A market economy tends to expand geographically, spilling over political boundaries and encompassing an ever-increasing fraction of the human race (Kuznets, 1953, p. 308). The demand for less expensive labor and resources causes economic development to spread (Johnson, 1965b, pp. 11–12). Over time, more and more of the nonmarket economic periphery is brought within the orbit of the market mechanism. The reasons for this expansionist tendency include efficiencies of scale, improvements in transportation, and growth of demand. Adam Smith had this in mind when he stated that both the division of labor and economic growth are dependent on the scale of the market (Smith, 1937 [1776], p. 17). In order to take advantage of increased efficiencies and to reduce costs, economic actors try to expand the extent and scale of the market.

Yet another characteristic of a market economy is a tendency to incorporate every aspect of society into the nexus of market relations. Through such "commercialization," the market generally brings all facets of traditional society into the orbit of the price mechanism. Land, labor, and other so-called factors of production become commodities to be exchanged; they are subject to the interplay of market forces (Heilbroner, 1985, p. 117). Stated more crudely, everything has its price and, as an economist friend is fond of saying, "its value *is* its price." As a consequence, markets have a profound and destabilizing impact on a society because they dissolve traditional structures and social relations (Goldthorpe, 1978, p. 194).

At both the domestic and international levels a market system also tends to create a hierarchical division of labor among producers, a division based principally on specialization and what economists call the law of comparative advantage (or costs). As a consequence of market forces, society (domestic or international) becomes reordered into a dynamic core and a dependent periphery. The core is characterized principally by its more advanced levels of technology and economic development; the periphery is, at least initially, dependent on the core as a market for its commodity exports and as a source of productive techniques. In the short term, as the core of a market economy grows, it incorporates into its orbit a larger and larger periphery; in the long term, however, due to the diffusion of productive technology and the growth process, new cores tend to form in the periphery and then to become growth centers in their own right. These tendencies for the core to expand and stimulate the rise of new cores have profound consequences for economic and political affairs (Friedmann, 1972).

The market economy also tends to redistribute wealth and economic activities within and among societies. Although everyone benefits in absolute terms as each gains wealth from participation in a market economy, some do gain more than others. The tendency is for markets, at least initially, to concentrate wealth in particular groups, classes, or regions. The reasons for this tendency are numerous: the achievement of economies of scale, the existence of monopoly rents, the effects of positive externalities (spillovers from one economic activity to another) and feedbacks, the benefits of learning and experience, and a host of other efficiencies that produce a cycle of "they who have get." Subsequently, however, markets tend to diffuse wealth throughout the system due to technology transfer, changes in comparative advantage, and other factors. It may also produce in certain societies a vicious cycle of decline, depending on their flexibility and capacity to adapt to changes. A diffusion of wealth and growth, however, does not take place evenly throughout the system; it tends to concentrate in those new cores or centers of growth where conditions are most favorable. As a consequence, a market economy tends to result in a process of uneven development in both domestic and international systems.

A market economy, if left to its own devices, has profound effects on the nature and organization of societies as well as on the political relations among them. Although many of these consequences may be beneficial and much desired by a society, others are detrimental to the desires and interests of powerful groups and states. The resulting tendency, therefore, is for states to intervene in economic activities in order to advance the effects of markets beneficial to themselves and to counter those that are detrimental.

Market Effects and Political Responses

In the abstract world of economists, the economy and other aspects of society exist in separate and distinct spheres. Economists hypothesize a theoretical universe composed of autonomous, homogeneous, and maximizing individuals who are free and able to respond to market forces in terms of their perceived self-interest. They assume that economic structures are flexible and behaviors change automatically and predictably in response to price signals (Little, 1982, ch. 2). Social classes, ethnic loyalties, and national boundaries are assumed not to exist. When once asked what was missing from his classic textbook, Nobel laureate Paul Samuelson is reported to have responded, "the class struggle." This puts the point well, although he could have added, without undue exaggeration or violation of the spirit of the text, "races, nation-states, and all the other social and political divisions."

The essence of economics and its implications for social and political organization, as viewed by economists, are contained in what Samuelson has called "the most beautiful idea" in economic theory, namely, David Ricardo's law of comparative advantage. The implication of this simple concept is that domestic and international society should be organized in terms of relative efficiencies. It implies a universal division of labor based on specialization, in which each participant benefits absolutely in accordance with his or her contribution to the whole. It is a world in which the most humble person and the most resource-poor nation can find a niche and eventually prosper. A fundamental harmony of interest among individuals, groups, and states is assumed to underlie the growth and expansion of the market and of economic interdependence.

In the real world, divided among many different and frequently conflicting groups and states, markets have an impact vastly different from that envisaged by economic theory, and they give rise to powerful political reactions. Economic activities affect the political, social, and economic well-being of various groups and states differentially. The real world is a universe of exclusive and frequently conflicting loyalties and political boundaries in which the division of labor and the distribution of its benefits are determined as much by power and good fortune as they are by the laws of the market and the operation of the price mechanism. The assumption of a fundamental harmony of interest is most frequently invalid, and the growth and expansion of markets in a socially and politically fragmented globe have profound consequences for the nature and functioning of international politics. What then are these consequences that give rise to political responses?

One consequence of a market economy for domestic and international politics is that it has highly disruptive effects on a society; the introduction of market forces and the price mechanism into a society tends to overwhelm and even dissolve traditional social relations and institutions. The competition of the efficient drives out the inefficient and forces all to adapt to new ways. As noted earlier, markets have an inherent tendency to expand and bring everything into their orbit. New demands are constantly stimulated and new sources of supply sought. Further, markets are subject to cyclical fluctuations and disturbances over which the society may have little control; specialization and its resulting dependencies increase vulnerabilities to untoward events. In short, markets constitute a powerful source of sociopolitical change and produce equally powerful responses as societies attempt to protect themselves against market forces (Polanyi, 1957). Therefore, no state, however liberal its predilections, permits the full and unregulated development of market forces.

Another consequence of a market economy is that it significantly affects the distribution of wealth and power within and among societies. In theory, all can take advantage of market opportunities to better themselves. In practice, however, individuals, groups, or states are differently endowed and situated to take advantage of these opportunities and therefore the growth of wealth and the spread of economic activities in a market system tends to be uneven, favoring one state or another. Thus, states attempt to guide market forces to benefit their own citizens, resulting, at least in the short run, in the unequal distribution of wealth and power among the participants in the market and the stratification of societies in the international political economy (Hawtrey, 1952).

Another important consequence of a market economy for states is due to the fact that economic interdependence establishes a power relationship among groups and societies. A market is not politically neutral; its existence creates economic power which one actor can use against another. Economic interdependence creates vulnerabilities that can be exploited and manipulated. In the words of Albert Hirschman, "the power to interrupt commercial or financial relations with any country . . . is the root cause of the influence or power position which a country acquires in other countries" through its market relations (Hirschman, 1945, p. 16). In varying degrees, then, economic interdependence establishes hierarchical, dependency, and power relations among groups and national societies. In response to this situation, states attempt to enhance their own independence and to increase the dependence of other states.

A market economy confers both benefits and costs on groups and societies. On the one hand, economic specialization and a division of labor foster economic growth and an increase in the wealth of market participants. Although gains are unevenly distributed, in general everyone benefits in absolute terms. Therefore few societies choose to absent themselves from participation in the world economic system. Yet, on the other hand, a market economy also imposes economic, social, and political costs on particular groups and societies, so that in relative terms, some benefit more than others. Thus, states seek to protect themselves and limit the costs to themselves and their citizens. The struggle among groups and states over the distribution of benefits and costs has become a major feature of international relations in the modern world.

Conclusion

The central concerns of [international political economy], then, are the impact of the world market economy on the relations of states and the ways in which states seek to influence market forces for their own advantage. Embedded in this relationship of state and market are three closely related issues of importance to the student of politics. The first is the way in which market interdependence affects and is affected by international politics and in particular by the presence or absence of political leadership. The second is the interaction of economic and political change that gives rise to an intense competition among states over the global location of economic activities, especially the so-called commanding heights of modern industry. The third is the effect of the world market on economic development and the consequent effort of states to control or at least to be in a position to influence the rules or regimes governing trade, foreign investment, and the international monetary system as well as other aspects of the international political economy.

Behind seemingly technical issues of trade or international money lurk significant political issues that profoundly influence the power, independence, and well-being of individual states. Thus, although trade may well be of mutual benefit, every state wants its own gains to be disproportionately to its advantage; it wants to move up the technological ladder to reap the highest value-added return from its own contribution to the international division of labor. Similarly, every state wants to have its say in decision making about the rules of the international monetary system. In every area of international economic affairs, economic and political issues are deeply entwined.

Scholars and other individuals differ, however, on the nature of the relationship between economic and political affairs. Although many positions can be identified, almost everyone tends to fall into one of three contrasting perspectives, ideologies, or schools of thought. They are liberalism, nationalism, and Marxism. . . .

Notes

1. The concepts of state and market used in this book are derived primarily from Max Weber (1978, vol. I, pp. 56, 82, and passim) .

2. Perhaps the first writer to address this theme systematically was Eugene Staley (1939).

3. Obviously, the choice of these three issues as the central ones will not meet with the approval of everyone in the field of international political economy. Many would quite rightly come up with another set. These issues exclude, for example, such topics as the making and substance of foreign economic policy. Although this subject is important, the principal focus of this book is on the structure, functioning, and interaction of the international economic and political systems. A parallel and not invidious distinction can be and usually is made between the study of the foreign policies of particular states and the study of the theory of international relations. Although these subjects are closely related, they ask different questions and are based on different assumptions. Gaddis (1982) and Waltz (1979) are respectively excellent examples of each approach.

4. Goldthorpe (1984, ch. 13); Giddens (1985), and Rostow (1975) are representative of these positions.

5. An excellent analysis of these various meanings is Cooper (1985, pp. 1196–1200).

References

Appleby, Joyce Oldham. 1978. *Economic Thought and Ideology in Seventeenth-Century England*. Princeton: Princeton University Press.

Condliffe, J. B. 1950. *The Commerce of Nations*. New York: W. W. Norton.

Cooper, Richard. 1985. "Economic Interdependence and Coordination of Economic Policies." In Jones and Kenen, Vol. 2, Chapter 23.

Craig, Gordon A. 1982. *The Germans*. New York: G. P. Putnam's Sons.

Friedmann, John. 1972. "A General Theory of Polarized Development." In Niles M. Hansen, ed., *Growth Centers in Regional Economic Development*. New York: Free Press.

Gaddis, John Lewis. 1982. *Strategies of Containment: A Critical Appraisal of Postwar American National Security Policy*. New York: Oxford University Press.

Giddens, Anthony. 1985. *A Contemporary Critique of Historical Materialism*. Vol. 2, *The Nation-State and Violence*. Berkeley: University of California Press.

Goldthorpe, John H. 1978. "The Current Inflation: Towards a Sociological Account." In Fred Hirsch and John H. Goldthorpe, eds., *The Political Economy of Inflation*. Cambridge: Harvard University Press.

Goldthorpe, John H., ed. 1984. *Order and Conflict in Contemporary Capitalism: Studies in the Political Economy of Western European Nations*. Oxford: Clarendon Press.

Hawtrey, Ralph G. 1952. *Economic Aspects of Sovereignty*. London: Longmans.

Heilbroner, Robert L. 1980. *Marxism: For and Against*. New York: W. W. Norton.

Heilbroner, Robert L. 1985. *The Nature and Logic of Capitalism*. New York: W. W. Norton.

Hirschman, Albert O. 1945. *National Power and the Structure of Foreign Trade*. Berkeley: University of California Press.

Johnson, Harry G. 1965b. *The World Economy at the Crossroads: A Survey of Current Problems of Money, Trade, and Economic Development*. New York: Oxford University Press.

Keohane, Robert O., and Joseph S. Nye, Jr., 1977. *Power and Interdependence: World Politics in Transition*. Boston: Little, Brown.

Kuznets, Simon. 1953. *Economic Change: Selected Essays in Business Cycles, National Income, and Economic Growth*. New York: W. W. Norton.

Little, Ian M. D. 1982. *Economic Development: Theory, Policy and International Relations*. New York: Basic Books.

McNeill, William H. 1982. *The Pursuit of Power: Technology, Armed Force, and Society since A.D. 1000*. Chicago: University of Chicago Press.

Polanyi, Karl. 1957. *The Great Transformation: The Political and Economic Origins of Our Time*. Boston: Beacon Press.

Rawls, John. 1971. *A Theory of Justice*. Cambridge: Harvard University Press.

Rostow, W. W. 1975. *How It All Began: Origins of the Modern Economy*. New York: McGraw-Hill.

Smith, Adam. 1937 [1776]. *An Inquiry into the Nature and Causes of the Wealth of Nations*. New York: Modern Library.

Staley, Eugene. 1939. *World Economy in Transition: Technology vs. Politics,*

Laissez-Faire vs. Planning, Power vs. Welfare. New York: Council on Foreign Relations.

Tooze, Roger. 1984. "Perspectives and Theory: A Consumers' Guide." In Susan Strange, ed., *Paths to International Political Economy.* London: George Allen and Unwin.

Waltz, Kenneth N. 1979. *Theory of International Politics.* Reading, Mass.: Addison-Wesley.

Weber, Max. 1978. *Economy and Society: An Outline of Interpretive Sociology.* 2 vols. Guenther Roth and Claus Wittich, eds. Berkeley: University of California Press.

2

International Politics and International Economics

Jeffry A. Frieden and David A. Lake

In the previous chapter, Robert Gilpin discussed the scope of international political economy and described the evolution of the state system and capitalism. This contribution by Jeffry Frieden and David Lake outlines the historical and philosophical foundations of liberalism, realism, and Marxism, which constitute the three paradigms or worldviews devised to interpret the international system and the behavior of the institutions and organizations created to govern it. Understanding the tenets and assumptions of these worldviews aids the student of international political economy in understanding why countries and institutions act the way they do, and why conflicts emerge between and among them.

Three Perspectives on International Political Economy

Nearly all studies in International Political Economy can be classified into one of three mutually exclusive perspectives: Liberalism, Marxism, and Realism. Each of the three perspectives has a unique set of simplifying assumptions used to render the world less complex and more readily understandable. Assumptions are assertions accepted as true for purposes of further investigations. The value of an assumption lies in the ability of the theory built upon it to explain observed phenomena. Thus, assumptions are neither true nor false, only useful or not useful.

The assumptions upon which each of these three perspectives is based lead international political economists to view the world in very different ways. Many Liberals regard foreign direct investment in less developed

countries, for instance, as a mutually rewarding exchange between entrepreneurs. Many Marxists, on the other hand, see the foreign firm as exploiting the less developed country. Consequently, a first step in studying
International Political Economy is to understand the assumptions made by
each of the three perspectives.

Liberalism

The Liberal perspective is drawn primarily from the field of economics and
can be traced to the writings of Adam Smith (1723–1790) and David
Ricardo (1772–1823). Smith and Ricardo were reacting to the pervasive
economic controls that existed under mercantilism between the sixteenth
and nineteenth centuries. In this period, the domestic and international
economies were tightly regulated by governments in order to expand
national power and wealth. Smith, Ricardo, and their followers argued that
the philosophy underlying this practice was mistaken. Rather, these
Liberals asserted that national wealth was best increased by allowing free
and unrestricted exchange among individuals in both the domestic and
international economies. As their ideas gained adherents in the early nineteenth century, many of the mercantilist trade restrictions were dismantled.

Smith and the nineteenth-century Liberals were the economic reformers of their era. In International Political Economy, advocates of free trade
and free markets are still referred to as Liberals. In twentieth-century
American domestic politics, on the other hand, the term has come to mean
just the opposite. In the United States today, "Conservatives" generally
support free markets and less government intervention, while "Liberals"
advocate greater governmental intervention in the market to stimulate
growth and mitigate inequalities. These contradictory uses of the term
"Liberal" may seem confusing, but in the readings below and elsewhere,
the context usually makes the author's meaning clear.

Three assumptions are central to the Liberal perspective. First, Liberals
assume that individuals are the principal actors within the political economy
and the proper unit of analysis. While this may seem obvious, as all social
activity can ultimately be traced back to individuals, this first assumption
gains its importance by comparison with Marxism and Realism, each of
which makes alternative assumptions (see below).

Second, Liberals assume that individuals are rational, utility-maximizing actors. Rational action means that individuals make cost-benefit calculations across a wide range of possible options. Actors are utility maximizers when, given a calculated range of benefits, they choose the option
which yields the highest level of subjective satisfaction. This does not
imply that individuals actually gain from every utility-maximizing choice.
In some circumstances, utility maximization implies that the individual will
choose the option that makes him or her least worse off.

Third, Liberals assume that individuals maximize utility by making trade-offs between goods. Consider the trade-off between clothing and jewelry. At high levels of clothing and low levels of jewelry some individuals—depending upon their desires for these two goods—might be willing to trade some of their wearing apparel for more jewelry. Likewise, if an individual possesses a great deal of jewelry but little clothing, he or she might be willing to trade jewelry for apparel. Individuals thus increase their utility, according to Liberals, by exchanging goods with others. Those who desire jewelry more strongly than clothing will trade the latter for the former. Others who prefer clothing over jewelry will trade jewelry for apparel. This process of exchange will occur until each individual, given the existing quantities of jewelry and clothing, is as well off as possible without making someone else worse off. At this point, all individuals in society will have maximized their uniquely defined utilities. Some will possess jewelry but no clothing. Others will possess only clothing. The vast majority of us, on the other hand, will possess varying mixes of both.

The Liberal argument has traditionally been applied primarily to the economy, in which it implies that there is no basis for conflict in the marketplace. Because market exchanges are voluntary, and if there are no impediments to trade among individuals, Liberals reason, everyone can be made as well off as possible given existing stocks of goods and services. All participants in the market, in other words, will be at their highest possible level of utility. Neo-classical economists, who are generally Liberals, believe firmly in the superiority of the market as the allocator of scarce resources.

Liberals therefore believe that the economic role of government should be quite limited. Many forms of government intervention in the economy, they argue, intentionally or unintentionally restrict the market and thereby prevent potentially rewarding trades from occurring.

Liberals do generally support the provision by government of certain "public goods," goods and services that make society better off but that would not be provided by private markets.[1] The government, for example, plays an important role in supplying the conditions necessary for the maintenance of a free and competitive market. Governments must provide for the defense of the country, protect property rights, and prevent unfair collusion or concentration of power within the market. The government should also, according to most Liberals, educate its citizens, build infrastructure, and provide and regulate a common currency. The proper role of government, in other words, is to provide the necessary foundation for the market.

At the level of the international economy, Liberals assert that a fundamental harmony of interests exists between as well as within countries. As Richard Cobden argued in the fight against trade protection in Great Britain during the early nineteenth century, all countries are best off when goods and services move freely across national borders in mutually rewarding exchanges. If universal free trade were to exist, Cobden reasoned, all coun-tries would enjoy the highest level of utility and there would be no econom-ic basis for international conflict and war.

Liberals also believe that governments should manage the international economy in much the same way as they manage their domestic economies. They should establish rules and regulations—often referred to as "interna-tional regimes"—to govern exchanges between different national curren-cies and ensure that no country or domestic group is damaged by "unfair" international competition.

Liberals realize, of course, that governments often do far more than this at both the domestic and international levels, and they have applied their theoretical tools to analyze patterns of government activity. As might be expected, the principal Liberal approach—known generally as "public choice" or "rational choice"—thinks of the political arena as a marketplace. Politicians compete among each other for the privilege of holding office; individuals and groups compete among each other to get support for their preferred policies from office-holders—with votes, campaign contribu-tions, and lobbying. This view, closely related to long-standing theories of interest-group pluralism, sees government action as the result of competi-tion among politicians, and among their constituents.

Marxism

Marxism originated with the writings of Karl Marx, a nineteenth-century political economist and perhaps capitalism's severest critic. Just as Liberalism emerged in reaction to mercantilism, Marxism was a response to the spread of Liberalism in the nineteenth century. Where for Liberals the market allows individuals to maximize their utility, Marx saw capital-ism and the market creating extremes of wealth for capitalists and poverty for workers. While everyone may have been better off than before, the cap-italists were clearly expanding their wealth more rapidly than all others. Marx rejected the assertion that exchange between individuals necessarily maximizes the welfare of the whole society. Accordingly, Marx perceived capitalism as an inherently conflictual system that both should and will be inevitably overthrown and replaced by socialism.

Marxism makes three essential assumptions. First, Marxists believe that classes are the dominant actors in the political economy and are the appropriate unit of analysis. Marxists identify two economically deter-mined aggregations of individuals, or classes, as central: capital, or the owners of the means of production, and labor, or workers.

Second, Marxists assume that classes act in their material economic interests. Just as Liberals assume that individuals act rationally to maxi-mize their utility, Marxists assume that each class acts to maximize the eco-nomic well-being of the class as a whole.

Third, Marxists assume that the basis of the capitalist economy is the exploitation of labor by capital. Marx's analysis began with the labor theory of value, which holds that the value of any product is determined by the amount of past and present labor used to produce it. Marx believed that under capitalism the value of any product could be broken down into three components: constant capital, or past labor as embodied in plant and equipment or the raw materials necessary to produce the good; variable capital, the wages paid to present labor to produce the item; and surplus value— defined as profits, rents, and interest—which was expropriated by or paid to the capitalist. The capitalists' expropriation of surplus value, according to Marx, denies labor the full return for its efforts.

This third assumption leads Marxists to see the political economy as necessarily conflictual, because the relationship between capitalists and workers is essentially antagonistic. Surplus value is not the capitalist's "reward" for investment, but something that is taken away from labor. Because the means of production are controlled by a minority within society—the capitalists—labor does not receive its full return; conflict between the classes will thus occur because of this exploitation. For Marx, the relationship between capital and labor is zero-sum; any gain for the capitalist must come at the expense of labor, and vice versa.

Starting with these three assumptions, Marx constructed a sophisticated theory of capitalist crisis. Such crisis would, Marx believed, ultimately lead to the overthrow of capitalism by labor and the erection of a socialist society in which the means of production would be owned jointly by all members of society and no surplus value would be expropriated.

While Marx wrote primarily about domestic political economy, or the dynamics and form of economic change within a single country, Lenin extended Marx's ideas to the international political economy to explain imperialism and war. Imperialism, Lenin argued, was endemic to modern capitalism. As capitalism decayed in the most developed nations, these nations would attempt to solve their problems by exporting capital abroad. As this capital required protection from both local and foreign challengers, governments would colonize regions to safeguard the interests of their foreign investors. When the area available for colonization began to shrink, capitalist countries would compete for control over these areas and intra-capitalist wars would eventually occur.

Today, Marxists who study the international political economy are primarily concerned with two sets of analytical and practical issues. The first concerns the fate of labor in a world of increasingly internationalized capital. With the growth of multinational corporations and the rise of globally integrated financial markets, the greater international mobility of capital appears to have weakened the economic and political power of labor. If workers in a particular country demand higher wages or improved health and safety measures, for example, the multinational capitalist can simply shift production to another country where labor is more compliant. As a result, many Marxists fear that labor's ability to negotiate with capital for a more equitable division of surplus value has been significantly undermined. Understanding how and in what ways labor has been weakened and how workers should respond to the increased mobility of capital is thus an important research agenda.

Second, Marxists are concerned with the poverty and continued underdevelopment of the Third World. Some Marxists argue that development is blocked by domestic ruling classes who pursue their own narrow interests at the expense of national economic progress. "Dependency" theorists, on the other hand, extend Marx's class-analytic framework to the level of the international economy. According to these Marxists, the global system is stratified into an area of autonomous self-sustaining growth, the "core" or First World, and a region of attenuated inhibited growth, the "periphery" or Third World. International capitalism, in this view, extracts surplus value from the periphery and concentrates it in the core, just as capitalists exploit workers within a single country. The principal questions here focus on the mechanisms of exploitation—whether they be multinational corporations, international financial markets and organizations, or trade—and the appropriate strategies for stimulating autonomous growth and development in the periphery.

While Liberals perceive the political economy as inherently harmonious, Marxists believe conflict is endemic. Marxists adopt different assumptions and derive a very different understanding of the world. For Marxists, economics determines politics. The nature of politics and the fundamental cleavages within and between societies, in other words, are rooted in economics.

Realism

Realism has perhaps the longest pedigree of the three principal perspectives in International Political Economy, starting with Thucydides's writings in 400 B.C. and including Niccolo Machiavelli, Thomas Hobbes, and the mercantilists Jean-Baptiste Colbert and Friedrich List. Discredited with the rise of Liberalism in the nineteenth century, Realism reemerged as an important perspective only in the aftermath of the Great Depression of the 1930s as scholars sought to understand the causes of the widespread economic warfare of "beggar-thy-neighbor" policies initiated in 1929. Realists believe that nation-states pursue power and shape the economy to this end. Unlike Liberals and Marxists, Realists perceive politics as determining economics.

Realism is based upon three assumptions. First, Realists assume that nation-states are the dominant actors within the international political economy and the proper unit of analysis. According to Realists, the international system is anarchical, a condition under which nation-states are sovereign, the sole judge of their own behaviors, and subject to no higher authority. If no authority is higher than the nation-state, Realists also believe that all actors are subordinate to the nation-state. While private citizens can interact with their counterparts in other countries, Realists assert that the basis for this interaction is legislated by the nation-state. Thus, where Liberals focus on individuals and Marxists on classes, Realists concentrate on nation-states.

Second, Realists assume that nation-states are power maximizers. Because the international system is based upon anarchy, the use of force or coercion by other nation-states is always a possibility and no other country or higher authority is obligated to come to the aid of a nation-state under attack. Nation-states are thus ultimately dependent upon their own resources for protection. For Realists, then, each nation-state must always be prepared to defend itself to the best of its ability. It must always seek to maximize its power; the failure to do so threatens the very existence of the nation-state and may make it vulnerable to others. Power is a relative concept. If one nation-state (or any other actor) expands its power over another, it can do so only at the expense of the second. Thus, for Realists, politics is a zero-sum game and by necessity conflictual. If one nation-state wins, another must lose.

Third, Realists assume that nation-states are rational actors in the same sense that Liberals assume individuals are rational. Nation-states are assumed to perform cost-benefit analyses and choose the option which yields the greatest value, in this case, the one which maximizes power.

It is the assumption of power maximization that gives Realism its distinctive approach to International Political Economy. While economic considerations may often complement power concerns, the former are—in the Realist view—subordinate to the latter. Liberals and Marxists see individuals and classes, respectively, as always seeking to maximize their economic well-being. Realists, on the other hand, allow for circumstances in which nation-states sacrifice economic gain to weaken their opponents or strengthen themselves in military or diplomatic terms. Thus, trade protection—which might reduce a country's overall income by restricting the market—may be adopted for reasons of national political power.

Given its assumptions, Realist political economy is primarily concerned with how changes in the distribution of international power affect the form and type of international economy. The best known Realist approach to this question is the "theory of hegemonic stability," which holds that an open international economy—that is, one characterized by the free exchange of goods, capital, and services—is most likely to exist when a single dominant or hegemonic power is present to stabilize the system and construct a strong regime. For Realists, then, politics underlies economics. In the pursuit of power, nation-states shape the international economy to best serve their desired ends.

Each of these three perspectives adopts different assumptions to simplify reality and render it more explicable. Liberals assume that individuals are the proper unit of analysis, while Marxists and Realists make similar assumptions for classes and nation-states, respectively. The three perspectives also differ on the inevitability of conflict within the political economy. Liberals believe economics and politics are largely autonomous spheres, Marxists maintain that economics determines politics, and Realists argue that politics determines economics.

These three perspectives lead to widely different explanations of specific events and general processes within the international political economy. Their differences have generated numerous debates in the field, many of which are contained in the readings herein. Overlying these perspectives are two additional debates on the relative importance of international and domestic factors, and of social or state forces, in determining economic policy. . . .

Note

1. More specifically, a public good is one that, in its purest form, is *nonrival in consumption* and *nonexcludable*. The first characteristic means that consumption of the good by one person does not reduce the opportunities for others to consume the good: clean air can be breathed by one without reducing its availability to others. The second characteristic means that nobody can be prevented from consuming the good—those who do not contribute to pollution control are still able to breathe clean air. These two conditions are fully met only rarely, but goods that come close to them are generally considered public goods.

3

Excerpts from *The Wealth of Nations*

Adam Smith

Adam Smith's The Wealth of Nations *(1776), along with the later works of David Ricardo, established the central concepts that are now recognized as classic liberalism. In this excerpt from* The Wealth of Nations, *Smith makes his case for free trade, arguing that goods should be purchased from the most efficient producer, regardless of the country of origin. The advantage of this type of trade is not only seen in the savings obtained for individuals and societies as a result of encouraging production by the most efficient producers; in addition, jobs will be shifted to the most efficient sectors of the economy. Unlike some contemporary proponents of free trade, Smith does not champion unconditional or unilateral free trade. Here he explains how national-security concerns led him to sympathize with the Navigation Acts. He also concedes that in some cases it may be wise to neutralize the advantages some foreign governments give to their producers. Such actions, Smith warns, may backfire and damage long-term trade relations.*

The importation of gold and silver is not the principal, much less the sole benefit which a nation derives from its foreign trade. Between whatever places foreign trade is carried on, they all of them derive two distinct benefits from it. It carries out that surplus part of the produce of their land and labour for which there is no demand among them, and brings back in return for it something else for which there is a demand. It gives a value to their superfluities, by exchanging them for something else, which may satisfy a part of their wants, and increase their enjoyments. By means of it, the narrowness of the home market does not hinder the division of labour in any particular branch of art or manufacture from being carried to the highest perfection. By opening a more extensive market for whatever part of the produce of their labour may exceed the home consumption, it encourages them to improve its productive powers, and to augment its annual produce to the utmost, and thereby to increase the real revenue and wealth of the society. These great and important services foreign trade is continually occupied in performing, to all the different countries between which it is carried on. They all derive great benefit from it, though that in which the merchant resides generally derives the greatest, as he is generally more employed in supplying the wants, and carrying out the superfluities of his own, than of any other particular country. To import the gold and silver which may be wanted, into the countries which have no mines, is, no doubt, a part of the business of foreign commerce. It is, however, a most insignificant part of it. A country which carried on foreign trade merely upon this account, could scarce have occasion to freight a ship in a century.

It is not by the importation of gold and silver, that the discovery of America has enriched Europe. By the abundance of the American mines, those metals have become cheaper. A service of plate can now be purchased for about a third part of the corn, or a third part of the labour, which it would have cost in the fifteenth century. With the same annual expence of labour and commodities, Europe can annually purchase about three times the quantity of plate which it could have purchased at that time. But when a commodity comes to be sold for a third part of what had been its usual price, not only those who purchased it before can purchase three times their former quantity, but it is brought down to the level of a greater number of purchasers, perhaps to more than ten, perhaps to more than twenty times the former number. So that there may be in Europe at present not only more than three times, but more than twenty or thirty times the quantity of plate which would have been in it, even in its present state of improvement, had the discovery of the American mines never been made. . . . By opening a new and inexhaustible market to all the commodities of Europe, [the American colonies] gave occasion to new divisions of labour and improvements of art, which, in the narrow circle of the ancient commerce, could never have taken place for want of a market to take off the greater part of their produce. The productive powers of labour were improved, and its produce increased in all the different countries of Europe, and together with it the real revenue and wealth of the inhabitants. . . .

The discovery of a passage to the East Indies, by the Cape of Good Hope, which happened much about the same time, opened, perhaps, a still more extensive range to foreign commerce than even that of America, notwithstanding the greater distance. There were but two nations in America, in any respect superior to savages, and these were destroyed almost as soon as discovered. The rest were savages. But the empires of China, Indostan, Japan, as well as several others in the East Indies, without having richer mines of gold or silver, were in every other respect much richer, better cultivated, and more advanced in all arts and manufactures than either Mexico or Peru, even though we should credit, what plainly deserves no credit, the exaggerated accounts of the Spanish writers, concerning the ancient state of those empires. But rich and civilized nations can always exchange to a much greater value with one another, than with savages and barbarians. Europe, however, has hitherto derived much less advantage from its commerce with the East Indies, than from that with America. The Portuguese monopolized the East India trade to themselves for about a century, and it was only indirectly and through them, that the other nations of Europe could either sent out or receive any goods from that country. When the Dutch, in the beginning of the last century, began to encroach upon them, they vested their whole East India commerce in an exclusive company. The English, French, Swedes, and Europe has ever yet had the benefit of a free commerce to the East Indies. No other reason need be assigned why it has never been so advantageous as the trade to America, which, between almost every nation of Europe and its own colonies, is free to all its subjects. . . .

What is prudence in the conduct of every private family, can scarce be folly in that of a great kingdom. If a foreign country can supply us with a commodity cheaper than we ourselves can make it, better buy it of them with some part of the produce of our own industry, employed in a way in which we have some advantage. The general industry of the country, being always in proportion to the capital which employs it, will not thereby be diminished, no more than that of the above-mentioned artificers; but only left to find out the way in which it can be employed with the greatest advantage. It is certainly not employed to the greatest advantage, when it is thus directed towards an object which it can buy cheaper than it can make. The value of its annual produce is certainly more or less diminished, when it is thus turned away from producing commodities evidently of more value than the commodity which it is directed to produce. According to the supposition, that commodity could be purchased from foreign countries cheaper than it can be made at home. It could, therefore, have been purchased with a part only of the commodities, or, what is the same thing, with a part only of the price of the commodities, which the industry employed by an equal capital would have produced at home, had it been left to follow its natural course. The industry of the country, therefore, is thus turned away from a more, to a less advantageous employment, and the exchangeable value of its annual produce, instead of being increased, according to the intention of the lawgiver, must necessarily be diminished by every such regulation.

By means of such regulations, indeed, a particular manufacture may sometimes be acquired sooner than it could have been otherwise, and after a certain time may be made at home as cheap or cheaper than in the foreign country. But though the industry of the society may be thus carried with advantage into a particular channel sooner than it could have been otherwise, it will by no means follow that the sum total, either of its industry, or of its revenue, can ever be augmented by any such regulation. The industry of the society can augment only in proportion as its capital augments, and its capital can augment only in proportion to what can be gradually saved out of its revenue. But the immediate effect of every such regulation is to diminish its revenue, and what diminishes its revenue is certainly not very likely to augment its capital faster than it would have augmented of its own accord, had both capital and industry been left to find out their natural employments.

Though for want of such regulations the society should never acquire the proposed manufacture, it would not, upon that account, necessarily be the poorer in any one period of its duration. In every period of its duration its whole capital and industry might still have been employed, though upon different objects, in the manner that was most advantageous at the time. In every period its revenue might have been the greatest which its capital could afford, and both capital and revenue might have been augmented with the greatest possible rapidity.

The natural advantages which one country has over another in producing particular commodities are sometimes so great, that it is acknowledged by all the world to be in vain to struggle with them. By means of glasses, hotbeds, and hotwalls, very good grapes can be raised in Scotland, and very good wine too can be made of them at about thirty times the expence for which at least equally good can be brought from foreign countries. Would it be a reasonable law to prohibit the importation of all foreign wines, merely to encourage the making of claret and burgundy in Scotland? But if there would be a manifest absurdity in turning towards any employment, thirty times more of the capital and industry of the country, than would be necessary to purchase from foreign countries an equal quantity of the commodities wanted, there must be an absurdity, though not altogether so glaring, yet exactly of the same kind, in turning towards any such employment a thirtieth, or even a three hundredth part more of either. Whether the advantages which one country has over another, be natural or acquired, is in this respect of no consequence. As long as the one country has those advantages, and the other wants them, it will always be more advantageous for the latter, rather to buy of the former than to make. It is an acquired advantage only, which one artificer has over his neighbour, who exercises another trade; and yet they both find it more advantageous to buy of one another, than to make what does not belong to their particular trades.

Merchants and manufacturers are the people who derive the greatest advantage from this monopoly of the home-market. The prohibition of the importation of foreign cattle, and of salt provisions, together with the high duties upon foreign corn, which in times of moderate plenty amount to a prohibition, are not near so advantageous to the graziers and farmers of Great Britain, as other regulations of the same kind are to its merchants and manufacturers. Manufactures, those of the finer kind especially, are more easily transported from one country to another than corn or cattle. It is in the fetching and carrying manufactures, accordingly, that foreign trade is chiefly employed. In manufactures, a very small advantage will enable foreigners to undersell our own workmen, even in the home market. It will require a very great one to enable them to do so in the rude produce of the soil. If the free importation of foreign manufactures were permitted, several of the home manufactures would probably suffer, and some of them, perhaps, go to ruin altogether, and a considerable part of the stock and industry at present employed in them, would be forced to find out some other employment. But the freest importation of the rude produce of the soil could have no such effect upon the agriculture of the country.

If the importation of foreign cattle, for example, were made ever so free, so few could be imported, that the grazing trade of Great Britain could be little affected by it. Live cattle are, perhaps, the only commodity of which the transportation is more expensive by sea than by land. By land they carry themselves to market. By sea, not only the cattle, but their food and their water too, must be carried at no small expence and inconveniency. The short sea between Ireland and Great Britain, indeed, renders the importation of Irish cattle more easy. But though the free importation of them, which was lately permitted only for a limited time, were rendered perpetual, it could have no considerable effect upon the interest of the graziers of Great Britain. Those parts of Great Britain which border upon the Irish sea are all grazing countries. Irish cattle could never be imported for their use, but must be drove through those very extensive countries, at no small expence and inconveniency, before they could arrive at their proper market. Fat cattle could not be drove so far. Lean cattle, therefore, only could be imported, and such importation could interfere, not with the interest of the feeding or fattening countries, to which, by reducing the price of lean cattle, it would rather be advantageous, but with that of the breeding countries only. The small number of Irish cattle imported since their importation was permitted, together with the good price at which lean cattle still continue to sell, seem to demonstrate that even the breeding countries of Great Britain are never likely to be much affected by the free importation of Irish cattle. The common people of Ireland, indeed, are said to have sometimes opposed with violence the exportation of their cattle. But if the exporters had found any great advantage in continuing the trade, they could easily, when the law was on their side, have conquered this mobbish opposition.

Feeding and fattening countries, besides, must always be highly improved, whereas breeding countries are generally uncultivated. The high price of lean cattle, by augmenting the value of uncultivated land, is like a bounty against improvement. To any country which was highly improved throughout, it would be more advantageous to import its lean cattle than to breed them. The province of Holland, accordingly, is said to follow this maxim at present. The mountains of Scotland, Wales and Northumberland, indeed, are countries not capable of much improvement, and seem destined by nature to be the breeding countries of Great Britain. The freest importation of foreign cattle could have no other effect than to hinder those breeding countries from taking advantage of the increasing population and improvement of the rest of the kingdom, from raising their price to an exorbitant height, and from laying a real tax upon all the more improved and cultivated parts of the country.

The freest importation of salt provisions, in the same manner, could have as little effect upon the interest of the graziers of Great Britain as that of live cattle. Salt provisions are not only a very bulky commodity, but when compared with fresh meat, they are a commodity both of worse quality, and as they cost more labour and expence, of higher price. They could never, therefore, come into competition with the fresh meat, though they might with the salt provisions of the country. They might be used for victualling ships for distant voyages, and such like uses, but could never make any considerable part of the food of the people. The small quantity of salt provisions imported from Ireland since their importation was rendered free, is an experimental proof that our graziers have nothing to apprehend from it. It does not appear that the price of butcher's-meat has ever been sensibly affected by it.

Even the free importation of foreign corn could very little affect the interest of the farmers of Great Britain. Corn is a much more bulky commodity than butcher's-meat. A pound of wheat at a penny is as dear as a pound of butcher's-meat at fourpence. The small quantity of foreign corn imported even in times of the greatest scarcity, may satisfy our farmers that they can have nothing to fear from the freest importation. The average quantity imported one year with another, amounts only, according to the very well informed author of the tracts upon the corn trade, to twenty-three thousand seven hundred and twenty-eight quarters of all sorts of grain, and does not exceed the five hundredth and seventy-one part of the annual consumption. But as the bounty upon corn occasions a greater exportation in years of plenty, so it must of consequence occasion a greater importation in years of scarcity, than in the actual state of tillage would otherwise take place. By means of it, the plenty of one year does not compensate the scarcity of another, and as the average quantity exported is necessarily augmented by it, so must likewise, in the actual state of tillage, the average quantity imported. If there were no bounty, as less corn would be exported, so it is probable that, one year with another, less would be imported than at present. The corn merchants, the fetchers and carriers of corn between Great Britain and foreign countries, would have much less employment, and might suffer considerably; but the country gentlemen and farmers could suffer very little. It is in the corn merchants accordingly, rather than in the country gentlemen and farmers, that I have observed the greatest anxiety for the renewal and continuation of the bounty.

Country gentlemen and farmers are, to their great honour, of all people, the least subject to the wretched spirit of monopoly. The undertaker of a great manufactory is sometimes alarmed if another work of the same kind is established within twenty miles of him. The Dutch undertaker of the woollen manufacture at Abbeville stipulated, that no work of the same kind should be established within thirty leagues of that city. Farmers and country gentlemen, on the contrary, are generally disposed rather to promote than to obstruct the cultivation and improvement of their neighbours' farms and estates. They have no secrets, such as those of the greater part of manufacturers, but are generally rather fond of communicating to their neighbours, and of extending as far as possible any new practice which they have found to be advantageous. *Pius Questus,* says old Cato, *stabilissimusque, minimeque invidiosus; minimeque male cogitantes sunt, qui in eo studio occupati sunt.* Country gentlemen and farmers, dispersed in different parts of the country, cannot so easily combine as merchants and manufacturers, who being collected into towns, and accustomed to that exclusive corporation spirit which prevails in them, naturally endeavour to obtain against all their countrymen, the same exclusive privilege which they generally possess against the inhabitants of their respective towns. They accordingly seem to have been the original inventors of those restraints upon the importation of foreign goods, which secure to them the monopoly of the home-market. It was probably in imitation of them, and to put themselves upon a level with those who, they found, were disposed to oppress them, that the country gentlemen and farmers of Great Britain so far forgot the generosity which is natural to their station, as to demand the exclusive privilege of supplying their countrymen with corn and butcher's-meat. They did not perhaps take time to consider, how much less their interest could be affected by the freedom of trade, than that of the people whose example they followed.

To prohibit by a perpetual law the importation of foreign corn and cattle, is in reality to enact, that the population and industry of the country shall at no time exceed what the rude produce of its own soil can maintain.

There seem, however, to be two cases in which it will generally be advantageous to lay some burden upon foreign, for the encouragement of domestic industry.

The first is, when some particular sort of industry is necessary for the defence of the country. The defence of Great Britain, for example, depends very much upon the number of its sailors and shipping. The act of navigation, therefore, very properly endeavours to give the sailors and shipping of Great Britain the monopoly of the trade of their own country, in some cases, by absolute prohibitions, and in others by heavy burdens upon the shipping of foreign countries. The following are the principal dispositions of this act.

First, all ships, of which the owners, masters, and three-fourths of the mariners are not British subjects, are prohibited, upon pain of forfeiting ship and cargo, from trading to the British settlements and plantations, or from being employed in the coasting trade of Great Britain.

Secondly, a great variety of the most bulky articles of importation can be brought into Great Britain only, either in such ships as are above described, or in ships of the country where those goods are produced, and of which the owners, masters, and three-fourths of the mariners, are of that particular country; and when imported even in ships of this latter kind, they are subject to double aliens duty. If imported in ships of any other country, the penalty is forfeiture of ship and goods. When this act was made, the Dutch were, what they still are, the great carriers of Europe, and by this regulation they were entirely excluded from being the carriers to Great Britain, or from importing to us the goods of any other European country.

Thirdly, a great variety of the most bulky articles of importation are prohibited from being imported, even in British ships, from any country but that in which they are produced; under pain of forfeiting ship and cargo. This regulation too was probably intended against the Dutch. Holland was then, as now, the great emporium for all European goods, and by this regulation, British ships were hindered from loading in Holland the goods of any other European country.

Fourthly, salt fish of all kinds, whale-fins, whale-bone, oil, and blubber, not caught by and cured on board British vessels, when imported into Great Britain, are subjected to double aliens duty. The Dutch, as they are still the principal, were then the only fishers in Europe that attempted to supply foreign nations with fish. By this regulation, a very heavy burden was laid upon their supplying Great Britain.

When the act of navigation was made, though England and Holland were not actually at war, the most violent animosity subsisted between the two nations. It had begun during the government of the long parliament, which first framed this act, and it broke out soon after in the Dutch wars during that of the Protector and of Charles the Second. It is not impossible, therefore, that some of the regulations of this famous act may have proceeded from national animosity. They are as wise, however, as if they had all been dictated by the most deliberate wisdom. National animosity at that particular time aimed at the very same object which the most deliberate wisdom would have recommended, the diminution of the naval power of Holland, the only naval power which could endanger the security of England.

The act of navigation is not favourable to foreign commerce, or to the growth of that opulence which can arise from it. The interest of a nation in its commercial relations to foreign nations is, like that of a merchant with regard to the different people with whom he deals, to buy as cheap and to sell as dear as possible. But it will be most likely to buy cheap, when by the most perfect freedom of trade it encourages all nations to bring to it the goods which it has occasion to purchase; and, for the same reason, it will be most likely to sell dear, when its markets are thus filled with the greatest number of buyers. The act of navigation, it is true, lays no burden upon foreign ships that come to export the produce of British industry. Even the ancient aliens duty, which used to be paid upon all goods exported as well as imported, has, by several subsequent acts, been taken off from the greater part of the articles of exportation. But if foreigners, either by prohibitions or high duties, are hindered from coming to sell, they cannot always afford to come to buy; because coming without a cargo, they must lose the freight from their own country to Great Britain. By diminishing the number of sellers, therefore, we necessarily diminish that of buyers, and are thus likely not only to buy foreign goods dearer, but to sell our own cheaper, than if there was a more perfect freedom of trade. As defence, however, is of much more importance than opulence, the act of navigation is, perhaps, the wisest of all the commercial regulations of England.

The second case, in which it will generally be advantageous to lay some burden upon foreign for the encouragement of domestic industry, is, when some tax is imposed at home upon the produce of the latter. In this case, it seems reasonable that an equal tax should be imposed upon the like produce of the former. This would not give the monopoly of the home market to domestic industry, nor turn towards a particular employment a greater share of the stock and labour of the country, than what would naturally go to it. It would only hinder any part of what would naturally go to it from being turned away by the tax, into a less natural direction, and would leave the competition between foreign and domestic industry, after the tax, as nearly as possible upon the same footing as before it. In Great Britain, when any such tax is laid upon the produce of domestic industry, it is usual at the same time, in order to stop the clamorous complaints of our merchants and manufacturers, that they will be undersold at home, to lay a much heavier duty upon the importation of all foreign goods of the same kind.

This second limitation of the freedom of trade according to some people should, upon some occasions, be extended much farther than to the precise foreign commodities which could come into competition with those which had been taxed at home. When the necessaries of life have been taxed in any country, it becomes proper, they pretend, to tax not only the like necessaries of life imported from other countries, but all sorts of foreign goods which can come into competition with any thing that is the produce of domestic industry. Subsistence, they say, becomes necessarily dearer in consequence of such taxes; and the price of labour must always rise with the price of the labourers subsistence. Every commodity, therefore, which is the produce of domestic industry, though not immediately taxed itself, becomes dearer in consequence of such taxes, because the labour which produces it becomes so. Such taxes, therefore, are really equivalent, they say, to a tax upon every particular commodity produced at home. In order to put domestic upon the same footing with foreign industry, therefore, it becomes necessary, they think, to lay some duty upon every foreign commodity, equal to this enhancement of the price of the home commodities with which it can come into competition.

Whether taxes upon the necessaries of life, such as those in Great Britain upon soap, salt, leather, candles, &c. necessarily raise the price of labour, and consequently that of all other commodities I shall consider hereafter, when I come to treat of taxes. Supposing, however, in the mean time, that they have this effect, and they have it undoubtedly, this general enhancement of the price of all commodities, in consequence of that of labour, is a case which differs in the two following respects from that of a particular commodity, of which the price was enhanced by a particular tax immediately imposed upon it.

First, it might always be known with great exactness how far the price of such a commodity could be enhanced by such a tax: but how far the general enhancement of the price of labour might affect that of every different commodity about which labour was employed, could never be known with any tolerable exactness. It would be impossible, therefore, to proportion with any tolerable exactness the tax upon every foreign, to this enhancement of the price of every home commodity.

Secondly, taxes upon the necessaries of life have nearly the same effect upon the circumstances of the people as a poor soil and a bad climate. Provisions are thereby rendered dearer in the same manner as if it required extraordinary labour and expence to raise them. As in the natural scarcity arising from soil and climate, it would be absurd to direct the people in what manner they ought to employ their capitals and industry, so is it likewise in the artificial scarcity arising from such taxes. To be left to accommodate, as well as they could, their industry to their situation, and to find out those employments in which, notwithstanding their unfavourable circumstances, they might have some advantage either in the home or in the foreign market, is what in both cases would evidently be most for their advantage. To lay a new tax upon them, because they are already overburdened with taxes, and because they already pay too dear for the necessaries of life, to make them likewise pay too dear for the greater part of other commodities, is certainly a most absurd way of making amends.

Such taxes, when they have grown up to a certain height, are a curse equal to the barrenness of the earth and the inclemency of the heavens; and yet it is in the richest and most industrious countries that they have been most generally imposed. No other countries could support so great a disorder. As the strongest bodies only can live and enjoy health, under an unwholesome regimen; so the nations only, that in every sort of industry have the greatest natural and acquired advantages, can subsist and prosper under such taxes. Holland is the country in Europe in which they abound most, and which from peculiar circumstances continues to prosper, not by means of them, as has been most absurdly supposed, but in spite of them.

As there are two cases in which it will generally be advantageous to lay some burden upon foreign, for the encouragement of domestic industry; so there are two others in which it may sometimes be a matter or deliberation; in the one, how far it is proper to continue the free importation of certain foreign goods; and in the other, how far, or in what manner, it may be proper to restore that free importation after it has been for some time interrupted.

The case in which it may sometimes be a matter of deliberation how far it is proper to continue the free importation of certain foreign goods, is, when some foreign nation restrains by high duties or prohibitions the importation of some of our manufactures into their country. Revenge in this case naturally dictates retaliation, and that we should impose the like duties and prohibitions upon the importation of some or all of their manufactures into ours. Nations accordingly seldom fail to retaliate in this manner. The French have been particularly forward to favour their own manufactures by restraining the importation of such foreign goods as could come into competition with them. In this consisted a great part of the policy of Mr. Colbert, who, notwithstanding his great abilities, seems in this case to have been imposed upon by the sophistry of merchants and manufacturers, who are always demanding a monopoly against their countrymen. It is at present the opinion of the most intelligent men in France that his operations of this kind have not been beneficial to his country. That minister, by the tariff of 1667, imposed very high duties upon a great number of foreign manufactures. Upon his refusing to moderate them in favour of the Dutch, they in 1671 prohibited the importation of the wines, brandies and manufactures of France. The war of 1672 seems to have been in part occasioned by this commercial dispute. The peace of Nimeguen put an end to it in 1678, by moderating some of those duties in favour of the Dutch, who in consequence took off their prohibition. It was about the same time that the French and English began mutually to oppress each other's industry, by the like duties and prohibitions, of which the French, however, seem to have set the first example. The spirit of hostility which has subsisted between the two nations ever since, has hitherto hindered them from being moderated on either side. In 1697 the English prohibited the importation of bonelace, the manufacture of Flanders. The government of that country, at that time under the dominion of Spain, prohibited in return the importation of English woollens. In 1700, the prohibition of importing bonelace into England, was taken off upon condition that the importation of English woollens into Flanders should be put on the same footing as before.

There may be good policy in retaliations of this kind, when there is a probability that they will procure the repeal of the high duties or prohibitions complained of. The recovery of a great foreign market will generally more than compensate the transitory inconveniency of paying dearer during a short time for some sorts of goods. To judge whether such retaliations are likely to produce such an effect, does not, perhaps, belong so much to the science of a legislator, whose deliberations ought to be governed by general principles which are always the same, as to the skill of that insidious and crafty animal, vulgarly called a statesman or politician, whose councils are directed by the momentary fluctuations of affairs. When there is no probability that any such repeal can be procured, it seems a bad method of compensating the injury done to certain classes of our people, to do another injury ourselves, not only to those classes, but to almost all the other classes of them. When our neighbours prohibit some manufacture of ours, we generally prohibit, not only the same, for that alone would seldom affect them considerably, but some other manufacture of theirs. This may no doubt give encouragement to some particular class of workmen among ourselves, and by excluding some of their rivals, may enable them to raise their price in the home-market. Those workmen, however, who suffered by our neighbours' prohibition will not be benefited by ours. On the contrary, they and almost all the other classes of our citizens will thereby be obliged to pay dearer than before for certain goods. Every such law, therefore, imposes a real tax upon the whole country, not in favour of that particular class of workmen who were injured by our neighbours' prohibition, but of some other class.

The case in which it may sometimes be a matter of deliberation, how far, or in what manner, it is proper to restore the free importation of foreign goods, after it has been for some time interrupted, is, when particular manufactures, by means of high duties or prohibitions upon all foreign goods which can come into competition with them, have been so far extended as to employ a great multitude of hands. Humanity may in this case require that the freedom of trade should be restored only by slow gradations, and with a good deal of reserve and circumspection. Were those high duties and prohibitions taken away all at once, cheaper foreign goods of the same kind might be poured so fast into the home market, as to deprive all at once many thousands of our people of their ordinary employment and means of subsistence. The disorder which this would occasion might no doubt be very considerable. It would in all probability, however, be much less than is commonly imagined, for the two following reasons:

First, all those manufactures, of which any part is commonly exported to other European countries without a bounty, could be very little affected by the freest importation of foreign goods. Such manufactures must be sold as cheap abroad as any other foreign goods of the same quality and kind, and consequently must be sold cheaper at home. They would still, therefore, keep possession of the home market, and though a capricious man of fashion might sometimes prefer foreign wares, merely because they were foreign, to cheaper and better goods of the same kind that were made at home, this folly could, from the nature of things, extend to so few, that it could make no sensible impression upon the general employment of the people. But a great part of all the different branches of our woollen manufacture, of our tanned leather, and of our hard-ware, are annually exported to other European countries without any bounty, and these are the manufactures which employ the greatest number of hands. The silk, perhaps, is the manufacture which would suffer the most by this freedom of trade, and after it the linen, though the latter much less than the former.

Secondly, though a great number of people should, by thus restoring the freedom of trade, be thrown all at once out of their ordinary employment and common method of subsistence, it would by no means follow that they would thereby be deprived either of employment or subsistence. By the reduction of the army and navy at the end of the late war, more than a hundred thousand soldiers and seamen, a number equal to what is employed in the greatest manufactures, were all at once thrown out of their ordinary employment; but, though they no doubt suffered some inconveniency, they were not thereby deprived of all employment and subsistence. The greater part of the seamen, it is probable, gradually betook themselves to the merchant-service as they could find occasion, and in the meantime both they and the soldiers were absorbed in the great mass of the people, and employed in a great variety of occupations. Not only no great convulsion, but no sensible disorder arose from so great a change in the situation of more than a hundred thousand men, all accustomed to the use of arms, and many of them to rapine and plunder. The number of vagrants was scarce any-where sensibly increased by it, even the wages of labour were not reduced by it in any occupation, so far as I have been able to learn, except in that of seamen in the merchant-service. But if we compare together the habits of a soldier and of any sort of manufacturer, we shall find that those of the latter do not tend so much to disqualify him from being employed in a new trade, as those of the former from being employed in any. The manufacturer has always been accustomed to look for his subsistence from his labour only: the soldier to expect it from his pay. Application and industry have been familiar to the one; idleness and dissipation to the other. But it is surely much easier to change the direction of industry from one sort of labour to another, than to turn idleness and dissipation to any. To the greater part of manufactures besides, it has already been observed, there are other collateral manufactures of so similar a nature, that a workman can easily transfer his industry from one of them to another. The greater part of such workmen too are occasionally employed in country labour. The stock which employed them in a particular manufacture before, will still remain in the country to employ an equal number of people in some other way. The capital of the country remaining the same, the demand for labour will likewise be the same, or very nearly the same, though it may be exerted in different places and for different occupations.

Soldiers and seamen, indeed, when discharged from.the king's service, are at liberty to exercise any trade, within any town or place of Great Britain or Ireland. Let the same natural liberty of exercising what species of industry they please, be restored to all his majesty's subjects, in the same manner as to soldiers and seamen; that is, break down the exclusive privileges of corporations, and repeal the statute of apprenticeship, both which are real encroachments upon natural liberty, and add to these the repeal of the law of settlements, so that a poor workman, when thrown out of employment either in one trade or in one place, may seek for it in another trade or in another place, without the fear either of a prosecution or of a removal, and neither the public nor the individuals will suffer much more from the occasional disbanding some particular classes of manufacturers, than from that of soldiers. Our manufacturers have no doubt great merit with their country, but they cannot have more than those who defend it with their blood, nor deserve to be treated with more delicacy.

To expect, indeed, that the freedom of trade should ever be entirely restored in Great Britain, is as absurd as to expect that an Oceana or Utopia should ever be established in it. Not only the prejudices of the public, but what is much more unconquerable, the private interests of many individuals, irresistibly oppose it. Were the officers of the army to oppose with the same zeal and unanimity any reduction in the number of forces, with which master manufacturers set themselves against every law that is likely to increase the number of their rivals in the home market; were the former to animate their soldiers, in the same manner as the latter enflame their workmen, to attack with violence and outrage the proposers of any such regulation; to attempt to reduce the army would be as dangerous as it has now become to attempt to diminish in any respect the monopoly which our manufacturers have obtained against us. This monopoly has so much increased the number of some particular tribes of them, that, like an overgrown standing army, they have become formidable to the government, and upon many occasions intimidate the legislature. The member of parliament who supports every proposal for strengthening this monopoly, is sure to acquire not only the reputation of understanding trade, but great popularity and influence with an order of men whose numbers and wealth render them of great importance. If he opposes them, on the contrary, and still more if he has authority enough to be able to thwart them, neither the most acknowledged probity, nor the highest rank, nor the greatest public services, can protect him from the most infamous abuse and detraction, from personal insults, nor sometimes from real danger, arising from the insolent outrage of furious and disappointed monopolists.

The undertaker of a great manufacture, who, by the home markets being suddenly laid open to the competition of foreigners, should be obliged to abandon his trade, would no doubt suffer very considerably. That part of his capital which had usually been employed in purchasing materials and in paying his workmen, might, without much difficulty, perhaps, find another employment. But that part of it which was fixed in workhouses, and in the instruments of trade, could scarce be disposed of without considerable loss. The equitable regard, therefore, to his interest requires that changes of this kind should never be introduced suddenly, but slowly, gradually, and after a very long warning. The legislature, were it possible that its deliberations could be always directed, not by the clamorous importunity of partial interests, but by an extensive view of the general good, ought upon this very account, perhaps, to be particularly careful neither to establish any new monopolies of this kind, nor to extend further those which are already established. Every such regulation introduces some degree of real disorder into the constitution of the state, which it will be difficult afterwards to cure without occasioning another disorder.

How far it may be proper to impose taxes upon the importation of foreign goods, in order, not to prevent their importation, but to raise a revenue for government, I shall consider hereafter when I come to treat of taxes. Taxes imposed with a view to prevent, or even to diminish importation, are evidently as destructive of the revenue of the customs as of the freedom of trade.

4

Realism and Complex Interdependence

Robert O. Keohane and Joseph S. Nye

*In this classic work, Robert Keohane and Joseph Nye offer a neoliberal cri-
tique of the realist worldview. They assert that in the post–World War II era
countries have become more and more intertwined economically. The
explosive growth in the size and number of transnational corporations has
blurred state boundaries, rendering traditional realist assumptions about
the centrality of the state questionable. Realists contend that the state is the
dominant actor in world politics and that military force and violence are
the primary means by which states achieve their goals. Keohane and Nye
propose an alternative ideal type—complex interdependence—that emphasizes cooperation rather than conflict. While the authors caution that violence and conflict have not disappeared, they point to the growing importance of non security-related issues such as international monetary
relations and global environmental concerns. To them the day-to-day
affairs of states have more to do with promoting cooperative economic
interactions than with military and security matters.*

One's assumptions about world politics profoundly affect what one sees
and how one constructs theories to explain events. We believe that the
assumptions of political realists, whose theories dominated the postwar
period, are often an inadequate basis for analyzing the politics of interdependence. The realist assumptions about world politics can be seen as
defining an extreme set of conditions or ideal type. One could also imagine
very different conditions. In this chapter, we shall construct another ideal

Reprinted with permission of the publisher from *Power and Interdependence:
World Politics in Transition*, 2d edition, by Robert O. Keohane and Joseph S. Nye
(Glenview, IL: Pearson Education, Inc.). Copyright © 1989 by Robert O. Keohane
and Joseph S. Nye, pp. 23–25; 29–37.

type, the opposite of realism. We call it *complex interdependence*. After establishing the differences between realism and complex interdependence, we shall argue that complex interdependence sometimes comes closer to reality than does realism. When it does, traditional explanations of change in international regimes become questionable and the search for new explanatory models becomes more urgent.

For political realists, international politics, like all other politics, is a struggle for power but, unlike domestic politics, a struggle dominated by organized violence. . . . Three assumptions are integral to the realist vision. First, states as coherent units are the dominant actors in world politics. This is a double assumption: states are predominant; and they act as coherent units. Second, realists assume that force is a usable and effective instrument of policy. Other instruments may also be employed, but using or threatening force is the most effective means of wielding power. Third, partly because of their second assumption, realists assume a hierarchy of issues in world politics, headed by questions of military security: the "high politics" of military security dominates the "low politics" of economic and social affairs.

These realist assumptions define an ideal type of world politics. They allow us to imagine a world in which politics is continually characterized by active or potential conflict among states, with the use of force possible at any time. Each state attempts to defend its territory and interests from real or perceived threats. Political integration among states is slight and lasts only as long as it serves the national interests of the most powerful states. Transnational actors either do not exist or are politically unimportant. Only the adept exercise of force or the threat of force permits states to survive, and only while statesmen succeed in adjusting their interests, as in a well-functioning balance of power, is the system stable.

Each of the realist assumptions can be challenged. If we challenge them all simultaneously, we can imagine a world in which actors other than states participate directly in world politics, in which a clear hierarchy of issues does not exist, and in which force is an ineffective instrument of policy. Under these conditions—which we call the characteristics of complex interdependence—one would expect world politics to be very different than under realist conditions.

The Characteristics of Complex Interdependence

Complex interdependence has three main characteristics:

1. *Multiple channels* connect societies, including: informal ties between governmental elites as well as formal foreign office arrangements; informal ties among nongovernmental elites (face-to-face and through telecommunications); and transnational organizations (such as multination-

al banks or corporations). These channels can be summarized as interstate, transgovernmental, and transnational relations. *Interstate* relations are the normal channels assumed by realists. *Transgovernmental* applies when we relax the realist assumption that states act coherently as units; *transnational* applies when we relax the assumption that states are the only units.

2. The agenda of interstate relationships consists of multiple issues that are not arranged in a clear or consistent hierarchy. This *absence of hierarchy among issues* means, among other things, that military security does not consistently dominate the agenda. Many issues arise from what used to be considered domestic policy, and the distinction between domestic and foreign issues becomes blurred. These issues are considered in several government departments (not just foreign offices), and at several levels. Inadequate policy coordination on these issues involves significant costs. Different issues generate different coalitions, both within governments and across them, and involve different degrees of conflict. Politics does not stop at the waters' edge.

3. Military force is not used by governments toward other governments within the region, or on the issues, when complex interdependence prevails. It may, however, be important in these governments' relations with governments outside that region, or on other issues. Military force could, for instance, be irrelevant to resolving disagreements on economic issues among members of an alliance, yet at the same time be very important for that alliance's political and military relations with a rival bloc. For the former relationships this condition of complex interdependence would be met; for the latter, it would not.

Traditional theories of international politics implicitly or explicitly deny the accuracy of these three assumptions. Traditionalists are therefore tempted also to deny the relevance of criticisms based on the complex interdependence ideal type. We believe, however, that our three conditions are fairly well approximated on some global issues of economic and ecological interdependence and that they come close to characterizing the entire relationship between some countries. One of our purposes here is to prove that contention. In [*Power and Interdependence: World Politics in Transition* we] examine complex interdependence in oceans policy and monetary policy and in the relationships of the United States to Canada and Australia. In this chapter, however, we shall try to convince you to take these criticisms of traditional assumptions seriously. . . .

The Political Processes of Complex Interdependence

The three main characteristics of complex interdependence give rise to distinctive political processes, which translate power resources into power as control of outcomes. As we argued earlier, something is usually lost or added in the translation. Under conditions of complex interdependence the translation will be different than under realist conditions, and our predictions about outcomes will need to be adjusted accordingly.

In the realist world, military security will be the dominant goal of states. It will even affect issues that are not directly involved with military power or territorial defense. Nonmilitary problems will not only be subordinated to military ones; they will be studied for their politico-military implications. Balance of payments issues, for instance, will be considered at least as much in the light of their implications for world power generally as for their purely financial ramifications. . . .

In a world of complex interdependence, however, one expects some officials, particularly at lower levels, to emphasize the *variety* of state goals that must be pursued. In the absence of a clear hierarchy of issues, goals will vary by issue, and may not be closely related. Each bureaucracy will pursue its own concerns; and although several agencies may reach compromises on issues that affect them all, they will find that a consistent pattern of policy is difficult to maintain. Moreover, transnational actors will introduce different goals into various groups of issues.

Linkage Strategies

Goals will therefore vary by issue area under complex interdependence, but so will the distribution of power and the typical political processes. Traditional analysis focuses on the international system, and leads us to anticipate similar political processes on a variety of issues. Militarily and economically strong states will dominate a variety of organizations and a variety of issues, by linking their own policies on some issues to other states' policies on other issues. By using their overall dominance to prevail on their weak issues, the strongest states will, in the traditional model, ensure a congruence between the overall structure of military and economic power and the pattern of outcomes on any one issue area. Thus world politics can be treated as a seamless web.

Under complex interdependence, such congruence is less likely to occur. As military force is devalued, militarily strong states will find it more difficult to use their overall dominance to control outcomes on issues in which they are weak. And since the distribution of power resources in trade, shipping, or oil, for example, may be quite different, patterns of outcomes and distinctive political processes are likely to vary from one set of issues to another. If force were readily applicable, and military security were the highest foreign policy goal, these variations in the issue structures of power would not matter very much. The linkages drawn from them to military issues would ensure consistent dominance by the overall strongest states. But when military force is largely immobilized, strong states will find that linkage is less effective. They may still attempt such links, but in the absence of a hierarchy of issues, their success will be problematic.

Dominant states may try to secure much the same result by using over-all economic power to affect results on other issues. If only economic objectives are at stake, they may succeed: money, after all, is fungible. But economic objectives have political implications, and economic linkage by the strong is limited by domestic, transnational, and transgovernmental actors who resist having their interests traded off. Furthermore, the international actors may be different on different issues, and the international organizations in which negotiations take place are often quite separate. Thus it is difficult, for example, to imagine a militarily or economically strong state linking concessions on monetary policy to reciprocal concessions in oceans policy. On the other hand, poor weak states are not similarly inhibited from linking unrelated issues, partly because their domestic interests are less complex. Linkage of unrelated issues is often a means of extracting concessions or side payments from rich and powerful states. And unlike powerful states whose instrument for linkage (military force) is often too costly to use, the linkage instrument used by poor, weak states—international organization—is available and inexpensive.

Thus as the utility of force declines, and as issues become more equal in importance, the distribution of power within each issue will become more important. If linkages become less effective on the whole, outcomes of political bargaining will increasingly vary by issue area.

The differentiation among issue areas in complex interdependence means that linkages among issues will become more problematic and will tend to reduce rather than reinforce international hierarchy. Linkage strategies, and defense against them, will pose critical strategic choices for states. Should issues be considered separately or as a package? If linkages are to be drawn, which issues should be linked, and on which of the linked issues should concessions be made? How far can one push a linkage before it becomes counterproductive? For instance, should one seek formal agreements or informal, but less politically sensitive, understandings? The fact that world politics under complex interdependence is not a seamless web leads us to expect that efforts to stitch seams together advantageously, as reflected in linkage strategies, will, very often, determine the shape of the fabric.

Agenda Setting

Our second assumption of complex interdependence, the lack of clear hierarchy among multiple issues, leads us to expect that the politics of agenda formation and control will become more important. Traditional analyses lead statesmen to focus on politico-military issues and to pay little attention to the broader politics of agenda formation. Statesmen assume that the agenda will be set by shifts in the balance of power, actual or anticipated, and by perceived threats to the security of states. Other issues will only be very important when they seem to affect security and military power. In these cases, agendas will be influenced strongly by considerations of the overall balance of power.

Yet, today, some nonmilitary issues are emphasized in interstate relations at one time, whereas others of seemingly equal importance are neglected or quietly handled at a technical level. International monetary politics, problems of commodity terms of trade, oil, food, and multinational corporations have all been important during the last decade; but not all have been high on interstate agendas throughout that period.

Traditional analysts of international politics have paid little attention to agenda formation: to how issues come to receive sustained attention by high officials. The traditional orientation toward military and security affairs implies that the crucial problems of foreign policy are imposed on states by the actions or threats of other states. These are high politics as opposed to the low politics of economic affairs. Yet, as the complexity of actors and issues in world politics increases, the utility of force declines and the line between domestic policy and foreign policy becomes blurred: as the conditions of complex interdependence are more closely approximated, the politics of agenda formation becomes more subtle and differentiated.

Under complex interdependence we can expect the agenda to be affected by the international and domestic problems created by economic growth and increasing sensitivity interdependence. . . . Discontented domestic groups will politicize issues and force more issues once considered domestic onto the interstate agenda. Shifts in the distribution of power resources within sets of issues will also affect agendas. During the early 1970s the increased power of oil-producing governments over the transnational corporations and the consumer countries dramatically altered the policy agenda. Moreover, agendas for one group of issues may change as a result of linkages from other groups in which power resources are changing; for example, the broader agenda of North-South trade issues changed after the OPEC price rises and the oil embargo of 1973–74. Even if capabilities among states do not change, agendas may be affected by shifts in the importance of transnational actors. The publicity surrounding multinational corporations in the early 1970s, coupled with their rapid growth over the past twenty years, put the regulation of such corporations higher on both the United Nations agenda and national agendas.

Transnational and Transgovernmental Relations

Our third condition of complex interdependence, multiple channels of contact among societies, further blurs the distinction between domestic and international politics. The availability of partners in political coalitions is not necessarily limited by national boundaries as traditional analysis assumes. The nearer a situation is to complex interdependence, the more we expect the outcomes of political bargaining to be affected by transnational relations. Multinational corporations may be significant both as independent actors and as instruments manipulated by governments. The attitudes and policy stands of domestic groups are likely to be affected by communications, organized or not, between them and their counterparts abroad.

Thus the existence of multiple channels of contact leads us to expect limits, beyond those normally found in domestic politics, on the ability of statesmen to calculate the manipulation of interdependence or follow a consistent strategy of linkage. Statesmen must consider differential as well as aggregate effects of interdependence strategies and their likely implications for politicization and agenda control. Transactions among societies—economic and social transactions more than security ones—affect groups differently. Opportunities and costs from increased transnational ties may be greater for certain groups—for instance, American workers in the textile or shoe industries—than for others. Some organizations or groups may interact directly with actors in other societies or with other governments to increase their benefits from a network of interaction. Some actors may therefore be less vulnerable as well as less sensitive to changes elsewhere in the network than are others, and this will affect patterns of political action.

The multiple channels of contact found in complex interdependence are not limited to nongovernmental actors. Contacts between governmental bureaucracies charged with similar tasks may not only alter their perspectives but lead to transgovernmental coalitions on particular policy questions. To improve their chances of success, government agencies attempt to bring actors from other governments into their own decision-making processes as allies. Agencies of powerful states such as the United States have used such coalitions to penetrate weaker governments in such countries as Turkey and Chile. They have also been used to help agencies of other governments penetrate the United States bureaucracy.[1] . . .

The existence of transgovernmental policy networks leads to a different interpretation of one of the standard propositions about international politics—that states act in their own interest. Under complex interdependence, this conventional wisdom begs two important questions: which self and which interest? A government agency may pursue its own interests under the guise of the national interest; and recurrent interactions can change official perceptions of their interests. . . .

The ambiguity of the national interest raises serious problems for the top political leaders of governments. As bureaucracies contact each other directly across national borders (without going through foreign offices), centralized control becomes more difficult. There is less assurance that the state will be united when dealing with foreign governments or that its components will interpret national interests similarly when negotiating with foreigners. The state may prove to be multifaceted, even schizophrenic. National interests will be defined differently on different issues, at different times, and by different governmental units. States that are better placed to maintain their coherence (because of a centralized political tradition such as France's) will be better able to manipulate uneven interdependence than fragmented states that at first glance seem to have more resources in an issue area.

Role of International Organizations

Finally, the existence of multiple channels leads one to predict a different and significant role for international organizations in world politics. Realists in the tradition of Hans J. Morgenthau have portrayed a world in which states, acting from self-interest, struggle for "power and peace." Security issues are dominant; war threatens. In such a world, one may assume that international institutions will have a minor role, limited by the rare congruence of such interests. International organizations are then clearly peripheral to world politics. But in a world of multiple issues imperfectly linked, in which coalitions are formed transnationally and transgovernmentally, the potential role of international institutions in political bargaining is greatly increased. In particular, they help set the international agenda, and act as catalysts for coalition-formation and as arenas for political initiatives and linkage by weak states.

Governments must organize themselves to cope with the flow of business generated by international organizations. By defining the salient issues, and deciding which issues can be grouped together, organizations may help to determine governmental priorities and the nature of interdepartmental committees and other arrangements within governments. The 1972 Stockholm Environment Conference strengthened the position of environmental agencies in various governments. The 1974 World Food Conference focused the attention of important parts of the United States government on prevention of food shortages. The September 1975 United Nations special session on proposals for a New International Economic Order generated an intragovernmental debate about policies toward the Third World in general. The International Monetary Fund and the General Agreement on Tariffs and Trade have focused governmental activity on money and trade instead of on

**Table 4.1   Political Processes Under Conditions of Realism and Complex
Interdependence**

	Realism	Complex Interdependence
Goals of actors	Military security will be the dominant goal.	Goals of states will vary by issue area. Transgovernmental politics will make goals difficult to define. Transnational actors will pursue their own goals.
Instruments of state policy	Military force will be most effective, although economic and other instruments will also be used.	Power resources specific to issue areas will be most relevant. Manipulation of interdependence, international organizations, and transnational actors will be major instruments.
Agenda formation	Potential shifts in the balance of power and security threats will set the agenda in high politics and will strongly influence other agendas.	Agenda will be affected by changes in the distribution of power resources within issue areas; the status of international regimes; changes in the importance of transnational actors; linkages from other issues and politicization as a result of rising sensitivity interdependence.
Linkages of issues	Linkages will reduce differences in outcomes among issue areas and reinforce international hierarchy.	Linkages by strong states will be more difficult to make since force will be ineffective. Linkages by weak states through international organizations will erode rather than reinforce hierarchy.
Roles of international organizations	Roles are minor, limited by state power and the importance of military force.	Organizations will set agendas, induce coalition-formation, and act as arenas for political action by weak states. Ability to choose the organizational forum for an issue and to mobilize votes will be an important political resource.

private direct investment, which has no comparable international organization.

By bringing officials together, international organizations help to activate potential coalitions in world politics. It is quite obvious that international organizations have been very important in bringing together representatives of less developed countries, most of which do not maintain embassies in one another's capitals. Third World strategies of solidarity among poor countries have been developed in and for a series of international conferences, mostly under the auspices of the United Nations.[2] International organizations also allow agencies of governments, which might not otherwise come into contact, to turn potential or tacit coalitions into explicit transgovernmental coalitions characterized by direct communications. In some cases, international secretariats deliberately promote this process by forming coalitions with groups of governments, or with units of governments, as well as with nongovernmental organizations having similar interests.[3]

International organizations are frequently congenial institutions for weak states. The one-state-one-vote norm of the United Nations system favors coalitions of the small and powerless. Secretariats are often responsive to Third World demands. Furthermore, the substantive norms of most international organizations, as they have developed over the years, stress social and economic equity as well as the equality of states. Past resolutions expressing Third World positions, sometimes agreed to with reservations by industrialized countries, are used to legitimize other demands. These agreements are rarely binding, but up to a point the norms of the institution make opposition look more harshly self-interested and less defensible. . . .

Complex interdependence therefore yields different political patterns than does the realist conception of the world. (Table 4.1 summarizes these differences.) Thus, one would expect traditional theories to fail to explain international regime change in situations of complex interdependence. But, for a situation that approximates realist conditions, traditional theories should be appropriate. . . .

Notes

1. For a more detailed discussion, see Robert O. Keohane and Joseph S. Nye, Jr., "Transgovernmental Relations and International Organizations," *World Politics* 27, no. 1 (October 1974): 39–62.

2. Branislav Gosovic and John Gerard Ruggie, "On the Creation of a New International Economic Order: Issue Linkage and the Seventh Special Session of the UN General Assembly," *International Organization* 30, no. 2 (Spring 1976): 309–46.

3. Robert W. Cox, "The Executive Head," *International Organization* 23, no. 2 (Spring 1969): 205–30.

5

The Invisible Hand vs. the Dead Hand

Brink Lindsey

Responding to charges that unrestrained market activity is to blame for many of today's economic and social problems, Brink Lindsey presents a forceful defense of the liberal IPE perspective. From his point of view, instability in the global economy and attendant suffering is due not to unchecked markets but to a larger global struggle between a failed ideology of "top-down control and central planning" and forces promoting a reinvigoration of market activity. Lindsey's contribution provides a strong defense of markets, which becomes a useful point of comparison and debate with other contributors to this volume, notably Robert Went and Samir Amin.

In the world economy today there are signs of struggle: financial crises in Asia, Russia, and Latin America; chronic double-digit unemployment in Europe; slowing growth in China; and slow-motion collapse in Japan. But what is the nature of the struggle?

Critics of economic liberalization believe that the world is in the grip of unrestrained market forces, and that those forces must be subdued if order is to be restored. They are profoundly wrong. It is not the invisible hand of market competition that the world is straining against, but the dead hand of a failed statist past—a past whose animating spirit is gone but whose malignant influence continues to weigh down on us.

Reprinted with permission of the publisher of *Global Fortune: The Stumble and Rise of Capitalism,* edited by Ian Vasquez. Washington, D.C.: The Cato Institute, 2000, pp. 43–53.

Polanyi's Disciples

To understand the historical context of the present situation, it is useful to review the arguments of those who claim that the present struggle represents a crisis of unrestrained capitalism. These arguments are illuminating in their almost perfect inversion of the truth.

In recent years critics of free markets from across the ideological spectrum have charged that "globalization"—the growing internationalization of market relations—is out of control. They claim that the various currency crashes of this decade bear witness to the inherent instability of markets. Meanwhile, in the rich industrialized countries, the pressures of unrestricted international competition are allegedly causing unemployment, dragging down living standards, and eroding hard-won social protections. A blind faith in laissez faire is to blame for these troubling developments, they say; governments must reassert control or catastrophe will ensue.

Pat Buchanan typifies this point of view when he denounces the dogmatic attachment to markets that supposedly holds sway at present: "What is wrong with the Global Economy is what is wrong with our politics," he contends; "It is rooted in the myth of Economic Man. It elevates economics above all else (Buchanan 1998: 287)."

"To worship the market," Buchanan argues, "is a form of idolatry no less than worshiping the state. The market should be made to work for man, not the other way around. 'What is the market? It is the law of the jungle, the law of nature. And what is civilization? It is the struggle against nature.' So declared France's Prime Minister Edouard Balladur at the close of the GATT negotiations in 1993; he is right" (Buchanan 1998:288).

If it is odd to hear "America Firster" Buchanan make common cause with a Frenchman, it is perhaps even stranger to hear a financier trash the markets in which he has made billions. But that is what George Soros does: "Financial markets are inherently unstable and there are social needs that cannot be met by giving market forces free rein. Unfortunately these defects are not recognized. Instead there is a widespread belief that markets are self-correcting and a global economy can flourish without any need for a global society . . . This idea was called laissez faire in the nineteenth century, but . . . I have found a better name for it: market fundamentalism" (Soros 1998: xx).

"[M]arket fundamentalism," Soros concludes in what even he concedes is a "shocking" contention, "is today a greater threat to open society than any totalitarian ideology" (Soros 1998: xxi).

Some of the critics of globalization cite historical parallels with the aborted world economy of the early 20th century. The internationalization of economic life at that time rivaled and in some respects exceeded our present situation, only to be swallowed up by the cataclysms of world war, depression, and totalitarianism. Capitalism self-destructed then allegedly because of its unregulated volatility and brutality; it was saved only when governments tamed its energies to the service of social goals. The utopian faith in self-regulating markets thus supposedly brought ruin in the past, and again threatens ruin today.

Left-wing journalist William Greider adopts this line in his book *One World, Ready or Not.*

> The gravest danger I perceive at this moment is the understandable inclination of people and societies to . . . replay the terrible conflicts of the twentieth century. . . .
> Assuming that the global economic system is not redirected toward a more moderate course, these weary political and class conflicts are sure to ripen, leading toward the same stalemate between markets and society in which fascism arose and flourished nearly a hundred years ago (Greider 1997: 309).

This last twist represents a revival of the historical analysis of Karl Polanyi, author of the 1944 book *The Great Transformation.* Polanyi argued that the catastrophes of his time could ultimately be traced back to the evils of laissez faire. "[T]he origins of the cataclysm," he wrote, "lay in the utopian endeavor of economic liberalism to set up a self-regulating market system" (Polanyi 1957: 29).

Here Polanyi elaborates:

> [T]he idea of a self-adjusting market implied a stark utopia. Such an institution could not exist for any length of time without annihilating the human and natural substance of society; it would have physically destroyed man and transformed his surroundings into a wilderness. Inevitably, society took measures to protect itself, but whatever measures it took impaired the self-regulation of the market, disorganized industrial life, and thus endangered society in yet another way. It was this dilemma which forced the development of the market system into a definite groove and finally disrupted the social organization based upon it (Polanyi 1957: 3).

The conflict between "society" and the market ultimately gave rise, in Polanyi's view, to totalitarianism: "The fascist solution of the *impasse* reached by liberal capitalism can be described as a reform of market economy achieved at the price of the extirpation of all democratic institutions, both in the industrial and the political realm" (Polanyi 1957: 237).

Karl Polanyi has been rescued from well-deserved obscurity to become a kind of patron saint of global capitalism's current critics. His influence is cited explicitly by both Greider and Soros; Dani Rodrik (1997) of Harvard University and author of *Has Globalization Gone Too Far?* refers to him frequently; as does John Gray (1998), a professor at the London School of Economics, who wrote *False Dawn: The Delusions of Global Capitalism.*

The Industrial Counterrevolution

Polanyi's analysis and its reappearance today turn history on its head. The destruction of the first global economy stemmed not from overreliance on markets, but from a pervasive loss of faith in them.

The spectacular wealth creation of the Industrial Revolution, made possible by the decentralized trial and error of market competition, was widely misinterpreted at the time and afterward as a triumph of top-down control and central planning. People believed that the new giant industrial enterprises demonstrated the superiority of consolidation and technocratic control over the haphazard wastefulness of market competition. They concluded that the logic of industrialization compelled an extension of the top-down rationality of the factory to the whole of society—in other words, social engineering.[1]

This tragic error gave rise to a social phenomenon that may be described as the Industrial Counterrevolution—an assault on the principles that brought modern technological society into being. This reactionary movement was far broader than any one ideology—it encompassed the "one best way" of "scientific management"; the cartelization of the "associative state"; the welfare state; the developmental "catch-up" state; and at the extreme, the totalitarian state.

The belief in technocratic control—and especially in vesting that control in the state—gained momentum steadily from around 1880 onward. Aside from the damage it wrought within national boundaries, its fundamental incompatibility with the liberal international order that developed during the 19th century meant that one of them had to give way. It was the latter that yielded: as societies closed, so did borders.

The great catastrophe from which the first world economy never recovered was World War I. But the roots of that carnage lay in the rise of economic nationalism and its international projection through imperialism. The free-trade order presided over by Great Britain fell on the defensive as the "newly industrializing countries" of the late 19th century—the United States, Germany, and Russia—were all explicitly protectionist. The spreading belief in zero-sum economic conflict among nations was strengthened by the combination of colonial land-grabs and systems of imperial trade preferences. The arms races and deepening antagonisms of the prewar period made sense only in a world in which political control over territory was necessary to gain access to its raw materials and markets.[2]

After the war, attempts were made to rebuild the old system; but the economic shock waves of inflation and debt that reverberated after the war, and the new political realities of social democracy and totalitarianism, rendered a return to antebellum stability impossible. Finally, the Great Depression and the protectionist spasms it provoked rang the death knell for the old liberal order. Indeed, for a dark time it appeared that any future international order would be totalitarian.

It is utterly preposterous to attribute this collapse, as did Polanyi and do his followers, to excessive faith in market competition. Throughout this period all the intellectual momentum was running in the opposite, collectivist direction. Polanyi's bogeyman—the minimal-state ideal of laissez faire—was so defunct as to be virtually without prominent adherents, much less practical influence over the course of events.

Twilight of the Idols

In the years after World War II there was a partial move back toward a liberal international order through the Bretton Woods system and tariff reductions under the General Agreement on Tariffs and Trade. But much of the world remained outside this reborn international economy: the Communist nations and most of the so-called Third World pursued economic policies of autarky and isolation. For the bulk of the world's population, the ascendancy of the Industrial Counterrevolution continued to squelch any significant participation in an international division of labor.

Only in the past couple of decades has the counterrevolutionary momentum exhausted itself in failure and collapse.[3] And as overweening state control has receded—with the opening of China, the dissolution of the Soviet bloc, and the abandonment by many developing countries of "import substitution"—market connections have been reestablished. So although globalization is charged with undermining the state, the more powerful flows of historical causation have actually been in the opposite direction: it is the retreat of the state that has allowed international market relationships to regain a foothold.

This is a point that bears some emphasis. The unprecedented degree of international economic integration that the world enjoys today is certainly attributable in part to steadily falling transportation costs, and a spectacular fall in the costs of processing and communicating information. But there would be no *global* economy today except that large parts of the globe decided to abandon economic policies of self-imposed isolation from international commerce. And this policy shift has been part of a much broader movement away from centralized state control in favor of the decentralized experimentation of the liberal market system.

In other words, the reunited world economy must be understood fundamentally as a *political* event: in particular, as a consequence of the death and repudiation of the old counterrevolutionary ideal of top-down planning. Critics of globalization portray the spread of markets as the impingement of blind economic forces upon otherwise functional policies. In fact, the dramatic changes in economic policy that have swept through the communist and Third Worlds over the past 20 years, of which one important element has been reintegration into the international economy, have been driven primarily by the recognition on the part of national political leaders that their state-dominated systems had failed—failed in absolute terms as billions of people remained mired in grinding poverty, and failed in relative terms by comparison with the prosperous West and the relatively open and thriving Pacific Rim.

Meanwhile, over the same period, the failures of interventionism have prompted a wave of economic reforms in the industrialized democracies as well. Tax cuts, privatizations, elimination of price and entry controls, and perhaps, most important, the repudiation of inflationary monetary policy—these steps in the direction of liberalization became politically possible only after the stagflation of the 1970s discredited the "mixed economy" and macroeconomic "fine tuning."

Thus, the reemergence of a global economy occurred at the same time as, and as one consequence of, a global disillusionment with top-down control and central planning. The critics of globalization thus get the temper of the times all wrong when they condemn the present era as one of market "idolatry" and dogmatic enthusiasm. This is a time of idol-smashing, not of setting up new gods.

Yes, Ronald Reagan and Margaret Thatcher were vigorous and eloquent spokespersons for free markets and limited government, though their rhetoric far outdistanced their accomplishments. But as ideological reformers they stand more or less alone. Nobody has done more to liberate more people than Deng Xiaoping—an ardent communist and veteran of the Long March. Mikhail Gorbachev, a loyal Leninist, inadvertently toppled the Soviet Empire. Argentina has rediscovered liberalism under Carlos Menem, a Peronist. New Zealand went from one of the most protectionist to one of the most open economies in the world under a Labor government. And so on and so on—around the world, pragmatism, not ideological zeal, has been the guiding spirit of liberalization.

Global Battle Lines

But this pragmatic process of unraveling state controls still has a long, long way to go. Although the belief in central planning has lost its utopian fire, its effects are still very much with us. Both friends and enemies of globalization have made breathless pronouncements about the unrestrained ascendancy of market forces in today's world economy, but such hype cannot bear scrutiny. The Industrial Counterrevolution may have expired as a living faith, but the dead hand of its accumulated institutions, mindsets, and vested interests still imposes a heavy and disfiguring burden.

Our present world situation, then, is far removed from the unchallenged triumph of markets that Buchanan, Soros, Greider et al. complain about. Rather, we live in the midst of an ongoing and uncertain struggle between the revitalization of markets on the one hand and the dead hand of top-down control on the other. Call it the invisible hand versus the dead hand. That struggle strains and distorts market and social development, and gives rise to occasional, crippling instability. Globalization is as a consequence an uncertain and uneven process, and subject to sudden and traumatic reverses and dislocations. Critics of globalization blame the distortions and volatility on free markets run amok; in fact, however, these problems are overwhelmingly due to the continuing bulking presence of anti-market policies and institutions.

Please note that this struggle cannot be reduced to a conflict between government *per se* and markets; it is not simply an issue of governments doing too much or too little. The problem is that governments are simultaneously doing too much *and* too little. By diverting so much of their attention to preempting and controlling voluntary, private activity, governments have often failed to do the necessary work of building and fostering the institutions within which voluntary, private activity can flourish.

The exact nature of the conflict between markets and the dead hand differs from country to country. Still, it is possible to identify certain broad battle lines. Together, they define the critical challenges facing the emerging world economy today.

The Monetary Trilemma

Critics of free markets blame the recent financial crises in Asia and Latin America on unregulated capital movements. This charge is partly true, in that the crises could not have occurred if capital flows had not been liberalized. But the whole story is that currency crashes happen when governments abuse their access to international capital markets by pursuing unsustainable monetary policies.

There are three desiderata of international monetary policy: free currency convertibility to ensure full access to global investment capital and opportunities; flexibility to respond to macroeconomic shocks; and stable exchange value to promote certainty and transparency in international transactions. Unfortunately, no monetary regime can pursue more than two out of three of these worthy objectives at any given time. Free capital flows and monetary flexibility come at the expense of exchange rate stability; free capital flows and exchange rate stability come at the expense of monetary flexibility; exchange rate stability and monetary flexibility come at the expense of free capital flows. In short, a country must either let its currency float, or fix it and abandon independent monetary policy, or else withdraw from full integration into the international economy (Krugman).

Currency crises happen when monetary authorities try to have their cake and eat it too—by pegging their rates but still pursuing an independent monetary policy. These currency crises have been wreaking havoc in the world economy over the past few years—up and down the Pacific Rim, in Russia, and then in Brazil. Each and every time, the explosion occurred because of an unsustainable overburdening of monetary policy.

Economic Gangrene

Commercial failure is an essential if unpleasant part of the market process. It allows poorly used resources to be redirected to more productive pursuits, and it signals to other enterprises what mistakes to avoid. When economic institutions do not recognize and respond to failure, growth and vitality can be undermined by a buildup of rot in the system. Specifically, unresolved bad debts and chronically loss-making state-owned enterprises plague today's world economy and threaten traumatic collapse and dislocation when the burden of necrosis becomes unbearable. For example, bad debt is at the root of Japan's economic malaise, while a wealth-destroying state-owned sector imperils China's continued rapid growth.

Hollow Capitalism

At the core of the capitalist market order are the institutions that direct the flow of capital from savers to investors. Around the world, those institutions are to a greater or lesser extent characterized by overcentralization and perverse incentives. Direct state intervention and politicized banking industries too often dominate capital allocation, while the legal structures that allow decentralized access to capital through bond and equity markets are underdeveloped or suppressed.

The problem is especially acute in the post-communist and developing world; in particular, even the most successful developing countries have achieved at most a kind of hollow capitalism, where state-directed mimicry of Western industrial development substitutes poorly for market-signaled investment. Anti-market policies afflict the financial systems of advanced countries as well—witness the U.S. savings and loan disaster and the flagging returns on capital in the bank-dominated systems of Europe and Japan. Wherever market-driven finance is frustrated, malinvestment and underperformance are the universal result.

The Rule of Lawlessness

An even more fundamental deformity in developing and transition economies is the failure of governments to provide reliable security for property and contract rights. This failure stems partially from corruption, partially from sheer fecklessness. Without stability and congruence in expectations regarding the present and future disposition of property, the ability to make long-term investments and construct intricate divisions of labor is seriously undermined. In addition to throttling domestic entrepreneurial initiative and discouraging foreign investment, the absence of a reliable rule of law can lead to horrendous environmental despoliation as resources of uncertain ownership are ruthlessly plundered.

Strangulation by Safety Net

However well-intentioned, policies to protect individuals from economic hardship too often backfire because of the perverse incentives they create. Nowhere is this more evident today than in Europe, where rigidities in the labor market and overindulgent welfare policies have resulted in chronic double-digit unemployment. In the United States, welfare policies have fostered the social pathologies of the inner cities, although now reform efforts give some cause for hope of improvement. Around the world, pay-as-you-go public pension systems rob the world of a massive pool of savings, while over the longer term their demographic inviability threatens fiscal breakdown.

Liberalization by Fits and Starts

What is the outlook for the ongoing struggle between the invisible hand and the dead hand? Will liberalization continue to gain ground? Or have the past couple of decades of worldwide reform been a kind of Prague spring, to be crushed sooner or later by a reassertion of anti-market policies—in the form of capital controls, protectionism, renationalizations, and the like?

By characterizing the anti-market forces as the dead hand, I have already given some clue as to my answer: I believe that the long-term advantage lies with the liberal cause. Since the collectivist, top-down ideal is moribund, there is at present only one viable model of economic development—the liberal model of markets and competition. Consequently, the ongoing struggle is not one between rival ideologies, but between what is and what works. Those terms of battle consign defenders of the dead hand to a perpetual rear-guard action.

Vested interests and sheer inertia will render existing dirigiste policies difficult to dislodge—there will be few easy victories. But as dysfunctional controls and restrictions cause acute crises and breakdowns or chronic underperformance relative to more open countries, national political leaders will find themselves recurrently under extreme pressure to act. When such points are reached, they must move either toward liberalization or toward ever more heavy-handed interventionism. The current intellectual climate strongly favors the former alternative.

The economic crises of the past couple of years illustrate this dynamic.

For the most part economic collapse has accelerated the process of pro-market reform. There have been exceptions—Russia, certainly, and to a lesser extent Malaysia—but by and large the dominant political response in the crisis-affected countries has been in a liberal direction. What real choice is there?

There is little cause, however, for liberal triumphalism. So-called reforms will all too often turn out to be weak half-measures, debilitated by political compromise. At the same time, the sheer poverty and backwardness of most of the world affords enormous opportunities for higher-than-Western catchup growth rates even when public policies are far from optimal. The ongoing availability of catchup growth, and the legitimacy it confers upon even deeply flawed policies, will weaken the incentives for thoroughgoing reform.

Liberalization's advances, then, will come in fits and starts. Crisis, reform, euphoria, disillusionment, and crisis and reform again—such is the dialectic of the invisible hand against the dead hand.

Notes

1. For an interesting examination of the rise of this idea in American history, see Jordan (1994).

2. "While under free trade and freedom of migration, no individual is concerned about the territorial size of his country, under the protective measures of economic nationalism nearly every citizen has a substantial interest in these territorial issues. The enlargement of the territory subject to the sovereignty of his own government means material improvement for him or at least relief from restrictions which a foreign government has imposed upon his well-being" (von Mises 1949: 824).

3. A number of recent books do a good job of narrating the worldwide sputtering of the Industrial Counterrevolution. See, for example, Skidelsky (1995), Yergin and Stanislaw (1998), and Henderson (1998).

References

Buchanan, Patrick J. 1998. *The Great Betrayal: How American Sovereignty and Social Justice Are Being Sacrificed to the Gods of the Global Economy.* Boston: Little, Brown and Company.

Gray, John. 1998. *False Dawn: The Delusions of Global Capitalism.* New York: The New Press.

Greider, William. 1997. *One World, Ready or Not: The Manic Logic of Global Capitalism.* New York: Simon & Schuster.

Henderson, David. 1998. *The Changing Fortunes of Economic Liberalism: Yesterday, Today and Tomorrow.* London: The Institute of Economic Affairs.

Jordan, John M. 1994. *Machine-Age Ideology: Social Engineering and American Liberalism, 1911–1939.* Chapel Hill: The University of North Carolina Press.

Krugman, Paul. *The Eternal Triangle.* Accessed at http://web.mit.edu/krugman/www/triangle.html.

von Mises, Ludwig. 1949. *Human Action.* Chicago: Contemporary Books.

Polanyi, Karl. 1957. *The Great Transformation: The Political and Economic Origins of Our Time.* Boston: Beacon Press.

Rodrik, Dani. 1997. *Has Globalization Gone Too Far?* Washington: Institute for International Economics, 1997.

Skidelsky, Robert. 1995. *The Road from Serfdom: The Economic and Political Consequences of the End of Communism.* New York: Penguin Books.

Soros, George. 1998. *The Crisis of Global Capitalism.* New York: Public Affairs.

Yergin, Daniel, and Joseph Stanislaw. 1998. *The Commanding Heights: The Battle Between Government and the Market That Is Remaking the Modern World.* New York: Simon & Schuster.

6

The Rise of the Virtual State

Richard Rosecrance

In this chapter Richard Rosecrance provides a liberal interpretation of recent trends in the international political economy. His thesis is a provocative one—that land is no longer important for a state's production and power. Rosecrance contends that the increased mobility of capital, labor, and information has undermined traditional state rationales for acquiring land. Such changes require new state strategies for building national wealth and power. In today's world, competitive economies are based less on production and more on knowledge. At home, states should boost support for education and create an environment conducive to attracting foreign capital; abroad, states should be negotiating entities seeking to expand access to foreign markets.

Territory Becomes Passé

Amid the supposed clamor of contending cultures and civilizations, a new reality is emerging. The nation-state is becoming a tighter, more vigorous unit capable of sustaining the pressures of worldwide competition. Developed states are putting aside military, political, and territorial ambitions as they struggle not for cultural dominance but for a greater share of world output. Countries are not uniting as civilizations and girding for conflict with one another. Instead, they are downsizing—in function if not in geographic form. Today and for the foreseeable future, the only international civilization worthy of the name is the governing economic culture of the world market. Despite the view of some contemporary observers, the forces of globalization have successfully resisted partition into cultural camps.

Reprinted with permission of *Foreign Affairs*, volume 75, number 4. Copyright © 1996 by the Council on Foreign Relations, Inc.

Yet the world's attention continues to be mistakenly focused on military and political struggles for territory. In beleaguered Bosnia, Serbian leaders sought to create an independent province with an allegiance to Belgrade. A few years ago Iraqi leader Saddam Hussein aimed to corner the world oil market through military aggression against Kuwait and, in all probability, Saudi Arabia; oil, a product of land, represented the supreme embodiment of his ambitions. In Kashmir, India and Pakistan are vying for territorial dominance over a population that neither may be fully able to control. Similar rivalries beset Rwanda and Burundi and the factions in Liberia.

These examples, however, look to the past. Less developed countries, still producing goods that are derived from land, continue to covet territory. In economies where capital, labor, and information are mobile and have risen to predominance, no land fetish remains. Developed countries would rather plumb the world market than acquire territory. The virtual state—a state that has downsized its territorially based production capability—is the logical consequence of this emancipation from the land.

In recent years the rise of the economic analogue of the virtual state— the virtual corporation—has been widely discussed. Firms have discovered the advantages of locating their production facilities wherever it is most profitable. Increasingly, this is not in the same location as corporate headquarters. Parts of a corporation are dispersed globally according to their specialties. But the more important development is the political one, the rise of the virtual state, the political counterpart of the virtual corporation.

The ascent of the trading state preceded that of the virtual state. After World War II, led by Japan and Germany, the most advanced nations shifted their efforts from controlling territory to augmenting their share of world trade. In that period, goods were more mobile than capital or labor, and selling abroad became the name of the game. As capital has become increasingly mobile, advanced nations have come to recognize that exporting is no longer the only means to economic growth; one can instead produce goods overseas for the foreign market.

As more production by domestic industries takes place abroad and land becomes less valuable than technology, knowledge, and direct investment, the function of the state is being further redefined. The state no longer commands resources as it did in mercantilist yesteryear; it negotiates with foreign and domestic capital and labor to lure them into its own economic sphere and stimulate its growth. A nation's economic strategy is now at least as important as its military strategy; its ambassadors have become foreign trade and investment representatives. Major foreign trade and investment deals command executive attention as political and military issues did two decades ago. The frantic two weeks in December 1994 when the White House outmaneuvered the French to secure for Raytheon Company a deal worth over $1 billion for the management of rainforests and air traffic in Brazil exemplifies the new international crisis.

Timeworn methods of augmenting national power and wealth are no longer effective. Like the headquarters of a virtual corporation, the virtual state determines overall strategy and invests in its people rather than amassing expensive production capacity. It contracts out other functions to states that specialize in or need them. Imperial Great Britain may have been the model for the nineteenth century, but Hong Kong will be the model for the twenty-first.

The virtual state is a country whose economy is reliant on mobile factors of production. Of course it houses virtual corporations and presides over foreign direct investment by its enterprises. But more than this, it encourages, stimulates, and to a degree even coordinates such activities. In formulating economic strategy, the virtual state recognizes that its own production does not have to take place at home; equally, it may play host to the capital and labor of other nations. Unlike imperial Germany, czarist Russia, and the United States of the Gilded Age—which aimed at nineteenth-century omnicompetence—it does not seek to combine or excel in all economic functions, from mining and agriculture to production and distribution. The virtual state specializes in modern technical and research services and derives its income not just from high-value manufacturing, but from product design, marketing, and financing. The rationale for its economy is efficiency attained through productive downsizing. Size no longer determines economic potential. Virtual nations hold the competitive key to greater wealth in the twenty-first century. They will likely supersede the continent-sized and self-sufficient units that prevailed in the past. Productive specialization will dominate internationally just as the reduced instruction set, or "RISC," computer chip has outmoded its more versatile but slower predecessors.

The Trading State

In the past, states were obsessed with land. The international system with its intermittent wars was founded on the assumption that land was the major factor in both production and power. States could improve their position by building empires or invading other nations to seize territory. To acquire land was a boon: a conquered province contained peasants and grain supplies, and its inhabitants rendered tribute to the new sovereign. Before the age of nationalism, a captured principality willingly obeyed its new ruler. Hence the Hapsburg monarchy, Spain, France, and Russia could become major powers through territorial expansion in Europe between the sixteenth and nineteenth centuries.

With the Industrial Revolution, however, capital and labor assumed new importance. Unlike land, they were mobile ingredients of productive strength. Great Britain innovated in discovering sophisticated uses for the new factors. Natural resources—especially coal, iron, and, later, oil—were still economically vital. Agricultural and mineral resources were critical to the development of the United States and other fledgling industrial nations like Australia, Canada, South Africa, and New Zealand in the nineteenth century. Not until late in the twentieth century did mobile factors of production become paramount.

By that time, land had declined in relative value and become harder for nations to hold. Colonial revolutions in the Third World since World War II have shown that nationalist mobilization of the population in developing societies impedes an imperialist or invader trying to extract resources. A nation may expend the effort to occupy new territory without gaining proportionate economic benefits.

In time, nationalist resistance and the shift in the basis of production should have an impact on the frequency of war. Land, which is fixed, can be physically captured, but labor, capital, and information are mobile and cannot be definitively seized; after an attack, these resources can slip away like quicksilver. Saddam Hussein ransacked the computers in downtown Kuwait City in August 1990 only to find that the cash in bank accounts had already been electronically transferred. Even though it had abandoned its territory, the Kuwaiti government could continue to spend billions of dollars to resist Hussein's conquest.

Today, for the wealthiest industrial countries such as Germany, the United States, and Japan, investment in land no longer pays the same dividends. Since mid-century, commodity prices have fallen nearly 40 percent relative to prices of manufactured goods (Grilli and Yang 1988). The returns from the manufacturing trade greatly exceed those from agricultural exports. As a result, the terms of trade for many developing nations have been deteriorating, and in recent years the rise in prices of international services has outpaced that for manufactured products. Land prices have been steeply discounted.

Amid this decline, the 1970s and 1980s brought a new political prototype: the trading state. Rather than territorial expansion, the trading state held trade to be its fundamental purpose. This shift in national strategy was driven by the declining value of fixed productive assets. Smaller states—those for which, initially at any rate, a military-territorial strategy was not feasible—also adopted trade-oriented strategies. Along with small European and East Asian states, Japan and West Germany moved strongly in a trading direction after World War II.

Countries tend to imitate those that are most powerful. Many states followed in the wake of Great Britain in the nineteenth century; in recent decades, numerous states seeking to improve their lot in the world have emulated Japan. Under Mikhail Gorbachev in the 1980s, even the Soviet

Union sought to move away from its emphasis on military spending and territorial expansion.

In recent years, however, a further stimulus has hastened this change. Faced with enhanced international competition in the late 1980s and early 1990s, corporations have opted for pervasive downsizing. They have trimmed the ratio of production workers to output, saving on costs. In some cases productivity increases resulted from pruning of the work force; in others output increased. These improvements have been highly effective; according to economist Stephen Roach in a 1994 paper published by the investment banking firm Morgan Stanley, they have nearly closed the widely noted productivity gap between services and manufacturing. The gap that remains is most likely due to measurement problems. The most efficient corporations are those that can maintain or increase output with a steady or declining amount of labor. Such corporations grew on a worldwide basis.

Meanwhile, corporations in Silicon Valley recognized that cost-cutting, productivity, and competitiveness could be enhanced still further by using the production lines of another company. The typical American plant at the time, such as Ford Motor Company's Willow Run factory in Michigan, was fully integrated, with headquarters, design offices, production workers, and factories located on substantial tracts of land. This comprehensive structure was expensive to maintain and operate, hence a firm that could employ someone else's production line could cut costs dramatically. Land and machines did not have to be bought, labor did not have to be hired, medical benefits did not have to be provided. These advantages could result from what are called economies of scope, with a firm turning out different products on the same production line or quality circle.

Or they might be the result of small, specialized firms' ability to perform exacting operations, such as the surface mounting of miniaturized components directly on circuit boards without the need for soldering or conventional wiring. In either case, the original equipment manufacturer would contract out its production to other firms. SCI Systems, Solectron, Merix, Flextronics, Smartflex, and Sanmina turn out products for Digital Equipment, Hewlett-Packard, and IBM. In addition, AT&T, Apple, IBM, Motorola, MCI, and Corning meet part of their production needs through other suppliers. TelePad, a company that makes pen-based computers, was launched with no manufacturing capability at all. Compaq's latest midrange computer is to be produced on another company's production line.

Thus was born the virtual corporation, an entity with research, development, design, marketing, financing, legal, and other headquarters functions, but few or no manufacturing facilities: a company with a head but no body. It represents the ultimate achievement of corporate downsizing, and the model is spreading rapidly from firm to firm. It is not surprising that the virtual corporation should catch on. "Concept" or "head" corporations can design new products for a range of different production facilities. Strategic alliances between firms, which increase specialization, are also very profitable. According to the October 2, 1995, *Financial Times,* firms that actively pursue strategic alliances are 50 percent more profitable than those that do not.

Toward the Virtual State

In a setting where the economic functions of the trading state have displaced the territorial functions of the expansionist nation, the newly pruned corporation has led to the emerging phenomenon of the virtual state. Downsizing has become an index of corporate efficiency and productivity gains. Now the national economy is also being downsized. Among the most efficient economies are those that possess limited production capacity. The archetype is Hong Kong, whose production facilities are now largely situated in southern China. This arrangement may change after 1997 with Hong Kong's reversion to the mainland, but it may not. It is just as probable that Hong Kong will continue to govern parts of the mainland economically as it is that Beijing will dictate to Hong Kong politically. The one country–two systems formula will likely prevail. In this context, it is important to remember that Britain governed Hong Kong politically and legally for 150 years, but it did not dictate its economics. Nor did this arrangement prevent Hong Kong Chinese from extending economic and quasi-political controls to areas outside their country.

The model of the virtual state suggests that political as well as economic strategy push toward a downsizing and relocation of production capabilities. The trend can be observed in Singapore as well. The successors of Lee Kuan Yew keep the country on a tight political rein but still depend economically on the inflow of foreign factors of production. Singapore's investment in China, Malaysia, and elsewhere is within others' jurisdictions. The virtual state is in this sense a negotiating entity. It depends as much or more on economic access abroad as it does on economic control at home. Despite its past reliance on domestic production, Korea no longer manufactures everything at home, and Japanese production (given the high yen) is now increasingly lodged abroad. In Europe, Switzerland is the leading virtual nation; as much as 98 percent of Nestle's production capacity, for instance, is located abroad. Holland now produces most of its goods outside its borders. England is also moving in tandem with the worldwide trend; according to the Belgian economic historian Paul Bairoch in 1994, Britain's foreign direct investment abroad was almost as large as America's. A remarkable 20 percent of the production of U.S. corporations now takes place outside the United States.

A reflection of how far these tendencies have gone is the growing portion of GDP consisting of high-value-added services, such as concept, design, consulting, and financial services. Services already constitute 70 percent of American GDP. Of the total, 63 percent are in the high-value category. Of course manufacturing matters, but it matters much less than it once did. As a proportion of foreign direct investment, service exports have grown strikingly in most highly industrialized economies. According to a 1994 World Bank report, Liberalizing International Transactions in Services, "The reorientation of [foreign direct investment] towards the services sector has occurred in almost all developed market economies, the principal exporters of services capital: in the most important among them, the share of the services sector is around 40 percent of the stock of outward FDI, and that share is rising."

Manufacturing, for these nations, will continue to decline in importance. If services productivity increases as much as it has in recent years, it will greatly strengthen U.S. competitiveness abroad. But it can no longer be assumed that services face no international competition. Efficient high-value services will be as important to a nation as the manufacturing of automobiles and electrical equipment once were (Ripoll 1996). Since 1959, services prices have increased more than three times as rapidly as industrial prices. This means that many nations will be able to prosper without major manufacturing capabilities.

Australia is an interesting example. Still reliant on the production of sheep and raw materials (both related to land), Australia has little or no industrial sector. Its largest export to the United States is meat for hamburgers. On the other hand, its service industries of media, finance, and telecommunications—represented most notably by the media magnate Rupert Murdoch—are the envy of the world. Canada represents a similar amalgam of raw materials and powerful service industries in newspapers, broadcast media, and telecommunications.

As a result of these trends, the world may increasingly become divided into "head" and "body" nations, or nations representing some combination of those two functions. While Australia and Canada stress the headquarters or head functions, China will be the twenty-first-century model of a body nation. Although China does not innately or immediately know what to produce for the world market, it has found success in joint ventures with foreign corporations. China will be an attractive place to produce manufactured goods, but only because sophisticated enterprises from other countries design, market, and finance the products China makes. At present China cannot chart its own industrial future.

Neither can Russia. Focusing on the products of land, the Russians are still prisoners of territorial fetishism. Their commercial laws do not yet permit the delicate and sophisticated arrangements that ensure that "body" manufacturers deliver quality goods for their foreign "head." Russia's transportation network is also primitive. These, however, are temporary obstacles. In time Russia, with China and India, will serve as an important locus of the world's production plant.

The Vestiges of Serfdom

The world is embarked on a progressive emancipation from land as a determinant of production and power. For the Third World, the past unchangeable strictures of comparative advantage can be overcome through the acquisition of a highly trained labor force. Africa and Latin America may not have to rely on the exporting of raw materials or agricultural products; through education, they can capitalize on an educated labor force, as India has in Bangalore and Ireland in Dublin. Investing in human capital can substitute for trying to foresee the vagaries of the commodities markets and avoid the constant threat of overproduction. Meanwhile, land continues to decline in value. Recent studies of 180 countries show that as population density rises, per capita GDP falls. In a new study, economist Deepak Lal notes that investment as well as growth is inversely related to landholdings (Garstka 1995, Lal 1996).

These findings are a dramatic reversal of past theories of power in international politics. In the 1930s the standard international relations textbook would have ranked the great powers in terms of key natural resources: oil, iron ore, coal, bauxite, copper, tungsten, and manganese. Analysts presumed that the state with the largest stock of raw materials and goods derived from land would prevail. CIA estimates during the Cold War were based on such conclusions. It turns out, however, that the most prosperous countries often have a negligible endowment of natural resources. For instance, Japan has shut down its coal industry and has no iron ore, bauxite, or oil. Except for most of its rice, it imports much of its food. Japan is richly endowed with human capital, however, and that makes all the difference.

The implications for the United States are equally striking. As capital, labor, and knowledge become more important than land in charting economic success, America can influence and possibly even reshape its pattern of comparative advantage. The "new trade theory," articulated clearly by the economist Paul Krugman, focuses on path dependence, the so-called QWERTY effect of past choices. The QWERTY keyboard was not the arrangement of letter-coded keys that produced the fastest typing, except perhaps for left-handers. But, as the VHS videotape format became the standard for video recording even though other formats were technically better, the QWERTY keyboard became the standard for the typewriter (and computer) industry, and everyone else had to adapt to it. Nations that invested from the start in production facilities for the 16-kilobyte computer memory chip also had great advantages down the line in 4- and 16-megabyte chips. Intervention at an early point in the chain of development can influence results later on, which suggests that the United States and other nations can and should deliberately alter their pattern of comparative advantage and choose their economic activity.

American college and graduate education, for example, has supported the decisive U.S. role in the international services industry in research and development, consulting, design, packaging, financing, and the marketing of new products. Mergers and acquisitions are American subspecialties that draw on the skills of financial analysts and attorneys. The American failure, rather, has been in the first 12 years of education. Unlike that of Germany and Japan (or even Taiwan, Korea, and Singapore), American elementary and secondary education falls well below the world standard.

Economics teaches that products should be valued according to their economic importance. For a long period, education was undervalued, socially and economically speaking, despite productivity studies by Edward Denison and others that showed its long-term importance to U.S. growth and innovation. Recent studies have underscored this importance. According to the World Bank, 64 percent of the world's wealth consists of human capital. But the social and economic valuation of kindergarten through 12th-grade education has still not appreciably increased. Educators, psychologists, and school boards debate how education should be structured, but Americans do not invest more money in it. Corporations have sought to upgrade the standards of teaching and learning in their regions, but localities and states have lagged behind, as has the federal government. Elementary and high school teachers should be rewarded as patient creators of high-value capital in the United States and elsewhere. In Switzerland, elementary school teachers are paid around $70,000 per year, about the salary of a starting lawyer at a New York firm. In international economic competition, human capital has turned out to be at least as important as other varieties of capital. In spite of their reduced functions, states liberated from the confines of their geography have been able, with appropriate education, to transform their industrial and economic futures.

The Reduced Danger of Conflict

As nations turn to the cultivation of human capital, what will a world of virtual states be like? Production for one company or country can now take place in many parts of the world. In the process of downsizing, corporations and nation-states will have to get used to reliance on others. Virtual corporations need other corporations' production facilities. Virtual nations need other states' production capabilities. As a result, economic relations between states will come to resemble nerves connecting heads in one place to bodies somewhere else. Naturally, producer nations will be working quickly to become the brains behind emerging industries elsewhere. But in time, few nations will have within their borders all the components of a technically advanced economic existence.

To sever the connections between states would undermine the organic unit. States joined in this way are therefore less likely to engage in conflict. In the past, international norms underlying the balance of power, the Concert of Europe, or even rule by the British Raj helped specify appropriate courses of action for parties in dispute. The international economy also rested partially on normative agreement. Free trade, open domestic economies, and, more recently, freedom of movement for capital were normative notions. In addition to specifying conditions for borrowing, the International Monetary Fund is a norm-setting agency that inculcates market economics in nations not fully ready to accept their international obligations.

Like national commercial strategies, these norms have been largely abstracted from the practices of successful nations. In the nineteenth century many countries emulated Great Britain and its precepts. In the British pantheon of virtues, free trade was a norm that could be extended to other nations without self-defeat. Success for one nation did not undermine the prospects for others. But the acquisition of empire did cause congestion for other nations on the paths to industrialization and growth. Once imperial Britain had taken the lion's share, there was little left for others. The inability of all nations to live up to the norms Britain established fomented conflict between them.

In a similar vein, Japan's current trading strategy could be emulated by many other countries. Its pacific principles and dependence on world markets and raw materials supplies have engendered greater economic cooperation among other countries. At the same time, Japan's insistence on maintaining a quasi-closed domestic economy and a foreign trade surplus cannot be successfully imitated by everyone; if some achieve the desired result, others necessarily will not. In this respect, Japan's recent practices and norms stand athwart progress and emulation by other nations.

President Clinton rightly argues that the newly capitalist developmental states, such as Korea and Taiwan, have simply modeled themselves on restrictionist Japan. If this precedent were extended to China, the results would endanger the long-term stability of the world economic and financial system. Accordingly, new norms calling for greater openness in trade, finance, and the movement of factors of production will be necessary to stabilize the international system. Appropriate norms reinforce economic incentives to reduce conflict between differentiated international units.

Defusing the Population Bomb

So long as the international system of nation-states lasts, there will be conflict among its members. States see events from different perspectives, and competition and struggle between them are endemic. The question is how far conflicts will proceed. Within a domestic system, conflicts between individuals need not escalate to the use of physical force. Law and settlement procedures usually reduce outbreaks of hostility. In international relations, however, no sovereign, regnant authority can discipline feuding states. International law sets a standard, but it is not always obeyed. The great powers constitute the executive committee of nation-states and can intervene from time to time to set things right. But, as Bosnia shows, they often do not, and they virtually never intervene in the absence of shared norms and ideologies.

In these circumstances, the economic substructure of international relations becomes exceedingly important. That structure can either impel or retard conflicts between nation-states. When land is the major factor of production, the temptation to strike another nation is great. When the key elements of production are less tangible, the situation changes. The taking of real estate does not result in the acquisition of knowledge, and aggressors cannot seize the needed capital. Workers may flee from an invader. Wars of aggression and wars of punishment are losing their impact and justification.

Eventually, however, contend critics such as Paul Ehrlich, author of *The Population Bomb,* land will become important once again. Oil supplies will be depleted; the quantity of fertile land will decline; water will run dry. Population will rise relative to the supply of natural resources and food. This process, it is claimed, could return the world to the eighteenth and nineteenth centuries, with clashes over territory once again the engine of conflict. The natural resources on which the world currently relies may one day run out, but, as before, there will be substitutes. One sometimes forgets that in the 1840s whale oil, which was the most common fuel for lighting, became unavailable. The harnessing of global energy and the production of food does not depend on particular bits of fluid, soil, or rock. The question, rather, is how to release the energy contained in abundant matter.

But suppose the productive value of land does rise. Whether that rise would augur a return to territorial competition would depend on whether the value of land rises relative to financial capital, human capital, and information. Given the rapid technological development of recent years, the primacy of the latter seems more likely. Few perturbing trends have altered the historical tendency toward the growing intangibility of value in social and economic terms. In the twenty-first century it seems scarcely possible that this process would suddenly reverse itself, and land would yield a better return than knowledge.

Diminishing their command of real estate and productive assets, nations are downsizing, in functional if not in geographic terms. Small nations have attained peak efficiency and competitiveness, and even large nations have begun to think small. If durable access to assets elsewhere can be assured, the need to physically possess them diminishes. Norms are potent reinforcements of such arrangements. Free movement of capital and goods, substantial international and domestic investment, and high levels of technical education have been the recipe for success in the industrial world of the late twentieth century. Those who depended on others did better than those who depended only on themselves. Can the result be different in the future? Virtual states, corporate alliances, and essential trading relationships augur peaceful times. They may not solve domestic problems, but the economic bonds that link virtual and other nations will help ease security concerns.

The Civic Crisis

Though peaceful in its international implications, the rise of the virtual state portends a crisis for democratic politics. Western democracies have traditionally believed that political reform, extension of suffrage, and economic restructuring could solve their problems. In the twenty-first century none of these measures can fully succeed. Domestic political change does not suffice because it has insufficient jurisdiction to deal with global problems. The people in a particular state cannot determine international outcomes by holding an election. Economic restructuring in one state does not necessarily affect others. And the political state is growing smaller, not larger.

If ethnic movements are victorious in Canada, Mexico, and elsewhere, they will divide the state into smaller entities. Even the powers of existing states are becoming circumscribed. In the United States, if Congress has its way, the federal government will lose authority. In response to such changes, the market fills the vacuum, gaining power.

As states downsize, malaise among working people is bound to spread. Employment may fluctuate and generally decline. President Clinton recently observed that the American public has fallen into a funk. The economy may temporarily be prosperous, but there is no guarantee that favorable conditions will last. The flow of international factors of production—technology, capital, and labor—will swamp the stock of economic power at home. The state will become just one of many players in the international marketplace and will have to negotiate directly with foreign factors of production to solve domestic economic problems. Countries must induce foreign capital to enter their domain. To keep such investment, national economic authorities will need to maintain low inflation, rising productivity, a strong currency, and a flexible and trained labor force. These demands will sometimes conflict with domestic interests that want more government spending, larger budget deficits, and more benefits. That conflict will result in continued domestic insecurity over jobs, welfare, and medical care. Unlike the remedies applied in the insulated and partly closed economies of the past, purely domestic policies can no longer solve these problems.

The Necessity of Internationalization

The state can compensate for its deficient jurisdiction by seeking to influence economic factors abroad. The domestic state therefore must not only become a negotiating state but must also be internationalized. This is a lesson already learned in Europe, and well on the way to codification in East Asia. Among the world's major economies and polities, only the United States remains, despite its potent economic sector, essentially introverted politically and culturally. Compared with their counterparts in other nations, citizens born in the United States know fewer foreign languages, understand less about foreign cultures, and live abroad reluctantly, if at all. In recent years, many English industrial workers who could not find jobs migrated to Germany, learning the language to work there. They had few American imitators.

The virtual state is an agile entity operating in twin jurisdictions: abroad and at home. It is as prepared to mine gains overseas as in the domestic economy. But in large countries, internationalization operates differentially. Political and economic decision-makers have begun to recast their horizons, but middle managers and workers lag behind. They expect too much and give and learn too little. That is why the dawn of the virtual state must also be the sunrise of international education and training. The virtual state cannot satisfy all its citizens. The possibility of commanding economic power in the sense of effective state control has greatly declined. Displaced workers and businesspeople must be willing to look abroad for opportunities. In the United States, they can do this only if American education prepares the way.

References

Garstka, Daniel. 1995. "Land and Economic Prowess." Unpublished mimeograph.
Grilli, Enzo R., and Maw Cheng Yang. 1998. "Primary Commodity Prices, Manufactured Goods Prices, and the Terms of Trade of Developing Countries: What the Long Run Shows." *The World Bank Economic Review*, 2:1.
Lal, Deepak. 1996. "Factor Endowments, Culture and Politics: On Economic Performance in the Long Run." Unpublished mimeograph.
Ripoll, Jose. 1996. *The Future of Trade in International Services.* Center for International Relations Working Paper, University of California at Los Angeles (January).

7

Excerpts from *Report on Manufactures*

Alexander Hamilton

Classic mercantilism involved extensive state regulation of the economy in the interest of national strength and development. At its core, it advocated policies of political and economic self-reliance and the building of wealth through trade policies that encouraged exports and discouraged imports. The strength of a country, according to the mercantilists, could be measured by its gold hoard; because trade debts were resolved in gold, a successful trade policy would swell government coffers and thus the strength of the government. As this excerpt from the Report on Manufactures *(1791) shows, Alexander Hamilton does not call for building a gold hoard to demonstrate governmental strength, but he does make the classic call for government action to aid in the development of the economy and the promotion of national self-reliance. Hamilton worries that during the war of independence the colonies had to rely upon foreign trade and armaments to maintain the war. If the United States wanted to be a country of consequence, Hamilton argues, it would have to spend public funds to encourage the emergence of manufactures and to protect these nascent domestic industries from foreign competition.*

The Secretary of the Treasury, in obedience to the order of ye House of Representatives, of the 15th day of January, 1790, has applied his attention, at as early a period as his other duties would permit, to the subject of Manufactures; and particularly to the means of promoting such as will tend to render the United States, independent on foreign nations for military and other essential supplies. And he thereupon respectfully submits the following Report.

The expediency of encouraging manufactures in the United States, which was not long since deemed very questionable, appears at this time to be pretty generally admitted. The embarrassments, which have obstructed the progress of our external trade, have led to serious reflections on the necessity of enlarging the sphere of our domestic commerce: the restrictive regulations, which in foreign markets abridge the vent of the increasing surplus of our Agricultural produce, serve to beget an earnest desire, that a more extensive demand for that surplus may be created at home: And the complete success, which was rewarded manufacturing enterprise, in some valuable branches, conspiring with the promising symptoms, which attend some less mature essays, in others, justify a hope, that the obstacles to the growth of this species of industry are less formidable than they were apprehended to be, and that it is not difficult to find, in its further extension, a full indemnification of any external disadvantages, which are or may be experienced, as well as an accession of resources, favorable to national independence and safety.

There still are, nevertheless, respectable patrons of opinions, unfriendly to the encouragement of manufactures. The following are, substantially, the arguments by, which these opinions are defended.

"In every country (say those who entertain them) Agriculture is the most beneficial and productive object of human industry. This position, generally, if not universally true, applies with peculiar emphasis to the United States, on account of their immense tracts of fertile territory, uninhabited and unimproved. Nothing can afford so advantageous an employment for capital and labour, as the conversion of this extensive wilderness into cultivated farms. Nothing equally with this, can contribute to the population, strength and real riches of the country.

"To endeavor, by the extraordinary patronage of Government, to accelerate the growth of manufactures, is, in fact, to endeavor, by force and art, to transfer the natural current of industry from a more, to a less beneficial channel. Whatever has such a tendency must necessarily be unwise. Indeed it can hardly ever be wise in a government, to attempt to give a direction to the industry of its citizens. This under the quick sighted guidance of private interest, will, if left to itself, infallibly find its own way to the most profitable employment: and 'tis by such employment, that the public prosperity will be most effectually promoted. To leave industry to itself, therefore, is, in almost every case, the soundest as well as the simplest policy. . . . "

It has been maintained that Agriculture is, not only, the most productive, but the only productive, species of industry. The reality of this suggestion in either aspect, has, however, not been verified by any accurate detail of facts and calculations; and the general arguments, which are adduced to prove it, are rather subtle and paradoxical, than solid or convincing. . . .

It might also be observed, with a contrary view, that the labor employed in Agriculture is in a great measure periodical and occasional, depending on seasons, liable to various and long intermissions; while that occupied in many manufactures is constant and regular, extending through the year, embracing in some instances night as well as day. It is also probable, that there are among the cultivators of land, more examples of remissness, than among artificers. The farmer, from the peculiar fertility of his land, or some other favorable circumstance, may frequently obtain a livelihood, even with a considerable degree of carelessness in the mode of cultivation; but the artisan can with difficulty effect the same object, without exerting himself pretty equally with all those who are engaged in the same pursuit. And if it may likewise be assumed as a fact, that manufactures open a wider field to exertions of ingenuity than agriculture, it would not be a strained conjecture, that the labour employed in the former, being at once more constant, more uniform and more ingenious, than that which is employed in the latter, will be found, at the same time more productive. . . .

The foregoing suggestions are not designed to inculcate an opinion that manufacturing industry is more productive than that of Agriculture. They are intended rather to show that the reverse of this proposition is not ascertained; that the general arguments which are brought to establish it are not satisfactory; and, consequently that a supposition of the superior productiveness of Tillage ought to be no obstacle to listening to any substantial inducements to the encouragement of manufactures, which may be otherwise perceived to exist, through an apprehension; that they may have a tendency to divert labour from a more to a less profitable employment. . . .

It is now proper to proceed a step further, and to enumerate the principal circumstances, from which it may be inferred that manufacturing establishments not only occasion a positive augmentation of the Produce and Revenue of the Society, but that they contribute essentially to rendering them greater than they could possibly be, without such establishments. These circumstances are—

1. The division of labour.
2. An extension of the use of Machinery.
3. Additional employment to classes of the community not ordinarily engaged in the business.
4. The promoting of emigration from foreign Countries.
5. The furnishing greater scope for the diversity of talents and dispositions which discriminate men from each other.
6. The affording a more ample and various field for enterprize.
7. The creating in some instances a new, and securing in all, a more certain and steady demand for the surplus produce of the soil.

Each of these circumstances has a considerable influence upon the total mass of industrious effort in a community: Together, they add to it a degree of energy and effect, which are not easily conceived. . . .

It is a primary object of the policy of nations, to be able to supply themselves with subsistence from their own soils; and manufacturing nations, as far as circumstances permit, endeavor to procure from the same source, the raw materials necessary for their own fabrics. This disposition, urged by the spirit of monopoly, is sometimes even carried to an injudicious extreme. It seems not always to be recollected, that nations who have neither mines nor manufactures, can only obtain the manufactured articles, of which they stand in need, by an exchange of the products of their soils; and that, if those who can best furnish them with such articles are unwilling to give a due course to this exchange, they must of necessity, make every possible effort to manufacture for themselves; the effect of which is that the manufacturing nations abridge the natural advantages of their situation, through an unwillingness to permit the Agricultural countries to enjoy the advantages of theirs, and sacrifice the interests of a mutually beneficial intercourse to the vain project of selling every thing and buying nothing.

But it is also a consequence of the policy, which has been noted, that the foreign demand for the products of Agricultural Countries is, in a great degree, rather casual and occasional, than certain or constant. To what extent injurious interruptions of the demand for some of the staple commodities of the United States, may have been experienced from that cause, must be referred to the judgment of those who are engaged in carrying on the commerce of the country; but it may be safely affirmed, that such interruptions are at times very inconveniently felt, and that cases not unfrequently occur, in which markets are so confined and restricted as to render the demand very unequal to the supply.

Independently likewise of the artificial impediments, which are created by the policy in question, there are natural causes tending to render the external demand for the surplus of Agricultural nations a precarious reliance. The differences of seasons, in the countries, which are the consumers, make immense differences in the produce of their own soils, in different years; and consequently in the degrees of their necessity for foreign supply. Plentiful harvests with them, especially if similar ones occur at the same time in the countries, which are the furnishers, occasion of course a glut in the markets of the latter. . . .

The foregoing considerations seem sufficient to establish, as general propositions, that it is the interest of nations to diversify the industrious pursuits of the individuals who compose them—that the establishment of manufactures is calculated not only to increase the general stock of useful and productive labour; but even to improve the state of Agriculture. . . .

If the system of perfect liberty to industry and commerce were the prevailing system of nations, the arguments which dissuade a country, in the predicament of the United States, from zealous pursuit of manufactures, would doubtless have great force. It will not be affirmed, that they might not be permitted, with few exceptions, to serve as a rule of national conduct. In such a state of things, each country would have the full benefit of its peculiar advantages to compensate for its deficiencies or disadvantages. If one nation were in a condition to supply manufactured articles on better terms than another, that other might find an abundant indemnification in a superior capacity to furnish the produce of the soil. And a free exchange, mutually beneficial, of the commodities which each was able to supply, on the best terms, might be carried on between them, supporting in full vigour the industry of each. And though the circumstances which have been mentioned and others, which will be unfolded hereafter render it probable, that nations merely Agricultural would not enjoy the same degree of opulence, in proportion to their numbers, as those which united manufactures with agriculture; yet the progressive improvement of the lands of the former might, in the end, atone for an inferior degree of opulence in the meantime; and in a case in which opposite considerations are pretty equally balanced, the option ought perhaps always to be, in favor of leaving Industry to its own direction.

But the system which has been mentioned, is far from characterising the general policy of Nations. The prevalent one has been regulated by an opposite spirit. The consequence of it is, that the United States are to a certain extent in the situation of a country precluded from foreign Commerce. They can indeed, without difficulty obtain from abroad the manufactured supplies of which they are in want; but they experience numerous and very injurious impediments to the emission and vent of their own commodities. Nor is this the case in reference to a single foreign nation only. The regulations of several countries, with which we have the most extensive intercourse, throw serious obstructions in the way of the principal staples of the United States.

In such a position of things, the United States cannot exchange with Europe on equal terms; and the want of reciprocity would render them the victim of a system which should induce them to confine their views to Agriculture, and refrain from Manufactures. A constant and increasing necessity, on their part, for the commodities of Europe, and only a partial and occasional demand for their own, in return, could not but expose them to a state of impoverishment, compared with the opulence to which their political and natural advantages authorise them to aspire.

Remarks of this kind are not made in the spirit of complaint. 'Tis for the nations, whose regulations are alluded to, to judge for themselves, whether, by aiming at too much, they do not lose more than they gain. It is for the United States to consider by what means they can render themselves least dependent on the combinations, right or wrong, of foreign policy.

It is no small consolation, that already the measures which have embarrassed our Trade, have accelerated internal improvements, which upon the whole have bettered our affairs. To diversify and extend these improvements is the surest and safest method of indemnifying ourselves for any inconveniences, which those or similar measures have a tendency to beget. If Europe will not take from us the products of our soil, upon terms consistent with our interest, the natural remedy is to contract as fast as possible our wants of her. . . .

The remaining objections to a particular encouragement of manufactures in the United States now require to be examined.

One of these turns on the proposition, that Industry, if left to itself, will naturally find its way to the most useful and profitable employment: whence it is inferred that manufactures without the aid of government will grow up as soon and as fast, as the natural state of things and the interest of the community may require. . . .

Experience teaches, that men are often so much governed by what they are accustomed to see and practise, that the simplest and most obvious improvements, in the most ordinary occupations, are adopted with hesitation, reluctance, and by slow gradations. . . . To produce the desirable changes as early as may be expedient, may therefore require the incitement and patronage of government. . . .

The superiority antecedently enjoyed by nations, who have preoccupied and perfected a branch of industry, constitutes a more formidable obstacle . . . to the introduction of the same branch into a country in which it did not before exist. To maintain between the recent establishments of one country and the long matured establishments of another country, a competition upon equal terms, both as to quality and price, is in most cases impracticable. The disparity, in the one or in the other, or in both, must necessarily be so considerable as to forbid a successful rivalship, without the extraordinary aid and protection of government.

But the greatest obstacle of all to the successful prosecution of a new branch of industry in a country, in which it was before unknown, consists, as far as the instances apply, in the bounties premiums and other aids which are granted, in a variety of cases, by the nations, in which the establishments to be imitated are previously introduced. It is well known . . . that certain nations grant bounties on the exportation of particular commodities, to enable their own workmen to undersell and supplant all competitors in the countries to which those commodities are sent. Hence the undertakers of a new manufacture have to contend not only with the natural disadvantages of a new undertaking, but with the gratuities and remunerations which other governments bestow. To be enabled to contend with success, it is evident that the interference and aid of their own governments are indispensable. . . .

There remains to be noticed an objection to the encouragement of manufactures, of a nature different from those which question the probability of success. This is derived from its supposed tendency to give a monopoly of advantages to particular classes, at the expense of the rest of the community, who, it is affirmed, would be able to procure the requisite supplies of manufactured articles on better terms from foreigners, than from our own Citizens, and who, it is alleged, are reduced to the necessity of paying an enhanced price for whatever they want, by every measure, which obstructs the free competition of foreign commodities.

It is not an unreasonable supposition, that measures, which serve to abridge the free competition of foreign Articles, have a tendency to occasion an enhancement of prices and it is not to be denied that such is the effect, in a number of Cases; but the fact does not uniformly correspond with the theory. A reduction of prices has, in several instances immediately succeeded the establishment of a domestic manufacture. Whether it be that foreign manufactures endeavour to supplant, by underselling our own, or whatever else be the cause, the effect has been such as is stated, and the reverse of what might have been expected.

But though it were true, that the immediate and certain effect of regulations controling the competition of foreign with domestic fabrics was an increase of Price, it is universally true, that the contrary is the ultimate effect with every successful manufacture. When a domestic manufacture has attained to perfection, and has engaged in the prosecution of it a competent number of Persons, it invariably becomes cheaper. Being free from the heavy charges which attend the importation of foreign commodities, it can be afforded, and accordingly seldom or never fails to be sold Cheaper, in process of time, than was the foreign Article for which it is a substitute. The internal competition which takes place, soon does away [with] every thing like Monopoly, and by degrees reduces the price of the Article to the minimum of a reasonable profit on the Capital employed. This accords with the reason of the thing, and with experience.

Whence it follows, that it is the interest of a community, with a view to eventual and permanent economy, to encourage the growth of manufactures. In a national view, a temporary enhancement of price must always be well compensated by a permanent reduction of it. . . .

[T]he uniform appearance of an abundance of specie, as the concomitant of a flourishing state of manufactures, and of the reverse, where they do not prevail, afford a strong presumption of their favorable operation upon the wealth of a Country.

Not only the wealth, but the independence and security of a Country, appear to be materially connected with the prosperity of manufactures. Every nation, with a view to those great objects, ought to endeavour to possess within itself all the essentials of national supply. These comprise the means of Subsistence, habitation, clothing, and defence.

The possession of these is necessary to the perfection of the body politic; to the safety as well as to the welfare of the society; the want of either is the want of an important Organ of political life and Motion; and in the various crises which await a state, it must severely feel the effects of any such deficiency. The extreme embarrassments of the United States during the late War, from an incapacity of supplying themselves, are still matter of keen recollection: A future war might be expected again to exemplify the mischiefs and dangers of a situation to which that incapacity is still too great a degree applicable, unless changed by timely and vigorous exertion. To effect this change, as fast as shall be prudent, merits all attention and all the Zeal of our Public Councils; 'tis the next great work to be accomplished.

The want of a Navy, to protect our external commerce, as long as it shall Continue, must render it a peculiarly precarious reliance, for the supply of essential articles, and must serve to strengthen prodigiously the arguments in favour of manufactures. . . .

In order to a better judgment of the Means proper to be resorted to by the United States, it will be of use to Advert to those which have been employed with success in other Countries. The principal of these are—

I. Protecting Duties—or Duties on Those Foreign Articles Which Are the Rivals of the Domestic Ones Intended to Be Encouraged

Duties of this nature evidently amount to a virtual bounty on the domestic fabrics since by enhancing the charges on foreign articles, they enable the National Manufacturers to undersell all their foreign Competitors. The propriety of this species of encouragement need not be dwelt upon, as it is not only a clear result from the numerous topics which have been suggested, but is sanctioned by the laws of the United States, in a variety of instances; it has the additional recommendation of being a resource of revenue. Indeed all the duties imposed on imported articles, though with an exclusive view to Revenue, have the effect in Contemplation, and except where they fall on raw materials wear a beneficent aspect toward the manufactures of the Country.

II. Prohibitions of Rival Articles, or Duties Equivalent to Prohibitions

Considering a monopoly of the domestic market to its own manufacturers as the reigning policy of manufacturing Nations, a similar policy on the part of the United States in every proper instance, is dictated, it might almost be said, by the principles of distributive justice; certainly, by the duty of endeavoring to secure to their own Citizens a reciprocity of advantages.

III. Prohibitions of the Exportation of the Materials of Manufactures

The desire of securing a cheap and plentiful supply for the national workmen, and where the article is either peculiar to the Country, or of peculiar quality there, the jealousy of enabling foreign workmen to rival those of the nation with its own Materials, are the leading motives to this species of regulation. It ought not to be affirmed, that it is in no instance proper, but it is, certainly one which ought to be adopted with great circumspection, and only in very plain Cases. . . .

IV. Pecuniary Bounties

This has been found one of the most efficacious means of encouraging manufactures, and, is in some views, the best. Though it has not yet been practiced upon by the Government of the United states (unless the allowance on the exportation of dried and pickled Fish and salted meat could be considered as a bounty), and though it is less favored by public Opinion than some other modes. . . .

A Question has been made concerning the Constitutional right of the Government of the United States to apply this species of encouragement, but there is certainly no good foundation for such a question. The National Legislature has express authority "To lay and Collect taxes, duties, imposts, and excises, to pay the Debts, and provide for the Common defence and general welfare." . . .

V. Premiums

These are of a nature allied to bounties, though distinguishable from them in some important features.

Bounties are applicable to the whole quantity of an article produced, or manufactured, or exported, and involve a correspondent expense. Premiums serve to reward some particular excellence or superiority, some extraordinary exertion or skill, and are dispensed only in a small number of cases. But their effect is to stimulate general effort, contrived so as to be both honorary and lucrative, they address themselves to different passions; touching the chords as well of emulation as of Interest. They are accordingly a very economical means of exciting the enterprise of a whole Community. . . .

VI. The Exemption of the Materials of Manufactures from Duties

The policy of that Exemption as a general rule particularly in reference to new Establishments is obvious. It can hardly ever be advisable to add the obstructions of fiscal burthens to the difficulties which naturally embarrass a new manufacture; and where it is matured and in condition to become an object of revenue it is generally speaking better that the fabric than the Material should be the subject of Taxation. . . .

VII. Drawbacks of the Duties Which Are Imposed on the Materials of Manufactures

It has already been observed as a general rule that duties on those materials ought with certain exceptions, to be forborne. Of these exceptions, three cases occur, which may serve as examples—one, where the material is itself an object of general or extensive consumption, and a lit and productive source of revenue: Another, where a manufacture of a simpler kind, the competition of which with a like domestic article is desired to be restrained, partakes of the Nature of a raw material, from being capable, by a further process to be converted into a manufacture of a different kind, the introduction or growth of which is desired to be encouraged; a third where the Material itself is a production of the country, and in sufficient abundance to furnish a cheap and plentiful supply to the national Manufacturers. . . .

VIII. The Encouragement of New Inventions and Discoveries, at Home, and of the Introduction into the United States of Such as May Have Been Made in Other Countries; Particularly Those Which Relate to Machinery

This is among the most useful and unexceptionable of the aids, which can be given to manufactures. The usual means of that encouragement are pecuniary rewards, and, for a time, exclusive privileges. The first must be employed according to the occasion, and the utility of the invention or discovery. For the last, so far as respects "authors and inventors," provision has been made by Law. But it is desirable, in regard to improvements, and secrets of extraordinary value, to be able to extend the same benefit to

Introducers, as well as Authors and Inventors; a policy which has been practiced with advantage in other countries. . . .

IX. Judicious Regulations for the Inspection of Manufactured Commodities

This is not among the least important of the means by which the prosperity of manufactures may be promoted. It is indeed in many cases one of the most essential. Contributing to prevent frauds upon consumers at home and exporters to foreign countries, to improve the quality and preserve the character of the national manufactures, it cannot fail to aid the expeditious and advantageous sale of them, and to serve as a guard against successful competition from other quarters. . . .

X. The Facilitating of Pecuniary Remittances from Place to Place

—is a point of considerable moment to trade in general, and to manufactures in particular; by rendering more easy the purchase of raw materials and provisions and the payment for manufactured supplies. A general circulation of Bank paper, which is expected from the institution lately established will be most valuable mean to this end. But much good would also accrue from some additional provisions respecting inland bills of exchange. If those drawn in one state payable in another were made negotiable, everywhere, and interest and damages allowed in case of protest, it would greatly promote negotiations between the Citizens of different states, by rendering them more secure; and, with it the convenience and advantage of the Merchants and manufacturers of each.

XI. The Facilitating of the Transportation of Commodities

Improvements favoring this object intimately concern all domestic interests of a community; but they may without impropriety be mentioned as having an important relation to manufactures. There is perhaps scarcely anything which has been better calculated to assist the manufacturers of Great Britain than the amelioration of the public roads of that Kingdom, and the great progress which has been of late made in opening canals. . . .

[After discussing the importance of a number of raw materials and industries—iron, copper, lead, fossil coal, wood, skins, grain, flax and hemp, cotton, wool, silk, glass, gunpowder, paper, printed books, refined sugars, and chocolate—Hamilton concludes his *Report on Manufactures.—Eds.*]

The foregoing heads comprise the most important of the several kinds of manufactures, which have occurred as requiring, and, at the same time, as most proper for public encouragement; and such measures for affording it, as have appeared best calculated to answer the end, have been suggested.

The observations, which have accompanied this delineation of objects, supersede the necessity of many supplementary remarks. One or two however may not be altogether superfluous.

Bounties are in various instances proposed as one species of encouragement.

It is a familiar objection to them, that they are difficult to be managed and liable to frauds. But neither that difficulty nor this danger seems sufficiently great to countervail the advantages of which they are productive, when rightly applied. And it is presumed to have been shown, that they are in some cases, particularly in the infancy of new enterprises, indispensable.

It will however be necessary to guard, with extraordinary circumspection, the manner of dispensing them. The requisite precautions have been thought of; but to enter into the detail would swell this report, already voluminous, to a size too inconvenient.

If the principle shall not be deemed inadmissable the means of avoiding an abuse of it will not be likely to present insurmountable obstacles. There are useful guides from practice in other quarters.

It shall therefore only be remarked here, in relations to this point, that any bounty, which may be applied to the manufacture of an article, cannot with safety extend beyond those manufactories, at which the making of the articles is a regular trade. . . .

The possibility of a diminution of the revenue may also present itself, as an objection to the arrangements, which have been submitted.

But there is no truth, which may be more firmly relied upon, than that the interests of the revenue are promoted, by whatever promotes an increase of National industry and wealth.

In proportion to the degree of these, is the capacity of every country to contribute to the public Treasury; and where the capacity to pay is increased, or even is not decreased, the only consequence of measures, which diminish any particular resource is a change of the object. If by encouraging the manufacture of an article at home, the revenue, which has been wont to accrue from its importation, should be lessened, an indemnification, can easily be found, either out of the manufacture itself, or from some other object, which may be deemed more convenient.

The measures however, which have been submitted, taken aggregately, will for a long time to come rather augment than decrease the public revenue.

There is little room to hope, that the progress of manufactures, will so equally keep pace with the progress of population, as to prevent, even, a gradual augmentation of the product of the duties on imported articles.

As, nevertheless, an abolition in some instances, and a reduction in others of duties, which have been pledged for the public debt, is proposed, it is essential, that it should be accompanied with a competent substitute. In order to this, it is requisite, that all the additional duties which shall be laid, be appropriated in the first instance, to replace all defalcations, which may proceed from any such abolition or diminution. It is evident, at first glance, that they will not only be adequate to this, but will yield a considerable surplus.

This surplus will serve:

First. To constitute a fund for paying the bounties which shall have been decreed.

Secondly. To constitute a fund for the operations of a Board to be established, for promoting Arts, Agriculture, Manufactures and Commerce. Of this institution, different intimations have been given, in the course of this report. An outline of a plan for it shall now be submitted.

Let a certain annual sum, be set apart, and placed under the management of Commissioners, not less than three, to consist of certain Officers of the Government and their Successors in Office.

Let these Commissioners be empowered to apply the fund confided to them to defray the expenses of the emigration of Artists and Manufacturers in particular branches of extraordinary importance—to induce the prosecution and introduction of useful discoveries, inventions, and improvements, by proportionate rewards, judiciously held out and applied—to encourage by premiums both honorable and lucrative the exertions of individuals, and of classes, in relation to the several objects they are charged with promoting—and to afford such other aids to those objects as may be generally designated by law.

The Commissioners to render to the Legislature an annual account of their transactions and disbursements; and all such sums as shall not have been applied to the purposes of their trust, at the end of every three years, to revert to the Treasury. It may also be enjoined upon them not to draw out the money, but for the purpose of some specific disbursement.

It may, moreover, be of use to authorize them to receive voluntary contributions, making it their duty to apply them to the particular objects for which they may have been made, if any shall have been designated by the donors.

There is reason to believe that the progress of particular manufactures has been much retarded by the want of skilful workmen. And it often happens, that the capitals employed are not equal to the purposes of bringing from abroad workmen of a superior kind. Here, in cases worthy of it, the auxiliary agency of Government would, in all probability, be useful. There are also valuable workmen in every branch, who are prevented from emigrating solely by the want of means. Occasional aids to such persons properly administered might be a source of valuable acquisitions to the country.

The propriety of stimulating by rewards, the invention and introduction of useful improvements, is admitted without difficulty. But the success of attempts in this way must evidently depend much on the manner of conducting them. It is probable, that the placing of the dispensation of those rewards under some proper discretionary direction, where they may be accompanied by collateral expedients, will serve to give them the surest efficacy. It seems impracticable to apportion, by general rules, specific compensations for discoveries of unknown and disproportionate utility.

The great use which may be made of a fund of this nature, to procure and import foreign improvements is particularly obvious. Among these, the article of machines would form a most important item.

The operation and utility of premiums have been adverted to; together with the advantages which have resulted from their dispensation, under the direction of certain public and private societies. Of this some experience has been had, in the instance of the Pennsylvania Society for Promotion of Manufactures and useful Arts; but the funds of that association have been too contracted to produce more than a very small portion of the good to which the principles of it would have led. It may confidently be affirmed that there is scarcely any thing which has been devised, better calculated to excite a general spirit of improvement than the institutions of this nature. They are truly invaluable.

In countries where there is great private wealth, much may be effected by the voluntary contributions of patriotic individuals; but in a community situated like that of the United States, the public purse must supply the deficiency of private resource. In what can it be so useful, as in prompting and improving the efforts of industry?

All which is humbly submitted.
Alexander Hamilton, Secy of the Treasury.

8

The Theory of Hegemonic Stability and Changes in International Economic Regimes, 1967–1977

Robert O. Keohane

When attempting to describe the neorealist version of hegemonic stability theory, scholars often cite this work by Robert Keohane because it offers a clear explanation of the tenets and assumptions of the theory. Neorealists, such as Robert Gilpin, believe the state is the most important actor in the international system and that states need a powerful leader to ensure compliance with the rules. If the hegemonic leader chooses to enforce a set of neoliberal rules, the international system will be characterized by monetary and exchange stability, free trade, and a high potential for global economic growth. When challengers to the hegemon arise, the system, according to neorealist thought, becomes economically unstable and violent. Keohane found some support for this theory. One of his primary criticisms surrounds the measurement of power. Hegemonic stability theorists, Keohane believes, lean too heavily upon tangible resources (gross domestic product, oil import dependence, and similar factors) in their measurements of power, whereas intangibles—such as confidence in a currency or in some political positions relative to others—receive too little attention or weight.

Europe and Japan had recovered impressively from World War II and during the 1960s the United States had been enjoying strong, sustained economic growth as well. Both unemployment and inflation in seven major industrialized countries stood at an average of only 2.8 percent. International trade had been growing even faster than output, which was expanding at about 5 percent annually; and direct investment abroad was

Reprinted with permission from "The Theory of Hegemonic Stability and Changes in International Regimes, 1967–1977," in *Changes in the International System,* eds. Ole Holsti, Randolph Siverson, and Alexander George. Boulder: Westview Press, 1980, pp. 131–132, 136–149, 151–152, 154–155.

increasing at an even faster rate.[1] The Kennedy Round of trade talks was successfully completed in June 1967; in the same month, the threat of an oil embargo by Arab countries in the wake of an Israeli-Arab war had been laughed off by the Western industrialized states. Fixed exchange rates prevailed; gold could still be obtained from the United States in exchange for dollars; and a prospective "international money," Special Drawing Rights (SDRs), was created in 1967 under the auspices of the International Monetary Fund (IMF). The United States, "astride the world like a colossus," felt confident enough of its power and position to deploy half a million men to settle the affairs of Vietnam. U.S. power and dynamism constituted the problem or the promise; "the American challenge" was global. Conservative and radical commentators alike regarded U.S. dominance as the central reality of contemporary world politics, although they differed as to whether its implications were benign or malign (Liska, 1967; Servan-Schreiber, 1969; Magdoff, 1969).

A decade later the situation was very different. Unemployment rates in the West had almost doubled while inflation rates had increased almost threefold. Surplus capacity had appeared in the steel, textiles, and ship-building industries, and was feared in others (Strange, 1979). Confidence that Keynesian policies could ensure uninterrupted growth had been undermined if not shattered. Meanwhile, the United States had been defeated in Vietnam and no longer seemed to have either the capability or inclination to extend its military domination to the far corners of the world. The inability of the United States to prevent or counteract the oil price increases of 1973–1974 seemed to symbolize the drastic changes that had taken place. . . .

Explaining Changes in International Regimes

A parsimonious theory of international regime change has recently been developed by a number of authors, notably Charles Kindleberger, Robert Gilpin, and Stephen Krasner. According to this theory, strong international economic regimes depend on hegemonic power. Fragmentation of power between competing countries leads to fragmentation of the international economic regime; concentration of power contributes to stability.[2] Hegemonic powers have the capabilities to maintain international regimes that they favor. They may use coercion to enforce adherence to rules; or they may rely largely on positive sanctions—the provision of benefits to those who cooperate. Both hegemonic power and the smaller states may have incentives to collaborate in maintaining a regime—the hegemonic power gains the ability to shape and dominate its international environment, while providing a sufficient flow of benefits to small middle powers to persuade them to acquiesce. Some international regimes can be seen partially as collective goods, whose benefits (such as stable money) can be consumed by all participants without detracting from others' enjoyment of them. Insofar as this is the case, economic theory leads us to expect that extremely large, dominant countries will be particularly willing to provide these goods, while relatively small participants will attempt to secure "free rides" by avoiding proportionate shares of payment. International systems with highly skewed distributions of capabilities will therefore tend to be more amply supplied with such collective goods than systems characterized by equality among actors.[3]

The particular concern of this chapter is the erosion of international economic regimes. The hegemonic stability theory seeks sources of erosion in changes in the relative capabilities of states. As the distribution of tangible resources, especially economic resources, becomes more equal, international regimes should weaken. One reason for this is that the capabilities of the hegemonial power will decline—it will become less capable of enforcing rules against unwilling participants, and it will have fewer resources with which to entice or bribe other states into remaining within the confines of the regime. Yet the incentives facing governments will also change. As the hegemonial state's margin of resource superiority over its partners declines, the costs of leadership will become more burdensome. Enforcement of rules will be more difficult and side payments will seem less justifiable. Should other states—now increasingly strong economic rivals—not have to contribute their "fair shares" to the collective enterprise? The hegemon (or former hegemon) is likely to seek to place additional burdens on its allies. At the same time, the incentives of the formerly subordinate secondary states will change. They will not only become more capable of reducing their support for the regime; they may acquire new interests in doing so. On the one hand, they will perceive the possibility of rising above their subordinate status, and they may even glimpse the prospect of reshaping the international regime in order better to suit their own interests. On the other hand, they may begin to worry that their efforts (and those of others) in chipping away at the hegemonial power and its regime may be too successful—that the regime itself may collapse. This fear, however, may lead them to take further action to hedge their bets, reducing their reliance on the hegemonial regime and perhaps attempting to set up alternative arrangements of their own.

As applied to the last century and a half, this theory—which will be referred to as the "hegemonic stability" theory—does well at identifying apparently necessary conditions for strong international economic regimes, but poorly at establishing sufficient conditions. International economic regimes have been most orderly and predictable where there was a single hegemonic state in the world system: Britain during the mid-nineteenth century in trade and until 1914 in international financial affairs; the United States after 1945. Yet although tangible U.S. power resources were large during the interwar period, international economic regimes were anything but orderly. High inequality of capabilities was not, therefore, a sufficient condition for strong international regimes; there was in the case of the United States a lag between its attainment of capabilities and its acquisition of a willingness to exert leadership, or of a taste for domination depending on point of view.[4]

The concern here is not with the validity of the hegemonic stability theory throughout the last 150 years, but with its ability to account for changes in international economic regimes during the decade between 1967 and 1977. Since the United States remained active during those years as the leading capitalist country, the problem of "leadership lag" does not exist, which raises difficulties for the interpretation of the interwar period. Thus the theory should apply to the 1967–1977 period. Insofar as "potential economic power" (Krasner's term) became more equally distributed—reducing the share of the United States—during the 1960s and early to mid-1970s, U.S.-created and U.S.-centered international economic regimes should also have suffered erosion or decline.

The hegemonic stability thesis is a power-as-resource theory, which attempts to link tangible state capabilities (conceptualized as "power resources") to behavior. In its simplest form, it is what James G. March calls a "basic force model" in which outcomes reflect the potential power (tangible and known capabilities) of actors. Basic force models typically fail to predict accurately particular political outcomes, in part because differential opportunity costs often lead competing actors to use different proportions of their potential power. Yet they offer clearer and more easily interpretable explanations than "force activation models," which incorporate assumptions about differential exercise of power.[5] Regarding tendencies rather than particular decisions, they are especially useful in establishing a baseline, a measure of what can be accounted for by the very parsimonious theory that tangible resources are directly related to outcomes, in this case to the nature of international regimes. The hegemonic stability theory, which is systemic and parsimonious, therefore seems to constitute a useful starting point for analysis, on the assumption that it is valuable to see how much can be learned from simple explanations before proceeding to more complex theoretical formulations.

Ultimately, it will be necessary to integrate systemic analysis with explanations at the level of foreign policy. Domestic forces help to explain changes in the international political structure; changes in the international political structure affect domestic institutions and preferences (Gourevitch, 1978: 881–912). This chapter focuses only on one part of the overall research problem: the relationship between international structure and international regimes. It examines to what extent changes in recent international economic regimes can be accounted for by changes in international power distributions within the relevant issue areas.

Changes in International Economic Regimes, 1967–1977

The dependent variable in this analysis is international regime change between 1967 and 1977 in three issues areas: international monetary relations, trade in manufactured goods, and the production and sale of petroleum. These are not the only important areas of international economic activity—for example, foreign investment is not included—but they are among the most important.[6] Descriptive contentions about international regime change in the three chosen areas are that (1) all three international regimes existing in 1967 became weaker during the subsequent decade; (2) this weakening was most pronounced in the petroleum area and in monetary relations, where the old norms were destroyed and very different practices emerged—it was less sudden and less decisive in the field of trade; and (3) in the areas of trade and money, the dominant political coalitions supporting the regime remained largely the same, although in money certain countries (especially Saudi Arabia) were added to the inner "club," whereas in the petroleum issue area, power shifted decisively from multinational oil companies and governments of major industrialized countries to producing governments. Taking all three dimensions into account, it is clear that regime change was most pronounced during the decade in oil and least pronounced in trade in manufactured goods, with the international monetary regime occupying an intermediate position.

These descriptive contentions will now be briefly documented and then interpreted, inquiring about the extent to which the hegemonic stability theory accounts for these changes in international economic regimes.

The international trade regime of the General Agreement on Tariffs and Trade was premised on the principles of reciprocity, liberalization, and nondiscrimination. Partly as a result of its success, world trade had increased since 1950 at a much more rapid rate than world production. Furthermore, tariff liberalization was continuing: in mid-1967 the Kennedy round was successfully completed, substantially reducing tariffs on a wide range of industrial products. Yet despite its obvious successes, the GATT trade regime in 1967 was already showing signs of stress. The reciprocity and nondiscrimination provisions of GATT were already breaking down. Tolerance for illegal trade restrictions had grown, few formal complaints were being processed, and by 1967 GATT did not even require states maintaining illegal quantitative restrictions to obtain formal waivers of the rules. The "general breakdown in GATT legal affairs" had gone very far indeed, largely as a result of toleration of illegal restrictions such as the variable levy of the European Economic Community (EEC), EEC association agreements, and export subsidies (Hudec, 1975: 256; Patterson, 1965). In addition, nontariff barriers, which were not dealt with effectively by GATT codes, were becoming more important. The trade regime in 1967 was thus strongest in the area of tariff liberalization, but less effective on nontariff barriers or in dealing with discrimination.

In the decade ending in 1967 the international monetary regime was explicit, formally institutionalized, and highly stable. Governments belonging to the International Monetary Fund were to maintain official par values for their currencies, which could be changed only to correct a "fundamental disequilibrium" and only in consultation with the IMF. During these nine years, the rules were largely followed; parity changes for major currencies were few and minor.[7] In response to large U.S. deficits in its overall liquidity balance of payments, the U.S. government introduced an Interest Equalization Tax in 1963 and voluntary capital controls in 1965; in addition, a variety of ingenious if somewhat ephemeral expedients had been devised, both to improve official U.S. balance of payments statements and to provide for cooperative actions by central banks or treasuries to counteract the effects of destabilizing capital flows. Until November 1967 even British devaluation (seen by many as imminent in 1964) had been avoided. Nevertheless, as in trade, signs of weakness in the system were apparent. U.S. deficits had to a limited extent already undermined confidence in the dollar; and the United States was fighting a costly war in Vietnam which it was attempting to finance without tax increases at home. Consequently, inflation was increasing in the United States (Shapiro, in Krause and Salant, 1977).

The international regime for oil was not explicitly defined by intergovernmental agreement in 1967. There was no global international organization supervising the energy regime. Yet, as mentioned above, the governing arrangements for international oil production and trade were rather clear. With the support of their home governments, the major international oil companies cooperated to control production and, within limits, price. The companies were unpopular in the host countries, and these host country governments put the companies on the defensive on particular issues, seeking increased revenue or increased control. However, as Turner puts it, "the critical fact is that the companies did not really lose control of their relationship with host governments until the 1970s, when the concessionary system finally came close to being swept away. The long preceding decade of the 1960s had seen only minimal improvement for the host governments in the terms under which the majors did business with them" (Turner, 1978: 70). The companies retained superior financial resources and capabilities in production, transportation, and marketing that the countries could not attain. Furthermore, the companies possessed superior information: "Whatever the weakness of company defences which is apparent in retrospect, the host governments did not realize it at the time. Their knowledge of the complexities of the industry was scanty, their experience of serious bargaining with the companies was limited and their awe of the companies was great" (Turner, 1978: 94–95).

In addition, and perhaps most important, the feudal and semifeudal elites that controlled many oil-producing countries until the end of the 1960s were more often concerned with their personal and family interests than with modernization or national interests on a larger scale.

Although the U.S. government did not participate directly in oil production or trade, it was the most influential actor in the system. The United States had moved decisively during and after World War II to ensure that U.S. companies would continue to control Saudi Arabian oil (Kolko, 1968: 294–307; Krasner, 1978: 190–205; Feis, 1944, 1947: 104; Shwadran, 1955: 302–309; U.S. GPO, 1943, 1944: v. 4: 941–948; v. 3: 94–111). Later, when the Anglo-Iranian Oil Company became unwelcome as sole concessionaire in Iran, the United States sponsored an arrangement by which U.S. firms received 40 percent of the consortium established in the wake of the U.S.-sponsored coup that overthrew Premier Mossadegh and restored the shah to his throne (Krasner, 1978: 119–128; Kolko, 1972: 413–420; Blair, 1976: 43–47, 78–80; U.S. Congress, 1974b). U.S. tax policy was changed in 1950 to permit U.S. oil companies to increase payments to producing governments without sacrificing profits, thus solidifying the U.S. position in the Middle East and Venezuela (U.S. Congress, 1974a: 84–110; Jenkins and Wright, 1975; Krasner, 1978: 205–213). The United States had provided military aid and political support to the rulers of Saudi Arabia and Iran, maintaining close relations with them throughout the first two postwar decades (except for the Mossadegh period in Iran). And in case of trouble—as in 1956–1957—the United States was willing to use its own reserves to supply Europe with petroleum (U.S. Congress, 1957; OECD, 1958; Eisenhower, 1957: 124). The governing arrangements for oil thus reflected the U.S. government's interests in an ample supply of oil at stable or declining prices, close political ties with conservative Middle Eastern governments, and profits for U.S.-based multinational companies.

The international economic regime of 1977 looked very different. Least affected was the trade regime, although even here important changes had taken place. Between 1967 and 1977, nontariff barriers to trade continued to proliferate, and the principle of nondiscrimination was further undermined. Restrictions on textile imports from less developed countries, originally limited to cotton textiles, were extended to woolen and manmade fabrics in 1974 (GATT, 1974; UNCTAD, 1977).[8] Nontariff barriers affecting world steel trade in the early 1970s included import licensing, foreign exchange restrictions, quotas, export limitations, domestic-biased procurement, subsidies, import surcharges, and antidumping measures (MacPhee, 1974). During the 1970s, "voluntary" export restraints, which had covered about one-eighth of U.S. imports in 1971, were further extended (Bergsten, 1975b). In late 1977, the United States devised a "trigger price system" to help protect the U.S. steel industry from low-priced imports. Contemporaneously, the European Economic Community launched an ambitious program to protect and rationalize some of its basic industries afflicted with surplus but relatively inefficient capacity, such as steel and shipbuilding. On the basis of a general survey, the GATT secretariat estimated tentatively in 1977 that import restrictions introduced or seriously threatened by industrially advanced countries since 1974 would affect 3–5 percent of world trade—$30 to $50 billion. The stresses on the international trade system, according to the director-general of GATT, "have now become such that they seriously threaten the whole fabric of postwar cooperation in international trade policy" (*IMF Survey,* 12 Dec. 1977: 373).

Nevertheless, the weakening of some aspects of the international trade regime had not led, by the end of 1977, to reductions in trade or to trade wars; in fact, after a 4 percent decline in 1975, the volume of world trade rose 11 percent in 1976 and 4 percent in 1977 (*IMF Survey,* 20 Mar. 1978: 81, and 18 Sept. 1978: 285). Furthermore, by 1977 the Tokyo round of trade negotiations was well underway; in 1979 agreement was reached on trade liberalizing measures that not only would (if put into effect) reduce tariffs on industrial products, but that would also limit or prohibit a wide range of nontariff barriers, including export subsidies, national preferences on government procurement, and excessively complex import licensing procedures (*New York Times,* 12 Apr. 1979). The weakening of elements of the old regime was therefore accompanied both by expanding trade (although at a lower rate than before 1973) and by efforts to strengthen the rules in a variety of areas.

By 1977 the international monetary regime had changed much more dramatically. The pegged-rate regime devised at Bretton Woods had collapsed in 1971, and its jerry-built successor had failed in 1973. Since then, major currencies had been floating against one another, their values affected both by market forces and frequently extensive governmental intervention. In 1976 international agreement was reached on amendments to the Articles of Agreement of the International Monetary Fund, yet this did not return the world to stable international exchange rates or multilateral rule making but merely provided for vaguely defined "multilateral surveillance" of floating exchange rates. Exchange rates have fluctuated quite sharply at times, and have certainly been more unpredictable than they were in the 1960s. Substantial secular changes have also taken place; nominal effective exchange rates on 15 May 1978, as a percentage of the rates prevailing in March 1973, ranged from 58.6 for Italy to 130.0 for Germany and 154.2 for Switzerland (Morgan Guaranty Trust Co., 1978).

In the oil area, the rules of the old regime were shattered between 1967 and 1977, as power shifted dramatically from the multinational oil companies and home governments (especially the United States and Britain), on the one hand, to producing countries' governments, on the other. The latter, organized since 1960 in the Organization of Petroleum Exporting Countries, secured a substantial price rise in negotiations at Teheran in

1971, then virtually quadrupled prices without negotiation after the Yom Kippur War of October 1973. Despite some blustering and various vague threats the United States could do little directly about this, although high rates of inflation in industrial countries and the decline of the dollar in 1977 helped to reduce substantially the real price of oil between 1974 and 1977 (Morgan Guaranty Trust Co., 1978).[9] By 1977 the United States had apparently conceded control of the regime for oil pricing and production to OPEC, and particularly to its key member, Saudi Arabia. OPEC made the rules in 1977, influenced (but not controlled) by the United States. Only in case of a crippling supply embargo would the United States be likely to act. The United States was still, with its military and economic strength, an influential actor, but it was no longer dominant.

Reviewing this evidence about three international economic regimes supports the generalizations offered earlier. Although all three old regimes became weaker during the decade, this was most pronounced for oil and money, least for trade. In oil, furthermore, dominant coalitions changed as well, so that by 1977 the regime that existed, dominated by OPEC countries, was essentially a new regime. The old petroleum regime had disappeared. By contrast, the 1977 trade regime was still a recognizable version of the regime existing in 1967; and the international monetary regime of 1977, although vastly different than in 1967, retained the same core of supportive states along with the same international organization, the IMF, as its monitoring agent. Since the rules had changed, the function of the IMF had also changed; but it persisted as an element, as well as a symbol, of continuity. In the oil area, the emergence of the International Energy Agency (IEA) after the oil embargo symbolized discontinuity: only after losing control of the pricing-production regime did it become necessary for the industrialized countries to construct their own formal international organization.

The Theory of Hegemonic Stability and International Regime Change

It should be apparent from the above account that a theory purporting to explain international economic regime change between 1967 and 1977 faces two tasks: first, to account for the general pattern of increasing weakness, and second, to explain why the oil regime experienced the most serious changes, followed by money and trade. Furthermore, hegemonic stability theory must show not only a correspondence between patterns of regime change and changes in tangible power resources, but it must be possible to provide at least a plausible account of how those resource changes could have caused the regime changes that we observe.

The most parsimonious version of a hegemonic stability theory would be that changes in the overall international economic structure account for the changes in international regimes that we have described. Under this interpretation, a decline in U.S. economic power (as measured crudely by gross domestic product) would be held responsible for changes in international economic regimes. Power in this view would be seen as a fungible set of tangible economic resources that can be used for a variety of purposes in world politics.

There are conceptual as well as empirical problems with this parsimonious overall structure theory. The notion that power resources are fungible—that they can be allocated to issues as policymakers choose, without losing efficacy—is not very plausible in world political economy. . . . A second problem with the overall structure version of the hegemonic stability thesis is itself contextual: since we have to account not only for the general pattern of increasing weakness but also for differential patterns by issue area, focusing on a single independent variable will clearly not suffice. Changes in the overall U.S. economic position will clearly not explain different patterns of regime change in different issue areas.

Table 8.1 indicates the gross domestic product of the United States and the four other major market economy countries. As the last column indicates, the U.S. share of gross domestic product (GDP) of all five countries fell between 1960 and 1975 from about two-thirds to about one-half of the total five-country GDP. This is consistent with the hegemonic stability thesis, although one can question whether such a moderate decline (leaving the United States more than triple the economic size of its nearest competitor) accounts very convincingly for the regime changes that have been observed. . . .

Table 8.2 summarizes the evidence about changes in the distribution of economic power resources in the areas of trade, money, and petroleum. For trade and money the same comparative measures are used, similar to those used in Table 8.1: the U.S. proportion of resources is compared to that of the top five market-economy countries taken as a group. This measure can

Table 8.1   Distribution of Overall Economic Resources Among the Five Major Market-Economy Countries, 1960–1975 (gross domestic product in billions of current U.S. dollars)

Year	United States	Germany	Britain	France	Japan	U.S. Percent of Top Five Countries
1960	507	72	71	61	43	67
1963	594	95	85	83	68	64
1970	981	185	122	141	197	60
1975	1526	419	229	335	491	51

Source: United Nations Statistical Yearbook, 1977, pp. 742–744. Last column calculated from these figures.

Table 8.2   Distribution of Economic Resources, by Issue Area, Among the Five Major Market-Economy Countries, 1960–1975

A. *Trade Resources (exports plus imports as percentage of world trade)*

Year	United States	Germany	Britain	France	Japan	U.S. as Percent of Top Five Countries
1960	13.4	8.1	8.7	4.9	3.3	35
1965	14.4	9.4	8.0	5.7	4.2	35
1970	15.0	11.0	6.9	6.3	6.2	33
1975	13.0	10.0	5.8	6.4	6.6	31

Source: Kenneth N. Waltz, *Theory of International Politics* (Reading, Mass.: Addison-Wesley, 1979), Appendix Table IV, p. 215. Last column calculated from these figures.

B. *Monetary Resources (reserves as percentage of world reserves)*

Year	United States	Germany	Britain	France	Japan	U.S. as Percent of Top Five Countries
1960	32.4	11.8	6.2	3.8	3.3	56
1965	21.8	10.5	4.2	9.0	3.0	45
1970	15.5	10.7	3.0	5.3	5.2	39
1975	7.0	13.6	2.4	5.5	5.6	21

Source: Calculated from *International Financial Statistics* (Washington, D.C.: IMF), Volume XXXI-5 (May, 1978), 1978 Supplement, pp. 34–35. Last column calculated from these percentages.

C. *Petroleum Resources*
   1. United States imports and excess production capacity in three crisis years

Year	U.S. Oil Imports as Percent of Oil Consumption	U.S. Excess Production Capacity as Percent of Oil Consumption	Ratio of U.S. to European Position
1956	11	25	+14
1967	19	25	+6
1973	35	10	−25

Source: Joel Darmstadter and Hans H. Landsberg, "The Economic Background," in Raymond Vernon, ed., *The Oil Crisis,* special issue of *Daedalus,* Fall 1975 (pp. 30–31).

   2. Oil imports as percentage of energy supply

Year	United States	Western Europe	Japan	Ratio of U.S. to European Dependence
1967	9	50	62	.18
1970	10	57	73	.18
1973	17	60	80	.28
1976	20	54	74	.37

Source: Kenneth N. Waltz, *Theory of International Politics* (Reading, Mass.: Addison-Wesley, 1979) Appendix Table X, p. 221. Last column calculated from these figures.

be justified on the grounds that only Germany, Britain, France and Japan were strong enough during this period to consider challenging the United States or attempting to thwart it in significant ways; they are the potential rivals against whom it is significant to measure U.S. resources. The measures have to be somewhat different for petroleum. The relevant resources here appear to be U.S. imports vs. excess production capacity (since in 1956–1957 and 1967 the United States helped to maintain the existing regime by shipping oil to Europe from its own wells), and oil imports as a percentage of energy supply, giving a measure of relative U.S. and European dependence on imports.[10]

None of these measures of "economic power" is perfect; indeed, they are quite crude. Often the composition of exports, for instance, may be as important as the amount; and the balance of trade may in some cases weigh as heavily as the combinations of imports and exports. Probably most deficient is the monetary measure, since reserves are not necessarily an indicator of a country's *net* positions. Measures of the U.S. net liquidity position, however, would also show a sharp decline (U.S. GPO, 1971: 40; *International Economic Report of the President,* 1977: 161).[11]

The figures on economic resources provide prima facie support for the hegemonic stability thesis. The U.S. proportion of trade, for the top five market-economy countries, fell only slightly between 1960 and 1975—much less than its proportion of gross domestic product, reflecting the rapid increases during these years in U.S. trade as a proportion of total product. As we saw, the international trade regime—already under pressure in 1967—changed less in the subsequent decade than the regimes for money and oil. U.S. financial resources in the form of reserves fell sharply, reflecting the shift from U.S. dominance in 1960 to the struggles over exchange rates of the 1970s. In view of the continued ability of the United States to finance its deficits with newly printed dollars and treasury bills rather than with reserves, Table 8.2, B should not over interpreted: it does *not* mean that Germany was "twice as powerful as the United States" in the monetary area by 1975. Yet it does, as indicated above, signal a very strong shift in the resource situation of the United States. Finally, the petroleum figures—especially in Table 8.2, C-1—are dramatic: the United States went from a large positive position in 1956 and a small positive position in 1967 to a very large petroleum deficit by 1973. The hegemonic stability theory accurately predicts from this data that U.S. power in the oil area and the stability of the old international oil regime would decline sharply during the 1970s.

These findings lend plausibility to the hegemonic stability theory by not disconfirming its predictions. They do not, however, establish its validity, before concluding that the theory accounts for the observed changes, to see whether plausible causal sequences can be constructed linking shifts in the international distribution of power to changes in international regimes.

The following sections of this [chapter] therefore consider the most plausible and well-founded particular accounts of changes in our three issue areas, to see whether the causal arguments in these accounts are consistent with the hegemonic stability theory. The ensuing discussion begins with oil, since it fits the theory so well, and then addresses the more difficult cases. . . .

Interpreting Changes in the Petroleum Regime

The hegemonic stability model leads us to expect a change in international petroleum arrangements during the mid-1970s: The dominance of the United States and other industrialized countries was increasingly being undermined, as OPEC members gained potential power resources at their expense. What the Yom Kippur War did was to make the Arab members of OPEC willing to take greater risks. When their actions succeeded in quadrupling the price of oil almost overnight, mutual confidence rose that members of the cartel who cut back production would not be "double-crossed" by other producers, but would rather benefit from the externalities (high prices as a result of supply shortages) created by others' similar actions. Calculations about externalities became positive and risks fell. A self-reinforcing cycle of underlying resource strength leading to success, to increased incentives to cooperate, and to greater strength was launched. . . .

Interpreting Changes in the International Monetary Regime

On the basis of the hegemonic stability theory, one would predict that the major financial powers would have had great difficulty reconstructing the international monetary regime after the events of 1971. Yet the theory's precise prediction would have been ambiguous. As Table 8.1 indicates, in the early 1970s the gross domestic product of the United States still exceeded the combined total of the four next largest market-economy countries. Unilateral U.S. actions, furthermore, had strengthened the U.S. position and made its weak official reserve position less relevant. Thus there was some reason to believe that it might have been possible to reconstruct a stable international monetary regime under U.S. leadership in 1971.

This, of course, failed to occur. The exchange rates established at the Smithsonian Institution in December 1971 collapsed within fifteen months. The United States was no more willing after 1971 to play a responsible, constrained international role than it had been during the six years before the destruction of the Bretton Woods regime. Indeed, the U.S. monetary expansion of 1972, which helped to secure Richard Nixon's reelection, implied a decision by the administration to abandon that role.[12] Had its own economic policies been tailored to international demands, the United States could probably in 1971 have resumed leadership of a reconstructed international monetary system; but the United States did not have sufficient power to compel others to accept a regime in which only it would have monetary autonomy. Between 1971 and 1976, the United States was the most influential actor in international monetary negotiations, and secured a weak flexible exchange rate regime that was closer to its own preferences than to those of its partners; but given its own penchant for monetary autonomy, it could not construct a strong, stable new regime. . . .

Interpreting Changes in the International Trade Regime

As has been seen, changes in the trade regime between 1967 and 1977 were broadly consistent with changes in potential power resources in the issue area. Power resources (as measured by shares of world trade among the industrialized countries) changed less in trade than in money or oil; and the regime changed less as well. So once again, the hegemonic stability theory is not disconfirmed.

The causal argument of the hegemonic stability theory, however, implies that the changes we do observe in trade (which are less than those in money and oil but are by no means insignificant) should be ascribable to changes in international political structure. Yet this does not appear to be the case. Protectionism is largely a grass-roots phenomenon, reflecting the desire of individuals for economic security and stability and of privileged groups for higher incomes than they would command in a free market. Adam Smith excoriated guilds for protecting the wages of their members at the expense of society (although to the advantage, he thought, of the towns) (Smith, 1776). Officials of the GATT now criticize labor unions and inefficient industries for seeking similar protection and attempt to refute their arguments that such actions would increase national as well as group income. Most governments of advanced capitalist states show little enthusiasm for protectionist policies, but have been increasingly goaded into them by domestic interests. . . .

To some extent, difficulties in maintaining liberal trade among the OECD countries do reflect erosion of U.S. hegemony, although this is more pronounced as compared with the 1950s than with the late 1960s. In the 1950s the United States was willing to open its markets to Japanese goods in order to integrate Japan into the world economic system, even when most European states refused to do so promptly or fully. This has been much less the case in recent years. Until the European Common Market came into existence, the United States dominated trade negotiations; but since the EEC has been active, it has successfully demanded numerous exceptions to GATT rules. Relative equality in trade-related power resources between the

EEC and the United States seems to have been a necessary, if not sufficient, condition for this shift.

On the whole, the hegemonic stability theory does not explain recent changes in international trade regimes as well as it explains changes in money or oil. The theory is not disconfirmed by the trade evidence, and correctly anticipates less regime change in trade than in money or oil; but it is also not very helpful in interpreting the changes that we do observe. Most major forces affecting the trade regime have little to do with the decline of U.S. power. For an adequate explanation of changes in trade, domestic political and economic patterns, and the strategies of domestic political actors, would have to be taken into account.

Hegemonic Stability and Complex Interdependence: A Conclusion

A structural approach to international regime change, differentiated by issue area, takes us some distance toward a sophisticated understanding of recent changes in the international politics of oil, money, and trade. Eroding U.S. hegemony helps to account for political reversals in petroleum politics, to a lesser extent for the disintegration of the Bretton Woods international monetary regime, and to a still lesser extent for the continuing decay of the GATT-based trade regime.

Table 8.3 summarizes the results of the analysis. There is a definite correspondence between the expectations of a hegemonic stability theory and the evidence presented here. Changes in tangible power resources by issue area and changes in regimes tend to go together. In terms of causal

Table 8.3   Hegemonic Stability and International Economic Regimes 1966–1977: An Analytic Summary

	Oil	Issue Area Money	Trade
Correspondence between changes in power resources and changes in international regimes:			
Extent of change in tangible power resources, 1965–1977 (rank orders)	1	2	3
Extent of change in regime, 1967–1977 (rank orders)	1	2	3
Causal links:			
Plausibility of causal argument linking tangible resource changes to changes in the regime	high	medium	low

analysis, however, the results are more mixed. In the petroleum area a plausible and compelling argument links changes in potential economic power resources directly with outcomes. With some significant caveats and qualifications, this is also true in international monetary politics; but in trade, the observed changes do not seem causally related to shifts in international political structure.

On the basis of this evidence, we should be cautious about putting the hegemonic stability theory forward as a powerful explanation of events. It is clearly useful as a first step; to ignore its congruence with reality, and its considerable explanatory power, would be foolish. Nevertheless, it carries with it the conceptual difficulties and ambiguities characteristic of power analysis. Power is viewed in terms of resources; if the theory is to be operationized, these resources have to be tangible. Gross domestic product, oil import dependence, international monetary reserves, and share of world trade are crude indicators of power in this sense. Less tangible resources such as confidence (in oneself or in a currency) or political position relative to other actors are not taken into account. Yet these sources of influence would seem to be conceptually as close to what is meant by "power resources" as are the more tangible and measurable factors listed above. Tangible resource models, therefore, are inherently crude and can hardly serve as more than first-cut approximations—very rough models that indicate the range of possible behavior or the probable path of change, rather than offering precise predictions.

Notes

1. For figures relating to these points, see McCracken et al. (1977) esp. pp. 41–42. Cited below as "McCracken Report."

2. For analysis along these lines, see the following: Kindleberger (1974); Gilpin (1975); and Krasner (1976) pp. 317–347.

3. Kindleberger relies most heavily on the theory of collective goods. See his "Systems of International Economic Organization," in Calleo (1976) pp. 19–20; and Kindleberger, *The World in Depression*, chap. 14. It is necessary to be cautious in viewing international regimes as "collective goods," since in many cases rivalry may exist (everyone may benefit from stable money but not everyone can benefit noncompetitively from an open U.S. market for imported electronic products) and countries can be excluded from many international regimes (as the debate over whether to give most-favored-nation status to the Soviet Union illustrates). On the provision of collective goods, a useful article is Olson and Zeckhauser (1966) 48:266–279, reprinted in Russett (1968). See also Ruggie (1972) 66. September: 874–893.

4. Both Krasner, "State Power," and Kindleberger, *World in Depression*, make this admission. The hegemonic stability theory is criticized by Calleo (1976) in his concluding essay in Rowland. Calleo dislikes hegemony and seems reluctant to admit its association with economic order; he therefore seeks both to reinterpret

the pre-1914 period as not "imperial," and to characterize the bloc system of the 1930s as having "worked relatively well." Harold van B. Cleveland and Benjamin Rowland make better differentiated arguments in the same volume that critique or qualify the hegemonic stability thesis.

5. The problem with "force activation models" is that such models can "save" virtually any hypothesis, since one can always think of reasons, after the fact, why an actor may not have used all available potential power. See March, in Easton (1966), esp. pp. 54–61. See also Harsanyi (1962): 67–80.

6. Recent work on foreign investment indicates that international regimes in this area have also changed since 1967. See Krasner (1978); and Lipson (forthcoming).

7. For good discussions, see Cohen (1977); Bergsten (1975a); Eckes, Jr. (1975); and Hirsch (1967).

8. This was accomplished by the Arrangement Regarding International Trade in Textiles, known as the "Multifiber Agreement," or MFA. For the text, see "Arrangement Regarding International Trade in Textiles" (GATT publication, 1974). UNCTAD has commented on implementation of the agreement in "International Trade in Textiles," Report by UNCTAD secretariat, 12 May 1977.

9. On the basis of an index with 1974 as 100, OPEC's terms of trade had declined by 1977 to 91.0 (and by 1978 to 81.0). In 1977 this reflected import prices that were 25 percent higher, compared with oil prices that had only increased by 14 percent. Morgan Guaranty Trust Company, *World Financial Markets*, December 1978.

10. Since excess U.S. capacity fell between 1967 and 1976, the figures in Table 8.2, part C-2, actually understate the increase in U.S. dependence on foreign oil during that nine-year period. In 1967 the United States could have withstood a complete embargo quite comfortably (apart from any obligations or desire it might have had to export oil), simply by increasing production from shut-in wells. In a sense, then, its real energy dependence increased from zero to 20 percent during the 1967–1976 period.

11. U.S. liquid liabilities to all foreigners began to exceed reserve assets in 1959 (not alarming for a country acting in many ways like a bank), and had reached five times reserve assets by 1971. U.S. Government Printing Office, *The United States in the Changing World Economy*, statistical background material (1971), chart 53, p. 40. However, total U.S. assets abroad remained about 50 percent higher than foreign assets in the United States in 1975 [*International Economic Report of the President* (January 1977), p. 161].

12. For a discussion of President Nixon's manipulation of U.S. monetary policy for electoral purposes in 1971–1972, see Tufte (1978), pp. 45–55.

References

Bergsten, C. Fred. 1975a. *Dilemmas of the Dollar.* New York: New York University Press.

———. 1975b. "On the Non-Equivalence of Import Quotas and 'Voluntary' Export Restraints," in Bergsten, ed., *Toward a New World Trade Policy: The Maidenhead Papers.* Lexington, Mass.: Lexington Books.

Blair, John M. 1976. *The Control of Oil.* New York: Pantheon Books, pp. 43–47, 78–80.

Calleo, David P. 1976. in Rowland, ed., *Balance of Power or Hegemony: The*

Interwar Monetary System. New York: New York University Press, published for the Lehrman Institute.

Cohen, Benjamin J. 1977. *Organizing the World's Money: The Political Economy of International Monetary Relations*. New York: Basic Books.

Eckes, Jr., Alfred E. 1975. *A Search for Solvency: Bretton Woods and the International Monetary System, 1941–1971*. Austin: University of Texas Press.

Eisenhower, Dwight D. 1957. *Public Papers of the President. News Conference of President Eisenhower*. Washington, D.C.: Government Printing Office, p. 124. 6 February.

Feis, Herbert. 1947. *Seen From E.A.:Three International Episodes*. New York: Alfred A. Knopf, pp. 104ff.

———. 1944. *Petroleum and American Foreign Policy*. Stanford, Calif.: Food Research Institute, Stanford University, March.

Gilpin, Robert. 1975. *U.S. Power and the Multinational Corporation*. New York: Basic Books.

Gourevitch, Peter A. 1978. "The Second Image Reversed," *International Organization* 32 Autumn: 881–912.

Harsanyi, John C. 1962. "Measurement of Social Power, Opportunity Costs, and the Theory of Two-Person Bargaining Games," *Behavioral Science* 7: 67–80.

Hirsch, Fred. 1967. *Money International*. London: Penguin Press.

Hudec, Robert E. 1975. *The GATT Legal System and World Trade Diplomacy* New York: Praeger Publishers, p. 256.

IMF Survey, 12 December 1977, p. 373; 20 March 1978, p. 81; and 18 September 1978, p. 285.

International Economic Report of the President (January 1977), p. 161.

Jenkins, Glenn P. and Brian D. Wright. 1975. "Taxation of Income of Multinational Corporations: The Case of the United States Petroleum Industry," *Review of Economics and Statistics* 17. February.

Kindleberger, Charles P. 1976. "Systems of International Economic Organization," in Calleo, ed., *Money and the Coming World Order*. New York: New York University Press for the Lehrman Institute, pp. 19–20

———. 1974. *The World in Depression, 1929–1939*. Berkeley: University of California Press, chap 14.

Kolko, Gabriel. 1968. *The Politics of War: 1943–45*. New York: Vintage Books, pp. 294–307.

Kolko, Joyce and Gabriel. 1972. *The Limits of Power: The World and American Foreign Policy, 1946–1954*. New York: Harper and Row, pp. 413–420.

Krasner, Stephen D. 1978. *Defending the National Interest: Raw Materials Investment and U.S. Foreign Policy*. Princeton, N.J.: Princeton University Press. pp. 119–128, 190–213.

———. 1976. "State Power and the Structure of International Trade," *World Politics* 28. April: pp. 317–347.

Lipson, Charles. forthcoming. *Standing Guard: The Protection of Foreign Investment*. Berkeley: University of California Press.

Liska, George. 1967. *Imperial America: The International Politics of Primacy*, no. 2. Washington, D.C.: Johns Hopkins Studies in International Affairs.

MacPhee, Craig R. 1974. *Restrictions on International Trade in Steel*. Lexington, Mass.: Lexington Books.

Magdoff, Harry. 1969. *The Age of Imperialism*. New York: Monthly Review Press.

March, James G. 1966. "The Power of Power," in Easton, ed., *Varieties of Political Theory*. New York: Prentice-Hall, esp. pp. 54–61.

McCracken, Paul et al. 1977. *Towards Full Employment and Price Stability.* Paris: Organization for Economic Cooperation and Development.

Morgan Guaranty Trust Company, *World Financial Markets*, May and December 1978.

New York Times, 12 April 1979.

OECD. 1958. *Europe's Need for Oil: Implications and Lessons of the Suez Crisis.* Paris.

Olson, Jr., Mancur and Richard Zeckhauser. 1966. "An Economic Theory of Alliances," *Review of Economics and Statistics* 48:266–279, reprinted in Russett, ed., 1968. *Economic Theories of International Politics.* Chicago: Markham Publishing Co.

Patterson, Gardner C. 1965. *Discrimination in International Trade.* Princeton, N.J.: Princeton University Press.

Ruggie, John Gerard. 1972. "Collective Goods and Future International Collaboration," *American Political Science Review* 66. September: 874–893.

Servan-Schreiber, J. J. 1969. *The American Challenge*, trans. Ronald Steel. New York: Avon Books.

Shapiro, Harold T. 1977. "Inflation in the United States," in Krause and Salant, eds., *Worldwide Inflation: Theory and Recent Experience.* Washington, D.C.: Brookings Institution.

Shwadran, Benjamin. 1955. *The Middle East, Oil and the Great Powers.* New York: Praeger Publishers, pp. 302–309.

Smith, Adam, 1776. *An Inquiry into the Nature and Causes of the Wealth of Nations*, book 1, part 2, chap. 10

Strange, Susan. 1979. "The Management of Surplus Capacity," *International Organization* 33. Summer.

Tufte, Edward R. 1978. *Political Control of the Economy.* Princeton, N.J.: Princeton University Press, pp. 45–55.

Turner, Louis. 1978. *Oil Companies in the International System.* London: George Allen and Unwin for the Royal Institute of International Affairs, p. 70, 94–95.

U.S. Congress: Senate, Committee on Foreign Relations, Subcommittee on Multinational Corporations. 1974a. *The International Petroleum Cartel, The Iranian Consortium and U.S. National Security*, Committee Print, 93rd Cong., 2d sess., 21 February.

———. 1974b. *Multinational Corporations and United States Foreign Policy*, Part 4, Hearings, 93rd Cong., 2d sess., 30 January, pp. 84–110.

U.S. Congress: Senate, Committee on the Judiciary and on Interior and Insular Affairs. 1957. *Emergency Oil Lift Program*, Hearings, 85th Cong., 1st sess. February.

U.S. Government Printing Office. 1971. *The United States in the Changing World Economy.* Washington, D.C.: U.S. GPO, chart 53, p. 40.

———. 1943 and 1944. *Foreign Relations of the United States.* Washington, D.C.: U.S. GPO. Vol. 4, pp. 941–948; vol.3, pp. 94–111.

9

States and Industrial Transformation

Peter Evans

Peter Evans offers a new interpretation of why state intervention in the process of industrialization works in some cases and produces disasters in others. To answer this question, Evans develops a framework based on theories of the state, bureaucratic politics, and development. This new approach demonstrates that successful state intervention requires an understanding of three critical issues of state structure and relationship: (1) the way states are organized, (2) their relationship to the global economy, and (3) the nature of their links to society that Evans calls "embedded autonomy." To support his contention, he presents an empirical analysis of state effectiveness in predatory states like Zaire, developmental states like Korea and intermediary states like Brazil and India. Evans offers an insightful analysis that brings "the state back in" to our understanding of the process of successful industrial transformation.

A perennially popular Brazilian joke about two lions evokes one way of seeing the state. Escapees from the zoo, the two lions take different paths. One goes to a wooded park and is apprehended as soon as he gets hungry and eats a passerby. The second remains at large for months. Finally captured, he returns to the zoo sleek and fat. His companion inquires with great interest, "Where did you find such a great hiding place?" "In one of the ministries" is the successful escapee's answer. "Every three days I ate a bureaucrat and no one noticed." "So how did you get caught?" "I ate the man who served coffee for the morning break," comes the sad reply.

The moral is clear: bureaucrats do nothing and are never missed; even other bureaucrats care more about their morning coffee than about anything their colleagues do. The joke is popular because it affirms the conviction that Third World states deliver little of value. It is also popular because it converts bureaucrats from predators to prey. Identifying with the lion, listeners reverse their usual self-perception as victims of the state.

For those with less sense of humor, the quotidian power of the state over their individual lives can take on disturbing proportions. As Anita Desai (1991:3–4) puts it, "In the present time, in which the laws and whims of politicians and bureaucrats are as pervasive and powerful as those of the gods, not only must a minister be propitiated before he will issue a license, allot a house, or award a pension, but so must every clerk through whose hands the relevant file passes." This is not a lament about dictatorship or authoritarian repression, it is a complaint about how the Third World state conducts "business as usual" in relation to ordinary citizens.

Identification with the escaped lion is natural, but until less hierarchical ways of avoiding a Hobbesian world are discovered, the state lies at the center of solutions to the problem of order. Without the state, markets, the other master institution of modern society, cannot function. We do not spend our valuable time standing in lines in front of the counters of bureaucrats because we are masochists. We stand there because we need what the state provides. We need predictable rules, and these in turn must have a concrete organizational structure behind them. We need some organizational reflection, however imperfect, of general as opposed to individual interests. We need something beyond caveat emptor to sustain the process of exchange. We need "collective goods" like sewage systems, roads, and schools.

Attempts to dismantle the state or make it wither away risk perverse consequences. Communist revolutionaries who fought to install a system that would lead to the state's "withering away" ended up constructing state apparatuses more powerfully repressive than those of the age of absolutism. Fervent calls for the dismantling of the state by late-twentieth-century capitalist free-marketeers served to derail the state's ability to act as an instrument of distributive justice, but not to reduce its overall importance.

From the poorest countries of the Third World to the most advanced exemplars of welfare capitalism, one of the few universals in the history of the twentieth century is the increasingly pervasive influence of the state as an institution and social actor.[1] None of which is to say that the existing states give us what we need. Too often we stand in line in vain. The contradiction between the ineradicable necessity of the state in contemporary social life and the grating imperfection with which states perform is a fundamental source of frustration. Dreams of cannibalizing bureaucrats are one response. Analyzing what makes some states more effective than others offers less immediate satisfaction but should be more useful in the long run.

Since analyzing states entails almost as much hubris as pretending to run them, it is important to place some boundaries on the endeavor. My boundaries are narrow and clear. I have focused on only one of the state's tasks—promoting industrial growth. The empirical discussion is even more specific—the growth of local information technology (IT) industries. In addition, I am primarily concerned with a particular set of states—newly industrializing countries (NICs). Within this set, the empirical narrative draws primarily on the experiences of Brazil, India, and Korea during the 1970s and 1980s. Despite the boundaries, the hubris remains. The underlying aim is to understand state structures and roles, relations between state and society, and how states contribute to development.

In this chapter I will try to do three things. I will begin with a brief excursus on how responsibility for economic transformation has become increasingly central to the state's role. Then I will set economic transformation at a national level in the context of a global division of labor. Finally, I will try to explain the conceptual approach and strategies of investigation that lie behind the analysis.

States and Economic Transformation

States remain, as Weber defined them, "compulsory associations claiming control over territories and the people within them,"[2] but Weber's definition does not reduce the complexities of analyzing what states do. The first step in making analysis manageable is separating out the different roles that states perform. Making war and ensuring internal order are the classic tasks. In the contemporary world, fostering economic transformation and guaranteeing minimal levels of welfare are not far behind.

"Realists" tell us that, as sovereign entities in an anarchic world, states must concern themselves above all with the conditions of military survival.[3] Gilpin (1987:85) puts it succinctly: "The modern nation-state is first and foremost a war-making machine that is the product of the exigencies of group survival in the condition of international anarchy." Historical analysis makes it clear that the task of war making, more than any other, drove the construction of the modern state.[4] War making is also the task that allows the state most easily to portray itself as the universal agent of societal interests.

War making is one justification for the state's monopoly on violence; avoiding Hobbesian chaos internally is the other. Here again the state projects itself as an agent of the universal interests of society. What happens when a state disintegrates demonstrates that the claim is at least partially valid, as the citizens of contemporary Somalia can bitterly attest. Yet the claim also masks other aspects of the state's role.

When it defends sovereignty and internal order, the state is also, as Charles Tilly (1985) puts it, running a "protection racket" on its own behalf. Classic Marxist analysis reminds us that states are instruments for dominating the societies they serve. State actions reflect and enforce disparities of social power on behalf of the privileged. When the state exercises its monopoly on violence internally, its identification with the interests of the nation is no longer automatic. All states would like to portray themselves as carrying out a project that benefits society as a whole,[5] but sustaining this image requires continuous effort.[6]

Making war and enforcing internal order are classic roles, shared by ancient and modern states. In modern times, a third role has increasingly stolen the limelight. As political survival and internal peace are more often defined in economic terms, states have become responsible for economic transformation. There was always a connection between economic success and the ability to make war; economic failure meant eventual geopolitical decline. Now the state's economic role goes beyond being a means to military ends. It is a source of legitimacy in itself as well as a means to accomplishing the classic goals of military survival and internal order.

Being involved in economic transformation has two different facets. First of all, it means becoming implicated in the process of capital accumulation. Wealth creation is no longer considered just a function of nature and markets; effective statecraft is involved as well. Eliciting entrepreneurship and facilitating the creation of new productive capacities require a more complicated involvement in the affairs of the citizenry than simply eliciting loyalty and enforcing good behavior. The capacity required for what I will call the state's "transformative role" is correspondingly greater.

Once the state is implicated in the process of capital accumulation, responsibility for economic hardship is less easily shifted to nature or markets. If the inegalitarian outcomes of market relations cannot be dismissed as "natural," the state becomes responsible for deprivation as well as oppression. Its involvement in conflicts over distribution and welfare is more explicit.[7]

Welfare and growth easily become entangled. Fostering growth is often portrayed as a substitute for addressing distributional issues. Equating the overall accumulation of productive capacity with the national interest makes it easier to claim the role of universal agent. Better a smaller share of an expanding pie than a larger piece of a shrinking one, the argument goes. In reality, of course, pieces often shrink faster than pieces grow, and losers ask whose interests transformation serves. Nonetheless, growth remains a prerequisite to delivering welfare in the long term. Finding new ways to generate growth is a preoccupation even for welfare states.

As they become increasingly involved in economic transformation, states increasingly look at the international system not just as a system of sovereign political entities but also as a division of labor.[8] The connection between internal accomplishment and external context becomes intimate and direct. The very possibilities and criteria of economic transformation depend on the international division of labor. Transformation is inescapably defined in global terms.

The Global Context

Modern nations must fit their economic aspirations and activities into a global division of labor. Some produce cotton, others weave cloth, others market high fashion. Some mine iron ore, others make automobiles, others sell insurance. As "world system" theorists have hammered home, each nation's place in production for global markets has powerful implications for its politics and the welfare of its citizens.[9]

Like any kind of differentiation, the international division of labor can be seen as a basis of enhanced welfare or as a hierarchy. The arguments for enhanced welfare are enshrined in the theory of comparative advantage: all countries will be better off if each concentrates on what it does best.[10] Compatibility with resource and factor endowments defines the activity most rewarding for each country. Trying to produce goods that other countries can deliver more efficiently will only lower everybody's welfare.

Poorer countries have always been suspicious of this argument. From Alexander Hamilton[11] to Friedrich List[12] to Raul Prebisch,[13] there has been the suspicion that position in the international division of labor was a cause of development, not just a result.[14]

No one denies that an interdependent global economy is an improvement over a system of autarky, even for those that occupy less desirable niches. Nor does anyone deny that countries should do what they do best, just as the theory of comparative advantage argues. Yet contemporary theorizing offers support for persistent convictions that trying to get into more desirable niches is an important part of the struggle to develop. Recent developments in trade theory suggest that profit rates can differ systematically and persistently across sectors. As Paul Krugman (1987: 230) puts it, "with imperfect competition sustained by economies of scale and entry barriers, some industries may be able to generate persistent excess returns." Differential profit rates are, however, only part of what is at stake.

As Albert Hirschman (1977) has argued persuasively, filling a particular niche in the international division of labor has dynamic implications as well as static ones. Some sectors create a "multidimensional conspiracy" in favor of development, inducing entrepreneurial energies, creating positive spillovers in the rest of the economy, and molding political interest groups into a developmental coalition (Hirschman 1977:96). Niches in the international division of labor are desirable not just because they may entail higher profits and more rapid accumulation of capital, but also because they facilitate the achievement of the social and welfare goals associated with "development" in the broadest sense of the term.

Ability to generate a "multidimensional conspiracy" in favor of development is not inherent in a product itself. It depends on how the product fits into a global array of sectoral possibilities. As such theorists of the "product cycle" as Vernon and Wells have shown, products also have developmental trajectories.[15] The country that catches them on their upswing will reap different rewards from one that inherits them on their downswing. Textiles offered eighteenth-century England a "multidimensional conspiracy," but they are unlikely to do the same for late-twentieth-century India. Autos and steel supported a "multidimensional conspiracy" in the United States during the first half of this century, but not in Brazil during the second half. One era's multidimensional conspiracy may become another's "lagging sector."

From this perspective, "development" is no longer just a local trajectory of transformation. It is also defined by the relation between local productive capacity and a changing global array of sectors. The countries that fill the most rewarding and dynamic sectoral niches are "developed." Being relegated to niches that are less rewarding or filling less desirable links in a "commodity chain" reduces the prospect of progressive change.[16] Insofar as the international division of labor is a hierarchy, worrying about development means worrying about your place in the hierarchy.

Accepting national development as enmeshed in a global economy in which some positions are more dynamic and rewarding than others forces us to ask another question: Are positions in the international division of labor structurally determined or is there room for agency? Put more simply, can countries deliberately change the position they fill in the international division of labor?

Traditional renditions of the theory of comparative advantage are adamantly on the side of structure. Countries that attempt activities other than those most compatible with their productive endowments simply saddle themselves with wasteful output and lose potential gains from trade. If you are sitting on copper deposits, you are stupid not to sell copper. If your climate allows you to grow superior coffee, you should take advantage of it. Whether these are privileged or disadvantaged sectors in the global economy is neither here nor there. Countries must do what they do best. To do otherwise is self-destructive. The international division of labor presents itself as a structural imperative.

Traditional renditions make most sense in a world where international trade consists of unprocessed raw materials. In a world where manufactures dominate global trade and even services are increasingly considered "tradables," choices about what to make and sell cannot be deduced from a simple reading of natural endowments. Constructing comparative advantage is no less plausible than taking it as given. In William Cline's formulation, "increasingly, trade in manufactures appears to reflect an exchange of goods in which one nation could be just as likely as another . . . to develop comparative advantage . . . ."[17] In a globalized economy where most value is added at several removes from natural resources, the global division of labor presents itself as an opportunity for agency, not just an exogenous constraint.

The idea of constructing comparative advantage is, in some ways, a natural extension of traditional theory. The original Ricardian version emphasized given natural endowments. Hecksher and Ohlin's refinements emphasized relative domestic scarcities of labor and capital that were themselves products of development rather than inherent features of a given national territory. The idea of constructing comparative advantage brings in social and institutional factors that are even more clearly consequences of the developmental process. Cline does not really mean that "one nation could be just as likely as another" to develop comparative advantage in a particular good. He means that a simple assessment of natural resource endowments or the relative scarcity of different factors of production cannot tell us who will have a competitive advantage in chemicals or computers or designer jeans. Social and political institutions must be analyzed as well.

Michael Porter's work makes the point more explicitly. Why should Switzerland specialize in textile equipment while Italy gains comparative advantage in machinery for injection molding? Why should Denmark be a leader in pharmaceutical exports while Sweden has a comparative advantage in heavy trucks (Porter 1990: 1, 149, 162, 314)? With hindsight, these specializations might be traced back to historical differences in endowments, but emergence of advantage depends on a complex evolution of competitive and cooperative ties among local firms, on government policies, and on a host of other social and political institutions.

Sociologists and historians have long postulated such connections between social and institutional endowments and subsequent positions in the international division of labor. Robert Brenner's (1976) classic analysis of the divergent roles taken by Eastern and Western Europe in the early modern period is a case in point. For Brenner, Eastern Europe's specialization in the production of commodity grains depended on the inability of the Eastern European peasantry to defend itself against the imposition of repressive labor control, while the more politically powerful peasantry of Western Europe forced agriculture into products that lent themselves to productivity-enhancing technological change. Maurice Zeitlin (1984) focuses more on the state and politics to explain Chile's relegation to the role of a producer of raw materials over the course of the first third of the twentieth century, but the argument is similar.[18] Dieter Senghaas's (1985) analysis of the evolution of Denmark's position in the international division of labor over the course of the nineteenth and twentieth centuries stresses how social and political factors facilitate state strategies, which in turn allow reconstruction of the country's niche in the global system.

In a world of constructed comparative advantage, social and political institutions—the state among them—shape international specialization.[19] State involvement must be taken as one of the sociopolitical determinants of what niche a country ends up occupying in the international division of labor.

States with transformative aspirations are, almost by definition, looking for ways to participate in "leading" sectors and shed "lagging" ones. Gilpin (1987) argues that "every state, rightly or wrongly, wants to be as close as possible to the innovative end of 'the product cycle' where, it is believed, the highest 'value-added' is located." These states are not just hoping to generate domestic sectors with higher profit rates. They are also hoping to generate the occupational and social structures associated with "high-technology industry." They are hoping to generate a multidimensional conspiracy in favor of development.

Even if states are committed to changing their positions in the international division of labor as Gilpin suggests, desire and capability have to be sharply separated. Constructing new kinds of comparative advantage may be possible, but it is not likely to be easy. If not immutable, the structure of the global hierarchy is certainly obdurate.[20] Explicit attempts to move within it are likely to be ineffective or even counterproductive. Aspiration without the requisite state capacity can lead to bungling that undercuts even the existing bases of comparative advantage. Efforts to reshape participation in the global economy are interesting, not just because they might succeed, but also because they reveal the limits of what states can do.

If institutional endowments and the exercise of agency can reshape the kinds of products a country produces, and if producing different kinds of products has broad implications for development, arguments about how and whether states might facilitate the local emergence of new sectors become centrally important to understanding states, national development, and ultimately the international division of labor itself.

The Argument

Sterile debates about "how much" states intervene have to be replaced with arguments about different kinds of involvement and their effects. Contrasts between "dirigiste" and "liberal" or "interventionist" and "noninterventionist" states focus attention on degrees of departure from ideal-typical competitive markets. They confuse the basic issue. In the contemporary world, withdrawal and involvement are not the alternatives. State involvement is a given. The appropriate question is not "how much" but "what kind."

Ideas about variations in state involvement have to be built on the historical examination of particular states. I chose the set of states for which the challenge of industrial transformation is most salient. This study focuses on "newly industrializing countries" (NICs), defined, not narrowly as the four East Asia tigers,[21] but broadly to include those developing countries large enough or advanced enough to support a full range of industrial production. NICs are particularly good cases because they are less thoroughly constrained than peripheral raw materials exporters and more desperate to achieve transformation than advanced industrial countries.

Within this group I focused on Brazil, India, and Korea. At first glance this is an unlikely threesome. At the beginning of the 1970s, Brazil was the archetype of "dependent development," a country whose rapid industrialization was propelled by a combination of investment by transnational corporations and the demand for consumer durables that depended on rising inequality. India was a "multinational subcontinent" of three-quarters of a billion people, the vast majority of whom still depended on peasant agriculture, renowned for its penchant for autarky. In Korea, peasants were no longer the majority, and export orientation was considered the only sound basis for industrial growth. Yet all three are countries where state involvement in industrial transformation is undeniable. For understanding why it is more important to ask "what kind" of state involvement rather than "how much," they are an excellent triplet.

Variations in state involvement must also be situated in specific arenas. I chose to look at the evolution of the information technology (IT) sector in each of these countries during the 1970s and 1980s.[22] The IT sector (also known as "informatics" or the computer industry) is of obvious interest because it is the sector most likely to spark a twenty-first-century conspiracy in favor of development. It is a particularly good case because it provides an exceptionally strong test of the proposition that state involvement can affect a country's place in the international division of labor.

The information technology sector is fascinating in itself, but the purpose of a sectoral lens is to allow the concrete investigation of general concepts. My aim is not to theorize the IT sector but rather to sharpen general ideas about state structures, state-society relations, and how they shape possibilities for industrial transformation.

My starting premise is that variations in involvement depend on variations in the states themselves. States are not generic. They vary dramatically in their internal structures and relations to society. Different kinds of state structures create different capacities for action. Structures define the range of roles that the state is capable of playing. Outcomes depend both on whether the roles fit the context and on how well they are executed.

How should we characterize variations in state structure and state-society relations? My strategy was to start by constructing two historically grounded ideal types: predatory and developmental states. Predatory states extract at the expense of society, undercutting development even in the narrow sense of capital accumulation. Developmental states not only have presided over industrial transformation but can be plausibly argued to have played a role in making it happen.

Associating different kinds of states with different outcomes is a start, but if the two ideal types consisted only in attaching appropriate labels to divergent outcomes, they would not get us very far. The trick is to establish a connection between developmental impact and the structural characteristics of states—their internal organization and relation to society. Fortunately, there are clear structural differences between predatory and developmental states.

Predatory states lack the ability to prevent individual incumbents from pursuing their own goals. Personal ties are the only source of cohesion, and individual maximization takes precedence over pursuit of collective goals. Ties to society are ties to individual incumbents, not connections between constituencies and the state as an organization. Predatory states are, in short, characterized by a dearth of bureaucracy as Weber defined it.

The internal organization of developmental states comes much closer to approximating a Weberian bureaucracy. Highly selective meritocratic recruitment and long-term career rewards create commitment and a sense of corporate coherence. Corporate coherence gives these apparatuses a certain kind of "autonomy." They are not, however, insulated from society as Weber suggested they should be. To the contrary, they are embedded in a concrete set of social ties that binds the state to society and provides institutionalized channels for the continual negotiation and renegotiation of goals and policies. Either side of the combination by itself would not work. A state that was only autonomous would lack both sources of intelligence and the ability to rely on decentralized private implementation. Dense connecting networks without a robust internal structure would leave the state incapable of resolving "collective action" problems, of transcending the individual interests of its private counterparts. Only when embeddedness and autonomy are joined together can a state be called developmental.

This apparently contradictory combination of corporate coherence and connectedness, which I call "embedded autonomy," provides the underlying structural basis for successful state involvement in industrial transformation. Unfortunately, few states can boast structures that approximate the ideal type. While Korea can legitimately be considered a version of embedded autonomy, Brazil and India are definitely intermediate cases, exhibiting partial and imperfect approximations of embedded autonomy. Their structures do not categorically preclude effective involvement, but they do not predict it either.

Structures confer potential for involvement, but potential has to be translated into action for states to have an effect. I talk about patterns of state involvement in terms of "roles." To convey what Brazil, Korea, and India were doing in the information technology industry, I needed some new terminology. Traditional ways of labeling the state roles make it too easy to slip back into the comfortable feeling that the parameters of state involvement are known and we need only worry about "how much." New words are flags, recurring reminders that the question should be "what kind." I ended up with four rubrics. The first two, "custodian" and "demiurge," represent variations on the conventional roles of regulator and producer. The second pair, which I call "midwifery" and "husbandry," focuses more on the relation between state agencies and private entrepreneurial groups.

The role of custodian highlights one aspect of the conventional role of regulator. All states formulate and enforce rules, but the thrust of rule-making varies. Some rules are primarily promotional, aimed at providing stimulus and incentives. Other regulatory schemas take the opposite tack, aiming to prevent or restrict the initiatives of private actors. The rubric "custodial" identifies regulatory efforts that privilege policing over promotion.

Just as being a custodian is one way of playing out the more generic role of regulator, the demiurge[23] is a specific way of playing the more generic role of producer. All states play the role of producer, taking direct responsibility for delivering certain types of goods. At the very least, states assume this role in relation to infrastructural goods assumed to have a collective or public character, like roads, bridges, and communications nets. The role of demiurge is based on a stronger assumption about the limitations of private capital. It presumes that private capital is incapable of successfully sustaining the developmentally necessary gamut of commodity production. Consequently, the state becomes a "demiurge," establishing enterprises that compete in markets for normal "private" goods.

Taking on the role of midwife is also a response to doubts about the vitality of private capital, but it is a response of a different sort. The capacities of the local entrepreneurial class are taken as malleable, not as given. Instead of substituting itself for private producers, the state tries to assist in the emergence of new entrepreneurial groups or to induce existing groups to venture into more challenging kinds of production. A variety of techniques and policies may be utilized. Erecting a "greenhouse" of tariffs to protect infant sectors from external competition is one. Providing subsidies and incentives is another. Helping local entrepreneurs bargain with transnational capital or even just signaling that a particular sector is considered important are other possibilities. Regardless of the specific technique, promotion rather than policing is the dominant mode of relating to private capital.

Even if private entrepreneurial groups are induced to tackle promising sectors, global changes will continually challenge local firms. Husbandry consists of cajoling and assisting private entrepreneurial groups in hopes of meeting these challenges. Like midwifery, it can take a variety of forms, from simple signaling to something as complex as setting up state organizations to take over risky complementary tasks, such as research and development. The techniques of husbandry overlap with those of midwifery.

Most states combine several roles in the same sector. Sectoral outcomes depend on how roles are combined. My expectations for the informatics sector are obvious from the descriptions of the roles themselves. Neither trying to replace private capital nor fixating on preventing it from doing undesirable things should work as well as trying to create synergistic promotional relations with entrepreneurs or potential entrepreneurs. Combining midwifery and husbandry should work better than combinations that rely more heavily on custodian or demiurge.

The evolution of information technology sectors in Brazil, India, and Korea provides a nice illustrative confirmation of this basic contention. The blend of roles varied across countries. The variations grew, at least in part, out of differences in state structure and state-society relations. Different role combinations were associated with differential effectiveness in the expected way.

The principal difference between Korea and the other two countries was that Korea was able to build on a base of firms with a broad range of related industrial prowess, fostered by prior midwifery. This allowed the state to shift easily to the combination of prodding and supporting that I have called husbandry. Brazil and India made less thoroughgoing use of midwifery, got bogged down in restrictive rule-making, and invested heavily in direct production of information technology goods by state-owned enterprises. Their efforts to play custodian and demiurge were politically costly and absorbed scarce state capacity, leaving them in a poor position to embark on a program of husbandry that would help sustain the local industries they had helped create.

The similarities among the three countries were as suggestive as the differences. In each, the vision of a local information technology sector began with individuals convinced of the value of local informatics production who managed to find positions of leverage within the state apparatus. Their ideas were eventually turned into policies and institutions designed to bring forth local production. Initial state policies in all three countries began with "greenhouses," which provided space for local entrepreneurs to experiment protected from transnational competition. The greenhouses were a fundamental part of playing the role of midwife. Midwifery bore fruits in all three. The local industrial panorama in the mid- to late 1980s represented an impressive transformation of the scenery that had been in place two decades earlier.

By the end of the 1980s, Korea's industry was the largest and most robust, but local producers could claim significant successes in all three countries. Brazil had put together a new set of diversified informatics corporations that were significant actors on the local industrial scene. They presided over what had become a multibillion-dollar local industry. Local entrepreneurs commanded experienced organizations that employed thousands of technically trained professionals. Local *técnicos*[24] had demonstrated their technological bravura and even managed to turn their talents into internationally competitive products in the financial automation sector. India could boast early design successes by local hardware firms and the prospect of growing participation in international markets for certain kinds of software engineering. In Korea, production of information technology products had become a cornerstone of the country's overall industrial strategy. The *chaebol*[25] were going head to head with the world's leading firms in memory chips and had succeeded, at least for a time, in becoming a force in the world personal computer (PC) market.

All three industries had serious weaknesses, but they did demonstrate that developing countries could be producers as well as consumers of information technology goods. Overall, it was an impressive set of accomplishments for three countries that conventional analysis at the end of the 1960s would have categorically excluded from a chance at real participation in the globe's leading sector.

If I had stopped following my three information technology sectors in 1986 or 1987, this would have been the story—complicated in its details, but still relatively straightforward in its overall lessons. Some states and some roles were definitely more effective than others, but states could make a difference, even in what was universally judged an extremely difficult sector to crack.

Trends in the latter part of the 1980s gave the story a different twist. If nationalist industrialization had been the leitmotif in the 1970s, a new internationalization was clearly taking hold at the end of the 1980s. The hallmark of this new internationalization was a new relation between transnational and local capital, epitomized by IBM's new joint venture in India.[26] This was accompanied by a new emphasis on connectedness to the global economy, in terms of both increased openness to imports and increased concern with exports.

The easy interpretation would have been that this was a case of "the empire strikes back,"[27] of maverick nationalist aspirations being brought back under the discipline of the global economy. In fact, the new internationalization was not simply the negation of earlier nationalist policies. In some ways it was a vindication. IBM provides the emblematic case. Its expansion in the 1990s was increasingly based on alliances with locally owned firms. This was in part because the nature of the industry had changed globally, but it was also because local greenhouses had produced Brazilian, Indian, and Korean firms whose organizational strength, human capital, and experience made them legitimate partners. The new internationalization was in part the product of successful midwifery.

What was most interesting about this change, from the point of view of my argument, was its contradictory implications for relations between the state and the industrial constituency it had helped create. Local entrepreneurial groups had been at first tempted entrants, then grateful clients, and eventually actors strong enough to attract transnational allies. It was the state's opposition to foreign entry that gave local capital its trump card in negotiating the initial alliances, but once alliances had been negotiated, relations between firms and states changed again. The state's leverage was undercut. Firms had, in effect, traded the rents associated with state protection of the local market for those associated with their transnational corporate allies' proprietary technology and global market power. The new alliance of local entrepreneurs and transnational corporations make it harder to sustain the old alliance between local capital and the state.

If shrinking political support for state action corresponded neatly to the increasing developmental irrelevance of state action, the equation would be balanced, but that is not what analysis of the new internationalization suggested. New alliances were prone to devolve back into de facto subsidiaries. New exports, like software from India or PC clones from Korea, opened avenues for mobility in the global division of labor, but they also had the potential to turn into low-return dead ends. Continued husbandry was crucial, but in a sector populated with firms more beholden to transnational alliances than to state support, the political viability of past patterns of state involvement was in doubt.

I began my investigation of informatics industries trying to understand how state initiative could reshape local industrial efforts. I ended up intrigued by the way in which the very success of state efforts could undercut the political possibilities for sustaining state involvement. The neo-utilitarian perspective prevalent in the 1980s predicted that state involvement would produce an economically stagnant, politically stable symbiosis between officials with the capacity to create rents and private actors anxious to take advantage of them. I had found the opposite. State involvement was associated with economic dynamism, and the result was political contestation, not symbiosis.

The argument at the sectoral level ends up combining a vision of how state initiatives might produce industrial transformation with ideas about how state-induced industrial transformation redefines the political possibilities for future state action. This sectoral argument in turn raises obvious questions for my societal-level analysis of state structures and state-society relations. If successfully fostering new entrepreneurial groups in a particular sector generates a new political relation between the state and the constituency it has helped create, should not the same logic hold more generally?

Reexamination of the evolution of state-society relations suggests that the same basic dynamic does apply more generally. There is evidence to suggest that the transformative project advanced under the aegis of embedded autonomy in Korea may have undercut its own political foundations. If this is true, future state involvement will require some sort of reconstruction of state-society relations.

In the original formulation, embedded autonomy implied dense links not with society in general but specifically with industrial capital. From the point of view of other social groups, it was an exclusionary arrangement. Could embeddedness be built around ties to multiple social groups? Comparative evidence suggests that sometimes it can be. One way of reconstructing state-society relations would be to include links with other social groups, like labor. The evolution of agrarian communism in Kerala state in India and European social democracy in Austria suggests that a broadly defined embeddedness may offer a more robust basis for transformation in the long run. This suggestive evidence argues for further exploration of potential variations in embedded autonomy.

The essential outline of my . . . argument can be recapitulated in three points. First, developmental outcomes depend on both the general character of state structures and the roles that states pursue. Second, state involvement can be associated with transformation even in a sector like information technology where conventional wisdom would suggest little chance of success. Finally, an analysis of states and industrial transformation cannot stop with the emergence of a new industrial landscape. Successful transformation changes the nature of the state's private counterparts, making effective future state involvement dependent on the reconstruction of state-society ties.

Notes

1. See, for example, Boli-Bennett (1980).
2. Skoçpol (1985:7). For Weber's original discussion of the state, see Weber (1968 [1904–1911], chaps. 10–13).
3. For a brief summary of the most influential version of the "neorealist aproach," see Waltz (1979, chap. 2).
4. See Tilly (1985); Mann (1984, 1986, 1993); Giddens (1987).
5. Thereby achieving something analogous to what Gramsci (1971) called "hegemony."
6. Compare with Rueschemeyer and Evans (1985).
7. Cf. Rueschemeyer and Evans (1985) on the state as "an arena of social conflict."
8. For Wallerstein, of course, the existence of a single division of labor that encompasses multiple cultural and political units is what sets "world-economies" like the contemporary capitalist world-system apart from "mini-systems" and "world-empires." See Wallerstein (1974b: 391).
9. See Chase-Dunn (1989) for a recent overview of the world-system approach.
10. For a brief, accessible summary of the theory of comparative advantage, see Todaro (1977: 277–291).

11. Hamilton's (1817) "Report on Manufactures" remains a classic defense of state support for "import-substituting industrialization."

12. List (1885) set out German suspicions that Ricardian formulations of comparative advantages represented England's interests rather than "objective" economics.

13. Prebisch (1950) and his Economic Commission on Latin America (ECLA) school of economists led the earliest attacks on comparative advantage from the perspective of the contemporary Third World.

14. This is, of course, the position of the dependency approach (see Cardoso and Faletto 1979) and world-system theory. Wallerstein paints the picture with the broadest strokes. In his vision, occupying different productive roles in the world-system entails a comprehensive set of sociopolitical differences ranging from the kind of labor control to the extent of division among dominant elites to the efficacy of the state. See Wallerstein (1974a, 1974b); Chase-Dunn (1989).

15. See Vernon (1966) and Wells (1972). The idea of the "product cycle" has been expanded from the more "economistic" versions of Vernon and Wells to a full-blown sociopolitical schema by Kurth (1979) and Cumings (1987).

16. "Niches" do not necessarily have to be equated with sectors or products. A "commodity chain" perspective suggests that the process of production and commercialization in any sector includes a set of interlinked niches, some of which are more desirable than others. See Gereffi (1991); Gereffi and Korzeniewicz (1990, 1993); Hopkins and Wallerstein (1986). In this perspective, it is not what you produce that counts so much as what role you play in producing it. The difference is one of emphasis, since the distribution of available "links" depends on the sector. Some sectors involve chains with very few high return links; others offer a variety of possibilities. Nonetheless, the commodity chain perspective is a good reminder that what is important in the final analysis is not the sector per se but the set of productive roles that go with it.

17. Cited in Wade (1990: 355).

18. Both authors emphasize the contrast between their arguments and a world-system approach that assumes that class relations and the character of the state are consequences rather than determinants of position in the international division of labor. See especially Zeitlin (1984: 217–237) and Brenner (1977).

19. Obviously, the reverse argument is also possible. In the same article that looks at sectors as "multidimensional conspiracies in favor of development," Hirschman (1977) also uses the term "micro-Marxism" to describe the idea that sectoral specialization shapes sociopolitical institutions. The implications of "micro-Marxism" are certainly worth exploring (cf. Evans 1986; Shafer 1990, 1994; Karl 1997). Nonetheless, in a world dominated by manufacturing and services rather than by primary production, single products rarely determine the shape of a country's economy. The degree of specialization required for a "sectoral determinist" argument to be plausible is increasingly hard to find.

20. See, for example, Arrighi and Drangel (1986), who found that only a handful of nations actually changed their general position in the international division of labor as defined in world-system terms (i.e., shifted between periphery and semiperiphery or semiperiphery and core) during the post–World War II period.

21. Korea, Taiwan, Singapore, and Hong Kong.

22. While the bulk of the analysis focuses on the 1970s and 1980s, the period actually begins in the late 1960s in India and runs into the beginning of the 1990s.

23. Since the "demiurge" in its original usage was the creator of material things, the term is an appropriate label for a state that takes on directly productive activities itself rather than leaving them to private capital. Credit for first applying

the term to the state should go, I believe, to Luciano Martins (1977), who used it to describe Brazil's national development bank. For a different usage of the demiurge rubric, see L. Frischtak (1992).

24. Tecnico translates roughly as a professional whose expertise is technical.

25. The chaebol are the large conglomerate firms that dominate Korea's industrial economy.

26. IBM actually came back in 1992, but the move was clearly in the works at the end of the 1980s.

27. Emanuel Adler (1986, 1987) uses this term in talking about Brazil.

References

Adler, Emanuel. 1986. "Ideological Guerrillas and the Quest for Technological Autonomy: Development of a Domestic Computer Industry in Brazil." *International Organization,* 40, no. 3 (Summer): 673–705.

———. 1987. *The Power of Ideology: The Quest for Technological Autonomy in Argentina and Brazil.* Berkeley and Los Angeles: University of California Press.

Arrighi, Giovanni, and Jessica Drangel. 1986. "The Stratification of the World Economy." *Review,* 10:9–74.

Boli-Bennett, John. 1980. "Global Integration and the Universal Increase of State Dominance: 1910–1970." In *Studies of the Modern World-System,* edited by Albert Bergesen, New York: Academic Press.

Brenner, Robert. 1976. "Agrarian Class Structure and Economic Development in Pre-industrial Europe." *Past and Present,* 70 (February): 30–75.

Cardoso, Fernando Henrique. 1975. *Autoritarismo E Democratizacao.* Rio de Janeiro: Paz e Terra.

Chase-Dunn, Christopher. 1989. *Global Formation: Structures of the World Economy.* Cambridge, Mass.: Basil Blackwell.

Cline, William. 1987. *Informatics and Development: Trade and Industrial Policy in Argentina, Brazil, and Mexico.* Washington, D.C.: Economics International, Inc.

Cumings, Bruce. 1987. "The Origins and Development of the Northeast Asian Political Economy: Industrial Sectors, Product Cycles, and Political Consequences." In *The Political Economy of the New Asian Industrialism,* edited by Frederic Deyo, Ithaca, N.Y.: Cornell University Press.

Desai, Anita. 1991. "India: The Seed of Destruction." *New York Review of Books* 38, no. 12 (June 27): 3–4.

Evans, Peter. 1986. "A Generalized Linkage Approach to Recent Industrial Development in Brazil: The Case of the Petrochemical Industry, 1967–1979." In *Development, Democracy and the Art of Trespassing: Essays in Honor of Albert Hirschman,* edited by Alexandro Foxley, Guillermo O'Donnell, and Michael McPherson, South Bend: University of Notre Dame Press.

Frischtak, Claudio. 1992. "The International Market and the Competitive Potential of National Producers of Equipment and Systems. In *High Technology and Third World Industrialization: Brazilian Computer Policy in Comparative Perspective,* edited by Peter Evans, Claudio Frischtak, and Paulo Tigre, Research Series, no. 85. Berkeley: International and Area Studies.

Gereffi, Gary. ed. 1991. *Manufacturing Miracles: Paths of Industrialization in Latin America and East Asia.* Princeton, N.J.: Princeton University Press.

Gereffi, Gary, and Miguel Korzeniewicz. 1990. "Commodity Chains and Footwear Exports in the Semiperiphery." In *Semiperipheral States in the World-Economy*, edited by William Martin, Westport, Conn.: Greenwood Press.

———. 1993. ed. *Commodity Chains and Global Capitalism*. Westport, Conn.: Praeger.

Giddens, Anthony. 1987. *The Nation State and Violence*. Berkeley and Los Angeles: University of California Press.

Gilpin, Robert. 1987. *The Political Economy of International Relations*. Princeton, N.J.: Princeton University Press.

Gramsci, Antonio. 1971. *Selections from the Prison Notebooks*. New York: International Publishers.

Hamilton, Alexander. 1817. *The Soundness of the Policy of Protecting Domestic Manufactures*. Philadelphia: J.R.A. Skerett.

Hirschman, Albert. 1977. "A Generalized Linkage Approach to Development, with Special Reference to Staples." *Economic Development and Cultural Change*, 25 (supplement): 67–98.

Hopkins, Terence, and Immanuel Wallerstein. 1986. *Processes of the World-System*. Beverly Hills: Sage Publications.

Karl, Terry. 1997. *The Paradox of Plenty: Oil Booms and Petrostates*. Studies in International Political Economy, No. 26. Berkeley and Los Angeles: University of California Press.

Krugman, Paul. 1987. "Strategic Sectors and International Competition." In *U.S. Trade Policies in a Changing World Economy*, edited by Robert M. Stern. Cambridge: MIT Press.

Kurth, James R. 1979. "Industrial Change and Political Change: A European Perspective." In *The New Authoritarianism in Latin America*, edited by David Collier. Princeton: Princeton University Press.

List, Friedrich. 1885 (1966). *The National System of Political Economy*. New York: Augustus M. Kelley.

Mann, Michael. 1984. "The Autonomous Power of the State: Its Origins, Mechanisms and Results." *Archives Europeennes de Sociologie* 25:185–213.

———. 1986. *The Sources of Social Power, Vol. 1: A History from the Beginning to A.D. 1760*. Cambridge: Cambridge University Press.

———. 1993. *The Sources of Social Power, Vol. 2: The Rise of Classes and Nation States, 1760–1914*. Cambridge: Cambridge University Press.

Martins, Luciano. 1977. *A expansao recente do estado no brasil: seus problemas e seus atores*. Research report to FINEP, Rio de Janeiro.

Porter, Michael E. 1990. *The Competitive Advantage of Nations*. New York: Free Press.

Prebisch, Raul. 1950. *The Economic Development of Latin America and Its Principal Problems*. New York: United Nations.

Rueschemeyer, Dietrich, and Peter Evans. 1985. "The State and Economic Transformation: Toward an Analysis of the Conditions Underlying Effective Intervention." In *Bringing the State Back In*, edited by Peter Evans, Dietrich Reuschemeyer, and Theda Skoçpol, Cambridge: Cambridge University Press.

Senghaas, Dieter. 1985. *The European Experience: A Historical Critique of Developmental Theory*. Translated from the German by K. H. Kimmig, Dover, N.H.: Berg Publishers.

Shafer, D. Michael. 1990. "Sectors, States, and Social Forces: Korea and Zambia Confront Economic Restructuring." *Comparative Politics* (January): 127–150.

———. 1994. *Winner and Losers: How Sectors Shape the Developmental Prospects of States*. Ithaca, N.Y.: Cornell University Press.

Skoçpol, Theda. 1985. "Bringing the State Back In: Strategies of Analysis in Current Research." In *Bringing the State Back In*, edited by Peter Evans, Dietrich Rueschemeyer, and Theda Skoçpol, Cambridge: Cambridge University Press.

Tilly, Charles. 1985. "War Making and State Making as Organized Crime." In *Bringing the State Back In,* edited by Peter Evans, Dietrich Rueschemeyer, and Theda Skocpol, Cambridge: Cambridge University Press.

Todaro, Michael. 1977. *Economic Development in the Third World: An Introduction to Problems and Policies in a Global Perspective*. London: Longman.

Vernon, Raymond. 1966. "International Investment and International Trade in the Product Cycle." *Quarterly Journal of Economics* 80:190–207.

Wade, Robert. 1990. *Governing the Market: Economic Theory and the Role of Government in East Asian Industrialization*. Princeton, N.J.: Princeton University Press.

Wallerstein, Immanuel. 1974a. *The Modern World-System, vol. 1: Capitalist Agriculture and the Origins of the European World-Economy in the Sixteenth Century*. New York: Academic Press.

———. 1974b. "The Rise and Future Demise of the Capitalist World System." *Comparative Studies in Society and History* 16, 4 (September): 387–415.

Waltz, Kenneth. 1979. *Theory of International Politics*. Reading, Mass.: Addison-Wesley.

Weber, Max. 1968 [1904–1911]. *Economy and Society*, edited by Guenter Roth and Claus Wittich, New York: Bedminster Press.

Wells, Louis T. 1972. *The Product Life Cycle and International Trade*. Boston: Graduate School of Business Administration, Harvard University.

Zeitlin, Maurice. 1984. *The Civil Wars in Chile, or the Bourgeois Revolutions that Never Were*. Princeton, N.J.: Princeton University Press.

10

Sovereignty

Stephen D. Krasner

*Stephen Krasner takes issue with the emergent opinion that "globaliza-
tion" is undermining traditional notions of state sovereignty. He argues
that the sovereign-state model will endure, adapting as it always has to
changing circumstances. He acknowledges that the globalization process is
narrowing the scope of state control in some areas but maintains that such
control is expanding in other spheres as a direct result of this same process.
As such, Krasner's contribution to this volume provides an important qualification to those who suggest that the sovereign state is falling victim to
increasing integration across national borders.*

The idea of states as autonomous, independent entities is collapsing under
the combined onslaught of monetary unions, CNN, the Internet, and nongovernmental organizations. But those who proclaim the death of sovereignty misread history. The nation-state has a keen instinct for survival and
has so far adapted to new challenges—even the challenge of globalization.

The Sovereign State Is Just About Dead

Very Wrong

Sovereignty was never quite as vibrant as many contemporary observers
suggest. The conventional norms of sovereignty have always been challenged. A few states, most notably the United States, have had autonomy,
control, and recognition for most of their existence, but most others have

Reprinted with permission from *Foreign Policy,* 122 (January/February 2001).
Copyright © 2001 by the Carnegie Endowment for International Peace.

not. The polities of many weaker states have been persistently penetrated, and stronger nations have not been immune to external influence. China was occupied. The constitutional arrangements of Japan and Germany were directed by the United States after World War II. The United Kingdom, despite its rejection of the euro, is part of the European Union.

Even for weaker states—whose domestic structures have been influenced by outside actors, and whose leaders have very little control over transborder movements or even activities within their own country—sovereignty remains attractive. Although sovereignty might provide little more than international recognition, that recognition guarantees access to international organizations and sometimes to international finance. It offers status to individual leaders. While the great powers of Europe have eschewed many elements of sovereignty, the United States, China, and Japan have neither the interest nor the inclination to abandon their usually effective claims to domestic autonomy.

In various parts of the world, national borders still represent the fault lines of conflict, whether it is Israelis and Palestinians fighting over the status of Jerusalem, Indians and Pakistanis threatening to go nuclear over Kashmir, or Ethiopia and Eritrea clashing over disputed territories. Yet commentators nowadays are mostly concerned about the erosion of national borders as a consequence of globalization. Governments and activists alike complain that multilateral institutions such as the United Nations, the World Trade Organization, and the International Monetary Fund overstep their authority by promoting universal standards for everything from human rights and the environment to monetary policy and immigration. However, the most important impact of economic globalization and transnational norms will be to alter the scope of state authority rather than to generate some fundamentally new way to organize political life.

Sovereignty Means Final Authority

Not Anymore, if Ever

When philosophers Jean Bodin and Thomas Hobbes first elaborated the notion of sovereignty in the 16th and 17th centuries, they were concerned with establishing the legitimacy of a single hierarchy of domestic authority. Although Bodin and Hobbes accepted the existence of divine and natural law, they both (especially Hobbes) believed the word of the sovereign was law. Subjects had no right to revolt. Bodin and Hobbes realized that imbuing the sovereign with such overweening power invited tyranny, but they were predominately concerned with maintaining domestic order, without which they believed there could be no justice. Both were writing in a world driven by sectarian strife. Bodin was almost killed in religious riots in

France in 1572. Hobbes published his seminal work, *Leviathan,* only a few years after parliament (composed of Britain's emerging wealthy middle class) had executed Charles I in a civil war that had sought to wrest state control from the monarchy.

This idea of supreme power was compelling, but irrelevant in practice. By the end of the 17th century, political authority in Britain was divided between king and parliament. In the United States, the Founding Fathers established a constitutional structure of checks and balances and multiple sovereignties distributed among local and national interests that were inconsistent with hierarchy and supremacy. The principles of justice, and especially order, so valued by Bodin and Hobbes, have best been provided by modern democratic states whose organizing principles are antithetical to the idea that sovereignty means uncontrolled domestic power.

If sovereignty does not mean a domestic order with a single hierarchy of authority, what does it mean? In the contemporary world, sovereignty primarily has been linked with the idea that states are autonomous and independent from each other. Within their own boundaries, the members of a polity are free to choose their own form of government. A necessary corollary of this claim is the principle of nonintervention: One state does not have a right to intervene in the internal affairs of another.

More recently, sovereignty has come to be associated with the idea of control over transborder movements. When contemporary observers assert that the sovereign state is just about dead, they do not mean that constitutional structures are about to disappear. Instead, they mean that technological change has made it very difficult, or perhaps impossible, for states to control movements across their borders of all kinds of material things (from coffee to cocaine) and not-so-material things (from Hollywood movies to capital flows).

Finally, sovereignty has meant that political authorities can enter into international agreements. They are free to endorse any contract they find attractive. Any treaty among states is legitimate provided that it has not been coerced.

The Peace of Westphalia Produced the Modern Sovereign State

No, It Came Later

Contemporary pundits often cite the 1648 Peace of Westphalia (actually two separate treaties, Münster and Osnabrück) as the political big bang that created the modern system of autonomous states. Westphalia—which ended the Thirty Years' War against the hegemonic power of the Holy Roman Empire—delegitimized the already waning transnational role of the Catholic Church and validated the idea that international relations should be driven by balance-of-power considerations rather than the ideals of Christendom. But Westphalia was first and foremost a new constitution for the Holy Roman Empire. The preexisting right of the principalities in the empire to make treaties was affirmed, but the Treaty of Münster stated that "such Alliances be not against the Emperor, and the Empire, nor against the Publick Peace, and this Treaty, and without prejudice to the Oath by which every one is bound to the Emperor and the Empire." The domestic political structures of the principalities remained embedded in the Holy Roman Empire. The Duke of Saxony, the Margrave of Brandenburg, the Count of Palatine, and the Duke of Bavaria were affirmed as electors who (along with the archbishops of Mainz, Trier, and Cologne) chose the emperor. They did not become or claim to be kings in their own right.

Perhaps most important, Westphalia established rules for religious tolerance in Germany. The treaties gave lip service to the principle (cuius regio, eius religio) that the prince could set the religion of his territory—and then went on to violate this very principle through many specific provisions. The signatories agreed that the religious rules already in effect would stay in place. Catholics and Protestants in German cities with mixed populations would share offices. Religious issues had to be settled by a majority of both Catholics and Protestants in the diet and courts of the empire. None of the major political leaders in Europe endorsed religious toleration in principle, but they recognized that religious conflicts were so volatile that it was essential to contain rather than repress sectarian differences. All in all, Westphalia is a pretty medieval document, and its biggest explicit innovation—provisions that undermined the power of princes to control religious affairs within their territories—was antithetical to the ideas of national sovereignty that later became associated with the so-called Westphalian system.

Universal Human Rights Are an Unprecedented Challenge to Sovereignty

Wrong

The struggle to establish international rules that compel leaders to treat their subjects in a certain way has been going on for a long time. Over the centuries the emphasis has shifted from religious toleration, to minority rights (often focusing on specific ethnic groups in specific countries), to human rights (emphasizing rights enjoyed by all or broad classes of individuals). In a few instances states have voluntarily embraced international supervision, but generally the weak have acceded to the preferences of the strong: The Vienna settlement following the Napoleonic wars guaranteed religious toleration for Catholics in the Netherlands. All of the successor states of the Ottoman Empire, beginning with Greece in 1832 and ending with Albania in 1913, had to accept provisions for civic and political equality for religious minorities as a condition for international recognition. The peace settlements following World War I included extensive provisions for the protection of minorities. Poland, for instance, agreed to refrain from holding elections on Saturday because such balloting would have violated the Jewish Sabbath. Individuals could bring complaints against governments through a minority rights bureau established within the League of Nations.

But as the Holocaust tragically demonstrated, interwar efforts at international constraints on domestic practices failed dismally. After World War II, human, rather than minority, rights became the focus of attention. The United Nations Charter endorsed both human rights and the classic sovereignty principle of nonintervention. The 20-plus human rights accords that have been signed during the last half century cover a wide range of issues including genocide, torture, slavery, refugees, stateless persons, women's rights, racial discrimination, children's rights, and forced labor. These U.N. agreements, however, have few enforcement mechanisms, and even their provisions for reporting violations are often ineffective.

The tragic and bloody disintegration of Yugoslavia in the 1990s revived earlier concerns with ethnic rights. International recognition of the Yugoslav successor states was conditional upon their acceptance of constitutional provisions guaranteeing minority rights. The Dayton accords established externally controlled authority structures in Bosnia, including a Human Rights Commission (a majority of whose members were appointed by the Western European states). NATO created a de facto protectorate in Kosovo.

The motivations for such interventions—humanitarianism and security—have hardly changed. Indeed, the considerations that brought the great powers into the Balkans following the wars of the 1870s were hardly different from those that engaged NATO and Russia in the 1990s.

Globalization Undermines State Control

No

State control could never be taken for granted. Technological changes over the last 200 years have increased the flow of people, goods, capital, and ideas—but the problems posed by such movements are not new. In many ways, states are better able to respond now than they were in the past.

The impact of the global media on political authority (the so-called CNN effect) pales in comparison to the havoc that followed the invention of the printing press. Within a decade after Martin Luther purportedly nailed his 95 theses to the Wittenberg church door, his ideas had circulated throughout Europe. Some political leaders seized upon the principles of the Protestant Reformation as a way to legitimize secular political authority. No sovereign monarch could contain the spread of these concepts, and some lost not only their lands but also their heads. The sectarian controversies of the 16th and 17th centuries were perhaps more politically consequential than any subsequent transnational flow of ideas.

In some ways, international capital movements were more significant in earlier periods than they are now. During the 19th century, Latin American states (and to a lesser extent Canada, the United States, and Europe) were beset by boom-and-bust cycles associated with global financial crises. The Great Depression, which had a powerful effect on the domestic politics of all major states, was precipitated by an international collapse of credit. The Asian financial crisis of the late 1990s was not nearly as devastating. Indeed, the speed with which countries recovered from the Asian flu reflects how a better working knowledge of economic theories and more effective central banks have made it easier for states to secure the advantages (while at the same time minimizing the risks) of being enmeshed in global financial markets.

In addition to attempting to control the flows of capital and ideas, states have long struggled to manage the impact of international trade. The opening of long-distance trade for bulk commodities in the 19th century created fundamental cleavages in all of the major states. Depression and plummeting grain prices made it possible for German Chancellor Otto von Bismarck to prod the landholding aristocracy into a protectionist alliance with urban heavy industry (this coalition of "iron and rye" dominated German politics for decades). The tariff question was a basic divide in U.S. politics for much of the last half of the 19th and first half of the 20th centuries. But, despite growing levels of imports and exports since 1950, the political salience of trade has receded because national governments have developed social welfare strategies that cushion the impact of international competition, and workers with higher skill levels are better able to adjust to changing international conditions. It has become easier, not harder, for states to manage the flow of goods and services.

Globalization Is Changing the Scope of State Control

Yes

The reach of the state has increased in some areas but contracted in others. Rulers have recognized that their effective control can be enhanced by walking away from issues they cannot resolve. For instance, beginning with the Peace of Westphalia, leaders chose to surrender their control over religion because it proved too volatile. Keeping religion within the scope of state authority undermined, rather than strengthened, political stability.

Monetary policy is an area where state control expanded and then ultimately contracted. Before the 20th century, states had neither the administrative competence nor the inclination to conduct independent monetary policies. The mid-20th-century effort to control monetary affairs, which was associated with Keynesian economics, has now been reversed due to the magnitude of short-term capital flows and the inability of some states to control inflation. With the exception of Great Britain, the major European states have established a single monetary authority. Confronting recurrent hyperinflation, Ecuador adopted the U.S. dollar as its currency in 2000.

Along with the erosion of national currencies, we now see the erosion of national citizenship—the notion that an individual should be a citizen of one and only one country, and that the state has exclusive claims to that person's loyalty. For many states, there is no longer a sharp distinction between citizens and noncitizens. Permanent residents, guest workers, refugees, and undocumented immigrants are entitled to some bundle of rights even if they cannot vote. The ease of travel and the desire of many countries to attract either capital or skilled workers have increased incentives to make citizenship a more flexible category.

Although government involvement in religion, monetary affairs, and claims to loyalty has declined, overall government activity, as reflected in taxation and government expenditures, has increased as a percentage of national income since the 1950s among the most economically advanced states. The extent of a country's social welfare programs tends to go hand in hand with its level of integration within the global economy. Crises of authority and control have been most pronounced in the states that have been the most isolated, with sub-Saharan Africa offering the largest number of unhappy examples.

NGOs Are Nibbling at National Sovereignty

To Some Extent

Transnational nongovernmental organizations (NGOs) have been around for quite awhile, especially if you include corporations. In the 18th century, the East India Company possessed political power (and even an expeditionary military force) that rivaled many national governments. Throughout the 19th century, there were transnational movements to abolish slavery, promote the rights of women, and improve conditions for workers.

The number of transnational NGOs, however, has grown tremendously, from around 200 in 1909 to over 17,000 today. The availability of inexpensive and very fast communications technology has made it easier for such groups to organize and make an impact on public policy and international law—the international agreement banning land mines being a recent case in point. Such groups prompt questions about sovereignty because they appear to threaten the integrity of domestic decision-making. Activists who lose on their home territory can pressure foreign governments, which may in turn influence decision makers in the activists' own nation.

But for all of the talk of growing NGO influence, their power to affect a country's domestic affairs has been limited when compared to governments, international organizations, and multinational corporations. The United Fruit Company had more influence in Central America in the early part of the 20th century than any NGO could hope to have anywhere in the contemporary world. The International Monetary Fund and other multilateral financial institutions now routinely negotiate conditionality agreements that involve not only specific economic targets but also domestic institutional changes, such as pledges to crack down on corruption and break up cartels.

Smaller, weaker states are the most frequent targets of external efforts to alter domestic institutions, but more powerful states are not immune. The openness of the U.S. political system means that not only NGOs, but also foreign governments, can play some role in political decisions. (The Mexican government, for instance, lobbied heavily for the passage of the North American Free Trade Agreement.) In fact, the permeability of the American polity makes the United States a less threatening partner; nations are more willing to sign on to U.S.-sponsored international arrangements because they have some confidence that they can play a role in U.S. decision making.

Sovereignty Blocks Conflict Resolution

Yes, Sometimes

Rulers as well as their constituents have some reasonably clear notion of what sovereignty means—exclusive control within a given territory—even if this norm has been challenged frequently by inconsistent principles (such as universal human rights) and violated in practice (the U.S.- and British-enforced no-fly zones over Iraq). In fact, the political importance of conventional sovereignty rules has made it harder to solve some problems. There is, for instance, no conventional sovereignty solution for Jerusalem, but it doesn't require much imagination to think of alternatives: Divide the city into small pieces; divide the Temple Mount vertically with the Palestinians controlling the top and the Israelis the bottom; establish some kind of international authority; divide control over different issues (religious practices versus taxation, for instance) among different authorities.

Any one of these solutions would be better for most Israelis and Palestinians than an ongoing stalemate, but political leaders on both sides have had trouble delivering a settlement because they are subject to attacks by counterelites who can wave the sovereignty flag.

Conventional rules have also been problematic for Tibet. Both the Chinese and the Tibetans might be better off if Tibet could regain some of the autonomy it had as a tributary state within the traditional Chinese empire. Tibet had extensive local control, but symbolically (and sometimes through tribute payments) recognized the supremacy of the emperor. Today, few on either side would even know what a tributary state is, and even if the leaders of Tibet worked out some kind of settlement that would give their country more self-government, there would be no guarantee that they could gain the support of their own constituents.

If, however, leaders can reach mutual agreements, bring along their constituents, or are willing to use coercion, sovereignty rules can be violated in inventive ways. The Chinese, for instance, made Hong Kong a special administrative region after the transfer from British rule, allowed a foreign judge to sit on the Court of Final Appeal, and secured acceptance by other states not only for Hong Kong's participation in a number of international organizations but also for separate visa agreements and recognition of a distinct Hong Kong passport. All of these measures violate conventional sovereignty rules since Hong Kong does not have juridical independence. Only by inventing a unique status for Hong Kong, which involved the acquiescence of other states, could China claim sovereignty while simultaneously preserving the confidence of the business community.

The European Union Is a
New Model for Supranational Governance

Yes, But Only for the Europeans

The European Union (EU) really is a new thing, far more interesting in terms of sovereignty than Hong Kong. It is not a conventional international organization because its member states are now so intimately linked with one another that withdrawal is not a viable option. It is not likely to become a "United States of Europe"—a large federal state that might look something like the United States of America—because the interests, cultures, economies, and domestic institutional arrangements of its members are too diverse. Widening the EU to include the former communist states of Central Europe would further complicate any efforts to move toward a political organization that looks like a conventional sovereign state.

The EU is inconsistent with conventional sovereignty rules. Its member states have created supranational institutions (the European Court of

Justice, the European Commission, and the Council of Ministers) that can make decisions opposed by some member states. The rulings of the court have direct effect and supremacy within national judicial systems, even though these doctrines were never explicitly endorsed in any treaty. The European Monetary Union created a central bank that now controls monetary affairs for three of the union's four largest states. The Single European Act and the Maastricht Treaty provide for majority or qualified majority, but not unanimous, voting in some issue areas. In one sense, the European Union is a product of state sovereignty because it has been created through voluntary agreements among its member states. But, in another sense, it fundamentally contradicts conventional understandings of sovereignty because these same agreements have undermined the juridical autonomy of its individual members.

The European Union, however, is not a model that other parts of the world can imitate. The initial moves toward integration could not have taken place without the political and economic support of the United States, which was, in the early years of the Cold War, much more interested in creating a strong alliance that could effectively oppose the Soviet Union than it was in any potential European challenge to U.S. leadership. Germany, one of the largest states in the European Union, has been the most consistent supporter of an institutional structure that would limit Berlin's own freedom of action, a reflection of the lessons of two devastating wars and the attractiveness of a European identity for a country still grappling with the sins of the Nazi era. It is hard to imagine that other regional powers such as China, Japan, or Brazil, much less the United States, would have any interest in tying their own hands in similar ways. (Regional trading agreements such as MERCOSUR and NAFTA have very limited supranational provisions and show few signs of evolving into broader monetary or political unions.) The EU is a new and unique institutional structure, but it will coexist with, not displace, the sovereign-state model.

Want to Know More?

For some examples of the conventional view that sovereignty is a mechanistic process that constrains state behavior, see Hedley Bull's classic *The Anarchical Society: A Study of Order in World Politics* (New York: Columbia University Press, 1977) and Robert Jackson's *Quasi-states: Sovereignty, International Relations and the Third World* (Cambridge: Cambridge University Press, 1990). The most forceful recent presentations of the constructivist perspective, which emphasizes the importance of ideas, are Alexander Wendt's *Social Theory of International Politics* (Cambridge: Cambridge University Press, 1999) and John Ruggie's

Constructing the World Polity: Essays on International Institutionalization (London: Routledge, 1998).

More skeptical views about the impact of sovereignty on state behavior can be found in Stephen D. Krasner's *Sovereignty: Organized Hypocrisy* (Princeton: Princeton University Press, 1999) and Michael Fowler and Julie Marie Bunck's *Law, Power, and the Sovereign State: The Evolution and Application of the Concept of Sovereignty* (University Park: Pennsylvania State University Press, 1995).

Hendrik Spruyt's *The Sovereign State and Its Competitors* (Princeton: Princeton University Press, 1994) and Charles Tilly's *Coercion, Capital, and European States, AD 990–1992* (Cambridge: Blackwell Publishers, 1992) emphasize economic and military considerations in their excellent historical analyses of the evolution of the sovereign-state system. Quentin Skinner's *The Foundations of Modern Political Thought, Volume 2, The Age of Reformation* (Cambridge: Cambridge University Press, 1978) is a superlative treatment of the relationship between the ideas of the Reformation and the development of the modern state.

Paul Gordon Lauren offers historical insight into international efforts to safeguard human rights in *The Evolution of International Human Rights: Visions Seen* (Philadelphia: University of Pennsylvania Press, 1998). For a treatment of the almost forgotten Versailles minority-rights regimes established after World War I, see Inis L. Claude, Jr.'s *National Minorities: An International Problem* (New York: Greenwood Press, 1969).

Margaret Keck and Kathryn Sikkink investigate the growing significance of transnational nongovernmental organizations in *Activists Beyond Borders: Advocacy Networks in International Politics* (Ithaca: Cornell University Press, 1998), and Jeremy Rabkin discusses the anxiety they provoke in *Why Sovereignty Matters* (Washington: AEI Press, 1998). Anyone interested in globalization and its national political underpinnings must read Kevin H. O'Rourke and Jeffrey G. Williamson's *Globalization and History: The Evolution of a Nineteenth-Century Atlantic Economy* (Cambridge: MIT Press, 1999).

11

Excerpts from *Capital* and *Communist Manifesto*

Karl Marx and Friedrich Engels

The following excerpts from the classic works of Karl Marx focus on Marx's critique of the nature of capitalism in the workplace and in society. In the selection from Capital *(1867), Marx outlines the division and specialization of labor under capitalistic conditions and the conversion of labor to commodity status. Marx contends that this division impoverishes and brutalizes the worker—the foundation of the notion of estrangement, or alienation, an enduring concept of the Marxist literature. The excerpt from the* Communist Manifesto *(1848) focuses on the capitalist class (the bourgeoisie) and its powerful and revolutionary impact on society, providing a summary glimpse of the Marxist view of the dialectical forces of history. The contradictions of capitalism become apparent in the pauperization of all classes except the capitalists and in the persistence of ever deeper crises in the impending clash of historical forces—the capitalist and proletarian classes. Many of Marx's ideas about capitalism, such as his analysis of alienation and of the distributional impact of capitalism, remain timely on the cusp of the twenty-first century.*

From *Capital*

The Detail Labourer and His Implements

If we now go more into detail, it is, in the first place, clear that a labourer who all his life performs one and the same simple operation, converts his whole body into the automatic, specialised implement of that operation. Consequently, he takes less time in doing it, than the artificer who performs a whole series of operations in succession. But the collective labourer, who constitutes the living mechanism of manufacture, is made up solely of such specialised detail labourers. Hence, in comparison with the independent handicraft, more is produced in a given time, or the productive power of labor is increased. Moreover, when once this fractional work is established as the exclusive function of one person, the methods it employs become perfected. The workman's continued repetition of the same simple act, and the concentration of his attention on it, teach him by experience how to attain the desired effects with the minimum of exertion. But since there are always several generations of labourers living at one time, and working together at the manufacture of a given article, the technical skill, the tricks of the trade thus acquired, become established, and are accumulated and handed down. Manufacture, in fact, produces the skill of the detail labourer, by reproducing, and systematically driving to an extreme within the workshop, the naturally developed differentiation of trades, which it found ready to hand in society at large. On the other hand, the conversion of fractional work into the life-calling of one man, corresponds to the tendency shown by earlier societies, to make trades hereditary; either to petrify them into castes, or whenever definite historical conditions beget in the individual a tendency to vary in a manner incompatible with the nature of castes, to ossify them into guilds. . . .

An artificer, who performs one after another the various fractional operations in the production of a finished article, must at one time change his place, at another his tools. The transition from one operation to another interrupts the flow of his labour, and creates, so to say, gaps in his working-day. These gaps close up so soon as he is tied to one and the same operation all day long; they vanish in proportion as the changes in his work diminish. The resulting increased productive power is owing either to an increased expenditure of labour-power in a given time—i.e., to increased intensity of labour—or to a decrease in the amount of labour-power unproductively consumed. The extra expenditure of power, demanded by every transition from rest to motion, is made up for by prolonging the duration of the normal velocity when once acquired. On the other hand, constant labour of one uniform kind disturbs the intensity and flow of a man's animal spirits, which had recreation and delight in mere change of activity. . . .

Early in the manufacturing period, the principle of lessening the necessary labour-time in the production of commodities, was adopted and formulated: and the use of machines, especially for certain simple first processes that have to be conducted on a very large scale, and with the application of great force, sprang up here and there. Thus, at an early period in paper manufacture, the tearing up of the rags was done by paper-mills; and in metal works, the pounding of the ores was effected by stamping mills. The Roman Empire had handed down the elementary form of all machinery in the water-wheel.

The handicraft period bequeathed to us the great inventions of the compass, of gunpowder, of type-printing, and of the automatic clock. But, on the whole, machinery played that subordinate part which Adam Smith assigns to it in comparison with division of labour. The sporadic use of machinery in the 17th century was of the greatest importance, because it supplied the great mathematicians of that time with a practical basis and stimulant to the creation of the science of mechanics.

The collective labourer, formed by the combination of a number of detail labourers, is the machinery specially characteristic of the manufacturing period. The various operations that are performed in turns by the producer of a commodity, and coalesce one with another during the progress of production, lay claim to him in various ways. In one operation he must exert more strength, in another more skill, in another more attention; and the same individual does not possess all these qualities in an equal degree. After Manufacture has once separated, made independent, and isolated the various operations, the labourers are divided, classified, and grouped according to their predominating qualities. If their natural endowments are, on the one hand, the foundation on which the division of labour is built up, on the other hand, Manufacture, once introduced, develops in them new powers that are by nature fitted only for limited and special functions. The collective labourer now possesses, in an equal degree of excellence, all the qualities requisite for production, and expends them in the most economical manner, by exclusively employing all his organs, consisting of particular labourers, or groups of labourers, in performing their special functions. The one-sidedness and the deficiencies of the detail labourer become perfections when he is a part of the collective labourer. The habit of doing only one thing converts him into a never failing instrument, while his connection with the whole mechanism compels him to work with the regularity of the parts of a machine. Since the collective labourer has functions, both simple and complex, both high and low, his members, the individual labour-powers, require different degrees of training, and must therefore have different values. Manufacture, therefore, develops a hierarchy of labour-powers, to which there corresponds a scale of wages. If, on the one hand, the individual labourers are appropriated and annexed for life by a limited function; on the other hand, the various operations of the hierarchy are parcelled out among the labourers according to both their natural and their acquired capabilities. Every process of production, however, requires certain simple manipulations, which every man is capable of doing. They too are now severed from their connection with the more pregnant moments of activity, and ossified into exclusive functions of specially appointed laborers. Hence, Manufacture suggests, ill every handicraft that it scizes upon, a class of so-called unskilled labourers, a class which handicraft industry strictly excluded. . . .

Section 4: Division of Labour
in Manufacture, and Division of Labour in Society

Division of labour in a society, and the corresponding tying down of individuals to a particular calling, develops itself, just as does the division of labour in manufacture, from opposite starting-points. Within a family, and after further development with a tribe, there springs up naturally a division of labour, caused by differences of sex and age, a division that is consequently based on a purely physiological foundation, which division enlarges its materials by the expansion of the community, by the increase of population, and more especially, by the conflicts between different tribes, and the subjugation of one tribe by another. On the other hand, as I have before remarked, the exchange of products springs up at the points where different families, tribes, communities, come in contact; for, in the beginning of civilisation, it is not private individuals but families, tribes, etc., that meet on an independent footing. Different communities find different means of production, and different means of subsistence in their natural environment. Hence, their modes of production, and of living, and their products are different. It is this spontaneously developed difference which, when different communities come in contact, calls forth the mutual exchange of products, and the consequent gradual conversion of those products into commodities.
. . .

The foundation of every division of labour that is well developed, and brought about by the exchange of commodities, is the separation between town and country. It may be said, that the whole economic history of society is summed up in the movement of this antithesis. We pass it over, however, for the present.

Just as a certain number of simultaneously employed labourers are the material pre-requisites for division of labour in manufacture, so are the number and density of the populations, which here correspond to the agglomeration in one workshop, a necessary condition for the division of labour in society. Nevertheless, this density is more or less relative. A relatively thinly populated country, with well-developed means of communication, has a denser population than a more numerously populated country, with badly-developed means of communication; and in this sense the Northern States of the American Union, for instance, are more thickly populated than India.

Since the production and the circulation of commodities are the general pre-requisites of the capitalist mode of production, division of labour in manufacture demands, that division of labour in society at large should previously have attained a certain degree of development. Inversely, the former division reacts upon and develops and multiplies the latter. Simultaneously, with the differentiation of the instruments of labour, the industries that produce these instruments, become more and more differentiated. If the manufacturing system seize upon an industry, which, previously, was carried on in connection with others, either as a chief or as a subordinate industry, and by one producer, these industries immediately separate their connection, and become independent. If it seize upon a particular stage in the production of a commodity, the other stages of its production become converted into so many independent industries. It has already been stated, that where the finished article consists merely of a number of parts fitted together, the detail operations may re-establish themselves as genuine and separate handicrafts. In order to carry out more perfectly the division of labour in manufacture, a single branch of production is, according to the varieties of its raw material, or the various forms that one and the same raw material may assume, split up into numerous, and to some extent, entirely new manufactures. Accordingly, in France alone, in the first half of the 18th century, over 100 different kinds of silk stuffs were woven, and, in Avignon, it was law, that "every apprentice should devote himself to only one sort of fabrication, and should not learn the separation of several kinds of stuff at once." The territorial division of labour, which confines special branches of production to special districts of a country, acquires fresh stimulus from the manufacturing system, which exploits every special advantage. The Colonial system and the opening out of the markets of the world, both of which are included in the general conditions of existence of the manufacturing period, furnish rich material for developing the division of labour in society. It is not the place, here, to go on to show how division of labour seizes upon, not only the economic, but every other sphere of society, and everywhere lays the foundation of that all engrossing system of specialising and sorting men, that development in a man of one single faculty at the expense of all other faculties, which caused A. Ferguson, the master of Adam Smith, to exclaim: "We make a nation of Helots, and have no free citizens."

But, in spite of the numerous analogies and links connecting them, division of labour in the interior of a society, and that in the interior of a workshop, differ not only in degree, but also in kind. The analogy appears most indisputable where there is an invisible bond uniting the various branches of trade. For instance the cattle-breeder produces hides, the tanner makes the hides into leather, and the shoemaker, the leather into boots. Here the thing produced by each of them is but a step towards the final form, which is the product of all their labours combined. There are, besides, all the various industries that supply the cattle-breeder, the tanner, and the shoemaker with the means of production. Now it is quite possible to imagine, with Adam Smith, that the difference between the above social division of labour, and the division in manufacture, is merely subjective, exists merely for the observer, who, in a manufacture, can see with one glance, all the numerous operations being performed on one spot, while in the instance given above, the spreading out of the work over great areas, and the great number of people employed in each branch of labour, obscure the connexion. But what is it that forms the bond between the independent labours of the cattle-breeder, the tanner, and the shoe-maker? It is the fact that their respective products are commodities. What, on the other hand, characterises division of labour in manufactures? The fact that the detail labourer produces no commodities. It is only the common product of all the detail labourers becomes a commodity. Division of labour in society is brought about by the purchase and sale of the products of different branches of industry, while the connection between the detail operations in a workshop, is due to the sale of the labour-power of several workmen to one capitalist, who applies it as combined labour-power. The division of labour in the workshop implies concentration of the means of production in the hands of one capitalist; the division of labour in society implies their dispersion among many independent producers of commodities. . . .

The same bourgeois mind denounces with equal vigour every conscious attempt to socially control and regulate the process of production, as an inroad upon such sacred things as the rights of property, freedom and unrestricted play for the bent of the individual capitalist. It is very characteristic that the enthusiastic apologists of the factory system have nothing more damning to urge against a general organisation of the labour of society, than that it would turn all society into one immense factory.

If, in a society with capitalist production, anarchy in the social division of labour and despotism in that of the workshop are mutual conditions the one of the other, we find, on the contrary, in those earlier forms of society in which the separation of trades has been spontaneously developed, then crystallised, and finally made permanent by law, on the one hand, a specimen of the organisation of the labour of society, in accordance with an approved and authoritative plan, and on the other, the entire exclusion of division of labour in the workshop, or at all events a mere dwarf-like or sporadic and accidental development of the same.

Those small and extremely ancient Indian communities, some of which have continued down to this day, are based on possession in common of the land, on the blending of agriculture and handicrafts, and on an unalterable division of labour, which serves, whenever a new community is started, as a plan and scheme ready cut and dried. . . . The law that regulates the division of labour in the community acts with the irresistible authority of a law of Nature, at the same time that each individual artificer, the smith, the carpenter, and so on, conducts in his workshop all the operations of his handicraft in the traditional way, but independently, and without recognising any authority over him. The simplicity of the organisation for production in these self-sufficing communities that constantly reproduce themselves in the same form, and when accidentally destroyed, spring up again on the spot and with the same name—this simplicity supplies the key to the secret of the unchangeableness of Asiatic societies, an unchangeableness in such striking contrast with the constant dissolution and refounding of Asiatic States, and the never-ceasing changes of dynasty. The structure of the economic elements of society remains untouched by the storm-clouds of the political sky. . . .

While division of labour in society at large; whether such division be brought about or not by exchange of commodities, is common to economic formulations of society the most diverse, division of labour in the workshop, as practised by manufacture, is a special creation of the capitalist mode of production alone.

Section 5: The Capitalistic Character of Manufacture

An increased number of labourers under the control of one capitalist is the natural starting-point, as well of co-operation generally, as of manufacture in particular. But the division of labour in manufacture makes this increase in the number of workmen a technical necessity. The minimum number that any given capitalist is bound to employ is here prescribed by the previously established division of labour. On the other hand, the advantages of further division are obtainable only by adding to the number of workmen, and this can be done only by adding multiples of the various detail groups. But an increase in the variable component of the capital employed necessitates an increase in its constant component, too, in the workshops, implements, etc., and, in particular, in the raw material, the call for which grows quicker than the number of workmen. The quantity of it consumed in a given time, by a given amount of labour, increases in the same ratio as does the productive power of that labour in consequence of its division. Hence, it is a law, based on the very nature of manufacture, that the minimum amount of capital, which is bound to be in the hands of each capitalist, must keep increasing; in other words, that the transformation into capital of the social means of production and subsistence must keep extending.

In manufacture, as well as in simple co-operation, the collective working organism is a form of existence of capital. The mechanism that is made up of numerous individual detail labourers belongs to the capitalist. Hence, the productive power resulting from a combination of labours appears to be the productive power of capital. Manufacture proper not only subjects the previously independent workman to the discipline and command of capital, but, in addition, creates a hierarchic gradation of the workmen themselves. While simple co-operation leaves the mode of working by the individual for the most part unchanged, manufacture thoroughly revolutionises it, and seizes labour-power by its very roots. It converts the labourer into a crippled monstrosity, by forcing his detail dexterity at the expense of a world of productive capabilities and instincts; just as in the States of La Plata they butcher a whole beast for the sake of his hide or his tallow. Not only is the detail work distributed to the different individuals, but the individual himself is made the automatic motor of a fractional operation, and the absurd fable of Menenius Agrippa, which makes man a mere fragment of his own body, becomes realised. If, at first, the workman sells his labour-power to capital, because the material means of producing a commodity fail him, now his very labour-power refuses its services unless it has been sold to capital. Its functions can be exercised only in an environment that exists in the workshop of the capitalist after the sale. By nature unfitted to make anything independently, the manufacturing labourer develops productive activity as a mere appendage of the capitalist's workshop. . . .

In manufacture, in order to make the collective labourer, and through him capital, rich in social productive power, each labourer must be made poor in individual productive powers. "Ignorance is the mother of industry as well as of superstition. Reflection and fancy are subject to err; but a habit of moving the hand or the foot is independent of either. Manufactures, accordingly, prosper most where the mind is least consulted, and where the workshop may . . . be considered as an engine, the parts of which are men." As a matter of fact, some few manufacturers in the middle of the 18th century preferred for certain operations that were trade secrets, to employ half-idiotic persons.

"The understandings of the greater part of men," says Adam Smith, "are necessarily formed by their ordinary employments. The man whose whole life is spent in performing a few simple operations . . . has no occasion to exert his understanding. . . . He generally becomes as stupid and ignorant as it is possible for a human creature to become." After describing the stupidity of the detail labourer he goes on: "The uniformity of his stationary life naturally corrupts the courage of his mind. . . . It corrupts even the activity of his body and renders him incapable of exerting his strength with vigour and perseverance in any other employments than that to which he has been bred. His dexterity at his own particular trade seems in this manner to be acquired at the expense of his intellectual, social, and martial virtues. But in every improved and civilised society, this is the state into which the labouring poor, that is, the great body of the people, must necessarily fall." For preventing the complete deterioration of the great mass of the people by division of labour, A. Smith recommends education of the people by the State, but prudently, and in homeopathic doses. . . .

Some crippling of body and mind is inseparable even from division of labour in society as a whole. Since, however, manufacture carries this social separation of branches of labour much further, and also, by its peculiar division, attacks the individual at the very roots of his life, it is the first to afford the materials for, and to give a start to, industrial pathology.

"To subdivide a man is to execute him, if he deserves the sentence, to assassinate him if he does not. . . . The subdivision of labour is the assassination of a people."

From *Communist Manifesto*

A spectre is haunting Europe—the spectre of Communism. All the Powers of old Europe have entered into a holy alliance to exorcise this spectre: Pope and Czar, Metternich and Guizot, French Radicals and German police-spies.

Where is the party in opposition that has not been decried as Communistic by its opponents in power? Where the Opposition that has not hurled back the branding reproach of Communism, against the more advanced opposition parties, as well as against its reactionary adversaries?

Two things result from this fact.

I.   Communism is already acknowledged by all European Powers to be itself a Power.

II.   It is high time that Communists should openly, in the face of the whole world, publish their views, their aims, their tendencies, and meet this nursery tale of the Spectre of Communism with a Manifesto of the party itself.

To this end, Communists of various nationalities have assembled in London, and sketched the following Manifesto, to be published in the English, French, German, Italian, Flemish and Danish languages.

I. Bourgeois and Proletarians

The history of all hitherto existing society is the history of class struggles.

Freeman and slave, patrician and plebeian, lord and serf, guild-master and journeyman, in a word, oppressor and oppressed, stood in constant opposition to one another, carried on an uninterrupted, now hidden, now open fight, a fight that each time ended, either in a revolutionary re-constitution of society at large, or in the common ruin of the contending classes.

In the earlier epochs of history, we find almost everywhere a complicated arrangement of society into various orders, a manifold gradation of social rank. In ancient Rome we have patricians, knights, plebeians, slaves; in the Middle Ages, feudal lords, vassals, guild-masters, journeymen, apprentices, serfs; in almost all of these classes, again, subordinate gradations.

The modern bourgeois society that has sprouted from the ruins of feudal society has not done away with class antagonisms. It has but established new classes, new conditions of oppression, new forms of struggle in place of the old ones.

Our epoch, the epoch of the bourgeoisie, possesses, however, this distinctive feature: it has simplified the class antagonisms: Society as a whole is more and more splitting up into two great hostile camps, into two great classes directly facing each other: Bourgeoisie and Proletariat.

From the serfs of the Middle Ages sprang the chartered burghers of the earliest towns. From these burgesses the first elements of the bourgeoisie were developed.

The discovery of America, the rounding of the Cape, opened up fresh ground for the rising bourgeoisie. The East-Indian and Chinese markets, the colonisation of America, trade with the colonies, the increase in the means of exchange and in commodities generally, gave to commerce, to navigation, to industry, an impulse never before known, and thereby, to the revolutionary element in the tottering feudal society, a rapid development.

The feudal system of industry, under which industrial production was monopolised by closed guilds, now no longer sufficed for the growing wants of the new markets. The manufacturing system took its place. The guild-masters were pushed on one side by the manufacturing middle class; division of labour between the different corporate guilds vanished in the face of division of labour in each single workshop.

Meantime the markets kept ever growing, the demand ever rising. Even manufacture no longer sufficed. Thereupon, steam and machinery revolutionised industrial production. The place of manufacture was taken by the giant, Modern Industry, the place of the industrial middle class, by industrial millionaires, the leaders of whole industrial armies, the modern bourgeois.

Modern industry has established the world-market, for which the discovery of America paved the way. This market has given an immense development to commerce, to navigation, to communication by land. This development has, in its turn, reacted on the extension of industry; and in proportion as industry, commerce, navigation, railways extended, in the same proportion the bourgeoisie developed, increased its capital, and pushed into the background every class handed down from the Middle Ages.

We see, therefore, how the modern bourgeoisie is itself the product of a long course of development, of a series of revolutions in the modes of production and of exchange.

Each step in the development of the bourgeoisie was accompanied by a corresponding political advance of that class. An oppressed class under the sway of the feudal nobility, an armed and self-governing association in the mediaeval commune; here independent urban republic (as in Italy and Germany), there taxable "third estate" of the monarchy (as in France), afterwards, in the period of manufacture proper, serving either the semi-feudal or the absolute monarchy as a counterpoise against the nobility, and, in fact, corner-stone of the great monarchies in general, the bourgeoisie has at last, since the establishment of Modern Industry and of the world-market, conquered for itself, in the modern representative State, exclusive political sway. The executive of the modern State is but a committee for managing the common affairs of the whole bourgeoisie.

The bourgeoisie, historically, has played a most revolutionary part.

The bourgeoisie, wherever it has got the upper hand, has put an end to all feudal, patriarchal, idyllic relations. It has pitilessly torn asunder the motley feudal ties that bound man to his "natural superiors," and has left remaining no other nexus between man and man than naked self-interest, than callous "cash payment." It has drowned the most heavenly ecstasies of religious fervour, of chivalrous enthusiasm, of philistine sentimentalism, in the icy water of egotistical calculation. It has resolved personal worth into exchange value, and in place of the numberless indefeasible chartered freedoms, has set up that single, unconscionable freedom—Free Trade. In one word, for exploitation, veiled by religious and political illusions, it has substituted naked, shameless, direct, brutal exploitation.

The bourgeoisie has stripped of its halo every occupation hitherto honoured and looked up to with reverent awe. It has converted the physician, the lawyer, the priest, the poet, the man of science, into its paid wage-labourers. The bourgeoisie has torn away from the family its sentimental veil, and has reduced the family relation to a mere money relation. The bourgeoisie has disclosed how it came to pass that the brutal display of vigour in the Middle Ages, which Reactionists so much admire, found its fitting complement in the most slothful indolence. It has been the first to show what man's activity can bring about. It has accomplished wonders far surpassing Egyptian pyramids, Roman aqueducts, and Gothic cathedrals; it has conducted expeditions that put in the shade all former Exoduses of nations and crusades.

The bourgeoisie cannot exist without constantly revolutionising the instruments of production, and thereby the relations of production, and with them the whole relations of society. Conservation of the old modes of production in unaltered form, was, on the contrary, the first condition of existence for all earlier industrial classes. Constant revolutionising of production, uninterrupted disturbance of all social conditions, everlasting uncertainty and agitation distinguish the bourgeois epoch from all earlier ones. All fixed, fast-frozen relations, with their train of ancient and venerable prejudices and opinions, are swept away, all new-formed ones become antiquated before they can ossify. All that is solid melts into air, all that is holy is profaned, and man is at last compelled to face with sober senses, his real conditions of life, and his relations with his kind.

The need of a constantly expanding market for its products chases the bourgeoisie over the whole surface of the globe. It must nestle everywhere, settle everywhere, establish connexions everywhere.

The bourgeoisie has through its exploitation of the world-market given a cosmopolitan character to production and consumption in every country. To the great chagrin of Reactionists, it has drawn from under the feet of industry the national ground on which it stood. All old-established national industries have been destroyed or are daily being destroyed. They are dislodged by new industries, whose introduction becomes a life and death question for all civilised nations, by industries that no longer work up indigenous raw material, but raw material drawn from the remotest zones; industries whose products are consumed, not only at home, but in every quarter of the globe. In place of the old wants, satisfied by the productions of the country, we find new wants, requiring for their satisfaction the products of distant lands and climes. In place of the old local and national seclusion and self-sufficiency, we have intercourse in every direction, universal inter-dependence of nations. And as in material, so also in intellectual production. The intellectual creations of individual nations become common property. National one-sidedness and narrow-mindedness become more and more impossible, and from the numerous national and local literatures, there arises a world literature.

The bourgeoisie, by the rapid improvement of all instruments of production, by the immensely facilitated means of communication, draws all, even the most barbarian, nations into civilisation. The cheap prices of its commodities are the heavy artillery with which it batters down all Chinese walls, with which it forces the barbarians' intensely obstinate hatred of foreigners to capitulate. It compels all nations, on pain of extinction, to adopt the bourgeois mode of production; it compels them to introduce what it calls civilisation into their midst, i.e., to become bourgeois themselves. In one word, it creates a world after its own image.

The bourgeoisie has subjected the country to the rule of the towns. It has created enormous cities, has greatly increased the urban population as compared with the rural, and has thus rescued a considerable part of the population from the idiocy of rural life. Just as it has made the country dependent on the towns, so it has made barbarian and semi-barbarian countries dependent on the civilised ones, nations of peasants on nations of bourgeois, the East on the West.

The bourgeoisie keeps more and more doing away with the scattered state of the population, of the means of production, and of property. It has agglomerated population, centralised means of production, and has concentrated property in a few hands. The necessary consequence of this was political centralisation. Independent, or but loosely connected provinces, with separate interests, laws, governments and systems of taxation, became lumped together into one nation, with one government, one code of laws, one national class-interest, one frontier and one customs-tariff.

The bourgeoisie, during its rule of scarce one hundred years, has created more massive and more colossal productive forces than have all preceding generations together. Subjection of Nature's forces to man, machinery, application of chemistry to industry and agriculture, steam-navigation, railways, electric telegraphs, clearing of whole continents for cultivation, canalisation of rivers, whole populations conjured out of the ground—what earlier century had even a presentiment that such productive forces slumbered in the lap of social labour?

We see then: the means of production and of exchange, on whose foundation the bourgeoisie built itself up, were generated in feudal society. At a certain stage in the development of these means of production and of exchange, the conditions under which feudal society produced and exchanged, the feudal organisation of agriculture and manufacturing industry, in one word, the feudal relations of property became no longer compatible with the already developed productive forces; they became so many fetters. They had to be burst asunder; they were burst asunder.

Into their place stepped free competition, accompanied by a social and political constitution adapted to it, and by the economical and political sway of the bourgeois class.

A similar movement is going on before our own eyes. Modern bourgeois society with its relations of production, of exchange and of property, a society that has conjured up such gigantic means of production and of exchange, is like the sorcerer, who is no longer able to control the powers of the nether world whom he has called up by his spells. For many a decade past the history of industry and commerce is but the history of the revolt of modern productive forces against modern conditions of production, against the property relations that are the conditions for the existence of the bourgeoisie and of its rule. It is enough to mention the commercial crises that by their periodical return put on its trial, each time more threateningly, the existence of the entire bourgeois society. In these crises a great part not only of the existing products, but also of the previously created productive forces, are periodically destroyed. In these crises there breaks out an epidemic that, in all earlier epochs, would have seemed an absurdity—the epidemic of over-production. Society suddenly finds itself put back into a state of momentary barbarism; it appears as if a famine, a universal war of devastation had cut off the supply of every means of subsistence; industry and commerce seem to be destroyed; and why? Because there is too much civilisation, too much means of subsistence, too much industry, too much commerce. The productive forces at the disposal of society no longer tend to further the development of the conditions of bourgeois property; on the contrary, they have become too powerful for these conditions, by which they are fettered, and so soon as they overcome these fetters, they bring disorder into the whole of bourgeois society, endanger the existence of bourgeois property. The conditions of bourgeois society are too narrow to comprise the wealth created by them. And how does the bourgeoisie get over these crises? On the one hand by enforced destruction of a mass of productive forces; on the other, by the conquest of new markets, and by the more thorough exploitation of the old ones. That is to say, by paving the way for more extensive and more destructive crises, and by diminishing the means whereby crises are prevented. The weapons with which the bourgeoisie felled feudalism to the ground are now turned against the bourgeoisie itself.

But not only has the bourgeoisie forged the weapons that bring death to itself; it has also called into existence the men who are to wield those weapons—the modern working class—the proletarians.

In proportion as the bourgeoisie, i.e., capital, is developed, in the same proportion is the proletariat, the modern working class, developed—a class of labourers, who live only so long as they find work and who had work only so long as their labour increases capital. These labourers, who must sell themselves piece-meal, are a commodity, like every other article of commerce, and are consequently exposed to all the vicissitudes of competition, to all the fluctuations of the market.

Owing to the extensive use of machinery and to division of labour, the work of the proletarians has lost all individual character, and consequently, all charm for the workman: He becomes an appendage of the machine, and it is only the most simple, most monotonous, and most easily acquired knack, that is required of him. Hence, the cost of production of a workman is restricted, almost entirely, to the means of subsistence that he requires for his maintenance, and for the propagation of his race. But the price of a commodity, and therefore also of labour, is equal to its cost of production. In proportion, therefore, as the repulsiveness of the work increases, the wage decreases. Nay more, in proportion as the use of machinery and division of labour increases, in the same proportion the burden of toil also increases, whether by prolongation of the working hours, by increase of the work exacted in a given time or by increased speed of the machinery, etc.

Modern industry has converted the little workshop of the patriarchal master into the great factory of the industrial capitalist. Masses of labourers, crowded into the factory, are organised like soldiers. As privates of the industrial army they are placed under the command of a perfect hierarchy of officers and sergeants. Not only are they slaves of the bourgeois class, and of the bourgeois State; they are daily and hourly enslaved by the machine, by the over-looker, and, above all, by the individual bourgeois manufacturer himself. The more openly this despotism proclaims gain to be its end and aim, the more petty, the more hateful and the more embittering it is.

The less the skill and exertion of strength implied in manual labour, in other words, the more modern industry becomes developed, the more is the labour of men superseded by that of women. Differences of age and sex have no longer any distinctive social validity for the working class. All are instruments of labour, more or less expensive to use, according to their age and sex.

No sooner is the exploitation of the labourer by the manufacturer, so far, at an end, that he receives his wages in cash, than he is set upon by the other portions of the bourgeoisie, the landlord, the shopkeeper, the pawnbroker, etc.

The lower strata of the middle class—the small tradespeople, shopkeepers, and retired tradesmen generally, the handicraftsmen and peasants—all these sink gradually into the proletariat, partly because their diminutive capital does not suffice for the scale on which Modern Industry is carried on, and is swamped in the competition with the large capitalists, partly because their specialised skill is rendered worthless by new methods of production. Thus the proletariat is recruited from all classes of the population. . . .

The essential condition for the existence, and for the sway of the bourgeois class, is the formation and augmentation of capital; the condition for capital is wage-labour. Wage-labour rests exclusively on competition between the labourers. The advance of industry, whose involuntary promoter is the bourgeoisie, replaces the isolation of the labourers, due to competition, by their revolutionary combination, due to association. The development of Modern Industry, therefore, cuts from under its feet the very foundation on which the bourgeoisie produces and appropriates products. What the bourgeoisie, therefore, produces, above all, is its own grave-diggers. Its fall and the victory of the proletariat are equally inevitable.

12

The Structure of Dependence

Theotonio dos Santos

In this chapter, Theotonio dos Santos, a Brazilian economist, crafts what is probably the most cited definition of dependence. Although some scholars argue that there is no such thing as a coherent dependency "theory," dos Santos presents many of the most commonly held tenets. He argues that dependence is difficult to define because it is conditioned by the characteristics of the dependent country and it has changed over time. Three basic forms of dependence have appeared: (1) colonial, (2) financial-industrial, and (3) multinational corporate. Dos Santos focuses on how the latest form, that arising out of the linkage between dependent countries and multinational corporations, limits the developmental potential of newly industrializing nations and is blamed for restricting the size of local markets and contributing to income inequality. Ultimately, according to dos Santos, dependent development will culminate in revolutionary movements of the left or the right.

This chapter attempts to demonstrate that the dependence of Latin American countries on other countries cannot be overcome without a qualitative change in their internal structures and external relations. We shall attempt to show that the relations of dependence to which these countries are subjected conform to a type of international and internal structure which leads them to underdevelopment or more precisely to a dependent structure that deepens and aggravates the fundamental problems of their peoples.

Reprinted with permission from *The American Economic Review*, vol. 60 (May 1970): 231–236.

I. What Is Dependence?

By dependence we mean a situation in which the economy of certain countries is conditioned by the development and expansion of another economy
to which the former is subjected. The relation of interdependence between
two or more economies, and between these and world trade, assumes the
form of dependence when some countries (the dominant ones) can expand
and can be self-sustaining, while other countries (the dependent ones) can
do this only as a reflection of that expansion, which can have either a positive or a negative effect on their immediate development (dos Santos,
1968b; p. 6).

The concept of dependence permits us to see the internal situation of
these countries as part of world economy. In the Marxian tradition, the theory of imperialism has been developed as a study of the process of expansion of the imperialist centers and of their world domination. In the epoch
of the revolutionary movement of the Third World, we have to develop the
theory of laws of internal development in those countries that are the object
of such expansion and are governed by them. This theoretical step tran-
scends the theory of development which seeks to explain the situation of
the underdeveloped countries as a product of their slowness or failure to
adopt the patterns of efficiency characteristic of developed countries (or to
"modernize" or "develop" themselves). Although capitalist development
theory admits the existence of an "external" dependence, it is unable to perceive underdevelopment in the way our present theory perceives it, as a
consequence and part of the process of the world expansion of capitalism—
a part that is necessary to and integrally linked with it.

In analyzing the process of constituting a world economy that inte-
grates the so-called "national economies" in a world market of commodities, capital, and even of labor power, we see that the relations produced
by this market are unequal and combined—unequal because development
of parts of the system occurs at the expense of other parts. Trade relations
are based on monopolistic control of the market, which leads to the transfer of surplus generated in the dependent countries to the dominant countries; financial relations are, from the viewpoint of the dominant powers,
based on loans and the export of capital, which permit them to receive
interest and profits, thus increasing their domestic surplus and strengthening their control over the economies of the other countries. For the
dependent countries these relations represent an export of profits and
interest which carries off part of the surplus generated domestically and
leads to a loss of control over their productive resources. In order to permit these disadvantageous relations, the dependent countries must generate large surpluses, not in such a way as to create higher levels of technology but rather creating superexploited manpower. The result is to limit the

development of their internal market and their technical and cultural capacity, as well as the moral and physical health of their people. We call this combined development because it is the combination of these inequalities and the transfer of resources from the most backward and dependent sectors to the most advanced and dominant ones which explains the inequality, deepens it, and transforms it into a necessary and structural element of the world economy.

II. Historic Forms of Dependence

Historic forms of dependence are conditioned by: (1) the basic forms of this world economy which has its own laws of development; (2) the type of economic relations dominant in the capitalist centers and the ways in which the latter expand outward; and (3) the types of economic relations existing inside the peripheral countries which are incorporated into the situation of dependence within the network of international economic relations generated by capitalist expansion. It is not within the purview of this chapter to study these forms in detail but only to distinguish broad characteristics of development.

Drawing on an earlier study, we may distinguish: (1) Colonial dependence, trade export in nature, in which commercial and financial capital in alliance with the colonialist state dominated the economic relations and the colonies by means of a trade monopoly, (2) Financial-industrial dependence, which consolidated itself at the end of the nineteenth century, characterized by the domination of big capital in the hegemonic centers, and its expansion abroad through investment in the production of raw materials and agricultural products for consumption in the hegemonic centers. A productive structure grew up in the dependent countries devoted to the export of these products (which I.V. Levin labeled export economies [Levin, 1964]; other analysis in other regions [Myrdal, 1968; Nkrumah, 1966]), producing what the Economic Commission for Latin America (ECLA) has called "foreign-oriented development" *(desarrollo hacia afuera)* (Cepal, 1968). (3) In the postwar period a new type of dependence has been consolidated, based on multinational corporations which began to invest in industries geared to the internal market of underdeveloped countries. This form of dependence is basically technological-industrial dependence (dos Santos, 1968a).

Each of these forms of dependence corresponds to a situation which conditioned not only the international relations of these countries but also their internal structures: the orientation of production, the forms of capital accumulation, the reproduction of the economy, and, simultaneously, their social and political structure.

III. The Export Economies

In forms (1) and (2) of dependence, production is geared to those products destined for export (gold, silver, and tropical products in the colonial epoch; raw materials and agricultural products in the epoch of industrial-financial dependence); i.e., production is determined by demand from the hegemonic centers. The internal productive structure is characterized by rigid specialization and monoculture in entire regions (the Caribbean, the Brazilian Northeast, etc.). Alongside these export sectors there grew up certain complementary economic activities (cattle-raising and some manufacturing, for example) which were dependent, in general, on the export sector to which they sell their products. There was a third, subsistence economy which provided manpower for the export sector under favorable conditions and toward which excess population shifted during periods unfavorable to international trade.

Under these conditions, the existing internal market was restricted by four factors: (1) Most of the national income was derived from export, which was used to purchase the inputs required by export production (slaves, for example) or luxury goods consumed by the hacienda- and mine-owners, and by the more prosperous employees. (2) The available manpower was subject to very arduous forms of superexploitation, which limited its consumption. (3) Part of the consumption of these workers was provided by the subsistence economy, which served as a complement to their income and as a refuge during periods of depression. (4) A fourth factor was to be found in those countries in which land and mines were in the hands of foreigners (cases of an enclave economy): a great part of the accumulated surplus was destined to be sent abroad in the form of profits, limiting not only internal consumption but also possibilities of reinvestment (Baran, 1967). In the case of enclave economies the relations of the foreign companies with the hegemonic center were even more exploitative and were complemented by the fact that purchases by the enclave were made directly abroad.

IV. The New Dependence

The new form of dependence, (3) above, is in process of developing and is conditioned by the exigencies of the international commodity and capital markets. The possibility of generating new investments depends on the existence of financial resources in foreign currency for the purchase of machinery and processed raw materials not produced domestically. Such purchases are subject to two limitations: the limit of resources generated by the export sector (reflected in the balance of payments, which includes not only trade but also service relations); and the limitations of monopoly on patents which leads monopolistic firms to prefer to transfer their machines in the form of capital rather than as commodities for sale. It is necessary to analyze these relations of dependence if we are to understand the fundamental structural limits they place on the development of these economies.

1. Industrial development is dependent on an export sector for the foreign currency to buy the inputs utilized by the industrial sector. The first consequence of this dependence is the need to preserve the traditional export sector, which limits economically the development of the internal market by the conservation of backward relations of production and signifies, politically, the maintenance of power by traditional decadent oligarchies. In the countries where these sectors are controlled by foreign capital, it signifies the remittance abroad of high profits, and political dependence on those interests. Only in rare instances does foreign capital not control at least the marketing of these products. In response to these limitations, dependent countries in the 1930s and 1940s developed a policy of exchange restrictions and taxes on the national and foreign export sector; today they tend toward the gradual nationalization of production and toward the imposition of certain timid limitations on foreign control of the marketing of exported products. Furthermore, they seek, still somewhat timidly, to obtain better terms for the sale of their products. In recent decades, they have created mechanisms for international price agreements, and today the United Nations Conference on Trade and Development (UNCTAD) and ECLA press to obtain more favorable tariff conditions for these products on the part of the hegemonic centers. It is important to point out that the industrial development of these countries is dependent on the situation of the export sector, the continued existence of which they are obliged to accept.

2. Industrial development is, then, strongly conditioned by fluctuations in the balance of payments. This leads toward deficit due to the relations of dependence themselves. The causes of the deficit are three:

a. Trade relations take place in a highly monopolized international market, which tends to lower the price of raw materials and to raise the prices of industrial products, particularly inputs. In the second place, there is a tendency in modern technology to replace various primary products with synthetic raw materials. Consequently, the balance of trade in these countries tends to be less favorable (even though they show a general surplus). The overall Latin American balance of trade from 1946 to 1968 shows a surplus for each of those years. The same thing happens in almost every underdeveloped country. However, the losses due to deterioration of the terms of trade (on the basis of data from ECLA and the International Monetary Fund), excluding Cuba, were $26,383 million for the 1951–66 period, taking 1950 prices as a base. If Cuba and Venezuela are excluded, the total is $15,925 million.

b. For the reasons already given, foreign capital retains control over the most dynamic sectors of the economy and repatriates a high volume of profit; consequently, capital accounts are highly unfavorable to dependent countries. The data show that the amount of capital leaving the country is much greater than the amount entering; this produces an enslaving deficit in capital accounts. To this must be added the deficit in certain services which are virtually under total foreign control—such as freight transport, royalty payments, technical aid, etc. Consequently, an important deficit is produced in the total balance of payments; thus limiting the possibility of importation of inputs for industrialization.

c. The result is that "foreign financing" becomes necessary, in two forms: to cover the existing deficit, and to "finance" development by means of loans for the stimulation of investments and to "supply" an internal economic surplus which was decapitalized to a large extent by the remittance of part of the surplus generated domestically and sent abroad as profits.

Foreign capital and foreign "aid" thus fill up the holes that they themselves created. The real value of this aid, however, is doubtful. If overcharges resulting from the restrictive terms of the aid are subtracted from the total amount of the grants, the average net flow, according to calculations of the Inter-American Economic and Social Council, is approximately 54 percent of the gross flow (Interamerican Economic and Social Council, 1969).

If we take account of certain further facts—that a high proportion of aid is paid in local currencies, that Latin American countries make contributions to international financial institutions, and that credits are often "tied"—we find a "real component of foreign aid" of 42.2 percent on a very favorable hypothesis and of 38.3 percent on a more realistic one (Interamerican Economic and Social Council, 1969, II, p. 33). The gravity of the situation becomes even clearer if we consider that these credits are used in large part to finance North American investments, to subsidize foreign imports which compete with national products, to introduce technology not adapted to the needs of underdeveloped countries, and to invest in low-priority sectors of the national economies. The hard truth is that the underdeveloped countries have to pay for all of the "aid" they receive. This situation is generating an enormous protest movement by Latin American governments seeking at least partial relief from such negative relations.

3. Finally, industrial development is strongly conditioned by the technological monopoly exercised by imperialist centers. We have seen that the underdeveloped countries depend on the importation of machinery and raw materials for the development of their industries. However, these goods are not freely available in the international market; they are patented and usually belong to the big companies. The big companies do not sell machinery and processed raw materials as simple merchandise: they demand either the payment of royalties, etc., for their utilization or, in most cases, they convert these goods into capital and introduce them in the form of their own

investments. This is how machinery which is replaced in the hegemonic centers by more advanced technology is sent to dependent countries as capital for the installation of affiliates. Let us pause and examine these relations in order to understand their oppressive and exploitative character.

The dependent countries do not have sufficient foreign currency, for the reasons given. Local businessmen have financing difficulties, and they must pay for the utilization of certain patented techniques. These factors oblige the national bourgeois governments to facilitate the entry of foreign capital in order to supply the restricted national market, which is strongly protected by high tariffs in order to promote industrialization. Thus, foreign capital enters with all the advantages: in many cases, it is given exemption from exchange controls for the importation of machinery; financing of sites for installation of industries is provided; government financing agencies facilitate industrialization; loans are available from foreign and domestic banks, which prefer such clients; foreign aid often subsidizes such investments and finances complementary public investments; after installation, high profits obtained in such favorable circumstances can be reinvested freely. Thus it is not surprising that the data of the U.S. Department of Commerce reveal that the percentage of capital brought in from abroad by these companies is but a part of the total amount of invested capital. These data show that in the period from 1946 to 1967 the new entries of capital into Latin America for direct investment amounted to $5,415 million, while the sum of reinvested profits was $4,424 million. On the other hand, the transfers of profits from Latin America to the United States amounted to $14,775 million. If we estimate total profits as approximately equal to transfers plus reinvestments we have the sum of $18,983 million. In spite of enormous transfers of profits to the United States, the book value of the United States's direct investment in Latin America went from $3,045 million in 1946 to $10,213 million in 1967. From these data it is clear that: (1) Of the new investments made by U.S. companies in Latin America for the period 1946–67, 55 percent corresponds to new entries of capital and 45 percent to reinvestment of profits; in recent years, the trend is more marked, with reinvestments between 1960 and 1966 representing more than 60 percent of new investments. (2) Remittances remained at about 10 percent of book value throughout the period. (3) The ratio of remitted capital to new flow is around 2.7 for the period 1946–67; that is, for each dollar that enters $2.70 leaves. In the 1960s this ratio roughly doubled, and in some years was considerably higher.

The *Survey of Current Business* data on sources and uses of funds for direct North American investment in Latin America in the period 1957–64 show that, of the total sources of direct investment in Latin America, only 11.8 percent came from the United States. The remainder is, in large part, the result of the activities of North American firms in Latin America (46.4

percent net income, 27.7 percent under the heading of depreciation), and from "sources located abroad" (14.1 percent). It is significant that the funds obtained abroad that are external to the companies are greater than the funds originating in the United States.

V. Effects on the Productive Structure

It is easy to grasp, even if only superficially, the effects that this dependent structure has on the productive system itself in these countries and the role of this structure in determining a specified type of development, characterized by its dependent nature.

The productive system in the underdeveloped countries is essentially determined by these international relations. In the first place, the need to conserve the agrarian or mining export structure generates a combination between more advanced economic centers that extract surplus value from the more backward sectors and internal "metropolitan" centers on the one hand, and internal interdependent "colonial" centers on the other (Frank, 1968). The unequal and combined character of capitalist development at the international level is reproduced internally in an acute form. In the second place the industrial and technological structure responds more closely to the interests of the multinational corporations than to internal developmental needs (conceived of not only in terms of the overall interests of the population, but also from the point of view of the interests of a national capitalist development). In the third place, the same technological and economic-financial concentration of the hegemonic economies is transferred without substantial alteration to very different economies and societies, giving rise to a highly unequal productive structure, a high concentration of incomes, underutilization of installed capacity, intensive exploitation of existing markets concentrated in large cities, etc.

The accumulation of capital in such circumstances assumes its own characteristics. In the first place, it is characterized by profound differences among domestic wage-levels, in the context of a local cheap labor market, combined with a capital-intensive technology. The result, from the point of view of relative surplus value, is a high rate of exploitation of labor power. (On measurements of forms of exploitation, see Casanova, 1969.)

This exploitation is further aggravated by the high prices of industrial products enforced by protectionism, exemptions and subsidies given by the national governments, and "aid" from hegemonic centers. Furthermore, since dependent accumulation is necessarily tied into the international economy, it is profoundly conditioned by the unequal and combined character of international capitalist economic relations, by the technological and financial control of the imperialist centers by the realities of the balance of payments, by the economic policies of the state, etc. The role of the state in the growth of national and foreign capital merits a much fuller analysis than can be made here. Using the analysis offered here as a point of departure, it is possible to understand the limits that this productive system imposes on the growth of the internal markets of these countries. The survival of traditional relations in the countryside is a serious limitation on the size of the market, since industrialization does not offer hopeful prospects. The productive structure created by dependent industrialization limits the growth of the internal market.

First, it subjects the labor force to highly exploitative relations which limit its purchasing power. Second, in adopting a technology of intensive capital use, it creates very few jobs in comparison with population growth, and limits the generation of new sources of income. These two limitations affect the growth of the consumer goods market. Third, the remittance abroad of profits carries away part of the economic surplus generated within the country. In all these ways limits are put on the possible creation of basic national industries which could provide a market for the capital goods this surplus would make possible if it were not remitted abroad.

From this cursory analysis we see that the alleged backwardness of these economies is not due to a lack of integration with capitalism but that, to the contrary, the most powerful obstacles to their full development come from the way in which they are joined to this international system and its laws of development.

VI. Some Conclusions: Dependent Reproduction

In order to understand the system of dependent reproduction and the socioeconomic institutions created by it, we must see it as part of a system of world economic relations based on monopolistic control of large-scale capital, on control of certain economic and financial centers over others, on a monopoly of complex technology that leads to unequal and combined development at a national and international level. Attempts to analyze backwardness as a failure to assimilate more advanced models of production or to modernize are nothing more than ideology disguised as science. The same is true of the attempts to analyze this international economy in terms of relations among elements in free competition, such as the theory of comparative costs which seeks to justify the inequalities of the world economic system and to conceal the relations of exploitation on which it is based (Palloix, 1969).

In reality we can understand what is happening in the underdeveloped countries only when we see that they develop within the framework of a process of dependent production and reproduction. This system is a dependent one because it reproduces a productive system whose development is limited by those world relations which necessarily lead to the development of only certain economic sectors, to trade under unequal conditions (Emmanuel, 1969), to domestic competition with international capital under unequal conditions, to the imposition of relations of superexploitation of the domestic labor force with a view to dividing the economic surplus thus generated between internal and external forces of domination. (On economic surplus and its utilization in the dependent countries, see Baran, 1967.)

In reproducing such a productive system and such international relations, the development of dependent capitalism reproduces the factors that prevent it from reaching a nationally and internationally advantageous situation; and it thus reproduces backwardness, misery, and social marginalization within its borders. The development that it produces benefits very narrow sectors, encounters unyielding domestic obstacles to its continued economic growth (with respect to both internal and foreign markets), and leads to the progressive accumulation of balance-of-payments deficits, which in turn generate more dependence and more superexploitation.

The political measures proposed by the developmentalists of ECLA, UNCTAD, Inter-American Development Bank (BID), etc., do not appear to permit destruction of these terrible chains imposed by dependent development. We have examined the alternative forms of development presented for Latin America and the dependent countries under such conditions elsewhere (dos Santos; 1969). Everything now indicates that what can be expected is a long process of sharp political and military confrontations and of profound social radicalization which will lead these countries to a dilemma: governments of force, which open the way to fascism, or popular revolutionary governments, which open the way to socialism. Intermediate solutions have proved to be, in such a contradictory reality, empty and utopian.

References

Paul Baran, *Political Economy of Growth* (Monthly Review Press, 1967).
Thomas Balogh, *Unequal Partners* (Basil Blackwell, 1963).
Pablo Gonzalez Casanova, *Sociología de la explotación, Siglo XXI* (Mexico, 1969).
CEPAL, *La CEPAL y el Análisis del Desarrollo Latinoamericano* (1968, Santiago, Chile).
Consejo Interamericano Economico Social (CIES) O.A.S., Interamerican Economic and Social Council, External Financing for Development in L.A. *El Financiamiento Externo para el Desarrollo de América Latina* (Pan-American Union, Washington,1969).
Theotonio dos Santos, *El nuevo carácter de la dependencia*, CESO (Santiago de Chile, 1968a).
———, *La crisis de la teoría del desarrollo y las relaciones de dependencia en América Latina*, Boletin del CESO, 3 (Santiago, Chile, 1968b).
———, *La dependencia económica y las alternotivas de cambio en América Latina*,

Ponencia al IX Congreso Latinoamericano de Sociología (México, Nov., 1969).

A. Emmanuel, *L'Echange Inégal* (Maspero, Paris, 1969).

Andre G. Frank, *Development and Underdevelopment in Latin America* (Monthly Review Press, 1968).

I. V. Levin, *The Export Economies* (Harvard Univ. Press, 1964).

Gunnar Myrdal, *Asian Drama* (Pantheon, 1968).

K. Nkrumah, *Neocolonialismo, última etapa del imperialismo* (Siglo XXI, Mexico, 1966).

Cristian Palloix, *Problemes de la Croissance en Economie Ouverte* (Maspero, Paris, 1969).

13

The Future of Global Polarization

Samir Amin

Samir Amin's essay is a pioneering study of the nature and consequences of the world capitalist system. It remains one of the driving intellectual discourses of the world system school of thought. With its roots in Marxist thought, Amin's arguments reveal the growing intensification of exploitation by the core (rich, industrialized, and militarily powerful) countries in the global capitalist system. He argues that the core countries' monopoly over technology, finance, natural resources, media and communications, and weapons of mass destruction and their stubborn resistance to lose control over their monopoly has perpetuated the center-periphery inequality and polarization. Samir Amin's prescription to deal with this inequality is to strengthen regional groupings on the periphery. By so doing, peripheral countries will increase their bargaining power and contribute positively toward the construction of a renewed global economic and financial system that he calls global socialism. His call for global socialism remains controversial yet thought provoking.

Unequal Development and the Historical Forms of Capitalism

History since antiquity has been characterized by the unequal development of regions. But it is only in the modern era that polarization has become the immanent by-product of the integration of the entire planet into the capitalist system.

Reprinted with permission of the publisher from *Capitalism in the Age of Globalization: The Management of Contemporary Society* by Samir Amin. London: Zed Books Ltd., 1997.

Modern (capitalist) polarization has appeared in successive forms during the evolution of the capitalist mode of production:

1. *The mercantilist form* (1500–1800) before the industrial revolution which was fashioned by the hegemony of merchant capital in the dominant Atlantic centers, and by the creation of the peripheral zones (the Americas) whose function involved their total compliance with the logic of accumulation of merchant capital.

2. *The so-called classical model* which grew out of the industrial revolution and henceforth defined the basic forms of capitalism. In contrast, the peripheries—progressively all of Asia (except for Japan) and Africa, which were added to Latin America remained rural, non-industrialized, and as a result their participation in the world division of labor took place via agriculture and mineral production. This important characteristic of polarization was accompanied by a second equally important one: the crystallization of core industrial systems as national autocentered systems which paralleled the construction of the national bourgeois states. Taken together, these two characteristics account for the dominant lines of the ideology of national liberation which was the response to the challenge of polarization: (i) the goal of industrialization as a synonym for a liberating progress and as a means of "catching up"; (ii) the goal of constructing nation-states inspired by the models of those in the core. This is how modernization ideology was conceived. From the industrial revolution (after 1800) up to the end of the Second World War the world system was characterized by this classical form of polarization.

3. *The postwar period* (1945–90) witnessed the progressive erosion of the above two characteristics. It was a period of industrialization of the peripheries, unequal and uneven to be sure. It was the dominant factor in Asia and Latin America, with the national liberation movement doing its best to accelerate the process within peripheral states which had recently regained their political autonomy. This period was simultaneously, however, one of the progressive dismantling of autocentric national production systems and their recomposition as constitutive elements of an integrated world production system. This double erosion was the new manifestation of the deepening of globalization.

4. *The most recent period* (since 1990) in which the accumulation of these transformations has resulted in the collapse of the equilibria characteristic of the postwar world system.

This evolution is not leading simply to a new world order characterized by new forms of polarization, but to global disorder. The chaos which confronts us today comes from a triple failure of the system: (i) it has not developed new forms of political and social organization going beyond the nation-state—a new requirement of the globalized system of production;

(ii) it has not developed economic and political relationships capable of reconciling the rise of industrialization in the newly competitive peripheral zones of Asia and Latin America with the pursuit of global growth; (iii) it has not developed a relationship, other than an exclusionary one, with the African periphery which is not engaged in competitive industrialization at all. This chaos is visible in all regions of the world and in all facets of the political, social and ideological crisis. It is at the root of the difficulties in the present construction of Europe and that continent's inability to pursue market integration and establish parallel integrative political structures. It is also the cause of the convulsions in all the peripheries in Eastern Europe, in the old semi-industrialized Third World and in the new marginalized Fourth World. Far from sustaining the progression of globalization, the current chaos reveals its extreme vulnerability.

The predominance of this chaos should not keep us from thinking about alternative scenarios for a new "world order" even if there are many different possible future "world orders." What I am trying to do here is to call attention to questions which have been glossed over by the triumphalism of inevitable globalization at the same time as its precariousness is revealed.

The reader will no doubt have discovered that this analysis of world capitalism is not centered on the question of hegemonies. I do not subscribe to the successive hegemonies school of historiography. The concept of hegemony is often sterile, and is unscientific because it has been so loosely defined. It does not seem to me that it should be the center of the debate. I have, in contrast, developed the idea that hegemony is the exception to the rule. The rule is conflict among partners which puts an end to hegemony. The hegemony of the United States, seemingly unchallenged today, perhaps by default, is as fragile and precarious as the globalization of the structures through which it operates.

The Present World System
and the Five Monopolies of the Center

In my opinion, the debate should start with an in-depth discussion of the new features in the present world system which are produced by the erosion of the previous one. In my opinion there are two new elements:

1. The erosion of the autocentered nation-state and the subsequent disappearance of the link between the arena of reproduction and accumulation together with the weakening of political and social control which up to now had been defined precisely by the frontiers of this autocentered nation-state;
2. The erosion of the great divide: industrialized center/non-industrial-

ized peripheral regions, and the emergence of new dimensions of polarization.

A country's position in the global hierarchy is defined by its capacity to compete in the world market. Recognizing this truism does not in any way imply sharing the bourgeois economist's view that this position is achieved as the result of rational measures—the said rationality being assessed by the yardstick of the so-called "objective laws of the market." On the contrary, I think that this competitiveness is a complex product of many economic, political and social factors. In this unequal fight the centers use what I call their "five monopolies." These monopolies constitute a challenge to social theory in its totality. They are:

1. *Technological monopoly.* This requires huge expenditures that only a large and wealthy state can envisage. Without the support of the state, especially through military spending—something liberal discourse doesn't mention—most of these monopolies would not last.

2. *Financial control of worldwide financial markets.* These monopolies have an unprecedented efficacy thanks to the liberalization of the rules governing their establishment. Not so long ago, the greater part of a nation's savings could circulate only within the largely national arena of its financial institutions. Today these savings are handled centrally by the institutions whose operations are worldwide. We are talking of finance capital: capital's most globalized component. Despite this, the logic of this globalization of finance could be called into question by a simple political decision to delink, even if delinking were limited to the domain of financial transfers. Moreover I think that the rules governing the free movement of finance capital have broken down. This system had been based in the past on the free floating of currencies on the market (according to the theory that money is a commodity like any other) with the dollar serving *de facto* as a universal currency. Regarding money as a commodity, however, is a theory that is unscientific and the pre-eminent position of the dollar is only *faute de mieux*. A national currency cannot fulfill the functions of an international currency unless there is a surplus of exports in the country whose currency purports to serve as an international currency, thus underwriting structural adjustment in the other countries. This was the case with Great Britain in the late-nineteenth century. This is not the case of the United States today which actually finances its deficit by the borrowing which the rest of the world is forced to accept. Nor indeed is this the case with the competitors of the United States: Japan's surplus (that of Germany disappeared after reunification in 1991) is not sufficient to meet the financial needs occasioned by the structural adjustment of the others. Under these conditions financial globalization, far from being a "natural" process, is an extremely fragile one. In the short run, it leads only to permanent instability

rather than to the stability necessary for the efficient operation of the processes of adjustment.

3. *Monopolistic access to the planet's natural resources.* The dangers of the reckless exploitation of these resources are now planet-wide. Capitalism, based on short-term rationality, cannot overcome these dangers posed by this reckless behavior, and it therefore reinforces the monopolies of already developed countries. The much-vaunted environmental concern of these countries is simply not to let others be equally irresponsible.

4. *Media and communication monopolies.* These not only lead to uniformity of culture but also open up new means of political manipulation. The expansion of the modern media market is already one of the major components in the erosion of democratic practices in the West itself.

5. *Monopolies over weapons of mass destruction.* Held in check by the postwar bipolarity, this monopoly is again, as in 1945, the sole domain of the United States. While it may be true that nuclear proliferation risks getting out of control, it is still the only way of fighting this unacceptable US monopoly in the absence of democratic international control.

These five monopolies, taken as a whole, define the framework within which the law of globalized value operates. The law of value is the condensed expression of all these conditions, and not the expression of objective, "pure" economic rationality. The conditioning of all of these processes annuls the impact of industrialization in the peripheries, devalues their productive work and overestimates the supposed value-added resulting from the activities of the new monopolies from which the centers profit. What results is a new hierarchy, more unequal than ever before, in the distribution of income on a world scale, subordinating the industries of the peripheries and reducing them to the role of subcontracting. This is the new foundation of polarization, presaging its future forms.

An Alternative Humanist Project of Globalization

In contrast to the dominant ideological discourse, I maintain that globalization via the market, is a reactionary utopia. We must counter it by developing an alternative humanistic project of globalization consistent with a socialist perspective.

Implied in the realization of such a project is the construction of a global political system which is not in the service of a global market, but one which defines its parameters in the same way as the nation-state represented historically the social framework of the national market and not merely its passive field of deployment. A global political system would thus have major responsibilities in each of the following four areas:

1. The organization of global disarmament at appropriate levels, thus liberating humanity from the menace of nuclear and other holocausts.
2. The organization of access to the planet's resources in an equitable manner so that there would be less inequality. There would have to be a global decision-making process with a valuation (tariffication) of resources which would make obligatory waste reduction and the more equitable distribution of the value and income from these resources. This could also be the beginning of a globalized fiscal system.
3. Negotiation of open, flexible economic relationships between the world's major regions which, currently, are unequally developed. This would reduce progressively the centers' technological and financial monopolies. This means, of course, the liquidation of the institutions presently running the global market (the so-called World Bank, the IMF, the World Trade Organization, etc.) and the creation of other systems for managing the global economy.
4. Starting negotiation for the correct management of the global/national dialectic in the areas of communication, culture and political policy. This implies the creation of political institutions which would represent social interests on a global scale—the beginning of a "world parliament" going beyond the inter-state mechanisms of the United Nations system that exist now.

Obstacles to the Realization of This Project

It is more than evident that current trends are not going in the direction described above and that humanist objectives are not those being fought for today. I am not surprised. The erosion of the old system of globalization is not able to prepare its own succession and can only lead to chaos. Dominant forces are developing their activities in the framework of these constraints, trying to maneuver for short-term gain and thereby aggravating the chaos. Their attempt to legitimate their choices by the stale ideology of the "self-regulating" market, or by affirming that "there is no alternative," or by pure and simple cynicism, is not the solution but part of the problem. The people's spontaneous responses to the degradation they experience, however, are not necessarily any more helpful. In a time of disarray, illusory solutions such as fundamentalism or chauvinism can be highly politically mobilizing. It is up to the Left—that is in fact its historic mission—to formulate, in theory and in practice, a humanistic response to the challenge. In its absence and until it is formulated, regressive and outright criminal scenarios will be the most likely order of the day.

The difficulties confronting the EU's European project right now are a good illustration of the impasse created by globalization through market mechanisms. In the first flush of enthusiasm over the European project no one foresaw these difficulties. Yet they were perfectly predictable by people who never believed that the Common Market by itself could create a united Europe. They said that a project as ambitious as this could not be accomplished without a Left capable of making it socially and culturally progressive. In the absence of that, it would remain fragile, and even a minor political accident could prove fatal. It was necessary, therefore, for the various European Lefts to make sure that each step of the integration was accompanied by a double series of measures: on the one hand, ensuring that profits went to the workers, thereby reinforcing their social power and their unity; and on the other, beginning the construction of a political system which would supersede the nation-state and could be the only unit that could effectively manage an enlarged market. This did not happen. The European project, in the hands of the Right, was reduced to purely mercantilist proportions, and the Left sooner or later simply offered its support without imposing any conditions. The result is what we see before us: the economic downturn has put the European partners in an adversarial position. They can only imagine solutions to their problems (notably unemployment) that are at the expense of others, and they don't even have effective tools for achieving those. They are increasingly tempted to retreat behind national barriers. Even the sincere efforts to avoid such action on the part of French and German politicians on both the Right and the Left have resulted only in rhetoric rather than effective pan-European action.

The EU's Europe is experiencing problems at the same time as the wider Europe is giving a new meaning to the challenge facing it. This ought to be an opportunity for the Left to rethink the European project as a whole and to begin the construction of a confederal political and "economic big" Europe that is anchored on the left by a reconstructed and united European labor force. But it has missed this opportunity and, on the contrary, has backed the forces of the Right which were in a hurry to profit from the collapse of the Soviet Empire by substituting a kind of unrestrained, wildcat capitalism. It is obvious that the present Latin Americanization of Eastern Europe can only weaken the chances of success of a left-leaning pan-European project. That in turn can only accentuate the disequilibrium within the Europe of the EU to the benefit of the only partner able to profit from this evolution: a reunited Germany.

The crisis of the European project is one of the major challenges confronting the construction of the new globalization. But these inward-looking manifestations, these inadequate and tragic responses to the challenge of the construction of a renewed global system, are not found exclusively in Europe. They are seen throughout the former Third World, especially in regions marginalized by the collapse of the old world order (sub-Saharan Africa and the Arab Islamic areas), and also in the new Third World of the

East (as in the former USSR and former Yugoslavia), where we see self-destructive involutions rather than valid responses to the challenge.

Possible Future Scenarios and Their Inadequacy

Given this background there are a few realistic scenarios, which can be proposed. I will examine several of them and show that they do not constitute adequate responses to the demands posed by the construction of an acceptable and stable world order. They therefore do not provide a way out from chaos.

The European question is at the center of theorizing about the future of globalization. With the breakdown of the European project and the threat of its disintegration, forces faithful to the European idea could find it useful, and possible, to regroup around their second-best position that is, a German Europe. There is reason to believe that in this scenario the British ship would sail close to American shores, keeping its distance from "continental Europe." We have already started down this path and some have even legitimated this choice by giving priority to the notion of the "neutral management of money" (a technocratic concept based on ignorance of the political meaning of monetary management), and conferring it (where else?) on the Bundesbank! I do not believe that this caricature of the original European project can be truly stable since several European countries will not accept the erosion of their positions which it implies.

To make matters worse, the preferential position of the United States is not challenged by this scenario of a German-led Europe. Nor is it clear that there is anything in this project that could challenge America in any of the areas of the five monopolies discussed above. A German-led Europe would remain within the American orbit.

There is another possible scenario—for lack of an alternative—a kind of second edition, American hegemony. There are many variations of this. The most likely one is a "sharing of the burden" associated with neo-imperialist regionalization: hitching Latin America to the US wagon and Africa to the German-European one (with some crumbs for France), and with the Gulf oil region and a "common market of the Middle East" remaining the domain of the United States. The American presence is already felt by its military occupation of the Gulf and less directly by its alliance with Israel. Finally, there might be a certain symmetry, with South and South-East Asia left open to Japanese expansion. But there is no equality implied in this division among the three centers: the United States would retain its privileged position. Here, too, I do not believe that neo-imperialist options of this kind would guarantee the stability of the system. They would be disputed periodically by revolts in Latin America, Asia and Africa.

We should therefore focus our attention on Asia, which has been largely outside the Euro-American conflict. It has often been observed that Asia—from Japan to Communist China, Korea, and to a lesser degree certain countries of South-East Asia (Singapore, Thailand and Malaysia) and even India—has not been affected by the present crisis, and that these countries have registered successes in terms of growth and efficiency (measured by their competitive position on the world market). Nevertheless, one cannot leap ahead and say that Asia will be the locus of the next hegemony. Asia may have more than half the world's population, but this is divided among distinct states. In place of a vague concept of global hegemony, one could substitute the notion of Asia becoming the principal region of capitalist accumulation. It remains to be described in detail how this may be occurring already: the articulation among the different Asian nations, and between them and the rest of the world. And there are variants of this model. The easiest to imagine—the domination of the region by Japanese imperialism—is, in my opinion, the least plausible. Admirers of Japan's recent success too often underestimate Japan's vulnerability. It is because of this weakness that Japan remains tied to the US. Nor is it probable that China, or even Korea, would accept being subordinated to Japan. Under these conditions the maintenance of an inter-Asian equilibrium would depend on forces external to the region, and here again only the United States is a candidate for this role, which would in turn prolong its primacy on the world scene.

Nonetheless it is highly probable that the positions of these Asian countries will be reinforced within the capitalist world system. How will the United States react to this? All alliance strategies will, in my opinion, revolve around this question. It goes almost without saying that the future development of China threatens all global equilibria. And that is why the United States will feel threatened by her development. In my opinion the United States and China will be the major antagonists in any future global conflict.

Renewing a Perspective of Global Socialism

Current developments suggest different possible scenarios, none of which questions the realities of North-South polarization. The commanding logic of the capitalist system perpetuates the center/periphery polarization. Its modes of operation are ever renewed and will in the future be founded on the five monopolies around which I have constructed my argument.

One could say that there is nothing new in this view because polarization is almost part of the natural order of things. I do not agree with this contention precisely because this polarization has been challenged over the past five centuries. Peoples peripheralized by capitalist world expansion, and who seemed for a long time to accept their fate, have over the past 50 years ceased accepting it, and they will refuse to do so more and more in the future. The positive political aspect of the universalization which capitalism inaugurated—and which can't get beyond its present truncated version—is the worm in the fruit. The Russian and Chinese revolutions began the attempt to go beyond the system on the basis of the revolts of peripheral people, and this will be continued in new versions. The final explanation for the instability of the world-system being built is found here. Of course, the conflicts that will occupy international attention in the future will, as always, not all be of equal importance. I would intuitively give determining priority to those involving the peoples of Asia and the dominant system. This doesn't mean others won't participate in this generalized revolt against polarization, just as it does not mean that transformations, and even progress, won't emanate from the very centers of the system.

In short, a humanistic response to the challenge of globalization inaugurated by capitalist expansion may be idealistic but it is not utopian. On the contrary, it is the only realistic project possible. If only we begin to develop it, powerful social forces will rally to it from all regions of the world.

This is the way to renew the perspective of global socialism. In preparation, ideological and political forces must regroup in order to be capable of combating the five monopolies, which reproduce capitalism. This struggle will create conditions for mutual adjustment. In it we have to reconsider fundamental questions on the ideological cultural front: (i) the dialectic between the universal and the particular; (ii) the relationship between political democracy and social progress; (iii) the dialectic of so-called economic efficiency (and the way it is expressed, "the market") and values of equality and fraternity; and (iv) the definition of a global socialist objective in the light of all the above.

On the political front we have to develop world organizational forms which are more authentically democratic so as to be capable of reshaping economic relations on the basis of diminishing inequality. In this perspective it seems to me that high priority should be given to reorganizing the global system around large areas which would group together scattered parts of the peripheries. This would be the place for the constitution of Latin American, Arab, African, South-East Asian regions, alongside China and India. I propose that this objective receive priority treatment in any new agenda of the Non-Aligned Movement. These regional groupings do not exclude others, such as Europe or the former USSR. The reason for this political call is simple: it is only by operating on this scale that one can effectively combat the five monopolies of our analysis. The construction, in turn, of a truly global economic and financial system becomes possible on this basis.

Of course the transformation of the world always begins by struggles at its base. Without changes in ideological, political and social systems at the national level, any discussion about challenging globalization and polarization remains a dead letter.

References

This chapter contains in condensed form conclusions from discussions developed in: Amin, Samir. 1993. *Empire of Chaos*. New York: Monthly Review Press.

————. 1994. *Re-reading the Post-War Period: An Intellectual Itinerary*. New York: Monthly Review Press.

————. 1993. *L'ethnicité à l'assaut des nations*. Paris: L'Harmattan.

————. 1993. *Mondialisation et accumulation*. Paris: L'Harmattan.

14

Globalization Under Fire

Robert Went

In sharp contrast to the arguments of Brink Lindsey, Robert Went puts forth a scathing indictment of the liberal free market model. His analysis blames increasing economic integration and attacks on state control of the economy for today's social, economic, and political problems. Not only does he explore the "perverse, anti-social logic" of global markets, he ends with an alternative vision for the global political economy. Went's contribution to this volume provides a structuralist interpretation of the globalization process and, from it, a positive plan for the future. As such, Went illuminates important dimensions of the globalization process ignored by the liberal and economic nationalist perspectives.

Will optimism about 21st century capitalism ultimately prove misguided? Hundreds of millions of people will not benefit from this new economic order. Victims include an older generation of unemployable Russians, the uprooted of India, and the newly idle of Europe and the U.S. In its most unbridled form, capitalism certainly delivers wealth but stumbles when it comes to distributing its rewards equitably enough. Resentment against capitalism could provoke a backlash against free trade and its sponsors. And few institutions now exist to regulate the excesses of global finance and post-cold-war geopolitics.

Business Week[1]

It is a bit hard to remember what the world looked like before globalization.

Paul Krugman (1999)

Reprinted with permission of the publisher from *Globalisation: Neoliberal Challenge, Radical Responses* by Robert Went. London: Pluto Press, 2000.

The collapse of bureaucratic regimes in Eastern Europe and the Soviet Union after 1989—beginning these countries' uneven, still incomplete integration into the world market—meant the disappearance of the main bloc in the world that functioned according to a non-capitalist logic. Together with the restructuring of global capitalism since the early 1980s, this has decreased the ability of countries, particularly in the Third World, to choose any model of economic development other than neoliberalism. It also removed one of the obstacles to attacks on the gains embodied in Western European welfare states.

Anyone who has opposed globalization in the last decade or two has risked not only being excluded from the discussion, but seeming cut off from reality. You have no choice but to adapt to globalization, organizations such as the OECD have insisted, whether you like it or not. According to the reigning economic orthodoxy, unhindered movement of capital, goods and services across national frontiers leads to an optimal and thus efficient allocation of scarce resources. True, as every first-year economics student learns, efficiency and fairness are not the same thing. But as in the decades after the First World War, when the world economy was also substantially integrated, the current acceleration of economic globalization has been solidly based on an international regime of free trade in combination with free movement of capital.

Since 1997, however, both these foundation stones of increasing international economic integration have once more been put in question. We have seen that the tendency towards growing internationalization of the world economy is real and forceful, but that the process of globalization is uneven, contradictory and certainly not linear. We have also seen that, despite the trends towards increasing globalization, no fully integrated world economy has come into existence. The world is considerably more globalized than 50 years ago, but considerably less than is theoretically conceivable.

In the coming years conflicts and contradictions will remain at work among countries, within countries, inside and among trading blocs and governments and with, among and inside institutions such as the IMF [International Monetary Fund], the EU [European Union], NAFTA [North American Free Trade Agreement], the World Bank, the G7 [Group of 7], the WTO [World Trade Organization] and the BIS [Bank of International Settlements]. Moreover, social movements and NGOs [non-governmental organizations] are increasingly globalizing *their* networks and activities in order to wage a worldwide fight against the social and ecological effects of free trade and against the dictatorship of the financial markets. The outcome of all these processes and clashes depends on many different developments and factors. In this chapter we examine what developments may be expected in the coming years.

Back to the Future?

For the time being, the tendency towards further globalization seems likely to continue. There are many contradictions and problems; neoliberalism's credibility has suffered from the series of crises since mid-1997; there is resistance in many countries to the consequences of the reigning international economic logic; but up until now that has not had major consequences for the overall direction in which the world economy is heading.

We are living in a new era, with an international economy that is being transformed into a true world economy. The Fordist organization of production, aimed at realising economies of scale, is being replaced in a growing number of companies and sectors with more flexible "just-in-time" production, in which "economies of scope" become more important (Smith 1994).[2] Examining the drastic changes in thinking about the role of the state in the economic process may give the clearest indication that a new period has arrived. Keynes has been buried and traded in for neoliberal neoclassicists (monetarists, supply-siders, rational-expectations adepts) who assume that it is best to leave as many decisions as possible to the market (Klein 1994). Although from time to time a plea is made for a new Bretton Woods–type international monetary order—in late 1998, for example, by the then German finance minister, Oskar Lafontaine, since resigned—few people seriously think that anything will come of it in the foreseeable future.

Is a return to the Golden Age possible? To ask this question is really to ask whether the economic, social, political and institutional constellation that led to the postwar period of prosperity—the postwar productive order—can come together again. In other words, to ask the question is to answer it: ...the postwar expansive phase was the result of specific factors that will not recur in that particular combination.[3] It is therefore extremely improbable that we are now headed back towards the Golden Age of postwar expansion. That period was exceptional in the history of capitalism, and even if the rate of profit recovered further it would not mean a return to the postwar order. Too much has changed in the organization and functioning of the world economy. As Joseph Schumpeter apparently once remarked: just as you can't restore the health of someone who's been run over by a truck by having the truck run him over in reverse, you can't restore an economy to health by reversing poor economic policies (Marglin and Bhaduri 1999).

To the extent that we *are* headed back to an earlier period, for much of the world population this means a return to the social relations of pre–Second World War capitalism or even longer ago. The effects of globalization . . . mean that for many people in the world *progress* is in fact *regression*. For a growing group of people in the OECD countries, postwar certainties like the right to a job, steadily increasing income, a good social system and decent public services no longer exist. For parts of the Third World as well, contrary to what is often thought and claimed, the postwar period until the early 1980s was more a time of progress (albeit minimal) than today (Rodrik 1999a). Real wages in Mexico, for example, were on average a full 10 per cent lower at the beginning of 1995—that is, *before* the announcement in January of President Ernesto Zedillo's plans to save the peso, which would lead to still lower wages—than they were in 1980— even though the IMF and the World Bank pointed to Mexico for years as an example for the rest of the Third World.

Advancing globalization will make its negative effects sharper and harder. That is, there will be a greater and more dominant dictatorship of the markets, particularly over countries that wish to attract capital; greater social inequality as a result of a dual process of polarization, within countries and on a world scale among countries; progressive levelling down of wages, working conditions and social security; ecological destruction and deterioration; a greater role for unaccountable international institutions and blocs; and a further undermining of democracy.

What will it all lead to? Not automatically to a new expansive phase, as we have seen; for that a major expansion of the market is necessary along with a considerable increase in the rate of surplus value. In the meantime, attacks on existing rights and gains continue (Tilly 1995). Some observers describe these attacks as a return to the elite tactics of the early nineteenth century, when the standard responses to popular discontent were indifference and repression—tactics that at least so far have proved quite successful almost two centuries later (Wallerstein 1995).

The counter-offensive is leading among other things to dismantling of the welfare state. But this is proceeding more slowly and with greater difficulty than many economists and politicians would like. The denial of existing rights and gains is happening bit by bit, mostly only a few small steps at a time. There has been considerable resistance.

In the Third World the economic orthodoxy of international organizations like the IMF and the World Bank has been leading for years to a form of social Darwinism (Bremen 1995). This barbarism is a daily reality for many people there. Even in the improbable event that all the IMF and World Bank's pro-market prescriptions are fully carried out, this will scarcely change. World Bank economists calculated in the early 1990s that in the best case the ratio between the world's richest 20 per cent and poorest 20 per cent would have declined by 2010 from 60:1 to 50:1. But if anything at all goes wrong, they wrote, the ratio can increase further, to 70:1 (Diwan and Revenga 1995). Since then large parts of the world have been hit by financial crises and thrown back decades in economic development. It can hardly be doubted that the more pessimistic scenario is the right one.

The First Crises of the Twenty-First Century

In the near future nothing seems able to stop the trend towards further globalization, with all the risks it entails. As we have seen in the late 1990s, the danger of a major international crisis is far from imaginary. The central problem is that little or no international regulation or control has been put in place to replace the national regulatory and control mechanisms eliminated by deregulation, privatization and, particularly, financial innovations. Problems requiring international action are myriad, and the responsibilities and authority of organizations like the OECD, the World Bank, the IMF, the WTO, the G7, the EU and the UN are being continually reshuffled. But in the foreseeable future none of these organizations will have the resources, facilities, room and authority to impose international regulations and controls.

In addition, the dominant paradigm is still that the market should in principle solve all problems and that the risks are not as great as all that. Many facts and incidents indicate the contrary: the October 1987 stock market crash; the European Monetary System crises; the dollar crises of 1977–79 and 1986–87; the Barings Bank scandals in Singapore and England; the various Japanese banking scandals; and the collapse of the Long-Term Capital Management hedge fund in 1998.[4] Instability has increased enormously in the financial sector in particular. Compared with the 1960s, when the Bretton Woods system kept exchange rates within narrow margins and capital flows were regulated, the volatility of the financial markets has grown and grown. "Financial crises seem now to happen with almost monotonous regularity": in addition to those just listed, "the bond market crashed in 1994; the Mexican crisis occurred late in the same year; East Asia went into turmoil in 1997; and Russia's default and associated shock waves shook the world in 1998."[5] No one really knows any more everything that is going on in the financial markets, what risks are being run and how great the odds are that a local crisis or stock market crash will spread, like an oil spill around the world.

The financial crises that broke out in Mexico in late 1994 and Asia in 1997 were the first major blows to the optimistic visions of progress held by globalization fans, and give a sense of the potential effects of future crises. In the Asian crisis in particular, economies that were considered powerhouses were thrown into a deep crisis from one day to the next because feelings among traders on financial markets turned against them. Millions of people suddenly lost their jobs, incomes and basic means of survival. All of the societies devastated by this crisis have experienced substantial "erosion of their social fabric, with social unrest, more crime, more violence in the home (UNDP 1999)." Now there are enthusiastic reports that growth rates and stock exchanges in these former Asian tigers are on the upswing. But it will be many years before the sharply increased unemployment and poverty can be brought back even to pre-crisis levels.

The Asian crisis is to students of financial markets what "the collapse of the Eastern Bloc was to Sovietologists (Eichengreen 1999)." Thanks to it, the position that financial markets are always efficient cannot be taken seriously. Traders' sheep-like behaviour and short-term thinking led in Asia and Latin America to "self-fulfilling crises" and overblown exchange rate fluctuations. Despite all the lovely stories and conferences about the necessity of reforming the "international financial architecture," nothing has changed. Everyone is just waiting for the next financial crisis.

Hardly anyone dared predict that neoliberal globalization would lead to such turmoil before the Mexican crisis—widely seen as the first crisis of the new globalized world—actually broke out in 1994. Mexico was the Rolls Royce among "emerging markets." In 1994 it was the first Third World country to be admitted to the OECD. That same year it joined the US and Canada to form the free-trade zone NAFTA. It was *the* example of successful neoliberal structural adjustment policies that the IMF and the World Bank preached to the South and East. But on 20 December 1994 the fairy tale was suddenly over. The peso lost over 40 per cent of its value, the stock market collapsed, and the government failed completely to stop capital flight, despite a tough austerity package. The crisis had arrived, and for the time being no end seemed in sight.

Politics and economics are always closely linked; but the Mexican power structure's reproach that the Zapatista uprising in Chiapas against NAFTA and single-party rule had caused the peso crisis was far too flattering. The Zapatistas' occupation of a few villages simply confirmed once more what the world already knew, that social inequality in Mexico is immense and that there are people there who refuse to accept it.[6] Perhaps this was shocking news for some investors and speculators. But the crisis's fundamental cause was something else: the fact that, from a strictly economic standpoint, the neoliberal project simply cannot work.

With far-reaching deregulation, privatization and market liberalization, Mexico has opened its doors wide to foreign capital. Everything is aimed at exports. But there are many other countries who also want to increase their share of export markets. Furthermore, inside NAFTA Mexico, as a Third World country, is in no way comparable to the world's premiere capitalist country, the US. As Mexican exports increased, its imports increased much more. The resulting balance of payments deficit rose to $28 billion, over 7 per cent of Mexico's GNP. The deficit was covered by capital imports; but much of the capital flowing into Latin America was speculative or was used to buy companies that were being sold cheap as part of privatization schemes. This was an extremely volatile, uncertain and unstable inward flow. The slightest upset turned the inward flow into an outward flow.

To save what was still savable President Zedillo announced a harsh austerity package. This was a rude awakening, particularly for those who had voted for him a few months before. Zedillo's campaign promises had been 4 per cent growth, many new jobs and "prosperity for your family." One of his slogans was: "He knows how to do it." Indeed, he did. The emergency package led to a recession, with higher interest rates, lower investment and consumption, problem-plagued banks and companies, sharply higher inflation and rapidly rising unemployment. A Brazilian weekly remarked shrewdly soon after the crisis broke out: "The real Mexico was a poor country that acted like a rich country. The party is over for the Mexican middle class. The party for the working class, that hadn't even begun, has been postponed indefinitely."[7]

In the wake of the Mexican crisis the stock market fell in Argentina, Brazil and Chile, and the exchange rates of many currencies such as the Brazilian real came under pressure. In Latin America they called this the "tequila effect," but the crisis had effects elsewhere as well. Government bond prices fell in Nigeria, Bulgaria, Morocco and Russia, while the US dollar also declined. This Mexican crisis "radiation" highlighted for the first time an explosive problem in the current world economy: thanks to the international regulatory vacuum, a crisis in one country can spread rapidly, and even lead to a worldwide financial crisis in which one stock market after another and one exchange rate after another threaten to fall like dominos. In 1997 and 1998 the same phenomenon was visible once more on an even greater scale.

While the reigning economic orthodoxy was and is that as much as possible must be left to the market, the time had come to lend the invisible hand a helping hand—since major financial institutions threatened to go under. On 31 January 1995 President Bill Clinton presented an international aid programme to contain the Mexican crisis—just in time, since the Mexican central bank had virtually exhausted its reserves and the moment was rapidly approaching when Mexico would have had to announce a moratorium on debt payments. That, according to IMF director Michel Camdessus, would have led to a true global catastrophe. The alarm was sounded, with even a touch of panic. Clinton was not managing to round up enough support in the US Senate for the rescue package he had announced immediately after the outbreak of the crisis.

At the World Economic Forum in Davos, where the world's top managers, central bankers and finance ministers gather each year, a discussion was organized on the question of where the next crisis would explode: Hungary, China, Argentina, Indonesia? Guru George Soros among others gave the opinion that a catastrophe was looming: a new stock market crash as in 1987, not just in Mexico but on Wall Street and in London, Frankfurt, Tokyo and Hong Kong. "Plan B" was hastily started up. Clinton did an end run around the Senate by using special presidential powers. The IMF and the BIS came forward with the largest amounts they had ever spent. All told, the Mexican government temporarily had over $50 billion to spend. Not that this was much of a gift: the money would have to be paid back, and would only be available when major cuts dictated by the IMF had been carried out. Mexico also had to pledge its oil revenues as security, and interest had to be paid on the loans. By the end of 1995 Mexico's foreign debt reached over $170 billion. In 1995 alone $57 billion in interest and principal payments were made: more than the total paid to foreign creditors from 1821 to 1976.

The package put together by Clinton was called many different things: "a disaster plan," "the last resort," "the emergency brake," and even, harking back to the Gulf War, "financial operation Desert Storm."[8] But the interesting question is: what were the world's richest countries really so anxious about? Why did they, together with the IMF and the BIS, put together the biggest aid package in history for a country like Mexico?

There were several reasons. First and foremost, they were afraid that the crisis would spread uncontrollably if Mexico stopped making payments. The "system risk" so feared by economists and bankers genuinely existed, thanks to the greatly increased integration of financial markets.

Second, the Mexican economy could not be allowed to collapse completely because it was the showcase example of the "emerging markets." Mexico was cited up until the day the peso crisis broke out as proof that IMF policies are the way to prosperity and happiness. Averting its collapse was seen as crucial to saving the IMF's credibility.

A third reason for the aid package had to do with the US position in the world. NAFTA could not be allowed to fail, because the free trade treaty's success and future enlargement is a major part of the US strategy to improve its position in the world economy. NAFTA's collapse would be very disadvantageous for the US's global economic role.

There was, finally, a fourth reason. Vast interests were at stake; if Mexico had had to announce a moratorium on its debt payments, investment funds, banks and speculators would have lost large sums of money. The aid package was in fact a gift from the taxpayers to the rich (Buiter 1995). One of the rich people in question was US Treasury Secretary Robert Rubin, who played a key role in arranging the aid programme. Before Rubin became secretary of the treasury he was vice-chairman of the board of Goldman Sachs, one of the US's largest brokerage houses. In 1992, Rubin's last year there, Goldman Sachs made a profit of $1.4 billion from, among other things investments in Mexico. The brokerage house was one of the largest donors to Clinton's presidential campaign, and Secretary Rubin had an estimated net worth of more than $150 million in 1995.

In the light of this background to the international aid programme, it is hardly surprising that all the anxiety over the state of the world economy did not include much concern for the effects on ordinary Mexicans. These effects have been immense. As a result of sharply higher interest rates, cuts in government spending and declining buying power Mexico went into a deep recession. More than a million Mexicans lost their jobs; more than half of Mexicans now live officially in poverty. Per capita income fell in 1995 from $3800 to $2600, the lowest level since 1989. No wonder that crime rates and suicide rates have risen rapidly and that many Mexicans must manage to survive by working in the informal sector.

The Mexican crisis showed how unstable and incalculable the world economy was. In its wake the G7 wrung its hands over the lack of "global governance." They decided that the IMF should work more closely with the World Bank and the WTO in order to signal more quickly where things risk going wrong. They also agreed to support initiatives that would give the IMF more funds so that it could react quickly in case of another Mexico. With the decision to give the IMF extra resources to act quickly when fresh disasters occur, the world's most important heads of government tacitly admitted that neither the IMF nor any other organization can *prevent* new crises.

This has since been confirmed many times over by the financial crises of 1997-98. In the months following the Mexican crisis commentators and analysts from international organizations warned that there would be more crises, though nobody knew where or when. Sooner than many expected it became clear that the next Mexicos were to be found in Asia, where from mid-1997 on one Tiger economy after another fell into a deep crisis. The crisis and its shock waves then spread to other continents, leading to dramatic impoverishment and lasting negative consequences for the growth perspectives of the world economy as a whole. It "prompted some radical new thinking," with well-known economists openly doubting central elements of the dominant orthodoxy of free trade and free capital flows (Eichengreen 1999).

The globalization of the Southeast Asian crisis came as a very unwelcome shock to protagonists of free trade and financial liberalization, who had presented the development of these Asian economies as the ultimate proof that their policies work better than old-style import-substitution strategies. To cite only one typical account by a free-trade champion (published ironically enough in 1997 under the title "How We Learn"):

> At the same time as evidence of the high costs of import-substitution regimes was accumulating, another important development occurred. Starting first in Taiwan, several East Asian economies began growing rapidly under policies diametrically opposite to those prevalent under import substitution . . . [T]he East Asian experiences demonstrated, as nothing else could have, the feasibility and viability of alternative trade policies . . . They also showed that rates of growth well above those realized even in the most rapidly growing import-substitution countries such as Brazil and Turkey could be realized (Krueger 1997).

In the light of these ideas, it is no accident that the IMF did not foresee the crisis in Asia. Less than three months before the crisis broke out in South Korea, it wrote: "Directors welcomed Korea's continued impressive macroeconomic performance and praised the authorities for their enviable fiscal record." With Thailand on the verge of financial collapse, it "strongly praised Thailand's remarkable economic performance and the authorities' consistent record of sound macroeconomic policies (Sachs 1997)." The same indestructible confidence in free trade and financial liberalization policies was expressed in the IMF negotiators' demands on countries in need of financial support. Even a mainstream economist notes that "once the crisis struck, Asian countries found their policies largely dictated by Washington—that is, by the International Monetary Fund and the U.S. Treasury (Krugman 1999)."

International organizations, economists and policymakers also seriously underestimated the consequences of the Asian crisis for the world economy as a whole. According to the Ten Commandments of neoliberal globalization that had become ever more rigid since the late 1970s, deregulation, privatization, trade liberalization, free capital movements, a shrinking social and public sector and more market discipline were supposed to ensure global prosperity and abundance. From this point of view a crisis here or there could not end the fun in the rest of the world. But those selling these neoliberal prayer beads threatened to become victims of their own success. The celebrated liberalization, deregulation and internationalization have created new forms of dependency, and in times of economic adversity they provide transmission routes along which crises spread and multiply. By 1998 one country after another, including Russia and Brazil, were hit by currency speculation, falling stock markets, capital flight, declining foreign investment and lower growth projections. The *Wall Street Journal* warned of a "financial Vietnam," while super-speculator George Soros spoke of a "crisis of globalized capitalism" (Soros 1998). Tens of millions lost their jobs in 1997–98, amidst reports of a major increase in child prostitution in many countries as they slid into poverty.

How did the IMF, backed by its shareholders, the world's rich countries, react? It made the situation still worse by posing sado-monetarist conditions for aid to countries in difficulties. An almost perfect inversion of the Keynesian compact lay at the core of the policies imposed by Washington over the last few years on one country after another: "faced with an economic crisis, countries are urged to raise interest rates, slash spending, and increase taxes." Apparently, no one except the all-too-eager hedge funds was responsible for these counterproductive policies. "The rules of the New World Order, it seemed, offered developing countries no way out. And so it was really nobody's fault that things turned out so badly" (Krugman 1999). The IMF makes demands that exacerbate crises, ones that are based simply on the market-based principle that countries must win back the "confidence" of the financial markets as quickly as possible.

No one could ask for a more telling illustration of the perverse, anti-social logic of today's neoliberal globalization. In order to offer speculators and investors a sufficient perspective of profits, governments on the threshold of the twenty-first century must deepen recessions, destroy jobs on a massive scale and slash away even more at social and other spending.

It has become steadily clearer in recent decades that the strategy of export-led growth proposed and imposed by the IMF, Wall Street and the rich countries' governments is unworkable for more and more "emerging markets." The financial markets have become all-powerful thanks to the far-reaching globalization of the world economy, and as a result the needs of the Third World's population are sacrificed. The globalizing world economy reproduces and reinforces domination by capital. Fortunately, the central building blocks of the neoliberal order—free movement of capital and free trade—are increasingly being challenged. In various countries and movements an alternative agenda is taking shape for a "negotiated and selective integration with the world economy" (Bello 1998), which means among other things: controls on capital flows; fiscal reforms based on a progressive tax system; land reform; priority for domestic development rather than exports; economic democracy, so as to let communities, citizens' groups and popular movements decide the main priorities for economic development; and priority to sustainability, given the major environmental problems in the countries in crisis. Until programmes of this kind based on a different economic and social logic are carried out, much of the world population will remain the plaything of financial market traders and multinational managers making decisions behind their backs.

Meanwhile, fresh financial crises can reinforce nationalist, chauvinist and protectionist tendencies, which are already on the rise, and lead to their triumph. Some observers say that contradictions between increasing globalization and the decreasing functionality of the national state are insoluble, and predict that they will mount until they result in chaos (Amin 1994). Others assume that contradictions among the big economic powers will grow, and suggest ominously that new military conflicts are possible. The fact that cooperation is rational should not lead us to conclude that the powers will in fact always cooperate:

> Only a few months before the guns opened fire in 1914, Norman Angell, a famous contemporary economic pundit, had predicted in his book *The Age of Illusion* that the degree of interdependence of the major European economies had made war no longer conceivable. (Glyn and Sutcliffe 1992)[9]

The outcome of a future crisis cannot be determined in advance, however; nor does it depend on any economic laws. It depends on the development of national and global struggles (Clarke 1992).

Towards a Different Economic Logic

Crises, chaos or the collapse of the international financial system are not the only ways by which the apparently unstoppable trend towards globalization can come to a halt. A less apocalyptic variant is also conceivable, one in which other economic and social priorities replace the profit-driven logic of capitalism. Many elements of such a positive alternative have been assembled in recent years by social movements North and South, East and West. The failure of the Multilateral Agreement on Investment and the 1999 WTO Seattle summit have increased their confidence that such an alternative may be attainable.

Neoliberals have responded to these setbacks by insisting even more shrilly that there is no alternative. The real losers in the Seattle conference's failure were the more than five billion inhabitants of the developing countries, they cried (Bello 1999).[10] But even demagogy has its limits: the US and EU negotiators who shed tears over the negative effects of the conference's failure on the world's poor were primarily interested in their own—in part clashing—interests and trading priorities. The EU, for example, wanted to put new items on the WTO agenda in order to eliminate barriers to Northern multinationals' access to Southern markets, while the EU itself still heavily subsidizes its agricultural exports. Progressives in the Third World tend in any event to see the Seattle conference's failure as a gain for developing countries, not a loss.

Can anything be done not just to slow down, but actually to counter the headlong rush towards globalization? Many proposals have been made in recent years to make the world somewhat less unjust and limit somewhat the power of financial markets and speculators, such as: cancellation (or reduction) of Third World countries' debts; an international tax on air travel, levied at each airport, to fund international development aid; an EU social charter guaranteeing basic rights such as health care, education, jobs and decent incomes for all Europeans; the "Tobin tax" of say 0.5 per cent proposed by Nobel Prize winner James Tobin on all currency transactions (Tobin 1978); controls and limits on capital flows; more regulation of derivatives trading; and so forth.

Is there any hope for such proposals in the globalized world economy? Some observers say that, while these proposals focus attention on the nature of the problem, "[p]ractical recommendations must acknowledge the powerful forces promoting the growth of capital flows" (Eichengreen 1999). But it is also practical to envisage the outright defeat of these "powerful forces." We have already seen that, while the functions of states have changed, states are definitely still playing a role and there are still choices to make about how they play it. Opponents of more regulation and active state intervention admit this. Even *The Economist* has rejected the idea that states are now powerless. Politicians are all too eager to use the drastic changes in the world to justify their abandonment of old political objectives and ideals. In reality, while it is not easy to rebuild fire walls that politicians have spent decades knocking down, it is far from impossible.[11]

A striking side effect of the Seattle fiasco is that assertions treated for years as knock-down, discussion-closing arguments are suddenly phrased in a more nuanced way. People now recall, for example, that "the first global economy" fell apart with the arrival of the First World War, even though everyone thought then as now that global economic integration was unstoppable (Krugman 2000). The progress of globalization no longer seems guaranteed. It seems possible after all that the strong technological forces propelling the world towards further economic integration "can be slowed, if not halted."[12]

Even the business press is making a bit of room now and then for a dissident who says that the forces of globalization not only can be stopped, but should be stopped. One columnist profaned the pages of *Business Week* with the headline, "The Seattle Protesters Got It Right," explaining: "The WTO agenda is set by the world's leading governments, which forgot that they are elected not only to advance the interests of multinational corporations but also those of citizens" (Kuttner 1999). One self-declared mainstream Harvard economist spoke up, not for the first time, against treating the means—trade—as if it were an end in itself. Instead of asking what kind of trading system is best for trade, he said, we should ask which is best to help people to uphold their values and reach their development objectives (Rodrik 1999b). These are not the kind of comments the WTO likes to hear. They imply, for example, that poor countries should have the right to prioritize fighting poverty instead of increasing exports.

It is clearly possible to throw a certain amount of sand in the machinery of globalization and market orthodoxy, if only the political will for it exists. However important such small changes and improvements can be—and they are in themselves very worthy of support—only symptoms are being combated and not the disease as long as the fundamental characteristics and laws of motion of the world capitalist system remain unaffected. Social inequality, ecological destruction, oppression and exploitation of the Third World, the further undermining of democracy and the leveling down of wages, working conditions and social security will continue to increase as long as the existing economic logic is not radically overhauled. The possibility of international crises, with possible regression towards nationalism, protectionism and chauvinism as a result, will also continue to exist.

It is not possible within the existing economic logic, in which profit maximization comes first, to solve the most important problems that humanity faces. Under capitalism, the individual interests of speculators, employers or investors determine what they do. The partial rationality of their actions clashes with the general social interest of present and future generations.

In fact, capitalism is becoming more and more irrational. The discrepancy between what is economically and socially possible and what is actually happening has never been greater than it is today. Criticisms of free-trade ideology are exposing year by year more and more of the system's flaws. For several years, for example, the environmental movement has been pointing out the ecological costs of unrestricted trade in the interest of profit maximization. How "free" are poor countries with enormous burdens of debt who earn money on the world's toxic waste market by allowing the dumping of poison from the rich West? The WTO, the IMF and the rich Western countries preach trade liberalization as a universally valid prescription; but movements in the North and the South are resisting the attack this implies for countries' democratic right, particularly in the Third World, to choose a development path in the interests of their own peoples.

The world could look very different if priorities were determined in a truly democratic way, instead of according to the principle of "one dollar, one vote." More and more people are arriving at the conclusion that revolutionary changes are both necessary and objectively possible.

Action by living, breathing social forces can transform even the most seemingly inextricable economic and political situation. More than ever before, an alternative must take into account a number of different dimensions:

- The political dimension. Although governments have deliberately cast aside a part of their regulatory functions to allow for the deregulation of capital flows, they can be pressured into reinstating these functions. It is a question of political will; if those in power cannot rise to the task, they can either step aside or be ousted.
- The dimensions of citizenship and class. Those "from below" and their organizations—whether from the labor movement born in the nineteenth century (parties, unions), from other grassroots movements or from new social movements born in the latter half of the twentieth century—must reclaim their right to intervene in society and exercise control over certain aspects of public life, to exert pressure on other political and economic players and to raise in concrete terms the question of hands-on political power.
- The economic dimension. Economic decisions lie at the core of all the other dimensions. Such decisions should be directed at placing restrictions on capital flows and on those that control them, the holders of capital. The recent evolution of capitalism has given renewed urgency to the debate on new forms of radicalism. (Toussaint 1998)

What would an alternative look like? As we have seen, many different ideas exist, but there are two core questions that must be answered in order to arrive at a different economic and social logic.[13] First, how and by what social forces should the priorities and direction of economic development be decided? Today this is done behind everyone's back by the "invisible hand" of the market and in multinationals' boardrooms. Second, what kind of relationship and engagement with the world market is wanted? This means that financial deregulation and fair trade must be put on the agenda. Developing an alternative means discussing the economic, social, political and institutional conditions under which the current downwards spiral—progress equals regression—can be reversed. This can happen only on the basis of a radically different starting point: that production should be organized not so as to make the highest possible profits, but to meet the needs of the whole world population.

The essence of what is necessary can really be summed up in one phrase: drastic redistribution and democratization of resources and structures. Many more collective debates, analyses, experiments and experiences, by workers, young people, women, activists and scholars in and with social movements, are needed to determine exactly what this means concretely. Their topics will undoubtedly include the following issues.

Reregulation of the Financial Sector

Bringing the financial sector under social control so as to put an end to speculation and economic sabotage, so that democratic decisions can be reached regarding how much resources should be devoted to what ends. Naturally, all small steps in this direction, such as the introduction of a Tobin tax on financial transactions, are worthy of support.

Cancellation of Third World Debt

A radical break with exploitation of the Third World, to be replaced with cooperation on the basis of mutual interest. This means the payment of fair prices for Third World products and the cancellation of Third World debt, which has already been repaid many times over (Toussaint & Drucker 1995).

Break with Export-Led Growth

A break with the export-led growth propagated and imposed all over the world by the IMF, the World Bank, the WTO and the OECD, so as to give priority to domestic development and the organising of production to meet local and regional needs.

Sustainable Production

A transition from the current wasteful and polluting ways of production to ecologically responsible, sustainable production. This requires a planned (how else could it be done?) global redivision of the world's environmental carrying capacity—that is, first, a prudent estimate of the maximum allowable annual usage of finite resources (like oil) and the maximum allowable annual level of activities (like car production) that would otherwise endanger the preservation of the biosphere; and, second, a democratically decided, equitable allocation of these annual maximums among the world's population.[14] By contrast with the current situation, economic growth will not be an end in itself within such an alternative logic, but will be subordinated to the planned satisfaction of the needs of the world's total current and future population.

Control over the Labor Process

A fundamental change in the current, management-dominated labor processes by introducing structures and processes controlled and initiated by all working people. Also giving a high priority to everyone's personal development and work satisfaction so as to make optimal use of the now largely unused creativity, knowledge and insights of the people who do the work every day (Smith 1994). Consumers and producers of goods and services can also ensure a far more sustainable satisfaction of needs.

Redistribution of Work

Drastic redistribution of paid work by introducing shorter working hours with no cut in pay, so that everyone can benefit from rising productivity instead of only a small minority as is now the case, and so that everyone who can and wants to work can have a job. Drastic redistribution of unpaid work as well through socialization of household tasks and through a shorter work week that gives everyone more time for caretaking tasks.

Redistribution of Income

Drastic redistribution of income and wealth from the small group of the most highly paid and rich people to those without assets and the lower-paid, and establishment of a maximum income alongside a global minimum income for everyone. Good, free, basic public services—education, health care, public transport, housing and culture—belong in this same framework.

Democracy and Planning

A break with the reigning orthodoxy of more and more market. Mechanisms and structures should be established for democratic discussion, decision-making and planning—that is, jointly by *everyone*—of the chief directions and priorities for economic development, in a socially and ecologically responsible way.[15]

Changes like these will require considerable social pressure, unrest, and the building of stronger organizations and movements. Without any doubt, there will be conflicts with the dominant elites that benefit from the status quo. Rebuilding the left, the trade union movement and other social movements is essential if these battles are to be won.

A new reinforcement of organizations and movements for social change requires more than recalling and defending past experiences. The world has changed in fundamental ways, and this will have consequences for the structure, themes and methods of work of opposition movements. The most important change that virtually all leftist organizations and social movements will have to make is a shift to functioning outside their old, almost exclusively national frameworks. In making this shift, they can take advantage of the great potential of new technologies like the Internet.

Paradoxically, the right and employers are far better organized internationally than the left and the unions, whose language is traditionally much more internationalist. In other social movements cross-border organizing is already more common. All over the world activists in environmental, solidarity, youth, immigrant, women's and lesbian/gay organizations are hard at work on globalization from below. There is also never an IMF, World Bank, OECD, EU or G8 summit without NGOs organizing a parallel counter-summit and all sorts of street actions. But when most organizations in the workers' movement draw up their budgets and work plans, international cooperation and solidarity are still an afterthought. As long as many unions and left-wing parties are protective of "national" interests, furthermore, the right and employers can easily play working and poor people in different countries off against each other. As long as this does not change there will be little social change, and even powerful organizations like the union movement are doomed to become more and more marginal.

That would be very serious. An effective response to the current neoliberal globalization must in the first place be economic, and thus must rely on the world's working and poor people. Interestingly, possibilities and points of departure for internationalizing trade union work are multiplying with each new forward surge of globalization. Since companies are organizing parts of their production, administration, assembly and sales internationally, and international takeovers, mergers and joint ventures are on the increase, new relations and contacts are being made between employees in different countries who all work for the same firm or are part of the same chain of production. Changes in the organization of labor (such as "just-in-time" production with the smallest possible inventories) also make production processes vulnerable in new ways to worker action. If a strike breaks out anywhere in the chain of production, within a few days other links will be paralyzed by parts shortages.

This increases the possibilities of connections and common interests in international trade union work. A fine example of where this can lead: when Ford factory workers in Cuatitlan, north of Mexico City, struck in 1994 against layoffs and for better working conditions, members of United Auto Workers in a US Ford factory sent money to support the action. Their reasoning was: if the Mexicans win, that's good for us as well as them because Ford won't be so quick to (threaten to) move production to Mexico.[16] There are many other such possibilities for intensive contacts and common actions by unions in different countries. The time is more than ripe for coordinating demands and actions in different parts of international concerns like Renault, Unilever and Shell. It is high time for at least a European trade union and welfare-recipient offensive in order to fight for a much shorter working week with no cut in pay and an expanded public sector.

It is also necessary and possible to go beyond internationalizing trade union work in single companies. Employers are playing workers off against each other everywhere and taking advantage of worsening working conditions at competing companies in order to lower their own companies' norms. This increases the objective possibilities of international trade union strategies for entire industries at a European or international level. Most industries are dominated by two or three companies; if wage earners in those few firms succeed in preventing workers in one company from being played off against workers in another, the race to the bottom in wages, benefits and working conditions can be slowed down or reversed. This would indeed require a radical change of course by most trade unions. Other social movements and leftist parties face the same task. In some countries we are beginning to see that more militant unions are developing into broader social movements. This may well become one of the most effective new responses to globalization (Moody 1997).

On the threshold of the twenty-first century the left, the trade union movement and other social movements face a fundamental challenge. In the face of cynicism, fatalism and the dominant market orthodoxy, a social, ecological, feminist and internationalist alternative must win back credibility and offer new hope by developing realistic utopias. We must show in practice that and how a different logic is possible. New experiences and initiatives, new forms of practical internationalism based on solidarity and educated self-interest, will be decisive to turning the tide.

Notes

1. *Financial Times*, 20 Dec. 1994.
2. This is definitely not a linear development. There are new sectors, particularly the service sector, in which Fordist and Taylorist methods are only now being introduced.

3. "Nostalgia for the stable, postwar compromise of the national welfare state is . . . misplaced and unrealistic. The historic compromise was based on the stable international order of the Cold War years. The new, post-1989 international order must be characterised above all as disordered. The national building blocks on which Keynes and Beveridge's welfare state rested were a homogeneous society, full employment regulated by Keynesian macroeconomic policy, a Fordist structure of production, centrally organised and very institutionalised interest groups of labour and capital, a self-confident interventionist state and the traditional family. None of these preconditions can be met today. Leaving aside the tremendous changes in the structure of production, Keynesian policies of demand stimulation are unworkable in a world of global competition and free capital markets. With the loss of its economic frontiers, the nation-state has lost its sovereignty over monetary and fiscal policy. This limits to a major extent the national welfare state's capacity to correct markets—even within an integrated European political economy. Under the deflationary criteria of the European Monetary Union, Keynesian policy prescriptions are not very realistic" (Hemerijk & Bakker, 1994).

4. A number of earlier crises and near-crises are described in Solomon (1995).

5. *Economist,* 12 June 1999.

6. For a description of the Chiapas rebellion and an analysis of the background to it, see, for example, Ross (1995).

7. *Veja.*

8. *Business Week,* 13 Feb. 1995.

9. Henk Overbeek pointed out to me that the same was true of Karl Kautsy in his article about "ultra-imperialism," published in August 1914 in *Die Neue Zeit.*

10. See, for example, *Economist,* 11 Dec. 1999.

11. "The myth of the powerless state," *Economist,* 7 Oct. 1995.

12. "Challenge of globalization," *Financial Times,* 28 Dec. 1999.

13. See, for example, G. Albo (1997), Altvater (1993), Amin (1994), Cassen (1994), Cavanagh, Wysham and Arruda (1994), Duchrow (1995), Engelen (1995), Fourth International (1985), Halimi, Michie, and Milne (1994), Husson (1994), Kassa (1994), Lang and Hines (1993), Mandel (1992, 1995), Norman (1987), Peet (1991), Smith (1994), Toussaint (1998), and Toussaint and Drucker (1995).

14. For an account of the irreconcilability of economics and ecology under capitalism, see, for example, Duchrow (1995) and Altvater (1993).

15. On a relationship between plan, market and democracy that would be an alternative to both capitalism and the old bureaucratically planned economies in Eastern Europe and the Soviet Union, see Altvater (1993), Mandel (1992), and Samary (1988, 2000).

16. "21st Century capitalism: How nations and industries will compete in the emerging global economy, part 2," *Business Week,* 19 Dec. 1994, p. 54.

References

Albo, G. 1997. "A World Market of Opportunities? Capitalist Obstacles and Left Economic Policy." In *Socialist Register 1997: Ruthless Criticism of All that Exists,* edited by Leo Panitch. London: Merlin Press.

Altvater, Elmar. 1993. *The Future of the Market: An Essay on the Regulation of Money and Nature after the Collapse of "Actually Existing Socialism."* London: Verso.

Amin, Samir. 1994. "De nieuwe wereldoverheersing van het kapitalisme: Problemen en vooruitzichten." *Vlaams Marxistisch Tijdschrift.* 28:3.

Bello, Walden. 1999. *Focus on Trade*, no. 42 (December).

———. 1998. "The End of the Asian Miracle." *Nation.* 12–19 January.

Breman, J. 1995. "Een laat-kapitalistisch manifest." *Volkskrant,* 7 October.

Buiter, Willem. 1995. *International Herald Tribune,* 2 February.

Cassen, Bernard. 1994. "Imperative transition vers une societe du temps libere." *Le Monde Diplomatique* (July).

Cavanagh, John, Daphne Wysham, and Marcos Arruda. 1994. *Beyond Bretton Woods: Alternatives to the Global Economic Order.* London: Pluto Press.

Clarke, Simon. 1992. "The Global Accumulation of Capital and the Periodization of the Capitalist State Form." In *Open Marxism I,* edited by Werner Bonefeld, Richard Gunn and Kosmo Psychopedis. London: Pluto Press.

Diwan, Ishac, and Ana Revenga. 1995. "The Outlook for Workers in the 21st Century." *Finance and Development* (September).

Duchrow, Ulrich. 1995. *Alternatives to Global Capitalism: Drawn from Biblical History, Designed for Political Action.* Utrecht: International Books.

Eichengreen, Barry. 1999. *Toward a New International Financial Architecture: A Practical Post-Asia Agenda.* Washington: Institute for International Economics.

Engelen, Ewald. 1995. *De mythe van de markt: Waarheid en leugen in de economie.* Amsterdam: Het Spinhuis.

Fourth International. 1985. "Dictatorship of the Proletariat and Socialist Democracy." *International Viewpoint* special issue: *Resolutions of the Twelfth World Congress of the Fourth International.*

Glyn, A. and B. Sutcliffe. 1992. "Global But Leaderless? The New Capitalist Order." In *Socialist Register 1992: New World Order?* edited by Ralph Miliband and Leo Panitch. London: Merlin Press.

Halimi, S., Jonathan Michie, and S. Milne. 1994. "The Mitterand Experience." In *Unemployment in Europe,* edited by Jonathan Michie and John Grieve Smith. London: Academic Press.

Hemerijk, Anton, and Wieger Bakker. 1994. "De pendule van perspectief: Convergentie en divergentie in het denken over de verzorgingsstaat." In *Zorgen in het Europese huis: Verkenningen over de grenzen van nationale verzorgingsstaten,* edited by Gottfried Engbersen, Anton Hemerijck & Wieger Bakker. Amsterdam: Boom.

Husson, Michel. 1994. "Face a la contrainte exterieure." In *Agir ensemble contre le chomage: Donnees et arguments,* Paris: Syllepse.

Kassa, 1994. *Nederland in spagaat: Pleidooi voor een andere ekonomiese logika.* Amsterdam: ISP.

Klein, Philip. 1994. "A Reassessment of Institutionalist-Mainstream Relations" *Journal of Economic Issues,* 28, no. 1.

Krueger, Anne. 1997. "Trade Policy and Economic Development: How We Learn." *American Economic Review,* 87:1.

Krugman, Paul. 2000. *New York Times,* 2 January.

———. 1999. *The Return of Depression Economics.* New York: W. W. Norton.

Kuttner, Robert. 1999. "Economic Viewpoint: The Seattle Protesters Got It Right." *Business Week,* 20 December.

Lang, Tim, and Colin Hines. 1993. *The New Protectionism: Protecting the Future against Free Trade.* London: Earthscan.

Mandel, Ernest. 1995. *Long Waves of Capitalist Development: A Marxist Interpretation.* London: Verso.

————. 1992. *Power and Money.* London: Verso.

Marglin, Stephan, and A. Bhaduri. 1991. "Profit Squeeze and Keynesian Theory." In *The Golden Age of Capitalism: Reinterpreting the Postwar Experience,* edited by Stephan Marglin and Juliet Schor. Oxford: Clarendon Press.

Moody, Kim. 1997. *Workers in a Lean World: Unions in the International Economy.* London: Verso.

Norman, Richard. 1987. *Free and Equal: A Philosophical Examination of Political Values.* Oxford: Oxford University Press.

Peet, Richard. 1991. *Global Capitalism: Theories of Societal Development.* London: Routledge.

Rodrik, Dani. 1999a. *The New Global Economy and Developing Countries: Making Openness Work.* Washington: Johns Hopkins University Press.

————. 1999b. "Wereldhandel mag geen doel op zichzelf zijn." *NRC Handelsblad,* 8 December.

Ross, John. 1995. *Rebellion from the Roots: Indian Uprising in Chiapas.* Monroe, ME: Common Courage Press.

Sachs, J. 1997. "Power unto Itself." *Financial Times.* 11 December.

Samary, Catherine. 2000. "Mandel's Views on the Transition to Socialism." In *The Marxism of Ernest Mandel,* edited by Gilbert Achcar. London: Verso.

————. 1988. *Plan, Market and Democracy: The Experience of the So-Called Socialist Countries.* Amsterdam: IIRE.

Smith, Tony. 1994. *Lean Production: A Capitalist Utopia?* Amsterdam: IIRE.

Solomon, Steven. 1995. *The Confidence Game: How Unelected Central Bankers Are Governing the Changed World Economy.* New York: Simon & Schuster.

Soros, George. 1998. *The Crisis of Global Capitalism: Open Society Endangered.* Boston: Little, Brown.

Tilly, Charles. 1995. "Globalization Threatens Labor's Rights." *International Labor and Working-Class History,* no. 47.

Tobin, James. 1978. "A Proposal for International Monetary Reform." *Eastern Economic Journal,* 4, nos. 3–4 (July–October).

Toussaint, Eric. 1998. *Your Money or Your Life! The Tyranny of Global Finance.* London: Pluto Press.

Toussaint, Eric, and Peter Drucker. 1995. *IMF/World Bank/WTO: The Free-Market Fiasco.* Amsterdam: IIRE.

United Nations Development Program (UNDP). 1999. *Human Development Report 1999.* New York: Oxford University Press.

Wallerstein, Immanuel. 1995. "Declining States, Declining Rights?" *International Labor and Working-Class History,* no. 47.

PART 2

INTERNATIONAL MONETARY RELATIONS

15

Monetary Governance in a Globalized World

Benjamin J. Cohen

With the introduction of the euro, the potential dollarization of several Latin American economies, and the plague of currency crises, monetary matters have moved to center stage among international economic issues. In this chapter, Benjamin Cohen examines the globalization of finance, arguing that it has fundamentally altered the traditional relationship between states and markets, ultimately undermining national monetary sovereignty. Cohen explores how money is governed by national authorities, highlighting how governance has been affected by the spread of currency competition. This chapter outlines four alternative strategies for governments as they respond to currency competition and the loss of national monetary sovereignty. Cohen concludes that states remain capable of exercising influence in currency matters, but within the tighter constraints of oligopolistic rivalry rather than as privileged local monopolists.

One of the hallmarks of globalization in the contemporary era is the ever-closer integration of national financial markets. Over the last half century, as barriers to international investment have gradually evaporated, capital mobility has accelerated to heights unseen since the days before World War I. Most informed observers agree that as a result, the traditional relationship between states and markets has been fundamentally altered. But how, precisely? At issue is the role of the state in the management of money. What does the globalization of finance mean for the convention of national monetary sovereignty? On this crucial question, not surprisingly, views differ. Where some analysts still see a potent role for government, ostensibly the ultimate locus of legitimate rule, others discern only constraint on political authority and a transfer of power to private societal actors. Who now rules, states or markets? To say the least, consensus remains elusive.

The aim of this chapter is to update our understanding of how money is governed in an increasingly globalized world. This will be done by shifting focus from capital mobility alone to the broader issue of substitutability between national monies—the accelerating competition among currencies across political borders, driven largely by market forces. Monetary sovereignty has been not so much lost as transformed by contemporary developments. Where once existed formal *monopoly,* with each state claiming absolute control over money within its own territory, we now find effective *oligopoly*—a finite number of autonomous suppliers, national governments, all vying ceaselessly to shape and manage demand. Globalized money, at its most basic, has become a political contest for market loyalty, posing extraordinarily difficult choices for policymakers.

In the first section, current thinking about monetary governance in a globalized world is briefly surveyed, followed by an outline of the basic parameters of cross-border currency competition today. The main benefits of national monetary sovereignty are then summarized, and the fourth section analyzes at some length the contemporary challenge to monetary sovereignty posed by the spread of currency competition. Following this analysis, we take up the tricky question of how governments may respond to their growing loss of monetary control. Four alternative strategies are discussed, defining the main options for policymakers. States, the chapter concludes, are still able today to exercise authority in currency matters but only within the constraints of oligopolistic rivalry rather than as privileged local monopolists. Many governments, as a result, can be expected to delegate their formal monetary authority elsewhere, either to a dominant foreign power or to the joint institutions of a currency union.

The Capital Mobility Hypothesis

That national monetary sovereignty has been significantly compromised by financial globalization is clear. Indeed, critical explorations of the political implications of financial globalization have become a staple—one might even say a cliché—of recent scholarly literature.[1] Overwhelmingly, analysts concur that governmental authority has to some extent been eroded by the remarkable increase of capital mobility in recent decades. Where consensus breaks down is over the question of degree. How much has public policy been constrained and what, if anything, can governments do about it?

The most popular view among specialists, labeled by David Andrews the Capital Mobility Hypothesis, is also the most pessimistic. In financial matters, it is said, states have become essentially impotent. As Andrews (1994: 197, 204) summarizes the proposition:

> The premise [is] that the constraints imposed on states by capital mobility are structural in nature, or at a minimum can usefully be construed as

structural by analysts. That is to say, the degree of international capital mobility systematically constrains state behavior by rewarding some actions and punishing others.

The underlying logic of the Capital Mobility Hypothesis is unexceptionable, deriving directly from the dilemma of what I have elsewhere termed the Unholy Trinity: the intrinsic incompatibility of currency stability, capital mobility, and national monetary autonomy (Cohen, 1993). Unless governments are willing to tolerate a virtually unlimited degree of exchange rate volatility, they must in a financially integrated world carefully tailor their policies to what is needed to avoid sudden or massive capital flows. The challenge to public authority is real, neither easy to withstand nor, typically, amenable to formal negotiation.

Dissent from the Capital Mobility Hypothesis usually takes two forms, either empirical or theoretical. At the empirical level, statistical evidence is cited to suggest that practical constraints on state behavior may in fact be rather less pronounced than suggested—particularly if one distinguishes between monetary policy, which does indeed tend to be negatively impacted, and fiscal policy, which could remain a potentially potent tool of policy. At the theoretical level, debate focuses mainly on the issue of reversibility. Has the constraint on monetary sovereignty really become something akin to a structural feature of the international system? In fact, we are reminded, financial globalization was a direct consequence of decisions taken at the national level to promote competition and deregulate markets. As Eric Helleiner (1994: vii) has written: "The contemporary open global financial order could not have emerged without the support and blessing of states." What governments have wrought, therefore, they might also undo should they so choose. Summarizes Louis Pauly (1995: 373): "Capital mobility constrains states, but not absolutely. . . . States can still defy markets. . . . The abrogation of the emergent regime of international capital mobility . . . may be unlikely and undesirable, but it is certainly not inconceivable."

Neither form of dissent, however, has put much of a dent in the popularity of the Capital Mobility Hypothesis, which remains the dominant paradigm for thinking about money in today's globalized world. Empirical caveats do not prove the proposition wrong, just less than complete. Theoretical arguments for reversibility, meanwhile, are challenged by real evidence of significant hysteresis in the development of financial markets. After several decades of worldwide liberalization and innovation, a vast network of private institutions and intermediaries has now come into existence that can be used—legally if possible, illegally when felt necessary—to evade intervention by public authorities. Though abrogation of the regime of capital mobility might still be conceivable in principle, it would not be easy and would surely be costly in practice.

But that hardly means that the Capital Mobility Hypothesis is without flaw. On the contrary, for all its insight and relevance, the proposition borders on caricature, seriously misrepresenting both the scope and the severity of the challenge to contemporary government. In fact, the view manages simultaneously both to understate and to overstate the constraints now imposed on the monetary powers of states.

Constraints are understated because a focus on capital mobility, emphasizing asset-market integration, highlights only one function of money: its use for store-of-value purposes. In fact, that is only part of the story. Change in currency markets has really been far more extensive, involving all the standard functions of money—not just the role of money as a private investment vehicle but also its use as a unit of account and, most critically, as a transactions medium—thus penetrating to the very core of what is meant by national monetary sovereignty. Much more is involved here than just borrowing and lending or trades of financial claims. It is, indeed, a matter of the basic effectiveness of government itself.

At the same time, the challenge is overstated because a focus on capital mobility, stressing the preferences of currency users, highlights only one side of the market: the demand side. That too ignores an important part of the story, namely supply, which even in an increasingly globalized world remains largely the privilege of the state. Governments are still the principal source of the monies that are now exchanged so easily across political frontiers. Hence the state, though challenged, still retains a considerable influence of its own in the governance of monetary affairs. The real issue is how governments choose to respond to the accelerating cross-border circulation and competition of currencies.

Cross-Border Currency Competition

When addressing issues of global finance, we are accustomed to thinking of money as effectively insular: each currency sovereign within the territorial frontiers of a single country or monetary union. In fact, nothing could be further from the truth.

For a currency to be truly "territorial," its functional domain would have to coincide precisely with the political jurisdiction of its issuing state—a very special case. The currency would have to exercise an exclusive claim to all the traditional roles of money within the domestic economy. There could be no other money accepted for transactions purposes or used for the denomination of contracts or financial assets. And the government would have to be able to exercise sole control over the operation of the monetary system, dominating market agents. In matters of commerce, the equivalent would be described as *autarky:* national self-sufficiency. In truth, however, autarky is no more commonly achieved in monetary matters than it is in trade.

As a practical matter, a surprising number of monies today have come to be employed widely outside their country of origin for transactions either between nations or within foreign states. The former is usually referred to as international currency use (or *currency internationalization*); the latter is typically described by the term *currency substitution* and may be referred to as foreign-domestic use.[2] Reciprocally, an even larger number of monies now routinely face growing competition at home from currencies originating abroad. It is simply wrong to deny that several currencies may circulate in the same state. In fact, the phenomenon is increasingly prevalent.

Both currency internationalization (CI) and currency substitution (CS) are a product of intense market rivalry—a kind of Darwinian process of natural selection, driven by the force of demand, in which some monies such as the U.S. dollar or the deutschemark (DM, now being succeeded by the euro) came to be viewed as more attractive than others for various commercial or financial purposes. Cross-border circulation of currencies was once quite common before the emergence of the modern state system. More recently, the practice has reemerged, as declining barriers to monetary exchange have greatly expanded the array of effective currency choice. Competition between national monies is accelerating rapidly. As a result, the domains within which individual currencies serve the standard functions of money now diverge more and more sharply from the legal jurisdictions of issuing governments. Money has become effectively deterritorialized.

Though cross-border use is known to be accelerating rapidly, its full dimensions cannot be measured precisely in the absence of comprehensive statistics on global currency circulation. Partial indicators, however, may be gleaned from a variety of sources to underscore the impressive orders of magnitude involved.

The clearest signal of the accelerated pace of CI is sent by the global foreign-exchange market where, according to the Bank for International Settlements (BIS, 1999), average daily turnover has accelerated from $590 billion in 1989 (the first year for which such data are available) to $1.5 trillion in 1998—a rate of increase in excess of 25 percent per annum. A parallel story is evident in international markets for financial claims, including bank deposits and loans as well as bonds and stocks, all of which have grown at double-digit rates for years. Using data from a variety of sources, Niels Thygesen and others (1995) calculated what they call "global financial wealth": the world's total portfolio of private international investments. From just over $1 trillion in 1981, aggregate cross-border holdings quadrupled to more than $4.5 trillion by 1993—an expansion far faster than that of world output or trade in goods and services. More recently, the International Monetary Fund (IMF, 1999) put the total of international portfolio investments (including equities, long- and short-term debt securities, and financial derivatives) at just over $6 trillion in 1997

The clearest signal of the accelerated pace of CS is sent by the rapid increase in the physical circulation of several major currencies, including especially the dollar, DM, and Japanese yen, outside their country of origin. For the dollar, an authoritative Federal Reserve study (Porter and Judson, 1996) put the value of U.S. banknotes in circulation abroad in 1995 at between 55 and 70 percent of the total outstanding stock—equivalent to perhaps $250 billion in all. The same study also reckoned that as much as three-quarters of the annual increase of U.S. notes now goes directly abroad, up from less than one-half in the 1980s and under one-third in the 1970s. Appetite for the greenback appears to be not only strong but growing. Using a comparable approach, Germany's central bank, the Bundesbank (1995), estimated deutschemark circulation outside Germany at the end of 1994, mainly in east-central Europe and the Balkans, at about 30 to 40 percent of total stock, equivalent to some DM 65–90 billion ($45–65 billion). The deutschemark's successor, the euro, is confidently expected to take over the DM's role in foreign-domestic use as euro notes enter circulation in 2002 and perhaps even to cut into the dollar's market share. Similarly, on the other side of the world, Bank of Japan officials have been privately reported to believe that of the total supply of yen banknotes, amounting to some $370 billion in 1993, as much as 10 percent was located in neighboring countries (Hale, 1995). Combining these diverse estimates suggests a minimum foreign circulation of the top currencies in the mid-1990s of at least $300 billion in all—by no means an inconsiderable sum and, judging from available evidence, apparently continuing to rise rapidly. According to another source (Krueger and Ha, 1996), as much as one-quarter to one-third of the world's paper money is now located outside its country of issue.

Deterritorialization is by no means universal, of course—at least not yet. But it is remarkably widespread. Russell Krueger and Jiming Ha (1996) estimate that foreign-currency notes in the mid-1990s accounted for 20 percent or more of the local money stock in as many as three dozen nations inhabited by at least one-third of the world's population. Most currency substitution is concentrated in Latin America, the Middle East, and republics of the former Soviet Union, where the dollar is favored, or in east-central Europe and the Balkans, where the DM has traditionally predominated. By a different measure, focusing on foreign-currency deposits rather than paper money, the IMF (Baliño et al., 1999) identifies some eighteen nations where by the mid-1990s another state's money accounted for at least 30 percent of broad money supply. The most extreme cases, with ratios above 50 percent, included Azerbaijan, Bolivia, Croatia, Nicaragua, Peru, and Uruguay. Another thirty-nine economies had ratios approaching 30 percent, indicating "moderate" penetration.

These numbers clearly confirm the growing importance of both international and foreign-domestic use of money. Two main messages stand out. First, the scale of cross-border currency use is manifestly extensive and growing rapidly, reflecting both the scope and intensity of market-driven competition. Monetary circulation really is no longer confined to the territories of issuing countries. Strict autarky in currency relations is becoming increasingly rare.

Second, while the number of monies actually employed for either international or foreign-domestic purposes tends to be rather small, the number of those routinely facing rivalry at home from currencies abroad appears to be remarkably large. Deterritorialization also means that there is no longer a functional equivalence among national monies. Even though all currencies of sovereign states enjoy nominally equal status as a matter of international law, some monies—to paraphrase George Orwell—clearly are far more equal than others as a matter of practical reality. Some monies, particularly in the developing world and so-called transition economies, face what amounts to a massive competitive invasion from abroad; others, especially those of the wealthiest industrial countries, are effectively immune from foreign rivalry at home. The population of the currency universe is in fact distinctly stratified.

Topping the charts, quite obviously, is the dollar, which remains by far the world's most popular choice for both CI and CS. In effect, the dollar's functional domain spans the globe, from the Western Hemisphere (where dollars circulate widely as a de facto parallel currency) to the former Soviet bloc and much of the Middle East. Next comes the DM—now being replaced by the euro—which has clearly dominated currency relations within much of the European neighborhood, including east-central Europe and the Balkans. And not far behind are the yen and a handful of other elite international monies such as the pound sterling and Swiss franc. Much lower ranked are the many currencies of poorer countries that are forced to struggle continuously for the loyalty of local users.

Add these two messages together and a picture emerges that is strikingly at variance with the conventional imagery of strictly territorial money: a universe of increasingly intense competition as well as distinct hierarchy among currencies. Individually, national monies confront market forces that are increasingly indifferent to the barriers posed by political frontiers. Collectively, therefore, governments face a challenge to their monetary sovereignty that is unprecedented in modern times.

Benefits of Monetary Sovereignty

Monetary sovereignty, of course, continues to exist as a constitutive rule. It is the exceptional government that does not still seek to preserve, as best it can, an effective monopoly over the issue and management of money within its own territory. Production of money may not be an essential attribute of state sovereignty; along with the raising of armies and the levying of taxes, however, it has long been regarded as such. As one observer (O'Mahony, 1984: 127) has commented, with just a touch of sarcasm: "A government that does not control money is a limited government. . . . No government likes to be limited. . . . Governments simply must monopolize money if they are to control it and they must control it if they really are to be governments."

It is easy to see why a monetary monopoly is so highly prized. Genuine power resides in the privilege that money represents. Four main benefits are derived from a strictly territorial currency: first, a potentially rich source of revenue to underwrite public expenditures; second, a possible instrument to manage the macroeconomic performance of the economy; third, a potent political symbol to promote a sense of national identity; and finally, a practical means to insulate the nation from foreign influence or constraint. Within each state, all four advantages privilege the interests of the government in relation to societal actors.

One of the best-known benefits of a territorial currency is *seigniorage*—the capacity a monetary monopoly gives governments to augment public spending at will. Technically defined as the excess of the nominal value of a currency over its cost of production, seigniorage can be understood as an alternative source of revenue for the state, beyond what can be raised via taxation or by borrowing from financial markets. Public spending financed by money creation in effect appropriates real resources at the expense of the private sector, whose purchasing power is correspondingly reduced by the ensuing increase of inflation—a privilege for government if there ever was one. Because of the inflationary implications involved, the process is also known popularly as the "inflation tax." But despite the economic disadvantages associated with inflation, the privilege of seigniorage makes sense from a political perspective as a kind of insurance policy against risk—a "revenue of last resort," as one source has called it (Goodhart, 1995: 452). Seigniorage is in fact the single most flexible instrument of taxation available to policymakers to mobilize resources in the event of a sudden crisis or threat to national security.

A second benefit derives from money's potential impact on "real" economic performance—aggregate output and employment—as well as prices. So long as governments can maintain control of currency supply within their own territory, they have the capacity, in principle at least, to influence and perhaps even manage the overall pace of market activity. Money may be used to promote the broad prosperity and strength of the state as well as the government's own narrowly drawn fiscal requirements. Two policy instruments become available. First is the money supply itself, which can be manipulated to increase or decrease levels of expenditure by residents. The second is the exchange rate—the price of home currency in terms of foreign currency—which can be adjusted to increase or decrease spending in the national economy through induced shifts between home and foreign goods. Neither instrument is infallible, of course; nor is either likely to attain a truly sustained impact on economic activity over the proverbial long term, if recent theoretical developments are to be believed. But over the shorter time horizons that are of most interest to public officials, monetary and exchange rate policies do manifest substantial influence as tools for macroeconomic management.

A third benefit is the vital symbolic role that a territorial currency can play for rulers wary of internal division or dissent. Centralization of political authority is facilitated insofar as citizens feel themselves bound together as members of a single social unit—all part of the same "imagined community," in Benedict Anderson's (1991) apt phrase. Anderson stresses that states are made not just through force but through loyalty, a voluntary commitment to a joint identity. The critical distinction between "us" and "them" can be heightened by all manner of tangible symbols: flags, anthems, postage stamps, public architecture, even national sports teams. Among the most potent of these tokens is money, which serves to enhance a sense of national identity in two ways. First, because it is issued by the government or its central bank, a currency acts as a daily reminder to citizens of their connection to the state and oneness with it. Second, by virtue of its universal use on a daily basis, the currency underscores the fact that everyone is part of the same social entity—a role not unlike that of a single national language, which many governments also actively promote for nationalistic reasons. A common money helps to homogenize diverse and often antagonistic social groups.

Finally, an important benefit is derived in a negative sense: from the enhanced ability a territorial money gives government to avoid dependence on some other provenance for this critical economic resource. Currency territoriality draws a clear economic boundary between the state and the rest of the world, promoting political authority. The closer government is able to come to achieving an absolute monetary monopoly, the better equipped it will be to insulate itself from outside influence or constraint in formulating and implementing policy. That sovereign states might use monetary relations coercively, given the opportunity, should come as no surprise. As Jonathan Kirshner (1995: 29, 31) recently reminded us: "Monetary power is a remarkably efficient component of state power . . . the most potent instrument of economic coercion available to states in a position to exercise it." Money, after all, is simply command over real resources. If a nation can be denied access to the means needed to purchase vital goods and services, it is clearly vulnerable in political terms. The lesson is simple: If you want political autonomy, don't rely on someone else's money.

The State as Oligopolist

Given these benefits, we should not be surprised that states cling so res-
olutely to the idea of monetary sovereignty. What matters, however, is not
formal principle but actual practice, and that depends not just on the supply
of money but also on demand, over which governments today have
decreasingly firm control. States exercise direct jurisdiction only over the
stock of national currency in circulation. In an increasingly globalized
world, not even the most authoritarian government can assure that its
money will always be preferred to currencies originating elsewhere.

Does that mean that where once governments exercised monetary sovereignty, the private sector now categorically rules? The answer, it should
be clear, is no, not so long as states remain the principal source of the currencies that today compete so vigorously across national frontiers. The
Darwinian struggle may be intense, but it is a struggle that, for now at least,
is limited on the supply side almost exclusively to official national monies.
Governments thus continue to play a role, albeit a lessened one, in the management of monetary affairs. The power of the state may be diminished; it
has not, however, been extinguished.

Rivals to state monies do exist, of course, but for the present mostly
take the form of very local private monies that are little different from institutionalized systems of barter.[3] One day, as I have suggested elsewhere
(Cohen, 2001), a new and more threatening kind of competitor may well be
generated in the developing world of cyberspace, if and when digital
entries in computers—electronic cash or "e-cash," as they are sometimes
called—begin to substitute for banknotes and checking accounts as custom-
ary means of payment. But even that threat will remain nothing more than
hypothetical until e-cash, once introduced, can command the same general
acceptability as conventional monies, a development that at the moment
would appear still to be well over the horizon. Until that day arrives, traditional state monies will continue to dominate the supply side of the market.

Thus not one but two sets of actors are intimately involved here: not
just the users of money but also its producers—governments. Neither one
side nor the other, therefore, is wholly in charge. Rather, as in any market
setting, it is supply and demand together, interacting symbiotically, that
determine final outcomes. The basic point was made many years ago by the
renowned English economist Alfred Marshall (1948: 348), commenting on
whether it is demand ("utility") or supply ("cost of production") that governs market results ("value"): "We might as reasonably dispute whether it
is the upper or the under blade of a pair of scissors that cuts a piece of
paper, as whether value is governed by utility or cost of production."
Likewise, in our own time we might as reasonably dispute whether it is the
state or society that governs. In reality, as with Marshall's scissors, it is
both, each playing a critical reciprocal role in an ongoing dialectical

process. The real question is what, if anything, governments can do about their loss of monetary authority.

With deterritorialization, governments have been deprived of the monopoly control they once claimed over demand. This is as true for countries at the top of the currency hierarchy as it is for those at the bottom. The reason is that today many transactors now have an alternative: the happy option of currency choice. Few states, therefore, are any longer in a position to *enforce* an exclusive role for their own money within established political frontiers. Governments do, however, still dominate the supply side of the market, retaining jurisdiction over the issue of money. Hence they are in a position still to *influence* demand insofar as they can successfully compete, inside and across borders, for the allegiance of market agents. Power is retained to the extent that user preferences can be swayed.

In essence, therefore, the role of states today is not unlike that of competing firms in an oligopolistic industry—the state as oligopolist—and no one has ever accused oligopolists of a lack of practical authority. In a world of increasing interpenetration of monetary domains, all governments find themselves driven to join the competitive fray, to preserve or promote market share for their product. Like oligopolistic firms, governments assert influence by doing what they can, consciously or unconsciously, to shape and manage demand.

Oligopoly provides a particularly apt analogy in this regard because of its two key structural characteristics of interdependence and uncertainty. Both are inherent features of the traditional state system as well. In the interstate system, as in an oligopolistic industry, actors are significantly few in number so that the behavior of any one of them has an appreciable effect on at least some of its competitors; in turn, the actions and reactions of other actors cannot be predicted with certainty. The result is an interdependence of decisionmaking that compels all states, like rival firms, to be noticeably preoccupied with considerations of long-term strategy. In this sense, producers of currency are essentially no different from producers of cars or computers.

Moreover, like producers of cars or computers, governments have been forced to implement their strategies via efforts to manage the demand side of the market—in effect, to "sell" their product. Their targets are the users of money, at home or abroad. Their aim is to sustain or enhance a currency's functional domain, almost as if monies were like goods to be sold under registered trademarks. As economist Robert Aliber (1987: 153) has quipped, "The dollar and Coca-Cola are both brand names." He continues: "Each national central bank produces its own brand of money . . . Each national money is a differentiated product. . . . Each central bank has a marketing strategy to strengthen the demand for its particular brand of money."

The task, of course, may not be easy. What strategies are available to governments to market their brand of money? Broadly speaking, economic theory distinguishes between two contrasting approaches to the formulation of competitive strategy in an oligopolistic setting. Firm behavior can be either defensive or offensive, that is, designed either to build defenses against existing competitive forces or, alternatively, to attack existing conditions in order to enhance market position. The former seeks to match the firm's strengths and weaknesses to its environment, taking the structure of the industry as given. The latter seeks to improve the firm's position in relation to its environment by actively influencing the balance of forces in the marketplace. Currency policy, too, can be either defensive or offensive, aiming either to preserve or promote market share.

In turn, each approach may be pursued either unilaterally or collusively, yielding a total of four possible broad strategies:

(1) *Market leadership*: an aggressive, unilateralist policy intended to maximize use of the national currency, analogous to predatory price leadership in an oligopoly.

(2) *Market alliance*: a collusive policy of sharing monetary sovereignty in a monetary or exchange rate union of some kind, analogous to a tacit or explicit cartel.

(3) *Market preservation*: a status-quo policy intended to defend, rather than augment, a previously acquired market position.

(4) *Market followership*: an acquiescent policy of subordinating monetary sovereignty to a stronger foreign currency via some form of exchange rate rule, analogous to passive price followership in an oligopoly.

Of these four, a strategy of market leadership is, of course, generally available only to governments with the most widely circulated currencies, such as the dollar, euro (succeeding the DM), or yen. For the vast majority of states with less-competitive monies, decisionmaking is limited to the remaining three options—a tricky tripartite choice.

Market Leaders

Start first with the small handful of states with the most attractive monies at the very peak of the international currency hierarchy. These are the Big Three: the United States, Europe, and Japan. For these privileged few there is little reason to doubt that a unilateralist strategy to maintain or enhance market position will be the preferred choice. The reason is simple. Much is at stake.

Though minimized by some (e.g., Wyplosz, 1999: 97–100), the benefits of leadership in currency affairs can in fact be considerable. Economists tend to focus primarily on the potential for international seigniorage: the implicit transfer, equivalent to an interest-free loan, that goes to a state whose money is widely used and held abroad. But in fact three other gains may also be anticipated. First is the increased flexibility of macroeconomic policy that is afforded by the privilege of being able to rely on one's own money to help finance external deficits. Second is the prestige that goes with market dominance. Broad circulation of a currency is a constant reminder of the issuing country's elevated rank in the community of nations. Foreign publics cannot help but be impressed when another nation's money successfully penetrates the domestic currency system and gains widespread acceptance. "Great powers have great currencies," Nobel laureate Robert Mundell once wrote (1993: 10). And third is the political power that derives from the monetary dependence of others. Not only is the issuing country better insulated from outside influence or coercion in the domestic policy arena; it is also better positioned to pursue foreign objectives without constraint or even to exercise a degree of influence or coercion internationally.

Admittedly, there are limits to these benefits. All are likely to be greatest in the early stages of cross-border use, when confidence in a money is at a peak. Later on, as external liabilities accumulate increasing supply relative to demand, gains may be eroded, particularly if an attractive alternative becomes available. Foreigners may legitimately worry about the risk of future devaluation or even restrictions on the usability of their holdings. As a result, the market leader's autonomy may eventually be constrained, to a degree, by a need to discourage sudden or substantial conversions through the exchange market. Both seigniorage income, on a net basis, and macroeconomic flexibility will be reduced if a sustained increase of interest rates is required to maintain market share. Likewise, overt exploitation of political power will be inhibited if foreigners can switch allegiance easily to another currency. Even admitting such limits, though, there seems little doubt that on balance these are advantages worth defending, as numerous sources acknowledge (e.g., Portes and Rey, 1998: 308–310). There is more than enough incentive here to motivate policymakers. Enhanced competition among the Big Three, therefore, should come as no surprise.

Consider Europe, for example. Officially, European aspirations remain modest. According to the European Central Bank (ECB), which has been given responsibility for management of the European Union's new common currency, the development of the euro as an international currency—to the extent it happens—will mainly be a market-driven process, simply one of many possible byproducts of the Economic and Monetary Union (EMU). In an authoritative statement, the European Central Bank (ECB) (1999: 31, 45) has declared that euro internationalization "is not a policy objective [and] will be neither fostered nor hindered by the Eurosystem. . . . The Eurosystem therefore adopts a neutral stance." But these carefully considered words may be dismissed as little more than diplomatic rhetoric, revealing nothing. Behind the scenes it is known that there is considerable disagreement among European policymakers, with the eventual direction of policy still unsettled. Many in Europe are indeed inclined to leave the future of the euro to the logic of market competition. But many others, aware of the strong incumbency advantages of the dollar, favor a more proactive stance to reinforce EMU's potential. The euro has long been viewed in some circles, particularly in France, as the European Union's best chance to challenge the long-resented hegemony of the greenback.

Much more revealing, therefore, is not what the ECB says but what it does. Especially suggestive is the bank's controversial decision to plan to issue euro notes in denominations as high as 100, 200, and 500—sums far greater than most Europeans are likely to find useful for everyday transactions. Why issue such large notes? Informed sources suggest that the plan may have been decided in order to reassure the German public, fearful of losing their beloved deutschemark, that notes comparable to existing high-denomination DM bills would be readily available. But that is hardly the whole story. As knowledgeable experts like Kenneth Rogoff (1998) and Charles Wyplosz (1999) observe, it is also likely that the decision had something to do with the familiar phenomenon of currency substitution: the already widespread circulation of large-denomination dollar notes, especially $100 notes, in various parts of the world. Market-driven dollarization translates conservatively into an interest saving for the U.S. government, a form of seigniorage earnings, of at least $15 billion a year (Blinder, 1996)—not a huge profit but nonetheless enough, apparently, to persuade EMU authorities to plan on offering a potentially attractive alternative. As Rogoff (1998: 264) has written: "Given the apparently overwhelming preference of foreign and underground users for large-denomination bills, the [ECB's] decision to issue large notes constitutes an aggressive step toward grabbing a large share of developing country demand for safe foreign currencies." Europeans who favor more widespread use of the euro have openly applauded the plan. Writes one: "The United States is able to obtain goods and services by simply giving foreigners pieces of green paper that cost pennies to print. . . . There is no reason why the United States should monopolize these benefits" (Hüfner, 2000: 25).

Or consider Japan, which has given every indication that it too intends to stay in the race, competing actively to preserve as much as possible of the yen's fragile international role—in Tokyo's own hinterland in East Asia at least, if not beyond. Unlike the Europeans, the Japanese have been uncharacteristically frank in articulating their aspirations. After rapid expansion during the heady years of Japanese economic growth, cross-border use of the yen actually declined in the 1990s following the bursting of Japan's "bubble" economy. Reversal of the currency's slide in standing was made an official policy objective in 1998 and was given further impetus the next year by a widely publicized report of a Ministry of Finance advisory group, the Council on Foreign Exchange and Other Transactions (1999). Declared the council (1999: 1–2): "Internationalization has not necessarily kept pace with what is warranted by the scale of the Japanese economy. . . . Recent economic and financial environments affecting Japan point to the need for the greater internationalization of the yen. . . . The question of what Japan must do to heighten the international role of the yen has reemerged as a vital issue."

One straw in the wind came as early as 1996, when Japan signed a series of agreements with nine neighboring countries to lend their central banks yen if needed to help stabilize exchange rates. Informed sources had no doubt that these pacts were deliberately designed to increase Japanese influence among members of an eventual yen bloc. "It's a manifest attempt to take leadership," said one bank economist in Tokyo (*New York Times*, 27 April 1996: 20). An even stronger indicator came in 1997, after the first shock waves of the great Asian financial crisis, when Tokyo seized upon the occasion to propose a new regional facility—what quickly came to be called the Asian Monetary Fund (AMF)—to help protect local currencies against speculative attack. The AMF proposal was by far the most ambitious effort yet by Japan to implement a strategy of market leadership in Asian finance. Tokyo's initiative was successfully blocked by the United States, which publicly expressed concern about a possible threat to the central role of the International Monetary Fund (IMF). Privately, it was clear that Washington officials were even more concerned about a possible threat to the dominance of the dollar in the region.

But Tokyo was undeterred, persisting in its efforts to promote its monetary role in Asia. In October 1998, Finance Minister Kiichi Miyazawa offered some $30 billion in fresh financial aid for neighboring countries in a plan soon labeled the "New Miyazawa Initiative"; two months later he made clear that Japan had every intention to revive its AMF proposal when the time seemed right. Similarly, in late 1999, Japanese authorities floated a plan to drop two zeros from the yen (which is currently valued at near one hundred yen for either the dollar or the euro), in order to facilitate its use in foreign transactions. Simplifying the currency's denomination, said one official, "might have a positive effect in that the yen would be more internationally easy to understand" (*New York Times*, 19 November 1999: C4). Commented a foreign banker in Tokyo: "If there's a liquid market in dollars and a liquid market in euros, there's a risk of Japan becoming a sort of second-string market. . . . They don't want the yen to become the Swiss franc of Asia" (*New York Times*, 19 November 1999: C4). Most recently, in May 2000, Tokyo engineered agreement among thirteen regional governments on a new network of swap arrangements centered on the yen. Clearly, Tokyo does not intend to allow further erosion of its currency's standing without a fight.

How will Washington react to such competition? Officially, the United

States remains unconcerned. Policy statements regarding prospective challenges from the euro or yen have been studiously neutral, avoiding provocation. EMU, for example, is said to be strictly Europe's business, not America's. "The emergence of the euro as an international currency should not be viewed with alarm," wrote Bill Clinton's Council of Economic Advisers (1999: 297). "It is unlikely that the dollar will be replaced anytime soon" (1999: 299). But such words also may be dismissed as diplomatic rhetoric, concealing as much as they reveal. As Richard Portes (1999: 34) writes: "It is difficult to believe that the American authorities are indifferent."

In fact, in Washington, too, there is much disagreement behind the scenes about what should be the eventual direction of policy. But much sentiment exists to respond in kind to any direct threat to the dollar's global predominance. The ECB's plans for large-denomination notes, for example, have already generated a counterproposal to issue a rival $500 Federal Reserve note, designed to preserve the U.S.'s seigniorage earnings abroad (Makinen, 2000: 5). Japan's efforts to revive the yen are no less likely to arouse opposition and even irritation in Washington. As even a yen enthusiast like David Hale (1995: 162) acknowledges, there is "a risk that [Japanese initiatives] will be interpreted as a threat by some Americans [and] could intensify the economic conflicts that are already straining U.S.-Japan relations." The probability is that aggressive policy measures from either Europe or Japan will ultimately provoke countermeasures from Washington, with all of the Big Three doing what they can to maximize market use.

All the Rest

But what about all the rest? In a landscape dominated by the market leaders, the basic challenge for other governments is plain. Should monetary sovereignty be defended, shared, or subordinated? Should policymakers seek, above all, to preserve their traditional monetary sovereignty (market preservation)? Or alternatively, should they consider delegating some or all of their formal authority elsewhere, either to a dominant foreign power (market followership) or to the joint institutions of a currency partnership (market alliance)? Involved is what one source (Litfin, 1997) calls a "sovereignty bargain"—a voluntary agreement to accept certain limitations on national authority in exchange for anticipated benefits. Monetary sovereignty is either pooled or surrendered, wholly or in part.[4] The former president of the Argentine central bank put the point bluntly (Pou, 1999: 244): "Should a [country] produce its own money, or should it buy it from a more efficient producer?" Buying from a more efficient producer necessarily implies a degree of regionalization in currency relations.

Market Preservation

Many governments, for the present at least, appear resolved to continue producing their own money, avoiding regionalization. They want to keep the national currency alive, no matter how uncompetitive it may be. Such an impulse is understandable, given the historical advantages of a formal monetary monopoly. But at what price? There is also a cost to defending monetary sovereignty. Under the pressure of growing cross-border competition among currencies, that cost is becoming increasingly prohibitive.

Defense of monetary sovereignty, as indicated, requires a sustained effort to "sell" the national brand of money. Tactics of persuasion are natural in an oligopoly, where competition compels suppliers to seek to manage the demand side of the market. In an industrial oligopoly, rival firms may enhance the appeal of their products via price cuts, quality improvements, aggressive advertising, or any number of similar marketing devices. In the global arena, states can try to do the same by investing in their money's reputation, acting to reinforce the attractiveness of a currency for any or all of the usual monetary purposes. The idea is to enhance confidence in the money's continued usefulness and reliability—the "confidence game," to recall Paul Krugman's (1998) name for it. The label is ironic because as in any con game, the effort to play may prove an exercise in futility.

Demand for a money may be strengthened in several ways. Most narrowly, currency policy may be transformed into an exercise in political symbolism. The competitive success of a more attractive foreign money can be treated as the equivalent of a military invasion, calling for allegiance to the local currency as an act of patriotism. This was, for example, one of the tactics adopted by Indonesia when the national currency, the rupiah, came under attack in 1997. Public-service advertisements appeared showing a currency trader wearing a terrorist mask made of U.S. $100 bills. "Defend the rupiah," the notices urged. "Defend Indonesia." In the end, however, Jakarta's campaign notably failed, suggesting that such a gambit is unlikely to suffice to restore confidence in a currency in the absence of other, more substantive policy actions.[5]

Beyond exhortation, use of a money might be encouraged by special tax advantages, convertibility guarantees, or higher rates of return on selected liquid assets. Most fundamentally, a money's reputation may be buttressed by a credible commitment to "sound" macroeconomic management. "Sound" in this context means a strong emphasis on stability, promising low inflation and open access for users. Highest priority is placed on placating the preferences of societal actors with the capacity and opportunity to choose among alternative currencies.

The merit of such an approach is that it enables governments to preserve at least some of the advantages of a national monetary monopoly—in particular, the political benefits of symbolism and insulation. The country's currency survives to continue promoting a sense of national identity, and policymakers are still able to hold down exposure to foreign influence or coercion. But there are also two distinct disadvantages, each essentially economic in nature. One is a limit on a government's access to seigniorage, a constraint on fiscal policy. Rational market agents are unlikely to be attracted to the currency of a government that cannot resist the temptation to willfully exploit the seigniorage privilege, which so often results in depreciation of a money's value. States that wish to avoid a flight from their currency must, in effect, practice a kind of fiscal self-denial—a "patience for revenue," as one economist puts it (Ritter, 1995: 134)—voluntarily limiting issue of their own money. The other disadvantage is a limit on a government's flexibility in managing prices and interest rates, a constraint on monetary policy. Rational market agents are also unlikely to be attracted to a currency that appears to be overused for expansionary purposes, a practice that can also result in depreciation of value. States wishing to rely on persuasion must therefore practice a kind of monetary self-denial too, stressing price stability above all in management of money supply and credit.

Together, these two constraints introduce a deflationary bias into policy that, once installed, will be difficult to remove. Reputation is not something that can be enhanced quickly, and certainly not without considerable, sustained effort. As one source has commented, "Monetary confidence cannot be created overnight [and] is not a free good" (Melvin, 1988: 440). Reputation is also something that is much easier to destroy than to build, given the constant vigilance of the market that banker Walter Wriston (1998: 340) likens to "a giant voting machine that records in real time, real world evaluations of . . . currencies." Market actors are understandably sensitive to even the slightest sign of recidivism by governments. A commitment to sound management, therefore, cannot be easily relaxed. States can never let down their guard if they are to establish and maintain a successful brand name for their money.

In fact, a deflationary bias is regarded as an imperative of sound management—simply the price to be paid for defending a currency's reputation. But that price can turn out to be remarkably high, as many governments in recent years have discovered. Nothing demonstrates the costliness of a market-preservation strategy more than the financial crisis that swept over East Asia following devaluation of Thailand's currency, the baht, in mid-1997. Instinctively, as shock waves of speculation hit the region, the impulse of governments was to go on the defensive, investing expensively in determined efforts to restore confidence in their currencies. User preferences, however, proved more resistant to tactics of persuasion than first anticipated, and governments that previously had taken pride in the competitiveness of their national monies suddenly found themselves unable to sustain market share. Strategies that once seemed adequate to manage demand now had to be reevaluated in the light of a worldwide "flight to quality" by mobile capital, forcing policymakers to institute the harshest possible measures to depress incomes and living standards. The same story of crisis and austerity has also been evident in many other countries around the world, from Mexico in 1994 to Brazil in 1999 to Argentina and Turkey in 2001.

Credibility, in short, does not come cheap. To be persuasive to market actors, states must literally put their money where their mouth is—and even then, they may not be successful in defending market share. Playing the confidence game is frustrating and may well prove futile, sacrificing both growth and employment. The rising cost of defending monetary sovereignty is real, a direct result of the growing deterritorialization of money. And as the cost continues to rise, the alternative of buying from a more efficient producer becomes increasingly appealing or, at least, less unappealing.

Market Followership

One alternative is simply to replace a country's own currency, either unilaterally or by agreement, with the already existing money of another, an approach typically described as full or formal dollarization.[6] Until recently, formal dollarization was seen as an option limited only to tiny enclaves or microstates like Monaco or the Marshall Islands. In all, during the modern era, only some dozen sovereign entities have traditionally used the currency of a larger neighbor or patron in lieu of a money of their own, including just two countries, Panama and Liberia, with populations exceeding one hundred thousand. Today, however, even nations as large as Argentina or Mexico are debating the merits of the approach.

The general advantages of dollarization are clear. Most important would be a reduction of transactions costs, reflecting an enhanced usefulness of money for all its basic functions (medium of exchange, unit of account, store of value). With replacement of the local money there is no longer a need to incur the expenses of currency conversion or hedging in trade and investment transactions between the partner economies. These are the standard economic benefits of monetary and financial integration. In addition, there might be a significant saving in administrative expenses, as the government would no longer need to incur the cost of maintaining an infrastructure dedicated solely to production and management of an independent national money. And there could also be a substantial reduction of interest rates, which now would no longer have to be kept at a high level to sustain market confidence. In all, efficiency gains could be considerable. But there are also obvious disadvantages, both economic and political. Adopting another country's currency means foregoing all the benefits of a monetary monopoly—forfeiture of both seigniorage and policy autonomy as well as a symbol of national identity and a degree of insulation from foreign influence. In effect, the state becomes a dependent client in a distinctly hierarchical relationship.

Nonetheless, the idea of formal dollarization has aroused widespread interest, particularly in Latin America, since Argentina's former president, Carlos Menem, spoke out publicly in its favor in early 1999. Weary of the high costs of the confidence game, Menem suggested formal adoption of the U.S. greenback as a way of resolving doubts about Argentina's money. "The dollar is the global currency *par excellence*," wrote one of his key advisers (Castro, 1999: 7, 16). Dollarization offers an opportunity "to gain comparative advantage in a global frame characterized by uncertainty and frequent financial turmoil." Though subsequently rejected by the government of Menem's successor, Fernando de la Rúa, the option did find favor elsewhere, most notably in Ecuador, which formally dollarized in 2000, and El Salvador, which followed a year later. The idea is also widely discussed in east-central Europe and the Mediterranean, where adoption of the euro— "euroization"—increasingly is touted as a natural path for countries with close ties to the European Union or hopes of joining the EU eventually.

Interest is also widespread in the alternative possibility of a currency board, a close equivalent of dollarization, such as has long existed in Brunei, Djibouti, and Hong Kong. With a currency board the home money is preserved and continues to account for a large, if not dominant, part of domestic money supply. Issue of the local money, however, is firmly tied to the availability of a designated foreign currency, usually referred to as the anchor currency. The exchange rate between the two monies is rigidly fixed, ostensibly irrevocably; both currencies circulate as legal tender in the dependent country; and any increase in the issue of local money must be fully backed by an equivalent increase of reserve holdings of the anchor currency. Effectively, the home money becomes little more than foreign money by another name—a proxy for the anchor currency, as it were.

Currency boards share many of the same disadvantages of dollarization, in particular the loss of both monetary autonomy and political insulation. But as compared with formally adopting another country's currency, creation of a currency board does allow a government to preserve a symbol of national identity as well as a measure of seigniorage revenue. Over the last decade new currency boards were established in a significant number of economies—including most notably Argentina, Bosnia, Bulgaria, Estonia, and Lithuania—and more are under consideration elsewhere.

How far might this process go? Market followership, by definition, whether in the form of formal dollarization or a currency board, has the effect of creating a regional currency zone; and with each additional government that chooses to go this route, the greater will be the appeal for others to join as well. In time, therefore, it is not at all difficult to imagine the gradual emergence of two giant monetary blocs, one centered on the dollar and one on the euro. (The question exists whether a third bloc would ever coalesce around the Japanese yen.) As one observer has predicted (Beddoes, 1999: 8): "By 2030 the world will have two major currency zones—one European, the other American. The euro will be used from Brest to Bucharest, and the dollar from Alaska to Argentina—perhaps even in Asia. These regional currencies will form the bedrock of the next century's financial stability." Regionalization of the world's monies along these lines has happened before, in medieval Europe and again during the nineteenth century, as Barry Eichengreen and Nathan Sussman (2000) remind us. Obviously, it could happen again.

Market Alliance

But the question remains: Will many governments really be prepared to surrender their monetary sovereignty to the degree required by dollarization or a currency board? Many might prefer instead a strategy of pooling sovereignty in a monetary alliance of some sort. One long-standing currency union, the CFA Franc Zone, already exists in Africa; another, the Eastern Caribbean Currency Union (ECCU), functions smoothly in the Caribbean; and since the Maastricht Treaty in 1991, which set the timetable for Europe's Economic and Monetary Union, prospects for more such alliances have been discussed in almost every region of the world. EMU is clearly viewed as a test case for a strategy of sharing rather than subordinating monetary sovereignty. If Europe's experiment comes to be seen as a success, it could have a powerful demonstration effect, encouraging similar initiatives elsewhere. This would be especially likely for groups of states already engaged in a common integration project such as South America's MERCOSUR, the Association of Southeast Asian Nations (ASEAN), or Australia and New Zealand, where a shared ANZAC dollar has been advocated (Grimes and Holmes, 2000). Alongside two (or three) major currency zones, a variety of new joint monies could also eventually come into existence in addition to the euro.

A strategy of alliance is highly demanding, owing to the strict political preconditions necessary for a monetary partnership to succeed. As I have written elsewhere (Cohen, 1998: 84–91), the lessons of history on this issue are clear. To be sustainable, a joint currency among sovereign states requires one of two prerequisites: either a local hegemon with the will and capacity to enforce discipline, by means of side-payments or sanctions, or else a broad network of institutional linkages sufficient to make surrender of monetary sovereignty fully acceptable to each partner. Such conditions are not impossible to attain, but neither are they easy, and they could take a considerable amount of time to bring into being. On the other hand, as compared with the alternative of market followership, an alliance approach offers several attractive advantages, including an opportunity to continue sharing in both seigniorage revenues and a role in macroeconomic management. Moreover, as compared with the frustrations of trying to defend an uncompetitive national currency, it offers the benefit of numbers and thus the hope that the whole might, in effect, be greater than the sum of the parts. Who could doubt, after all, that one joint money might be more attractive than a myriad of weak separate currencies? The incentive for governments to go this route, therefore, is strong.

Conclusion

States, we may thus conclude, face difficult choices in today's increasingly globalized world. As the traditional notion of monetary sovereignty has come to be more and more contested by competitive market forces, governments have been forced to adapt to a dramatic transformation of their status, from monopoly to oligopoly. As a result, scenarios of currency regionalization have come to seem not only plausible but even likely—indeed, for many states, arguably the most reasonable outcome to be expected from today's accelerating deterritorialization of money. Among informed observers today it is rapidly becoming conventional wisdom that the number of currencies in the world will soon decline.[7] "Convergence on regional monies is a no-brainer," writes Rudi Dornbusch (2001: 9). The logic of oligopolistic competition suggests that many governments will eventually yield to the market power of more efficient producers, replacing national monies with regional currencies of some kind. Indeed, for Ricardo Hausmann, formerly chief economist of the Inter-American Development Bank, the process has an almost historical inevitability about it: "National currencies are a phenomenon of the twentieth century; supranational currencies are the solution of the future" (Hausmann, 1999: 96). That formulation may be a bit too deterministic. Nonetheless, there is little doubt that in many instances the locus of monetary governance is beginning to shift away from national governments, where it has historically resided.

Notes

This discussion draws on several previous publications, including Cohen 1998, 2000a, 2000b, and 2002b.

1. For a recent survey, see Cohen (2002a).

2. Useful sources on currency internationalization include Krugman (1992) and Black (1993). For general introductions to currency substitution, see Giovannini and Turtelboom (1994); Mizen and Pentecost (1996).

3. Literally hundreds of private monies exist around the world, particularly in English-speaking countries, but none trades in any significant amount across national frontiers. For some discussion, see Solomon (1996) and Douthwaite (1999).

4. The distinction between pooling and surrender of sovereignty, which is generic to the question of how to organize political authority, is of course a familiar one in political science and is used in a variety of contexts—in analyzing differences between confederal states and empires, for instance.

5. As part of the same campaign, stickers appeared declaring "I love the rupiah." Responded one citizen (as quoted in *The Economist,* 24 January 1998: 38): "Never mind the rupiah, I love money."

6. The adjectives "full" or "formal" are frequently added to distinguish this policy choice from the market-driven process of currency substitution, which in the past was also often popularly labeled dollarization (now unofficial or informal dollarization). Dollarization, of course, does not necessarily require the dollar. Some other currency, such as the euro or yen, may also be chosen to replace a country's currency.

7. See, for example, Alesina and Barro (2001); Fischer (2001); Rogoff (2001).

References

Alesina, Alberto and Robert J. Barro. 2001. "Dollarization." *American Economic Review* 91, 2 (May): 381–385.

Aliber, Robert Z. 1987. *The International Money Game*, 5th ed. New York: Basic Books.

Anderson, Benedict. 1991. *Imagined Communities: Reflections on the Origins and Spread of Nationalism.* Revised ed. London: Verso.

Andrews, David M. 1994. "Capital Mobility and State Autonomy: Toward a Structural Theory of International Monetary Relations." *International Studies Quarterly* 38, 2 (June): 193–218.

Baliño, Tomás J. T., Adam Bennett, and Eduardo Borensztein. 1999. *Monetary Policy in Dollarized Economies.* Washington, DC: International Monetary Fund.

Bank for International Settlements. (BIS) 1999. *Central Bank Survey of Foreign Exchange and Derivatives Market Activity 1998.* Basel, Switzerland: The Bank.

Beddoes, Zanny Minton. 1999. "From EMU to AMU? The Case for Regional Currencies." *Foreign Affairs* 78, 4 (July/August): 8–13.

Black, Stanley W. 1993. "The International Use of Currencies." In Dilip K. Das, ed., *International Finance.* London: Routledge.

Blinder, Alan S. 1996. "The Role of the Dollar as an International Currency." *Eastern Economic Journal* 22, 2 (Spring): 127–136.

Bundesbank. 1995. "The Circulation of Deutsche Mark Abroad." *Monthly Report* 47, 7 (July): 65–71.

Castro, Jorge. 1999. "Basis of the Dollarization Strategy and a Treaty of Monetary Association." Working paper submitted by the Secretary of State for Strategic Planning. Buenos Aires: Secretariat of Strategic Planning.

Cohen, Benjamin J. 1993. "The Triad and the Unholy Trinity: Lessons for the Pacific Region." In Richard Higgott, Richard Leaver, and John Ravenhill, eds., *Pacific Economic Relations in the 1990s: Cooperation or Conflict?* 133–158. Boulder, CO: Lynne Rienner.

———. 1998. *The Geography of Money.* Ithaca, NY: Cornell University Press.

———. 2000a. "Life at the Top: International Currencies in the Twenty-First

Century." *Essays in International Economics* 221. Princeton, NJ: Princeton University, International Finance Section.

————. 2000b. "Money in a Globalized World." In Ngaire Woods, ed., *The Political Economy of Globalization*. London: Macmillan.

————. 2001. "Electronic Money: New Day or False Dawn?" *Review of International Political Economy* 8, 2 (Summer).

————. 2002a. "International Finance and International Relations Theory" In Walter Carlsnaes, Thomas Risse, and Beth A. Simmons, eds., *Handbook of International Relations*. London: Sage Publications, forthcoming.

————. 2002b. "Monetary Governance in a World of Regional Currencies." Manuscript.

Council of Economic Advisers. 1999. *Annual Report*. Washington, DC: U.S. Government Printing Office.

Council on Foreign Exchange and Other Transactions. 1999. "Internationalization of the Yen for the 21st Century." Tokyo, April 20, available at: www.mof.go.jp/english/if/e1b064a.htm

Dornbusch, Rudi. 2001. *Fewer Monies, Better Monies*. Working paper W8324. Cambridge, MA: National Bureau of Economic Research.

Douthwaite, Richard. 1999. *The Ecology of Money*. Totnes, UK: Green Books.

Eichengreen, Barry and Nathan Sussman. 2000. "The International Monetary System in the (Very) Long Run." In *World Economic Outlook Supporting Studies*. Washington, DC: International Monetary Fund.

European Central Bank. 1999. "The International Role of the Euro," *ECB Monthly Bulletin* (August), 31–53.

Fischer, Stanley. 2001. "Exchange Rate Regimes: Is the Bipolar View Correct?" *Journal of Economic Perspectives* 15, 2 (Spring): 3–24.

Giovannini, Alberto and Bart Turtelboom. 1994. "Currency Substitution." In Frederick Van Der Ploeg, ed., *The Handbook of International Macroeconomics*. Oxford: Basil Blackwell.

Goodhart, Charles A. E. 1995. "The Political Economy of Monetary Union." In Peter B. Kenen, ed., *Understanding Interdependence: The Macroeconomics of the Open Economy*. Princeton: Princeton University Press.

Grimes, Arthur and Frank Holmes. 2000. *An ANZAC Dollar? Currency Union and Business Development*. Wellington, NZ: Victoria University of Wellington, Institute of Policy Studies.

Hale, David D. 1995. "Is It a Yen or a Dollar Crisis in the Currency Market?" *Washington Quarterly* 18, 4 (Autumn): 145–171.

Hausmann, Ricardo. 1999. "Why the Interest in Reform?" In Jane Sneddon Little and Giovanni P. Olivei, eds., *Rethinking the International Monetary System*, 94–96. Boston, MA: Federal Reserve Bank of Boston.

Helleiner, Eric. 1994. *States and the Reemergence of Global Finance*. Ithaca, NY: Cornell University Press.

Hüfner, Martin. 2000. "Give the Euro Greater Currency." *The International Economy* (November/December): 24–25, 50.

International Monetary Fund. 1999. *Results of the 1997 Coordinated Portfolio Investment Survey*. Washington, DC: IMF.

Kirshner, Jonathan. 1995. *Currency and Coercion: The Political Economy of International Monetary Power*. Princeton, NJ: Princeton University Press.

Krueger, Russell and Jiming Ha. 1996. "Measurement of Cocirculation of Currencies." In Paul D. Mizen and Eric J. Pentecost, eds., *The Macroeconomics of International Currencies: Theory, Policy and Evidence*. Brookfield, VT: Edward Elgar.

Krugman, Paul R. 1992. "The International Role of the Dollar: Theory and Prospect," in his *Currencies and Crises*. Cambridge, MA: MIT Press.

———. 1998. "The Confidence Game." *The New Republic* 5 (October): 23–25.

Litfin, Karen. 1997. "Sovereignty in World Ecopolitics." *Mershon International Studies Review* 41: 167–204.

Makinen, Gail E. 2000. "Euro Currency: How Much Could It Cost the United States?" CRS Report 98-998E, updated. Washington, DC: Congressional Research Service.

Marshall, Alfred. 1948. *Principles of Economics*. 8th ed. New York: Macmillan.

Melvin, Michael. 1988. "Monetary Confidence, Privately Produced Monies, and Domestic and International Monetary Reform." In Thomas D. Willett, ed., *Political Business Cycles: The Political Economy of Money, Inflation, and Unemployment*. Durham, NC: Duke University Press.

Mizen, Paul D. and Eric J. Pentecost. 1996. *The Macroeconomics of International Currencies: Theory, Policy and Evidence*. Brookfield, VT: Edward Elgar.

Mundell, Robert A. 1993. "EMU and the International Monetary System: A Transatlantic Perspective." Working paper 13. Vienna: Austrian National Bank.

O'Mahony, David. 1984. "Past Justifications for Public Interventions." In Pascal Salin, ed., *Currency Competition and Monetary Union*, 127–130. The Hague: Martinus Nijhoff.

Pauly, Louis W. 1995. "Capital Mobility, State Autonomy and Political Legitimacy." *Journal of International Affairs* 48, 2 (Winter): 369–388.

Porter, Richard D. and Ruth A. Judson. 1996. "The Location of U.S. Currency: How Much Is Abroad?" *Federal Reserve Bulletin* 82, 10 (October): 883–903.

Portes, Richard. 1999. "Global Financial Markets and Financial Stability: Europe's Role." Discussion paper 2298. London: Centre for Economic Policy Research.

Portes, Richard and Hélène Rey. 1998. "The Emergence of the Euro as an International Currency." In David Begg, Jürgen von Hagen, Charles Wyplosz, and Klaus F. Zimmermann, eds., *EMU: Prospects and Challenges for the Euro*, 307–343. Oxford. Blackwell.

Pou, Pedro. 1999. "Is Globalization Really to Blame?" In Jane Sneddon Little and Giovanni P. Olivei, eds., *Rethinking the International Monetary System*, 243–250. Boston, MA: Federal Reserve Bank of Boston.

Ritter, Joseph A. 1995. "The Transition from Barter to Fiat Money." *American Economic Review* 85, 1 (March): 134–149.

Rogoff, Kenneth. 1998. "Blessing or Curse? Foreign and Underground Demand for Euro Notes." In David Begg, Jürgen von Hagen, Charles Wyplosz, and Klaus F. Zimmerman, eds., *EMU: Prospects and Challenges for the Euro*, 261–303. Oxford: Blackwell.

———. 2001. "Why Not a Global Currency?" *American Economic Review* 91, 2 (May): 243–247.

Solomon, Lewis D. 1996. *Rethinking Our Centralized Monetary System: The Case for a System of Local Currencies*. Westport, CT: Praeger.

Thygesen, Niels et al. 1995. *International Currency Competition and the Future Role of the Single European Currency*. Final report of a working group on European Monetary Union–International Monetary System. London: Kluwer Law International.

Wriston, Walter B. 1998. "Dumb Networks and Smart Capital." *Cato Journal* 17, 3 (Winter): 333–344.

Wyplosz, Charles. 1999. "An International Role for the Euro?" In Jean Dermine and Pierre Hillion, eds., *European Capital Markets with a Single Currency*. Oxford: Oxford University Press.

16

The International Monetary Fund

C. Roe Goddard

In this chapter, C. Roe Goddard provides a detailed overview of the evolution of the International Monetary Fund (IMF) and its lending. Goddard notes that—although the IMF's original mandate was limited to monitoring currencies and maintaining currency stability—the explosive growth in the international economy, its increased complexity, and the frequent appearance of system-threatening crises and disequilibrium in the international monetary system have led to an expansion in the nature and scope of the IMF's functions. Under these evolving circumstances and crises, the IMF has come forward and provided a broad array of new forms of lending to deal with the special needs of developing and, more recently, the so-called transitional economies. Most recently, in response to the Asian financial crisis, the IMF has made funding available for countries experiencing exchange rate volatility and has reevaluated the assistance it provides to the most heavily indebted poor countries.

In July 1944, two key multilateral institutions in the international political economy, the International Monetary Fund (IMF or the Fund) and the International Bank for Reconstruction and Development (World Bank), were created. Delegates from forty-five countries attended the meeting in Bretton Woods, New Hampshire, where negotiations over the design and the ultimate birth of the post–World War II monetary system took place. The objective of the Bretton Woods conference was to establish the ground rules for all of international trade and finance. Moreover, it was at the Bretton Woods conference that the multilateral institutions were designed to provide stability to trade and monetary relations and oppose the ever-present potential for a rise of system-threatening economic nationalism. The overriding objective was to prevent the reappearance of virulent economic nationalism, which scholars and policymakers alike had identified as a leading cause of World War II.

The IMF came into official existence on December 27, 1945. Succinctly, its mandate was to stabilize and establish a clear and unequivocal value for each currency, encourage the unrestricted conversion of one currency into another, and oppose practices such as competitive devaluations that had stifled investment flows and brought trade to a virtual halt in the 1930s. Attacking the problem piecemeal, the IMF's immediate postwar objective was to restore exchange rate stability among the currencies of the combatant countries and to provide the basis for peaceful economic exchange. Once monetary stability had been achieved and the foundation set for the expansion of postwar trade, the IMF's charge shifted to ensuring exchange rate stability among all of the world's trading countries.

Since the Bretton Woods conference, the responsibilities of the IMF have grown as new and unforeseen challenges to international monetary stability have appeared. As the lead agency for the international monetary system, it is now entrusted with a wide array of responsibilities for the smooth functioning of the system. Under a number of different scenarios since 1945, the Fund has been called upon to provide financial assistance and preserve the system's stability. For example, countries experiencing severe balance-of-payments problems following the quadrupling of oil prices in 1973–1974 received special assistance. Similarly, the IMF created a special lending facility for countries in need of access to key currencies to counter speculative attacks on their currencies. The IMF has also assisted the most impoverished countries with debt relief and financed the transition to market economies of former Soviet bloc countries. Despite these broader responsibilities and interventions, its fundamental purposes remain to assist in the establishment of a multilateral system of payments; to provide temporary resources to members experiencing balance-of-payments difficulties; and to shorten the duration and lessen the degree of disequilibrium in the international balance of payments of its members.

IMF Organization

The Articles of Agreement, which took effect in December 1945, not only outlined the functions of the Fund but also specified its organizational structure. It has remained largely the same to this day. The Articles of Agreement provide for a Board of Governors, an Executive Board, a managing director, a staff of international civil servants, and a council.

The ultimate governing authority within the Fund is the Board of Governors, which presently consists of 183 governors. The individual board members are recruited from the highest echelons of their governments' economic policymaking organizations, often concurrently serving as ministers of finance or as heads of the central banks. The Board of Governors meets only once each year during the combined annual meeting of the IMF and the World Bank. During the remainder of the year, the governors communicate the wishes of their governments to their representatives on the IMF's Executive Board.

Conducting the day-to-day business of the IMF is the Executive Board. It is the organization's locus of power and its permanent decisionmaking organ. The Executive Board is composed of twenty-four executive directors. Currently, there are eight executive directors representing individual countries—China, France, Germany, Japan, Russia, Saudi Arabia, the United Kingdom, and the United States—and sixteen others who each represent groupings of the remaining countries. The Executive Board selects as its chair the managing director of the IMF. The board meets a minimum of three times per week to address a wide variety of policy, operational, and administrative matters, including surveillance of members' exchange rate policies, provision of financial assistance to member countries, consultations with members, and comprehensive studies on issues of importance to the membership. To minimize confrontation and the potential politicization of sensitive lending decisions, decisions made by the board are based on consensus rather than a formal voting process. Executive Board members and their voting power as of February 8, 2002, are listed in Table 16.1.

The responsibilities of the managing director, the administrative head of the organization, include chairing the Executive Board, participating in the combined annual IMF–World Bank meetings, advising the Group of Seven (G7) or, where relevant, the Group of Eight (G8) leading industrialized countries, and overseeing the Fund's professional staff. Although the managing director is the official head of the organization, the position bestows the director no real power. The director cannot even cast a vote when chairing meetings of the Executive Board.

Historically, the managing director of the IMF has been European, and the president of the World Bank has been a U.S. citizen. While not codified in the original constitution, and certainly subject to change with the increasing economic power of many non-European and non–North American countries, this at least has been the pattern to date. If the recent leadership struggle over the selection of a new director-general for the World Trade Organization (WTO) is a precursor of things to come, we can expect that U.S. and European dominance of the leadership positions of the Bretton Woods institutions will change.

The managing director is chairman of the Executive Board and heads the IMF's staff. Known for its economic expertise, the IMF staff is composed of twenty-five hundred professional employees from 133 countries. The staff is composed mainly of international economists, but it also includes professionals in taxation and public finance, statistics, linguistics, writing, and research. The staff carries out the policies and instructions of the Executive Board, including oversight of borrowers. The majority of staff members work at IMF headquarters in Washington, D.C.; however, a small number are employed in IMF offices in Paris, Geneva, and at the United Nations in New York.

Table 16.1   IMF Executive Directors and Voting Power (as of February 8, 2002)

Director *Alternate*	Casting Votes of	Votes by Country	Total Votes[a]	Percent of Fund Total[b]
APPOINTED				
Randal Quarles	United States	371,743	371,743	17.16
Meg Lundsager				
Ken Yagi	Japan	133,378	133,378	6.16
Haruyuki Toyama				
Karlheinz Bischofberger	Germany	130,332	130,332	6.02
Ruediger von Kleist				
Pierre Duquesne	France	107,635	107,635	4.97
Sébastien Boitreaud				
Tom Scholar	United Kingdom	107,635	107,635	4.97
Martin Brooke				
ELECTED				
Willy Kiekens	Austria	18,973		
(Belgium)	Belarus	4,114		
Johann Prader	Belgium	46,302		
(Austria)	Czech Republic	8,443		
	Hungary	10,634		
	Kazakhstan	3,907		
	Luxembourg	3,041		
	Slovak Republic	3,825		
	Slovenia	2,567		
	Turkey	9,890	111,696	5.16
J. de Beaufort Wijnholds	Armenia	1,170		
(Netherlands)	Bosnia and Herzegovina	1,941		
Yuriy G. Yakusha	Bulgaria	6,652		
(Ukraine)	Croatia	3,901		
	Cyprus	1,646		
	Georgia	1,753		
	Israel	9,532		
	Macedonia, former Yugoslav Republic of	939		
	Moldova	1,482		
	Netherlands	51,874		
	Romania	10,552		
	Ukraine	13,970	105,412	4.87
Fernando Varela	Costa Rica	1,891		
(Venezuela)	El Salvador	1,963		
Hernán Oyarzábal	Guatemala	2,352		
(Spain)	Honduras	1,545		
	Mexico	26,108		
	Nicaragua	1,550		
	Spain	30,739		
	Venezuela	26,841	92,989	4.29
Pier Carlo Padoan	Albania	737		
(Italy)	Greece	8,480		
Harilaos Vittas	Italy	70,805		
(Greece)	Malta	1,270		

Table 16.1   Continued

Director *Alternate*	Casting Votes of	Votes by Country	Total Votes[a]	Percent of Fund Total[b]
	Portugal	8,924		
	San Marino	420	90,636	4.18
Ian E. Bennett	Antigua and Barbuda	385		
(Canada)	Bahamas, The	1,553		
Nioclás A. O'Murchú	Barbados	925		
(Ireland)	Belize	438		
	Canada	63,942		
	Dominica	332		
	Grenada	367		
	Ireland	8,634		
	Jamaica	2,985		
	St. Kitts and Nevis	339		
	St. Lucia	403		
	St. Vincent and the Grenadines	333	80,636	3.72
Ólafur Ísleifsson	Denmark	16,678		
(Iceland)	Estonia	902		
Benny Andersen	Finland	12,888		
(Denmark)	Iceland	1,426		
	Latvia	1,518		
	Lithuania	1,692		
	Norway	16,967		
	Sweden	24,205	76,276	3.52
Michael J. Callaghan	Australia	32,614		
(Australia)	Kiribati	306		
Diwa Guinigundo	Korea	16,586		
(Philippines)	Marshall Islands	275		
	Micronesia, Federated States of	301		
	Mongolia	761		
	New Zealand	9,196		
	Palau	281		
	Papua New Guinea	1,566		
	Philippines	9,049		
	Samoa	366		
	Seychelles	338		
	Solomon Islands	354		
	Vanuatu	420	72,413	3.34
Sulaiman M. Al-Turki	Saudi Arabia	70,105	70,105	3.24
(Saudi Arabia)				
Ahmed Saleh Alosaimi				
(Saudi Arabia)				
Cyrus D. R. Rustomjee	Angola	3,113		
(South Africa)	Botswana	880		
Ismaila Usman	Burundi	1,020		
(Nigeria)	Eritrea	409		

(continues)

Table 16.1   Continued

Director Alternate	Casting Votes of	Votes by Country	Total Votes[a]	Percent of Fund Total[b]
	Ethiopia	1,587		
	Gambia, The	561		
	Kenya	2,964		
	Lesotho	599		
	Liberia	963		
	Malawi	944		
	Mozambique	1,386		
	Namibia	1,616		
	Nigeria	17,782		
	Sierra Leone	1,287		
	South Africa	18,935		
	Sudan	1,947		
	Swaziland	757		
	Tanzania	2,239		
	Uganda	2,055		
	Zambia	5,141		
	Zimbabwe	3,784	69,968	3.23
Dono Iskandar Djojosubroto (Indonesia) *Kwok Mun Low* *(Singapore)*	Brunei Darussalam	1,750		
	Cambodia	1,125		
	Fiji	953		
	Indonesia	21,043		
	Lao People's Democratic Republic	779		
	Malaysia	15,116		
	Myanmar	2,834		
	Nepal	963		
	Singapore	8,875		
	Thailand	11,069		
	Tonga	319		
	Vietnam	3,541	68,367	3.16
A. Shakour Shaalan (Egypt) *Mohamad Chatah* *(Lebanon)*	Bahrain	1,600		
	Egypt	9,687		
	Iraq	5,290		
	Jordan	1,955		
	Kuwait	14,061		
	Lebanon	2,280		
	Libya	11,487		
	Maldives	332		
	Oman	2,190		
	Qatar	2,888		
	Syrian Arab Republic	3,186		
	United Arab Emirates	6,367		
	Yemen, Republic of	2,685	64,008	2.95
Wei Benhua (China) *Jin Qi* *(China)*	China	63,942	63,942	2.95

Table 16.1   Continued

Director *Alternate*	Casting Votes of	Votes by Country	Total Votes[a]	Percent of Fund Total[b]
Aleksei V. Mozhin (Russia) *Andrei Lushin* *(Russia)*	Russia	59,704	59,704	2.76
Roberto F. Cippa (Switzerland) *Wieslaw Szczuka* *(Poland)*	Azerbaijan Kyrgyz Republic Poland Switzerland Tajikistan Turkmenistan Uzbekistan	1,859 1,138 13,940 34,835 1,120 1,002 3,006	 56,900	 2.63
Murilo Portugal (Brazil) *Roberto Junguito* *(Colombia)*	Brazil Colombia Dominican Republic Ecuador Guyana Haiti Panama Suriname Trinidad and Tobago	30,611 7,990 2,439 3,273 1,159 857 2,316 1,171 3,606	 53,422	 2.47
Vijay L. Kelkar (India) *R.A. Jayatissa* *(Sri Lanka)*	Bangladesh Bhutan India Sri Lanka	5,583 313 41,832 4,384	 52,112	 2.41
Abbas Mirakhor (Islamic Republic of Iran) *Mohammed Daïri* *(Morocco)*	Algeria Ghana Iran, Islamic Republic of Morocco Pakistan Tunisia	12,797 3,940 15,222 6,132 10,587 3,115	 51,793	 2.39
A. Guillermo Zoccali (Argentina) *Guillermo Le Fort* *(Chile)*	Argentina Bolivia Chile Paraguay Peru Uruguay	21,421 1,965 8,811 1,249 6,634 3,315	 43,395	 2.00
Alexandre Barro Chambrier (Gabon) *Damian Ondo Mañe* *(Equatorial Guinea)*	Benin Burkina Faso Cameroon Cape Verde Central African Republic Chad Comoros Congo, Republic of Côte d'Ivoire	869 852 2,107 346 807 810 339 1,096 3,502		

(continues)

Table 16.1   Continued

	Casting Votes of	Votes by Country	Total Votes[a]	Percent of Fund Total[b]
	Djibouti	409		
	Equatorial Guinea	576		
	Gabon	1,793		
	Guinea	1,321		
	Guinea-Bissau	392		
	Madagascar	1,472		
	Mali	1,183		
	Mauritania	894		
	Mauritius	1,266		
	Niger	908		
	Rwanda	1,051		
	São Tomé and Príncipe	324		
	Senegal	1,868		
	Togo	984	<u>25,169</u>	<u>1.16</u>
			2,159,666[c,d]	99.71[e]

Notes: a. Voting power varies on certain matters pertaining to the General Department with use of the Fund's resources in that department.

b. Percentages of total votes 2,166,739 in the General Department and the Special Drawing Rights Department.

c. This total does not include the votes of the Islamic State of Afghanistan, Somalia, and the Federal Republic of Yugoslavia, which did not participate in the 2000 regular election of executive directors. The total votes of these members is 7,073—0.33 percent of those in the General Department and Special Drawing Rights Department.

d. This total does not include the votes of the Democratic Republic of the Congo which were suspended effective June 2, 1994, pursuant to Article XXVI, Section 2(b) of the Articles of Agreement.

e. This figure may differ from the sum of the percentages shown for individual Directors because of rounding.

Source: "IMF Executive Members and Voting Power," http://www.imf.org/external/np/see/memdir/eds.htm [accessed February 15, 2002].

Funding the IMF

The Quota System

The IMF is, in effect, "owned" by its members, with ownership distributed in accordance with a system of quotas. The size of each member's quota is determined by a complex formula that incorporates the size of the economy, the percentage of the economy involved in international trade, and the value of foreign-exchange holdings. This quota is the most fundamental element of a member's voting power in the IMF. The number of votes a country possesses is determined on the basis of one vote for each IMF 100,000 currency units (Special Drawing Rights, or SDRs), plus the 250 basic votes each member is automatically granted. Effectively, the system of quotas and voting weights power heavily and favorably toward members with large gross national products (GNPs). In addition to determining voting power, a member's quota also determines the maximum amount of IMF financing to which the country has access. In January 1999, the IMF called for a 45 percent increase in quotas that totaled SDR 212 billion or U.S.$269 billion. The 2002 U.S. quota was just under 18 percent of the total. Together, the industrial countries possess a majority of votes and thus dominate the decisions of the Executive Board.

General Arrangements to Borrow, Special Drawing Rights, and the New Arrangements to Borrow

When the IMF was established in 1944, each member's quota was assumed adequate to provide access to enough international currencies to meet any balance-of-payments problems that might develop; however, the negotiators at Bretton Woods failed to anticipate the explosive growth in world trade flows that occurred after World War II. As trade in global aggregate terms has grown, so has the potential magnitude of current account surpluses and, more worrisome, deficits. To ensure adequate liquidity and keep pace with the growth in world trade and potential balance-of-payments financing needs, the IMF has had to periodically increase members' quotas, a strategy that worked fairly well until the late 1950s. At that time, with quotas alone no longer capable of providing adequate liquidity for the balance-of-payments financing needs of the member countries, a second source of funding known as the General Arrangements to Borrow (GAB) was created to meet heightened liquidity needs.

The GAB, established in 1962, allows the IMF to borrow from the eleven participating countries, the Group of Ten (G-10) industrialized countries, and Switzerland. By matching the interest rate and the maturity of its borrowing and lending, the IMF enhances international liquidity by serving as a conduit for the transfer of funds from countries that possess reserve assets, presumably the G-10 countries, to those that wish to borrow. The G-10 countries, the wealthiest, most industrialized countries in the world, are presumably in the best position to provide the needed additional liquidity.

In addition to the GAB as a source of funding for the IMF, Saudi Arabia and other oil-exporting countries have provided significant resources derived from their balance-of-payments surpluses. When oil prices quadrupled in 1973–1974, the IMF used assets from the surpluses of the oil-exporting countries to provide assistance to countries that faced a significant increase in the cost of energy imports.

Special Drawing Rights as a Source of Liquidity. With the continuing explosive growth in the magnitude of world trade flows, by the mid-1960s the quotas and the GAB combined were no longer adequate to meet burgeoning financing needs. In response, a new reserve asset known as the Special Drawing Right (SDR) was created in 1969. SDRs can best be understood as an international reserve asset. They can be exchanged at an agreed-upon value in lieu of currency. SDRs do not widely circulate and are not in general usage, but they are exchangeable among IMF member countries in transactions among themselves.

Since their introduction, SDRs have generated their share of controversy and opponents. Concerns about SDRs focus on the ease with which a potentially inflationary mechanism was introduced into the system. In the words of Henry Hazlitt, "These SDRs were created out of thin air, by a stroke of the pen" (Hazlitt, 1984: 15). The specific concern is that the introduction of "paper gold," while providing needed liquidity, will undermine moral hazard and substitute for the necessary belt-tightening measures countries experiencing balance-of-payments problems should be undertaking. At the heart of the unease about SDRs is the fear that an expansion of IMF financial resources will lead to an internationalization of individual countries' debt problems, shifting the burden of adjustment from the debtor country to the international community.

Despite these concerns, SDRs have become an accepted mechanism for interjecting additional liquidity into the system. Highlighting its acceptance among the IMF's member countries, countries now pay 25 percent of their quota subscriptions in SDRs, and as of 2001, several IMF members had chosen the SDR as the standard for valuing their currencies, replacing other traditional valuing standards such as the U.S. dollar and Japanese yen.

Initially, the monetary authorities chose to base the value of SDRs on a weighted "basket" of sixteen currencies. The number of currencies composing this basket has diminished over time. In 1981, the basket was reduced to the currencies of the G5 countries. As of January 1, 1999, there were only four currencies in the basket, and their respective weights were the dollar (45 percent), euro (29 percent), yen (15 percent), and pound sterling (11 percent). The precise value of the SDR is determined daily. Its value is more stable than that of any single currency in the basket, given that changes in the value of any of the basket currencies are to a degree offset by changes in the values of other currencies.

New Agreement to Borrow. The newest source of IMF funding is the New Agreement to Borrow (NAB) introduced in 1998. Its creation was largely in response to the crippling and contagious effects of currency and balance-of-payments crises that struck emerging markets in Mexico (1994), East Asia (1997), and Russia and Brazil (1998). The purpose of making these additional funds available is to counter excessive swings in currency values. Rapid access to a considerable sum of foreign currency, in times when the member country's currency is experiencing significant downward pressure from the selling of its currency in the currency markets, allows the country to intervene in the market, purchase its own currency with the foreign currency, lower its supply in the marketplace, and thereby quell excessive swings in the currency's value. In a related situation, under the NAB, funds have also been made available to member countries as precautionary lines of defense against sudden and disruptive losses of market confidence in their currencies because of contagion from difficulties in other countries.

The NAB was established with the participation of twenty-five member countries. Creation of the NAB represents a significant expansion in liquidity, doubling the amount of GAB resources to U.S.$44 billion. Table 16.2 lists the member countries participating in the NAB and their respective credit amounts.

Borrowing from the Fund

In its early years, IMF lending was limited to countries experiencing traditional balance-of-payment problems, but in the more than fifty years since its creation, the organization has responded to a number of disruptive challenges to the smooth operation of the international monetary system and expanded the range of purposes for which it lends. These challenges have included periodic Fund liquidity problems because of aggregate member needs exceeding available assets; the financial dislocation associated with oil price hikes in 1973–1974 and 1978–1979; the debt crisis of the 1980s; currency/capital flight crises of the 1990s; and the special needs of countries making the transition from centrally planned socialist economies to market-based economies.

To address this array of anticipated and unanticipated contingencies, the Fund gives financial assistance to countries under three broad sets of programs. The first program provides balance-of-payments financing through unconditional and conditional tranches. Standby arrangements (SBAs) form the core of the IMF's traditional lending programs. First used in 1952, they are designed to address short-term balance-of-payments problems. The second program provides funding under special facilities for countries that have specific needs and circumstances. The third program provides concessional financing for low-income member countries.

Mainstay of IMF Lending: The Tranche System

A member country approaches the IMF and requests balance-of-payments assistance when its foreign-exchange reserves have been depleted. Most

Table 16.2   NAB Participants and Credit Amounts

Participant	Amount (millions of SDRs)
Australia	810
Austria	412
Belgium	967
Canada	1,396
Denmark	371
Deutsche Bundesbank	3,557
Finland	340
France	2,577
Hong Kong Monetary Authority	340
Italy	1,772
Japan	3,557
Korea	340
Kuwait	345
Luxembourg	340
Malaysia	340
Netherlands	1,316
Norway	383
Saudi Arabia	1,780
Singapore	340
Spain	672
Sveriges Riksbank	859
Swiss National Bank	1,557
Thailand	340
United Kingdom	2,577
United States	6,712
Total	34,000

Source: "The General Arrangements and the New Arrangements to Borrow—A Fact Sheet," August 2001, http://www.imf.org/external/np/exr/facts/gabnab.htm [accessed February 15, 2002].

countries earn adequate foreign exchange to finance their imports and never approach the IMF for assistance. There are several means by which the country can gain foreign exchange. The sale of goods or services in the export market, receipts from foreign tourists, foreign direct investment (FDI) and portfolio flows, or international loans can all generate a foreign-exchange inflow. However, if the combined inflow from these sources fail to equal or exceed imports and foreign debt-servicing needs, the country's foreign-exchange reserves will gradually decline. Upon the depletion of these reserves, the country could experience an abrupt halt to its imports. This is harmful not only to the importing country but to its trading partners as well who have now lost an export market. Through the "lender of last resort" function the IMF attempts to temporarily fill the void by providing balance-of-payments assistance (foreign exchange) to the member country.

This will allow a less abrupt adjustment on the part of the borrowing country and maintain export markets for its trading partners.

Gold or Reserve Tranche. The first option for a country experiencing balance-of-payments problems is accessing that system. Within the tranche system, the country will first access the gold or reserve tranche. A tranche is a slice or a portion, up to one-quarter, of the country's quota denominated in a currency of its choosing or in SDRs. Because of the prominent role the U.S. dollar has played in world trade and the willingness of most trading partners to accept it in exchange, members often request, but are not limited to, the dollar. Historically, other key currencies widely accessed because of their acceptance in international trade transactions are the Japanese yen, British pound, German deutschemark, and more recently, the euro.

When a member country goes to the IMF to obtain balance-of-payments assistance and make a purchase from the first tranche, the currency of choice or SDRs are given with minimal conditions. The only expectation is that the purchasing country will make a "reasonable effort" to overcome its balance-of-payments problems. According to John Williamson, "A member requesting a drawing limited to the first credit tranche was expected to have in place a program representing reasonable efforts to overcome its balance of payments difficulties, but what constitutes reasonable efforts is in practice left to the borrower's discretion, since a country applying for such a drawing is given the overwhelming benefit of the doubt in any difference of view between the member and the Fund" (Williamson, 1982: 65). This remains true today.

After accessing the first tranche, if the purchasing country fails to make the adjustments necessary to earn enough foreign exchange to balance its accounts, it will purchase from the second, the third, and possibly the fourth tranches. Countries drawing on all four tranches can purchase up to 100 percent of their quotas.

Upper Level or Conditional Tranches. The first tranche is known as an unconditional tranche because of the minimal performance requirements placed on the borrower. The second, third, and fourth are conditional tranches with progressively more rigorous requirements for borrowing. When a country seeks to borrow from these conditional tranches, it must comply with specific macroeconomic policies put forth by the IMF. Purchasing from these tranches has generated the most controversy for the IMF, because of the obvious loss of sovereignty in economic policymaking and the progressive intrusion of IMF demands on the borrower.

By imposing these progressively strenuous conditions on borrowers, the IMF seeks to ensure that a country that purchases foreign currencies,

SDRs, or both will be able to overcome its balance-of-payments difficulties and repay the borrowed amount in a timely manner, thereby preserving the revolving nature of IMF resources and ensuring that resources will be available to other countries in time of need. Another reason for imposing stringent conditions is to combat the free-rider problem and ensure that the burden of adjustment is not shifted to the international community.

Before access to the upper tranches is granted, meetings are held between the country's economic leaders and IMF representatives to establish performance criteria for the borrowing country. Following these meetings, a letter of intent is exchanged. The letter outlines the macroeconomic policies that the country has agreed to institute to alleviate its balance-of-payments problems and establishes the performance criteria to be used to measure the country's progress. Keeping the country on a short leash, upper-level or conditional tranche drawings are made in installments and are released when the country has implemented those policies specified in the negotiated agreement and has reached similarly specified performance targets.

Standby Arrangements.　The drawings on the conditional tranches, along with their negotiated agreements and set performance targets, are known as standby arrangements. Standby arrangements are designed to meet the trade financing needs for a twelve- to eighteen-month period. Repayment of standby arrangements is to be made within three-and-a-quarter to five years of each drawing. By September 30, 2001, the number of countries with standby arrangements had been reduced to fourteen from a peak of twenty-two in August 1994. It is also important to note that by September 2001, a large part of the IMF member countries (39 in total) had opted for arrangements under the Poverty Reduction Growth Facility (PRGF), even though the total amount of credit granted was much less than the total credit amount under traditional standby arrangements.[1] The attraction of the Poverty Reduction and Growth Facility is because, unlike other IMF programs, it includes the opportunity for debt forgiveness in its lending program. Table 16.3 lists countries and the amount of IMF assistance they have received under standby arrangements, the extended Fund facility, and the Poverty Reduction and Growth Facility.

Controversial Nature of the Fund's Conditional Lending

Of all of the lending activities of the International Monetary Fund, the conditional lending has been the most controversial and has increasingly placed the IMF in the public spotlight. The IMF historically has been a target of vehement criticism from both the left and the right.

From the left, critics argue that Fund programs are driven solely by ideology, specifically a singular commitment to liberal economic theory and its orthodoxy concerning the limitations of the state and the virtues of

Table 16.3   Standby, EFF, and PRGF Arrangements as of September 30, 2001

Member	Date of arrangement (million SDRs)	Expiration date	Amount approved	Undrawn balance
Standby Arrangements				
Argentina[a]	March 10, 2000	March 9, 2003	16,936.80	7,180.49
Brazil[a]	September 14, 2001	December 13, 2002	12,144.40	8,468.32
Croatia	March 19, 2001	May 18, 2002	200.00	200.00
Ecuador	April 19, 2000	December 31, 2001	226.73	75.58
Gabon	October 23, 2000	April 22, 2002	92.58	79.36
Latvia	April 20, 2001	December 19, 2002	33.00	33.00
Lithuania	August 30, 2001	March 29, 2003	86.52	86.52
Nigeria	August 4, 2000	October 31, 2001	788.94	788.94
Panama	June 30, 2000	March 29, 2002	64.00	64.00
Peru	March 12, 2001	March 11, 2002	128.00	128.00
Serbia/Montenegro	June 11, 2001	March 31, 2002	200.00	100.00
Sri Lanka	April 20, 2001	June 19, 2002	200.00	96.65
Turkey[a]	December 22, 1999	December 21, 2002	15,038.40	5,702.36
Uruguay	May 31, 2000	March 31, 2002	150.00	150.00
Total			46,289.37	23,153.72
EFF Arrangements				
Colombia	December 20, 1999	December 19, 2002	1,957.00	1,957.00
FYR Macedonia	November 29, 2000	November 28, 2003	24.12	22.97
Indonesia	February 4, 2000	December 31, 2002	3,638.00	2,477.20
Jordan	April 15, 1999	April 14, 2002	127.88	60.89
Kazakhstan	December 13, 1999	December 12, 2002	329.10	329.10
Ukraine	September 4, 1998	August 15, 2002	1,919.95	726.95
Yemen	October 29, 1997	October 28, 2001	72.90	26.40
Total			8,068.95	5,600.51
PRGF Arrangements				
Armenia	May 23, 2001	May 22, 2004	69.00	59.00
Azerbaijan	July 6, 2001	July 5, 2004	80.45	72.40
Benin	July 17, 2000	July 16, 2003	27.00	16.16
Bolivia	September 18, 1998	June 7, 2002	100.96	37.10
Burkina Faso	September 10, 1999	September 9, 2002	39.12	16.76
Cambodia	October 22, 1999	October 21, 2002	58.50	25.07
Cameroon	December 21, 2000	December 20, 2003	111.42	79.58
Central-African Republic	July 20, 1998	January 19, 2002	49.44	24.96
Chad	January 7, 2000	January 6, 2003	42.00	20.80
Djibouti	October 18, 1999	October 17, 2002	19.08	13.63
Ethiopia	March 22, 2001	March 21, 2004	86.90	52.14
FYR Macedonia	November 29, 2000	December 17, 2003	10.34	8.61
Gambia, The	June 29, 1998	December 31, 2001	20.61	3.44
Georgia	January 12, 2001	January 11, 2004	108.00	90.00
Ghana	May 3,1999	May 2, 2002	228.80	105.17
Guinea	May 2, 2001	May 1, 2004	64.26	51.41
Guinea-Bissau	December 15, 2000	December 14, 2003	14.20	9.12
Honduras	March 26, 1999	March 25, 2002	156.75	64.60
Kenya	August 4, 2000	August 3, 2003	190.00	156.40
Lao People's Democratic Republic	April 25, 2001	April 24, 2004	31.70	27.17
Lesotho	March 9, 2001	March 8, 2004	24.50	17.50
Madagascar	March 1, 2001	March 1, 2004	79.43	68.08
Malawi	December 21, 2000	December 20, 2003	45.11	38.67

Table 16.3 (continues)

Table 16.3   Continued

Member	Date of arrangement (million SDRs)	Expiration date	Amount approved	Undrawn balance
Mali	August 6, 1999	August 5, 2002	6.65	21.74
Mauritania	July 21, 1999	July 20, 2002	42.49	18.21
Moldova	December 15, 2000	December 20, 2003	110.88	92.40
Mozambique	June 28, 1999	June 27, 2002	87.20	33.60
Nicaragua	March 18, 1998	March 17, 2002	148.96	33.64
Niger	December 14, 2000	December 21, 2003	59.20	42.28
Rwanda	June 24, 1998	January 31, 2002	71.40	19.04
São Tomé and Príncipe	April 28, 2000	April 28, 2003	6.66	4.76
Senegal	April 20, 1998	April 19, 2002	107.01	28.54
Sierra Leone	September 26, 2001	September 25, 2004	130.84	84.00
Tajikistan	June 24, 1998	December 24, 2001	100.30	22.02
Tanzania	March, 31, 2000	April 3, 2003	135:00	75.03
Vietnam	April 13, 2001	April 12, 2004	290.00	248.60
Yemen	October 29, 1997	October 28, 2001	264.75	94.75
Zambia	March 25, 1999	March 28, 2003	254.45	199.51
Total			3,513.36	2,075.86
Grand total			57,871.68	30,830.09

Source: "Stand-By, EFF and PRGF Arrangements as of September 30," *IMF Survey,* October 22, 2001, p. 330.
Note: a. Includes amounts under Supplemental Reserve Facility.
EFF = Extended Fund Facility.
PRGF = Poverty Reduction and Growth Facility
Figures may not add to totals owing to rounding.
Data: IMF Treasurer's Department.

the market. As a corollary, critics charge that the IMF imposes a single policy framework, or "adjustment recipe," on all borrowers regardless of specific and unique economic and political conditions characteristic of each member country. This straightjacket of policy prescriptions is said to unfairly target the lowest-income strata in society and contribute to social unrest and political instability. The Fund is also accused of using the country's need for foreign exchange as a means of further liberalizing the country's foreign direct investment regulations. This, in turn, provides large, well-endowed foreign multinational corporations the opportunity to purchase or outcompete local firms, resulting in deeper foreign ownership of the national economy. Finally, the Fund is charged with contributing to the destruction of the environment by encouraging countries to exploit their natural resources to gain much needed foreign exchange.

According to the Fund, the logic behind its policy prescriptions associated with conditional lending is straightforward and sound. At a minimum, most of its critics will agree that it is ideologically consistent. By proposing free-market solutions, it seeks to institute macroeconomic policy changes that will unleash the pent-up productive capability of free capital, product, and labor markets. The IMF believes that this, in turn, will increase domestic production and enhance export competitiveness, generate foreign exchange, and thereby return the country to balance-of-payments equilibrium.

The task of increasing exports, balancing the trade account, and returning the country to equilibrium is the primary objective central to all IMF policy prescriptions. It is to achieve this end that the IMF's conditions and policy prescriptions on the exchange rate, monetary policy, fiscal expenditures, privatization, and the regulation of foreign direct investment and trade are oriented.

While overwhelmingly embracing free-market economics and endorsing market-determined prices, there is one area where the IMF makes a slight exception—in valuing the currency. Given the perceived severity of the country's condition and the IMF's mandate to expeditiously return the country to a balance-of-payments equilibrium, a slightly undervalued currency is prescribed. The effect of this is twofold, and both are desirable from the IMF's perspective. First, it lowers the cost of domestic relative to foreign goods and thereby enhances the price competitiveness of the country's exports. Second, the undervalued currency simultaneously decreases the demand for imported goods by making them more expensive. Both of these effects of an undervalued currency assist the country in earning and keeping foreign exchange.

The IMF also prescribes specific policies regarding traditional fiscal and monetary policy tools. Reduced government spending and a contraction of the money supply are intended to reduce inflation by lessening domestic demand. The Fund argues that combating domestic inflation is a critical task. By increasing the cost of labor and other product inputs, inflation decreases the price competitiveness in the international marketplace of domestically produced goods. The loss of price competitiveness means fewer exports and diminishing foreign exchange.

Reduced government spending also has the desirable effect of lessening the crowding-out effect of excessive government drawing on the capital markets, thus freeing up more capital for the presumably more productive and export-income-earning private sector. Finally, consistent with its free-market ideology, the Fund supports the liberalization of foreign investment regulations and trade restrictions to promote capital inflows and allow market forces to further rationalize the economy.

Whatever the truth regarding the effectiveness of IMF conditional lending and policy prescriptions, concerned nongovernmental organizations and borrowing country elites continue to chafe under the discipline imposed by IMF programs. Well-publicized and well-attended demonstrations now plague the annual meetings of the IMF and other multilateral organizations.

Although it stands firm in its commitment to orthodox economic principles, the Fund has not been impervious to public concerns. During the 1980s, closer collaboration between the IMF and the World Bank permitted the latter to make loans designed, in part, to mitigate some of the adverse social consequences of Fund stabilization programs. Both the IMF and the World Bank have sought to make their lending programs more environmentally sensitive by incorporating environmental impact audits as a component of all lending decisions. Nevertheless, the IMF continues to be the focal point for much dissension in the world community about the desirability of globalization and the benefits of free-market reform.

Special Facilities of the IMF

In the fifty years since its creation, the IMF has periodically created special facilities to provide credit that extends beyond its traditional focus on short-term, balance-of-payments adjustment lending. These facilities vary in terms of the nature or source of the problem they are designed to address and the terms and conditions of the financing they make available. A representative sample of Fund facilities that have provided financial assistance beyond the scope of the IMF's traditional standby arrangments are: the compensatory contingency financing facility (CCFF) (1963), the extended Fund facility (EFF) (1974), and the systemic transformation facility (STF) (1993). Over the years developing countries and now the formerly socialist Soviet republics have made use of this grouping of special facilities.

Beginning operations in 1963, the CCFF was created to provide a member country with resources to help compensate for temporary shortfalls in export earnings and temporary excesses in cereal import costs that arise from events largely beyond the country's control. Financial assistance under the CCFF is provided to cover unpredictable deviations in highly volatile and easily identifiable key variables that directly affect the member's current account, including main export or import prices and international interest rates.

The EFF provides assistance to member countries for longer periods and in larger amounts than are available under credit tranche policies. Financial assistance under the EFF is generally aimed at overcoming balance-of-payments difficulties stemming from structural problems that require a longer period of adjustment. Countries must repay EFF currencies within four-and-a-half to ten years of the drawing. As in the majority of IMF loans, specific conditions and performance criteria are similar to those of standby arrangements.

The CCFF and EFF and their borrowing terms are of particular consequence for the nonindustrial members. First, borrowing through the CCFF does not include conditionality. Second, their presence reflects an important adjustment in the institutional culture of the IMF in accepting the notion that members specializing in primary product exports face special problems inherent in the global marketplace. These problems stem from imperfect supply-side responses to price cues and the extreme volatility and long-term decline of primary product prices relative to manufactures. These facilities legitimize the economic argument that questions the neutrality of market forces and run explicitly counter to free-market doctrine and the assumption of the infallibility of the unfettered marketplace.

Finally, the systemic transformation facility was created in response to the needs of the nations of central Europe, the Baltic countries, Russia, and the other countries of the Commonwealth of Independent States in making the transition from centrally planned economies to market economies. Under the STF, assistance was provided to members experiencing balance-of-payments difficulties as a result of severe disruptions in their traditional arrangements in trade and payments. Member countries experiencing a sharp fall in total export earnings or a permanent increase in import costs during the transition from significant reliance on bilateral trading at non-market prices by bureaucratic agents to multilateral, market-based trade by private agents, qualified for assistance under the STF.

Assistance under the STF was not provided without qualification. To have received assistance under the STF, the Fund had to be satisfied that the country would cooperate in solving its balance-of-payments problems and would continue to reform its policies. When requesting Fund assistance under the STF, the member submitted a written description of the objectives of its economic policies, its macroeconomic policy projections, and the structural, fiscal, monetary, and exchange measures it would implement over the following twelve months. The member was also required not to tighten exchange or trade restrictions or introduce new restrictions or multiple currency practices.

In addition to the financial assistance provided under the STF, the IMF has provided technical expertise to the transitional economies to assist them in establishing the financial and economic architectures viewed as foundational for a market economy to function. IMF staff played a crucial role in creating many of the basic institutions of a capitalist system, such as central banks, fiscal systems, and legal codes. While the STF is no longer operating and providing assistance, it is a testimony to the breadth of purposes to which IMF support has been provided.[2]

Concessional Facilities

The Structural Adjustment Facility (SAF) (1986) and its successor, the Enhanced Structural Adjustment Facility (ESAF) (1987), were created in response to the debt crisis and its impact on developing countries. Through these facilities, numerous low-income countries have accessed concessional loans providing longer-term payback periods up to ten years. While these facilities were the cornerstone of IMF concessional aid during the 1980s and most of the 1990s, a renewed effort to address the problems of the most impoverished member countries has resulted in the creation of the Poverty Reduction and Growth Facility. This facility replaced the ESAF in November 1999.

The IMF and the International Debt Crisis. The catalyst behind the IMF's targeting of the poorest member countries was the declining economic conditions in the developing world rooted in the 1980s debt crisis. The international debt crisis that led to the creation of the Structural Adjustment Facilities posed a particular challenge to the IMF and its management of the international monetary and financial system.

The crisis itself was complex in that it involved hundreds of international banks, dozens of borrowing countries, creditor governments, and the IMF. The creditors were the commercial banks of the industrialized countries, and the debtors were the oil-importing countries of the less-developed world. The magnitude of the debt, the degree to which the lending banks were leveraged to the sovereign debtors, and the potentially devastating impact that a single country's default could have on a major bank's balance sheet all contributed to fear of a financial panic and meltdown should default occur. This brought the debt crisis to the attention of creditor governments and the IMF.

The IMF played a pivotal role in the management and ultimate resolution of the international debt crisis. As the crisis broke in 1982—and continuing throughout the multiple renegotiations of sovereign countries' debts that followed—the creditor governments of the industrial world and the international banks consistently made their support for rescheduling and additional lending contingent on first having a standby arrangement in place between the IMF and the debtor country. Negotiations focused on the terms for rescheduling the original short- and medium-term loans to long-term loans and for extending new loans. The new lending agreement would then be negotiated between the private banks and the borrowing country with the IMF acting as intermediary. Such renegotiations frequently stretched over many months and sometimes more than a year. Virtually all renegotiated loan packages were predicated on a standby arrangement in place with the IMF.

A contentious aspect of these renegotiations concerned new loans in the form of fresh funds as compared with new loans in the form of rolling over old debt. Naturally, many banks were hesitant to lend additional money as a part of the restructuring package when the debtor countries were already experiencing difficulty servicing their existing debt. From the perspective of the banks, this was simply "throwing good money after bad." On the other hand, the debtor countries argued that some fresh funds, along with the lengthening of the payback period and the accompanying lowering of annual debt-service payments, were necessary to provide needed liquidity and return the countries to a path of stable, long-term growth.

The IMF stepped in to resolve this standoff, meet country needs for fresh capital, and propel the renegotiations forward. The SAF and the ESAF provided the additional liquidity, allowing the IMF, along with the World Bank, to extend such funds to heavily indebted borrowers and thereby facilitate the process of debt renegotiation. Countries that borrowed under the SAF and the ESAF committed to a set of long-term conditions or structural changes outlined in a policy framework paper (PFP). These structural changes included the typical IMF policies outlined earlier, as well as more long-term structural changes such as privatization, deregulation, and the elimination of discriminatory practices toward foreign investors. It is this partnering of the IMF and the World Bank in offering long-term structural adjustment loans that blurred the two institutions' functions and contributed to criticisms of mission creep. It is also the conditions associated with these new, longer-term loans that gave confidence to the private banking community and led to the successful renegotiating of country loans.

IMF Lending Under the Poverty Reduction and Growth Facility

While the IMF has been providing some form of concessional lending to help the poorest member countries achieve economic vitality, sustainable economic growth, and improved living standards since the late 1970s, the recently created Poverty Reduction and Growth Facility incorporates some innovative elements in lending to the poorest member countries.

Recently, the IMF and the World Bank have responded to calls within the larger international community for special assistance for the twenty-four so-called heavily indebted poor countries (HIPCs). This international chorus for special assistance for the world's most impoverished countries simply recognizes the obvious. Clearly, there is a subset of countries in the world that, whether due to internal strife, poor agricultural conditions, the devastating impact of the AIDS epidemic, or a combination of causes, fundamentally have lacked the ability to achieve the gains needed for lasting poverty reduction. These countries continue to borrow from the international community with little hope under present circumstances for long-term prosperity. Considering that Africa is the continent that has been most lacking in social and economic development, twenty of the twenty-four HIPC countries are located there.

In the final analysis, this initiative will allow impoverished and indebted countries to allocate more of their expenditures as a percentage of GDP on social, health, and education expenditures rather than on debt-service payments. In order to accomplish this, approximately 50 percent of each country's total debt will be relieved, translating to $36 billion in debt relief.

The most important aspect of this initiative is that the IMF is not acting alone. It is a multilateral approach to debt relief involving the development agencies of the advanced industrialized countries and the World Bank. The Paris Club, an organization composed of official creditors, is also participating in this effort.

Particularly unique and new about this form of IMF lending is the explicit focus on poverty reduction. The intent is clearly to ensure that the needs of the poor get addressed first in public policy debates. Also new is the effort to put countries in the driver's seat of their own development. Visions and goals for poverty reduction are to be articulated by the countries themselves, which assists them in owning the strategy and committing fully to its success.

To achieve their goals, participating countries design their own master plan embodied in a Poverty Reduction Strategy Paper (PRSP). This plan makes it easier for the IMF and other lending institutions to provide effective support. Although the countries are at the helm in designing their own PRSPs, debt forgiveness will remain contingent on the country meeting traditional IMF macroeconomic policy conditions.[3] More specifically, eligibility for forgiveness and assistance under the HIPC program requires of the countries certain steps outlined in the four phases of the program:

First phase.   To qualify for assistance, the country must adopt adjustment and reform programs supported by the IMF and the World Bank and establish a satisfactory track record in meeting agreed-upon macroeconomic targets. During that time, the country will continue to receive traditional concessional assistance from all the relevant donors and multilateral institutions, as well as debt relief from bilateral creditors (including the Paris Club).

Decision point.   At the end of the first phase, a debt sustainability analysis will be carried out to determine the current external debt situation of the country. If the external debt ratio for that country after traditional debt-relief mechanisms is above 150 percent for the net present value of debt to exports, it qualifies for assistance under the poverty reduction initiative. In the special case of very open economies (exports-to-GDP ratio above 30 percent) with a high debt burden in relation to fiscal revenues, despite strong revenue collection (above 15 percent of GDP), the net present value of debt-to-exports target may be set below 150 percent. In such cases, the target is set so that the net present value of debt must exceed 250 percent of fiscal revenues to qualify.

At the decision point, the Executive Boards of the IMF and World Bank will formally decide on a country's eligibility. If the decision is favorable, the international community is committed to provide sufficient assistance by the completion point (see below) for the country to achieve debt sustainability calculated at the decision point. The Fund's and the Bank's delivery of assistance is predicated on assurances of action by other creditors.

Second phase.   Once eligible for support under the initiative, the country must establish a further track record of good performance under IMF/World Bank–supported programs. The duration of this second period under the enhanced framework is not time bound but depends on the satisfactory implementation of key structural policy reforms agreed at the decision point, the maintenance of macroeconomic stability, and the adoption and implementation of a poverty reduction strategy developed through a broad-based participatory process. Broad-based participation is required in order to ensure buy-in by the borrowing country, thereby increasing its likely success. The use of "floating" completion points would permit strong performers to reach their completion point earlier. During this second phase, official and commercial creditors are generally expected to reschedule obligations coming due, with a 90 percent reduction in net present value. Both the World Bank and the IMF are expected to provide "interim relief" between the decision and completion points.

Completion point.   Remaining assistance will be provided at this point. This will imply the following:

1. For bilateral and commercial creditors: a reduction in the net present value of the stock of debt proportional to their overall exposure to the HIPC. Many bilateral creditors have announced they will also provide debt forgiveness over and above HIPC initiative assistance, particularly on official debt.
2. For multilateral creditors (the IMF, the World Bank, and the other multilateral institutions): a further reduction in the net present value of their claims on the country is expected, sufficient to reduce the country's debt to a sustainable level.[4]

In the post–World War II era there have been numerous calls for debt relief for the most impoverished countries. Debt relief has been an integral element in the demands of the new international economic order dating back to the early 1960s. It has consistently been a central element of economic reform proposals emanating from less-developed-country organizations and the United Nations Conference on Trade and Development (UNCTAD). The puzzling question is why at this particular juncture in history the IMF is aggressively pursuing poverty and debt reduction strategies. There are numerous reasons for the IMF's current focus on poverty reduction; two of the more convincing ones are increasing awareness of poverty reduction and promotion among other players in the international system such as the Roman Catholic Church (Jubilee 2000 Movement), the activities of international NGOs, and entertainment celebrities of worldwide status; and growing concern among IMF member nations, rich and poor, that increasing income disparity will destabilize political systems and undermine national support for the international capitalist system.

The poverty reduction initiative has already achieved some measurable success in reducing the burden of debt servicing as a portion of the participating country's fiscal expenditures. A declining debt burden enhances the HIPC's ability to increase its expenditures in areas of social and economic development. Table 16.4, incorporating a representative sample of HIPCs, provides a glimpse of the impact debt reduction has had on participating countries' fiscal expenditures.

IMF Services for Member Countries

The IMF provides a number of services for its members in addition to its primary responsibilities of supervising the international monetary system and providing financial support. It operates training courses in Washington, D.C., and Vienna, Austria, and issues a wide variety of publications relating to international monetary affairs.

Training

Since its founding in Washington, D.C., in 1964, the IMF Institute has trained approximately thirteen thousand officials from almost all of its 184 member countries, most of whom are employed in ministries of finance, central banks, and other government financial agencies. In addition to giving participants an understanding of the international monetary system and the role of the IMF within that system, the institute through its training has helped to standardize methods of gathering and presenting monetary, balance-of-payments, and financial statistics. The institute has also provided training in highly technical areas of public finance and central banking. Members have frequently relied on the IMF for assistance in such areas when domestic expertise was lacking, particularly in the 1960s and the 1970s, when for the first time a large number of newly independent nations were establishing central banks, issuing new currencies, and devising tax systems (Driscoll, 1994: 21). Since 1996, the IMF has also established the Internal Economics Program, which is designed to provide its staff economists and special invites with training in updated trends in economics and finance methodology. Not shying away from the digital age, as of 2000, the IMF also established its Distance Learning Center in an effort to find a more cost-effective way to serve its trainees all over the globe in a timely fashion.

Table 16.4 Debt Service for Select Individual HIPCs that Reached Decision Points, by Country, 1998-2005 (In million of US dollars, unless otherwise indicated)

	1998	1999	2000	2001	2002	2003	2004	2005
Bolivia								
Debt service paid	390	250						
Debt service due after enhanced HIPC initiative relief[a]			260	225	238	234	235	266
Debt service/exports (in percent)	29	20	18	14	14	12	11	12
Debt service/ government revenue (in percent)	19	13	14	11	12	11	10	10
Debt service/GDP (in percent)	5	3	3	3	3	2	2	2
Cameroon[b]								
Debt service paid[c]	401	401	312					
Debt service due after enhanced HIPC initiative relief[a]				226	242	291	328	347
Debt service/exports (in percent)	18	15	11	8	8	9	9	9
Debt service/ government revenue (in percent)	28	24	18	12	12	13	13	12
Debt service/GDP (in percent)	4	4	3	2	2	3	3	3
Ethiopia[b]								
Debt service paid [d]	104	91	161					
Debt service due after enhanced HIPC initiative relief[a]				105	74	85	100	100
Debt service/exports (in percent)	11	9	17	10	7	7	8	7
Debt service/government revenue (in percent)	9	8	13	7	7	6	5	5
Debt service/GDP (in percent)	2	1	2	2	1	1	1	1
Nicaragua								
Debt service paid[c]	198	108	126					
Debt service due after enhanced HIPC initiative relief				117	188	153	123	127
Debt service/exports (in percent)	24	13	13	11	17	12	9	9
Debt service/ government revenue (in percent)	37	19	20	16	26	21	13	12
Debt service/GDP (in percent)	9	5	6	5	7	5	4	4

Sources: HIPC country documents; World Bank and IMF staff estimates; "The Impact of Debt Reduction Under the HIPC Initiative on External Debt Service and Social Expenditures," http://www.imf.org/external/np/hipc/2001/impact/update/111601.htm [accessed March 6, 2002].

Notes: a. Debt service due after the full use of traditional debt-relief mechanism and assistance under the enhanced HIPC initiative.

b. On fiscal year basis (i.e., 2000 column shows FY 2000/01).

c. The debt-service figures for 2000 largely reflect pre-HIPC relief debt service because these countries did not reach their decision point until late in 2000. Thus the full impact of relief for them will not be felt until 2001 and thereafter.

d. Debt service for 2000 is pre-HIPC, as decision point was reached in 2001.

IMF Publications

The IMF is an important conduit of data on members' fiscal, monetary, and external debt positions. Since its early years, the IMF has issued statistical publications, such as *International Financial Statistics,* that keep members informed of the financial position of other members and provide an unmatched source of statistical information for the financial community, universities, research organizations, and the media. Other IMF publications include the semiannual *World Economic Outlook;* occasional papers on longer-term issues of finance and trade; economic reviews of countries; the *IMF Survey,* a biweekly publication featuring articles on international finance and national economies; a quarterly academic journal entitled *Staff Papers;* the joint IMF–World Bank quarterly *Finance and Development;* and a number of books on the international monetary system. Although very technical in nature, the Fund also publishes a report prepared by each member nation entitled, *Country's Policy Intention Documents,* which describe a member country's "policy intentions in respect of use of Fund resources or staff-monitored programs."[5] Additionally, and relevant to the issue of HIPCs, the IMF has recently published poverty reduction strategy papers of each member country involved in this initiative.

Conclusion

The IMF's relationship to member countries has changed dramatically since 1947. Its main purpose—serving as a lender of last resort in containing currency value fluctuations within the fixed but flexible peg-and-band system—evaporated with the breakdown of that system in 1971. Under the new, flexible exchange rate system, the IMF has the responsibility to monitor country compliance with the rules of the managed float system and limit national use of competitive devaluations for trade purposes. As this chapter has outlined, the Fund's responsibilities have also broadened in response to international crises member countries' needs for additional liquidity.

In a further expansion of the Fund's influence, since 1982 the IMF has participated in G7, now G8 meetings, at which the managing director and staff members brief the G8 regarding the short- and medium-term outlooks for the global economy. The IMF has worked with the G8 in developing a set of indicators for possible coordination of macroeconomic policy.

Simultaneously, the Fund's involvement in and influence on less-developed countries have increased as many of these countries have become increasingly dependent on Fund assistance in managing their heavy debt and frequent balance-of-payments disequilibria. This is particularly true in the case of the smaller countries with weak economies and very few exports. In such cases, the Fund has become a major policy influence and, together with the World Bank, oversees the developmental strategies and trajectories of dozens of states. The HIPC initiative, as well as recent IMF proposals on creating a national bankruptcy plan, are crucial steps toward helping countries resolve unrelenting long-term debt burdens and represent the latest of the IMF's major initiatives.

Notes

1. "IMF's Financial Assistance," http://www.imf.org/external/np/exr/facts/glance.htm [Accessed March 10, 2002].
2. Ibid.
3. "Debt Relief Under the Heavily Indebted Poor Countries (HIPC) Initiative, a Fact Sheet," http://www.imf.org/external/np/exr/facts/hipc.htm [accessed March 5, 2002].
4. Ibid.
5. "IMF Technical Assistance—A Fact Sheet," http://www.imf.org/external/np/exr/facts/tech.htm [accessed March 11, 2002].

References

Chandavarkar, Anand G. 1984. *The International Monetary Fund: Its Financial Organization and Activities*. Washington, DC: International Monetary Fund.
Driscoll, David D. 1994. *What Is the International Monetary Fund?* Washington, DC: International Monetary Fund.
Hazlitt, Henry. 1984. *From Bretton Woods to World Inflation*. Chicago: Regnery Gateway Press.
IMF Survey. May 1992. Washington, DC: International Monetary Fund.
IMF Survey. May 31, 1993. Washington, DC: International Monetary Fund.
IMF Survey. August 1994. Washington, DC: International Monetary Fund.
IMF Survey. October 22, 2001. Washington, DC: International Monetary Fund.
IMF Survey. March 5, 2002. Washington, DC: International Monetary Fund.
Williamson, John. 1982. *The Lending Policies of the International Monetary Fund*. Washington, DC: Institute for International Economics.

17

The Asian Economic Crisis and the Role of the IMF

Kishore C. Dash

What caused the Asian economic crisis in 1997? What role did the International Monetary Fund (IMF) play in managing it? What are the lessons of this crisis for the Asian countries in particular and emerging economies in general? In answering these questions, Kishore Dash stresses the need to complement existing economic explanations with an institutional approach. His political economy analysis provides a framework for understanding the origins and impact of the Asian crisis. In doing so, it also highlights key policy issues facing Asian governments and the IMF in the aftermath of the crisis.

The Asian economic crisis of 1997–1998 challenged the "East Asian miracle" thesis advanced by the World Bank and most neoliberal developmental economists (World Bank, 1993).[1] Once described as economic superachievers,[2] why did the East Asian and Southeast Asian countries suddenly experience a set of serious economic crises in 1997 and 1998? What went wrong? What caused the crisis? What role did the International Monetary Fund (IMF) play in dealing with this crisis? What are the lessons of this crisis for the Asian countries in particular and emerging economies in general?

Most literature on the Asian financial crisis focuses on economic factors to answer these questions. This chapter departs from such an emphasis and argues for the need to include political explanations in order to understand the causes and consequences of the crisis more adequately. Excessive reliance on economic explanations neglects a critical examination of the institutional framework within which economic activity in East Asia and Southeast Asia was carried out. The chapter begins with the political and economic explanations of the crisis in the three most severely impacted Asian economies: Thailand, Indonesia, and South Korea. The focus then shifts to the role of the IMF and the specific measures it took to manage the crisis. The third section evaluates the IMF's role in managing the crisis from the perspectives of both market fundamentalists and pragmatic liberals.[3] The market fundamentalist approach holds that the Asian crisis resulted primarily from the market-distorting policies of the governments of Asia: nontransparent accounting practices, credit allocation on the basis of political reasons rather than sound economic rationales, and inadequate provision of financial and legal systems necessary for a modern capitalist economy. The pragmatic liberal approach, on the other hand, holds that the most immediate and important cause of the crisis was a reversal in investors' beliefs about the future economic prospects of the Asian countries and subsequent rapid withdrawal of huge amounts of capital from these countries. Describing the Asian crisis as a liquidity crisis, pragmatic liberals criticize the IMF's exclusive reliance on market-oriented policies to manage this crisis. The final section concludes with some lessons for Asia and other emerging economies.

Economic Causes of the Crisis

What caused the crisis? At least three important macroeconomic factors can be identified to explain the Asian economic crisis: (1) erosion of international competitiveness contributing to growing current account deficits and declines in foreign-exchange reserves; (2) poor quality of investment; and (3) contagion.

Decline in International Competitiveness

The maintenance of a pegged currency system or semifixed exchange rate regimes by Thailand, South Korea, and Indonesia contributed to the erosion of their international competitiveness. The pegged currency dynamics provided confidence to international investors, leading to a massive inflow of foreign capital—in the form of foreign direct investment in the mid-1980s and mostly portfolio investment[4] in the early 1990s—to these countries.[5] An important cause for this inflow was the Plaza Accord of 1985, where the G7 countries decided to halt and reverse the U.S. dollar's rise against the world's other major currencies, the Japanese yen and the German deutschemark. As a result, the dollar declined steadily over the next ten years. As most of the currencies of the Asian developing countries were pegged to the dollar, their currencies also declined, making their exports more competitive. The change in the value of the dollar had two contradictory effects on the Asian current account situation: (1) by increasing export competitiveness it contributed to a rise in foreign exchange reserves; and (2) by attracting massive, Japanese foreign direct investment it contributed to an increase in local wages and prices, which later hurt Asia's international competitiveness.

The appreciation of the Japanese yen made production in Japan more expensive in dollar terms and, consequently, pushed the Japanese labor-intensive manufacturing firms to relocate to the Southeast Asian region. Between 1985 and 1990, about $15 billion of Japanese foreign direct investment flowed into the region in one of the "largest and swiftest movements of capital to the developing world in recent history" (Bello, 1998: 427). These large external financial inflows led to unsustainable increases in domestic prices and wage levels in these countries, making their exports more costly. Additionally, when the U.S. dollar appreciated sharply relative to the Japanese yen and European currencies in 1995 and 1996, the currencies of Southeast Asian countries appreciated alongside the dollar, eroding their international competitiveness. Finally, the devaluation of the Chinese yuan (renminbi) in 1994 further decreased the export competitiveness of these countries (Steinfeld, 1998). As a result, the Southeast Asian countries started to suffer significant current account deficits due to the sharp decline in their exports during 1995 and 1996 (Table 17.1). The pegged currency arrangements with the U.S. dollar also made it difficult for these countries to adjust to forces of supply and demand in the currency markets when the countries started to experience large current account deficits.

These current account deficits put enormous downward pressure on the Asian currencies and led to a rapid depletion of their foreign-exchange reserves.[6] In order to reverse this situation and defend the value of their currencies, the Asian countries started to borrow from international lenders on a short-term basis. But such a strategy could not continue for too long, as a country's export earnings limit its debt capacity. Short-term foreign debts usually prove disastrous for the value of a currency when foreign lending eventually stops. The significant decline in the currency values of

Table 17.1   Asian Export Growth Trends, 1995–1996 (percent)

	1995	1996
Thailand	23.1	0.5
Indonesia	13.4	9.7
Malaysia	20.3	6.5
Singapore	13.7	5.3
South Korea	30.3	3.7
Taiwan	20.0	3.8

Source: International Monetary Fund, *World Economic Outlook* (Washington, DC: IMF, 1998).

Thailand, Indonesia, and South Korea clearly reflected such a situation (Aggarwal, 1999).

Quality of Investment

A second factor that contributed to Asia's economic crisis is related to the quality of investment. In Southeast Asia, particularly in Thailand, domestic banks borrowed a huge amount of dollar-denominated, short-term loans and re-lent it to speculative real estate projects.[7] Since real estate investments are always long term in nature, they hardly help a country's immediate, short-term foreign-exchange needs. Moreover, when the rental income on real estate investment is in local currencies and the country has to pay debt service in dollars after devaluing its currency, it has an adverse impact on the foreign-exchange reserve situation. Also, there was a clear overinvestment in sectors such as electronics and semiconductors by Korean conglomerates, or *chaebols*. A cyclical slump in international demand for electronics and semiconductors proved disastrous to the South Korean, Taiwanese, and Malaysian economies, which were among the world's top offshore electronic assemblers. Finally, Indonesia, under former President Suharto, misallocated funds to crony projects such as the abortive national car program linked to family members.

Contagion

Contagion played an important role in quickly spreading the crisis from one country to another and even from one region to another. There were two channels of contagion in Asia. The first was what Morris Goldstein (1998: 18–20) describes as the "wake-up call hypothesis." According to this hypothesis, Thailand acted as a wake-up call for international investors to reassess the creditworthiness of Asian countries. This reassessment concluded that most Southeast Asian and some East Asian economies shared similar features of Thailand's economic condition: weak financial sectors, large external deficits, appreciating real exchange rates, declining exports, and poor quality of investment. As countries were written down by investors to reflect the new assessment, the crisis spread and caused a panicky outflow of international capital (Sachs and Radelet, 1998). Another channel of contagion in Asia was the competitive dynamics of devaluation (Goldstein, 1998: 19–21). According to this thesis, when one country after another in a region depreciates its currency, that increases the lack of competitiveness of other countries. A country's declining export earnings combined with low foreign-exchange reserves make its currency more susceptible to speculative attacks. Thus, while the currencies of Thailand, Indonesia, and South Korea were attacked by financial markets, Hong

Kong, China, and Singapore, with large foreign-exchange reserves, emerged relatively unscathed during 1997–1998 (Feldstein, 1998: 31).

Political Factors Underlying the Asian Crisis

While economic factors can explain why the crisis occurred, the timing and subsequent management of the crisis in Asia can only be explained by domestic political factors. In particular, the structure and role of political institutions are critical to explain why some governments were able to take effective policy decisions faster than others, and why some governments' policies enjoyed more credibility among investors than others. The focus of Stephan Haggard and Robert Kaufman (1992) on *credibility* and *decisiveness* of political institutions in explaining the Latin American crisis in the 1980s provides a useful framework to explain the financial crisis in Thailand, Indonesia, and Korea. Credibility refers to the confidence among investors that a government will not reverse its policy commitments. Credibility of policy commitments is high when the governmental structure and other institutional features make policy reversal difficult. Decisiveness is found when governments can take decisions without much delay (Haggard, 1990). Decisiveness is a casualty when there is a lack of elite cohesiveness and when multiple veto points exist in the decisionmaking process of a political system.

Thailand

Thailand provides an illustration of the importance of decisiveness in a policymaking process. Thailand had been experiencing economic problems since the late 1980s. This was evident in the country's gradual decline in export competitiveness, the continuing fall in foreign reserves, and the slow collapse of the stock market (Haggard and MacIntyre, 1998; Bello, 1998). What Thailand required was strong and effective leadership to address this problem, but this was not possible because of the formation of successive shaky coalition governments in Thailand since the late 1980s, which was a result of the country's constitutional arrangements and electoral rules. Thailand's electoral rules encouraged politicians to pursue individualized campaign strategies rather than identifying with their political parties. Such a system allowed undue influence on the campaigns by various business groups and other dominant domestic actors like the military and made politicians extremely vulnerable to their pressure. As a result, vote buying, frequent changes of political parties by politicians, and ministerial payoffs to support a policy decision had become endemic problems in Thailand's corrupt political system following the departure of Prime Minister Prem

Tinsulanonda in 1988 (Overholt, 1999). Given the high political transaction costs of coalition governments (Dixit, 1997),[8] Thailand's successive coalition governments—including the government of former army general Chavalit Yongchaiyudh, who was elected prime minister in November 1996—found it extremely difficult to initiate and implement effective, tough economic policies. Chavalit Yongchaiyudh was the leader of the New Aspiration Party (NAP), which spent an enormous amount of money on vote buying in the northeastern and central region. Yet Chavalit was not able to win a majority of seats in the parliament and had to form a coalition government of six political parties. No wonder his government, like his predecessors, remained ineffective. Accelerating corruption and ineffective leadership began eroding Thailand's underlying competitiveness during 1996–1997. Despite a growing current account deficit and economic downturn, Thailand maintained a pegged foreign-exchange rate from November 1996 to April 1997 due to increasing pressure from the business groups in the six-party coalition government of Chavalit. The Bank of Thailand (BoT) continued to defend the pegged baht by keeping interest rates high. By May 1997, the BoT reportedly spent U.S.$27 billion in defending the baht's value. The Chavalit government's decision finally to devalue the baht on July 2, 1997, came after a prolonged cabinet discussion. The subsequent collapse of the baht led the government to conclude an agreement with the IMF in August 1997 (see Table 17.2). But Chavalit found it difficult to implement the agreement because of his coalition partners' opposition to the loan's conditions. His cabinet failed to approve emergency measures that were necessary to put the financial restructuring plans in motion and delayed identifying financial companies for closure under the IMF agreement. When Thailand's finance minister Thanong Bidaya resigned over the issue of rescinding a gas tax that was a condition of the IMF program, the government's credibility reached its lowest point. The ensuing collapse of economic and public confidence led the Chavalit government to resign in November 1997. Following the resignation, a new parliamentary coalition built around Chuan Leekpai's Democratic Party came to power. Under the premiership of Chuan Leekpai, the Thai government announced it was going to close down fifty-six of the fifty-eight ailing finance companies that the IMF demanded on December 7, 1997. More important, with the critical support of the king, Chuan was able to bring about some changes in Thailand's constitution (Overholt, 1999: 1027–1031). But despite the constitutional changes, Thailand's institutionally rooted problems of indecisiveness were far from over.

Indonesia

Unlike Thailand, the Indonesian government under President Suharto did not suffer from any institutional constraints, and thus indecisiveness was

Table 17.2   IMF Intervention in Thailand

Dates	IMF Measures
8/97	• Approve U.S.$3.9b credit
	• Restructure financial sector—identify and close 56 insolvent finance companies
	• Target positive growth of 2.5% in 1997 and 3.5% in 1998
	• Maintain gross official reserve at equivalent of 4.2 months of imports in 1997 and 4.4 months in 1998
	• Limit rate of inflation to 9.5% in 1997 and 5% in 1998
	• Target overall fiscal surplus (1–2% of GDP) by 1998 through increase in rate of value-added tax (VAT)
	• Selectively cut public spending (average 19% cut)
11/97	• Second IMF package approved as baht rapidly appreciates
	• Tighten bank licensing rules
	• Maintain fiscal surplus of 1% GDP
	• Establish timetable for financial sector restructuring
12/97	• Disburse U.S.$810m
2/98	• Change fiscal policy target from surplus of 1% of GDP to deficit of 2% of GDP
6/98	• Disburse US$135m
	• Prepare restructuring and privatization plan for banks
	• Gradually reduce interest rates
	• Higher monetary growth rates
	• Target fiscal deficit at 3% of GDP
	• Accelerate corporate debt restructuring
12/98	• Completely dispose of assets of 56 finance companies
	• Implement stronger rules governing disclosure and accounting practices

Source: Thailand's Letter of Intent to the IMF (25 November 1997; 24 February 1999); *Bangkok Post* (13 February 1998); *Financial Times* (1 July 1998); *The Wall Street Journal* (5 August 1997).

not an issue. Executive authority in Indonesia is highly centralized around the presidency, which allowed Suharto's administration to take a series of bold and decisive measures to deal with the crisis initially. For example, within two months after the crisis started in Thailand in March 1997, the Indonesian government moved quickly to float the rupiah, raised interest rates, reduced tariffs on foreign imports, removed foreign ownership limits on the stock exchange, and canceled a number of high-cost infrastructure projects (Haggard and MacIntyre, 1998). Such measures won high praise in the financial community, including the IMF. Not surprisingly, the IMF promptly approved a multilateral financial package in October 1997 to help stabilize Indonesia's financial system.

Why, then, did Indonesia's condition become much worse than any other country in Asia? The answer lies clearly in the credibility of the Suharto government. For more than two decades, President Suharto practiced what is often referred to as "crony capitalism." Suharto's sons, daughters, and close friends directly controlled several huge infrastructure projects in Indonesia. For example, Indonesia's national car project was run by Suharto's youngest son, and the much-envied aircraft project was run by

Table 17.3 IMF Intervention in Indonesia

Dates	IMF Measures
10/97	• Approve U.S.$23b multilateral financial package involving World Bank and Asian Development Bank to help stabilize Indonesia's financial system

11/97	• Approve U.S.$10b standby credit and release disbursement of US$3b
	• Close 16 insolvent banks
	• Implement structural reforms to enhance economic efficiency and transparency
	  – Liberalize foreign trade and investment
	  – Dismantle monopolies and privatization
	• Stabilize rupiah through tight monetary policy
	• Implement fiscal surplus of 1% of GDP in 1997/98 and 2% of GDP in 1998/99
	• Place weak regional development banks under Bank of Indonesia supervision
	• Postpone costly infrastructure projects

1/98	• Approve second package • Change fiscal policy target from surplus of 1% of GDP to deficit of 1% of GDP • Dismantle government monopolies • Postpone infrastructure projects • Close insolvent banks • Establish Indonesia Bank Restructuring Agency (IBRA)
2/98	• Transfer 54 weak banks to IBRA • Establish new loan classification and banking rules based on international standards
5/98	• Disburse U.S.$1b to Indonesia • Require stricter enforcement of reform provisions
6/98	• Frame additional IMF-Indonesia agreement in light of worsening economic situation and changing political climate • Increase social expenditure to 7.5% of GDP • Target budget deficit at 8.5% of GDP • Merge two state-owned banks • Implement legislation to privatize state banks and remove limits on private ownership of banks
7/98	• Disburse U.S.$1b to Indonesia • At Indonesia's request, cancel existing arrangement with IMF and replace with new extended arrangement
8/98	• Approve extended facility with longer repayment period • Disburse U.S.$1b to Indonesia

Source: Indonesia's *Letter of Intent to the IMF* (15 January 1998; 10 April 1998); *Jakarta Post* (17 January 1998); *Financial Times* (1 July 1998); *Wall Street Journal* (5 August 1997).

Suharto's closest friend, B. J. Habibie, who was later appointed vice president of Indonesia by Suharto to deal with the financial crisis (Bullard, Bello, and Malhotra, 1998: 94). As long as the economy was doing reasonably well, nobody really cared about Suharto's family domination of Indonesia's political and economic landscape. But when the economy started to deteriorate toward the end of 1997, Suharto's practice of connected lending came under increased scrutiny, from both the international financial community and the Indonesian public.

In addition, serious doubts about Suharto's physical condition and growing uncertainty about the process of political succession contributed to a rapid erosion of confidence in his leadership. His inability to contain widespread violence and looting directed against ethnic Chinese in March 1997, which caused many to send their money offshore to safer havens in Singapore and Hong Kong, became a critically contested national issue, putting enormous pressure on the effectiveness of Suharto's leadership. With a sudden collapse of confidence in Suharto, his government's policies and promises of wide-range economic reforms lacked credibility. This lack of credibility contributed to further capital flight from Indonesia, leading to a downward decline of the Indonesian economy.

South Korea

In South Korea, political power is less diffused than in the case of Thailand. However, unlike Indonesia, executive authority is not highly centralized around the presidency of Korea. Since South Korea's transition to democracy in 1987, the president's power has been limited, and South Korea has become a divided government with power split between the executive branch and the legislature.[9] One of the institutional weaknesses of the presidency is that the president is not eligible to seek reelection. The one-term limit reflects the aversion of the South Korean people to excessive centralization of executive authority and the potential abuse of power by the president. On the other hand, the one-term limit makes him a lame-duck president toward the end of his term. An important consequence of this is lack of confidence among investors that a succeeding government will adhere to the preceding government's policy commitments. Policy continuity becomes a serious issue particularly at a time of economic crisis and, more critically, in the context of South Korea's institutional framework of corporate governance.

South Korea's rapid industrialization was a result of a close relationship between the private sector and state. During the 1960s and 1970s, the South Korean state practiced what is often referred to as a targeting system. In such a system, the state identifies priority strategic sectors and industries, provides the large business groups known as chaebols with subsidized credit through a government-directed banking system, protects them from competition from foreign corporations in the domestic market, and forces the chaebols to export to the global market. This export-led growth strategy was enormously successful until the late 1980s. But by the beginning of the 1990s, the Korean economy had started to slow down due to growing inefficiencies and corruption in the state-bank-chaebol nexus.

By 1997, South Korea's economic problems were mounting. In the midst of this situation, the country experienced three major political issues that contributed to investors' lack of confidence in the Korean economy and government policies. First, the upcoming Korean presidential election was scheduled for December 1997, making the outgoing president Kim

Young Sam (1993–1998) a lame-duck president. This, coupled with serious internal party opposition to his leadership, diminished his credibility and the government's effectiveness. As a result, both international and domestic investors became wary about his ability to take quick decisions to put the Korean economy on the right track. Second, a corruption scandal broke out in which President Kim Young Sam was accused of securing huge loans for the bankrupt Hanbo corporation, a giant steelmaker and the fourteenth largest chaebol in Korea. This scandal and internal party opposition to his indifference toward the bankruptcy of the Kia group, the eighth largest chaebol, weakened his presidency. Finally, the opposition party led by Kim Dae Jung sought to generate maximum political capital out of the weak presidency of Kim Young Sam by announcing that, if he were elected, he would renegotiate the IMF program. This announcement sent negative signals to investors and plunged Korea into a deep economic crisis.

Kim Dae Jung won the election by a narrow margin. Although he faced a divided government, he was able to implement some difficult reforms vis-à-vis the chaebols and financial sector because of his credibility as a reformer and large initial support from labor unions and the middle class (Haggard and MacIntyre, 1998: 388).

The IMF's response

The Asian crisis provided the IMF with a new opportunity to play a leading role in an international effort to stave off a global financial crisis. The IMF's prescriptions for the crisis affecting Asian countries such as Thailand, Indonesia, and Korea were based on two key postulates: (1) the need to reform their economies, with particular emphasis on fiscal discipline and banking sector restructuring, and (2) the need to maintain high interest rates to avoid capital flight and further speculative attacks on their currencies. While the first principle was devised to address Asia's infamous corporate–governance system, the latter principle was a condition imposed on every loan-recipient country.

The IMF's condition to raise interest rates seems to be based on a virtuous cycle logic. Raising interest rates would attract capital inflows to crisis-stricken countries, preventing the competitive devaluation of their currencies, easing domestic liquidity, stimulating investments, and eliminating panic. But such outcomes, as discussed below, hardly took place in the crisis-stricken countries in Asia.

The important IMF measures taken between July 1997 and August 1998 (Tables 17.2, 17.3, 17.4) suggest that the IMF had changed its loan conditionality more than once in response to deteriorating economic conditions in Thailand, Indonesia, and Korea. While the market fundamentalists argue that such changes in the IMF approach represent signs of flexibility

Table 17.4   IMF Intervention in South Korea

Dates	IMF Measures
12/97	• Approve U.S.$21b standby credit for Korea and release disbursement of U.S.$5.6b • Target GDP growth of 2.5% in 1998 • Suspend 9 insolvent merchant banks • Target balanced budget • Dismantle nontransparent and inefficient ties among government banks and business • Implement trade and capital account liberalization • Implement labor market reforms • Publish and disseminate key economic data • Korean government allowed *won* to float • Release second disbursement of U.S.$3.5b to Korea • Debt rescheduling by international commercial banks as critical to Korea's recovery • Third disbursement of U.S.$2b to Korea
1/98	• Fourth disbursement of U.S.$2b to Korea • International lenders agree on IMF plan to roll over Korea's short-term debt • Close 10 merchant banks
2/98	• Third IMF program to Korea announced • Lower GDP growth to 1% • Fiscal deficit set at 1% of GDP growth • Disburse U.S.$2b to Korea
5/98	• Further negotiation with IMF and growth forecasts for 1998 revised downward to −2% • Larger fiscal deficit of 2% of GDP in 1998 • Disburse U.S.$2b to Korea • Establish agencies at Ministry of Finance and Economy and under Financial Supervisory Board to coordinate and monitor bank restructuring and provision of public funds
8/98	• Further ease macroeconomic policies • Larger fiscal deficit of 5% of GDP for 1998 • Bolster social expenditure program • Disburse U.S.$1b to Korea

Source: Korea's *Letter of Intent to the IMF* (25 November 1997, 24 February 1999); *Financial Times* (1 July 1998).

and openmindedness, the pragmatic liberals focus on the fundamentally flawed thinking of IMF policymakers, influenced by the Washington Consensus, with its emphasis on market-oriented policies (Gore, 2000: 789–790).[10] The next section evaluates the market fundamentalists' and pragmatic liberals' perspectives on IMF recipes to deal with the Asian crisis.

The IMF as Crisis Manager: Pragmatic Liberals' Perspectives

The pragmatic liberals argue that the short-term policies imposed by the IMF were misguided and inefficient. According to this school of thought, the adjustment programs negotiated with the Fund by the crisis countries unnecessarily worsened their economic condition, intensifying panic and causing steep rises in bankruptcies and unemployment (Carvalho, 2001: 237). The central criticism of this group is that the IMF failed to recognize the Asian crisis as primarily a liquidity crisis (Radelet and Sachs, 1998; Stiglitz, 2001). The appropriate policy response to a liquidity crisis is to supply additional liquidity so that investors do not lose confidence in the capacity of a country to pay back its liabilities when investments mature. Instead, the IMF insisted on monetary tightening and fiscal austerity policies. The net effects of these policies in Asia can be explained in terms of a vicious circle: interest rate hikes led to the credit crunch, bringing severe financial losses to otherwise solvent companies; and the fall in profitability contributed to higher levels of nonperforming loans, which caused a further contraction in the supply of credit. Higher interest rates and lower aggregate demand as a result of fiscal contraction could not slow down currency depreciation in Asia. Rather, these policies worsened the crisis by leading to widespread banking and corporate bankruptcies in Korea, Indonesia, and Thailand.

The IMF's prescription of long-term financial reforms—particularly capital account convertibility—for the Asian countries in order to ensure steady capital flows into the region has also been criticized by the pragmatic liberal group. For instance, Joseph Stiglitz (2001) argues that the IMF-sponsored capitalism—that is, the IMF's push for global financial integration, removing barriers to any kind of capital flow and liberalizing capital transactions through the establishment of capital account convertibility—is an ill-conceived policy.[11] He finds little support for the Fund's absolute faith in the efficiency of capital markets. As many research analyses have shown, capital markets, after all, can fall victim to information asymmetries that cannot realistically be eliminated in either developed or developing countries (Eichengreen et al., 1999). After examining a large set of empirical data, Dani Rodrik (1998) argues that capital controls are essentially uncorrelated with a country's economic performance. Even assuming that IMF-type structural reforms can lead to the establishment of an efficient market economy, Stiglitz (1998) argues that it is not desirable to implement those policies in the middle of a short-term liquidity crisis. In his view, the IMF insistence on the closure of banks in Thailand and Indonesia actually exacerbated the panic situation in these countries (Stiglitz, 1998).

A final stream of criticisms from the pragmatic liberal perspective focuses on the congruence between the IMF's structural adjustment policies and the interests of its largest shareholder, the United States (Bello, 1998; Stiglitz, 2001).[12] Given its veto power over the decisionmaking process of the IMF,[13] the United States consistently pushed for its agenda of trade liberalization in Asia.[14] It is not surprising that the U.S. Treasury Department strongly supported the IMF-led role and structural adjustment policies in Asia during the crisis.[15] The role of the United States in derailing Japan's proposal to establish an Asian Monetary Fund (AMF), capitalized by U.S.$100 billion and designed to respond quickly to currency and market volatility in Asia, is an illustration of how much influence the United States exerts within the IMF. Of course, Japan had its own interests in proposing an AMF for two principal reasons: (1) heavy exposure of Japanese banks to the currency markets of Thailand, Indonesia, and South Korea, and (2) deep integration of the Japanese economy with the Southeast Asian economies. Thus any slowdown or collapse of the economy in this region would adversely impact the prospects for recovery in the Japanese economy, which has been in recession since the early 1990s.

Being a pioneer of the state-led development model (infamously known as Japan Inc.) in Asia,[16] Japan has long suggested that the Washington Consensus of rapid deregulation, which reduces the role of the state in economic development and liberalization of capital flows, may not be the best policy approach for Asian countries. The idea of establishing an AMF to provide long-term soft loans to the crisis-stricken countries in Asia with less-stringent conditionality than the IMF-imposed ones was rooted in the logic, "an Asian response to an Asian crisis." But Japan had to retreat from this proposal in the face of strong opposition from the IMF and the U.S. Treasury Department, most notably from then–Deputy Secretary Lawrence Summers. Thus the central role of the IMF in the Asian financial bailout was reaffirmed with strong support from the U.S. Treasury Department (Altbach, 1997).

The IMF as Crisis Manager:
Market Fundamentalists' Perspectives

The criticisms of the market fundamentalists regarding the IMF role in Asia revolved around two central issues. First, contrary to the pragmatic liberals' perspectives, this group argues that the Asian crisis was not a liquidity crisis but bank insolvency one, which resulted from years of incorrect structural policies by corrupt and inefficient governments in Asia (Burnside, Eichenbaum, and Rebelo, 1998; Schwartz, 1998). The market fundamentalists point to nontransparent accounting practices, bank loan decisions based on political reasons rather than sound economic rationales, and weak and nonindependent legal infrastructures as primary reasons for Asia's financial crisis (Halcomb and Marshall, 2001). Their prescription is that since the Asian governments caused the crisis, they should bear the cost of correcting their policies and not the IMF. The IMF, according to this group, should not have provided any short- or long-term rescue packages to the Asian countries and should have refrained from any engagement in bailing out these countries in the wake of their financial crisis.

Second, many analysts, led by Allan Meltzer (1998), argue that bailout packages by the IMF create the risk of moral hazard.[17] The central point of the moral hazard argument, which is based on the experience of the Mexican bailout of 1995, is that if international investors and creditors are convinced that the IMF will guarantee the availability of dollars to meet foreign-exchange obligations of a debtor country, they will not carefully examine the country's risk level in making their lending and investment decisions. It is also possible that governments in debtor countries may pursue unnecessarily risky courses of action under a false sense of security that the IMF will ultimately bail them out. While people in the crisis countries suffer misery because of the crisis-induced recession, creditors and investors do not bear a fair share of the burden of the crisis, as the IMF-guaranteed rescue packages can eventually bail them out.

While the logic of the moral hazard argument is valid, the evidence from Asia suggests that it is not empirically relevant. For example, there is no direct evidence to suggest that the massive inflow of foreign capital into the Asian region after 1995 was related to expectations of international bailouts in the aftermath of the Mexican rescue package (Corsetti, Presenti, and Roubini, 1998: 20). Also, the IMF has repeatedly pointed out that by the end of 1997, foreign investors had lost nearly three-quarters of their equity holdings in Thailand, Indonesia, and Korea (Lane et al., 1999).

Conclusions and Lessons

This analysis shows that while economic factors can explain why the Asian crisis occurred, the timing and subsequent management of the crisis can only be explained by domestic political factors. In particular, the structure and role of political institutions are critical to explain why political leaders in Thailand were not able to take effective and quick policy decisions and why political leaders in Korea and Indonesia lacked credibility. While the spread of the crisis in Indonesia and Korea can be attributed to a lack of credibility of political leaders, Thailand's crisis clearly reflects its government's indecisiveness and ineffective leadership due to political conditions.

The role of the IMF in managing the crisis has raised many questions from the market fundamentalists and the pragmatic liberals. Both schools of thought have criticized how the IMF managed the crisis, albeit on different grounds. The market fundamentalists have criticized the wrong structural policies of the inefficient and corrupt governments in Asia and the potential creation of moral hazard by the IMF bailout packages. The pragmatic liberals, on the other hand, have focused on the IMF's failure to diagnose the Asian crisis as a liquidity crisis and the consequent inappropriate policies it pursued to address the crisis.

With the deepening of the crisis in Korea, Indonesia, and Thailand, the IMF in January 1999 acknowledged for the first time that the Asian crisis was, in fact, a liquidity crisis due to the accumulation of short-term liabilities (Lane et al., 1999).[18] It also recognized the social costs of implementing its structural reform policies. Not surprisingly, the IMF showed a willingness to renegotiate some of its reform packages with Indonesia, Thailand, and Korea during the later part of the crisis. But with evidence of a Korean recovery in late 1999, the IMF began reasserting that rising interest rates and tight fiscal policies were essential in preventing capital flight. It also insisted that without structural reforms, sustained recovery for the Asian countries would not be possible.[19]

While the debate on the efficacy and appropriateness of the IMF's structural reform policies is likely to continue, the analysis of the Asian financial crisis here suggests at least five lessons. First, although the benefits of free capital mobility are numerous (Fischer, 1997), capital account liberalization will have to be gradual, cautiously and carefully managed by policymakers in emerging economies. As long as these countries' financial systems are weak, poorly regulated, and subject to political distortions, any hasty move for capital account liberalization will be counterproductive and produce destabilizing effects on the economy. As evident from Latin America, freeing capital flows may even lead to capital flight, which will be very destructive for less-developed countries (Carvalho, 2001). It is particularly unwise to undertake capital account liberalization during a currency crisis. The main reason why China and India were not so adversely affected by the financial crisis in Asia was because of their policies of currency inconvertibility and capital controls.[20] Malaysia also was able to deal with the financial crisis more effectively than Indonesia and Thailand because of its policy of selective capital controls. Thus capital controls may not be a bad idea until emerging economies are able to develop strong financial, regulatory, and institutional systems.

Second, the Asian crisis clearly demonstrated the need for strengthening domestic banking and financial systems to achieve sustainable economic growth. Deficiency in the banking sectors and poor banking oversight, a lack of transparency about each bank's operations, and conditions and connected lending contributed to the severity of the crisis in Asia. To protect their markets from short-term investment boom and undesirable shifts of capital flows, policymakers in emerging economies need to devise an appropriately prudent regulatory and supervisory framework that covers capital adequacy, lending standards, asset valuation, transparency in operations, bankruptcy laws, and other aspects of governance.

Third, when countries come to the IMF with a severe macroeconomic crisis, they are subject to painful and comprehensive reform conditions.

Emerging economies can take two proactive measures to escape from the politically hazardous IMF austerity conditions. First, they can approach the IMF for technical advice and modest financial help long before their economies reach a crisis point. By so doing, they may be able to negotiate IMF loans with less-stringent conditions. If denied the IMF loan, their relatively healthy economic conditions will enable them to explore alternative loan facilities from private banks that are not often available to debtor countries in more severe macroeconomic crisis. Second, developing countries should try to spend their export earnings prudently and seek to accumulate large foreign currency reserves to avoid any speculative currency attacks. Using their scarce foreign exchange for any unproductive expenditure, like politically expedient projects, is almost always a recipe for economic disaster.

The fourth lesson is that the global legitimacy of the IMF would be stronger if less-developed countries come to perceive it as a genuine friend when in need rather than as an institution seeking to pursue the trade and investment agenda of the G7 countries. The IMF should avoid using currency crises as opportunities to impose long-term structural and institutional reforms on troubled countries. If a troubled country's problem is one of short-term liquidity, the IMF should come out with a financial package to deal with it quickly rather than insisting on long-term structural reform. IMF's long-term structural reform conditions, which are based on the Washington Consensus principles, usually take a long time to negotiate and implement, resulting in a loss of precious time and making a bad situation worse.

Finally, the IMF should assume more of a crisis prevention role rather than that of a crisis manager. In order to accomplish this goal, it must provide technical and financial help and advice to those countries that are not yet experiencing a full-blown currency crisis. The important task is to encourage preemptive actions that will prevent a large current account deficit or excessive short-term debt that could later precipitate a crisis. The IMF must focus on this agenda rather than bailing out international lenders and domestic borrowers after a currency crisis has occurred. Ultimately, the most critical challenge for the IMF is to reverse its image from that of an irresponsive imposer of painful structural reform policies, intruding into a country's sovereign policymaking process, to one of a supportive, multilateral financial institution interested in the debtor country's monetary stability and economic progress. That is not a difficult goal to achieve, provided the major creditor countries show willingness to assume greater responsibility for making the IMF more responsive to the changing needs and goals of the emerging economies rather than perpetuating their own agenda. After all, it is in the interests of all Fund members to maintain the stability of the international financial architecture.

Notes

1. For a critical review of the Asian miracle thesis, see Krugman (1994); Baer, Miles, and Moran (1999).

2. The economies of Korea, Thailand, Indonesia, and Malaysia had for many years been seen as miracles of economic growth, with average annual growth rate since 1970 ranging from 6.9 percent in Indonesia to 8.4 percent in South Korea (Berg and Pattillo, 2000).

3. For the sake of argument, I include the following analysts in the market fundamentalist group: Anna J. Schwartz of Cato Institute, Professor Allan Meltzer, Craig Burnside, Martin Eichenbaum, and Sergio Rebelo. In the pragmatic liberal group, I include Jeffrey Sachs, Joseph Stiglitz, Dani Rodrik, and Walden Bello, to cite just a few.

4. According to the Bank of Thailand (BoT *Quarterly Bulletin,* 1996: 83), Thailand's portfolio investment increased sixfold from 23.5 billion baht in 1992 to 138 billion baht in 1993.

5. The ratio of foreign investment to GDP rose to around 40 percent during the early 1990s. Net private inflows to Indonesia, Malaysia, South Korea, Thailand, and the Philippines jumped from $40.5 billion in 1994 to $92.8 billion in 1996, then changed to a $12 billion outflow in 1997 (Wolf, 1997). In Thailand alone during 1990–1996, the investment ratio (gross domestic investment as a percentage of GDP) was between 40 percent and 44 percent, compared to average investment ratios of 25 percent and 30 percent during the 1980–1984 and 1985–1989 periods respectively (OBI, 1996: 3). Also see the analysis by Jeffrey Sachs and Wing Thye Woo (2000: 9).

6. Current account deficits occur when a country's imports exceed its exports. Large and growing current account deficits have two adverse consequences for a soft currency country. Unlike hard currencies such as the dollar, the euro, and the yen, soft currency is not internationally convertible. First, the country experiences a sharp decline in the value of its local currency because foreign creditors and domestic investors become concerned that the borrower will be unable to service its debt. As a result of this loss of confidence, speculative attacks on the currency and flight of capital may take place. As investors buy hard currencies and release more local currencies, an increase in the money supply occurs; with an increase in the money supply, the value of the local currency tends to depreciate further. Second, in order to defend the value of their currency, governments use their forex reserves. Extensive usage of forex reserves combined with a lack of adequate export earnings lead to a rapid depletion of foreign-exchange reserves.

7. The term *casino capitalism* (Strange, 1986) describes well this practice of short-term borrowing and lending in Thailand. Given high interest rates in Thailand (compared to low interest rates in Japan and the United States) and a fixed exchange rate policy, foreign investors were eager to provide short-term loans to Thai banks. Foreign and domestic investors were able to borrow at an interest rate of 5–8 percent from abroad and deposit in Thai banks to obtain 10–11 percent interest rates. Thus they could earn money simply by borrowing from abroad and depositing in Thai banks. As a consequence, too much offshore, short-term borrowing went on in Thailand. Thailand's external debt increased from $40 billion in 1992 to $80 billion in March 1997. Thailand's total outstanding debt as a share of GDP increased from 34 percent in 1990 to 51 percent in 1996. See Lauridsen (1998: 138–139).

8. Political transaction cost refers to alliances between the government, business, labor unions, opposition parties, and other dominant domestic groups such as

military and religious groups to take and implement policy decisions. Weak governments often fail to take and implement economic reform decisions quickly because of the nature of this alliance.

9. Before 1988, South Korea had a highly centralized political system. Under the 1988 constitution, South Korea became a multiparty democratic system with powers shared between the president and legislature. The president, elected for a term of five years by direct popular vote, is chief of state, head of the executive branch, and commander-in-chief of the armed forces. The legislative power is vested in the unicameral national assembly, which consists of 299 members who are elected to four-year terms.

10. Broadly speaking, the Washington Consensus approach recommends that governments pursue the following policies to achieve economic growth: (1) maintain macroeconomic stability by controlling inflation and reducing fiscal deficits; (2) undertake trade and capital account liberalization; and (3) liberalize domestic product and factor markets through privatization and deregulation.

11. Joseph Stiglitz, the Nobel Prize winner in economics, resigned as World Bank chief economist in 2000 as a result of his differences with the policies of the IMF in general and on the Asia crisis in particular.

12. See the interview of Joseph Stiglitz in *Business Week*, 19 November 2001. Also see the informative commentary by Pete Engardio in *Business Week*, 26 November 2001.

13. In the IMF's lending decisions, the United States alone enjoys a little over 17 percent of the total vote, and the dominant G5 coalition (United States, Japan, France, Germany, and United Kingdom) controls 39 percent. For the IMF's lending decisions, 85 percent of the total vote is necessary. Thus, either the G5 countries together or the United States alone can effectively veto a loan decision. See http://www.imf.org/external/np/sec/memdir/eds.htm

14. In her testimony to a U.S. House Ways and Means subcommittee, former U.S. trade representative Charlene Barshefsky succinctly summed up how U.S. interests could be furthered by the IMF's policies in Asia. She argued, "Many of the structural reform components of the IMF packages will contribute directly to improvements in the trade regimes in those countries. If effectively implemented, these programs will complement and reinforce our trade policy goals." USTR website, http://www.ustr.gov/pdf/1998tpa_ix.pdf (24 February 1998).

15. See the arguments of the Treasury secretary, Lawrence Summers, about the role of the IMF in Asia in *Treasury News*, RR 2226 (1998).

16. The Japan Inc. model focuses on links between state actors, business groups, and banking institutions to promote industrial development. Essentially, in this model the government guides banks to lend to favored industries in exchange for an implicit guarantee of the loans. Thus equity capital for new industrial projects comes from state-supported, soft banking loans rather than from the markets. This is the dynamic of the capitalist developmental states in Asia, particularly in Japan, South Korea, Taiwan, and Singapore.

17. The moral hazard argument was most clearly articulated by Allan Meltzer in 1997, in what is known as the Meltzer Report. This report was produced by a special committee of the U.S. House of Representatives, under the chairmanship of Meltzer.

18. In January 1999, the IMF published a preliminary assessment paper on the Asian crisis by Lane et al. on its web ite. In this paper, the authors defended the IMF's tight monetary policies, such as raising interest rates, but they also acknowledged that the Asian crisis was largely a liquidity crisis and that the IMF made a wrong diagnosis of the Asian economies on which its structural adjustment pro-

grams were formulated. Significantly, a summary of the comments made by the IMF's Executive Board on this issue appeared in the text of this paper. It was later published as an IMF occasional paper in June 1999.

19. The former managing director of the IMF, Michel Camdessus, is a champion of this view. See Camdessus (1998).

20. Krugman (1998) makes this point quite emphatically.

References

Aggarwal, Raj. 1999. "Assessing the Recent Asian Economic Crisis: The Role of Virtuous and Vicious Cycles." *Journal of World Business* 31, 4 (Winter): 1–14.

Altbach, Eric. 1997. "The Asian Monetary Fund Proposal: A Case Study of Japanese Regional Leadership." *Japan Economic Institute Report* 47A (December 19).

Baer, Werner, William R. Miles, and Allen B. Moran. 1999. "The End of the Asian Myth: Why Were the Experts Fooled?" *World Development* 27, 10: 1735–1747.

Bangkok Post. 1998. "IMF Agrees to Relax Condition." (13 February).

Bank of Thailand (BoT). 1996. *Quarterly Bulletin* (June).

Bello, Walden. 1998. "East Asia: On the Eve of Great Transformation?" *Review of International Political Economy* 5, 3 (Autumn): 424–444.

Berg, Andrew and Catherine Pattillo. 2000. *The Challenge of Predicting Economic Crises.* Washington, DC: International Monetary Fund Publication Services.

Brauchi, Marcus, Darren McDermott and David Wessel. 1997. "Southeast Asia Seems Still on Track to Grow Despite Currency Slide. *Wall Street Journal* (5 August).

Bullard, Nicola, Walden Bello, and Kamal Malhotra. 1998. "Taming the Tigers: The IMF and the Asian Crisis." In K. S. Jomo, ed., *Tigers in Trouble: Financial Governance, Liberalization and Crisis in East Asia,* 85–132. London: Zed Books Ltd.

Burnside, Craig, Martin Eichenbaum, and Sergio Rebelo. 1998. "Prospective Deficits and Asian Currency Crisis." Federal Reserve Bank of Chicago, Working paper WP-98-5.

Business Week. 2001. "Nobel Laureate, IMF Protester." (19 November).

Camdessus, Michel. 1998. "Crisis in Emerging Market Economics: The Road to Recovery," www.imf.org/external/np/speeches/1998/091598.htm.

Carvalho, Cardim de. 2001. "The IMF as Crisis Manager: An Assessment of the Strategy in Asia and Its Criticisms." *Journal of Post Keynesian Economics* 23, 2 (Winter): 235–267.

Corsetti, Giancarlo, Paolo Presenti, and Nouriel Roubini. 1998. "What Caused the Asian Currency and Financial Crisis?" In *Financial Crisis: Contagion and Market Volatility.* Papers presented at the CEPR–World Bank conference, University of Washington, May.

Dixit, Avinash. 1997. *The Making of Economic Policy: A Transaction Cost Politics Perspective.* Cambridge, MA: MIT Press.

Eichengreen, Barry, Michael Mussa, Giovanni Dell Ariccia, Enrica Detragiache, Gian Maria Milesi-Ferretti, and Andrew Tweedie. 1999. "Liberalizing Capital Movements: Some Analytical Issues." *IMF Economic Issues* 17. (February).

Engardio, Pete. 2001. "Commentary: Don't Use the IMF to Push U.S. Foreign Policy." *Business Week,* (26 November).

Feldstein, Martin. 1998. "Refocusing the IMF." *Foreign Affairs* 77, 2 (March/April): 20–33.

Fischer, Stanley. 1997. "Capital Account Liberalization and the Role of the IMF." *IMF Economic Issues* (September).

Goldstein, Morris. 1998. *The Asian Financial Crisis: Causes, Cures, and Systemic Implications.* Washington, DC: Institute for International Economics.

Gore, Charles, 2000. "The Rise and Fall of the Washington Consensus as a Paradigm for Developing Countries," *World Development,* vol. 28, no. 5, 789–804.

Haggard, Stephan. 1990. *Pathways from the Periphery: The Politics of Growth in Newly Industrializing Countries.* Ithaca, NY: Cornell University Press.

Haggard, Stephan and Robert Kaufman. 1992. "Institutions and Economic Adjustment. In Stephan Haggard and Robert Kaufman, eds., *The Politics of Economic Adjustment: International Constraints, Distributive Politics, and the State.* Princeton, NJ: Princeton University Press.

Haggard, Stephen and Andrew MacIntyre. 1998. "The Political Economy of the Asian Economic Crisis." *Review of International Political Economy* 5, 3 (Autumn): 381–392.

Halcomb, Darrin and David Marshall. 2001. "A Retrospective on the Asian Crisis of 1997: Was It Foreseen?" *Chicago Fed Letter* 161 (January).

International Monetary Fund. 1998. *World Economic Outlook.* Washington, DC: IMF.

Jakarta Post. 1998. "Indonesia–Memorandum of Economic and Financial Policies." (17 January).

Krugman, Paul. 1994. "The Myth of Asia's Miracle." *Foreign Affairs* 74: 62–78.

———. 1998. "What Happened to Asia?" MIT, Working paper, available at: http://web.mit.edu/krugman/www/

Lane, Timothy, Atish Ghosh, Javier Hamann, Steven Phillips, Marianne Schultze-Ghattas, Tsidi Tsikata. 1999. "IMF-supported Programs in Indonesia, Korea, and Thailand." IMF Occasional paper 178 (June), available at: www.imf.org/external/pubs/ft/op/op178/index.htm

Lauridsen, Laurids S. 1998. "Thailand: Causes, Conduct, Consequences." In K. S. Jomo, ed., *Tigers in Trouble: Financial Governance, Liberalization and Crisis in East Asia,* 138–161. London: Zed Books Ltd.

Meltzer, Allan H. 1998. *Moral Hazard Goes Global: The IMF, Mexico, and Asia.* Washington, DC: American Enterprise Institute.

Montagnon, Peter and Ted Bardacke. 1998. "A Year of Reckoning." *Financial Times* (1 July).

OBI Report (Office of the Board of Investment). 1996. "Key Investment Indicators in Thailand." Royal Thai Government (May): 1–44.

Overholt, William H. 1999. "Thailand's Financial and Political Systems: Crisis and Rejuvenation." *Asian Survey* 39, 6 (November/December): 1009–1035.

Rodrik, Dani. 1998. "Who Needs Capital Account Convertibility?" *Essays in International Finance* 207 (May). Princeton, NJ: Princeton University, International Finance Section.

Sachs, Jeffrey and Steven Radelet. 1998. *The Onset of the East Asian Financial Crisis.* Cambridge, MA: Harvard Institute for International Development (HIID).

Sachs, Jeffrey and Wing Thye Woo. 2000. "The Asian Financial Crisis: What Happened, and What Is To Be Done." In *The Asia Competitiveness Report 1999.* World Economic Forum Reports and Publications (29 November).

Schwartz, Anna J. 1998. "A Time to Terminate the ESF and the IMF." Institute.

Cato Foreign Policy Brief 48 (August), available at: http://www.ciaonet.org/pbei/cato/sza01.html

Steinfeld, Edward S. 1998. "The Asian Financial Crisis: Beijing's Year of Reckoning." *The Washington Quarterly* 21, 3 (Summer): 37–51.

Stiglitz, Joseph E. 1998. "Macroeconomic Dimensions of the East Asian Crisis." In Robert Chote, ed., *Financial Crises and Asia*. London: Center for Economic Policy Research.

———. 2001. "Failure of the Fund: Rethinking the IMF Response." *Harvard International Review* 23, 2 (Summer): 14–18.

Strange, Susan. 1998. *Casino Capitalism*. Oxford: Blackwell.

Summers, Lawrence. 1998. The Role of Multilateral Institutions in Preserving International Financial Stability. *Treasury News*, RR 2226.

Wolf, Martin. 1997. "Flow and Blows." *Financial Times*, 3 March.

World Bank. 1993. *The East Asian Miracle*. New York: Oxford University Press.

18

The Euro Debuts:
European Money, Global Money, or Both?

Olufemi A. Babarinde

In the history of regional economic integration schemes, the European experience has been the most visible and successful. Olufemi Babarinde provides a detailed account of Europe's march toward monetary integration. Beginning with the adoption of the Werner Plan in 1970, his chapter traces the many forward steps and setbacks leading to European monetary union and the introduction of the euro in early 2002. He clarifies the political and economic rationale for a single currency, the stages and policy actions taken to promote convergence among the EU economies, the costs and benefits of participating in the monetary arrangement, and the interstate conflicts and sovereignty issues surrounding the management of the euro. For the reader not intimately familiar with the concepts and dynamics of international monetary relations, this chapter provides a substantive foundation within the context of intra-European affairs.

On January 1, 2002, the European single currency, otherwise known as the euro, made its debut in twelve of the fifteen member countries of the European Union (EU).[1] This marked the commencement of the second transition in the EU's inexorable and steady march toward Economic and Monetary Union (EMU). The first was begun on January 1, 1999, when the euro was effectively launched, albeit in abstraction, that is, for invoicing, bookkeeping, and contractual purposes. The first transition, which terminated at the end of 2001, was designed to gradually promote the single currency and to enable consumers in Europe and beyond to acclimatize to the eventual arrival of the physical euro.[2] The second transition began with the distribution and availability of euro notes and coins throughout the "euro zone" and effectively ended on March 1, 2002, the day the euro became the sole legal tender of "Euroland."[3] The arrival of the physical euro was kicked off by "The Euro: Our Money" campaign in August 2001.

The introduction of euro banknotes and coins in Euroland constituted

291

one of the most extraordinary, captivating, and far-reaching watersheds in the evolution of European integration, especially since the end of the Cold War and the reunification of Germany in October 1990. The development was extraordinary because it amounted to the most significant transfer of sovereignty by EU member states to date. It was equally captivating because it was an adventure into uncharted waters by so many countries at the same time, all trying to dance to the same tune. The launch of the euro also implied numerous, far-reaching implications, touching virtually every facet of society within the euro zone and beyond. The arrival of the physical euro tested the logistical and coordinating deftness of the EU as it distributed 38 billion coins and 6.5 billion banknotes. Furthermore, the inauguration of euro notes and coins was a vindication of the stage-by-stage, gradualist strategy that was prescribed by Jean Monnet and Robert Schuman, the progenitors of the European Union, some four decades earlier (Schuman, 1998; Monnet, 1962, 1978).

In any event, despite the gradual inauguration of the euro since 1999, the palpable anticipation of its arrival, and its successful debut, it is still greeted with skepticism in some parts of Europe and elsewhere, especially in the United States. The cynicism is about the euro's viability and credibility as a European currency, let alone as a currency for international commerce. For example, despite the smooth introduction of euro banknotes and coins, the euro is still being greeted with caution in international financial markets.[4]

Is the enterprise of creating a single currency for Europe, therefore, nothing more than a quixotic undertaking and an ill-advised idea that is doomed to fail? Will the euro dream turn into a terrible nightmare for its architects and practitioners? Will the euro gain international acceptance and respectability as a credible alternative and rival to the U.S. dollar? What are the implications of the advent of the euro for international commerce, businesses of varied sizes, governments of Europe, and so on? How is the euro to be managed and by which institutions/individuals? These and other questions will be the focus of this inquiry.

The discourse here is intended to explain the nuances, evolution, challenges, and inception of the euro. It is designed to address lingering concerns in some quarters that it is a flawed undertaking by the EU. It aims to debunk the perception by skeptics that the euro initiative was hastily engineered and doomed to fail. It will be argued that the evolution of the euro spanned roughly three decades of diligent and meticulous planning by its architects, and thus it is likely to succeed.

Rationales for the (Euro) Single Currency

It is fitting to reflect on the underlying rationales for the EU's adoption of a single currency. Broadly, the justifications are both political and economic. Four specific imperatives of the euro are as follow:

The Single European Market (SEM) Imperative

In the mid-1980s, the EU launched an initiative that was designed to create a single market from its member states' differing economies, thereby enabling factor mobility and the free movement of goods and services by January 1, 1993. A single currency is widely believed, especially in the EU, to be a natural and logical complement of a unified European market. According to the European Commission and others, without a single currency the full benefits of a single market may not be realized (Commission of the European Communities, 1992; Emerson et al., 1992; Padoa-Schioppa, 1987). Moreover, it is absurd to speak of a single market without a single currency or its own money. Besides, according to various estimates (Cecchini, 1988), by themselves the SEM and the euro are expected to significantly boost Europe's gross domestic product (GDP). Together, however, both initiatives are expected to boost growth in the EU even more and reduce unemployment therein (Temperton, 1998). Additionally, the euro is expected to boost both intra- and extra-Euroland trade (Rose, 2000).

The Optimal Currency Area Imperative

According to the theory of optimal currency area (OCA), which dates back to the early 1960s, two or more countries should consider a single currency on the basis of the following considerations (Mundell, 1961; Kenen, 1969): first, if they are economically identical and their business cycles are synchronized; second, if the countries in question are advanced/industrialized and enjoy a high degree of economic diversification; third, if the countries enjoy factor mobility among themselves but factor immobility with third countries; and fourth, if the countries are relatively open and enjoy high bilateral trade intensity. On the basis of these conditions, it is arguable that EU economies are fairly identical, given their comparable affluence. As well, there is evidence of a common business cycle, at least for some member states of the euro zone.[5] They share the common traits of being mature, industrial, and diversified economies (Apel, 1998; Bini-Smaghi and Vori, 1993).[6] Furthermore, factor mobility is more of a possibility/reality nowadays, especially since the advent of the SEM, and member states' economies are fairly open. Given these commonalities, the case for a single currency within the EU may be equal to that for a single currency in the United States (Taylor, 1995; Emerson et al., 1992; Caparole, 1993).[7]

The European Peace Imperative

As with virtually every facet of European integration since its foundation was laid in 1951 in the Treaty of Paris, the desire to preserve and strengthen the peace in Europe remains the most basic political justification for the euro. The presumption is that adoption of the euro will strengthen European identity, bolster European solidarity, and contribute to the peace that has existed in the EU since World War II. This political imperative thus derives from an abiding raison d'être of European integration, which is to forge an ever closer union among the peoples of Europe, whereby war between member states will not only be improbable but also unthinkable. For some, "The Euro is much more than just a currency. It is a symbol of European integration in every sense of the word."[8]

The German Reunification Imperative

The other political justification is the abrupt fall of the Iron Curtain and the concomitant rapid collapse of communist governments in Eastern Europe in 1989–1990, which profoundly altered the European landscape. It meant that German reunification was now more attainable than at any time since its partition after World War II. There was, however, increasing angst in some EU capitals that reunification would tilt the German government "eastward," and it would be less committed to the European integration agenda. France, in particular, sought and obtained Germany's support for the single currency in exchange for dropping its objections to German reunification (Temperton, 1998: 8). For France, the EMU initiative would, in no small measure, further tie Germany to the EU agenda and keep European integration on Germany's radar screen. In other words, the quid pro quo was essentially a political arrangement between two old foes that further reinforces the significance of their alliance as the most important and most resilient in the European integration enterprise.

Evolution of the Euro: From Conception to Inception

The Werner Plan

The birth of the euro is the culmination of a long and arduous march toward EMU in Europe, commenced more than three decades earlier. The journey effectively started in 1969, when a powerful committee chaired by Pierre Werner, the prime minister of Luxembourg, was appointed by the EU to explore how EMU could be achieved. In 1971, the European Council of Heads of Government and of State subsequently adopted the committee's 1970 report as the "Werner Plan" (Apel, 1998; Watson, 1997; Taylor, 1995; Britto and Mayes, 1992; Barrell, 1992). It proposed a blueprint for achieving EMU by 1980, including the possible adoption of a single currency. As with regional integration in general and with everything about the EU in particular, EMU would be established in stages, beginning with the narrowing of the permissible exchange rate margin of fluctuation against the U.S. dollar and the strengthening of the coordination of domestic/economic policies by participating European countries. Following a transition phase,

EMU would ultimately be established when exchange rates were totally fixed and barriers to the movement of capital were completely eradicated. The plan envisaged an EMU that would facilitate factor mobility, free movement of goods and services, and a more united Europe.

The timing could not have been more inauspicious for the implementation of the Werner Plan, because developments in the international currency/capital markets hindered its implementation. Specifically, speculative pressures on the U.S. dollar in May 1971 eventually led to the U.S. government's decision in August to suspend the dollar's convertibility into gold. The six EU member states reacted differently to both external developments. First, in response to speculative attacks against the dollar and the subsequent large inflows of short-term capital to Europe, the Belgian, German, and Dutch bourses were closed. In response to the collapse of the Bretton Woods system in August 1971, Germany and four other EU countries temporarily floated their currencies against the dollar, while France maintained the parity of the franc against the dollar, albeit coupled with a two-tier foreign-exchange market and new restrictions on capital inflows.

The Snake in the Tunnel

The crumbling of the Bretton Woods system, which unleashed currency volatility in Europe and in the global market, further convinced European leaders of the need for EMU. Accordingly, in April 1972 and in reaction to what they deemed an unacceptable Smithsonian Agreement,[9] they limited the fluctuation margins of their currencies against one another to 2.25 percent. Otherwise known as the Basel Agreement, the pact created the so-called snake-in-the-tunnel regime, because it maintained a maximum fluctuation band of 2.25 percent between any two EU currencies (the "snake") while simultaneously maintaining the Smithsonian 4.5 percent fluctuation spread against the dollar (the "tunnel") (Apel, 1998; Watson, 1997; Taylor, 1995; Britto and Mayes, 1992; Barrell, 1992). The EU regime was thus designed both to facilitate EMU in Europe and to comply with the Smithsonian Agreement. Although designed to restore currency stability in the EU in the wake of the economic crises of the early 1970s, the regime was considered too strict and untenable because of its limited margin for maneuver. In fact, the regime was regularly breached with impunity by participating countries because they found it difficult to cope with speculative attacks on their currencies. Moreover, the energy crisis of the early 1970s and the attendant stagflation and increasing unemployment exacerbated the economic climate. The regime was thus abandoned in 1978.[10]

The European Monetary System

In its stead, a new regime, the European Monetary System (EMS), was launched in 1979 to create a zone of internal and external monetary stability by halting uncontrollable exchange rate fluctuations. It was also designed to combat inflation, unemployment, and other economic maladies of the late 1970s, as well as to promote macroeconomic policy coordination and the convergence of economic performances. The EMS, which was designed to foster intra-EU trade and advance European integration, also created an exchange rate mechanism (ERM) that added a wider fluctuating band (±6 percent around the bilateral central rate) to the ±2.25 percent band of the previous regime. The wider band was intended to encourage maximum and enduring participation by member states, including countries with weaker currencies (e.g., Italy), and thus enhance the credibility of the system. The ERM also included a 75 percent divergence intervention threshold that determined when the central banks and governments of participating states could rescue a currency in trouble. It was further endowed with a credit mechanism to provide short-term monetary support and medium-term financial assistance to needy participating countries. Additionally, the EMS introduced the European currency unit (ECU), which was a basket of currencies that reflected the relative strengths of participating currencies.[11] The EMS was a movement from the totally fixed exchange rate system of the past toward a "dirty" floating regime of sorts, because participating currencies were allowed to float against other currencies, and participating central banks periodically intervened when deemed necessary.

Whereas virtually all EU member states joined the EMS as soon as they were eligible to do so, some waited before acceding to the ERM. The learning curve from the snake regime facilitated a zone of monetary stability, encouraging Spain (1989), Norway and the UK (1990), Finland and Sweden (1991), and Portugal and Cyprus (1992) to join the ERM. By most accounts, the EMS was fairly successful in achieving its objectives during its first decade of operations. There was evidence of reduced volatility in intra-EMS exchange rates, decreasing exchange rate risk, reduced inflation rates, economic convergence, and increased policy cooperation (Frömmel and Menkhoff, 2001; McDonald and Zis, 1989; Apel, 1998: 72–77).[12]

The Delors Report

Encouraged by the favorable results of the EMS and the economic upswing in Europe during the early 1980s, the EU launched its SEM initiative in 1985 in its bid to establish a bona fide common market by January 1, 1993 (Commission of the European Communities, 1985). The completion of the internal market basically entailed the removal of all outstanding barriers to factor mobility, goods, and services, the harmonization of laws, and the coordination of policies. With the SEM program on course and buoyed by the generally favorable performance of the EMS, the European Council appointed a special committee in 1988 to explore and propose concrete stages that could result in the realization of EMU. The committee was comprised of the central bank governors of member states and five other experts, including Jacques Delors—then president of the European Commission—as its chair. In what amounted to a blueprint for EMU, the recommendations of the committee were published in 1989 in what is widely known as the "Delors Report" (Commission of the European Communities, 1989). Like the Werner Plan, it, too, proposed a three-stage approach but generally avoided the minefield of a timetable with fixed deadlines. It proposed, however, that the first stage should begin no later than July 1, 1990, when a previous agreement on the liberalization of capital movement was due to enter into effect.

Stage I required the participation of all EU members in the ERM at the ±2.25 percent margin, the removal of remaining barriers to the movement of capital in the EU, and increased cooperation among EU governments and their central banks over monetary and macroeconomic policies. In Stage II, intervention in the ERM would be limited only to when significant deviations occurred, and a European System of Central Banks (ESCB) would be gradually established. In Stage III, a totally fixed exchange rate system that could eventually lead to a single currency would be created, and the ESCB would assume unmitigated jurisdiction over EU monetary policies. It is noteworthy that the Delors Report identified the ESCB's principal purpose as price stability, a clear reflection of the influence of the Bundesbank—the German central bank—on the committee and the desire to assuage German concerns that the new arrangement would adequately fight inflation.

At its June 1989 summit, the European Council endorsed the Delors Report and took the decision to begin Stage I of EMU on July 1, 1990. At another European Council meeting in June 1990, it was agreed that two intergovernmental conferences (IGCs) would convene in December 1990 to negotiate and conclude separate agreements on EMU and European Political Union (EPU). That decision was later followed by another European Council announcement in October 1990 that Stage II of EMU would commence on January 1, 1994. Finally, at its December 1990 summit, the European Council inaugurated the two IGCs. It took virtually all of 1991 for both IGCs to barely complete the sometimes contentious negotiations. The resultant draft treaty that was signed in December 1991 required ratification by all member states.

The process hit a snag in June 1992, when Danish voters by a thin margin rejected the treaty in a referendum, partly due to concerns about EMU and loss of sovereignty and national identity. Additional discomforts in the EU by mid-1992 included evidence of economic recession in the wake of the 1991 Gulf War and the Bundesbank's decision to maintain high interest rates as a countervailing measure to the reunification of Germany. To the extent that ERM countries had pegged their currencies to the deutschemark and had de facto relinquished sovereignty over monetary policy to the

Bundesbank, most EU countries were at the mercy of the Bundesbank. Mounting expectations that the independent Bundesbank would cut its long-term rates were routinely dashed as rates were instead increased, much to the dismay and discomfort of Germany's EMS partners. Efforts by the Kohl government in Bonn to persuade the Bundesbank to lower rates in order to help its EMS partners were to no avail (Smith and Sandholtz, 1995).[13] Ironically, the Bundesbank's decisions to raise rates stemmed from concerns that the government was indulging in excessive spending to prop up the economies of the five states (*Länder*) of eastern Germany. Besides, whereas the easing of interest rates might have boded well for Germany's partners, such a move could potentially have nudged inflation upward in Germany. This steadfast anti-inflationary policy by the Germans was not without cost, because it seemed in early September 1992 that the French electorate would not ratify the Maastricht Treaty in a referendum.[14]

In light of these developments, currency traders unleashed unrelenting attacks on the Italian lira and the British pound. Following unsuccessful and embarrassing currency realignments to fend off further attacks on their currencies, Italy and the UK withdrew from the ERM in September 1992. Shortly thereafter, the Spanish, Portuguese, and Irish currencies became the new targets of currency speculators and were devalued. Finally, in summer 1993, the French franc came under ferocious attacks from currency speculators, which almost led to withdrawal of the French from the ERM, a move that would have in effect meant the demise of the EMS and possibly of the EMU dream. Instead, a political compromise was expeditiously reached after marathon meetings mainly in Paris to replace the 2.25 percent and the 6 percent bands with a ±15 percent band, largely to neutralize currency speculators and accommodate the French. Normalcy was thereafter restored, and the EMU agenda was saved.

The Maastricht Treaty and the Last Stretch to EMU

The Treaty on European Union (TEU), otherwise known as the Maastricht Treaty, entered into force on November 1, 1993, after eventual ratification by the then twelve member states.[15] The treaty, inter alia, essentially codified the three-stage EMU plan of the Delors Report but was more specific in a number of areas, including the explicit support of a single European currency as the culmination of an EMU.[16] Stage I of the Delors Report, on the liberalization of capital movement within the EU, had commenced on July 1, 1990. In accordance with Article 109e of the treaty, Stage II began on January 1, 1994, with the inauguration of the European Monetary Institute (EMI) as the forerunner of the European Central Bank (ECB). Afterward, at a December 1995 summit in Spain, the European Council chose the euro as the name of the new currency.

In keeping with the TEU, the European Council met at a specially convened summit in Brussels on May 1–3, 1998, to determine and announce those member states that qualified for single currency participation/membership. On the basis of criteria established in the treaty, the European Commission and the EMI recommended eleven of the EU countries to the council. Denmark and the UK exercised their previously negotiated option not to participate in the single currency as yet, while Greece and Sweden were adjudged not to have fulfilled the convergence criteria.[17] The TEU essentially stipulated six criteria—four quantifiable (inflation, interest rate, budget deficit, and public debt) and two nonquantifiable (currency stability and central bank independence)—purposely to facilitate economic convergence ahead of monetary union.[18] They were:

- Price stability: average rate of inflation during the preceding year must not exceed by more than 1.5 percent that of the three best-performing member states;
- Interest rate: average, nominal long-term interest rate over the previous year must not exceed by more than 2 percent that of the three member states with the lowest rates;
- Budget deficit: national budget deficit must not exceed 3 percent of the country's GDP;
- Public debt: public debt must not be in excess of 60 percent of the GDP;
- Currency stability: participation in the normal fluctuation margins in the ERM necessary for at least two years "without severe tensions," that is, without devaluation;
- Central bank: statutory steps must be undertaken before consideration for membership to ensure the independence of the central bank/monetary institutions.

It was announced that eleven EU member states had been admitted to the "euro zone."[19] It was further announced at the summit that a three-year transition period had been agreed upon between the irrevocable fixing of exchange rates and the appearance of the physical euro as a legal tender in the participating countries. In further compliance with the Maastricht Treaty, Willem Duisenberg, president of the EMI, was eventually appointed the first president of the ECB. The appointment was, however, preceded by an acrimonious debate, which pitted France against its EU partners.[20] Five other bankers were appointed to the Executive Board of the ECB, one of them as vice president and the others as members.[21] All of the appointees are reputed anti-inflation bankers, judging by their antecedents within their respective national banking systems. The appointment of an executive board for the ECB effectively meant that the ESCB is comprised of member states' national central banks (NCBs) and the ECB.

Managing the Euro

The Institutions

As noted earlier, the management of the euro and ancillary monetary policies, such as money supply, interest rate, and so on, of the euro zone is the responsibility of the ESCB and the ECB. In addition to overseeing the smooth operation of payment systems, the ESCB is responsible for managing the official foreign reserves and the foreign-exchange operations of the euro zone countries. It bears repeating that "the primary objective of the ESCB is to maintain price stability," it is to be an independent system, and it is to be governed by the decisionmaking institutions of the ECB. Additionally, it is obligated to conduct open market operations and offer standing facilities, and it could require credit institutions to maintain minimum reserves on account with it.

The ECB is comprised of a triumvirate of organs: the Executive Board, the Governing Council, and the General Council. The ECB's Governing Council is comprised of the Executive Board plus the governors of the NCBs of the euro zone countries. The General Council is comprised of the ECB's president and vice president plus the governors of the NCBs of all EU countries. The primary responsibility for executing the ECB's decisions falls on the NCBs. In late 1998, the ECB identified the pursuit of price stability as its primary task in accordance with the TEU, which it defined as less than 2 percent annual inflation within Euroland.

The Stabilization and Growth Pact

The German government feared that Euroland countries might respond to periods of economic downturn by indulging in excessive spending and incurring budget deficits. In the absence of a supranational government per se, especially since the EU is not a bona fide nation-state government, it is therefore imperative to have a credible fiscal policy. Thus, in order to complement the independent ECB and its monetary policy decisions, the Council of the European Union for Finance is regarded as the watchdog of participating governments' fiscal policies. Largely at the insistence of Germany and to ensure continued fiscal discipline by Euroland countries after doing their utmost to qualify for membership, the European Council agreed on a "Stability and Growth Pact" (SGP) at its June 1997 summit. According to this fiscal dimension of the EMU, those Euroland countries that allow their budget deficits to run amuck and fail to rectify the situation within a reasonable time frame could be fined up to 0.5 percent of their GDP.

It is instructive to note that the SGP was previously known as the "Stability Pact." A new left-of-center government in France in 1997, headed by Lionel Jospin, feared that qualifying for the euro might mean the pursuit of budgetary responsibility at the expense of employment considerations.[22] To accommodate French antipathy and placate other concerned EU members, the council reached a consensus to add "Growth" to the stability pact and consequently adopted a "Resolution on Growth and Employment" as a signal that employment issues would stay atop the EU's agenda. The SGP thus obliges participating countries to submit their stability and growth initiatives for annual peer reviews in order to determine their compliance with Euroland's medium-term SGP targets.

The Exchange Rate Mechanism

In addition to endorsing the design for euro notes and coins at its June 1997 summit, the European Council floated the idea of an ERM II, which would link the currency of any non-Euroland countries to the euro. The ECB's Governing Council subsequently worked out the modalities and agreed on the principles and principal components of the successor mechanism in September 1998. It is designed to prepare for the eventual accession of other currencies in the future. To that end, ERM II initially linked the Danish krone at the narrow ±2.25 percent fluctuation band and the Greek drachma to the euro at the wider ±15 percent fluctuation margin. Greece has since acceded to the euro zone.

In managing the euro, monetary reference, inflation target, and a potpourri of additional indicators guide the ECB's monetary policy. Moreover, the established rule that governed the euro during the transition period was that there would be "no compulsion, no prohibition" to use the new currency.[23] Additionally, conversion from one participating currency to another during the transition period had to go through what was known as "triangulation."[24] Finally, before the launching of the euro in 1999, the ECB and other EU institutions took measures to ensure that contractual obligations would not be affected by its advent. Specifically, a council regulation (legislation) was adopted to preserve the terms and obligations of contracts that were denominated in national currencies. The regulation specified that all references to the national currencies of Euroland countries and/or to the ECU in any existing contracts would be replaced by references to the euro at the fixed exchange rates.

The Euro Zone Profiled

On January 1, 1999, Greece began the process of joining the euro zone, when it (along with Denmark) joined the ERM II. On the basis of the convergence criteria, it was cleared for membership by the European Commission in April 2000[25] and thus became the first country since May

1998 to be admitted into Euroland on January 1, 2001. Currently, the euro zone is comprised of Austria, Belgium, Finland, France, Germany, Greece, Ireland, Italy, Luxembourg, the Netherlands, Portugal, and Spain. Together, they represent a combined population of over 300 million consumers, an aggregated GDP of almost 6 trillion euros ($6.6 trillion), and an estimated 20 percent of world trade and world GDP. This is an impressive market. Danish voters rejected a bid by the government to join the euro zone in a September 2000 referendum, and the governments of Sweden and the UK have yet to decide on euro membership, albeit strident opponents and supporters of the euro keep the debate alive in the UK.

Consequences of the Euro—A Benefits-Costs Analysis

Benefits of the Euro

One of the most important benefits of the adoption of the euro is that it has facilitated economic convergence in Euroland, at least on the basis of the convergence criteria. As well, in their bid to qualify for the euro, some Euroland governments that were not known for budgetary discipline have been compelled to pursue tough austerity measures. In other words, the euro has tamed renowned spendthrift governments in the euro zone. For example, but for the desire to qualify for the euro, the Italian, Spanish, Portuguese, and Greek governments might not have undertaken stringent austerity measures. Thus, to the extent that there is economic convergence in Euroland, the advent of the euro has contributed to an ever closer union in the EU.

Another widely cited benefit of the inception of the euro for consumers and economic actors in Euroland and beyond is price transparency. From the perspective of consumers, both individuals and businesses, pricing in the euro affords them the opportunity to compare (e.g., automobile) prices across national frontiers. It also enables price comparability of invoices and contracts by consumers/buyers, particularly businesses. Some large businesses are even demanding that suppliers domiciled outside of Euroland must submit bids in euros. With the euro, wage/salary comparability is also easier to accomplish. Two interrelated benefits of the comparability of salaries and prices are intensified competition and falling prices.[26]

Another benefit of the euro since 1999 has been the reduction of transaction costs with the removal of exchange rate risks and hedging against currency fluctuations. Considering a scenario of changing one U.S. dollar into the currencies of all fifteen EU states without buying anything vividly drives this point home. At the end of the exercise, one is typically left with less than half a dollar, due to transaction costs and commissions that are associated with changing money from one currency to another. Of course, these conversion and ancillary savings will be felt and appreciated more by individual consumers and small businesses that indulge in small transactions than by conglomerates and industrialists that have the wherewithal to hedge and engage in large transactions. In addition to saving on currency conversion, travelers are no longer saddled with coins and notes left over from trips across Euroland.

To the extent that the euro is being managed by an independent ECB, an institution whose primary objective is price stability, coupled with a sanction-supported SGP, the market can expect to benefit from low and stable inflation, as well as low interest rates in Euroland. Again, the evidence is that temporally and spatially this has been the case for some euro zone countries, especially in Southern Europe, where both interest rates and inflation are at their lowest in quite a while.

Costs of the Euro

Conversely, a major cost of adopting the euro is the loss of sovereignty, especially over monetary policy, and the ceding of that vital power to a centralized ECB in Frankfurt am Main.[27] Specifically, euro zone membership automatically deprives most member governments of the ability to manipulate interest rates and to devalue their currency in order to reinvigorate their economies. Additionally, by virtue of their Euroland "citizenship" and the SGP, member governments are equally deprived of utilizing fiscal measures to manage their economies. In short, national governments no longer enjoy, at their disposal, two major instruments of demand and cost management. As well, there has also been a seigniorage[28] shift from national governments.

The one monetary policy fits all that presumes a synchronized business cycle among Euroland members, even over the long run, may be too optimistic. The fear is that asymmetric shocks could have differential effects on Euroland members, especially in the absence of a synchronized business cycle. Some have even suggested that asymmetric shocks will likely desynchronize Euroland economies in the future (Taylor, 1995). A related cost of adopting the euro is associated with the possibility of an insignificant labor mobility, which could condemn some parts of the euro zone to perpetual poverty, high unemployment, and anemic economic performances.[29] As well, wage comparability could complicate wage negotiations under the auspices of collective bargaining for employers and thus prompt inflation.

One of the most obvious costs of adopting the euro is the cost of switching to a new currency by current or future members. On the one hand, billions of new banknotes and billions of new coins were to be distributed across Euroland and beyond by January 1, 2002, and afterward.[30] In and of itself, this constituted a logistical challenge for the ECB, the EU, and member states. The process required all of the authorities' logistical acumen to ferry the bulk of new notes and coins mainly to banks. It was expected to be an expensive undertaking, partly because authorities had to hire security personnel, since they could ill afford to have the process compromised by (large-scale) theft, as has already been reported in some quarters.[31] On the other hand, some companies expended a lot of their scarce resources preparing for e-Day. Among others, they had to switch millions of prices, redesign cash-dispensing machines, parking meters, vending machines, and convert databases. The process was expensive, not least because of personnel training. In addition, one of the most noticeable and inevitable consequences of the new currency was dual pricing on products and bookkeeping in two currencies, that is, in the local currency and in the euro until February 28, 2002.[32]

Intra–Euro Zone Dynamics

Even the best-laid plans in life do not always work. Despite the extensive planning that preceded the single European currency, the euro depreciated against the U.S. dollar by about 25 percent from January 1, 1999 to early 2002. One of the reasons that could be adduced for the euro's downward slide is its newness and its aspiration to be an alternative currency to the dollar for international transactions, store of value, and so on. The downward slide may amount to an inevitable progression of a new currency, whose credibility is being tested by the market, especially in the short term. It is perhaps inching toward its true market value, particularly if it was overvalued at its inception in the first place.

Political Interference/Uncertainties

The weakening of the euro, however, may also be due to sometimes unavoidable social, economic, and political signals being sent to the international currency market. The first adverse signal was sent at the May 1998 meeting of the European Council in the selection of Willem Duisenberg to head the ECB. At best, the messy compromise at the rancorous meeting seemed like a "political fix," as already discussed above. Another negative signal to the market was sent in September 1998, when the new socialist government in Germany, led by Gerhard Schröder, pressured the Bundesbank and ECB to lower interest rates, ostensibly to resuscitate its ailing economy. Later, on March 15, 1999, all twenty commissioners of the EU's executive arm resigned en masse following allegations of mismanagement, impropriety, fraud, and nepotism leveled at some of its members. These events prompted Duisenberg to remark at a March 25, 1999, European Council summit that increased uncertainty regarding political support for a stability-based monetary and fiscal policy had contributed to the weakening of the euro.

Confusion in Euroland?

Other factors account for the weakening of the euro. For example, Euroland and EU actors did not initially speak with one voice on euro-related issues, as responses were usually incoherent and uncoordinated. As the institutions and personnel in charge of the euro tried to find their rhythm, many of their remarks about euro-related exigencies were initially contradictory and confusing to the market. Consider the following chronology of reactions mired in contradictions. On March 11, 1999, Eugenio Solans, an ECB Executive Board member, wondered aloud if the bank was paying too much attention to the exchange rate level. Then on April 8, the ECB cut its main interest rate by half a percentage point to stimulate economic growth in Euroland and eventually shore up the value of the euro,[33] a decision the bank's president said was not approved by members of the Governing Council "with equal enthusiasm." On April 19, Duisenberg remarked that he was not bothered by the euro's continued slide, which he characterized as a "benign neglect" policy. At a subsequent gathering on May 3 of central bankers and finance ministers from G7 countries in Washington, D.C., Hans Tietmeyer, president of the Bundesbank, pointed out, as though to correct the ECB head, that "a policy of neglect would be inappropriate." He further remarked that a weakening euro would be unacceptable, a position he repeated on June 3 during a public lecture in the UK, when he opined that the decline of the euro's external value over the preceding few days had not been good for the currency. The euro had slid in value in reaction to the ECOFIN's decision at its May 26 meeting to allow Italy to increase its 1999 budget deficit from the SGP target of 1 percent to 2.4 percent of GDP.

Meanwhile, at the June 3–4 European Council meeting in Germany, because it did not see cause for alarm, the council made a concerted effort to downplay the ebbing value of the euro. However, on June 21, the then president-designate of the European Commission, Romano Prodi, alarmed the market when he suggested that Italy might have to depart the euro zone if it failed to match the competitiveness of its partners. The market's concern was who spoke for the euro? After all, in the United States (and in pre-euro Germany), the chairman of the Federal Reserve Bank (Bundesbank president) and the secretary of treasury (finance minister) typically commented about the dollar (deutschemark).

Weak Economic Performance and Structural Deficiencies

An abiding reason for the sliding euro is the lackluster economic performance of Euroland, which has, on the average, fallen short of forecasts. At the core of the anemic economic performance and the concomitant unemployment problem in Euroland are deep-seated structural deficiencies. Without undertaking unavoidable structural reforms, which involve the labor market, tax regimes, social security and welfare systems, and so forth, the pressure on the euro will continue unabated. These reforms are necessary for job creation, reversing capital flight, reducing reliance on monetary instruments, and easing pressures on the budget.

A slightly related though different episode that affected the value of the euro was an open dispute in February 2001 that led the European Commission and the ECOFIN to reprimand the Irish government over its expansionary budget. By most accounts, the commission's censure of Dublin over its decision to cut taxes was actually a warning to the incoming Italian government of Silvio Beluscoi not to pursue a tax-cutting agenda that could undermine the SGP. However, when Germany encountered some budgetary difficulties in July 2001, its finance minister, Hans Eichel, mooted the idea of revising the SGP and basing it on government spending instead of budget deficit.[34] Indeed, when in early 2002 Germany and Portugal edged dangerously close to violating the SGP, the German government lobbied its euro zone partners against a formal reprimand, contrary to the wishes of the EU commissioner for economic and financial affairs, Pedro Solbes, who preferred a formal censure.

Other events that seemed to have sent negative signals to the market were the rejection of a proposal by Danish voters for early entry into Euroland and the rejection of the Nice Treaty by Irish voters in May 2001. Another cloud over the euro is the enduring confusion vis-à-vis the ECB presidency. Duisenberg announced in early February 2002 that he would step down on July 9, 2003, but who will be his successor? His anointed successor, Jean-Claude Trichet—France's Central Bank governor—is the subject of a legal inquiry in France, a process that could go on a while. Additionally, ECOFIN is under pressure to announce a replacement for the European Central Bank vice president, Christian Noyer of France, whose term expires at the end of May 2002.

Prospects of the Euro as a Global Currency

In view of the foregoing, will the euro eventually ascend to the stature of an international currency? What are its prospects of rivaling the U.S. dollar as the currency of choice for international transactions anytime soon? Does it even matter whether the euro evolves into an important currency for international transactions, or is the internationalization of the euro a policy objective of the ECB?

The U.S. dollar remains very popular with fund managers, international investors, and international traders and will likely remain so in the near future, notwithstanding the economic slowdown in the United States in 2001. After all, more than three-fourths of all foreign-exchange transactions involve the dollar, at least half of official reserves are held in dollars, and almost half of global exports are still denominated in the dollar (Portes and Rey, 1998; Temperton, 1998).

The euro, however, could still emerge as the first serious rival to the dollar in almost a century for a variety of reasons. Among them, a large economic and population base that is comparable to the United States, and can only get bigger with enlargement, ceteris paribus, backs the euro. As noted earlier, Euroland at present boasts an aggregate GDP of roughly 6 trillion euros and a population of over 300 million. Economic actors, especially international traders domiciled in Euroland-cum-EU have been invoicing partially or exclusively in euros since January 2002. The foregoing factors could bolster the confidence of international investors and treasury managers in the nascent currency.

In that same vein, political, historical, and geographical factors could also enhance the international visibility of the euro. For example, the governments of former colonies of some Euroland members may decide to increase their euro-denominated reserve holdings with the debut of the physical euro or may, like the CFA franc zones of Central and West Africa, decide to peg their currencies to the euro.[35] Similarly, the euro is becoming a de facto regional currency to the extent that Eastern and Central European countries are opting to hold their reserves in the euro and are pegging their currencies to the euro, especially if they feel that doing so will enhance and expedite their accession to the EU and Euroland. In other words, the increased integration of Eastern and Central Europe with the EU is already enhancing the role and visibility of the Euro as an important international unit of account.

The euro could also evolve into an important international currency if the ECB does not officially obstruct its internationalization. Already, the ECB has warned that non-Euroland countries would not be allowed to unilaterally adopt the euro as a parallel legal tender in the manner that some East and Central European countries adopted the deutschemark in the late 1990s and 2000. The fear within the ECB is that there is a large amount of deutschemark holdings outside of the euro zone (roughly 40 billion euros), largely in Eastern Europe, that could destabilize the market due to inflationary pressures. We could infer from such a policy stance that the ECB could quietly impede the euro's internationalization in many ways. After all, it is common knowledge that the Bundesbank, an influential member of the ESCB, systematically and actively resisted the internationalization of the deutschemark for official reserve holdings during the boom years of the postwar era.

In addition, in order for the euro to become an important international currency beyond Euroland and the EU, it must be perceived by international investors, fund managers, and others to exude stability and be supported by a strong exchange rate. In other words, holding assets in the euro must not be a losing or highly risky proposition for investors. Likewise, the European financial markets must be well integrated, and the regulatory agencies must be sound enough to enable economic actors to liquidate or diversify their portfolio. Still, international financial institutions by nature are conservative and slow to change. In any case, the international respectability and visibility of the euro is likely to increase with the following scenarios. First, the euro is increasingly being employed as a means of payment in transactions between third currencies. Second, the euro is being used as a reference currency for the quotation of commodities.[36] Third, more governments around the world are linking their currencies in the manner of adjustable pegs, dirty floats, and so on to the euro. Fourth, the euro is increasingly being used as a store of value in terms of the official reserves, composition of official debt, and so forth.

Lingering Euro Issues

By January 1, 2002, roughly 6.5 billion euro banknotes worth 134 billion euros and almost 38 billion coins with a total value of 12.4 billion euros had been frontloaded and distributed mainly to credit institutions and central banks inside and outside of Euroland, thus facilitating a smooth changeover, especially within the EU. By the end of the day on January 1, more than 80 percent of automated teller machines (ATMs) were dispensing euros, and by January 6, the conversion of all ATMs in the euro zone had been completed. Additionally, the euro progress ratio (EPR), which measures the rate of substitution of national/legacy banknotes by euro banknotes, steadily increased from 33 percent (January 1) to 45 percent (January 8), 65 percent (January 24), and 85.2 percent (January 26). Although there were scattered reports of some ATMs in the euro zone running out of cash on January 1, as well as many vending machines yet to convert completely to the euro, the switchover was by most accounts smooth and even surpassed the expectations of the ECB. National central banks will continue to exchange national banknotes and currencies for euros, sometimes for a fee, for the next ten years or indefinitely, depending on the country.[37]

Perhaps after debuting as notes and coins and becoming the sole legal tender of the euro zone from March 1, 2002, on, the euro will ascend to the status of a respectable international currency. Possibly now that Europeans and the rest of the world are able to hold euro banknotes and coins in their hands and tucked away in their wallets/purses, the resultant psychological boost will eventually assure the euro a spot alongside the dollar. Still, some critical issues about the future of the euro persist.

First, will the euro be short-lived or endure? The educated response is that it is here to stay simply because the price of failure is prohibitively high for the EU in general and for the euro zone countries in particular.

Given the meticulous planning that preceded the launching of the euro, it is unlikely that as a currency it will be short-lived. Besides, abandoning the budding euro would have catastrophic consequences for the EU. Should it collapse, the ramifications would not be confined to EMU. Rather it would trigger ripple effects in other aspects of European integration and could potentially undermine previous achievements of integration. Clearly, if the euro can be abandoned, why not other contentious aspects of integration, such as the Schengen Agreement that opened up the internal frontiers of many EU states or even the SEM initiative—the philosophical underpinning of the euro?

More important, the collapse of the euro would unleash an unacceptable legal and political chaos in the international capital markets. EU politicians would be seriously embarrassed by such a development. Nonetheless, it is conceivable that the euro could break up under extraordinary circumstances in the euro zone or in the global economy. For example, the euro would be practically dead should a prolonged recession and/or other economic difficulties force either Germany or France or both to exit the arrangement. Even if such circumstances did unfold, serious attempts would certainly be undertaken by EU leaders to remedy the problem(s) and accommodate the two largest European economies.

A second lingering issue is that of British participation in the euro. Will it eventually join or will it stay out of the euro zone? It cannot be doubted that UK participation would add credibility to the inchoate currency, given its status as the third largest economy in Europe with a gross national output in excess of 1.5 trillion euros and an estimated population of sixty million. On the one hand, there is pressure on the UK to join the euro zone, largely because an estimated 60 percent of its trade is with the EU/euro zone. The pressure also stems from concerns that the longer the UK stays away from the euro, the less likely it can influence the euro's operational rules; it is also more likely that it would inherit rules determined by others if and when it eventually joined. On the other hand, a UK accession could destabilize the euro, especially given the history of the UK with European integration in general—combative, reluctant, skeptical, and so on. As with Italy, the UK would be coming aboard with the baggage of having pulled out of the ERM in fall 1992, and it could do so again, only this time it would be withdrawing from the euro. This possibility could prompt speculators to incessantly bet on the UK's likely withdrawal from the euro zone, which could further undermine the value of the currency. Even though it is widely believed that the issue of British participation in the euro will have to be resolved by a plebiscite, it is almost impossible to envisage a scenario that would compel the British electorate or prime minister to jettison the pound sterling in favor of the euro.

The third important issue is whether a currency can exist without a state (government)? Thus far and in the foreseeable future, the euro will not be owned by a nation-state. Rather, being jointly owned by a group of dissonant national and supranational authorities, it is no wonder the market seems skittish about the euro, because no "government" owns or speaks for it. It is also not surprising that the German government initiated a debate in summer 2000 regarding the adoption of a constitution for the EU that would mimic the German Basic Law. A federal structure was proposed, much like the ESCB and the ECB were modeled on the German monetary system and the Bundesbank. Predictably, the responses across the EU have ranged from opposed or lukewarm (UK and France) to supportive (Belgium).[38] Nonetheless, on February 28, 2002—coincidentally, the very day that national (legacy) currencies within the euro zone last served as legal tenders—the EU launched a European constitutional convention to debate the future institutional shape of the EU.[39] An abiding lesson of regional integration in general and the EU in particular is that in the end, "integration" is about shared sovereignty. Only time will tell if the euro will eventually have its own government.

Notes

1. Since its inception in the early 1950s, the European Union (EU) has had to change its name a few times with the deepening of integration. The evolution commenced when the 1951 Treaty of Paris created the European Coal and Steel Community (ECSC), which was followed in 1957 by the Treaty of Rome that established the European Atomic Energy Community (EAEC) and the European Economic Community (EEC). Of the three communities, the EEC was the best known and most often cited until 1967, when all three communities were merged into the European Communities (EC). Beginning in November 1993, the name changed yet again to the EU when the 1991 Treaty of Maastricht entered into force, and the Council of Ministers—the EU's principal decisionmaking body—changed its name to the Council of the European Union. The term has, however, been variously (mis)used because the EU has not legally supplanted the EC. Meanwhile, over the years the EU has steadily grown from six countries in 1951 to its present fifteen member states. Given that the target audiences of this volume are students in international political economy (IPE) courses and would likely have a limited understanding of the intricacies of the EU, the common usage of the EU will be employed in references to the development of the European Union in the generic sense as a continuity stretching from the 1950s to the present. Where deemed necessary and appropriate, the applicable name for that period (e.g., EEC, EC, etc.) will be used.

2. In fact, according to the *Eurobarometer*, a publication of the European Commission (the EU's bureaucracy and executive arm) that periodically tracks public opinion on varied issues in the EU, average support for the euro has remained at almost 70 percent in the twelve participating countries (*Eurobarometer* 55 [October 2001]: 46).

3. The terms *Euroland* and the *euro zone* are employed interchangeably in this chapter to refer to the twelve participating EU countries.

4. For instance, on the eve of the debut of the physical euro, it has weakened

by roughly 25 percent against major currencies since 1999, when it was introduced at the conversion rate of e1:$1.17.

5. See, for example, "The Euro: Europe's New Currency," http://pacific. commerce.ubc.ca/xr/euro/euro.html

6. Bini-Smaghi and Vori, for example, reported evidence of more product diversification in the EU than in the United States in the manufacturing sector.

7. Admittedly, many economists do not consider the EU an OCA, but the basis for their conclusion has equally been challenged.

8. This remark was made by the president of the European Central Bank (ECB), Willem Duisenberg, at the launching of the physical euro. "The Euro-Launch: The Biggest Monetary Change in History," *Business Credit* (October 2001): 42.

9. The Smithsonian Agreement was reached in December 1971 by the ten largest economies in the world to change the parity values against the U.S. dollar and to widen the margins of fluctuation from ±1 percent to ±2.25 percent, that is, a 4.5 percent spread. The EU considered the widened margins of fluctuations against the dollar "unacceptable," because they implied a maximum bilateral spread of 9 percent between any two EU currencies.

10. Some European countries either withdrew in less than two months of participation (the UK, Ireland, and Denmark) or entered and exited the regime at will (France and Denmark). By the time France left permanently in March 1976, what was left was essentially a "deutschemark zone" comprised of Germany and a number of smaller EU and non-EU countries with strong trade links to Germany.

11. The ECU was modeled after the Special Drawing Rights regime that was created by the IMF in 1969. See, for example, Mehmert (1992) for an in-depth discussion of the ECU.

12. See also "The European Monetary System: Ten Years of Progress in Monetary Cooperation," *Europe* (April 1989): 23, 47.

13. See also "Bundesbank Faces Pressure Not to Raise Rates," *Financial Times*, 16 July 1992.

14. It is noteworthy that the announcement by the French president to call a referendum to ratify the Maastricht Treaty came in the wake of the 1992 Danish rejection of it. Per French law, a three-fifths majority of the bicameral legislature would have been sufficient to ratify the treaty, and the French government seemed to have the votes. However, President Mitterrand decided on the referendum route, ostensibly because of perceived support by the French electorate, and a comfortable ratification would have counteracted the "no" vote by the Danes.

15. The Danes eventually ratified the treaty in May 1993, again by a slim margin. As in France, which also ratified it in a referendum in September 1992, although by a slim margin, the ratification of the treaty in both the UK and Germany was equally eventful and contentious.

16. Title VI of the treaty and appended protocols contain relevant provisions on the completion of EMU. For details, see http://Europa.eu.int/en/record/mt/top.html

17. European Monetary Institute, *Convergence Report* (Frankfurt am Main: European Monetary Institute, 1998); and "Commission Recommends 11 Member States for EMU," *Eurecom* (April 1998): 1.

18. The criteria are variously stipulated in Articles 109e, 109j, and in appended pertinent protocols.

19. The eleven countries were Austria, Belgium, Finland, France, Germany, Ireland, Italy, Luxembourg, the Netherlands, Portugal, and Spain.

20. The row at the meeting was not entirely a surprise, because President

Jacques Chirac of France had mooted his preference for a French citizen at the helm of the ECB as early as November 1997. Whereas it was widely believed in the EU that Willem Duisenberg, the head of the EMI, would be appointed the ECB's first president, the French government thought otherwise. Chirac interpreted such an appointment as ceding further ground to the Germans, because Duisenberg, although a Dutch central banker, was seen in Paris as a "German candidate." Who was appointed to the coveted position mattered to the French, because Germany had already won the battle to locate the ECB in Frankfurt am Main. The row was "resolved" when it was agreed that Duisenberg would step down of his own volition halfway through the mandated eight-year term, and Jean-Claude Trichet, France's central bank governor, would take over. See, among others, Lionel Barber, "War of Nerves in EU's Battle of the Bank," *Financial Times*, 22 April 1998, p. 2; John Vinocur, "Paris-Bonn Fight: It's About More Than Banker's Name," *International Herald Tribune*, 22 April 1998, p. 1; Wolfgang Münchau and Graham Bowley, "Paris and Bonn Dig in Their Heels over Rivals for European Bank," *Financial Times*, 30 April 1998, p. 1; and "EU Leaders Agree on EMU Countries and Central Bank President," *Eurecom* (May 1998): 1.

21. Christian Noyer (France) was appointed vice president, and he oversees the directorates-general (DGs) for administration/personnel and legal services. Eugenio Domingo Solans (Spain) manages the DGs for information systems and statistics, while Sirkka Hämäläinen (Finland) supervises the DG for operations. Otmar Issing (Germany) oversees the DGs for research and economics, and Tommaso Padoa-Schioppa (Italy) manages the DGs for international and European relations and payment systems.

22. The emergence of a new government was consequent to the outcome of national parliamentary elections in spring 1997, in which the Socialists gained control of the national assembly. Since the conservative President Chirac did not have to stand for reelection yet, a "cohabitation" government had to be formed, whereby a Conservative president and a Socialist prime minister shared executive powers.

23. "No compulsion" plainly meant that businesses were not obliged to use the euro in transactions until January 1, 2002, when the euro became a legal tender in Euroland. "No prohibition" basically meant that should an entity prefer transactions in the euro, it should be able to do so, irrespective of whether it was within or outside of Euroland.

24. Until December 31, 1998, if one wanted to convert, for example, the Spanish peseta to Italian lira, a direct and easy method of conversion using their exchange rate was employed. Following the debut of the euro in 1999, however, an indirect method involving the euro was required. Using the scenario described above, the fixed conversion rate of the peseta would first be used to convert to the euro. The second step entailed converting the euro to the lira, again utilizing the fixed conversion factor.

25. See "Greece Eligible to Join Euro," *Eurecom* (May, 2000): 2.

26. Admittedly, price transparency or falling prices have not been universally evident in all sectors of the Euroland economy or felt by all its consumers, but with time, as information becomes more readily accessible and as consumers become more sophisticated, that should change. Prices have not fallen as much as projected, in part because other factors, such as transportation/distribution costs and demand factors influence prices. Additionally, wage comparability could also pose a problem for employers during wage negotiations by nudging wages upward, thus triggering inflation in the euro zone.

27. It should be noted, however, that the adoption of the euro and the inception of the ESCB have allowed Euroland governments to have more say on monetary

policy instruments, such as setting interest rates, monetary targets, and so on, than they did when the Bundesbank unilaterally set interest rates before July 1, 1998. At least, through their surrogates the NCBs, Euroland governments now have a presence at the table where vital monetary policy decisions are being made.

28. Seigniorage refers to profit made by a central bank/government from issuing coins. It is the difference between the bullion price (intrinsic worth of the metal) and the face value of the coins.

29. One is, however, comforted by the awareness that the EU has a slew of funds (e.g., regional development, cohesion, etc.), which are likely to be deployed in the affected euro zone areas.

30. Rebecca Wright, "Will It Be €-Day or D-Day for Europe?" *EuroBusiness* (April 2001): 27–28; and "The Euro Launch: The Biggest Monetary Change in History," *Business Credit* (October 2001): 42.

31. For further discussions on the projected costs of switching to the euro, see "Ready, Set, euros," *Business Week*, 2 July 2001, pp. 48–50; James Blitz, "Armed Gang Steals Thousands of New Euro Coins in Italy," *Financial Times*, 24 September 2001, p. 1; and Carolyn Aldred, "Euro Transition Mints New Risks," *Business Insurance*, 9 July 2001, pp. 17–19.

32. The concern was largely responsible for advancing the date to complete the second transition from June 30, 2002, to February 28, 2002. For more on how the switchover is impacting businesses, see Allyson Stewart-Allen, "Changeover to Euro Has Hidden Expenses," *Marketing News*, 30 July 2001, p. 6.

33. The euro's decline had been largely due to investors' fears that Euroland's economy was weakening. If those same investors believed that the euro zone's economic growth would pick up after the rate cut, then they would likely make more euro investments, which would prompt the inchoate currency's value to rise.

34. Eichel later backtracked from the idea. "Eichel Rocks (and rolls)," *Economist*, 25 August 2001, p. 60.

35. It must be borne in mind that the CFA franc zones had been linked to the French franc before 1999.

36. Although (for purely political reasons) President Saddam Hussein and the Iraqi government insisted on being paid in euros for Iraqi crude oil exports under the United Nations sanctions program, it is doubtful that Euroland officials would cite it as a sign of the euro's increasing international respectability.

37. See http://www.ecb.int/press/02 for various press releases of the ECB.

38. Tobias Buck, "Germans Rally to Schröder's Blueprint," *Financial Times*, 1 May 2001, p. 2; Robert Graham, "Paris Regards Proposals as Ideas Rather Than Policy," *Financial Times*, 1 May 2001, p. 2; and Andrew Parker, "London Lays Sress on Difference of Opinion," *Financial Times*, 1 May 2001, p. 2.

39. See, for example, "European Convention Starts Debate EU's Future," *Eurecom* (March 2002): 4–5.

References

Apel, Emmanuel. 1998. *European Monetary Integration: 1958–2002*. London: Routledge.

Barrell, Ray, ed. 1992. *Economic Convergence and Monetary Union in Europe*. London: Sage.

Bini-Smaghi, L. and S. Vori. 1993. "Rating the EU as an Optimal Currency Area." *Banca d'Italia Temi di Discussione* 187.

Britto, Andrew and David Mayes. 1992. *Achieving Monetary Union in Europe*. London: Sage.

Caparole, G. 1993. "Is Europe an Optimum Currency Area? Symmetric Versus Asymmetric Shocks in the EC." *National Institute Economic Review* (May).

Cecchini, Paolo. 1988. *The European Challenge 1992: The Benefits of a Single Market*. Aldershot, UK: Wildwood House.

Commission of the European Communities. 1989. *Report on Economic and Monetary Union in the European Community*. Luxembourg: Office for Official Publications of the European Communities.

———. 1992. *From Single Market to European Union*. Luxembourg: Office for Official Publications of the European Communities.

Commission of the European Communities. 1985. *Completing the Internal Market*. White paper from the Commission to the European Council. Luxembourg: Office for Official Publications of the European Communities.

Emerson, E. et al. 1992. *One Market, One Money*. Oxford: Oxford University Press.

Frömmel, Michael, and Lukas Menkhoff. 2001. "Risk Reduction in EMS? Evidence from Trends in Exchange Rates Properties." *Journal of Common Market Studies* 39: 285–306.

Kenen, P.B. 1969. "The Theory of Optimal Currency Areas: An Eclectic View." In R. A. Mundell and A. K. Swoboda, eds., *Monetary Problems of the International Economy*. Chicago: University of Chicago Press.

McDonald, Frank and George Zis. 1989. "The European Monetary System: Towards 1992 and Beyond." *Journal of Common Market Studies* 27: 183–202.

Mehmert, Ralph. 1992. *User's Guide to the ECU*. London: Graham and Trotman.

Monnet, Jean. 1962. "A Ferment of Change." *Journal of Common Market Studies* 1: 203–211.

———. 1978. *Memoirs*. London: Collins.

Mundell, R. A. 1961. "A Theory of Optimum Currency Areas." *American Economic Review* 51: 657–665.

Padoa-Schioppa, Tomaso, ed. 1987. *Efficiency, Stability and Equity: A Strategy for the Evolution of the Economic System of the EC*. Luxembourg: Office for Official Publications of the European Communities.

Portes, Richard and Helene Rey. 1998. "The Emergence of the Euro as an International Currency." In David Begg et al., eds., *EMU: Prospects and Challenges for the Euro*. Oxford: Blackwell Publishers.

Rose, Andrew. 2000. "Does a Currency Union Boost International Trade?" *California Management Review* 42: 52–62.

Schuman, Robert. 1998. "The Schuman Declaration." In Brent Nelsen and Alexander Stubb, eds., *The European Union*. Boulder: Lynne Rienner.

Smith, Michael and Wayne Sandholtz. 1995. "Institutions and Leadership: Germany, Maastricht, and the ERM Crisis." In C. Rhodes and S. Mazey, eds., *The State of the European Union: Building a European Polity?* Boulder: Lynne Rienner.

Taylor, Christopher. 1995. *EMU 2000? Prospects for European Monetary Union*. London: Royal Institute of International Affairs.

Temperton, Paul, ed. 1998. *The Euro*. New York: John Wiley and Sons.

Watson, Alison. 1997. *Aspects of European Monetary Integration: The Politics of Convergence*. New York: St. Martin's Press.

PART 3

DEVELOPMENT AND THE WORLD BANK

19

The Rise and Fall of the Washington Consensus as a Paradigm for Developing Countries

Charles Gore

In recent decades, the Washington Consensus, with its emphasis on market-oriented policies, has influenced the basic parameters of development policies in both developed and developing countries. Charles Gore succinctly analyzes inherent contradictions in this model and identifies an emerging challenger, which he terms the Southern Consensus. This latter approach is based on the convergence of East Asian developmentalism and Latin American neostructuralism. Combining explanatory and normative frameworks, Gore offers a powerful and persuasive argument about the inevitable demise of the Washington Consensus and why the Southern Consensus will shape the future development agenda.

Introduction

Developing countries is an international practice. The essence of this practice is the mobilization and allocation of resources, and the design of institutions, to transform national economies and societies, in an orderly way, from a state and status of being less developed to one of being more developed. The agencies engaged in this practice include national governments of less-developed countries, which have adopted "development" as a purpose to which State power is put, and governments of richer countries, which disburse official development aid to support and influence this process: a variety of non-governmental organizations concerned to animate and channel popular concerns: and international intergovernmental organizations, such as the organs of the United Nations and the World Bank, many of which have been expressly set up to resolve various development

Reprinted with permission of the publisher from *World Development*, volume 28, number 3, pp. 789–804. Oxford, UK: Elsevier Science, 2000.

problems. Often it is the last group who have acted as the avant-garde of development practice. It is because of their activities, as well as the widespread tendency of governments to copy successful practice elsewhere, that it is appropriate to describe developing countries as an international practice. But it is by no means global in scope. Indeed the practice of developing countries is only done in a particular set of countries—those which in the 1950s and 1960s were generally called "underdeveloped" or "less-developed" countries, but which now generally identify themselves, and are identified by others, as "developing countries."

This paper discusses trends in the body of knowledge which guides and justifies the practice of development. It examines, in particular, the ideas propagated by international development agencies, and focuses on the shift in thinking which occurred in the 1980s with the introduction and widespread adoption of an approach to the practice of developing countries known as the "Washington Consensus." In broad terms, this approach recommends that governments should reform their policies and, in particular: (a) pursue macroeconomic stability by controlling inflation and reducing fiscal deficits: (b) open their economies to the rest of the world through trade and capital account liberalization: and (c) liberalize domestic product and factor markets through privatization and deregulation. Propagated through the stabilization and structural adjustment policies of the International Monetary Fund (IMF) and World Bank, this has been the dominant approach to development from the early 1980s to the present. The paper examines the introduction of the Washington Consensus as a paradigm shift, and assesses the configuration of development thinking in the 1990s and pressures for a further paradigm shift, particularly in the light of the East Asian financial crisis and recent attempts to construct a "post-Washington Consensus."

The paradigmatic nature of the Washington Consensus is most clearly evident in the work of John Williamson (1990 1993 1997), who coined the name and also set out a specific formulation of the approach at the end of the 1980s. This formulation was founded on an attempt to summarize, with particular reference to policy reform in Latin America, "the conventional wisdom of the day among the economically influential bits of Washington, meaning US government and the international financial institutions" (Williamson 1993: 1329). Williamson never explicitly identifies the Washington Consensus as a paradigm. But the way he describes the approach conforms in many respects with Thomas Kuhn's notion of one.[1] Thus, he argued that the Washington Consensus is a "universal convergence," and that it constitutes "the common core of wisdom embraced by all serious economists" (Williamson 1993: 1334). He codified the approach as a set of 10 axiomatic generalizations which, given certain values, are generally shared by scholars and practitioners concerned with economic growth in developing countries; and he listed remaining analytical problems on which normal economic science needs to focus. Finally, he dismissed those who challenged the consensus view as "cranks" (1993: 1330). As he put it:

> (T)he superior economic performance of countries that establish and maintain outward-oriented market economies subject to macro-economic discipline is essentially a positive question. The proof may not be quite as conclusive as the proof that the Earth is not flat, but it is sufficiently well established as to give sensible people better things to do with their time than to challenge its veracity. (1993: 1330)

The structure of the revolution in thinking which occurred with the introduction of Washington Consensus policies is usually seen as a shift from state-led *dirigisme* to market-oriented policies. Such a switch undoubtedly occurred. But it is not a sufficient description of the nature of the change as a paradigm shift. As Kuhn shows, when paradigms change, there are usually significant changes in the "methods, problem-field, and standards of solution" which are accepted by a community of practitioners (Kuhn 1970:103). As a consequence, "the proponents of competing paradigms practice their trades in different worlds . . . [they] see different things when they look from the same point in the same direction" (Kuhn 1970: 150). In examining the introduction of the Washington Consensus as a paradigm shift, what matters is not simply the substantive differences with earlier approaches, but also the nature of the change in the disciplinary matrix and world-view.

Here it will be argued that together with the swing to market-oriented policies, there was a deeper shift in the way development problems were framed and in the types of explanation through which development policies were justified. This involved changes in the spatial and temporal frame of reference of development policy analysis. In brief, these changes were: the partial globalization of development policy analysis; and a shift from historicism to ahistorical performance assessment.

The Partial Globalization of Development Policy Analysis

Specifying development policy problems involves both explanations of development trends and normative judgments about how the world should be. For each of these activities, an important decision which must be made is deciding the policy frame, i.e., what elements should be included when viewing a problem and what elements excluded.[2] The framing of policy issues has various aspects but, one which critically affects the practice of developing countries is whether policy problems are seen within a global or national frame of reference. Explanations and normative judgments can each be elaborated within a national or global frame of reference, and so the thinking which underpins the practice of developing countries can be wholly national, wholly global, or some combination of both (Figure 19.1). The full globalization of development policy analysis will be understood here to mean a shift from a national to a global frame of reference both for explanations and normative evaluations. Before the propagation of the Washington Consensus in the 1980s, mainstream explanations of the development process and evaluative judgments of the goals of development were both conducted within a national frame of reference. First, economic and social trends within countries were explained, in the mainstream, on the basis of conditions within the countries themselves, i.e., as a result of national factors. Particular external relations might be necessary to start the process, or to close "gaps" which threatened its breakdown. But the key ingredients of a successful development process were usually identified through analyses of sequences of change within already industrialized countries, which were then applied in less developed countries without any reference to their different external situation. Second, development policies were geared toward the achievement of national objectives. This orientation was often simply taken for granted in development policy analysis. But it was also influenced, more or less strongly, by political and economic nationalism. According to Johnson (1967), key features of economic policy in new States—namely, the desire for greater self-sufficiency and early industrialization, the preference for economic planning and public control, and hostility to foreign investment—can all be traced to the mutual supporting relations between nationalism, aid policy, and ideas about the development problem formed in the 1930s. Those ideas became part of a common understanding and language of national and international policy-makers after WWII.

There were, of course, major controversies both over the meaning of development and the means of achieving it. In the 1950s and 1960s there were debates about development strategy (for example, balanced or unbalanced growth), the nature of dualistic development processes, and the role

Figure 19.1   Four Main Combinations of Explanatory and Normative Framework in Development Policy Analysis

		Normative Framework	
		National	*Global*
Explanatory Framework	*National*	Wholly National	Global Norms/ National Explanations
	Global	Global Explanations/ National Norms	Wholly Global

of human capital. Moreover, in the 1970s the earlier focus on economic growth with structural change was strongly challenged by those who pointed to the need to focus on social objectives, notably income distribution, poverty, employment and basic needs satisfaction.[3] But these disputes actually served to reinforce the normative and explanatory frames of development policy analysis as being national. Whatever objectives were taken to be central, national objectives were the focal concern. Moreover the development strategy debates essentially examined the articulation and sequencing of internal (national) ingredients which could facilitate or accelerate the national development process.

An important countercurrent to mainstream development policy analysis before the 1980s came from structuralist and dependency theories elaborated in Latin America (see Kay, 1989). Like the dominant approach the normative concern of these theories was national, and indeed strongly informed by nationalist concerns. But their analytical perspective was global in scope, and this underpinned their critiques of mainstream thinking. Both structuralist and dependency theorists emphasized the importance of center-periphery relations as determining or conditioning the national development process. But some strands within dependency theory, instead of indicating how national development was affected by the articulation between internal and external factors, simply put forward an antithesis to the mainstream approach, arguing that external factors were the only ones that mattered, and then deduced that by delinking from the world economy, an "authentic" development process, solely founded on internal factors, could be made to occur.

In the late 1970s and early 1980s, the growth rate of most developing countries, with the notable exception of some countries in East Asia, collapsed. The economic crises which beset most developing countries lent weight to arguments that mainstream development practice had failed. But at the same time the East Asian success neutralized those versions of dependency theory which argued that development would always be blocked on the periphery, and also Latin American structuralism, which allegedly was wedded to inward-oriented import-substitution policies in contrast to East Asia's alleged outward-orientation. In this situation, arguments which emphasized the positive role of free markets in development attracted greater attention. These ideas had always been an element within development policy analysis, represented, for example, by early critiques of protectionism, such as G. Haberler and H. Myint, Milton Friedman's support of free enterprise, and P. T. Bauer's dissection of mainstream thinking (Bauer 1971). The uptake of these ideas was not strong however until the late 1970s and early 1980s, when a new approach to developing countries, which was later labeled the Washington Consensus, emerged as the main alternative to national developmentalism.[4]

The frame of reference for this new approach was, like the Latin

American countercurrents of the pre-1980s, partially global and partially national. But rather than combining normative economic nationalism with a methodological internationalism, the Washington Consensus was its mirror image. It combined normative economic internationalism with a methodologically nationalist form of explanation which attributed what was happening within countries mainly to national factors and policies (Figure 19.2).

In this new approach, the key norms which played the decisive role in defining development practice were the norms of a liberal international economic order (LIEO). In most general terms, these norms involve a commitment to free markets, private property and individual incentives, and a circumscribed role for government. But they can be specified in different ways, according to different interpretations of the precise content of the LIEO. For example, in the early 1980s, laissez-faire liberalism was strongly advocated. This entailed liberalization of both external and domestic economic relations. But at the start of the 1990s, this extreme market fundamentalism was softened with the emergence of the so-called market-friendly approach to development (see, notably, World Bank 1991). This continued strongly to advocate liberalization of external trade and capital movements. But, the scope of domestic economic liberalization was limited, in particular, by recognizing more fully the legitimacy of state intervention in cases of market failure.

These norms were propagated through two types of persuasive argument: first, arguments about the intrinsic ethical superiority of economic liberalism; and second, theoretical and empirical analyses which demonstrate that conformity to the norms of a LIEO (variously defined) would lead to better outcomes, not simply for the world community as a whole, but also for individual nation-states within it. The latter, which have served

Figure 19.2   The Configuration of Development Policy Analysis, 1950–1990

		Normative Framework	
		National	*Global*
Explanatory Framework	*National*	Competing Mainstream Develop. Paradigms Pre-1982 e.g., Balanced vs. Unbalanced Growth	Dominant Development Paradigm Post-1982: Washington Consensus
	Global	Main Countercurrents Pre-1982: Latin American Structuralism and Dependency Theory	

as the principal form of argument supporting the new approach, have mainly been articulated on a terrain in which promoting the national interest has been narrowly equated with promoting economic growth and increasing personal economic welfare. Important developmentalist concerns such as constructing national unity and realizing national sovereignty are thus excluded. On this narrowed ground, attention and publicity has been given to analyses which show that national policies which are in conflict with the norms of LIEO, including many elements at the heart of earlier development practice, such as protection of infant industries, managed interest rates and selective credit, have been harmful to national interests, and thus constituted domestic mismanagement and "irrationalities." At the same time, the policies of the East Asian newly industrializing economies which had actually achieved rapid and sustained growth have been described in ways which suggest that they conformed to the requisite liberal norms.[5] For both conflicting and conforming policies, their impact on the efficiency of resource allocation has been identified as the main mechanism by which domestic policies affect economic growth.

While the normative frame of reference of the new᾽ approach was global in scope, the explanatory arguments which sought to prove the instrumental superiority of the LIEO were characterized by methodological nationalism. That is to say, in explaining economic trends within countries, they partitioned influences into external and internal factors and attributed most of what was happening to internal (national) factors, and in particular, to domestic policy.[6] In making the case for trade liberalization and export promotion, for example, conditions of global demand are generally ignored and, through the "small country" assumption, it is typically assumed that foreign markets are always available, and at prices largely independent of a country's exports. Empirically, the most common approach to prove the dynamic benefits of outward-orientation has been cross-country regression analyses which establish the statistical relationships between indicators of national economic change and a series of national variables, which include, in particular, indicators of national policy. The essence of this methodology is a real correlation between dependent and independent variables, to identify the extent to which variation in the former between a given set of national territories matches variation in the latter between the same territories. This can be done at a certain point in time or for periods of time (e.g., by using growth rates over 20 years). In either case, specific histories are filtered out and it is assumed that relationships which pertained in the past will continue into the future. Economic trends are necessarily attributed to the behavior of the national factors.

In the 1990s, changes in the nature of the external environment are increasingly being used to explain why liberalization, coupled with the right macroeconomic fundamentals, "works." Thus it is argued that in an increasingly globalized world economy, in which there is the globalization of production systems, increasing reliance on trade and increased availability of external financial flows, countries which do not follow Washington Consensus policies will be especially penalized, as they will be cut off and thus excluded from the intensifying (and implicitly beneficial) global field of flows. Concomitantly, those countries which do follow the right policies will be rewarded, as they can capture foreign direct investment which brings technology and market access, and they can also supplement national savings with international capital flows, thus reaping the benefits of the new external environment. In this way, the case for liberalization is rooted in the rhetoric of the globalization. But the analysis remains methodologically nationalist as it retains the distinction between external and internal factors, and still attributes country trends largely to domestic policy (see, for example, IMF 1997; World Bank 1997). Globalization is something which is happening to the external economic environment of countries; it is outside them.

The Shift from Historicism to Ahistorical Performance Assessment

The curious combination of global liberalism[7] and methodological nationalism which underpins the way in which development is seen in the new paradigm has been buttressed by a second key shift which occurred in development policy analysis at the end of the 1970s. This can be characterized as a shift from historicism to ahistorical performance assessment.

Theorizing on development strategy from the 1950s to the 1970s was historicist in the general sense that it was founded on an attempt to understand rhythms, patterns and laws of development.[8] This understanding was based on historical analysis of long-term sequences of economic and social change, which had occurred in the past in already-industrialized countries and which were expected to reoccur, particularly if the right policy interventions were made, in "less-developed" countries. Such theorizing most typically understood development as a societal and economy-wide transition from a "traditional" (rural, backward, agricultural) society to a "modern" (urban, advanced, industrial) society. This process was seen as a sequence of stages of growth, a process of modernization, or recurrent patterns of structural transformation.[9] All countries were expected to go through such patterns of development, and development agencies sought to ensure or accelerate the arrival of a better future for whole societies through interventions in these long-term processes of historical transformation.

With the shift to ahistorical performance assessment, the focal object of enquiry has been to describe and explain national "performances" of various types. Not surprisingly but now taken-for-granted, the key word in the discourse propagated by international development agencies since the start of the 1980s has been "performance." Attention has been particularly paid to economic performance, but also agricultural performance, industrial performance, trade performance, financial performance, fiscal performance, poverty performance, human development performance and so on. Using these various standards, countries have been partitioned into good and bad performers, and ranked according to their performance in various new leagues of nations. Moreover comparative performances have been explained by reference to national factors and national policy.

It is according to these performance standards that past development policies have been criticized because they do not "work" and narratives have been constructed about the effectiveness of the Washington Consensus. A succession of countries which have undertaken policy reform in the requisite way and achieved good short-term growth results have also been identified as, and dubbed, "success stories." These stories have acted as exemplars for the new paradigm, providing not only practical rules-of-thumb guidance on how policy reform should be undertaken, but also proof of the validity of the Washington Consensus.

The transition from historicism to ahistorical performance assessment started in the 1970s, and was initially animated by those who sought to refine the definition of development by adding social aspects. Efforts to measure poverty based on the quality of life and satisfaction of basic needs were particularly important in this regard. Michael Lipton's book *Why Poor People Stay Poor* was a key text in propagating a performance-oriented approach. The uptake of the notion of urban bias, a concept which was forged within debates about how to achieve redistribution with growth but which became central to the neoliberal paradigm, can be attributed to its performance-based definition, and the vitriolic debates of the late 1970s, particularly with Byres, can be interpreted as an attempt to sustain a historicist view (Byres 1979). In the 1980s, these initial moves toward performance assessment were overtaken by, and later incorporated in, the discourse and practice of structural adjustment. Adjustment involved improving the performance of national economies by increasing the efficiency of resource allocation. The central criterion used to measure performance was current or recent GDP growth rate, and macroeconomic stability, indicated by fiscal and external payments balance and low inflation. The dynamics of long-term transformations of economies and societies slipped from view and attention was placed on short-term growth and reestablishing financial balances.

The shift to ahistorical performance assessment can be interpreted as a form of the post-modernization of development policy analysis. It reflects, in particular, the questioning of grand narratives of historical transformation which was central to the appeal of the post-modern ethos in the 1980s.[10] Before the shift, development agencies acted as handmaidens of "progress," "modernization," "industrialisation," or the emancipation of people from oppression, exploitation, disease and drudgery. After it, most agencies reoriented their work to monitor and seek to improve "performance," often through local problem-solving and local social engineering designed to make economic and social institutions "work" better. Adjustment also entailed the abandonment of grand long-term government-directed designs for whole societies and a shift to decentralized decision-making, laissez-faire and local social engineering. But ironically, this shift away from holism could not be achieved without a holistic approach. Everything has been made subject to the rules and discipline of the market. The vision of the liberation of people and peoples, which animated development practice in the 1950s and 1960s, has thus been replaced by the vision of the liberalization of economies. The goal of structural transformation has been replaced with the goal of spatial integration.

The Configuration of Development Policy Analysis in the 1990s

The collapse of communism in Eastern Europe and the Soviet Union has served as confirmation of arguments which predicted the impossibility of central planning and reinforced the apparent superiority of a market-oriented development approach. Since the late 1980s however there have developed two important challenges to the Washington Consensus. The first is the UNDP's sustainable human development (SHD) approach. This approach takes up some of the themes of the UNICEF critique of the dominant approach, *Adjustment with a Human Face,* originally published in 1987, and has been elaborated through the annual *Human Development Report,* which first appeared in 1990 (UNDP various years). The second is a latent "Southern Consensus," which is founded on analyses made from the perspective of countries undertaking late industrialization and seeking to catch up with richer countries in the global economy. This Southern Consensus does not exist as a political reality. Nor has it, as yet, been articulated analytically. Its existence is apparent however in the convergence between the policy conclusions of Latin American neostructuralism, initially set out by ECLAC in 1990, and the deeper understanding of East Asian development models, which is described in ESCAP (1990), but has been most thoroughly reconstructed by UNCTAD in its annual *Trade and Development Report* (particularly 1994 part 2, chapter 1; 1996 part two; 1997 part 2, chapters V and VI; and 1998 part 1 chapter 3).[11]

These two challenges to the Washington Consensus have shaped development thinking and practice in different ways. Indeed development policy analysis is now characterized by a double dialectic. The clash between the Washington Consensus and the sustainable human development approach acts to reinforce and conserve the key elements of the current paradigm, and in particular its ahistorical approach and its combination of normative internationalism with methodological nationalism, whilst the clash between the Washington Consensus and ideas within the two strands of the Southern Consensus serves to undermine these elements and creates tensions and pressures for a further paradigm shift.

The key feature of the sustainable human development approach which distinguishes it from the Washington Consensus, is that it espouses a different set of values. Whereas the Washington Consensus focuses on the promotion of GDP growth, and has been implemented through a top-down, donor-conditionality-driven and outside-expert-led, approach, the sustainable human development approach argues that the ultimate test of development practice is that it should improve the nature of people's lives, and advocates that it should be founded on participation and a more equal partnership between developing countries and aid donors.

This "people-centered" approach, which explicitly identifies itself as an alternative paradigm (ul Haq 1995 Part 1), has been quite influential. An important strand of development research in the early 1990s has sought to refute its challenge by showing that Washington Consensus policies in fact serve to reduce poverty, increase employment and can, in themselves, deliver growth with equity, and that therefore social concerns are already adequately addressed by the mainstream approach. But the SHD alternative has promoted the introduction of poverty reduction as a key goal of development practice and increasing attention to possible LIEO-compatible relaxation of Washington Consensus policies in order better to achieve poverty objectives (see World Bank 1990).

These changes have certainly made the Washington Consensus more humane. But at the same time, the SHD approach has had the effect of conserving key features of the world-view of the dominant paradigm. Although its different values have emphasized different indicators and weighting systems, particularly to capture levels of human development and poverty, these measures have reinforced a focus on short-term performance assessment. The substitution of multidimensional indicators of poverty for simple income poverty, for example, has added greater reality to the description of deprivation and more leverage for moral outrage, but at the cost of crippling effective analysis of the dynamics of change. Significantly also, the analytical basis of the SHD approach, which is itself somewhat loose, is methodologically nationalist. A central focus is the mismatch between economic growth performance and social performance and the ways in which domestic policy can rectify this mismatch to deliver more social achievements for any given level of GDP per capita. Even the apparent difference in values between the SHD approach and the Washington Consensus is less clear-cut than it appears. This applies whether human development is specified rigorously, as in Amartya Sen's capability approach which underpins the human development index, or through a vaguer focus on decentralization and participation. Sen's capability concept emphasizes freedom of choice which is quite consonant with the liberal perspective.[12] Moreover the project of making economic and social institutions work better through decentralization and the use of local knowledge, indigenous management practices and the participation, not of the masses, but of "local people" and "small communities," can be, and has easily been, fused into a kind of neoliberal populism.[13]

Whereas the SHD approach has made a moral critique of the Washington Consensus, the two strands of the Southern Consensus, Latin American neostructuralism and East Asian developmentalism, remain focused on economic growth as the central objective.[14] They offer however a different economic analysis of how growth occurs in late industrializing countries and on this basis propose a different policy orientation to the dominant paradigm.

From the Southern perspective, national economic growth involves a process of catching-up, in which national enterprises build up production capabilities and international competitiveness in a range of activities undertaken in more advanced countries. The structure of the economy changes as the relative importance of agriculture and natural resource exploitation declines while that of manufacturing activities increases, and as production progresses from less to more skill-, technology-, and capital-intensive activities. At the macrolevel, growth, structural change and productive upgrading is driven by a rapid pace of capital accumulation, which depends on increased domestic savings, investment, and exports, linked together in a virtuous circle of cumulative causation (ECLAC 1990: 48–49; ESCAP 1990: 13–14, 115, 151; UNCTAD 1996: 108–112). At the microlevel, this process is founded on imitation, adaptation and learning of internationally available technologies in order to reduce costs, improve quality, and introduce goods and services not existing in the country, and the diffusion of best practices from more advanced to less advanced enterprises within the country, including from foreign-owned to locally owned firms (ESCAP 1990: 15–17 and 92–95; ECLAC 1990: 64–71).

An important feature of the Southern Consensus is that it rejects the idea that growth with late industrialization can be animated using a general blueprint. Policy measures have to be adapted to initial conditions and the external environment, and change over time as an economy matures (ECLAC 1990: 97–102; UNCTAD 1996: 133–134; ESCAP 1990: 21–23, 140–141). It is possible however, to identify some general policy orientations which apply in all circumstances.[15]

First, the process of growth and structural change is best achieved through the "strategic integration" of the national economy into the international economy rather than either delinking from the rest of the world or rapid across-the-board opening up of the economy to imports and external capital. This means that the timing, speed and sequencing of opening, in relation to different types of international flows, should be decided on the basis of how they support the national interest in terms of promoting economic growth and structural change (Singh 1994). Multilateral norms are not disregarded (ECLAC 1996:86; UNCTAD 1996:156–157). As far as possible, however, import liberalization should be gradual—to enable national enterprises to build up production capabilities and thus face external competition—and selective. Tariffs should also be complemented by special measures to promote exports (ECLAC 1990: 103–107; ECLAC 1995, chapter V1; and for East Asian policies, UNCTAD 1994:58–59). Capital account liberalization should also be gradual and should be managed, in coordination with domestic financial development, to ensure that capital flows are, as much as possible, additional to, rather than a substitute for, domestic resources, that they support increased investment rather than consumption, and that they do not undermine macroeconomic stability (ECLAC 1995:285–291, UNCTAD 1998:75–76, 101–106). Inward FDI should support the buildup of domestic production capabilities and exports, and this is not automatic but requires specific domestic policies (ESCAP 1990:132; ECLAC 1990:45, UNCTAD 1996:131–133).

Secondly, growth and structural change is best promoted through a combination of a macroeconomic policy and what Latin American neostructuralists describe as a "productive development policy." The macroeconomic policy is growth oriented. It seeks to reduce inflation and fiscal deficits, but also aims to ensure full utilization of production capacity and encourage the pace of capital formation (ECLAC 1996 chapter V; ESCAP 1990:17–19). The productive development policy involves a range of measures, coordinated with the trade policy, which are designed to improve the supply capabilities of the economy as a whole and also specific sectors within it, and to help private enterprise identify and acquire competitive advantages. These measures are founded on a dynamic interpretation of the principle of comparative advantage. In this forward-looking approach, the opportunities of current relative cost advantages are exploited to the full, but efforts are made at the same time to promote investment and learning in economic activities where comparative advantage can realistically be expected to lie in the immediate future as the economy develops and as other late industrializing countries catch up (ESCAP 1990:148–149, OECF 1991, UNCTAD 1996: 112–123, ECLAC 1995:132–135, 159).

Elements of a productive development policy include: technology policy, financial policy, human resource development, physical infrastructure development, and industrial organization and competition policy (UNCTAD 1994:57–69; ECLAC 1990:107–148, ECLAC 1995:161–190, ESCAP 1990 chapter V:149–150). These elements can form part of, but they should not be simply equated with, a selective industrial policy. They are directed at improving productivity and competitiveness in agriculture and natural resource–based activities as well as manufacturing (ESCAP 1990: 22, 70–

75, ECLAC 1990:126–137). They entail a mix of sectorally neutral as well as selective policies. Moreover, their main goal is to accelerate the rate of capital accumulation and learning throughout the economy.

Third, the successful implementation of these development policies requires government-business cooperation within the framework of a pragmatic developmental State. The policies are implemented, as far as possible, through private initiative rather than public ownership, and through the market mechanism rather than administrative controls. But government plays a key role both in animating the "animal spirits" of the private sector and harnessing the aggressive pursuit of profits, which are the motor of the system, to the realization of the national interest. This requires the enhancement of state capacities rather than state minimalism. Policy should be formulated by a capable and pragmatic economic bureaucracy which, through various formal and informal ties with business, develops a common vision of development objectives and targets, and a common understanding of how these can best be achieved (ECLAC 1990:94–96, Evans 1998). But government must ensure that any support or protection for the private sector is conditional on investment, export or productivity targets, and also temporary. Policies should also focus on overcoming specific problems which impede the achievement of national development objectives, notably, missing markets and the lack of an entrepreneurial base, imperfections in technology and capital markets, risks of exporting, and dynamic complementarities between sectors which render competitiveness systemic rather than just dependent on firm-level capabilities (UNCTAD 1994:50, 69, ECLAC 1995:152–157, ECLAC 1996 Box V1.1, JDB/JERI 1993:53–56).

Fourth, distributional dimensions of the growth process are managed in order to ensure the legitimacy of the overall growth process. This is primarily achieved through a production-oriented approach rather than redistributive transfers. That is to say, the main bases for a more equitable and inclusive growth process are wide asset ownership and the expansion of productive employment. Important policies in this regard are: agrarian reform and rural development policies, high rates of reinvestment of profits and the establishment of profit-related payment systems, support for small and medium enterprises, particularly through financial policies, and broad-based human resource development (Campos & Root 1996, ECLAC 1992:15–27, UNCTAD 1997:183–189).

Finally, regional integration and cooperation policies are identified as an important element of strategic integration (ECLAC 1990 chapter VI, ECLAC 1994:9–19, ESCAP 1990:24–25, UNCTAD 1996 Part 11, chapter 1: 75–79, 92–94). Such policies should support the goal of increased international competitiveness, for example, by promoting regional production chains, and also nurture the development of regional markets in order to reduce demand-side constraints on growth.

These substantive features of the Southern Consensus arise because Latin American neostructuralism and East Asian developmentalism are rooted in a totally different world-view to the Washington Consensus (Figure 19.3). This does not reject performance standards as a guide to policy, but actions are founded on historical analysis, particularly of long-term processes of late industrialization in the periphery of the world economy. A global analytical perspective is adopted and this has a realist rather than idealist view of the way in which market economies work. This recognizes vulnerabilities associated with integration into the international economy and also external constraints due to restrictions in access to advanced country markets, falling terms of trade for primary commodities and simple manufactures, cartelization in global markets, difficulties in gaining access to technology, and instabilities of the international financial system. Finally, the approach is normatively rooted in a distinctive form of economic nationalism. This is not ideologically committed to self-sufficiency or public ownership, nor hostile to foreign ownership in and of itself. It does not seek the appearance of catching up, through either imitating consumption standards, or setting up showcase industries. It respects multilateral rules and arrangements, engaging in their design, negotiation and interpretation. But its aim is to build international competitiveness as part of a long-term national economic project founded on the development of national capabilities.

Of the two strands of the Southern Consensus, the challenge from the East Asian development models has proved to be most powerful because these models have, in terms of their performance and according to the criterion of economic growth, "worked" spectacularly well. Since the early 1990s, the major fault line in development policy analysis has thus been the discrepancy between the policies which have been pursued in rapidly growing and industrializing East Asian economies and the policies advocated by the Washington Consensus.[16]

Figure 19.3   The Configuration of Development Police Analysis, 1990s and Beyond

		Normative Framework	
		National	*Global*
Explanatory Framework	*National*		• Washington Consensus • Sustainable Human Development
	Global	Southern Consensus • East Asian Models • Latin American Neostructuralism	Coming Paradigm Shift

Kuhn argues that the questioning of a paradigm begins when anomalies arise between paradigmatic expectations and actual events, and shows that numerous ad hoc modifications typically are made to maintain an old paradigm before the accumulation of anomalies requires, and the availability of a superior alternative paradigm enables, a paradigm shift. With increasing awareness of the discrepancy between Washington Consensus recommendations and East Asian development practices, such a process has occurred with the Washington Consensus. The discrepancy has been a key factor which has impelled the shift in the Washington Consensus from laissez-faire liberalization to the market-friendly approach. But more fundamental change has, at the same time, been slowed by semantic ambiguities, particularly centered on the key words "outward-oriented" and "openness" (see Gore, 1996a), and also further work to re-describe the East Asian experience as being compatible with the norms of the market-friendly LIEO. The World Bank's East Asian Miracle study—which was prompted by disagreements between the Japanese government and the World Bank on specific development policy mechanisms and which Wade (1996) has explicitly dubbed an exercise in the "art of paradigm maintenance"—is a particularly significant example of the latter (World Bank 1993).

These re-descriptions have, like earlier characterizations, now been shown to have inconsistencies and ambiguities (Arnsden, 1994; Rodrik, 1994). But the debate has taken yet another turn with the financial crisis in East Asia, and the apparent fall of the newly industrializing economies which hitherto had been claimed on all sides as "legitimating angels."

The Coming Paradigm Shift

The financial crisis in East Asia is significant for the future directions in development thinking and practice. Economic growth has fallen dramatically in developing countries and, just as there was during the crisis of the early 1980s, there is now increasing reason to call into question the effectiveness of dominant policies. Commentators of every persuasion have been quick to argue that events confirm their analysis. Some of those who support the Washington Consensus have reversed their earlier description of East Asian policies as market-friendly, and identified domestic mismanagement, in the guise of crony capitalism and excessive government intervention, as responsible for the crisis. On the other side, it is argued that the crisis is mainly due to speculative financial flows and contagion. But domestic policy, particularly fast financial liberalization, is also said to have played a role. The abandonment of government coordination of capacity expansion has led to overinvestment, and the lack of government supervision of the scale of the foreign debts of domestic companies has precipitated overexposure to external debt. Finally, the IMF bailout packages are said to have exacerbated the problem. At best they are seen as a misdiagnosis; at worst, an attempt to use the crisis further to impose in a deeper way LIEO norms on domestic economic activity.

Although these debates are still playing themselves out, it is becoming increasingly unconvincing to attribute the crisis solely to domestic mismanagement (Chang, Palmer & Whittaker 1998), or analytically to separate external and internal factors. Moreover the Washington Consensus has cracked in the practical sense that real differences of opinion have emerged in Washington, between the IMF and the World Bank, on the causes of the crisis and how best to handle it. One important opinion-leader, Paul Krugman (1995), has already written the obituary of the Washington Consensus. After the Mexican crisis of 1994, he argued that the major mechanism through which its policies have worked is a speculative bubble in emerging markets in which policy reforms attracted private capital flows, and the attraction of the flows stimulated policy reforms, and that this bubble had now burst. In effect, he exposed market-friendly policies as actually being markets-friendly—financial markets, that is. Similarly, Joseph Stiglitz (1998a,b) has argued that there is a need for a "post-Washington Consensus," a new paradigm. This should seek to achieve broader objectives—embracing a focus on the living standards of people and the promotion of equitable, sustainable and democratic development. It should use a wider range of instruments to build markets as well as to correct market failure, and to foster competition as well as liberalization and privatization. It should also adopt limited forms of regulation, if necessary controlling short-term international capital flows. Finally, change should not be imposed from outside but requires ownership, participation, partnership and consensus-building.

It may be too early yet to announce the fall of the Washington Consensus. Stiglitz's proposed new paradigm contains some important shifts on values, continuing the incorporation of the goals and implementation style advocated by SHD, and, perhaps more significantly, it argues for a return to the notion of a development strategy, based on a long-term perspective, respecting historical specificities and with a more holistic approach centered on the transformation of societies. Development should no longer be a monopoly of economists. But the proposed post–Washington Consensus consensus can also be interpreted as simply a change to preserve the old order by making it more effective as well as more humane. In elaborating the new paradigm, Stiglitz (1998b: 34) explicitly states that a key task is to lessen the momentum of an expected swing of the pendulum of opinion against openness. The proposal retains a strong commitment to the fundamental principles of a LIEO founded on open trade regimes, competitive markets and open societies. But, by delinking trade and financial liberalization and then analytically separating short-term from long-term international capital flows, it reduces the risk that in the aftermath of the financial crisis the liberalization of external economic transactions will be called into question as a whole. Through this analytical splitting, what previously was propagated as a total package can now be taken to be a more flexible menu of options, and any possible backlash against liberalization can be more easily contained.

Whether or not Stiglitz's courageous intervention is a rupture with the past or the preservation of the old regime, more profound change is inevitable. This is because the forced marriage of global liberalism and methodological nationalism, the latter providing the empirical justification for the internalization in domestic policy of the prescribed international norms of the former, is inherently unsustainable. The only circumstances under which methodological nationalism is a completely coherent approach to explanation is if national economies are completely isolated and closed from outside influences. The more that the norms of a LIEO are adhered to, the more that national economies become open to outside influences, the less tenable methodological nationalism becomes as a form of explanation. The dominant paradigm is thus unstable. Its ideology and methodology are in contradiction.

The coming paradigm shift will be driven by the main "workable" alternative, East Asian models, politically strengthened through their convergence with Latin America neostructuralism, and extended to Africa and the least developed countries. But while this approach can offer a more effective way of developing countries than the Washington Consensus, it does not, as it stands, provide an ideal alternative paradigm. This is not because the current financial crisis has somehow nullified the development transformation which has occurred in East Asia—though the crisis demands closer consideration of the issue of "development strategy in the age of global money."[17] Rather, it is because it remains a moot point whether it is possible to achieve similar results to those achieved by East Asian countries in their high-growth period, given the widespread, simultaneous adoption of past East Asia–type policies. Moreover, though exaggerated, some new global rules, particularly concerning technological borrowing and adaptation, may inhibit the replication of some of these policies.

In the future, the full globalization of development policy analysis seems inevitable (Figure 19.3). This will entail the explanation of national development trends in a global context, and also the elaboration of alternative normative principles for the international regimes which constrain and enable national policy choices. Signs that such a spatial frame shift is now occurring are evident in diverse and unconnected analytical arenas. These include: attempts to link international trade theory to labor market performance (Wood 1994), the development of the new economic geography (Ottavino & Puga 1998) and sociological analysis of global production chains (Gereffi 1995), work on global environmental commons, and the emergence of social exclusion as a concept of deprivation (Gore 1996b).

The spatial frame shift is likely to be linked to the re-introduction of a historical perspective, which is already becoming evident, for example, in analyses of the history of globalization of economic activity (Bairoch 1993, Bairoch & Kozul-Wright 1998, Brenner 1998). But with the rejection of grand narratives, bringing history back in should not presage a return to the old teleological historicism, but rather identify alternative situations and possible development paths, and thereby inform a pragmatic commitment to progressive change in favor of present as well as future generations. The values which will glue together the new way of seeing the world are, like the methods of global analysis, as yet unclear. The most likely prospect is that we shall be blown into the future facing backward, embracing a form of embedded communitarian liberalism, which seeks to reconcile the achievement of national, regional and global objectives, and to marry universal values with a respect for diversity. But this is still waiting to be born.

Notes

1. That is, a constellation of beliefs, values, techniques and group commitments shared by members of a given community, founded in particular on a set of shared axioms, models and exemplars (see Kuhn 1970). The term "paradigm" is used in this sense throughout this paper.

2. For an extended discussion of the importance of frames in policy analysis, see Schon and Rein (1994). The notion of the frame is also pivotal in Amartya Sen's work on development evaluation, though he uses the term "informational basis" of evaluative judgments rather than "frame."

3. For deeper discussion of these debates, and the role of international development agencies in them, see Arndt (1987), chapters 3 and 4.

4. This was a complex historical process. As Kuhn (1970) explains, the timing of paradigm shifts is influenced not simply by scientific and policy debate, but also broader political and ideological configurations. These broader changes, which include the election of conservative political leaders in the United Kingdom, United States and Germany in the late 1970s and early 1980s, will not be dealt with here. For a subtle account, which locates changes in development thinking and practice within a broader counter-revolution against Keynesian economic policies, see Toye (1993).

5. For these two lines of argument, see various *World Development Reports*, particularly World Bank (1983, 1986, 1987). The last, as well as criticizing deviant policies, is an exemplar of the mobilization of East Asian experience to support key principles of a LIEO.

6. For an extended discussion of methodological nationalism, see Gore (1996a).

7. The term "global liberalism" is used here as shorthand for various types of LIEO, which may or may not allow a circumscribed role for national government intervention in market processes.

8. The term "historicism" is used here in the most general sense given by Popper (1960: 3). It does not imply that planning which aims at arresting, accelerating or controlling development processes is impossible, though some historicisms would adopt this stronger position (Popper 1960: 44–45).

9. Exemplars are Rostow (1960) and Chenery and Syrquin (1975).

10. Lyotard sees the main criterion which is used to legitimate knowledge after the questioning of the grand narratives as "performativity," which is understood as assessment of the performance of systems in terms of the best input/output relations (1984: 46).

11. Various academic books and articles are associated with these policy reports. Key elements of Latin American neostructuralism, which developed as a response to the weaknesses of both neoliberalism and import-substitution industrialization, are set out in Bitar (1988), Ffrench-Davies (1988), Sunkel and Zuleta (1990), Fajnzylber (1990) and Sunkel (1993), and are surveyed in Kay (1998). A Japanese view of the contrast between East Asian developmentalism and the Washington Consensus is set out in OECF (1990), whilst Okudo (1993) and JDB/JERI (1993) discuss the Japanese approach, focusing on two important policy mechanisms which diverge from the tenets of the dominant approach—two-step loans and policy-based lending. UNCTAD's reconstruction of East Asian developmentalism, which was elaborated independently of Latin American neostructuralism, draws on analyses of the Japanese development experience, particularly Akamatsu (1961, 1962) and Shinohara (1982), and key elements are set out in Akyuz and Gore (1996) and Akyuz (1998).

12. For an outline of this approach see, inter alia, Sen (1993), and an analysis of the limits of its moral individualism is made in Gore (1997).

13. For examples of a loose approach to poverty analysis based on the concept of sustainable human development, see UNDP (1995a,b); but Banuri et al. (1994) attempt to give a more rigorous specification of the concept through the notion of social capital. An interesting recent development has been to link sustainable human development to the promotion of human rights discourse, which some see as an alternative global ethics to neoliberalism. The increasing incorporation of the voice of nongovernment organizations (NGOs) into or alongside UN social deliberations is also affecting the SHD approach. A good discussion of some of the notions which animate these discussions is Nederveen Pierterse (1998).

14. It is difficult to identify an African strand to the Southern Consensus, but Mkandawire and Soludo (1999) seek to develop an African alternative to the Washington Consensus, and UNCTAD (1998 part 2) has drawn implications of the East Asian development experience for Africa.

15. There are some divergences between the East Asian and Latin American approaches. The latter gives more prominence to environment and democracy, is less committed to aggressive sectoral targeting (ECLAC 1996: 70–71, Ocampo 1999), and has a more refined policy analysis of the process of financial integration than East Asian developmentalism (ECLAC 1995, Part 3). But their similarities, and common disagreements with the Washington Consensus, are more striking.

16. For an interesting alternative interpretation of this fault line, see Yanagihara (1997) who contrasts an ingredients approach and a framework approach and seeks ways of synthesizing them.

17. To paraphrase Yanagihara and Sambommatsu (1996).

References

Akamatsu, K. 1961. "A Theory of Unbalanced Growth in the World Economy." *Weltwirtschaftliches Archiv*, 86:196–215.
Akamatsu, K. 1962. "A Historical Pattern of Economic Growth in Developing Countries." *The Developing Economies, 1,* no.1:3–25.

Akyüz, Y. 1998. "New Perspectives on East Asia." *Journal* of *Development Studies (special issue)* 34, no. 6.

Akyüz, Y. and C.G. Gore. 1996. "The Investment-Profits Nexus in East Asian Industrialization." *World Development*, 24, no. 3: 461–470.

Amsden, A. 1994. "Why Isn't the Whole World Experimenting with the East Asian Model to Develop? Review of the East Asian Miracle." *World Development*, 22, no.4:627–634.

Arndt, H. W. 1987. *Economic Development: The History of an Idea.* Chicago: University of Chicago Press.

Bairoch, P. 1993. *Economic and World History.* Brighton, UK: Wheatsheaf.

Bairoch, P. and R. Kozul-Wright. 1998. "Globalization Myths: Some Historical Reflections on Integration, Industrialization and Growth in the World Economy. In R. Kozul-Wright and R. Rowthorn, *Transnational Corporations and the Global Economy,* London: Macmillan; New York: St. Martin's Press.

Banuri, T., et al. 1994. *Defining and Operationalizing Sustainable Human Development: A Guide for Practitioners.* Bureau for Programme Policy and Evaluation. New York: UNDP.

Bauer, P. T. 1971. *Dissent on Development: Studies and Debates in Development Economics.* London: Weidenfeld and Nicolson.

Bitar, S. 1988. Neo-Conservatism Versus Neo-Structuralism in Latin America." *CEPAL Review,* 34:45–62.

Brenner, R. 1998. "The Economics of Global Turbulence: A Special Report on the World Economy, 1950–98," *New Left Review,* 229 (May/June).

Byres, T. J. 1979. "Of Neopopulist Pipedreams: Daedalus in the Third World and the Myth of Urban Bias." *Journal of Peasant Studies, 6,* no. 2:210–244.

Campos, J. E., and H. L. Root. 1996. *The Key to the Asian Miracle: Making Shared Growth Credible.* Washington, DC: The Brookings Institution.

Chang, H. J., G. Palmer, and D. Hugh Whittaker. 1998. "The Asian Crisis." *Cambridge Journal of Economics* (special issue), 22.

Chenery, H. B. and M. Syrquin. 1975. *Patterns of Development, 1950–70.* London: Oxford University Press.

ECLAC. 1990. *Changing Production Patterns with Social Equity: The Prime Task of Latin America and Caribbean Development in the 1990s.* Santiago: ECLAC.

———. 1992. *Social Equity and Changing Production Patterns: An Integrated Approach.* Santiago: ECLAC.

———. 1994. *Open Regionalism in Latin America and the Caribbean: Economic Integration as a Contribution to Changing Production Patterns with Social Equity.* Santiago: ECLAC.

———. 1995. *Policies to Improve Linkages with the Global Economy.* Santiago: ECLAC.

———. 1996. *Strengthening Development: The Interplay of Macro- and Microeconomics.* Santiago: ECLAC.

ESCAP. 1990. *Restructuring the Developing Economies of Asia and the Pacific in the 1990s.* United Nations: New York.

Evans, P. 1998. "Transferable Lessons? Re-examining the Institutional Prerequisites of East Asian Economic Policies." *Journal of Development Studies,* 34, no.6:66–86.

Fajnzylber, F. 1990. "Industrialization in Latin America: From the "Black Box" to the 'Empty Box.'" *Cuardenos de la CEPAL,* 60, CEPAL, Santiago.

Ffrench-Davies, R. 1988. "An Outline of a Neo-Structuralist Approach." *CEPAL Review. 34, 371.*

Gereffi. G. 1995. "Contending Paradigms for Cross-Regional Comparison: Development Strategies and Commodity Chains in East Asia and Latin

America." In P. H. Smith, *Latin America in Comparative Perspective: New Approaches to Methods and Analysis.* Boulder, CO: Westview Press: 33–58.

Gore. C. G. 1996a. "Methodological Nationalism and the Misunderstanding of East Asian Industrialization." *European Journal of Development Research,* 8, no.1: 77–122.

———. 1996b. "Social Exclusion, Globalization, and the Trade-Off Between Efficiency and Equity." In G. Kohler *et al., Questioning Development: Essays in the Theory, Policies and Practice of Development Interventions.* Metropolis Verlag, Marburg: 103–116.

———. 1997. "Irreducibly Social Goods and the Informational Basis of Amartya Sen's Capability Approach." *Journal of International Development. 9,* no. 2: 235–250.

Haq, M. ul. 1995. *Reflections on Human Development.* Oxford: Oxford University Press.

IMF. *World Economic Outlook.* 1997. *Globalization: Opportunities and Challenges.* Washington, DC: IMF.

JDB/JERI (Japan Development Bank and Japan Economic Research Institute). 1993. *Policy-Based Finance: The Experience of Postwar Japan.* Final Report to the World Bank, Washington, DC.

Johnson, H. J. 1967. "The Ideology of Economic Policy in the New States." In H. G. Johnson, ed., *Economic Nationalism in Old and New States.* Chicago: University of Chicago Press: 124–141.

Kay, C. 1989. *Latin American Theories of Development and Underdevelopment.* London: Routledge.

———. 1998. *Relevance of Structuralist and Dependency Theories in the Neoliberal Period: A Latin American Perspective.* Working Paper Series No. 281. The Hague: Institute of Social Studies.

Krugman, P. 1995. "Dutch Tulips and Emerging Markets." *Foreign Affairs.* 74, no. 4: 28–44.

Kuhn, T. 1970. "The Structure of Scientific Revolutions," 2d ed. In International *Encylopaedia of Unified Science* 2, no.2. Chicago: University of Chicago Press.

Lyotard, J. F. 1984. *The Post-Modern Condition: A Report on Knowledge.* Manchester: Manchester University Press.

Mkandawire, T. and C. Soludo. 1999. *Our Continent, Our Future: African Perspectives on Structural Adjustment.* Trenton, N.J. and Asmara, Eritrea: Africa World Press.

Nederveen Pierterse, J. 1998. "My Paradigm or Yours? Alternative Development, Post-Development, Reflexive Development." *Development and Change.* 29: 343–373.

Ocampo, J. A. 1999. *Beyond the Washington Consensus: An ECLAC perspective.* Paper prepared for the conference Beyond the Washington Consensus: Net Assessment and Prospects for New Approach, organized by the Department of Comparative Research on Development of the Ecole des Hautes Etudes en Sciences Sociales, Paris, and MOST of UNESCO. June 1999, Paris.

OECF. 1990. Issues Related to the World Bank's Approach to Structural Adjustment—Proposal from a Major Partner. OECF Discussion Paper No. 1.

Okudo, H. 1993. "Japanese Two-Step Loans: The Japanese Approach to Development Finance." *Hitorsubashi Journal of Economics,* 34: 67–85.

Ottavino. G. I. P. and D. Puga. 1998. "Agglomeration in the Global Economy: A Survey of the 'New Economic Geography.'" *The World Economy,* 21, no. 6: 707–732.

Popper, K. R. 1960. *The Poverty of Historicism,* 2nd ed. London: Routledge and Kegan Paul.

Rodrik, D. 1994. *King Kong Meets Godzilla: The World Bank and the East Asian Miracle.* CEPR Discussion Paper. No. 944, CEPR: Oxford.

Rostow, W. 1960. *The Stages of Economic Growth: A Non-Communist Manifesto.* Cambridge: Cambridge University Press.

Schön, D. and M. Rein. 1994. *Frame Refection: Towards the Resolution of Intractable Policy Controversies.* New York: Basic Books.

Sen, A. 1993. "Capability and Well-Being." In M. Nussbaum and A. Sen, eds., *The Quality of Life.* Oxford: Clarendon Press: 30–54.

Shinohara, M. 1982. *Industrial Growth, Trade and Dynamic Patterns in the Japanese Economy.* Tokyo: Tokyo University Press.

Singh, A. 1994. "Openness and the Market-Friendly Approach to Development: Learning the Right Lessons from Development Experience." *World Development,* 22, no. 12:1811–1823.

Stiglitz, J. 1998a. "More Instruments and Broader Goals: Moving Toward the Post-Washington Consensus." The WIDER Annual Lecture. Helsinki, Finland (January 7).

———. 1998b. "Towards a New Paradigm for Development: Strategies, Policies, and Processes." Prebisch Lecture given at UNCTAD, Geneva (October 19).

Sunkel, O. 1993. *Development From Within: Toward a Neostructuralist Approach for Latin America.* Boulder, CO: Lynne Rienner Publishers.

Sunkel, O. and G. Zuleta. 1990. "Neo-Structuralism Versus Neo-Liberalism in the 1990s. *CEPAL Review,* 41:36–51.

Toye, J. 1993. *Dilemmas of Development: Reflections on the Counter-Revolution in Development Theory and Practice,* 2nd ed. Oxford: Blackwell.

UNCTAD. various years. *Trade and Development Report.* Geneva: United Nations.

UNDP. various years. *Human Development Report.* New York: Oxford University Press.

———. 1995a. *Poverty Eradication: A Policy Framework for Country Strategies.* New York: UNDP.

———. 1995b. *From Poverty to Equity: An Empowering and Enabling Strategy.* New York: UNDP.

Wade, R. 1996. The World Bank and the art of paradigm maintenance: The East Asian Miracle in political perspective. *New Left Review. 117*: 3–36.

Williamson, J. 1990. "What Washington Means by Policy Reform." In J. Williamson, ed., *Latin American Adjustment: How Much Has Happened.* Washington DC: Institute of International Economics: 5–20.

———. 1993. "Democracy and the 'Washington Consensus.'" *World Development,* 11 no. 8: 1329–1336.

———. 1997. "The Washington Consensus Revisited." In L. Emmerij, ed., *Economic and Social Development into the XXI Century.* Washington, D.C.: Inter-American Development Bank (distributed by John Hopkins University Press, Baltimore):48–61.

Wood, A. 1994. *North-South Trade, Employment and Inequality: Changing Fortunes in a Skill-Driven World.* Oxford: Clarendon Press.

World Bank. various years. *World development report.* New York: Oxford University Press.

———. 1993. *The East Asian Miracle.* New York: Oxford University Press.

———. 1997. *Global Economic Prospects and the Developing Countries.* Washington, DC: World Bank.

Yanagihara, T. 1997. "Economic System Approach and Its Applicability." In T.

Yanagihara and S. Sambommatsu, *East Asian Development Experience: Economic System Approach and Its Applicability*. Tokyo: Institute for Developing Economies: 1–35.

Yanagihara. T. and S. Sambommatsu. 1996. "Exchange Rate Gluctuations and Asian Responses: Growth Strategy in the Age of Global Money." *IDE Spot Survey*. Tokyo: Institute for Developing Economies.

20

A New World Bank for a New Century

Robert Picciotto

The World Bank is the target of strident criticisms from the antiglobaliza-tion left and the market triumphalist right. In this chapter, presenting a pragmatic neoliberal argument, Robert Picciotto defends the World Bank and its shifting agenda. Picciotto argues that the Bank's reorientation from macroeconomic management toward governance, financial-sector reform, social development, and social protection is in tune with the changing times. This new orientation will distinguish the Bank from the International Monetary Fund and serve the development needs of low-income countries more appropriately and effectively. Picciotto identifies two critical chal-lenges: (1) the implementation of poverty reduction strategies and debt reduction programs in the least-developed countries, and (2) multilateral cooperation in the wake of the terrorist attacks of September 11, 2001. Both, he argues, will propel the World Bank and its operations into greater significance. In a highly fragmented development assistance architecture, he concludes, the role of the World Bank assumes even more critical impor-tance to address the issue of development partnership between the rich and poor countries.

The development effectiveness of the World Bank's operations has improved greatly in the past several years. Its organization is more respon-sive to country needs and stakeholder concerns. More than a money bank, it is also a knowledge bank and a partnership bank. And its operational agen-da is more comprehensive. Why? Because its business has changed, and it is being called on to deliver wholesaling services to the development com-munity.

This transition has been demanding for the Bank. Greater relevance has been achieved at the cost of budgetary stress, management-staff ten-sions, and organizational overload. Internal management arrangements have had to be revisited. Risk management has become a major challenge.

Accordingly, the World Bank may well be entering a period of consolidation, greater selectivity, and tighter internal controls. But there is no turning back: the new operational emphases of the World Bank are here to stay because they reflect the needs of the new century.

A New Role in the Development Architecture

The changes in the Bank's corporate strategies (and the massive challenges that remain) reflect the evolution of the environment for development. More than five billion people live in market economies today, up from one billion fifteen years ago. The information revolution is opening enormous opportunities for new products, new markets, and new production techniques. Yet failed and failing states, rampant corruption, and increased inequalities in income distribution among and within countries reduce the developmental benefits of more open trade and freer capital flows.

The share of the poor in the world population has declined, but this has largely been because of progress by China and India. Poverty trends have been very disappointing in Africa, Latin America, and the former Soviet Union. As a result, the development movement lost much public support in the 1990s, and the volume of development assistance as a share of GNP in developed countries came down by 40 percent. Just as the private sector and the civil society have adapted to globalization, so must the development assistance system.

All aid agencies are seeking greater development effectiveness through a more robust attack on the sources of poverty in developing countries (governance malfunctions, policy weaknesses, and inadequate levels of social expenditures). The "one size fits all" Washington Consensus has given way to a sober realization of the importance of building institutions and nurturing domestic ownership of reforms before administering shock therapies. Evaluation evidence has also pointed to the risks of operations imposed through top-down conditionality. The principles of effective aid endorsed by the OECD Development Assistance Committee (as well as the Comprehensive Development Framework championed by the Bank) reflect these lessons of experience.

To restore public confidence in aid and help protect the benefits of globalization, bilateral aid donors must give greater weight to country performance, harmonize their practices, reduce the transaction costs imposed on fragile recipient administrations, and focus on results within the framework of common international development goals. By endorsing these goals, the Bank has signaled its readiness to forge closer linkages with its development assistance partners and to play a leading role in helping to streamline a rococo development assistance architecture no longer adapted to global needs.

Conversely, most other multilateral and bilateral aid givers have given full support to the joint Bank-Fund initiative for poverty reduction strategies. They have also welcomed harmonization of aid practices across the development system (procurement, financial management, environmental assessment). And they are placing greater reliance on the due diligence analytical work of the Bank.

No organization can be expected to lead in all facets of development. That is why the Bank opted to reorient its operational emphases away from macroeconomic management toward governance, financial-sector reform, social development, and social protection—to distinguish its operations more sharply from those of the IMF. At the same time, the Bank began to reshape itself from a retail organization focused on projects to a wholesaling platform for development partnerships, filling a gap at the center of a highly fragmented development assistance architecture.

Reshaping the Bank

Responsiveness to the client has been the centerpiece of recent Bank reforms. A change of personnel at the top together with executive development training, "knowledge fairs," and new partnerships with governments, business, and voluntary organizations have induced deep changes in values and attitudes. The Bank is now more fluid and innovative. Management practices are less hierarchical. Partnership, ownership, and a results orientation have replaced projects, adjustment, and conditionality as the dominant themes of Bank operations. The normative, project-oriented Bank is giving way to a service-oriented development institution focused on the multiple challenges of poverty reduction.

Responsiveness to the increasingly differentiated needs of borrowing member countries underlies the logic of the Bank's country-based organization. The resulting organizational and budget process changes have been many and complex. They share a common characteristic: a determination to get closer to the client. This bias for proactive engagement also explains the fivefold expansion in development training activities of the World Bank Institute, the diversification of the Bank's instruments, and the new focus on development partnerships.

The advent of a matrix organization, the increased participation of the civil society in Bank operations, the tighter monitoring of safeguard policies, and the enhanced quality assurance efforts have come at a price. The cost of doing business with the Bank has been rising. Staff stress has grown. Budget pressures have become more intense and lending volume has come down after a remarkable spurt in the wake of the East Asia financial crisis—from $21.5 billion in FY96 to $29 billion in FY99 and down to $15.3 billion in FY00. But these are inevitable transition difficulties, and the general operational policy directions adopted by the Bank have been fully in line with the consensus of its membership.

The setup of an independent inspection panel, the renewal of the Operations Evaluation Department, and the setup of a board committee on development effectiveness have helped fill evaluation gaps and have made evaluation activities more timely and influential. Systemic links have been forged with the board's oversight of business processes not only at the project level but also at the level of country assistance strategies, sector strategy papers, and policy formulation.

In parallel, Bank management has invested heavily in self-evaluation and control activities. In particular, it has enhanced financial management and internal auditing and created the Quality Assurance Group, an anticorruption investigation unit, and a new operational policy and country services group. Because "what gets measured gets done," these reforms have paid off. The share of satisfactory outcomes for Bank projects has risen from two-thirds to three-fourths. This is all the more impressive given that the complexity and "demandingness" of Bank operations rose by more than 50 percent over the past decade.

Diversifying the Client Base

Borrowing governments have always been the Bank's main clients. But given the growing pluralism of the global operating environment, the Bank has had to build bridges to the private sector, civil society, and other development assistance agencies. The pressure for the Bank to change and broaden the scope of its assistance has come from rapidly evolving and increasingly diversified client needs.

As a result—and paradoxically for a global development agency—the Bank acts more locally now than ever before. For example, lending for policy reform to provinces and subnational entities has become the thrust of country assistance strategies in such large federal countries as India. And community-based projects have become a dynamic element of the Bank's lending program throughout the world. More often than not, the disappointment expressed by clients has to do with the Bank doing too little rather than too much.

The Bank has thus positioned itself as the indispensable financing platform for global poverty reduction. In partnership with the IMF, it is now the undisputed focal point of debt reduction programs. And it has taken the lead in multidonor partnerships in support of equitable and sustainable development in low-income countries. In parallel, it has secured the support of its governors for a continuing role in middle-income countries.

Adjusting to Market Realities

The globalization of capital markets has had a major impact on the Bank's financial intermediation role. The rise of private financial flows toward the developing world has led to a drop in the share of international financial institutions in capital flows from 40 percent in 1986 to only a few percent today. Net flows from the Bank in 2000 stood at $7.4 billion; IMF net flows were negative to the tune of $10.7 billion, while official development finance in 2000 stood at $39 billion and private flows at $257 billion, with $178 billion in foreign direct investment.

As long as private flows remain volatile and concentrated on relatively few countries, there will be a role for the Bank in middle-income countries. In effect, the higher the financial risks incurred by borrowing members in the global marketplace due to weak domestic institutions, the more relevant the financial intermediation and market stabilization roles of the Bank. Access to private capital is closely linked to variable public perceptions of the political stability and quality of economic management of individual countries.

A basic justification for continued Bank lending to middle-income countries is the herd tendency of private investors and the instability of global markets. Sovereign bond yields are highly volatile—a clear justification for nurturing long-term lending relationships between middle-income countries and the Bank. Many if not most middle-income countries have immature financial institutions, distorted social policies, badly designed social-safety nets, and limited, costly, and unreliable access to private capital markets. They will need development assistance from the World Bank for decades to come.

Managing Risks

With the global operating environment riskier and less stable, financial risk administration has become more demanding as key, large-country portfolios reach prudential ceilings. And for poor, highly indebted countries, debt reduction operations have become an indispensable addition to the Bank's tool kit.

The Bank's ten environmental and social safeguards have become benchmarks for the rest of the development system as well as touchstones of the Bank's own accountability and transparency. Weaknesses in oversight of safeguard policies have been identified and internal quality assurance strengthened to ensure that the Bank practices what it preaches, displays a human face in the operations it finances, and improves the management of its development risks. Today's World Bank has a human face.

Risk management does not mean risk avoidance. The regional and ethnic conflicts unleashed by the end of the Cold War have reconfirmed the validity of the Bank's original reconstruction mandate. The past decade has witnessed a proliferation of armed conflicts in low-income countries, most of which are domestic and affect civilian populations. Ten highly indebted African countries are affected by conflict. In addition to responding to increasingly frequent and destructive natural disasters, the Bank has become a leading player in postconflict rehabilitation, an entirely different reconstruction one from the role it played following the end of World War II: the current postconflict challenge centers on the restoration of institutional capacities in deeply wounded societies.

Connecting to the Private Sector

The collapse of communism has accelerated a trend toward a reduced role for public investment in developing countries. The growing realization that national wealth depends on setting up the right market institutions and policies has led to a greater appreciation by developing countries of the Bank's policy advice and capacity development services.

The advisory services delivered by the Bank have helped connect developing countries to the engine of the global market. Privatization, trade liberalization, financial-sector reform, improved judicial and regulatory frameworks, anticorruption programs, and other enhancements of the enabling investment climate have become a staple of the country dialogue. In particular, the Bank validates the soundness of structural and social policies, the appropriateness of public expenditures programs, and the quality of the fiduciary framework. A variety of Bank/business partnerships have sprouted to pilot new ways of reaching the poor through private enterprise.

In parallel, the two private-sector arms of the Bank—the International Finance Corporation (IFC) and the Multilateral Investment Guarantee Agency (MIGA)—have increased the scope of their operations. They now encompass infrastructure and social-sector activities previously handled exclusively by the Bank. Both IFC and MIGA are more active in "frontier" sectors and countries where risks and rewards are high and the signaling impact of the Bank Group is substantial. Assistance to small and medium-size industries and microcredit schemes is receiving more resources. Good corporate citizenship and leadership in environmental and social sustainability now lie at the core of the corporate private-sector development strategy.

Responding to Global Challenges

The growing realization that global issues need better management has induced a more explicit Bank role in multicountry collaborative programs.

From six billion people today, the world's population will expand to ten billion people over the next four decades. Food production will have to triple just as the land frontier disappears. The risks of global warming, deforestation, desertification, and infectious diseases will intensify. Environmental stress, already high, will rise further, and sustainable livelihoods will be threatened as natural resources get depleted.

To bring the cross-boundary dimension of these problems to the attention of policymakers, large numbers of informal policy networks have emerged to advocate collective action against deforestation, whaling, land mines, large dams, and corrupt practices. In parallel, hybrid forms of organization are emerging. They combine the innovative energies of the private sector, the altruism of voluntary agencies, and the regulatory clout of nation-states.

Partnership is part of the solution to the high transaction costs implicit in a multiplicity of national regulatory frameworks for oversight of financial transactions, corporate governance, and telecommunications. The challenge is to create effective global networks, to improve communication among governments, to help set standards, and to implement collaborative multicountry programs. This is the context in which amplifying the voices of the poor in international debates and mediating principled solutions to global policy issues have become growing business lines for the Bank. Already, the Bank has demonstrated a pragmatic capacity to act as a transgovernmental network. Over the past five years, it has participated in new multicountry initiatives to assist the least-developed countries in trade negotiations, combat HIV/AIDS, malaria, and tuberculosis, and develop new vaccines for tropical diseases. Partnerships have also been created to fight deforestation and protect biodiversity hotspots: 60 percent of all species are found on 1.4 percent of the planet's surface. The Bank has also financed distance learning centers, encouraged the spread of new information technologies, created a network of policy research institutes, and funded an African Virtual University.

All in all, the Bank is involved in more than ninety global and regional programs. Criticisms have been levied about the proliferation of these initiatives, the lack of clear criteria for entry, the weak resort to exit, and the tendency to take on work that does not always respect the Bank's comparative advantage. Tighter management of these activities is a clear priority. But given global trends, the Bank will continue to be called on to provide partnership services and knowledge platforms to deal with the critical problems and amazing opportunities associated with globalization.

Operating in the Wake of Terror

The terrorist attacks of September 11, 2001, have disrupted global transportation patterns, reduced trade flows, induced risk aversion among investors, undermined consumer confidence, and aggravated an already difficult economic situation for most developing countries. But they may also induce far greater economic cooperation among nations as isolationist doctrines lose ground and multilateralism gains in acceptance. The developed countries, given the sudden realization that they cannot be shielded from chaos at the periphery, will probably pay more attention to the zones of turmoil and development, where 85 percent of the world's people live. It is even conceivable that measures to liberalize trade, increase aid flows, and deal with regional conflicts will move up on their domestic policy agendas.

What does this mean for the World Bank? First, a sharply increased need for long-term financial assistance. Second, intensified demand for knowledge and advisory services to deal with the crisis. Third, a likely increase in the need for postconflict reconstruction assistance. Fourth, more interest in harmonizing practices among donors, improving aid coordination, and accelerating the implementation of poverty reduction strategies and debt reduction programs in the least-developed countries.

Of course, the greater potential rewards from World Bank activities bring higher risks. Social stresses and political constraints may undermine the momentum of policy reform by borrowers.

More than ever, the world needs a global financial institution well connected to its developing member countries, to the private sector, and to the development assistance community. For middle-income countries, the countercyclical need for World Bank assistance has become self-evident. For low-income countries, the unique poverty reduction instrument of the International Development Association (IDA), the World Bank's concessional lending window, is more visible and critical than ever.

Box 20.1   Shifting Opinions About the World Bank

Entering the new century, the World Bank has been the target of strident criticism from the antiglobalization left and the market triumphalist right. The radical street demonstrators perceive the Bank as a supine instrument of global capitalism. The "Chicago school" economists view it as a hindrance to the beneficial interplay of free-market forces. Both groups favor a drastic reduction in the Bank's role. By contrast, a broad-based—and sometimes less vocal—majority of the Bank's membership has been highly supportive of the Bank's new operational emphases.

Clearly, today's World Bank does not please everyone—and it never could. Recent organizational developments—the decentralization of country leadership, the proliferation of professional networks, and the vast increase in the number of corporate initiatives—have reinforced public perceptions of a highly decentralized, multifaceted, somewhat diffuse World Bank.

The Bank tries to do too much for too many clients? Satisfying a far wider range of constituencies and involving voluntary organizations and the private sector in Bank operations are a direct consequence of the state's reduced role in the new global economy. Inevitably, this has opened the Bank to a much wider range of influences over its policies. And it has made it harder for Bank managers to be selective given the high demand for a broad range of services by a diversity of stakeholders.

The Bank's operations encourage corruption? Quite the reverse: the Bank is a leader in the fight against corruption worldwide. Since 1996, it has launched more than six hundred anticorruption programs and government initiatives in almost one hundred countries. The Bank is also committed to keeping all Bank projects free of corruption, putting in place stringent guidelines and a hotline for complaints of abuses.

The Bank doesn't learn from its mistakes? For thirty years the Bank's operations have been independently evaluated. And because of new and unprecedented risks, the Bank now has a multifaceted evaluation system unique among development institutions. The independent Operations Evaluation Department (OED) provides a wide range of reports to the Board of Executive Directors and tracks the development effectiveness of the Bank. The Internal Audit Department assesses the effectiveness and efficiency of management controls. The independent inspection panel provides a voice to local communities that may be adversely affected by Bank-supported activities. The Quality Assurance Group (QAG) does real-time assessment of operational work. The Quality Assurance Group and Compliance Unit (QACU) addresses compliance with safeguard policies. The regional quality assurance teams are charged with all aspects of operational quality. The Oversight Committee on Fraud and Corruption oversees implementation of the Bank's anticorruption policies and strategies. And a new Department of Institutional Integrity investigates allegations of fraud and corruption.

The Bank doesn't really help the poor? Having provided $30 billion for education projects, the Bank is the world's largest external funder of education. With new commitments of $1.3 billion a year for health, nutrition, and population projects, it is also the world's largest external funder of health programs and the world's largest funder in the fight against HIV/AIDS. The Bank is also leading the initiative to reduce the debt of the world's poorest countries that have high debt burdens, tying the reductions to strategies to reduce poverty.

Box 20.2   Getting more effective

World Bank project performance has improved significantly over the past five years, according to a recent review by the World Bank's independent Operations Evaluation Department (OED). Three of every four recently completed Bank projects satisfactorily achieved their development objectives, hitting the Bank's target of 75 percent set five years ago.

Projects are evaluated on whether they did the right things (relevance to the country's development goals) and whether they did things right (the efficiency and effectiveness of implementation). Early analysis by OED confirms that Bank projects completed in fiscal year 2000 (June 30) have achieved a record level of satisfactory performance. The Bank has seen an upward trend in the quality of performance over the last five years, with performance climbing from 66 percent satisfactory (for 1990–1994), to 71 percent (for 1995–1998), 72 percent in 1999, and 77 percent for FY00 (based on partial sample). A solid 86 percent of adjustment lending outcomes were satisfactory, according to OED.

These findings suggest that the Bank's efforts to improve project design and supervision are showing results. The improvements are all the more impressive considering that Bank projects have become more complex and more demanding, especially in low-income countries. Projects now have multiple objectives and stronger requirements for such priorities as environmental safeguards.

Development outcome ratings capture not just whether the project implemented its planned investments but also whether it is likely to contribute to development and poverty alleviation over the medium to long term. The outcome rating is thus the main measure of a project's performance.

OED complements the outcome ratings with assessments of the project's contribution to strengthening institutions at the national or community level (institutional development), and a forward-looking assessment of whether project benefits are likely to be sustained (sustainability). Among recently evaluated projects, OED has determined that only 20 percent of all projects are unlikely to be sustained. The Bank's performance in institutional development has also improved over the past five years.

Notes

1. Robert Picciotto is director-general of Operations Evaluation for the World Bank Group. The views expressed here are his; they do not necessarily reflect those of the World Bank Group, the Board of Executive Directors, or the Operations Evaluation Department.

21

Still Waiting:
The Failure of Reform at the World Bank

Bruce Rich

In this essay, Bruce Rich provides a critical assessment of the World Bank's reform agenda for the twenty-first century. According to Rich, World Bank President James Wolfensohn's Comprehensive Development Framework, touted as a new paradigm for development, has failed to deliver any concrete results. He asserts that the World Bank's raison d'être—i.e., environmentally sustainable poverty alleviation—is no longer relevant as the Bank continues to serve the interests of rich countries and their corporate clients. Criticizing the Bank's culture of corruption, corporate welfare agenda, and lack of operational transparency and accountability, Rich argues that the Bank has clearly lost its relevance as a development institution. He provides a sharply contrasting perspective with that of Robert Picciotto in the previous chapter.

When James D. Wolfensohn became President of the World Bank in June 1995, he appeared to be the institution's last, best chance. A cello player, former Olympic fencer, and Medici-like financier, he could also outperform the most self-righteous non-governmental organisations (NGOs) in his public protestations of concern for the poor. In his own words, "the real test of development can be measured not by the bureaucratic approval process, but by the smile on a child's face . . . We must organise ourselves . . . to deliver on that smile."

From his first day in office, Wolfensohn promised to revolutionise the World Bank. He pledged to change the institution's long embedded internal culture from one of loan approval—where staff were rewarded above all for pushing money—to a culture of "development effectiveness" and "account-

Reprinted with permission of the publisher from *The Ecologist,* volume 30, number 6, 200. London: The Ecologist, www.theecologist.org.

ability," where economic, social and environmental results in the field would be top priorities. Making the World Bank more effective in helping the poor while protecting the environment would mean putting a priority on more intensive preparation, monitoring and supervision of Bank projects, as well as a much greater willingness to halt loan disbursements to governments—the Bank's major borrowers—that do not comply with Bank policies and loan conditions.

However, an effect of many of Wolfensohn's changes has been to make the Bank more amenable to its official governmental and corporate clients and weaken internal mechanisms for quality control. Moreover, the most rapidly growing area of Bank operations in the late 1990s has been in support for the private sector, and over the past two years, in huge, non-project emergency bail-out packages. Both priorities have even less connection to directly helping the poorest of the poor than more traditional Bank project loans. Worse, more and more evidence is coming to light that the approval culture has and is fostering systematic graft and the diversion of billions of dollars by corrupt politicians and bureaucrats in major Bank borrowers.

An Institution in Crisis

James Wolfensohn inherited an institution that was in crisis. Ever since the early 1980s, NGOs concerned with poverty alleviation and the environment have criticised the Bank relentlessly for financing development disasters in numerous countries. New Bank policies on environment and poverty alleviation, and increased staff did little to mute the criticism, since many Bank operations in the field appeared to go forward in violation of these policies.

The principal finding of the 1992 Independent Commission report into the Bank-financed Sardar Sarovar dam on the Narmada River in India, for example, was that the Bank and the Indian Government were culpable of "gross delinquency" in their implementation of the project, particularly concerning the forced resettlement of over 200,000 poor farmers. The Bank was found to be "more concerned to accommodate the pressures emanating from its borrowers than to guarantee implementation of its policies." The Wapenhans Report, released in 1992, confirmed that a "culture of loan approval" was deeply embedded in senior Bank management and had caused a relentless decline in the performance and quality of Bank operations. This was also documented in countless reports of the Bank's internal Operations Evaluation Department (OED), and ignored for over a decade by the World Bank's management and Executive Board. These deep-rooted institutional problems had been brewing for the better part of two decades and were unresolved when Wolfensohn began his tenure.

Failure of Poverty and Environmental Assessments

The Bank under Wolfensohn responded by trying to address all of these concerns simultaneously. He and Bank management maintained that there was no inherent contradiction in what amounted to promising all things to all constituencies. He thus promised to change the Bank's internal culture to better implement policies and to deliver better developmental results on the ground, but also to streamline Bank lending procedures to shorten loan processing and to increase the volume of lending.

The flaws in this approach soon became apparent in a crucial area. In the summer of 1996, two studies by the OED revealed the massive failure of the Bank to implement effectively its key poverty alleviation and environmental policy instruments—Poverty Assessments and Environmental Assessments (PAs and EAs).

Beginning in 1988 the Bank began to conduct Poverty Assessments of its borrowing nations to serve as a basis for better incorporating poverty reduction elements in the Bank's main country lending strategy documents, the Country Assistance Strategies (CASs). The Poverty Assessments were supposed to promote increased collaboration between the Bank and borrowers in poverty reduction, and to identify specific poverty reduction lending initiatives. The Bank's major donor governments made preparation of these Poverty Assessments, for the period 1994–96, a condition of the $18 billion funding replenishment of the International Development Association (IDA)—the part of the World Bank that makes low interest loans to the poorest countries. Bank staff prepared a voluminous *Poverty Reduction Handbook* to guide staff and management in carrying out Poverty Assessments and poverty reduction lending. By December 1994, 46 Poverty Assessments had been completed.

The OED review, however, concluded that the Poverty Assessments were a failure in influencing lending priorities and project design. The Poverty Assessments had little impact on Country Assistance Strategies— and this impact was supposed to be the single most important reason for their existence. The OED report found that "CASs focused overwhelmingly on broad macro-economic stabilisation and structural reform issues, with few references to the status or causes of poverty, or to approaches to poverty reduction." Not surprisingly, "Poverty Assessments have so far had little influence on the volume of lending targeted on reducing poverty." The OED report indicated that many of the Bank's borrowing governments did not in any case view poverty reduction as a goal or priority.

Perhaps the most interesting insight into the real role of concern for poverty in the Bank's institutional culture can be gleaned from the report's characterisation of comments by Bank staff familiar with the Poverty Assessment initiatives. They were able to express their opinions anonymously on Bank electronic meeting software:

> *Poverty Assessments are believed to lack influence with borrowers because poverty reduction is often not the overarching operational objective . . . Within the Bank, Poverty Assessments are not influential because they are believed not to be taken seriously by senior management . . . The Program of Targeted Interventions [increased loans to reduce poverty] (PTI) . . . has little support and generates a degree of cynicism. Too often the PTI designation is merely a label applied to projects that have little genuine poverty-reducing influence to meet an imposed requirement.*

The OED's environmental report's main findings were equally damning, concluding that most full EAs (required for so-called "Category A" projects) "generate massive documents that are of little use in project design and during implementation." Most EAs were undertaken too late in the project cycle, so that "very few EAs actually influence project design"; as a result, public consultation and information disclosure, also required by the Bank's public information policy, was also weak, and when it occurred often happened too late in the project cycle to be effective. Moreover, "most Category A project EAs have failed to give serious consideration to alternative designs and technologies as called for in the Operational Directive, and those that do often explore weak, superficial or easily dismissed options." Recommendations and environmental action plans contained in EAs were often not implemented, and Bank supervision of the environmental components of projects was often lax or non-existent. Environmental Assessments, the report continued, "are often not understood by project implementation staff and, in many instances, not even available in project offices."

The report also pointed out that if the single most important problem undermining the effectiveness of the EAs was their tardy preparation in the project cycle, Wolfensohn's efforts to speed up loan approval would worsen the problem: "if the Bank continues to reduce the number of days available for project preparation and appraisal, finding time for meaningful consultation (and quality control of EA reports) will be increasingly problematic..."

As with other OED reports, the analysis on both Poverty and Environmental Assessments was devastating, but the follow-up by Bank management virtually non-existent.

Amnesia, "Clientitis," and Unaccountability

The new internal review entity called the Quality Assurance Group—touted by Wolfensohn and Bank management as one of the key institutional changes that would bring about the much heralded "culture of development effectiveness"—concluded in April 1997, a year long review of key areas of the Bank's ongoing lending portfolio. It examined 150 projects in detail across 14 major areas. The *Synthesis Report* summarising these reviews was an indictment of the Bank's chronic, institution-wide inability to learn from past experience, the lessons of which were "well known but generally ignored," the report noted, in new lending operations. In the words of the Quality Assurance Group, the Bank had pervasive "institutional amnesia."

One of the factors behind this was that the thrust of the cultural change Wolfensohn claimed to promote was, once again, contradictory: improved project quality and, simultaneously, more responsiveness to the Bank's clients. But the Bank's clients have always been, and will in large part remain, borrowing governments and government agencies. The crisis of the culture of approval had become so overwhelming precisely because of the Bank's desire to please or not offend its government borrowing clients.

This problem is compounded by the lack of adequate accountability for socially and environmentally detrimental project violations that have arisen as a result. Only the Independent Inspection Panel is willing to undertake credible efforts to hold Bank management accountable for violations. But it has a debilitating Achilles' heel: the requirement that all investigations be approved by the Bank's Executive Board made up of developing country members who lobby heavily not to have the performance of their governments scrutinised.

Thus, when massive violations of Bank policy were alleged in the implementation of the Rondonia Natural Resources Management Project in Brazil, the Bank's Board, in January 1996, rejected a full investigation by the Panel, allowing it to review the project only after periods of six and 18 months. When it did, it found: "Deforestation has continued at high historical levels," and "illegal timber cutting and settlement in protected areas" continue. It also found "little progress in implementing a sustainable health plan for indigenous people." Similar results arose from complaints about two massively mismanaged projects in Brazil and India: the Itaparica dam resettlement project (the single most expensive resettlement project in Bank history, with $63,000 allotted per family, almost all which disappeared in corruption), and the National Thermal Power Sector Loan, (which involved pouring billions into a vast coal-fired power development at Singrauli, with disastrous neglect of resettlement and environmental conditions). Again, the governments of Brazil and India lobbied furiously against inspections of abuses. The Brazilian government succeeded in mobilising all of the borrowing countries in opposing the Panel (after all, any one of them could be the next target of the Panel . . .), as well as Italy, France, Belgium and Korea. The inspection was squelched, with countries holding 52 percent of the Bank's shares voting against, and 48 percent in favour. In the case of Singrauli, the Board approved an investigation, but prohibited the Panel from any site visits in India, limiting it to a desk-bound review of Bank documents in Washington.

The struggles of the Inspection Panel make it clear that the World Bank's accountability crisis is not only rooted in an entrenched, recalcitrant senior management, and in a remarkably impervious institutional culture, but equally in the lack of accountability and responsibility of many of its member governments, particularly borrowers. The institutional amnesia, culture of approval, lack of transparency and accountability are in reality comfortable arrangements supported by most governments, for all the wrong reasons.

Corporate Welfare or Poverty Alleviation?

Although he regularly reiterates the Bank's commitments to poverty allevi- ation and to the environment, Wolfensohn has simultaneously strengthened the institution's shift to supporting private corporations. In what the Bank's 1995 Annual Report called "a dramatic departure from what had been Bank policy for half a century," Wolfensohn has committed the Bank to increase the scale of the International Finance Corporation (IFC), the Multilateral Investment Guarantee Agency (MIGA), and to devote increasing amounts of IBRD capital to guaranteeing private sector investment, as opposed to direct lending to governments.

The key question is whether growing use of the Bank's financial resources to support such corporate investment is really a good, or optimal use of public funds to help the poor and conserve the environment. The answer, as far as many grassroots development and environmental groups are concerned, is that the growing focus on the private sector is little more than corporate welfare with little direct connection to improving the lot of the poor.

The Bank's private sector financial services do principally help larger corporations, many of them with headquarters in rich donor countries, including some of the largest multinationals on earth. In 1996, 1997 and 1998, MIGA and the IFC approved loans and insurance for Coca Cola bot- tling plants in Kyrgyzstan and Azerbaijan, respectively. Since 1997 the Bank has been preparing a huge IBRD/IFC project to assist Exxon-Mobil, Chevron and Petronas in oil field development and pipeline construction in Chad and Cameroon. MIGA guarantees have helped to support huge gold mining operations in Indonesian Irian Java and Papua New Guinea run by giant multinational mining operations with execrable environmental records: Freeport McMoran and Rio Tinto Zinc.

In Mexico, a *Wall Street Journal* article in September 1997 noted, "over the past 18 months the recipients of IFC money have been a who's who of the country's publicly listed blue chips." Among several examples, the *Journal* cited a 1997 IFC investment in a fund sponsored by Carlos Slim, a multibillionaire who is one of the developing world's richest men. In Brazil the IFC's latest investments include stakes in multi-billion dollar companies that are partners of large US multinationals such as Wal-Mart Stores and GTE Corporation.

Another area of dubious developmental benefits for the poor that has attracted IFC (and MIGA) investment is four- and five-star luxury hotels of well-known international chains such as Inter-Continental, Westin and Marriott. One would assume at the very least IFC investments in such hotels would be financially sound. Surprisingly, the IFC Annual Performance Review—FY1998 lists two such investments that have performed so poorly they have required major restructuring: the Camino Real hotel in the beach resort of Ixtapa, Mexico, and two hotels in Zambia operated by Intercontinental Hotels.

MIGA's 1998 Annual Report includes guarantees of about $29 million each for a Dutch beer company to build breweries in Moscow and near Bucharest, and guarantees totaling $34.3 million to construct a Marriott hotel in Miraflores, Lima, one of the richest, most expensive residential districts in all of Latin America. In 1998 MIGA issued four guarantees totaling $75 million to expand Citibank operations in Turkey and the Dominican Republic; four guarantees totaling $64 million to expand operations of the two biggest banks in the Netherlands, the ING and ABN Amro groups, in Turkey and Ecuador; and a $90 million guarantee to expand the branch bank of the Banque Nationale de Paris in St Petersburg. Banco Santander, one of the biggest banks in Spain, was the beneficiary of three guarantees totaling $64.1 million to expand its operations in Uruguay and Peru, and Lloyd's Bank of London also received a guarantee of $13.9 million to expand lending in its Argentinian branch office. These operations accounted for nearly half (48 percent) of MIGA's 1998 commitments.

How indeed were projects like these helping the poor or protecting the environment? The Bank's key argument was that by supporting private sector investment in capital-intensive areas, especially infrastructure, "fiscal space" would be opened up for governments to devote proportionally more resources to social and environmental services. In practice, however, this was often not the case: in many countries where the Bank promoted privatisation, and helped finance private sector investment, governments had cut social expenditures under Bank-supported structural adjustment programmes. The promised land of export-led, private sector growth that would raise the living standards of the poor often receded further in the future with each new Bank loan: Mexico had been a model pupil through the '80s and early '90s, and the living standard of more than half the population was lower in 1996 than it had been in 1980.

The Bank's other standard response, apart from the "fiscal space" rationale, was that its projects promoted growth and created employment— an assertion that could justify almost any project. But even on these grounds the record is suspect. In 1997 MIGA claimed that the 70 guarantees it approved facilitated some $4.7 billion in foreign direct investment, creating 4,000 jobs in host countries. This amounts to $1.175 million dollars in investment per job. If the goal is job creation for the poorest of the poor, this is a bankrupt strategy.

At the same time, it became increasingly clear that using more and more Bank resources for private sector finance is pushing the institution into an area where its record of poor project quality and inability to carry out its environmental and social policies is even worse than in its main lending operations to governments.

The IFC, for example, supports such projects as that of the Canadian Kumtor mining corporation in Kyrgyzstan, which was responsible for three toxic spills in the last two years, the first of which resulted in two tonnes of cyanide pouring into the Barskoon River (the only source of drinking water and irrigation for local communities). The IFC has also supported the Pangue dam on the Bio-Bio River in Chile, about which Chilean NGOs brought a complaint before the Independent Inspection Panel. The Panel has no mandate to examine the Bank's private sector projects, but to Wolfensohn's credit, he called for Jay Hair—President-Emeritus of the US National Wildlife Federation—to conduct an independent review.

Hair accused key IFC staff of "fail[ing] to disclose key documents to the IFC Board of Directors (and perhaps senior management) . . . At each stage of the project approval process, key decision-support documents often did not faithfully or accurately reflect the contents of underlying environmental studies." In fact, "there was no evidence that specific standards or criteria had been established by the IFC or discussed with Pangue SA as to what levels of environmental and social impacts for the Pangue Project were 'acceptable to the World Bank' or IFC." Thus:

> . . . from an environmental and social perspective IFC added little, if any value to the Pangue Project. Its failure to adequately supervise the project—from beginning to end—significantly increased the business risks and diminished the public credibility for both the World Bank Group (particularly IFC) and its private sector partner. There is no indication at this time (April 1997) that IFC has in place the necessary institutional operating systems, or clarity in its policy and procedural mandate, to manage complicated projects such as Pangue in a manner that complies consistently with World Bank Group environmental and social requirements . . .

The Hair report's conclusions were an indictment not just of the Pangue project, but of the IFC's ability to contribute to the World Bank Group's stated developmental goals. Certainly a reconsideration of the Bank's private sector financing would be in order, but the Hair Report did nothing to staunch the accelerating pace of Bank private sector lending. Although the IFC has recently clarified its environmental and public-disclosure policies, there is no evidence that its ability to adequately implement these policies has changed since the completion of the Hair report. Whatever the theory, under Wolfensohn the Bank's poverty alleviation and private sector priorities in practice have grown more contradictory.

The Culture of Corruption

Another major problem with operations at the Bank is the way in which its culture encourages systematic diversion of funds and corruption in a number of the Bank's major borrowers.

The Bank under Wolfensohn, while proclaiming a more visible role in fighting corruption in developing countries, has done little to address the fundamental source of the corruption associated with World Bank lending. That source is the internal pressure to keep lending in spite of poor compliance with World Bank policies—not just concerning poverty alleviation and the environment—but concerning the Bank's most basic fiduciary duty to ensure its funds are not misappropriated from their intended uses. If the Bank is serious about knowing—and changing—how its money is really used, much more is needed than Wolfensohn's initiatives to hire a private accounting firm to conduct spot audits in a handful of countries, and, more recently, firing a few staff caught in acts of flagrant corruption and disqualifying the few companies that are caught red-handed in procurement irregularities.

In the summer of 1997, the consequences of years of Bank complicity in the corruption of its major borrowers finally began to surface in Russia and Indonesia. *Business Week* alleged that "at least $100 million" from a $500 million Russian coal sector loan was either misspent or could not even be accounted for. Noting that the Bank was preparing a new half-billion dollar loan for the Russian coal sector, *Business Week* observed that "World Bank officials seem surprisingly unperturbed by the misspending. They contend offering loans to spur change is better than micromanaging expenditures." A little over a year later, the *Financial Times* estimated the amount stolen in the coal sector loan to be much higher, as much as $250 million.

In the case of Indonesia, Northwestern University professor Jeffrey Winters alleged in a Jakarta press conference in July 1997 that shoddy accounting practices by the World Bank had allowed corrupt Indonesian officials to steal as much as 30 percent of Bank loans over the past 30 years—a mind-boggling total of over $8 billion. At about the same time, the Bank's Jakarta Office commissioned an internal study of corruption in World Bank lending programmes to Indonesia. But the findings and recommendations of the study, which confirmed many of Winters' charges, were never acted on by World Bank senior management, and Wolfensohn learned of the existence of the report only in July 1998 a year after its completion.

In the 15 months after the publication of the report, the Bank committed and disbursed over $1.3 billion more to Indonesia without any effective measures to contain the "leakage" detailed in the study. In October 1998, with plans to commit and disburse two billion dollars more over the next nine months a second Bank mission, headed by Jane Loos, recorded the following:

> *Our mission confirms earlier reports on corruption in Indonesia: that it is pervasive, institutionalised, and a significant deterrent to overall growth of the economy and effectiveness of the Bank's assistance . . . there is significant leakage from Bank funds . . . Bank procedures/standards are not being applied uniformly . . . The [World Bank] auditing requirements have been allowed to deteriorate into a superficial exercise . . .*

The full consequences for development effectiveness of the inability to root out the "culture of approval" were spelled out in an unusually candid re-evaluation of the entire 10-year record of the Bank in Indonesia conducted by the OED and circulated internally (and leaked to the press) in February 1999. The Bank for years had touted Indonesia as one of its great success stories ("widely perceived within the Bank to be a miracle and a symbol of the Bank's success"), but the OED report concludes that reluctance to offend a major borrower, a refusal to address corruption, and a dysfunctional internal Bank culture that punishes staff for identifying problems that could slow down lending all contributed to the propagation of what the original draft of the OED report called the "myth of the Indonesian miracle." (The final report omitted this phrase in response to the objection of the Indonesian Government.) The OED report rates Bank and Indonesian government achievements as only "marginally satisfactory" for the past three decades, contradicting numerous previous evaluations of Bank involvement in Indonesia as a leading example, at least relatively, of development effectiveness.

One of the more revealing analyses in the report describes how the culture of approval and perverse Bank career incentives that punish staff who contradict the party line led to disastrous consequences in lending for the financial sector. As the Indonesian melt-down was brewing, supervision reports indicated the Bank's single biggest financial sector project, the Financial Sector Development Project, was riddled with problems.

> *A thorough supervision effort in August 1996 not only found the project outcome to be unsatisfactory on all counts, but concluded that Indonesia's State Banking Sector was in disarray, riddled with insolvency . . . the Bank downplayed the evidence presented in the supervision report and rejected the proposed cancellation of the loan for several months, arguing that such action would do serious damage to the Bank/Government relationship. This process also triggered perceptions of unjustified penalties to career prospects of some Bank staff who had brought the issues to light.*

The staff proposals for in-depth [financial] sector work were shelved;
ESW [Economic and Sector Work] in the finance sector dropped from
1.76 staff years in FY95 [Financial Year 1995], to 0.55 in FY96, and 0.10
in FY97. Coverage of financial sector issues in the July 1997 CAS was
minimal. The Bank's readiness to address the subsequent financial crisis
in Indonesia was seriously impaired.

The report also recounts how the reorganisation of the Bank under
Wolfensohn and his "Strategic Compact" further undermined the ability of
the Bank to respond to the Indonesian crisis in 1997–98: "The far-reaching
1997 reorganisation detracted attention from economic development
issues," and "complicated the ability of the Bank to respond to the crisis
. . ." The major recommendations of the OED Indonesia study of February
1999 echo the conclusions of countless reports past, particularly the 1992
Morse Commission and Wapenhans reports. If country monitoring is to be
effective, there must be "major changes in the Bank's internal culture."
Once again:

. . . warning signals were either ignored or played down by senior man-
agers in their effort to maintain the country relationship. Some staff
feared the potential negative impact on their opportunities that might
result from challenging mainstream Regional thinking.

One of the biggest obstacles to improved development effectiveness,
and a major factor in the culture of loan approval, once again, is the chronic
"clientitis" of the Bank, the desire to keep lending to maintain the "country
relationship" often to the direct detriment of the poor the Bank purports it
is trying to help. The current Bank reorganisation is making this clientitis
worse, not better. The OED Indonesia report makes clear that in many cases
a choice has to be made: "Bank strategy should look at the importance of
the issues to the country's development, and not whether the country relationship may be jeopardised."

Failing to Deliver the Results

The World Bank's *raison d'être,* in its own words, is environmentally sustainable poverty alleviation; it is really the only reason why taxpayers in
the industrialised world, already faced with a shrinking domestic social
safety net, should support such an institution.

Yet, as the Bank works through its sixth decade of trying to promote
something called "development," the poor in most of its borrowing countries are in worse shape than they were a decade and a half before.
According to the United Nations Development Programme (UNDP), since
1980, "economic decline or stagnation has affected 100 countries, reducing

the incomes of 1.6 billion people." For 70 of these countries, average incomes are less in the mid 1990s than in 1980, and for 43, less than in 1970. In the early 1990s incomes fell by 20 percent or more in 21 countries, mainly in the former Soviet Empire. The poorest fifth of the world's population has seen its share of global income fall from 2.3 percent to 1.4 percent over the past 30 years.

Even according to the Bank's Operations Evaluation Department's latest *Annual Review of Development Effectiveness 1999,* "poverty trends have worsened . . . The number of poor people living on less than US $1 a day rose from 1,197 million in 1987 to 1,214 million in 1997. Excluding China, there are 100 million more poor people in developing countries than a decade ago." Furthermore, since 1990 life expectancy has declined in 33 countries.

What difference then, has the World Bank made? The Bank now claims a higher overall success rate for its projects (up to 72 percent from 64 percent in 1991), but part of the reason for that is that the Bank's evaluation process for projects is not very credible. In Bank evaluation of what it calls "successful outcomes," very little importance (five percent) is attached to a project's likelihood of maintaining its results over its intended useful life, which is central to progress in the developing world. This is a serious omission given that the Bank's own internal audits reveal an astonishing 51 percent failure rate to achieve sustainable results in fiscal years (Fy) 1998–99, a performance that has not changed appreciably in the last decade. This failure rate is even more acute in the poorest countries and in the developmentally most critical sectors. In Africa, for Fy 1998–99 only 34 percent of evaluated projects are of likely sustainability, and only 26 percent of likely "institutional development impact." In the Social Sector, the OED found sustainability declined from 25 percent in 1994–97 to 20 percent in 1998–99. For Population, Health and Nutrition lending, sustainability declined from 55 percent in 1994–97 to 50 percent in 1998–99. In the Environment Sector, sustainability declined from 55 percent in 1994–97 to 50 percent in 1998–99.

Hence, under Wolfensohn, an already abysmally low performance in the social and environment sectors has become even worse, according to the Bank's very latest publicly released figures. This is particularly significant because if a project doesn't produce lasting benefits beyond or even during its lifetime, the increased debt burden that borrowing from the Bank incurs is nothing more than a drag on the economies of poor countries. From the borrowers' standpoint, the Bank thus becomes as much a contributor to their problems as a solution.

Yet World Bank management faces no consequences for such poor performance; on the contrary, it means more business. Heavily indebted poor countries need still more World Bank loans, followed by debt relief paid for by the taxpayers of the industrialised countries. Meanwhile, the octopus-like bureaucracy emits an ever greater cloud of reports espousing its concern for the poor and sustainable development.

Conclusion

The key word for understanding the World Bank in the 1990s is "Disconnect"—the disconnect between its alleged purposes and its record, the disconnect between Wolfensohn's proclamations to change the Bank's culture, and the actual internal reforms needed to address the Bank's systematic failure to implement its most basic policies concerning poverty alleviation and environmental assessment. There is the disconnect between speeding up loan approval, weakening Bank policies, and claiming to root out the "culture of [loan] approval." There is a widely noted disconnect between claiming to use public funds and guarantees to help the poor and the rapid growth of the IFC and MIGA with a preponderance of clients among large multinational corporations and international money centre banks. Their activities, moreover, provide little direct economic benefit—and too often a negative environmental and social impact—on poor populations in developing countries.

Over the past two years, the external pressures placed on the Bank to funnel large, quick-disbursing non-project loans to major borrowers as a consequence of the Asian financial crisis have heightened still further the tension and contradiction between development effectiveness and the "loan approval culture." Recent trends are troubling. In 1998, nearly 40 percent of new IBRD/IDA commitments were large, non-project, quick disbursing loans and credits (double the amount of the previous year), and in 1999 the figure rose to 63 percent. The Bank cannot promote improved development effectiveness and be an automatic teller machine for the much criticised structural adjustment bail-out deals of the IMF at the same time. Claims that such loans are effective tools for promoting needed policy reforms in crisis situations are hollow, indeed disingenuous.

In the final analysis the Bank's prospects in promoting greater development effectiveness means not trying to be all things to all people, but choosing priorities, particularly choosing to focus on quality, not quantity in its lending, rewarding staff first and foremost for ensuring that its policies relating to poverty alleviation, participation, and the environment are carried out in the design and implementation of operations. To make this choice, the question of who the Bank's real clients are is critical and decisive. In a session between Wolfensohn and 300 senior managers on 12 March 1996, a Bank manager identified the fundamental contradiction in the entire "cultural change" Wolfensohn is trying to promote:

> *Mr. President, the second-most recurrent theme in your appeals . . . is client responsiveness, which can be rephrased as "Why can't we be more like merchant banks, which are quick in providing what their customers ask . . . We keep assuming the client is the government . . . we can't have our cake and eat it too. We have to make a choice. Either we treat our governments as clients and we behave like merchant banks, in which case we owe it—again, to ourselves, in the first place, and to our counterparts, second—to stop talking about the environment, about women in development, about poverty alleviation, and so on, as priorities . . . If the government is not our client . . . the client is the people of the countries we work with, and the governments are agencies, instruments, with whom we work to meet our clients' needs.*

Wolfensohn did not have a coherent rejoinder, because the contradiction is real, and perhaps insurmountable. Perhaps this response can best be seen in the most recent Bank scandal, the so-called China Western Poverty Reduction Project which Wolfensohn attempted to keep alive to the bitter end.

Beneath its intensified public relations efforts, the World Bank under Wolfensohn has fatally reinforced a longstanding and pervasive bureaucratic 'culture of loan approval'. Reports continue to be produced that for 20 years have identified the same problems, but they like all their predecessors have no lasting operational consequences. Without fundamental reform, the institution risks mutating into an entity for which public support may be harder and harder to justify: a government-subsidised bank that serves not the poor, but a variety of state and corporate interests, and which is completely insulated from the financial consequences—not to speak of the political and moral aftermath—of its actions.

PART 4

INTERNATIONAL TRADE RELATIONS

22

The Doha Round: Prospects for the Rules-Based Trading System

Patrick Cronin

A multilateral commitment to freer trade has been a cornerstone of the post–World War II liberal international economic order. Patrick Cronin's contribution provides an analysis of the stresses on the international trading system that now threaten to rupture the postwar liberal consensus. He identifies a fundamental tension between the economic logic of free markets and the political logic of the nation-state system. A confluence of factors, many tied to increasing economic integration, has combined in recent decades to deepen the strains between these two logics. Preservation of a rules-based system will require states, particularly the most powerful ones, to make difficult and painful choices.

> All politics is local.
>> *Tip O'Neill,*
>> former Speaker of the U.S. House of Representatives

> All economics is international.
>> *Peter Drucker[1]*

In November 2001, the 142 members of the World Trade Organization (WTO) unanimously agreed to launch the ninth in a series of multilateral negotiations to promote a global free trade system (dubbed the Doha Round). A widely shared sense of relief following the decision stemmed from a growing series of fissures that threaten to fracture the post–World War II consensus in favor of a multilateral, rules-based trading system. The genesis of the problem, expressed in the quotes above, is a conflict between the economic logic of free markets and the political logic of the state-based international system.

The tension between these two logics has always been present, but only in the past several decades has it threatened to tear the rules-based system apart. The catalysts accelerating and deepening the strains on the system are several. They include, ironically, earlier successes in lowering tariff barriers, a larger number of issues being raised for inclusion on the negotiation tables, a substantial increase in the number of countries taking an active interest in the negotiation process, a governance process struggling to reconcile competing national interests, and an increased willingness by WTO members to engage in bilateral and regional trade arrangements. Outside the WTO, increasing civic concern about the social impact of free trade (and of "globalization" generally) is creating problems as well. Spurred by trade's perceived threat to jobs, communities, the environment, and human rights, to name just the most often cited linkages, protestors are calling for changes in the rules-based trading system. For some, the solution is to disband the WTO and allow states to set their own rules on trade. For others, the answer is to open up the organization to "public" participation, to make its actions more transparent and accountable, and to incorporate values such as environmental protection and worker rights that critics claim are now ignored in favor of free trade.

While the issues facing the multilateral trading system are significant, it would be a mistake to conclude that all hope is lost. WTO members can still arrive at a successful conclusion to the Doha Round, but doing so will require governments to face down powerful and entrenched domestic interests favoring trade protection. This is especially the case for governments in the world's largest markets: the United States, Europe, and Japan. Developing countries, in particular, are flexing new negotiating muscles and demanding important concessions in order to reach an agreement. Given the stakes involved and the process by which the negotiations will take place, the self-imposed deadline to conclude negotiations by the end of 2004 looks unrealistic.

Dueling Logics

Liberal economists forcefully argue that free trade among nations leads to positive-sum (win-win) outcomes for all countries when based on the principle of comparative advantage. As David Ricardo (1973) so elegantly demonstrated, societal welfare is maximized when countries specialize in producing goods that best use their given mix of factor endowments, such as land, labor, and capital, and then trade their surplus for goods produced by other countries.

With the benefits of free trade firmly etched in their minds, liberal economists must view the global trading system with obvious frustration. It is true that the system is much more open than it was before World War II. Global trade and financial flows are significantly higher in absolute terms and embrace more parts of the globe than at any other point in history. In that sense, economic integration in the past fifty years has truly stitched the world's economies together, such that "all economics *is* international" (Jackson, 1998; emphasis added). But at the same time, markets could be much freer than they are currently. Trade protectionism not only abounds today but appears to be increasing, a trend that runs counter to one of the most fundamental "truths" of liberal economics.

What explains the failure of governments to seize the benefits from free trade? After all, if a government finds it difficult to persuade other countries to open up their markets, then at least it can remove its own barriers to trade. Its citizens will be winners with access to more products and at cheaper prices. Moreover, increased import flows will inject competitive pressures into the domestic economy, raising efficiency levels as a whole. But nowhere do we see governments unilaterally removing all barriers to trade. Instead, liberalization efforts are often used as bargaining chips for access to foreign markets while protectionism, in various guises, is given to favored industries.

Standing in stark contrast to the liberal logic of trade is the fact that international economic transactions take place in a world of nation-states. With no supranational authority to dictate trade rules, much less enforce them, state trade policies are driven primarily by domestic concerns.[2] Since the appearance of nation-states centuries ago, governments have often approached trade from a mercantilist point of view—in terms of relative gains (how much my state gains relative to another state) and with careful attention to trade's domestic costs. The question of who gains more was always important given the absence of a "globo-cop" to enforce international peace. In an anarchic international environment, each state is forced to rely upon itself for its security. Trade becomes an obvious tool for the accumulation of wealth and power by one's own country—and by potential enemies as well. Further, with increased trade flows come job losses and plant closures. While liberals hail this as a process leading to a more efficient allocation of society's resources, politicians are acutely aware of the political costs to be paid if the losers from trade are ignored. As a result, governments conduct trade negotiations with the goal of gaining as much market access abroad while conceding as little as possible at home.

The influence of this economic nationalist view of the trading system was reflected in the very foundations of the post–World War II trading system. While the General Agreement on Tariffs and Trade (GATT) was created to facilitate a movement toward global free trade, its negotiation principles included the concept of reciprocity. Countries offering greater access to their domestic economies could demand that other countries provide increased access to theirs. No country was expected to offer unilateral concessions. As a result, within the GATT the liberal goal of free trade has been pursued through this mercantilist negotiating process.

The GATT: Victim of Its Own Success

Between 1947 and 1994, the member states of the GATT concluded eight sets of negotiations leading to dramatic reductions in average tariff levels (Table 22.1). Because of these efforts, throughout the 1950s and 1960s world trade volumes and living standards increased substantially—to many a validation of liberal ideas on the benefits of trade. Many of the tariff reductions were accomplished in the first two decades of the GATT's existence. For instance, following the conclusion of the Dillon Round in 1961, average tariffs had been reduced by almost 75 percent from their postwar peaks. The subsequent Kennedy Round achieved a further reduction of 35 percent (Spero and Hart, 1997: 57). Because developed countries dominated the GATT's membership at inception, it should come as no surprise that tariff negotiations focused primarily on manufactured products—goods of common interest within this group of nations. By mutual agreement, agriculture was kept off the table from the very beginning, labeled too sensitive to liberalize. Indeed, after the war U.S. senators favoring continued financial support for U.S. agricultural products scuttled the proposed International Trade Organization (ITO). These economic nationalists feared that the ITO would infringe on U.S. sovereignty by ordering an end to farm support programs.

It is important to note that liberalization efforts were facilitated by the willingness of the United States to play a leading role in pushing the negotiation process forward. Freer trade was part of a larger geopolitical strategy to help rebuild the U.S.'s Cold War allies Japan and Western Europe. In this context, the United States tacitly agreed to accept asymmetrical (lower) benefits from the liberalization process compared to its trading partners.

Over time, however, increasing levels of import competition began to affect traditionally dominant industries in the developed world. In the

Table 22.1   GATT/WTO Rounds, 1947–2001

Year	Name of Round	Number of Participants
1947	Geneva	23
1949	Annecy	13
1950	Torquay	38
1956	Geneva	26
1960–1961	Dillon	26
1962–1967	Kennedy	62
1973–1979	Tokyo	99
1986–1993	Uruguay	125
2001– ?	Doha	144[a]

Source: Spero and Hart (1997); Doha Round information added by author.
Note: a. As of January 1, 2002.

United States, industries such as textiles and apparel, electronics, automobiles, and steel came under substantial pressure from foreign producers. The erosion of U.S. economic hegemony following World War II was an inevitable consequence of the rebuilding of the war-torn economies of Japan and Western Europe as well as shifts in comparative advantage to these and other countries.[3]

Companies and workers in the affected sectors appealed to their governments for protection. In a variety of cases they found obliging politicians unwilling to allow economically and politically important sectors to wither away. The prospect of tens of thousands of jobless voters streaming to the polls at election time was often too much to bear.

The GATT's rules largely prohibited governments from raising tariff barriers to stem import competition. As a result, a proliferation of other forms of trade protection occurred as governments looked for creative ways to help their companies and workers. These measures included persuading foreign producers to limit exports (voluntary export restraints or VERs), quantitative restrictions on imports (import quotas), and nontariff barriers (NTBs)—a catchall term encompassing health and safety standards, labeling requirements, customs procedures, government procurement policies, and licensing requirements, among other measures. In the case of quotas (import and VERs), the protectionist intent was clear. But for other trade barriers like health and safety standards for imported products, it was often hard to know where legitimate nontrade concerns ended and trade protection began. This ambiguity only served to make disputes over the use of these measures harder to settle.

Contributing to growing trade tensions among GATT members was the inability of the GATT's dispute settlement mechanism (DSM) to effectively adjudicate these disputes. In many cases the new forms of protectionism lay outside of the GATT's purview. When disputes did fall under GATT rules, the organization's principle of unanimous consent proved an insurmountable obstacle. The defendant country in a complaint had the power to veto the formation of a dispute panel or to prevent the organization from adopting its findings. With a governance process like this, it is no surprise that members viewed the DSM as ineffectual.

A Proliferation of Issues

By the early 1980s, it was increasingly clear that the GATT's rules would need to expand to include not only these new forms of protectionism but also a growing list of other trade-related issues. At the top of the list was agriculture. During the 1970s, large surpluses in production due to favorable weather conditions and government aid created trade conflicts over the use of export subsidies to dispose of the excess. At the same time, structural changes in the economies of developed countries led to an upsurge in the export of services such as telecommunications, banking, and insurance. These were areas that many countries traditionally protected due to their perceived strategic importance. As a result, companies venturing abroad often ran into a variety of barriers including limits or outright bans on foreign participation. With the growing spread of multinational corporations around the world came pressures to include not only trade in services but also issues like intellectual property rights (IPRs) and investment law. Companies argued that both were trade-related since foreign direct investment (and the protection of technology transferred in the process) affected trade flows among countries. Businesses hoped that the creation of global standards in these two areas would make it easier to manage overseas operations, particularly in the developing world where IPRs were not well respected and where local investment codes often limited management's flexibility.[4]

The emergence of issues such as these split the GATT's membership along a variety of lines both within and across the developed/developing country divide. While a broader range of items for negotiation would seem to offer the best hopes for reaching a compromise, the politically sensitive nature of these issue areas led members to take strong positions in favor of or against them. Because of this, issues relating to agriculture and to new forms of protectionism proved too controversial to reach agreement on or were only addressed in a limited way until the Uruguay Round.

The Large "N" Problem and the GATT/WTO Governance Process

Compounding negotiation problems tied to the broader agenda was a significant increase in the GATT's (and now WTO's) membership in recent decades, particularly from developing countries.[5] Each of these countries brought to the table its own set of national interests—those issues it wanted to see on the trade agenda and those it opposed. As a group, developing countries are now taking a much more active role in the WTO and challenging the organization's traditional decisionmaking processes that have favored developed countries' interests.

As Table 22.1 shows, the number of countries at the negotiation table doubled between the Kennedy and Uruguay Rounds. When the latter round began in 1986, the GATT had eighty members, only forty to fifty of which took an active role in the formation of the negotiation agenda. By the late 1990s, membership in the WTO had risen to 135 following an influx of developing and "transition" (formerly communist) states (Laird, 2001; Odell, 2001).

The dramatic rise in the number of developing country members was driven by a number of factors. Perhaps the most important reason was a generalized trend toward the adoption of export-oriented development strategies in response to liberal pressures to remove barriers to international trade and investment (Odell, 2001). Instrumental in the policy change process was the leverage exerted by organizations like the International Monetary Fund (IMF) and World Bank that used their resources to promote a free-market approach to development. Now with outward-looking development policies, developing countries acquired an intense interest in market access and in the rule-making body that promoted it. For smaller economies, an organization furthering the development of a global, rules-based trading system was attractive. More than anything, it served as an alternative to a power-based trading system in which larger countries were free to bully smaller ones. It also offered an opportunity to shape the rules in ways that would promote the interests of developing countries. A final reason explaining the rise in developing country membership levels was a decision made for the Uruguay Round negotiations that any agreement would be adopted as a "single undertaking." In contrast to previous GATT rounds, members would now have to agree to adhere to all provisions in an agreement instead of being able to selectively choose which portions to respect. The practical effect of this all-or-nothing approach to deal making was that countries could no longer free ride on the willingness of other members to extend nonreciprocal trade concessions (Schott and Watal, 2000). As a result, members now had an interest in all issues under discussion.

The increase in WTO membership levels had a profound effect on the organization. Not only did it bring many new interests to the negotiation table, but it also exposed weaknesses in the organization's governance structure, creating what Jeffrey Schott (2000) terms the "consensus-building problem." From its founding, the GATT adopted a governance process based on the principle of consensus. This suggests that any agreement must necessarily reflect the interests of all members, potentially difficult to achieve as more and more countries join in the negotiation process. With more states at the table, the size of the win set (or the common concessions all are willing to make) is likely to decrease. As John G. Conklin (1996) notes, this system of governance generates least-common-denominator outcomes.

Despite formal governance rules that made agreement challenging, informal practices helped the GATT's members conclude successful negotiations through the 1970s. Reflecting the distribution of global power, the so-called Quad countries (United States, Canada, Japan, Europe) exercised a decisive amount of influence on agenda formation and the subsequent negotiation process in each round (Schott and Watal, 2000). Successful rounds were facilitated not only by Quad leadership but also by the small number of members, their mutual interest in the liberalization of manufactured products, and by economic structures dissimilar enough that tariff liberalization before the 1970s did not lead to substantial amounts of trade competition.[6]

This decisionmaking process came under strain once Quad unity fragmented in the face of disputes over agriculture and barriers to markets' access. While these did not preclude an agreement in the Tokyo Round, they proved to be substantial problems in the Uruguay Round. This was especially true in the context of an influx of developing countries into the GATT. Both existing and new developing country members began to participate more actively in the negotiation process.

Today, the problem of numbers is exacerbated by the continued accession of new members (over twenty since the conclusion of the Uruguay Round) and a determination by least-developed countries to make sure their views are adequately reflected in any future agreement. Although larger developing countries played important roles in negotiating a variety of the provisions of the Uruguay Round agreement, many of the least-developed countries felt that the final accord was forced upon them by the world's major trading states (Finger and Schuler, 2000).

This fragmentation of strongly held interests within and across levels of development was amply illustrated in the highly public fight over selection of the WTO's first director-general and in negotiations over how the Doha Round would be conducted. In the first case, crosscutting coalitions of developed and developing countries formed around New Zealand's Mike Moore and Thailand's Supachai Panitchpakdi. Members in each coalition felt strongly that their candidate best represented their national interests. Unwilling to concede, both sides compromised by splitting the job into two three-year periods with Moore having the first turn. Developing countries' resentment at past governance practices was displayed in the process to decide how the Doha Round negotiations would be carried out. A coalition of the WTO's least-developed countries, along with relatively wealthier developing countries like Egypt and Pakistan, called for all final decisions to be made in the WTO General Council and for no informal, closed-door negotiations talks to take place (Intl. Centre for Trade, 2002). This practice of using so-called green-room talks, named after the meeting room adjacent to the WTO director-general's office, to conduct "negotiations within the negotiations" came to a head during the Seattle ministerial meeting in 1999. Many of the smaller developing countries accused the host U.S. delegation of trying to promote its interests via the use of a green-room process that excluded them. While agreeing that informal consultations and negotiations can serve a useful purpose, they continue to insist that any informal talks be publicized and open to all members.

China's December 2001 accession to the WTO only exacerbates the numbers problem. With its large and growing economy, China's government will be able to exercise an important degree of influence over the course of any deliberations. However, how China will choose to wield its power is unclear at this early stage. During its first months as a member, Chinese officials supported proposals from various developing countries to limit Quad influence over the Doha talks. In that sense, early signs suggest that China may end up, deliberately or not, being a champion of developing country interests vis-à-vis a more democratic decisionmaking process within the WTO. This stance is consistent with China's national interest in strengthening its relative position at the global level.

The impact of China's accession—positively or negatively for the rules-based system—may ultimately be decided by its willingness to play by the rules and by other countries playing fairly with it. China is in the midst of a profound restructuring of its economy, with significant social dislocation already taking place. As it implements its commitments to the WTO, these costs will only rise. If the level of social unrest were to threaten the Communist Party's control of the political system, it is possible that China could reverse earlier liberalization efforts. More likely, however, is a China that will act like other powerful members of the WTO: using the rules to promote its own interests while complying with its obligations to the extent that domestic politics allow. This is likely to mean an increase in the number of disputes brought to the WTO with China either as complainant or defendant.[7]

In one sense, this increased use of the WTO's dispute settlement mechanism would be a positive sign for the future of the rules-based system—so long as the WTO is able to resolve these problems in an amicable fashion. More worrisome in recent years is an accumulation of cases in which powerful countries have chosen not to respect adverse rulings. These include the EU's loss with respect to the importation of hormone-fed beef from the United States and the U.S.'s loss to the EU over the issue of taxation of export earnings.[8] If China's entry to the WTO simply adds another major power unwilling to comply when it loses important cases or, alternatively, finds others stubbornly resisting when it wins, then this bodes ill for the rules-based system. Ultimately, the system's ability to survive and prosper will depend on the willingness of the world's major trading nations to comply with their obligations. In turn, this will necessitate being willing to ignore the pleas of powerful domestic interests favoring protectionism.

Prospects for Success

The inability of WTO members to launch a new round in Seattle and their difficult—but ultimately successful—struggle to do so in Doha two years later was due to stark differences among the membership over the direction and content of the negotiations.[9] Compounding these problems was strong resentment among many developing countries that the Quad powers were, as usual, trying to shape the agenda to suit their interests at the expense of everyone else's. Rather than capitulate, developing countries made a strong statement in Seattle by publicly condemning the use of green-room tactics and refusing to sign off on an agenda that did not adequately reflect their input. There were other important reasons for the failure in Seattle, including deep divisions among the Quad countries themselves, particularly over agriculture.[10] At the Seattle ministerial meeting, developing countries sent an unprecedented statement that they would use the principle of unanimous consent to block the talks unless their varied (and sometimes conflicting) interests were given space at the table. No longer would the Quad countries be able to informally dictate the terms under which negotiations would be held and agreements reached.

The issues and positions leading up to the Doha meeting closely paralleled those in Seattle. The key differences explaining success in the former case and failure in the latter can be tied to commonly held perceptions that the WTO and the multilateral trading system would suffer irreparable damage if members failed a second time. Adding to the pressure to bridge members' differences over an agenda was a global recession and attendant worries about resurgent protectionism, as well as the terrorist attacks in New York and Washington, D.C., in September 2001. In the weeks prior to the Doha meeting, it was widely believed that the attacks would further damage an already suffering U.S. economy. Despite these new forces for compromise, the Doha meeting almost failed, a testament to the difficulty in finding an acceptable agenda. The final result left all sides claiming victory; however, skeptics felt that the language of the declaration launching the round was sufficiently ambiguous to paper over important differences—divisions that may yet prevent a final agreement. The discussion below offers a look at contentious areas of the negotiation agenda and the difficulties to be faced in successfully concluding the latest round.

Industrial Tariff Reductions

No round would be complete without tariff reductions on industrial products. Developing countries, especially the poorest, are worried that new tariff reduction commitments (in percentage terms) will require them to reduce their protection rates relatively more than developed countries since the former have rates higher than the latter. Given the great sensitivity with which developing countries approach the issue of market access to Quad-country markets, these developing countries are likely to resist further concessions, at least and until they see greater market access for their own exports. Since the latter are often blocked by nontariff forms of protection, by antidumping actions, and by trade barriers on nonindustrial products (especially in agriculture), developing countries will require prompt and measurable concessions in other issue areas.

Antidumping Measures

The Doha declaration calls for negotiations "aimed at clarifying and improving" current rules on the use of subsidies and countervailing measures (SCM), especially antidumping measures. Ostensibly designed to allow countries to legally raise barriers to trade to counter unfair trade practices by others, many countries targeted by these measures feel that they are no more than disguised protection cloaked in an aura of legitimacy. Led by South Korea, Japan, the European Union (EU), and many developing countries, this item was placed on the agenda despite the vigorous opposition of the United States, a heavy user of such measures. This is an issue area ripe for discussion given a global upsurge in the use of these measures by rich and poor countries alike. However, the United Stastes is unlikely to sign off on a final agreement unless it extracts concessions on other issues. Complicating any trade-off will be U.S. domestic politics. The U.S. Congress, constitutionally charged with control of trade policy, has put the Bush administration on notice that it will not tolerate any interference in the U.S.'s antidumping mechanism. Supporting this stance are a variety of powerful domestic lobbies that benefit from it as well as congressmen who object to having a supranational organization dictate what the United States can and cannot do with its trade policy.

Agriculture

Agriculture is historically the most difficult issue to deal with in international trade, and the Doha Round will be no different in this respect. Negotiators will face four main issues: expanding market access, "substantial reductions" in trade-distorting domestic supports, reducing "with a view to phasing out" export subsidies, and providing "special and differential" treatment for developing countries (WTO, 2001a). Opposing each other on each of these issues are various coalitions of countries, often cutting across levels of development.

In general, developing countries have a strong interest in phasing out barriers to accessing the Quad markets. While the Uruguay Round's agricultural commitments included the transformation of nontariff barriers to tariffs, the resulting tariff levels often offered at least as much protection as before. Among those countries supporting greater market access as well as an end to export subsidies are the Cairns Group of fourteen developed and developing countries with a natural comparative advantage in agricultural products.[11] Against EU objections, this group successfully pushed for the goal of phasing out export subsidies. Internally, the EU's high level of domestic support and export subsidies for agriculture has placed it in opposition to calls for freer markcts in agricultural trade. Also resistant to market-opening measures and reductions in domestic support are countries like

Japan and South Korea that would prefer to continue to protect various agricultural products. In all cases, politically strong domestic lobbies underpin their decades-long protectionist stances.

Within the EU, the region's support for agriculture and its protectionist stance reflects the strong influence of countries like France. Any concessions here will require tough intra-EU bargaining, an agreement that might be more possible in light of the region's impending enlargement and the strains it will place on the region's budget for agricultural support. In an effort to avoid intra-EU disputes, EU negotiators unsuccessfully pushed for recognition of agriculture as a "multifunctional" activity. Under this rubric, countries could presumably continue to protect their sectors under the guise of preserving a rural way of life ("rural development") or the environment. Further, the continent's recent scare over mad cow disease has only deepened public pressures on politicians to allow countries to conduct their agricultural policies in ways that protect their citizens. The EU is already embroiled in a trade dispute over the banning of U.S. exports of hormone-fed beef. Although no scientific evidence has been produced to support the thesis, EU regulators claim that such beef is unhealthy for consumers and should be banned. Moreover, EU negotiators have argued (unsuccessfully to date) for inclusion of a "precautionary principle" in trade under which imported products can be banned if they are thought to be harmful despite a lack of evidence (or in the interim until such evidence can be developed). From the point of view of exporters seeking better access to EU markets, these positions smack of protectionism in other guises. Although EU efforts have been successfully resisted, agricultural exporters enter the Doha negotiations fearing that the EU seeks to take back with one hand what it may give with the other.

The United States has conflicting interests on agriculture as well. While not formally a member of the Cairns Group, it supports the group's position on market access and export subsidies. U.S. exporters believe the United States will benefit (at the EU's expense) if trade-distorting subsidies are removed from exports. When it comes to domestic supports, however, domestic politics have opened up a gap between rhetoric and practice. The 1996 U.S. Federal Agriculture Improvement and Reform Act was seen by liberals as an important step toward the reduction of U.S. agricultural supports that distorted prices for agricultural products. Under this law, farmers would no longer be paid according to government price supports for particular commodities or paid to not produce certain crops; rather they would be paid direct and diminishing amounts of money unconnected to what crops they produced. The liberal hope was that this form of protection would reduce price distortion while overall support levels would end over time. Good intentions have been upset by bad weather and domestic politics. In the intervening years, both major parties in the U.S. Congress have come together to authorize significant increases in farm aid in a bid to attract political support in farming areas hard hit by drought and other problems. It is unclear at this stage how U.S. negotiators will be able to reconcile the actions and attitude of Congress with a need to offer concessions in this area to trading partners.

Finally, developing countries themselves are split on the issue of agriculture and liberalization (Watal, 2000). Net-exporting countries such as Argentina and Thailand are vigorous supporters of greater market access and an end to subsidies. But net-importers like Egypt and Pakistan favor special treatment that will allow developing countries to protect in the name of food security and rural development. For the latter group of countries, liberalization forcing tens (or hundreds) of thousands of uncompetitive farmers and their families into cities in search of work would be a political nightmare and potential social catastrophe. Net-importers have pushed hard for the inclusion of special and differential treatment provisions and are unlikely to settle for provisions that do not substantially address their concerns.

Investment Policy and Competition Law

These issues are at the core of the so-called Singapore issues promoted by the EU and Japan.[12] The process of developing a core set of standards for host countries to follow in their treatment of foreign multinationals began with a partial set of rules agreed to in the Uruguay Round. Developed countries, home to most of the world's direct investors, have a strong interest in setting rules that give their corporations maximum flexibility in managing of their operations abroad. At the same time, developing countries have a history of imposing a variety of restrictions, for example, local content or trade balancing requirements, to help ensure that the host country captures as many of the benefits from this investment as possible. Efforts to establish global standards exposed a deep developed/developing country rift, with the latter naturally opposed to rules that restrict a host's ability to regulate companies within its borders.[13] The trade-related investment measures (TRIMs) provision of the Uruguay Round provided a first cut at outlawing a small number of these practices. Timetables were established to end the use of domestic-content requirements and certain export performance standards on foreign investment (Moran, 2000). Many developing countries would like to see these deadlines extended or repealed, while developed countries would like to expand the list to include other types of host-imposed rules on foreign direct investment.

Proposals to create an explicit link between competition law and the WTO created splits within the developed world, with the United States in opposition to negotiations on this issue area.[14] Developed countries see this as a mechanism to promote exports abroad in cases where domestic competition laws are absent or not enforced in the target market (Hoekman and

Holmes, 1999). Thus their concerns are not with the promotion of liberal, welfare-enhancing policies abroad but with market-access goals driven by mercantilistic concerns. Other aspects of competition law, such as those concerning improper behavior of foreign exporters or direct investors (e.g., export cartels or the use of transfer pricing), do not appear to be a priority for those countries pressing to include this issue on the WTO negotiation agenda. While supportive of the goals underlying the EU and Japanese proposal, the United States opposes it, apparently believing that U.S. interests are better promoted through the use of unilateral and bilateral approaches (Hoekman and Holmes, 1999). To bolster their case against a WTO-based mechanism, U.S. competition authorities suggest that ceding authority to the WTO might expose the organization to capture by export interests, that the WTO's evidentiary standards fall below those in the United States, and that the WTO lacks sufficient expertise to handle such issues (Graham, 2000). As with investment law, many developing countries stand in strong opposition to the EU and Japanese proposal. While many supported the establishment of a working group within the WTO to study these issues in 1996, few are willing to agree to the launch of negotiations (Watal, 2000; Graham, 2000).

Because negotiations on the Singapore issues are so important to the EU, they emerged as a major source of tension in discussions over the Doha Round agenda. With the EU appearing to concede important ground in agriculture (agreeing to negotiations with a goal of phasing out export subsidies), the region likely expected reciprocity on other issues, especially in this area. Nevertheless, opposition to including these issues on the agenda was strong enough that the Doha Declaration compromised, with agreement to continue to study the issues until the WTO's Fifth Ministerial Conference in 2003. However, even then negotiations were only to begin if the agenda for them was agreed to "by explicit consensus." The chair of the Doha discussions on this issue provided a public statement that in his view explicit consensus meant that any WTO member could unilaterally block the launch of negotiations if it was unhappy with their mandated goals. Wrangling over this issue and the reference to explicit consensus reflects past resentment felt by many developing countries regarding their lack of control over the agenda and the outcome of past rounds. They are determined to exploit the unanimity principle to ensure that their voices are heard on issues of importance to them. The finessing of the Singapore issues in Doha merely postpones the hard bargaining and trade-offs leading to the launch of negotiations on these issues that will likely be needed to keep the Europeans at the table.

Linking Trade to Environmental and Labor Standards

More than any other issue, proposals to tie international trade rules more firmly to global standards on the environment and labor practices have aroused substantial opposition both inside and outside the WTO. Inside, developing countries have consistently blocked U.S. attempts, beginning with the 1996 Singapore ministerial meeting, to create a working group on trade and labor. In the face of such resistance, U.S. authorities agreed that the issue would not be on the agenda for the next round and, further, that the WTO lacked competence to discuss it. Nevertheless, fears continued to run deep that the United States was trying to place it on the agenda in order to create new mechanisms to deny developing countries' exporters access to developed country markets. Indeed, such suspicions appeared confirmed by U.S. President Bill Clinton's ill-timed remark in favor of linking trade and labor standards just prior to the Seattle meeting (Laird, 2001). Clinton's statement was motivated by strong domestic pressures from trade unions affected by import competition and labor activists seeking to improve working conditions abroad, groups that were prominently protesting the WTO in the streets outside the meeting. Clinton's actions, which appeared to renege on earlier promises, significantly poisoned the atmosphere inside the hall. In the run-up to the Doha meeting, the U.S. government, under a Republican president much less beholden to labor interests, has not made this an important issue. The only WTO action has been to "take note" of the work by the International Labour Organization on the social dimensions of globalization (WTO, 2001a).

Efforts, particularly by the EU, to link trade rules more closely with the environment have also elicited strong criticism from the developing world. As with the United States on labor, EU negotiators are under strong domestic pressures to incorporate environmental concerns more closely into the work of the WTO. Some demands are driven by environmentalists critical of the impact of globalization on environmental conditions around the globe, while others spring from concerns over the health of the food supply. Still other efforts to link trade and the environment, however, are motivated more by domestic producers seeking new means to protect themselves in light of competition from developing countries, which generally have minimal environmental standards. Debate within the WTO has been as acrimonious on this issue as with labor. Developing country opposition forced the EU to scale back its expectations significantly. Nevertheless, in the bargaining at Doha the EU won agreement to begin immediate negotiations in three issue areas: to clarify the relationship between WTO rules and specific trade obligations in existing multilateral environmental agreements (MEA); to promote procedures for the regular information exchange between MEA secretariats and relevant WTO committees; and to reduce or eliminate tariff and nontariff barriers to the importation of environmental goods and services. Environmentalists criticized this outcome for its focus only on rule clarification and not rule change. Thus developing countries appear to have given away only limited concessions on an issue area of great importance to the EU. Environmentalists were cheered by agreement to begin negotiations to "clarify and improve" rules on fisheries subsidies that, in their opinion, have contributed to overfishing and the collapse of fish stocks in various parts of the world.

Development and "Implementation" Issues

With their newfound voice, developing countries have been making a variety of demands. Their willingness to walk away from the Seattle meeting without an agreement and their tough bargaining stances in the intervening years to Doha forced the Quad countries to take notice of their interests. Quad negotiators now understand that developing countries' interests have to figure prominently in any new agreement.

Helping to strengthen this conviction was the position taken by a group of developing countries regarding "implementation" issues. They argued that developing countries had yet to receive expected benefits from the Uruguay Round agreement and that this imbalance must be rectified before they would support a new round. From a developing country point of view, concessions on intellectual property rights and investment measures were to be offset by Quad agreement to open up their textile, apparel, and agricultural markets and to grant developing countries "special and differential" treatment. While developing countries walked away from the Uruguay Round negotiating table expecting measurable benefits in a short period of time, the reality is that the Quad countries scheduled many of their market-opening measures in textiles and apparel for the end of the allowed ten-year implementation period (1996–2005). Although the Quad countries are legally within the letter of the agreement, they are accused of violating its spirit (Laird, 2001). Adding insult to injury, Quad countries have used antidumping measures, along with other actions such as tariff escalation, to offset expected benefits to developing countries.[15]

Developing countries are also concerned about the costs of complying with their Uruguay Round commitments, particularly in areas such as investment law and customs procedures. Estimates show that the poorest countries may need to spend the equivalent of a year's worth of development monies simply to come into compliance (Finger and Schuler, 2000). As the extent of the costs became apparent, more and more developing countries called for extensions of the deadlines.

A third implementation issue revolves around the practical meaning of the Quad commitment to extend special and differential treatment. As Sam Laird (2001) relates, much to developing countries' dismay, this has turned out to be more rhetoric than substance and has focused largely on giving developing countries more time and technical assistance to comply with a single set of trading rules instead of offering them different and lesser obligations.

With these concerns in mind, the developing world has called for a "development" round to address their interests. Developing countries won a number of important victories in this regard at the Doha meeting. Most notably, they wrung a statement from the Quad powers that the existing IPR obligations would not stand in the way of efforts to deal with public health problems in developing countries (WTO, 2001b). At issue were growing attempts led by Brazil and South Africa to force brand-name drug-makers to offer AIDS drugs at a reasonable cost. Lacking the resources to pay prices propped up by patents but facing a serious health crisis, these countries argued that patent protection should not take precedence over public health. Facilitating the Doha statement was the anthrax scare in the United States. Facing a sudden need for millions of doses of the drug Cipro, U.S. and Canadian authorities threatened to override the patent held by the German pharmaceutical company Bayer unless prices were reduced. Traditionally strong support by these Quad countries for international intellectual property rights' protection melted away almost overnight when this public health threat turned up unexpectedly in their own backyards. Pointing out this apparent double standard, developing countries won over global opinion on this issue.[16]

Beyond the issue of IPRs, developing countries won other concessions. These include a WTO waiver of the Cotonou agreement under which the EU grants preferential market access to the seventy-eight members of the African, Caribbean, and Pacific (ACP) group of countries.[17] Composed largely of former European colonies and entirely of developing countries, this group includes fifty-six members of the WTO. To forestall objections, ACP members made it clear that acceptance of the waiver was important to their support for any future negotiations, especially relating to the Singapore issues, the environment, or labor (Intl. Centre for Trade, 2001).[18] Additionally, developing countries won a pledge that the WTO would provide sufficient technical assistance and capacity-building programs to ensure that developing countries were adequately trained for the Doha negotiations.[19] Further, WTO members agreed to establish working groups on debt and finance and on technology transfer, two issues of great importance to the developing world. All WTO members committed themselves to the objective of duty-free and quota-free access for products from the least-developed countries. Finally, the Doha declaration recognized the existence of developing country proposals to create a framework agreement on special and differential treatment, although no specific action was proposed. Instead, members agreed that all existing special and differential provisions of the WTO rules "shall be reviewed with a view to strengthening them and making them more precise, effective, and operational" (WTO, 2001c).

Developing countries were unsuccessful in getting implementation issues into a single negotiation area by themselves. In its place, members agreed to look favorably on requests for technical assistance and deadline extensions by developing countries and to take up these and other issues in the existing, relevant WTO committees (WTO, 2001d).

Dispute Settlement Mechanism

The Uruguay Round agreement created a stronger and more controversial Dispute Settlement Mechanism (DSM). Instead of one member being able to veto the resolution process, new rules stated that all members would have to agree to dismiss a case. With this and other changes, many observers concur that the DSM is much stronger than under the GATT. Economic nationalists are strongly critical of the new DSM. They object to the DSM's ability to erode state sovereignty, charging that it forces members to sacrifice environmental, health, and other concerns in favor of free trade (Public Citizen, 1999). They further argue that the WTO's DSM is run in a nondemocratic manner with little transparency or accountability to the outside world. Interestingly, liberals too have been critical but on different grounds. As Bernard Hoekman and Petros Mavroidis (1999) note, there have been no cases brought to the DSM by a least-developed country. In these authors' opinion, this is tied to asymmetric incentives to bring cases and enforce decisions (e.g., for fear of reprisal) and resource limitations tied to the cost and time needed to pursue a case. Supporters of free trade raise other issues including how to deal with an increasing number of cases of noncompliance (which leads to more protectionism via retaliation and less free trade) and concerns over the method of retaliation. This latter issue is tied to a U.S. threat to use a "carousel" approach in implementing authorized retaliation (Bhagwati, 2002).[20]

Negotiations on "improvements and clarifications" to the DSM are more likely to satisfy liberal concerns than nationalist ones since member states will be at the negotiating table rather than nongovernmental organizations. Smaller countries see the DSM as a way to constrain large-state behavior and have a strong interest in making the system work as effectively as possible. The Quad countries can also benefit from strengthening the system since each has won cases where compliance became an issue. Despite being on the outside looking in, nongovernmental critics have brought sufficient pressure on the organization that even some liberals acknowledge it would be wise to improve transparency if only to make a stronger case for free trade (Crook, 2001).[21] Unlike all other issues in the Doha Round, negotiations on the DSM are not part of the "single undertaking."

Regional Trade Arrangements

There has been a proliferation of Regional Trade Arrangements (RTAs) around the world in the past fifteen years, reaching 113 in 2000 (de Jonquieres, 2001). The forces promoting such an expansion are several, as Robert Lawrence explains elsewhere in this volume. Since its inception, the GATT allowed limited exceptions to the principle of nondiscrimination, which such agreements ostensibly violate. However, the dramatic increase in RTAs in recent years has increasingly called into question whether such arrangements are welfare enhancing or welfare reducing from a global efficiency standpoint. More and more liberal economists are branding RTAs as mercantilist-inspired impediments to the goal of global free trade. Analysts suspect that RTAs could be undermining the commitment of WTO members to the global trading system. If RTAs are in place with major trading partners, states may be less interested in supporting an international, rules-based trading system (Laird, 2001).

In an effort to reinforce support for global rules, WTO members agreed in Doha to begin negotiations to "clarify and improve" rules and procedures relating to RTAs. While liberals hope these efforts will be successful, the fact remains that it is the WTO's own members engaging in RTA creation. The chapter by Lawrence argues that deep-seated changes to the global economic system are driving the move toward regionalism, suggesting that the WTO may need to implicitly or explicitly condone RTA activity.

Conclusion

The multilateral, rules-based trading system faces its biggest challenges to date. The tension between the economic logic of free trade and the political logic of the state-based trading system is greater than ever before and threatens to unravel support for the system. Driving this dynamic is the WTO's governance structure, the size of its membership, the intensity with which all sides are pushing their own interests, and the politically sensitive nature of many of the issues on the agenda.

As the discussion above details, these are not insurmountable problems, and the bargaining in Doha suggests that sufficient room still exists for trade-offs across issue areas. But the hard part has now begun, and meeting the stated end-of-2004 deadline is unlikely to happen without some major shock to the global economy that forces countries to look beyond their own particularistic interests. If past history is a guide, WTO members will engage in zero-sum negotiation strategies unless and until the prospect of failure prompts members to compromise. Even then the organization has shown a willingness to negotiate years beyond established deadlines before reaching a make-or-break point. Crucial to the round's success will be a package that allows a large majority of members to walk away from the table feeling that their interests were reflected in the final agreement. With more and more countries at the table and participating actively, such a deal will require all countries to make significant concessions. This is especially the case for the system's most powerful members. U.S., Japanese, and EU governments will each need to stare down powerful domestic lobbies and concede important ground, not only to settle differences within the Quad but also to satisfy developing countries that now will accept nothing less.

Notes

1. Cited in Jackson (1998: 104).

2. Used here, I am referring to an organization that can, independent of nation-state influence, determine and effectively enforce a set of trade rules. While the WTO is often criticized as a powerful supranational organization that infringes on state sovereignty, the reality is that it cannot—on its own—enforce the rules entrusted to it. Instead, it can only verbally reprimand rule violators and, if need be, authorize states to retaliate in the face of unfair trade practices. The WTO cannot force states to change their behavior. Furthermore, the rules it does attempt to enforce were written and agreed to by the member states themselves.

3. What drove these changes in comparative advantage is in some cases the matter of bitter dispute. For liberals, these shifts were market-driven phenomena. For others, however, countries such as Japan used state intervention in the economy to create such advantages. For more on this latter view, see Krugman (1986) on strategic trade theory.

4. Common mandates relate to the use of domestically produced inputs, exporting, and technology transfer.

5. Ratification of the Uruguay Round brought with it the creation of the World Trade Organization in 1995.

6. Regarding differences in industrial structures, see Thurow (1992).

7. China filed its first complaint of unfair trade practices (against the EU) within a month of joining the WTO.

8. Another long-running dispute over the EU's banana import policy dragged on for years, leading the United States to impose retaliatory trade duties. An agreement was reached in 2001 only because both sides saw the conflict as an obstacle to launching a new WTO round.

9. As in Seattle two years earlier, Doha negotiators had not agreed on a text outlining the shape of a new round when the scheduled deadline expired. In contrast to the earlier meeting, officials in Doha continued their deliberations and hammered out an agenda for the negotiations the following day.

10. See Odell (2001), Laird (2001) and Schott (2000) for a variety of explanations for the collapse of the Seattle talks.

11. The Cairns Group members are Argentina, Australia, Brazil, Canada, Chile, Colombia, Fiji, Indonesia, New Zealand, Paraguay, Philippines, South Africa, Thailand, and Uruguay.

12. These items, along with government procurement and trade facilitation, were introduced at the 1996 WTO ministerial meeting in Singapore for possible inclusion on the trade agenda.

13. See Moran (1998) for an analysis of actual vs. expected benefits from these measures.

14. As Hoekman and Holmes (1999: 876–887) define it, competition (or antitrust) *law* is "a set of rules and disciplines maintained by governments relating either to agreements between firms that restrict competition or the abuse of dominant market position (including attempts to create dominant position through merger)." Competition *policy* is a broader concept encompassing rules and instruments

that define the "conditions of competition" in the marketplace. Thus competition law is a subset of competition policy but also includes actions relating to privatization, deregulation, and subsidies, among other areas.

15. Tariff escalation refers to the use of higher tariffs for items at later stages of production. This discourages exporters from developing an export capacity in downstream activities that often have higher value added at those stages and are more profitable.

16. Unresolved by this statement is the key issue of defining which health problems qualify for overriding patents.

17. This waiver is necessary because such an agreement violates WTO rules.

18. Some developing countries outside the ACP group, such as the Philippines and Thailand, did initially object to the deal (and the waiver) because of expected discrimination against their exports to the EU.

19. This is an important issue for the poorest developing countries. As Laird (2001) details, many developing countries find it fiscally difficult to staff an office in Geneva with a sufficient number of trained personnel to represent their interests among the many international organizations headquartered in that city. Of the fifty-five new members joining the WTO between 1986 and 1999, about forty were unable to fund an office at all.

20. Under this approach U.S. authorities would raise (and then lower) tariffs on different imported products over time. This is designed to hurt as many exporting sectors in the target country as possible, putting maximum pressure on their government to come into compliance with WTO rules.

21. The liberal hope is that greater transparency will do two things: force governments away from their mercantilist bargaining strategies while creating incentives for politicians to rally support for free trade based upon its economic benefits.

References

Bhagwati, Jagdish. 2002. "Trade: The Unwinnable War." *Financial Times* (London), 29 January.

Conklin, John G. 1996. "From GATT to the World Trade Organization: Prospects for a Rule-Integrity Regime." In C. Roe Goddard, John T. Passé-Smith, and John G. Conklin, eds., *International Political Economy: State-Market Relations in the Changing Global Order.* Boulder: Lynne Rienner Publishers.

Crook, Clive. 2001. "Who Elected the WTO?" *Economist,* 29 September, special section on "The Case for Globalization" p. 26.

de Jonquieres, Guy. 2001. "Popular Trend Is at Odds with Global Free Trade." *Financial Times,* 30 November, special section, p. v.

Finger, J. Michael and Phillip Schuler. "Implementation of Uruguay Round Commitments: The Development Challenge." *World Economy* 23, 4 (April): 511–525.

Graham, Edward. 2000. "Trade, Competition, and the WTO Agenda." In Jeffrey H. Schott, ed., *The WTO After Seattle,* 205–222. Washington, DC: Institute for International Economics.

Hoekman, Bernard and Peter Holmes. 1999. "Competition Policy, Developing Countries and the WTO." *World Economy* 22, 6 (August): 875–893.

Hoekman, Bernard M. and Petros C. Mavroidis. 2000. "WTO Dispute Settlement, Transparency, and Surveillance." *World Economy* 23, 4 (April): 527–542.

International Centre for Trade and Sustainable Development. 2001. "Comprehensive Trade Round Broadens Scope of Discussions in the WTO." In *BRIDGES Weekly Trade News Digest* 5, 39 (November 15). Accessed March 6, 2002, at http://www.newsbulletin.org

———. 2002. "Countries Struggle over How to Negotiate WTO Doha Mandate." In *BRIDGES Weekly Trade News Digest* 6, 1 (January 16). Accessed March 10, 2002, at http://www.newsbulletin.org

Jackson, John H. 1998. *The World Trade Organization: Constitution and Jurisprudence*. London: Royal Institute of International Affairs.

Krugman, Paul R., ed. 1986. *Strategic Trade Policy and the New International Economics*. Cambridge, MA: MIT Press.

Laird, Sam. 2001. "Dolphins, Turtles, Mad Cows and Butterflies—A Look at the Multilateral Trading System in the 21st Century." *World Economy* 24, 4 (April): 453–481.

Moran, Theodore. 1998. *Foreign Direct Investment and Development: The New Policy Agenda for Developing Countries and Economies in Transition*. Washington, DC: Institute for International Economics.

———. 2000. "Investment Issues." In Jeffrey H. Schott, ed., *The WTO After Seattle*, 223–242. Washington, DC: Institute for International Economics.

Odell, John. 2001. "The Seattle Impasse and Its Implications for the World Trade Organization." Paper presented at the 2001 convention of the International Studies Association. Chicago, IL, February 20. Accessible at www-rcf.usc.edu/~odell/papers.html

Public Citizen. 1999. *A Citizen's Guide to the World Trade Organization: Everything You Need to Know to Fight for Fair Trade*. New York: Apex Press.

Ricardo, David. 1973. *Principles of Policial Economy and Taxation*. London: Dent.

Schott, Jeffrey J. 2000. "The WTO After Seattle." In Jeffrey H. Schott, ed., *The WTO After Seattle,* 3–40. Washington, DC: Institute for International Economics.

Schott, Jeffrey J. and Jayashree Watal. 2000. "Decision Making in the WTO." In Jeffrey H. Schott, ed., *The WTO After Seattle*. 283–292. Washington, DC: Institute for International Economics.

Spero, Joan E. and Jeffrey A. Hart. 1997. *The Political Economy of International Economic Relations*. 5th ed. New York: St. Martin's Press.

Thurow, Lester. 1992. *Head to Head: The Coming Economic Battle Among Japan, Europe and America*. New York: William Morrow and Co.

Watal, Jayashree. 2000. "Developing Countries' Interests in a 'Development Round.'" In Jeffrey H. Schott, ed., *The WTO After Seattle*. 71–84. Washington, DC: Institute for International Economics.

World Trade Organization (WTO). 2001a. "Declaration of the Fourth Ministerial Conference." November 14. Accessed March 10, 2002, at www.wto.org/english/thewto_e/minist_e/min01_e/mindecl_e.htm

———. 2001b. "Declaration on the TRIPs Agreement and Public Health." November 14. Accessed March 10, 2002, at http://www.wto.org/english/thewto_e/minist_e/min01_e/mindecl_trips_e.htm

———. 2001c. "Implementation-Related Issues and Concerns." November 14. Accessed March 10, 2002, at www.wto.org/english/thewto_e/minist_e/min01_e/mindecl_implementation_e.htm

———. 2001d. "Procedures for Extensions Under Article 27.4 for Certain Developing Country Members." November 14. Accessed March 10, 2002, at http://www.wto.org/english/thewto_e/minist_e/min01_e/mindecl_scm_e.htm

23

Regionalism, Multilateralism, and Deeper Integration: Changing Paradigms for Developing Countries

Robert Z. Lawrence

*The proliferation of regional trading arrangements in the 1990s has gener-
ated significant debate regarding its implications for the multilateral trading system and for nation-states within it. Robert Lawrence addresses these
important issues from the point of view of developing countries. His analysis shows how post–World War II assumptions regarding the global trade
system and developing country participation in it have shifted in important
ways. At the same time, new forces within the private sector have emerged
in favor of deeper forms of regional integration. In the chapter below,
Lawrence provides an accessible political economy analysis of the merits
of regional, multilateral, and deeper integration from a developing country
perspective.*

There is a profound tension in our world. Increasingly the economy is global, but the world is organized politically into nation-states. This process of
globalization has raised two fundamental questions about how we should
be governed. First, to what degree should policies be decided by nations
independently, and to what degree should they be subject to international
agreement? And second, if international agreement is required, should it be
regional or multilateral? This chapter addresses the relevance of these questions to trade policy, adopting the perspective of developing countries. The
first part describes the historical shifts in the focus of trade policies in global systems during the period after World War II and then explores specifically how these shifts have given regionalism today its distinctive charac-

Reprinted with permission of the publisher from *Trade Rules in the Making:
Challenges in Regional and Multilateral Negotiations,* edited by Miguel Rodriguez
Mendoza, Patrick Low, and Barbara Kotschwar. Washington, D.C.: Brookings
Institution Press, 1999.

teristics. The second part considers several strategic trade policy questions from the perspective of developing countries. In particular, what are the merits of regional and multilateral agreements in achieving liberalization and to what extent should coverage of these agreements deal with more than border barriers?

The Changing Approaches to International Trade Policy

When barriers at nations' borders were high, as they were in the immediate postwar period, governments and citizens could sharply differentiate international policies from domestic policies. International policies dealt with at the—border barriers, but nations were sovereign over domestic policies without regard to the impact on other nations. In its original form, the General Agreement on Tariffs and Trade (GATT), which was signed in the 1940s, emphasized this approach. Tariffs were to be reduced on a most favored nation basis, and discrimination against foreign goods was to be avoided by according them with national treatment. But the rules of the trading system, by and large, left nations free to pursue domestic policies in other areas such as competition, environment, taxation, intellectual property, and regulatory standards.[1] To the degree that there were international agreements in other policy areas—indeed there were international multilateral agreements on business practices, labor standards, intellectual property, and the environment—these were made outside the GATT, and compliance was typically voluntary. This was the case, for example, when nations signed the conventions on international labor standards of the International Labor Organization (ILO) or the codes of conduct for multinational corporations of the United Nations.

In the 1950s and 1960s there was also a widely held view that in order to develop, developing countries should separate themselves from the world economy. In part this view was a response to the disastrous international environment that had prevailed in the 1930s. In part it reflected a skepticism regarding the potential of market forces and a faith in the capacity of governments to plan development and allocate resources. There was a view that political factors, such as neocolonialism, had created a system biased against developing countries, particularly producers of primary products. As a result, for the most part developing countries adopted import substitution policies and maintained high tariff barriers and restrictive quotas.

For developing countries the GATT approach of reducing tariffs on a most favored nation basis was attractive, particularly when it was amended to provide for special and differential treatment of countries. In principle, developing countries had considerable freedom to pursue whatever policies they chose. Specifically, developing countries were granted leniency in the use of infant industry protection and trade restrictions for purposes of balancing payments, and they were given special market access under the Generalized System of Preferences (GSP). They were also able to receive most favored nation treatment from other member nations without undertaking much liberalization at home.[2]

In sum, there were three widely accepted principles in the period immediately after World War II that help explain the overall thrust of the policies developed. First, trade agreements should concentrate on lowering border barriers; second, developing countries should try to develop with only limited engagement in the world economy; and third, when they do engage, they should be given special treatment. Over time, however, these principles have been increasingly challenged.

In the first place, starting in relationships among developed countries, pressures began building for deeper international integration—that is, for the harmonization and reconciliation of domestic policies. A host of new issues emerged as part of the international negotiating agenda. These included such issues as services trade, intellectual property, rules for foreign investors, product standards, competition policies, and labor and environmental standards. The increased scope of international trade agreements could be seen in bilateral agreements such as the Structural Impediments Initiative (SII) between Japan and the United States, which emphasized issues such as Japan's spending on infrastructure, its distribution system, and its antitrust policy; in regional arrangements such as the single-market initiative EC92 in Europe, which emphasized increased harmonization and mutual recognition of national standards and social dimensions; and in multilateral agreements such as the Uruguay Round, which resulted in the formation of the World Trade Organization (WTO), the adoption of rules on intellectual property rights, the liberalization of services and agriculture, the adoption of trade-related investment measures, and the development of a more powerful dispute resolution system. The new emphasis is also clear in discussions on the post–Uruguay Round agenda, with some nations calling for agreements to cover issues such as competition policy, labor standards, and the environment.

Why This Shift to Deeper Integration?

There are both political and functional forces driving this trend. When nations were separated by high border barriers and had little trade with each other, they could overlook each other's domestic affairs. As the barriers have come down, however, the impact of different domestic policies has become apparent. Improvements in communications and increased travel have made countries increasingly aware of foreign practices. In addition, as international competition has intensified, firms, workers, and citizens have become increasingly aware that different national policies have international effects. Increasingly, therefore, the call is for a level playing field.

The major political actors in society are business, labor, and environmentalists. When these groups see national rules affecting trade that are different from those of their countries, they are moved to cry foul. Pejorative terms are used to describe abhorrent foreign practices. For business the problem is dumping; for labor it is "social dumping"; and for environmentalists it is "ecodumping." All three groups are therefore seeking to achieve their goals, either by directly changing the trading rules or by using trade as a weapon to enforce agreements achieved elsewhere. In some cases groups put forward these arguments as a pretext for protectionism. Their real goals are not an integrated international system based on rules, but a world economy fragmented on the pretext that national differences preclude fair competition. In other cases, however, there are more widely held social concerns about the impact of unfair competition, low labor standards, and lax environmental standards. One argument is that once markets and competition are global there is a strong case for the rules defining fair competition to be global. Similarly, as the world becomes increasingly aware of shared environmental problems such as global warming and the depletion of the ozone layer, the case for international coordination of environmental policies becomes stronger. Likewise, as labor markets become linked through immigration and trade and international humanitarian concerns are raised because of improved publicity and communications—the CNN effect—the call for basic standards becomes stronger.

In addition to these political forces, there are even more powerful functional reasons behind the trend toward deeper integration. Foreign trade and foreign investment have become increasingly complementary. Access to foreign markets has become vital for competitive success not only for products, but also for foreign investment. To sell sophisticated products requires a significant domestic presence to provide marketing, sales, and service. The ability to follow market trends, respond to customer needs, and acquire innovative small foreign firms in all major markets has become vital for competitive success. These factors all lead companies to pay increasing attention not only to trade barriers, but also to foreign domestic practices that hinder their operation. This, in turn, leads to frictions resulting from different systems of corporate governance and rules of operation. Even absent trade barriers, other factors—for example, the weak enforcement of antitrust policies—can lead to collusion by domestic firms that limits new firms' entry into the market. International investment in services industries stimulated in part by deregulation, privatization, and liberalization has contributed to these trends. Once foreign firms operate in regulated sectors, they become increasingly interested in the rules that govern their behavior.

From Closed to Open Domestic Markets

The second basic premise of the early postwar system—that developing countries should develop behind high trade barriers—has also been questioned. In the 1980s developing nations responded both to success and to failure by moving toward liberalization and outward orientation. In Asia success led to external pressures on Taiwan and Korea to liberalize; elsewhere shifts toward an outward orientation were induced by debt problems, the Asian example, the encouragement of the International Monetary Fund (IMF) and the World Bank, and the need to attract new capital in new forms. The collapse of communism brought a large new group of nations into the international marketplace. China, the world's largest developing country and also its most rapidly growing, is only the most visible of these nations. Although complete removal of border barriers has not been achieved, the leaders of most nations can agree in principle that free trade is desirable, and many are prepared to commit their countries to achieving it in the foreseeable future. In late 1994, for example, thirty-four nations in the Western Hemisphere and eighteen members of the Asia Pacific Economic Cooperation (APEC) Forum committed themselves to eventual full regional free trade and investment.

From Special to Reciprocal Treatment

As developing countries have sought to liberalize and attract foreign investment, the pressures driving deeper integration have led to erosion of another part of the postwar consensus about how developing countries should be treated. In particular, there has been a turn away from the idea of preferential treatment. This is the logical implication of the shift toward deeper integration. It is straightforward to provide special treatment when an agreement relates to barriers at the border. The developed countries simply adopt lower tariffs than developing countries. But often when the agreement relates to adherence to a common rule—whether the rule is adopted or it is not—it is more difficult to have an agreement that does not involve reciprocal obligations. In addition, developing countries have increasingly seen the adoption of such commitments to be in their interest, as their efforts have been directed toward internal reforms that can be reinforced by international agreements.

Again, this development is evident in both multilateral and regional arrangements. In the Uruguay Round, although developing countries were given longer periods of time in which to adopt new disciplines such as those related to intellectual property, they were generally not exempted to anywhere near the same degree as they had been earlier. Likewise, in traditional regional arrangements such as the Lomé Convention between the European Union (EU) and developing nations in Africa and the Caribbean, manufactured goods from developing countries were granted duty-free access, but these countries were not expected to reciprocate. By contrast, the more recent agreements signed by the EU with eastern European nations and those from the Middle East and North Africa are markedly different. These agreements envisage much more complete reciprocity. Similarly, in the North American Free Trade Agreement (NAFTA), after the transition period the obligations assumed by Mexico and the more developed NAFTA partners are reciprocal. Likewise, in the APEC agreements, although developing countries are given an additional ten years (until 2020) to adopt complete free trade and investment, their obligations are similar to those of their developed counterparts.

As countries have turned toward global markets, a paradoxical consequence has been the development of pressures toward increased regional integration. Increased global competition has led multinational firms to develop regional strategies to compete globally. To be internationally competitive, firms must have access to key inputs at the lowest prices. This leads to sourcing from nearby trading partners whose comparative advantage lies in such inputs. Similarly, firms seek to enjoy scale economies by selling to large regional trading partners.

In North America, for example, outwardly oriented policies by one of the "natural" trading partners of the United States, Canada, led to free trade arrangements to secure market access and lure foreign investment with the prospect of servicing a rich regional market. Meanwhile, U.S. manufacturing firms were attracted by the possibility of escaping restrictions on investment in Canada, which would allow them to rationalize their North American strategies. In Europe the initiative to establish a single market by 1992 was led by Eurocrats who were motivated by the goals of political union and stimulating growth. However, it was also supported by European firms whose executives felt that even fairly large domestic markets such as those of Germany, France, and the United Kingdom were inadequate home bases for global competition. The EC92 initiative was successful not simply in removing barriers, but also in reorienting the strategies of European firms that now treat Europe as a single market and as a single production base from which to service global markets. These strategies have been reflected in decisions regarding investment, plant location, and mergers and acquisitions. The changed emphasis in policies on trade liberalization and deeper integration provides an important context for evaluating current regional trading arrangements and comparing them to those that emerged earlier.

In the 1950s and 1960s developing countries concluded preferential trading agreements among themselves as part of their trade policy strategies, but these agreements often failed miserably (Hazlewood 1979). This might have been expected given their motivation; many of these agreements were driven by purely political rather than economic considerations.

To the degree that economic objectives were involved, the agreements were usually an extension to the regional level of domestic import substitution and planning policies that were proposed to achieve scale economies for protectionist policies. The theory was that participating countries would become more specialized and by relying on regional markets could develop international competitiveness. In practice, however, given the general philosophy of trying to produce everything at home, members tended to give each other access to their markets only for those products they imported from the rest of the world. In other words, the region as a whole became more self-sufficient, but in a most inefficient manner—by maximizing trade diversion.

Under these circumstances it was no surprise that preferential trading agreements among developing countries often failed. This was especially true when countries had similar patterns of specialization so that there were few opportunities for avoiding competition. However, even where there was scope for such specialization, once the extraregional trade was diverted the impact of the agreements was exhausted. It is difficult, if not impossible, to plan resource allocation in a single economy. It is even more complicated, if not impossible, to do so when there are several countries and resource allocation decisions are highly politicized (Langhammer 1992).

The forces driving these developments differ radically from those driving previous waves of regionalization in this century. Unlike those of the 1930s, most of the current initiatives represent efforts to facilitate their members' participation in the world economy rather than their withdrawal from it. Unlike those of the 1950s and 1960s, the initiatives involving developing countries are part of a strategy to liberalize the economies of such countries in general and to open their economies to implement policies driven by exports and foreign investment rather than to promote import substitution. The current moves toward regionalization are, by and large, not meant to thwart the allocative process of the market, but to strengthen its operation. They represent efforts to fill the functional needs of international trade and investment and the requirements of international governance and cooperation to which globalization gives rise. In addition, many important regional initiatives are not developing as arrangements with exclusive memberships in which insiders limit their contacts with outsiders. On the contrary, they are developing as inclusive arrangements in which members either allow outsiders to join or independently join them in developing similar arrangements.

Some major aspects of the new regionalism are listed in Table 23.1. It is striking that recent regional agreements have been strongly supported by corporate leaders. In Europe the initiative to establish a single market was promoted by large European firms that argued that a fragmented Europe deprived them of the scale economies they needed to be competitive. Similarly, the NAFTA was boosted by U.S. businesses both large (repre-

Table 23.1   Regionalism: Old and New

Old	New
Import substitution—withdraw from world economy.	Export orientation—integrate into world economy.
Planned and political allocation of resources.	Market allocation of resources.
Driven by governments.	Driven by private firms.
Mainly industrial products.	All goods and services, as well as investment.
Deal with border barriers.	Aimed at deeper integration.
Preferential treatment for less-developed nations.	Equal rules (different adjustment periods) for all nations.

sented by the Business Round Table) and small (represented by the U.S. Chamber of Commerce) (Fishlow and Haggard 1992). Major supporters of a free trade agreement in Canada were the Business Council on National Issues and the Canadian Manufacturers Association (CMA), and large Mexican industrial groups strongly backed the NAFTA. Private foreign investors have led the informal regional integration in Asia. In addition, in the APEC political leaders have explicitly institutionalized the role of business by creating an advisory Pacific Business Forum, which was established in June 1994. Both large and small firms from the eighteen member countries are represented in this forum, which is charged with providing proposals for facilitating trade and investment within the region.

Clearly, many multinational corporations view these regional arrangements as promoting their interests. This view reflects the role of these arrangements as responses to the functional demands of multinational firms in the current economic environment. In particular it is noteworthy that these initiatives are concerned with services and foreign direct investment (FDI), as well as goods trade. Also, for reasons outlined earlier, they focus on internal rules and regulations and on institutional mechanisms to ensure implementation and enforcement as well as removal of border barriers.

As they seek to attract capital and at the same time pursue programs based on export-driven growth, foreign firms become increasingly attractive to developing countries. They bring knowledge about the latest technologies and ready-made access to major markets. Moreover, in many developing countries. accompanying the shift toward more open trade policies has been a reduction in the role of the state through privatization. In this context foreign investors have become increasingly attractive as providers of capital, technology, and operational skills.

The demand for foreign investment emanating from the developing countries has corresponded with an increased supply from multinational corporations. As international competition intensifies, small cost advantages may have large consequences. Particular national locations are not necessarily well suited to the complete manufacture of complex products. With improvements in communications and transportation, firms are increasingly able to produce products by sourcing from multiple locations. Raw materials might best be sourced in one country, labor-intensive processes performed in a second, and technologically sophisticated processes performed in a third. Multinationals from many nations are therefore expanding their foreign investments.

Traditionally, FDI in developing countries was made to gain access to raw materials. Later, in countries following protectionist import-substitution policies, it was attracted by the prospects of selling behind trade barriers in a large internal market.[3] Although the motive of an attractive domestic market persists, as developing countries have lowered their trade barriers, investment has increasingly been motivated toward providing service to export markets (Wells 1992). Those able to offer export platforms have become most successful in attracting FDI.[4]

Implications

The increased importance of international investment naturally shifts attention from trade to investment barriers and focuses attention on national differences in the degree of ease with which foreign firms can enter new markets through both acquisition and new establishment, and on the effects of domestic regulations and taxes on the conditions under which such firms can operate. Similarly, firms that plan to source in one country and sell in others need security about the rules and mechanisms governing trade. Such firms also prefer secure intellectual property rights as well as technical standards and regulations that are compatible.

For developing countries, particularly those that were previously inhospitable toward foreign investment, establishing the credibility of new policies to attract investment and securing access to markets for exports has come to be of major importance. In addition, for some developing countries it may be easier to "import" new institutions and regulatory systems than to develop them independently. Although such institutions may not have the virtue of matching domestic conditions precisely, they offer the advantages of having been pretested and of providing international compatibility. For nations in eastern Europe, for example, adopting policies that conform to EU norms is particularly attractive because they can be seen as the first steps toward full membership in the EU. Finally, entering international negotiations can affect an internal debate, tilting it in favor of one side and against another. In many cases domestic forces interested in liberalization will find their hands strengthened if they can present their policies as part of an international liberalization agreement (Haggard 1995).

Given these developments, the reasons for the distinctive character of the emerging regional arrangements become clearer. They are motivated by the desire to facilitate international investment and the operations of multinational firms as much as by the desire to promote trade. Although liberalization to permit trade requires the removal of border barriers—a relatively shallow form of integration—the development of regional production systems and the promotion of investment in services require deeper forms of international integration of national regulatory systems and policies. One example is eliminating differences in national production and product standards that make regionally integrated production costly. Investment also requires credible and secure governance mechanisms, and it requires secure access to large foreign markets that is unhindered either by customs officials or by domestic actions such as the adoption of antidumping policies. Since much of the investment relates to the provision of services, the regulatory regimes governing establishment and operation become the focus of attention. In sum, regionalism is a natural outgrowth of the shift toward globalization in developing countries.

Strategic Challenges

Almost all developing countries today are committed in principle to policies of increased trade and financial liberalization. But there remain important questions about the appropriate approaches to achieving these goals. One set of issues must be faced by countries individually. One key question is at what pace and in what order should liberalization be pursued? In particular, what kinds of institutional and competitive capacity need to be in place prior to full liberalization? This issue, which will not be explored in depth in this chapter, has been the subject of considerable debate, and there appears to be an emerging consensus that trade liberalization and domestic financial reform should precede liberalization of the capital account. A second question is what are the appropriate means for achieving liberalization? In particular, to what degree should countries act unilaterally and independently in setting their trade policies, to what degree should they pursue regional free trade agreements, and to what degree should they act only multilaterally? A third question relates to the nature of agreements that are signed. Should they cover only border barriers, or should they deal with the issues of deeper integration? Each of these issues is covered in turn.

International Agreements

Why do countries sign international trade agreements that constrain their behavior? If free trade is in a nation's interest, why not simply move unilaterally to remove border barriers? In particular, why would a sovereign state want to constrain its own behavior and subject itself to the possibilities of international sanction?

First, even though a nation may benefit from removing its own trade barriers, it can do even better if its trading partners also remove theirs, raising the demand for the nation's exports and improving its international buying power. Developing countries that sign agreements such as the GATT or regional agreements may gain improved access to foreign markets for their exports.

Second, international negotiations can strengthen the influence of the parties that gain from free trade. Although trade may benefit the nation, it may create losers in industries that compete with imports. If these losers are politically powerful, they may prevent a unilateral reduction in barriers. Trade negotiations help mobilize one group of domestic producers— exporters who gain from liberalization abroad—to offset the influence of producers and workers who compete with imports and thus make it politically easier for national leaders to adopt policies in the nation's interest.

Third, international agreements may make a nation's liberal trade policies more credible. Before firms will undertake the investments necessary to serve foreign markets, they need to be confident that access to these markets will be forthcoming. When countries, particularly those with a long history of protection, proclaim their newfound allegiance to policies of open trade and investment, foreign investors often react quite skeptically. By accepting commitments that could lead to international sanctions if broken, countries can persuade others of the permanence of their changes. Therefore, even small countries that are unable to change the behavior of their trading partners may gain from the lock-in effects of signing international trade agreements.

Fourth, international agreements and constraints can also prove useful where there is compelling evidence that international markets deviate markedly from the competitive model. One such type of market failure occurs when firms have monopoly or market power. Market failures may result if countries adopt policies that enhance the market power of their firms—so-called strategic trade policies—or raise their export prices by imposing the so-called optimal tariff. International oversight or rules that inhibit such behavior could, in principle, improve global welfare. Externalities or spillovers are a second source of market failure. As in a single nation's economy, some activities, such as pollution, may lead to inefficient outcomes when the polluters fail to take account of the social costs of their behavior. In an international economy there may be international environmental problems such as acid rain and depletion of the ozone layer that would not be countered efficiently if countries acted only independently.

Finally, agreements may allow for exploitation of economies of scale. One route calls for harmonization; another could entail mutual recognition. Where these benefits are great they may involve a trade-off. On the one hand, specific local regulations may match preferences more closely; on the other hand, international norms may yield benefits from scale economies.

These considerations all create the need for international agreements. Nations that are members of the WTO have agreed to bargain multilaterally to negotiate reductions in trade barriers. To ensure that these negotiations are credible, members have agreed to permit sanctions in the event they renege. To ensure that reductions are not undermined by domestic policies, they have also agreed not to harmonize policies, but to avoid measures that discriminate against foreign goods and to achieve their goals in the least trade-restricting way possible. In addition, efforts have been made to prevent firms from gaining monopoly power through predatory practices by means of rules against dumping and against nations' applying subsidies that may nullify their tariff reductions and inflict harm on their trading partners through the codes for subsidies. It is noteworthy, however, that although the GATT is based on nondiscrimination between its members (the principle of most favored nation treatment) and nondiscrimination between domestic and imported goods (the principle of national treatment), it does not require nations to have tariffs at similar levels or to adopt the same policies. Even with respect to border barriers, there is no level playing field. Aside from export subsidies, the GATT allows nations to respond to foreign subsidies and dumping only when these are seen to cause injury. It is not the goal of harmonization to create a level playing field that lies behind the trade rules, the goal is to make markets internationally contestable so that the benefits of international specialization can be most fully realized.

Given the existence of a forum for multilateral trade agreements and the ability to join the WTO, why might countries want to sign regional trade agreements? In particular, trade theory indicates that such agreements do not necessarily enhance welfare, since they may both divert and create trade, and indeed it has been argued that this effect could be quite powerful in the case of some Latin American countries that have high trade barriers.

However, those who point to the dangers of trade diversion generally compare liberalization with a preferential arrangement that entails complete multilateral liberalization. A more realistic comparison is between multilateral liberalization that is only partial and preferential trade liberalization, which could be much more complete. Under these circumstances, both measures are "second best," and we know that partial multilateral liberalization could actually reduce the efficiency of resource allocation. This can be seen easily in terms of the theory of effective protection, in which the reduction of tariffs on primary commodity inputs can actually increase effective protection on final products. In fact, during the postwar period, the world has moved toward free trade through two means. One, the multilateral, in which there has been full participation but partial liberalization and the other, preferential arrangements, in which there has been (almost) full liberalization but partial participation. In practice the two approaches have not been incompatible.

One reason for the coexistence of these approaches is that from a political standpoint it might be easier to persuade a government to liberalize with respect to neighbors than to do so multilaterally. Political feasibility may channel liberalization toward regional initiatives. This might particularly be the case in instances such as that of the European Common Market, in which political motivations made a European Customs Union feasible, whereas complete multilateral liberalization was not. Free trade opponents of preferential trading agreements assume that in the absence of regional free trade agreements multilateral liberalization will take place. However, there may be cases in which it is possible to liberalize in a free trade area when it is not possible to do so unilaterally or multilaterally.

It is generally agreed that because firms can act collectively more easily than consumers, firms are more powerful politically than consumers. This makes import liberalization politically difficult, because even in cases where the country as a whole will gain, the benefits will be enjoyed by consumers in the form of lower prices, while the costs will be born by firms that compete with imports. If consumers are poorly organized, import-competing firms lobbying for protection might have the upper hand. To offset this advantage, it might be necessary to have another group of producers—namely exporters—also supporting liberalization.

Indeed, we should generally expect exporting firms to support liberalization, but liberalization by participating in multilateral negotiations is not particularly attractive for exporting interests originating in small countries.[5] The offers of other nations are not likely to be influenced by the liberalization in a single country. Therefore, particularly in a system such as that imposed by the GATT in which all members are given most favored nation treatment unconditionally, it will be hard for exporters to see it as worth their while to lobby for domestic liberalization. Moreover, since the GATT has operated on the principle of special and differential treatment for developing countries, exporters from small developing countries have even less reason to promote domestic liberalization. This tendency toward free riding creates problems for exporters from large countries. These considerations are different in preferential trading agreements. Exporters will see gains in the form of more open foreign markets that are contingent on domestic liberalization, and are therefore likely to lobby more enthusiastically for such agreements.[6] If scale economies are important, the benefits from liberalization may be greater for small countries than for large countries. Accordingly, the bargaining power of large countries may be greater in regional negotiations. Indeed, Bhagwati and others argue that this can lead to placing undesirable demands on small countries under these circumstances (Bhagwati and Kreuger 1995).

Countries may also join regional arrangements for defensive reasons. For example, once Mexico joined the NAFTA the Caribbean economies that are highly dependent on the U.S. market felt a disadvantage, and they have been driven to seek mitigation. Therefore, countries that suffer from trade diversion could be better off joining such an agreement than staying out. Countries excluded from a preferential agreement may have incentives to join it. If the agreement is open to newcomers, there could be an expanding preferential arrangement that will eventually encompass the world. The incentive to join may increase as an agreement grows and becomes more effective. Richard Baldwin (1993) describes this as the domino effect. He shows how the trade diversion (and the increased efficiency) of countries forming an agreement can raise the costs for other competitors of not joining. This can increase the interest of export firms in the excluded country in joining the agreement, thereby spreading the process of liberalization. Key issues under these circumstances are the conditions under which accession is granted.

The domino effect Baldwin has identified may well be combined with another that may lead liberalization to proliferate—the incentives for a country that is prepared to liberalize to do so in a piecemeal fashion by joining a number of free trade agreements. Countries benefit from being the hub of a network of free trade agreements. Israel has free trade agreements with both the United States and the EU. Firms exporting from Israel, for example, receive preferential access to both the United States and the EU. By contrast, firms in the United States and the EU receive preferences only in the Israeli market. At the same time, by being open to more than one trading partner Israel experiences less trade diversion than it would have had it joined just one such agreement. Ultimately, in fact, the best situation for a single small country is to enjoy preferential access to all markets in the world while having open borders. If these incentives are present for every country, the system could move to free trade.

Countries trying to achieve this state face complicated timing decisions. It is necessary to have some preferences remaining to bargain away for access to each new partner, and as countries conclude these agreements the value of the preferences they confer diminishes. One of the advantages of simultaneous multilateral liberalization is that it reduces the incentive to hold back, since a country can keep track of all the concessions it receives in return for its own.

If full free trade is the outcome, why do the countries not get together and coordinate their actions? This may eventually happen, but particularly at the start there is a temporary advantage to the first movers from the preferential access they achieve. Indeed, a noteworthy aspect of liberalization, particularly in Latin America, has been the tendency of countries to join several free trade agreements simultaneously.[7] In the Western Hemisphere it appears that these will now be consolidated into a single Free Trade Area of the Americas.

Another fear is that in a customs union insiders with a stake in higher protection will capture the decision-making process of a more powerful entity and thus have increased power to thwart liberalization. This will particularly be the case for customs unions in which trade policy decisions require unanimity. For example, assume Spain and Poland compete in producing product A. If both are outside the EU they will lobby the EU to lower its tariffs on A. Once Spain achieves access, however, its incentives will change, and to preserve its preferential access it might oppose lower tariffs for Poland.

Moreover, a multilateral system with a few large players could be more susceptible to such foot-draggers. For a long time France opposed agricultural liberalization during the Uruguay Round. Since France was able to affect the position of the European Community (EC) as a whole, reaching agreement proved difficult. By contrast, had France been isolated an arrangement that simply bypassed or excluded it might have been possible.

However, larger customs union arrangements may be more difficult to capture than arrangements between single nations, because they are more likely to contain countervailing interests. It is true that France might have been opposed to agricultural liberalization, but other nations within the EU were not. Indeed, in the end France was forced to compromise, partly because of pressures from other members of the EU with an interest in agricultural liberalization. Moreover, a customs union such as the EU has relatively low external tariffs, and accession by more protectionist countries makes them more liberal. This was the case for Spain and Portugal, for example, in most industrial products.[8]

A third concern is the diversion of scarce political capital. Trade policymakers involved in negotiating and operating regional agreements will have less time and fewer resources available for multilateral negotiations. A related worry is that advocates for free trade with particular interests may be satisfied by liberalization with a few key countries and therefore not support multilateral liberalization. The United States is the market Mexican exporters most care about. If the only way the Mexican glass industry could sell in this market were for the United States to lower its tariffs multilaterally in accordance with the GATT, Mexican glass exporters might work hard for a GATT agreement. In a coalition with other exporters, they might tilt Mexican support for the GATT. If they gained access to the U.S. market through the NAFTA, however, their interest in the GATT might subside, and the lobby for multilateral liberalization would be weakened.

However, a regional arrangement might actually build up the political support for liberalization by doing it gradually rather than all at once. A regional arrangement might reduce the number of import-competing sectors and increase the number of exporters. This could, in turn, tilt the internal domestic political debate in favor of full liberalization.

It is of course not necessarily the case that countries are forced to choose between regional and multilateral liberalization. Indeed, both types of liberalization can be achieved simultaneously, and they could be complementary strategies. Nonetheless, there is also a danger that countries could join customs unions in particular, and thus retard the pace of their multilateral liberalization because of the opposition of such liberalization by other members of the union.

Deeper Integration

Should these issues of deeper integration become part of the regional or multilateral trading agenda? Consider first the multilateral agenda. For developing countries the stakes in how these new issues of deeper integration are handled in the international system are exceptionally high. Many in developing countries resisted the idea that the rules of the GATT should be extended to cover services and intellectual property and were willing to agree only in return for concessions in areas such agriculture and textiles. Likewise, many are understandably wary that adopting measures on the environment or labor could actually retard their development.

A second concern is that these issues could become a pretext for protectionism that denies developing countries access to international markets. This could be the result unless sufficient recognition is given to the limited capacities of many developing countries to implement standards, regulations, and other policies in these areas. As a result of these concerns, a common response by developing countries has been to resist the introduction of these issues into the multilateral trade agenda. It is common, for example, on issues of both environmental and labor standards for developing countries to point out that when they were poor, the developed countries of today did not adhere to the standards they are trying to require of others. Similarly, others feel that in a world dominated by developed-country multinationals the adoption of tough competition rules and international investment standards could preclude government assistance for firms headquartered in developing countries.

However, there are problems with these rejection responses because, as countries without much international power, developing countries have an interest in seeing these issues decided in a multilateral setting with their participation. The absence of clear international rules could well provide opportunities for protectionists to influence their domestic policies. In addition, developing countries themselves have interests in a more competitive international market, a cleaner world, and labor standards that enhance welfare. Therefore, there appears to be a need for compromise in this area that is not easy to attain.

A second arena for deeper integration is regionalism. Traditional theorizing about regionalism considers these arrangements in the context of a paradigm in which trade policy is characterized by changes to border barriers. Regional arrangements are modeled either as customs unions (in which members have free trade internally and a common external tariff) or as free trade areas (internal barriers are eliminated, while external tariffs differ). In the view of traditional analysis, therefore, the dominant goal is the maximization of global welfare, and this will be achieved in a competitive international economy by multilateral free trade. Against this paradigm, preferential free trade arrangements are judged to be "second best" and therefore inferior to multilateral free trade.

Although the removal of internal border barriers is certainly an important feature of these arrangements, focusing only on these barriers overlooks much of what regional arrangements are about. The traditional perspective is at best incomplete and at worst misleading. A more comprehensive view of these emerging arrangements acknowledges that they are also about achieving deeper integration of international competition and investment. Once tariffs are removed there remain complex problems between nations relating to different regulatory policies. In a national context there is an extensive theory dealing with the question of how to assign authority over different aspects of fiscal policy to different levels of government—the literature on fiscal federalism.

No single answer seems to result from a general consideration of the factors that will affect this choice. There will inevitably be tensions between, on the one hand, realizing scale economies and internalization by increasing the scope of governance and, on the other hand, realizing more precise matching of tastes and choices by reducing that scope. What does seem clear, however, is that the answer will not always be the nation-state or the world. It is bound to differ, depending on the nature of the activity to be regulated. In some cases—for example, reducing global warming or establishing global financial networks—the appropriate level may be the world; in other cases, it could be the local community. The answers to this question are ambiguous, and they will not be independent of technology, history, incomes, and tastes. Indeed, there is no reason, a priori, to assume that the provision of regulatory regimes and other public goods should be the sole responsibility of the nation-state. Some goods and rules are better provided locally, although bilateral and plurilateral international arrangements may be more appropriate for providing others.

Recognizing the deeper nature of these agreements also provides challenges for appraising their effects on welfare. The nature of policy changes under these arrangements suggests that the normal presumptions about trade creation and diversion may not hold. It is generally presumed, for example, that preferential trading arrangements will reduce exports from outside the region. However, deeper internal agreements could actually stimulate such trade. For example, if members were to agree on tougher pollution controls or labor standards, their imports of products from nations with more lenient standards could rise. Similarly, the adoption of a common standard in a regional arrangement might make it less costly not only for domestic producers, but also for producers outside the region to sell their products. Likewise, the adoption of constraints on national state aids would provide benefits for both internal and external producers that compete with firms that might once have received such subsidies. Tougher enforcement of antitrust policies could provide improved market access for both internal and external producers.

In empirical studies a reduction of external trade is generally an indication of trade diversion—that is, that a member of an agreement is buying products from a less-efficient internal source. However, deeper agreements could actually make regional firms more efficient. This might lead to a reduction of external trade, but it would not represent trade diversion that would reduce welfare. For example, changes in domestic regulations could give internal firms cost advantages over outsiders that would result both in fewer imports from outside the region and in lower internal costs. This concept has important implications for proposals that outsiders be compensated for their loss of trading opportunities when preferential trading arrangements are formed.

It is also possible, however, that even without raising border barriers or increasing internal trade, deeper regional agreements could become more closed to outsiders. One example would be the adoption of a common standard discriminating against external imports and raising internal costs. Another might be the adoption of common cartel-like industrial policies in the region as a whole, which would limit external producer access.

As these examples indicate, from an efficiency standpoint deeper international agreements could be better or worse than the domestic policies they replace or discipline. Deeper does not necessarily mean better or more efficient. First, the choice of the level of government is a matter of judgment and of balancing the costs and benefits of more centralized government. Mistakes could be made, and policies implemented by international agreement could violate the principle of subsidiarity. Second, much depends on the specific policies adopted. It could be much worse to harmonize on the wrong policy than to retain national policies that are not linked.

The European example is illustrative of the argument that deep integration—that is, the achievement of harmonized regional policies—could lead to either more or less protection depending on the specific nature of the policies. In particular, the EC's choice of trying to thwart market pressures in sectors such as agriculture, steel, and coal led to a Europe that was more protectionist to the outside world. In addition, the efforts by the EC to wrest control of external voluntary restraint arrangement (VRA) policies away from individual countries have probably also led to more protection for the EC as a whole. Similarly, the availability of antidumping rules has permitted producers to enjoy one-stop shopping for protection that might have been more difficult to achieve in markets that were more fragmented. There is therefore ample evidence of contamination.

On the other hand, market-conforming measures have had the opposite effect, leading to increased trade opportunities both internally and externally. European disciplines regarding state aids and other measures, which favor domestic producers, provide benefits for all who compete within Europe. Similarly, the achievement of common standards reduces costs for all who wish to sell in the market.

In sum, although traditional trade theory provides us with interesting insights into both the benefits and the costs of regional arrangements and their dynamics, the deeper aspects of these agreements suggest that they need to be viewed through more than the narrow prism of conventional trade theory. Some emerging regional arrangements are moving to deal with measures that have not been dealt with by the GATT. Some opponents of these regional arrangements actually see the "deeper" integrative aspects of these arrangements as pernicious and undesirable. They view these as mechanisms for foisting inappropriate rules and restraints on weaker, smaller—and, in particular, developing—countries. Jagdish Bhagwati, a free trade opponent of regional arrangements, views them as "a process by which a hegemonic power seeks (and often manages) to satisfy its multiple trade-unrelated demands on other weaker trading nations more easily than through Multilateralism." Free trade arrangements seriously damage the multilateral trade liberalization process by facilitating the capture of it by extraneous demands that aim not to reduce trade barriers, but to increase them (as when countries seek to deny market access on grounds such as ecodumping and social dumping) (Perroni and Whalley 1994; Bhagwati and Krueger 1995).

It is indeed likely that in negotiations between countries of differing market sizes an asymmetrical power relationship will exist. However, this does not mean that poor, small countries will lose in these associations. Indeed the power asymmetries reflect the fact that the gains, particularly those from realizing scale economies, are likely to be relatively larger for the smaller countries. Similarly, economic integration generally leads to convergence, with poorer economies growing more rapidly than richer economies. Moreover, small countries join these agreements voluntarily.

Indeed, if the NAFTA or the Canada-U.S. Free Trade Agreement (CUSTA) had been seen as U.S. initiatives, they would have been doomed politically from the start. In both cases the governments and firms of these countries saw these agreements as in their own interests, and not simply because they feared American protectionism. The same is true of the eastern European nations that are voluntarily seeking to join the EU and those in Latin America that are seeking a hemispheric arrangement with the United States. Finally, particularly in agreements with the EU, aid has been made part of the package.

Moreover, although countries seeking to join these arrangements may have to make "concessions" by adopting some rules and institutions that may not suit their needs perfectly, they also enjoy benefits from adopting institutions without having to incur the costs of developing them. Just as several European countries have sought to import the anti-inflation credibility enjoyed by the Bundesbank by pegging their exchange rates to the German mark, so countries can make their regulatory policies more credible through international cooperation.

The strong role played by corporations in promoting regional integration has been noted. Recognizing this role provides insight into both the promise of and the problems with the current regional initiatives. The promise is represented by moves toward deeper economic integration than is currently feasible under the GATT. Regional agreements can make progress in harmonizing domestic policies and providing more credible and more effective supranational governance mechanisms than the WTO. On the other hand, there is the concern of regulatory capture: that under the influence of companies new systems of rules will be set to help insiders and hurt outsiders. Skeptics such as Bernard Hoekman (1992), Anne Kreuger (1993), and Raymond Vernon (1994) are particularly concerned that although they masquerade as free trade agreements, the new arrangements have been severely compromised by intricate rules of origin and other loopholes that may actually represent a retreat from freer trade rather than a movement toward it.

In addition to the traditional problem of trade diversion, there are two other major risks with regional agreements. The first is that they could implement new forms of protection not by erecting new tariffs, but by implementing rules of origin and administering antidumping and countervailing duties that have protectionist effects. The second is that some countries may join regional arrangements even when the rules they provide are inappropriate for their levels of development.

Notes

1. Originally the charter for the International Trade Organization covered a broader range of issues, including restrictive business practices and labor standards, but it was never adopted.

2. To be sure, these principles were not always fulfilled, as exemplified by the failures to liberalize agricultural trade and the discriminatory treatment of exports of textiles by developing countries in the Multi-Fiber Arrangement.

3. In the 1970s, therefore, the developing countries receiving the largest foreign investment flows were Brazil ($1.3 billion annual average inflow), Mexico ($600 million), Egypt ($300 million), Malaysia ($300 million), Nigeria ($300 million), and Singapore ($300 million). See United Nations Center on Transnational Corporations (1992: 317). Of these only Singapore was an open export-oriented economy.

4. Between 1980 and 1990 the list of developing countries receiving the largest annual average inflows of FDI was headed by Singapore ($2.3 billion), followed by Mexico ($1.9 billion), Brazil ($1.8 billion), China ($1.7 billion), Hong Kong ($1.1 billion), and Malaysia ($1.1 billion). Of these only Brazil has not emphasized export-oriented investment.

5. Economic theory tells us that letting in more imports will tend to stimulate exports through various channels. First, increased imports could lower the exchange rate and promote exports. Second, cheap imported inputs could improve export competitiveness. Third, if resources are freed from import activities, they can be used in export industries. These arguments are very subtle, and effects operate through indirect channels that are not readily appreciated. This makes unilateral liberalization politically difficult even when it is economically beneficial.

6. The same would be true for multilateral liberalization if it was made conditional rather than unconditional.

7. Between 1990 and 1994 Chile signed free trade agreements with Mexico, Argentina, Bolivia, Venezuela, Colombia, and Ecuador; Mexico signed NAFTA and free trade agreements with Chile, the Caribbean Community (CARICOM), Costa Rica, Bolivia, Colombia, and Venezuela; Argentina signed agreements with Brazil, Chile, Bolivia, Venezuela, Ecuador, and the MERCOSUR; and Bolivia signed agreements with Uruguay, Argentina, Peru, Chile, and Brazil. See Inter-American Development Bank (1995: 217).

8. In the case of some agricultural products, the United States and other nations demanded compensation.

References

Baldwin, Richard. 1993. *A Domino Theory of Regionalism.* Working Paper 4465. Cambridge, Mass.: National Bureau of Economic Research.

Bhagwati, Jagdish, and Anne O. Kreuger. 1995. *The Dangerous Drift to Preferential Trade Agreements.* Washington, D.C.: American Enterprise Institute.

Fishlow, Albert, and Stephan Haggard. 1992. *The United States and the Regionalization of the World Economy.* Paris: Organization for Economic Cooperation and Development Development Center.

Haggard, Stephan. 1995. *Developing Nations and the Politics of Global Integration.* Washington, D.C.: Brookings Institution.

Hazlewood, Arthur. 1979. "The End of the East African Community: What Are the Lessons for Regional Integration Schemes?" *Journal of Common Market Studies* (September): 40–58.

Hoekman, Bernard M. 1992. *Regional Versus Multilateral Liberalization of Trade in Services.* Discussion Paper 749. London: Centre for Economic Policy Research.

Inter-American Development Bank. 1995. *Economic Integration in the Americas.* Washington, D.C.: IADB.

Kreuger, Anne O. 1993. *Free Trade Agreements as Protectionist Devices: Rules of Origin.* Working Paper 4352. Cambridge, Mass.: National Bureau of Economic Research.

Langhammer, Rolf J. 1992. "The Developing Countries and Regionalism." *Journal of Common Market Studies* 30 (July): 211–231.

Lawrence, Robert Z. 1996. *Regionalism, Multilateralism, and Deeper Integration.* Washington, D.C.: Brookings Institution.

Perroni, Carlo, and John Whalley. 1994. *The New Regionalism: Trade Liberalization or Insurance?* Working Paper 4626. Cambridge, Mass.: National Bureau of Economic Research.

United Nations Center on Transnational Corporations. 1992. *World Investment Report 1992.* New York: United Nations.

Vernon, Raymond. 1994. "Multinationals and Governments: Key Actors in

NAFTA." In *Multinationals in North America,* edited by Lorraine Eden, Ottawa: Investment Canada, pp. 25–52.

Wells, Louis T. 1992. "Mobile Exporters: The New Investors in East Asia." Paper presented at National Bureau of Economic Research Conference on Foreign Direct Investment.

PART 5

TRANSNATIONAL ENTERPRISES AND INTERNATIONAL PRODUCTION

24

Theoretical Perspectives on the Transnational Corporation

Rhys Jenkins

Rhys Jenkins reviews the fundamental tenets and policymaking implications of four major perspectives—neoliberal, global reach, neoimperialist, and neofundamentalism—on transnational corporations (TNCs). According to Jenkins, the neoliberal perspective emphasizes the relative efficiency of the TNC and its capacity to rectify market imperfections, particularly in the South where such imperfections are more pervasive and extreme. The global reach perspective emphasizes the oligopolistic nature of TNCs, which possess the power to create and benefit from market imperfections. Proponents of this perspective warn that governments need to be cautious in their relations with TNCs and to use regulation to ensure that the host state benefits from the presence and economic activities of TNCs. The neoimperialist perspective views the TNC as an obstacle to the socialist transformation of society. TNCs drain host-state resources, create monopolistic structures within the host state, and eviscerate the national bourgeoisie. The result in the South has been perpetual underdevelopment. Neofundamentalists are Marxists or neo-Marxists who view TNCs as positive and progressive agents of social change. Like Marx, they believe only the dynamic processes of capitalist production are capable of providing the material base for socialism. Analytically, the neofundamentalists have much in common with the neoliberals but with a different outcome.

Introduction

Not surprisingly, the intense debate over the impact of TNCs in the Third World has generated a vast literature and throws up a large number of con-

Reprinted with permission by the publisher of *Transnational Corporations and Uneven Development*, by Rhys Jenkins. New York: Routledge Press, 1987, pp. 17–37.

flicting arguments and positions. In order to bring some order to this literature, a number of writers have attempted to identify different approaches to
the TNCs (Lall, 1974; Hood and Young, 1979, ch. 8). It is obviously useful
to distinguish between those writers whose main emphasis is on the positive
benefits which TNCs bring to Third World countries and those who adopt a
more critical approach, stressing the disadvantages of TNC activities (although in practice there is a continuum with many writers discussing both
costs and benefits and differing primarily over the degree to which state intervention is necessary to ensure that the benefits outweigh the costs). Although some writers have been content to adopt a twofold classification
along these lines (e.g., Biersteker, 1978) this fails to recognize the very real
methodological differences between Marxists and non-Marxists writers,
which have important implications for their analysis of the TNC. Since
Marxists and non-Marxist alike adopt different positions *vis-à-vis* the TNC,
it is appropriate to start with a fourfold classification of approaches towards
the TNC.

	Pro-TNC	TNC Critics
Non-Marxist	Neo-classical (Reuber, Meier, Vernon, Rugman, Balasubramanyam)	Global Reach (Barnet and Muller, Streeten, Lall, Vaitsos, Helleiner, Newfarmer)
Marxist	Neo-fundamentalist (Warren, Emmanuel, Schiffer)	Neo-imperialist (Baran, Sweezy, Magdoff, Girvan, Sunkel, Frank)

The above table identifies four main perspectives on the transnational
corporation—the neo-classical, the Global Reach, the neo-fundamentalist
and the neo-imperialist—and some of the leading exponents of each approach amongst writers concerned with the impact of TNCs in the Third
World. . . . The purpose of this chapter is to sketch in broad outline the
main features of each perspective.

Neo-Classical Views

Most advocates of the benefits of foreign investment by TNCs base their arguments on neo-classical economic theory. Although the neo-classical case
has developed considerably over the past twenty-five years, a common
theme runs through all these writings. It is that the TNCs act as efficient al-
locators of resources internationally so as to maximize world welfare. The
distribution of the benefits from TNC operations is either assumed to accrue to both home and host countries, or is not addressed directly. . . .

Internalization

In the last ten years a new neo-classical synthesis for analysing trade and investment by TNCs has emerged. . . . It has become the approach adopted by most pro-TNC writers in recent years. The major proponents of internalization are quite specific in seeing it as a general theory within which previous contributions can be incorporated (Buckley and Casson, 1976; Rugman, 1981), regarding it as a synthesis not only of earlier neo-classical contributions but also of some of the critical studies discussed below.

The central argument of this approach is that TNCs exist because of market imperfections. If all markets operated perfectly there would be no incentive for firms to go to the trouble of controlling subsidiaries in different countries and to internalize markets between them, rather than engaging in arm's length transactions with independent firms. Internalization then is a way of bypassing imperfections in external markets.

Imperfections in a number of areas are regarded as being important in explaining the existence of TNCs. Markets for intangible assets such as technology or marketing skills are notoriously imperfect because of their public good nature, imperfect knowledge and uncertainty. This makes it difficult for the seller to appropriate fully the rent from such assets through external market transactions and creates an incentive to internalize. Similarly in vertically integrated industries such as oil or aluminium there are gains from internalization because of the existence of small numbers of oligopolistic firms and large investments which take a long time to mature. Internalization avoids the difficulties of determining market prices and the uncertainties associated with arm's length transactions in such a situation. A further important source of market imperfections internationally is government intervention. The existence of trade barriers, restrictions on capital movements or differences in tax rates between countries provide a further incentive to internalize since intra-firm prices can be set to minimize the effects of such controls.

The analysis of the consequences of the growth of TNCs follows from the view that they are essentially an efficient means of overcoming market failure. They therefore act to increase efficiency in the world economy. As with the product cycle theory, technology or information plays a central role in internalization theory. In analysing the gains to host countries these are not primarily related to the transfer of capital, as in the traditional neo-classical model, but to transfers of technology which would not otherwise take place because of external market imperfections (Casson, 1979: 5). More generally it is argued that the activity of TNCs makes both goods and financial markets more efficient than they would otherwise be (Rugman, 1981: 36). It has even been suggested that since market imperfections are more pervasive in the Third World than in the advanced capitalist countries, Third World countries are in a position to gain even more through TNC operations which circumvent such imperfections (Agmon and Hirsch, 1979).

A crucial assumption of this application of internalization theory to TNC operations is that market imperfections are exogenous, either "natural" or government induced, and that TNCs do not themselves generate such imperfections. As Rugman (1981: 33) points out:

> The multinational firm is able to circumvent most exogenous market imperfections. Concerns about its alleged market power are valid only when it is able to close a market or generate endogenous imperfections. In practice these events rarely occur.

It is here that the contrast between internalization and the Global Reach approach derived from Hymer's work with its emphasis on the creation of market imperfections by TNCs (see below) is most apparent.

Policy Implications

Although internalization theory provides a considerably more sophisticated analysis of TNCs than the earlier neo-classical theories of foreign investment, the policy prescriptions of both approaches are extremely similar. Any problems which TNC operations create are generally ascribed to misguided government policies. Thus a major recommendation is the removal of government induced distortions such as high protective tariffs (Reuber, 1973: 247–8; Rugman, 1981: 138). Such tariffs may give rise to a situation where direct foreign investment reduces income in the host country but the TNCs themselves are not to blame for this.

It follows that since there is, in the absence of misconceived government policies, a net gain to the host country from direct foreign investment (whether through inflows of capital or technology or through more efficient allocation of resources as a result of the elimination of market imperfections) host countries should generally encourage foreign investment, providing a "favourable climate for investment" (although not to the extent of introducing new distortions by granting large subsidies). In some cases the use of cost-benefit analysis to evaluate major projects is advocated but there should be in general a minimum of red tape. Government efforts to regulate the operations of TNCs are strongly discouraged. "Regulation is always inefficient. Multinationals are always efficient," as Rugman puts it (1981: 156–7). Reuber (1973: 248–9) agrees that government attempts to control TNCs probably do more harm than good.

Conclusion

A common thread which runs through the pro-TNC approaches to foreign investment is a primary concern with efficiency in resource allocation. This is of course quite explicit in internalization theory and is the underlying value premise of neo-classical analysis. A second common thread is the belief that direct foreign investment by TNCs is superior to all feasible alternatives. Here one faces the problem of the counterfactual which is at the heart of many of the debates about TNCs, i.e. what would have happened in the absence of direct foreign investment. The assumption of most neo-classical thinking on the subject is that the alternative to DFI is the complete absence of local production. Internalization theory on the other hand emphasizes local licensing as an alternative. Both of these alternatives are generally regarded as inferior to foreign investment.

Global Reach

A sharply contrasting view of the impact of TNCs is given in the writings of those authors who emphasize the oligopolistic nature of the TNCs. This approach has again been given different labels, for example the "nationalist approach" (Lall, 1974). . . . A rather more snappy title which captures the essence of this perspective is "Global Reach," after the title of the best seller on TNCs by Richard Barnet and Ronald Müller (1974).

Central to this approach is the view that foreign investment should be seen as part of the strategy of oligopolistic firms and not simply as a resource flow. Its roots can be traced back to industrial organization theory and the U.S. anti-trust tradition which was first applied to the analysis of DFI by Steve Hymer in the early 1960s. Hymer (1976) identified two major reasons leading firms to control subsidiaries in foreign countries: (i) in order to make use of a specific advantage which the firm enjoys over foreign firms; (ii) in order to remove competition between the firms concerned and to eliminate conflict. While most recent orthodox writings on TNCs have accepted the first point, it is only the Global Reach approach that has continued Hymer's emphasis on foreign investment as a means of restraining competition.

The main focus of attention of this approach is the market power of TNCs. This is seen as deriving from a number of oligopolistic advantages possessed by TNCs particularly access to capital (both internal to the firm and external); control of technology (both product and process technology); marketing through advertising and product differentiation; and privileged access to raw materials. (See Lall and Streeten, 1977: 20–9, and Hood and Young, 1979: 48–54, for a fuller discussion of these advantages.)

The existence of oligopolistic markets means that firms enjoy considerable discretionary powers rather than being the atomistic firms of neo-classical theory which respond to market conditions. Consequently much of the Global Reach literature focuses on the TNCs as *institutions*, their strategies and tactics. A leading proponent of this approach, Constantine Vaitsos, brings this out clearly in discussing the provision of "collective inputs" (i.e. a package) as a means of preserving monopoly rents. He concludes, "Thus a technological monopoly is transformed into an *institutional* one. *Viewed in this light the product cycle theory is seen as a theory of monopoly cycles*" (Vaitsos, 1974a: 18; emphasis in the original).

Whereas for neo-classical writers on the TNCs, particularly internalization theorists, market imperfections are exogenous, arising from government intervention or the nature of certain products such as technology, for the Global Reach view the TNCs are themselves major factors creating imperfect markets. Far from TNCs increasing global efficiency through overcoming market failure, they reduce efficiency by making markets less perfect as a result of their oligopolistic strategies.

The Global Reach approach has highlighted a number of consequences of the market power of TNCs for host countries. . . .

Market structure.　TNCs have tended to invest in oligopolistic markets in host Third World countries and it has been suggested that they tend to contribute to increased concentration.

Monopoly profits.　The market power of TNCs enables them to earn monopoly profits in host countries. These profits, however, do not always appear in the tax returns of the foreign subsidiaries because of various accounting procedures used by TNCs, particularly transfer pricing. There is also the question of how such monopoly rents are distributed between the TNCs and the host countries in which they operate.

Abuse of market power—restrictive business practices.　Individually and collectively TNCs act in order to restrict competition in various ways. Individually they impose restrictive clauses on subsidiaries and licenses through technology contracts. These include tying inputs of raw materials, machinery, etc., to the technology supplier or restricting exports in order to divide world markets. Collectively they form cartels or engage in informal collusion through market sharing agreements or the allocation of spheres of influence.

Demand creation.　TNCs use their market power to create demand for their products rather than responding to consumer preferences expressed through the market. This leads to "taste transfer" via the TNC and the expansion of the market for products which are inappropriate for local conditions.

Factor displacements.　The package nature of DFI and the monopoly power of the TNCs leads to situations where at least part of the package displaces local inputs (Hirschman, 1969). Importing technology which is not available locally and hence supplements local resources could also bring with it imports of capital and management which displace local capital and entrepreneurship. This has led to concern over the denationalization (i.e. the extension of control by foreign subsidiaries) of local industry, which is seen as a reflection of the market power of TNCs rather than their inherently greater efficiency compared to local firms.

Policy Implications

A major implication of this view of foreign investment is the need for state control of TNCs. These controls may be imposed either on a national or international basis. The areas which have been particularly emphasized as requiring regulation are transfer pricing and restrictive business practices. Governments in a number of countries have set up agencies to control foreign investment and technology transfer since the early 1970s, with a view to eliminating practices such as export restrictions and tied inputs, and monitoring TNC behavior. There have also been steps to develop codes of conduct on TNCs and technology transfer by various international agencies.

The emphasis on TNCs as oligopolists which generate monopoly rents in their activities has also led to the view that the state in the Third World should actively intervene in bargaining with TNCs in order to ensure that a greater share of such rents accrue to the host country. There are two areas in which such an emphasis on bargaining has been of particular significance. First in the extractive industries where host governments have negotiated with TNCs to increase their share of revenue through taxation of profits, royalties, share ownership, etc. Secondly in technology transfer where government agencies have intervened in negotiations often between two private parties in order to reduce the level of royalty payments and hence the outflow of foreign exchange.

A corollary of this emphasis on monopoly rents and the scope for bargaining is that foreign investment projects cannot be analysed along the "take-it-or-leave-it" lines of conventional cost-benefit analysis. Any such project will itself be subject to bargaining over the distribution of returns with a range of possible outcomes. Thus government policy should not be directed primarily at evaluating whether a proposed foreign investment project has a positive net present value, but rather at getting the best possible terms from the foreign investor.

Insofar as the packaged nature of DFI is seen as an important source of monopoly rents for TNCs, there is a case for "unpackaging" direct investment into its constituent elements. In other words rather than acquiring capital, technology, intermediate inputs, brand names, management skills all from the same TNC supplier, efforts can be made to acquire each component individually. This would permit each to be obtained at the lowest possible cost and for those elements for which domestic substitutes exist to be acquired locally. Such a call for unpackaging has become common in recent discussion of TNCs and technology transfer.

A further implication often drawn from this approach is that the state should give preferential treatment to national capital, e.g. in terms of access to local sources of credit. This derives from the view that TNCs tend to displace local firms primarily because of their market power rather than because of greater productive efficiency. The state should therefore attempt to redress the balance in favour of local capital. Indeed it provides a theoretical rationale for forms of bourgeois nationalism as well as greater state intervention in the economy.

Conclusion

The overall framework of this approach contrasts with the pro-TNC writings discussed above in a number of key respects. First, TNCs are seen as important creators of market imperfections rather than as competitive firms or as an efficient response to exogenous imperfections. Secondly, TNCs often substitute rather than complement local factors. In other words the alternative of production under local control is more feasible than pro-TNC authors admit. Thirdly, there is a greater concern with the distributive effects of TNCs both internationally and internally.

Neo-Imperialist Views

The best known Marxist or neo-Marxist approach to TNCs is that represented by the Monthly Review School (especially Baran, Sweezy, O'Connor and Magdoff) and those writers on dependency most influenced by the Monthly Review approach (for example Frank and Girvan). These authors view the TNCs as a major mechanism blocking development in the Third World and an important obstacle to socialist transformation.

The origins of this approach can be traced back to the classical Marxist writings on imperialism in the early twentieth century with their stress on the concentration and centralization of capital and the link between monopolization of industry, capital export and imperialism (Lenin, 1917; Bukharin, 1917). A central element in the argument was that the monopolization of industry led to a growing mass of profit in the major capitalist countries, while at the same time limiting the possibilities of accumulation at home because of the restrictions imposed on expansion by cartels and trusts. This led capital to seek outlets for this relative surplus of capital overseas (see Olle and Schoeller, 1982 for a critique of this view). Furthermore Lenin particularly emphasized the parasitic nature of imperialism stressing that the development of monopoly inhibits technical progress and leads to a tendency to stagnation and decay (Lenin, 1917, ch. viii).

This leads to the question of the impact of capital export or more generally imperialism in the countries on the receiving end. Marx himself had stressed the progressive nature of these processes and this view was accepted (although only mentioned in passing) by the major Marxist authors writing on imperialism. However, as Warren (1980: 81–3) has stressed, the implication of this view of a parasitic, decaying monopoly capitalism was that imperialism could no longer play a progressive role in the colonies. It was not surprising therefore that imperialism was recognized as a major obstacle to industrialization of the colonies at the 1928 Congress of the Comintern.

The recent neo-imperialist literature continues Lenin's and Bukharin's emphasis on the rise of monopolies as a cause of TNC expansion, either by reference to the classical theories of imperialism or through the new version of the surplus capital theory proposed by Baran and Sweezy (1966). They argued that a major characteristic of U.S. capitalism was the tendency for the economic surplus, defined as the difference between total output and the socially necessary costs of producing total output, to rise over time. The major cause of this rising surplus was the growth of monopoly and the consequent decline of price competition with the result that increases in productivity did not lead to falling prices as under competitive capitalism, and that the gap between prices and production costs tended to widen. While the surplus tended to rise, the monopolization of the economy limited the opportunities for investment because of the need to maintain monopoly prices (Sweezy and Magdoff, 1969: 1). There is therefore a chronic tendency to underconsumption and stagnation under monopoly capitalism.

One of the possible outlets for the surplus identified by Baran and Sweezy was foreign investment. (Others discussed were advertising, government expenditure and militarism.) Thus, although only alleviating temporarily the problem of the rising surplus, because the return flow of profits and dividends to the United States soon exceeded the outflow of new investment, capital export and the overseas expansion of U.S. firms was seen as primarily a consequence of the existence of large monopoly profits and the need to go slow on expanding productive capacity directed at existing markets. Two solutions offered themselves—international expansion or conglomerate expansion (i.e. diversification into new industries in the domestic market) (Sweezy and Magdoff, 1969; O'Connor, 1970).

It is worth noting in passing that this emphasis on monopoly and the tendency to underemphasize the competitiveness of the oligopolies (cf. Barratt Brown, 1974: 217) was also accompanied by the view that the United States enjoyed undisputed hegemony within the international capitalist system. This view characterized by Rowthorn (1975) as "super-imperialism" plays down the increasing competition between the United States, Western Europe and Japan, both politically and economically which

underlies the alternative "inter-imperialist rivalry" view of international relations. The downplaying of conflicts between capitals and between advanced capitalist states also tended to go hand in hand with a "Third
Worldist" view which stressed that the struggle against capitalism and imperialism would primarily take place in the underdeveloped countries.

Foreign investment in the Third World is seen as contributing to the
"blocking development" (Amin, 1977) or the "development of underdevelopment" (A.G. Frank, 1969). Three principal mechanisms link foreign capital to underdevelopment. Considerable emphasis is placed on the so-called
"drain of surplus" from the underdeveloped countries in direct opposition
to the claim of neo-classical economists that foreign capital supplements
foreign exchange earnings and local savings. Thus surplus transfers which
add to the problems of surplus absorption in the advanced capitalist countries at the same time deprive the countries of the Third World of the necessary resources for economic progress. The TNCs are viewed as a "vast
suction-pump" for obtaining resources from the periphery. At the same
time they are a major part of the balance of payments problems which are
so chronic in most Third World countries.

While much of the empirical analysis of the impact of TNCs concentrated on the outflow of capital from the Third World, equal or even greater
importance was attached to the impact of foreign investment on the economic and social structures of the underdeveloped countries. As Baran puts
it

> The worst of it is, however, that it is very hard to say what has been the
> greater evil as far as the economic development of underdeveloped coun-
> tries is concerned: the removal of the economic surplus by foreign capital
> or its reinvestment by foreign enterprise (Baran, 1973: 325).

The extension of TNC operations to the underdeveloped countries has
also led to the extension of the monopolistic or oligopolistic structures of
advanced capitalism to these areas (Dos Santos, 1968 on Brazil; Caputto
and Pizarro, 1970: ch. 11.5 on Chile). Given the association of monopoly
with stagnation in the United States, it is unlikely that monopolistic subsidiaries of U.S. firms operating in the periphery will be a major dynamic
force. Thus monopolistic firms with high profit rates will tend to repatri-
ate profits, intensifying the drain of surplus and limiting the rate of capital accumulation within the host economies.

Insofar as TNCs do reinvest profits locally, they are likely to expand
by displacing or acquiring local competitors or moving into new areas of
activity (diversification). Thus the twin spectres arise of denationalization
(i.e. increasing foreign control over the economy) and the reduction of the
spheres available to local capital which is confined to the most competitive
and least profitable sectors of the economy. This brings us to a central
point of the argument against foreign capital, namely that it reduces the

local bourgeoisie in the Third World to the subordinate status of a "comprador" or "dependent" bourgeoisie which is consequently incapable of playing its historical role in promoting capitalist development. Baran writing in the 1950s emphasized the strengthening of local merchant capital by foreign capital which was mainly directed towards the export sector, and the consequent blocking of the development of industrial capitalism (Baran, 1973: 337). Latin American dependency writers in the 1960s argued that a local industrial bourgeoisie did exist in the region but that its interests were closely tied to those of foreign capital and that it would not provide the basis for a strategy of national development. The crucial decisions on production and accumulation would be made in the light of the global interests of the parent companies of the foreign subsidiaries, and not in the interest of local economic development, a situation which local capital would be unwilling or powerless to alter.

While the drain of surplus, the creation of monopolistic structures and the emergence of a dependent bourgeoisie were the three main ways in which foreign capital contributed to underdevelopment, they were by no means the only consequences of TNC expansion. A common argument is that a foreign capital far from supplying basic goods for the mass of the population tends to concentrate on the production of luxuries for a small élite. The extensive activities of the car TNCs are often cited as an example (Frank, 1969: 168–9). The tendency for foreign subsidiaries to generate links primarily with the parent company or other affiliates and only to a very limited extent with local suppliers, leads to the development of an economic structure which is not integrated at the local level (Sunkel, 1972). Moreover, the TNCs are able to use their political influence in order that public expenditure is allocated to support their investment through the provision of infrastructure.

Political Implications

The political conclusion that generally follows from this analysis is the need to break out of the capitalist system in order to transcend underdevelopment. Hostility to TNCs is directed at them as the prime representatives of capitalism in the post-war period. In any case the lack of an authentic national bourgeoisie capable of leading the process, renders national capitalist development in the Third World impossible. Thus only through a socialist revolution can the situation of the periphery be fundamentally altered. Such a socialist transformation will however inevitably have to face the hostility of the TNCs and their home states.

Conclusion

Although many of the neo-imperialist arguments concerning the impact of TNCs in the Third World are similar to those of the Global Reach approach, and the two groups of writers are sometimes considered together (for example by Biersteker, 1978), the political conclusions drawn are quite different. This derives from a very different evaluation of the role of the local bourgeoisie in Third World countries and the possibility of state action to control the TNCs.

Neo-Fundamentalist Marxists

In the last decade some Marxists have begun to develop a very different view of the TNCs to that discussed in the last section, arguing that their impact on the Third World is overwhelmingly positive. This is presented as part of a more general picture of the progressive role played by capitalism in developing the forces of production and providing the material basis for a socialist society. These authors trace their roots back to Marx's view (for example in some of his writings on India) that the impact of imperialism in destroying pre-capitalist structures and laying the basis for the development of capitalism was progressive. The clearest exponent of such a position was Bill Warren (1973, 1980; see also Schiffer, 1981).

Warren stresses the continued competitive nature of the capitalist system going as far as suggesting that competition internationally has intensified since the loss of Britain's position of world hegemony, despite the rise of oligopolistic market structures within individual countries (Warren, 1980: 79–80). Thus he rejects the Leninist view of surplus capital as a cause of capital export and implicitly sees the geographic extension of capitalism as a consequence primarily of the competition of capitals (for a succinct presentation of this view see Cypher, 1979).

The main thrust of his thesis is to argue that the impact of imperialism on the Third World is progressive, in the sense that it is developing the productive forces in these areas. As part of this thesis he argues that "private foreign investment in the LDCs is economically beneficial irrespective of measures of government control" and "must normally be regarded not as a cause of dependence but rather as a means of fortification and diversification of the host countries. It thereby reduces 'dependence' in the long run" (Warren, 1980: 176).

The arguments on which he bases this thesis reproduce virtually point by point the claims made by bourgeois advocates of the TNCs discussed above. The three major assumptions of the neo-classical view of foreign investment are all accepted by Warren. First, foreign capital is seen in the main as complementary to local capital rather than displacing indigenous efforts (Warren, 1973: 37). Secondly, he points to increasing international competition particularly amongst manufacturing TNCs (Warren, 1980: 175), which has increased the bargaining power of Third World states enabling them to reduce the monopoly rents earned by the companies and to obtain technology on more favourable terms. Finally, Warren accepts the neo-classical view that TNCs not only supplement existing local resources but also generate additional local resources or utilize resources previously unutilized (Warren, 1980: 173, n. 31).

Not only does Warren share the main assumptions of pro-capitalist TNC advocates, but even on points of detail he reproduces the same arguments. Thus for instance TNCs are seen as playing a major role in opening up advanced country markets for Third World exports (Warren, 1973: 26–8), while the "drain of surplus" view of foreign investment is criticized on exactly the same grounds used by neo-classical economists (Warren, 1980: 140–3).

While Warren's position is an extreme one amongst Marxists, other writers who wish to stress that the problem of underdevelopment is a consequence of capitalism and not of TNCs *per se,* and that the foreign or local ownership of capital is not a major factor, come close to his position. Thus Emmanuel in pursuing this line of argument states that "Whenever we find . . . that in any particular aspect the behavior of the MNC differs from that of the traditional capitalist undertaking, the specific character of the MNC is generally to its (i.e. development's) advantage" (Emmanuel, 1976: 763). Emmanuel stresses primarily the technological contribution of TNCs emphasizing particularly the low cost of imported technology and rejecting arguments of the "inappropriate technology" variety (Emmanuel, 1976, 1982).

Political Implications

A major explicit political conclusion of this analysis is the need to distinguish carefully between anti-TNC rhetoric used to serve the interests of an expanding local bourgeoisie in the Third World, and true anti-capitalist struggles. As Warren (1973: 44) concludes, "Unless this distinction is clearly grasped the Left will find itself directly supporting bourgeois regimes which, as in Peru and Egypt, exploit and oppress workers and peasants while employing anti-imperialist rhetoric." However, the implicit conclusion to which Warren's analysis points is that capitalist development in the Third World should be actively supported since it is removing many of the internal obstacles to growth, and that the TNCs are playing a significant role in this process.

Conclusion

In recent years Marxist views of the TNCs have polarized around two positions which are, in terms of many of their arguments, not very different from those found amongst non-Marxist writers. The neo-imperialist view stresses the qualitative transformations which have taken place within capitalism with the rise of monopoly, and emphasizes the regressive nature of imperialist expansion, particularly the appropriation of surplus value from the peripheral areas. In contrast the neo-fundamentalist view stresses the essentially competitive nature of capitalism despite the concentration and centralization of capital and sees the international expansion of capital as playing a predominantly progressive role in breaking down pre-capitalist structures, and laying the basis for capitalist development.

The Internationalization of Capital

Although most of the current literature on TNCs and the Third World falls more or less neatly into the four categories discussed so far, and this exhausts the typology laid out at the beginning of this chapter, it is my view that none of these approaches offers a completely satisfactory treatment of the TNCs. . . .

Each of the approaches discussed so far is partial in that it emphasizes one level of analysis. The neo-classical, Global Reach and neo-imperialist approaches all focus on the sphere of circulation, that is on relations of exchange and distribution. Obviously this is the case with the neo-classical view of the firm responding to market forces, but it is also true of the Global Reach concern with *market* power and with income distribution both nationally and internationally. Similarly the neo-imperialist approach has also been described elsewhere as exchange-based (Cypher, 1979) in view of its emphasis on surplus transfer. On the other hand, the neo-fundamentalist view is a "productionist" approach (Jenkins, 1984b; Hoogvelt, 1982: 188–9). Its main concern is with the development of the forces of production and in so far as social relations are considered at all these are derived in a highly mechanistic way from the level of development of the forces of production. None of these approaches is able to successfully integrate the spheres of circulation and production.

Not only are these approaches partial in failing to take account of both the sphere of circulation and the sphere of production, but they also fail to integrate the analysis of TNCs as institutions with a broader analysis of the capitalist system. For both the neo-classical and the neo-fundamentalist approaches with their focus on markets and the forces of production respectively, structural and institutional concerns are largely absent. On the other hand, critics of the TNCs reacting against this neglect "have gone too far in lodging the laws with which they are concerned in firms as institutions, rather than treating the latter as the forms through which the laws of the market are manifested" (Murray, 1972). It is the failure to do this which has led to the position of many Marxist critics of the TNCs who "having first isolated the MNC as the characteristic evil of the century, they study it concretely as an excrescence of the system" (Emmanuel 1976: 769) which logically should lead them to the conclusion that a reformed capitalism without the TNCs would be perfectly acceptable.

A further unsatisfactory aspect of these approaches is their tendency to reduce a contradictory reality to one or other side of a false dichotomy. TNCs are regarded as either competitive or monopolistic. In the Third World they either contribute to development or increase dependence. TNC-state relations are either harmonious or conflictual and the Third World state is either "nationalist" or "comprador." The dominant tendency in the world economy is either towards greater internationalization or the strengthening of nation states. . . .

The point that needs to be emphasized here is that these polarities around which the debate on TNCs has often revolved can lead to a misunderstanding of the real issues.

Some writers, however, notably Palloix and Murray, have attempted to develop a Marxist framework for analysing TNCs which overcomes these three limitations. Although the term is often used very loosely, I shall refer to this as the "internationalization of capital approach." It is far less well represented in the literature on TNCs than any of the other approaches except the neo-fundamentalist position. . . .

In contrast to other critical writings on the TNCs, the starting point of this approach is not the TNCs *per se* but the self-expansion of capital which can be traced through the circuits of capital discussed by Marx in Volume II of *Capital* (see Fine 1975, ch. 7 for a brief exposition of the circuits of capital). The different aspects of the internationalization of capital are identified with the internationalization of the three circuits of capital. The circuits of commodity capital, money capital and productive capital were for Marx three different aspects of the process of self-expansion of capital. In the context of the internationalization of capital these three circuits have been identified with the growth of world trade, the growth of international capital movements, and the growth of the operations of TNCs and the international circulation of products within such firms, respectively (Palloix, 1975). The circuits of capital comprise both the sphere of circulation and the sphere of production.

The growth of TNCs therefore is seen not as a phenomenon in its own right, but as an aspect of a broader process of internationalization of capital which tends to create a more integrated world economy. The driving force which underlies international expansion is capitalist competition (Cypher, 1979). It is important to stress that despite concentration and centralization of capital, the TNCs remain subject to the compulsion of competition. . . .

This approach stresses the highly uneven nature of development brought about by TNC expansion. Foreign investment has tended to be heavily concentrated in a relatively small number of Third World countries (Weisskopf, 1978). Moreover, far from the underdeveloped countries representing a homogeneous block, there is a process of increasing economic differentiation within the Third World with some countries emerging as "newly industrializing countries" or forming the intermediate "semi-periphery" (Marcussen and Torp, 1982: 28–30; Evans, 1979: 291).

Despite the highly uneven nature of its impact, the internationalization of capital is leading to an ever more integrated capitalist world economy. This implies transformations in the relations of production as new areas are incorporated into the circuits of capital. In some cases this involves the extension of fully capitalist relations of production and a corresponding growth of the working class. In other areas it involves modifications to or the reinforcing of existing social relations. The impact of the growth of transnational agribusiness on the relations of production in agriculture provides many examples of such processes as does the incorporation of petty-commodity producers through the use of sub-contracting in manufacturing. Social relations at the periphery are neither frozen into the existing mould by TNC expansion, nor can they be totally neglected. Rather they are being continuously transformed and redefined by the internationalization of capital, but not in any simple or universal way. The creation of a unified capitalist world economy is accompanied by the extension of the competitive process of standardization and differentiation on a world scale. In other words there is a growing tendency for the products and production techniques of TNCs to become similar, while at the same time as part of the competitive struggle capital seeks to differentiate itself attaining super profits through the introduction of new products or new techniques, or taking advantage of different local and national conditions.

A feature of these analyses of the internationalization of capital and dependent development is the role attributed to the Third World state. There is an emphasis on the alliance created between the state, TNCs and local capital which is central to the dynamic expansion of certain Third World economies (Evans, 1979; Weisskopf, 1978). However, it is also recognized that such an alliance is inherently unstable because of the contradictory position both of the local state and the local bourgeoisie.

Political Implications

The analysis of the internationalization of capital focuses attention on two crucial areas of struggle. One is the need to develop international links between workers so that labour is able to combine internationally in order to limit the power of international capital to divide it along national lines (Picciotto and Radice, 1971). The second area for struggle is the state itself. In dependent development the state has come to play a central role not only in regulating but also participating directly in the accumulation process. The alliance of foreign capital, local capital and the state is by no means immutable and both internal and international developments put it under stress.

Conclusion

The key features of the internationalization of capital approach are its attempt to locate the TNCs within a broader framework of capitalist development and its integration of the spheres of circulation and production. This enables it to provide a more comprehensive view of the TNC phenomenon which like capitalism itself is recognized as being contradictory in many respects.

Further Reading

The typology of theories concerning TNCs and the Third World used in this chapter is not the only possible one by any means. Other attempts to classify different approaches to the TNCs can be found in Lall (1974), Emmanuel (1976), Hood and Young (1979, ch. 8) and Biersteker (1978). The most useful short summary of the neo-classical view of TNCs in relation to the Third World which takes account of the most recent developments is Balasubramanyam (1980). More detail summaries of all the neo-classical theories discussed can be found in Hood and Young (1979, chs. 2 and 5). A useful critique of the neo-classical approach and particularly of Reuber (1973) can be found in Lall (1974). Rugman (1981) is recommended on internalization theory because it goes beyond the tedious discussions found in some of the earlier literature to bring out the normative implications of the approach.

For the Global Reach approach, the book of that name by Barnet and Müller (1974) is very readable and Chapters 6 and 7 are relevant to the discussion in this chapter. For a more academic presentation of this view, Lall and Streeten (1977; chs. 2 and 3) is particularly recommended. For criticism of this approach generally and of Lall and Streeten in particular see Lal (1978).

The best critical summary of the neo-imperialist position as exemplified by the works of Baran and Sweezy is Brewer (1980, ch. 6). See also Cohen (1973, ch. IV) for a critical account from a different perspective. Sweezy and Magdoff (1969) provide a short analysis of the TNCs. Sunkel (1972) discusses the impact of TNCs in the Third World, particularly Latin America.

The neo-fundamentalist position is summarized in Emmanuel (1976). It is also found in scattered discussion of the TNC in Warren (1973) and (1980, chs. 6 and 7).

Few of the writings of Palloix are available in English and they are in any case extremely dense and difficult to follow. See for example his article in Radice (1975). Cypher (1979) is useful in some respects in contrasting the internationalization of capital with what he terms the Monthly Review School, although he includes Warren in the former. For the contradictory impact of the internationalization of capital on the periphery see Weisskopf (1978) and Cardoso (1972).

References

Agmon, T. and S. Hirsch. 1979. "Multinational Corporations and the Developing Economies: Potential Gains in a World of Imperfect Markets and Uncertainty," *Oxford Bulletin of Economics and Statistics*, November.

Amin, S. 1977. *Imperialism and Unequal Development*, Hassocks: Harvester.

Balasubramanyam, V. N. 1980. *Multinational Enterprises and the Third World*. London: Trade Policy Research Center, Thames Essay no. 26.

Baran, P. 1973. *The Political Economy of Growth*, Harmondsworth: Penguin.

Baran P. and P. Sweezy. 1966. *Monopoly Capital: An Essay on the American Economic and Social Order*, Harmondsworth: Penguin.

Barnet, R. and R. Müller. 1974. *Global Reach: The Power of Multinational Corporations*. New York: Simon and Schuster.

Barratt Brown, M. 1974. *Economics of Imperialism*, Harmondsworth: Penguin.

Biersteker, T. J. 1978. *Distortion or Development? Contending Perspectives on the Multinational Corporation*. Cambridge, MA: MIT Press.

Brewer, A. 1980. *Marxist Theories of Imperialism: A Critical Survey*. London: Rutledge and Kegan Paul.

Buckley, P. and M. Casson. 1976. *The Future of Multinational Enterprise*. London: Macmillan.

Bukharin, N. 1917. *Imperialism and World Economy*, London: Merlin.

Caputto, O. and R. Pizarro. 1970. *Desarrollismo y Capital Extranjero*, Santiago de Chile, Ediciones de la Universidad Tecnica del Estado.

Cardoso, F. H. 1972. "Dependency and development in Latin America," *New Left Review*, 74.

Casson, M. 1979. *Alternatives to the Multinational Enterprise*, London: Macmillan.

Cohen, B. 1973. *The Question of Imperialism: the Political Economy of Dominance and Dependence*. London: Macmillan.

Cypher, J. 1979. "The Internationalization of Capital and the Transformation of Social Formations: A Critique of the Monthly Review School," *The Review of Radical Political Economics*, 11: 4.

Dos Santos, T. 1968. "Foreign Investment and the Large Enterprise in Latin America: The Brazilian Case," in J. Petras and M. Zeitlin (eds.), *Latin America: Reform or Revolution?* Greenwich: Fawcett Publications.

Emmanuel, A. 1976. "The Multinational Corporations and Inequality of Development," *International Social Science Journal*, XXVIII.

Emmanuel, A. 1982. *Appropriate or Underdeveloped Technology?* Chichester: Wiley/IRM Series on Multinationals.

Evans, P. 1979. *Dependent Development: The Alliance of Multinational State and Local Capital in Brazil*. Princeton University Press.

Fine, B. 1975. *Marx's Capital*. London: Macmillan.

Frank, A. G. 1969. *Capitalism and Underdevelopment in Latin America*. New York: Monthly Review Press.

Hirschman, A. O. 1969. "How to Divest in Latin America and Why," *Essays in International Finance*, 76, Princeton University Press.

Hood, N., and S. Young. 1979. *The Economics of Multinational Enterprise*, London, Longman.

Hoogvelt, A. 1982. *The Third World in Global Development*. London: Macmillan.

Hymer, Stephen H. 1976. *The International Operations of National Firms: A Study of Direct Foreign Investment*. Cambridge, MA and London, England: MIT Press.

Jenkins, R. O. 1984b. "Divisions over the international division of labor," *Capital and Class*, 22.

Lal, D. 1978. "On the multinationals," *ODI Review,* 2.

Lall, S. 1974. "Less-developed Countries and Private Foreign Direct Investment: A Review Article," *World Development*, 2, 4 and 5.

Lall, S., and P. Streeten. 1977. *Foreign Investment, Transnationals and Developing Countries*, London: Macmillan.

Lenin. V. I. 1917. *Imperialism: The Highest Stage of Capitalism*, Moscow, Progress Publishers.

Marcussen, H. and J. Torp. 1982. *Internalization of Capital: Prospects for the Third World*. London: Zed Books.

Murray, R. 1972. "Underdevelopment, the international firm and the international division of labor," in *Society for International Development, Towards a New World Economy*. Potterdam University Press.

O'Connor, J. 1970. "International Corporations and Economic Underdevelopment," *Science and Society*, 32.

Olle, W. and W. Schoeller. 1982. "Direct Investment and Monopoly Theories of Imperialism," *Capital and Class*, 16.

Palloix, C. 1975. "The internationalization of capital and the circuit of social capital," in Radice (ed.) *International Firms and Modern Imperialism*. Harmondsworth: Penguin.

Picciotto, S. and Radice, H. 1971. "European integration, capital and the state," *Bulletin of the Conference of Socialist Economists*. 1: 1.

Reuber, G. L. 1973. *Private Foreign Investment in Development*. Oxford: Clarendon Press.

Rowthorn, B. 1975. "Imperialism in the 1970s—Unity or Rivalry?", in H. Radice (ed.), *International Firms and Modern Imperialism*. Harmondsworth: Penguin.

Rugman, A. M. 1981. *Inside the Multinationals: The Economics of Internal Markets*. London: Croom Helm.

Schiffer, J. 1981. "The Changing Post-War Pattern of Development: The Accumulated Wisdom of Samir Amin," *World Development* 9: 6.

Sunkel, O. 1972. "Big Business and 'Dependencia': A Latin American View." *Foreign Affairs*. 50: 517–31.

Sweezy, P., and H. Magdoff. 1969. "Notes on the Multinational Corporation," *Monthly Review*, 22, 5 and 6.

Vaitsos, C. 1974a. *Inter-Country Income Distribution and Transnational Enterprises*. Oxford: Clarendon Press.

Warren, B. 1973. "Imperialism and Capitalist Industrialization," *New Left Review*, 81.

Warren, B. 1980. *Imperialism: Pioneer of Capitalism*. London: Verso.

Weisskopf, T. 1978. "Imperialism and the economic development of the Third World." in R. G. Edwards, M. Reich and T. Weisskopf (eds.). *The Capitalist System*. Englewood Cliffs, N.J.: Prentice Hall.

25

Defining the Transnational Corporation in the Era of Globalization

C. Roe Goddard

With the exception of the nation-state, the transnational corporation (TNC) generates more controversy and attention in international political economy than any other single actor. While Rhys Jenkins in the previous chapter explores the multiple perspectives on the TNC, highlighting its controversial nature, C. Roe Goddard focuses on defining the TNC, assessing its role as the primary instrument of globalization and tracing the changing motivations and patterns of foreign direct investment (FDI) in the post World War II era. Goddard takes us inside the TNC to examine the complex and diverse mix of factors that motivate corporations to invest outside their home country and how these factors have changed over time. In addition to debunking common misperceptions about the motivations behind FDI, he examines FDI flows, emphasizing the role of the advanced industrialized countries as historically both providers and recipients of FDI, as well as the recent, increasing flow of investment into a limited number of developing countries.

As key agents in international political economy, transnational corporations (TNCs) are controversial and frequently misunderstood. Widely held beliefs about the nature of TNCs' activities, their motivations for investing outside the home country, and the patterns of international investments are often misinformed or too simplistic.

The reasons for this are several. First, the emotion and conflicting viewpoints surrounding the globalization debate often overshadow and inhibit a close examination of both globalization and TNCs. Both are highly politicized subjects, such that their mention elicits a barrage of often vehement responses from all sides of the political spectrum. It is under the "antiglobalization" umbrella that a disparate group composed of environmentalists, labor activists, human rights organizations, communists, as well as right-wing nationalists have found common cause or at least a common enemy.

Second, globalization and TNCs as concepts defy clarity. The multiple levels of aggregation at which we can speak about globalization (international, country, industry, firm) and the tremendous variability among TNCs make defining these concepts problematic (Govindarajan and Gupta, 2001).[1]

And third, traditional distinctions among academic disciplines and the artificial segmentation of scholarly investigation complicate obtaining a fully formed and complete understanding of TNCs. While scholars in international political economy tend to focus on the effects of TNCs and the political and distributional implications of their activities en masse, researchers from the management discipline emphasize the internal management or strategic issues of individual firms. Scholars of international political economy are often rightly accused of glaring generalizations regarding the motivations of TNCs in expanding internationally; equally so, their management colleagues fall victim to tunnel vision and the failure to recognize the fundamental conflict of interest between states and TNCs.

The primary objective of this chapter is to overcome these shortcomings, by bridging the disciplines of international political economy and management, and closely examine the TNC. To that end, the first section explores some of the controversy surrounding the TNC. At the root of the unease about TNCs is a fundamental incongruence between the interests of TNCs and those of the nation-state. This is further complicated by the proliferation of strategic alliances and the attendant, increasingly obscure boundaries of firm interests. The concentration of economic power among TNCs, long-term dispute over transfer pricing, and recent highly visible disclosures of excessive executive compensation and legally questionable accounting practices have fueled distrust in TNCs and undermined their standing in society.

With the controversies surrounding the TNC explored, the second section shifts to the challenging task of defining them. A one-size-fits-all definition of TNCs is problematic; they are quite diverse entities and belie simple definitions or classification schemes. Nevertheless, a number of important dimensions by which TNCs can be distinguished are highlighted and explained.

The third section searches for a theory of why firms invest outside their home country. Researchers focusing on corporate strategy and decision-making have not yet discovered a single elegant theory of why firms invest internationally; however, decades of research have produced several useful theories and frameworks. In particular, product life cycle theory and the ownership-locational-internalization (OLI) framework are highlighted as useful tools for understanding why firms invest abroad.

Finally, attention shifts to exploring the changing patterns of foreign direct investment (FDI) flows in the post–World War II era. The focus is on which countries' firms are investing in what other countries. Particular attention is paid to the role of the developed and developing world in providing and receiving foreign direct investment flows. The intent is to provide a global picture of investment flows, both inward and outward.

Controversial Nature of Transnational Corporations

Just as globalization has spurred its share of critics and controversy, it naturally follows that the TNC, the major vehicle for the globalization of international production, has generated opponents as well. When TNCs first became visible to the public and academic community in the 1960s and 1970s, there was uproar over the dangers they were perceived to pose to national sovereignty and labor around the world. As globalization has deepened and as the presence and activities of TNCs have grown, voices expressing concern have grown louder. Specific concerns regarding the TNC are the incongruence between the geographically dispersed activities and interests of the TNC and the geographically defined nation-state, most clearly illustrated by the transfer pricing issue; and the concentration of economic power in a limited number of TNCs.

Tensions in the System: TNCs and the Nation-State

At the root of the controversies surrounding the TNC are fundamental incompatibilities and inevitable tensions between TNCs and nation-states. At issue is the disconnect between an international economy dominated by TNCs, with their own set of distinct motivations and financial interests—largely determined by their geographically dispersed stockholders—and a global political system composed of geographically defined nation-states. Whereas the TNC's primary motivation is to maximize the profitability of the firm, the nation-state focuses on the nature and relative level of economic activity that occurs within its geographical space. At odds are two distinctive regimes, each with their own set of constituents and potentially incompatible objectives. Heightening the tension, the objectives of both TNCs and nation-states are widely perceived to be legitimate and constructive (Vernon, 1998: 28).

Given the incompatibility between these two regimes, achieving reconciliation and reducing the unease about TNCs will be difficult. Short of a retreat into isolationism and extreme nationalism, with the attendant devolution of TNCs into solely national firms, perhaps the best hope for restoring equilibrium is an enlargement of political society to a new level of organization capable of bringing TNCs under jurisdictional control. The unavoidable reality is that virtually all nation-states are now too small to control their own economic fate. No nation's jurisdiction comes close to matching the worldwide scope of most TNCs. Multilateral organizations, international agreements, and supranational governing bodies for regional economic pacts may be effective vehicles for reasserting some degree of control over TNCs. However, to date they have not replaced the functions of the traditional nation-state, and while possessing regional reach, they still lack the global reach of many TNCs. Calls for an amalgamation of political society may seem farfetched, but until a new equilibrium is obtained between the level of political organization and the nature of international production, the inevitable frictions will continue.

Strategic alliances: Blurring the boundaries. Adding to the unease about TNCs, recent changes in the nature of international production and the activities of TNCs in response to competitive challenges in the marketplace have further undermined the efficacy of the nation-state. The rising number of interfirm "strategic alliances" has blurred the boundaries of the interests of the enterprises involved, making their regulation or control more difficult and their activities more suspect. Observing the TNC from the perspective of a national government, environmental group, or a labor union, the formation of strategic alliances has made it more difficult to confidently assess the interests and influence of TNCs.

Strategic alliances, whether for technology-sharing purposes or to construct a manufacturing plant, have considerable variation in their range and depth. This contrasts to earlier and more traditional TNCs where their boundaries and interests were very discernible. These TNCs were composed of a parent company and subsidiaries, all operating under strict control with a clear line of separation between the company and outside interests. With the proliferation of strategic alliances, it is now much more difficult to define discrete boundaries between the interests of firms (Vernon, 1998: 26).

The Enduring Controversy over Transfer Pricing

While the obscure nature of strategic alliances complicates distinguishing between TNC and nation-state interests, nowhere is the fundamental incongruence more pointed and publicly visible than in the issue of taxation.

Determining taxable income is particularly difficult when the output of a particular subsidiary is part of a much larger production process incorporating other subsidiaries operating in other countries. Confounding host-state tax authorities is the task of assigning global profits to a specific geographic locale, when you consider that at issue is not just the transfer of goods and services between them but also the sharing of research gains, patents, trademarks, and copyrights among the firm's affiliates. Neither will this issue disappear. In fact, given the percentage of international trade flows that are associated with intrafirm trade, now estimated to be one-third of total aggregate global trade flows and growing, the issue of transfer pricing is likely to become even more salient in disputes between TNCs and their host-state regulators (Vernon, 1998: 39).

Transfer pricing defined. Central to tensions over determining tax liability is the transfer-pricing issue. Specifically at issue is the assignment of price and value to products that are traded within the firm. Given the tax differentials among different nation-states, it is in the TNCs' interests to transfer income from the high-tax country to the low-tax country to lower the tax liability of the parent corporation at large. This can be done by manipulating the price charged to individual affiliates for products or services traded among them. If country A's subsidiary operates in a tax locale that has a higher tax rate than country B where another subsidiary is located, and if products and services are traded among these two subsidiaries, all other things being equal, it is in the interest of the parent firm to minimize its tax exposure in the country with the higher tax rate, in this case country A. To do this the subsidiary in country A would decrease the internal price charged to country B's subsidiaries for products or services it provided, or conversely, the subsidiary in country A would agree to pay a higher price for the products and services it purchases from country B's subsidiary. In the end, country A's subsidiary's earnings are deflated, lessening taxable income, and country B's subsidiary's earnings are inflated, raising taxable income but at a lower tax rate than in country A.

The challenge is for the host-state tax authorities to garner their fair share of taxes. To achieve that and to stop what they perceive as an illegitimate exploitation of international reach by the TNC, the host state must determine a credible arm's-length price for the individual transactions. However, resolving the transfer-pricing controversy and determining an arm's-length price is no easy task. Despite being the subject of numerous congressional hearings, close examination by multilateral bodies, and the efforts of motivated armies of corporate comptrollers, tax accountants, and regulatory officials asserting their respective interests, setting an international standard or even achieving consistency in practice on transfer pricing and taxation remain out of reach. To this day it is arguably the most contentious issue in TNC–host-state relations, pointedly illustrating the fundamental incongruence between the interests of TNCs and nation-states (Vernon, 1998: 40).

The Concentration of Economic Power

Clearly adding to the unease over TNCs is the concentration of economic power they represent. By 2000, international production by TNCs spanned virtually all countries and economic activities. However, it is the concentration of economic power in a limited number of TNCs from a narrow range of countries that creates the most discomfort.

Annual sales for the largest TNCs exceed the gross national product of many of the countries in which they operate. It is estimated that a mere 1 percent of TNCs own half the total of all existing foreign assets. For the largest 1 percent of TNCs, in 1998 the $2 trillion in assets of their foreign affiliates accounted for one-eighth of the total assets of all foreign affiliates worldwide.

Adding to concerns over the concentration of economic power, while TNC activities may be dispersed throughout most of the countries in the world, they originate and are headquartered in a very limited number of advanced industrial countries. The world's top one hundred nonfinancial firms are disproportionately headquartered in the advanced industrialized countries of the United States, Britain, Germany, France, and Japan (*World Investment Report,* 2000: xv).

Recent Events and the Standing of the Transnational Corporation in Society

Recent events and activities of TNCs have added new fodder to the litany of complaints and undermined the standing of the corporation in society. Given the high visibility of TNCs, they are often the subject of public investigation and disclosure of their practices. While traditionally, TNCs have been accused of exploiting natural resources, using their international mobility to pit labor against labor, and intervening in local politics, recent activities have drawn attention to issues of compensation and ethics.

Particularly tarnishing the corporation's image have been recent public disclosures of the exorbitant salaries paid to upper management. In June 2001, *Fortune* magazine's cover story, by Geoffrey Colvin, titled "The Great CEO Pay Heist," chronicled the astronomical rise in compensation packages of U.S. CEOs (*Fortune,* 2001). The number-one earners in each of the past five years received packages averaging $274 million each. (*Fortune,* 2001: 66). Neither have the exorbitant salaries and the resulting public dismay been limited to cases involving American CEOs. Percy Barnevik, founder and former chairman of Asea Brown Boveri (ABB) and once the darling of the international corporate world, and Goran Lindahl, a former chief executive of ABB, were forced to return more than half of the controversial pension and severance benefits (estimated at $140 million between them) they received on leaving the company. The ABB debacle and the issue of executive compensation are particularly sensitive in egalitarian-minded Sweden.

Adding fuel to the flame, at a time when downsizing is rampant and the notion of cradle-to-grave employment in exchange for loyalty and commitment are dim recollections from a distant past, these disclosures seem particularly disconcerting. Recent corporate emphasis on providing employees with "portable skills," at the same time of these massive payouts, seems shallow and self-serving. In addition to soaring executive compensation, the Enron debacle and the collapse of Arthur Andersen amidst charges of corruption and obstruction of justice, as well as rogue traders have further undermined the position of TNCs within society. Over the long term, these events are likely to be more consequential than executive salaries in influencing regulatorial control over TNCs.

Defining the Transnational Corporation

Because of their tremendous diversity, TNCs resist definition and a simple classification scheme. A textbook definition of a TNC is an organization that has its productive activities in two or more countries. As a base definition this might serve a purpose, but it provides little insight into the rich variability among them. The TNC is simply a more disparate entity than a single definition can capture. Nevertheless, identifying the central and more consequential dimensions on which they differ will provide insight into the diverse universe of the TNC. Critical dimensions on which they differ are the nature of the TNCs' industry, segmentation of the value-chain, range and scope of product lines, and the varied relationships with subsidiaries.

Adding difficulty to defining the TNC is the ambiguity surrounding the issue of control. The varied equity stakes that parent companies have in their subsidiaries and the recent growth in more loosely knit alliances compounds efforts at determining the boundaries of the firm's interests.

Nature of the Industry

An important difference among TNCs is in the nature of the products they produce or services they provide. There is considerable breadth in the nature of activities in which TNCs are engaged. TNCs can be producers of finished, intermediate, capital, or consumer goods, extractors of natural resources, or providers of a service. Within a particular product or service line, TNCs may produce either a segment of the value-chain of the product or produce it in its entirety. Nike is an excellent illustration of the former; it focuses almost exclusively on the marketing and sale of the product—sport shoes in this instance—and subcontracts all of the manufacturing to firms mostly in East Asia. While it is surprising and seems somewhat deceptive that Nike does not manufacture any of its own shoes, involving itself with only a small segment of sport shoes' value-chain, the segmentation of functions is highly common and spans virtually all manufacturing and service sectors.

Driving the increased outsourcing of segment functions and the narrowing of the range of firm activity is intensifying competition. Since the 1970s, firms have increasingly shed stages of the value-chain in the production of goods in order to focus more exclusively on a particular stage of the production process. This focus on "core competence" is such now that the extensive division of the value-chain among firms is more the norm than the exception. If a simple, relatively low-technology product like sports shoes has multiple segments and suppliers in its value-chain, one can imagine the large number of suppliers and subdivisions of the production process that occurs in the more technology-intensive automotive, telecommunications, information technology, and aerospace industries.

Outsourcing has extended beyond hard components within the value-chain. It is also becoming commonplace for TNCs to outsource administrative functions such as billing, training, and even entire human resource functions. As firms have shed these various production and administrative functions, building collaborative and closer-knit relationships with suppliers and customers has taken on added importance for firm profitability. Changes in the organization of production, occurring to various degrees among most TNCs, have made the universe of TNCs even more diverse and have complicated attempts to define them.

Relationship Among Subsidiaries

Another dimension along which we can examine TNCs is the relationship among subsidiaries and the related range of products each affiliate produces. One mechanism for differentiating among TNCs categorizes them as being either horizontally integrated, vertically integrated, or diversified firms. Horizontally integrated firms produce broadly the same line of goods from their affiliates in each of its geographical markets. These subsidiaries operate as relatively self-contained entities, producing similar products that are consumed in the same location as they were produced. Thus, in the horizontally integrated firm there is minimal interaction among the subsidiaries.

In contrast, vertically integrated firms produce outputs in some of their plants that serve as inputs to activities in other plants. The subsidiaries are tightly coordinated in an attempt to achieve a seamless manufacturing process, benefit from economies of scale, and minimize duplication of effort. A third type of TNC in this scheme is the diversified firm that is neither vertically nor horizontally integrated. Subsidiary products are neither components for other subsidiaries nor are they similar in nature (Caves, 1996: 2). This particular firm type is noted for the unrelated and diverse nature of the products it produces.

Foreign Direct Investment and the Issue of Control

Adding to the challenge of defining the TNC is the difficulty of determining what constitutes the minimum amount of a firm's overseas activity for it to be considered multinational, and the uncertainty surrounding the parent firm's control over its affiliates. According to Richard Caves, the minimum "plant" abroad needed to make an enterprise multinational is a matter of judgment. The transition from being purely a foreign sales subsidiary or a technology licensee to a producing subsidiary is not always a clearly identifiable shift in function or status.

Compounding the challenge of establishing functional minimums for plants overseas to qualify as multinational, what constitutes control over a foreign establishment is another judgmental issue. Many foreign affiliates of TNCs are not wholly foreign-owned enterprises (WFOE). In fact, the TNC may own only a small equity stake in the production facility and be one of several partners in a joint venture relationship. For accounting and tax purposes, countries differ with regard to the minimum percentage of equity that is required to engender control and therefore represent FDI and not portfolio investment. Without a universally accepted minimum, the deciding factor in qualifying as FDI is whether the investor is engaged in an ongoing manner in the long-term management of the enterprise. To qualify as FDI, the intent of the investor must be to control significant strategic and operational decisions (Caves, 1996: 1). Examples of FDI would be Caterpillar investing in a plant to manufacture diesel engines in Shanghai, Toyota investing in an assembly plant in Poland, or Morgan Stanley setting up a branch office in São Paolo, Brazil.

Determinants of Foreign Direct Investment

There is no single elegant theory that can by itself capture and explain why firms invest outside their home country. This is not for lack of research; a vast literature base has sought to explain the motivations behind foreign direct investment.

We do know that the nature of competition among TNCs is one of movement and activity. This means that TNCs are constantly engaged in a range of activities to identify rivals and weaken them, penetrate new markets, access higher quality and less-expensive sources of supply, or develop new products and services. A decision to invest outside the home country can be the outcome of one or a combination of these activities (Vernon, 1998: 22). The diversity of these activities highlight the breadth of objectives that can occupy the TNCs' energies and the plausibility of achieving a single theory on why firms invest. Despite the lack of a single succinct explanation for why firms invest abroad and the multitude of potential motivations, decades of research have provided useful concepts and a framework for examining the driving forces behind foreign direct investment.

Product Life Cycle Theory

One of the more classic and enduring explanations of why firms invest abroad is Raymond Vernon's classic product life cycle theory (Vernon, 1966).[2] Notions of the product life cycle have been used to explain the evolution of demand for single products as well as the motivations for corporations to expand internationally. The basic idea of the product life cycle theory is that following the introduction of a new technology—whether a product, manufacturing process, or business technique—the high profit margins obtained will attract new entrants into the market. This undermines the "monopoly windfall for the early starter" (Vernon, 1966). With the initial expansion in demand, production becomes more standardized, which lessens uncertainty for competitors entering the market, imitators appear, and initial monopoly profits begin to disappear as price competition intensifies. With profit margins lessening, the firm is motivated to expand the sale or use of the technology into new markets where similar products or processes have not yet materialized.

According to Vernon, the firm attempts to capitalize on its own experience and knowledge by introducing the technology in its home market, where it has already proven itself by past profits, and seeks out markets with a similar economic profile in which to duplicate that experience. Given that the preponderance of new technologies originate in developed countries where most of the world's TNCs reside, the firm seeks to export the technology to similar high-income and high labor cost countries. Whereas introduction of the technology into the home market was relatively easy, with a lengthy introductory period during which profit margins were high, introducing this technology into a foreign market is more challenging for a number of reasons. Whether because of increased costs of transporting the product to the foreign market, a slower market-penetration rate due to peculiar consumer tastes and preferences, less familiarity with the vagaries of operating in the foreign market, or the lack of adequate patent or trademark protection for the firm's process or products, indigenous producers quickly threaten the technology's margins as they develop similar products.

Should the firm be committed to establishing a presence for this technology in the new market, it is at a major decision point that ultimately may require committing significant financial capital to enter the market. In many ways, this decision point is commonplace and is confronted by all firms in the evolutionary process of expanding internationally. The decision is, in the face of rising indigenous competition, whether the firm sould continue simply to export the product from the home market or increase its commitment and establish a more permanent manufacturing presence in the foreign market.

In lieu of the significant commitment of financial capital required to build a plant is the option of licensing the technology to a local producer. Establishing a relationship with a local manufacturer, licensing the technology to the firm, and allowing them to use the firm's technology in exchange for a royalty on all sales or goods produced by that technology does create a local ally interested in the technology's success. However, for most firms this is a second-best option given the loss of control over the technology, product quality concerns, and the sharing of profits with the local licensee. Consequently, finding the licensing option less desirable and convinced that for a variety of reasons the firm should be present in this market, the firm commits significant capital by either building or acquiring a manufacturing capability in the target country.

According to product life cycle theory, the firm's expansion into developing countries occurs after the technology has been introduced into the high-margin and high-labor-cost market. Less-developed countries become involved in the international production of goods by two routes. First, as imitators enter the high-income and high labor cost market, profit margins are squeezed, and the firm begins seeking ways to lower production costs. To do this, the production process of the good is segmented into component parts. As stages in the value-chain are identified, low-cost producers of individual components are sought out. Whereas the developing country might lack both the market for the finished good and the ability to manage the entire production process, it could produce select, individual component parts that would then be transported to the target market for final assembly. Or conversely, the developing country could perform the minimal value-added final assembly of the good, and the production of critical technology-intensive components would remain in the more industrially advanced target market.

At first, it is likely the parent firm will simply seek out local suppliers in the less-developed countries. But as time progresses and demand for the product or similar products grows, it is commonplace for firms to internalize the production of that good either by acquiring critical suppliers in the developing country or by investing in a manufacturing plant for the component that is independent and in competition with their traditional suppliers.

Vernon and product life cycle theorists identify a second route by which firms expand into developing country markets. This explanation is more central to the fundamental idea of the "product" in product life cycle theory itself. As markets in the high-margin and high labor cost countries become increasingly competitive with new entrants, and as profit margins lessen and new products offer incremental but worthwhile improvements over the original product, the monopoly position of the original producer disappears. Unable to achieve the high margins of the earlier stage in the product's life cycle, the original producer seeks new markets where the product can be introduced and thus reproduce the gains associated with being a unique or differentiated product or process. In an overall sense, the whole thrust of expansion into new markets also allows firms to further dilute their fixed costs over a larger number of products sold and to recoup their initial investment in research and development. All of these variables, in total, provide further motivation for the firm to expand into new markets.

The OLI Framework

To this day Vernon's product life cycle theory continues to be one of the most widely accepted explanations for why TNCs invest internationally. In the wake of Vernon's seminal work, considerable research has been conducted on motivations behind FDI. With the additional research, a framework has emerged that organizes the determinants of FDI in terms of firms seeking to exploit ownership (O), locational (L), and internalization (I) advantages (Dunning, 1993: 53).[3]

Firm-specific or ownership determinants of FDI. While there is no final agreement among scholars on which of the three determinants is most important in investment decisions, the most frequently cited explanation for why firms invest is that the firm possesses some firm-specific or ownership competitive advantage that will allow it to prevail in competition in foreign markets. Given the added difficulties and cost of doing business outside the firm's home market where it has knowledge and experience, this advantage must not be possessed by others, and in particular by firms operating in the target market. Indigenous firms within the target market are perceived to have certain home-court advantages, including established contacts, intimate knowledge of the customers, and brand recognition, all of which could place the foreign investor in an inferior position without possession of some unique product or process knowledge. If the potential investor has some knowledge or experience in the market through previous exports to that market, or if it has past licensing agreements, operates a sales office, or has enlisted a local marketing representative, these can lessen the home-court advantage of the indigenous firm. Not to be overlooked, transaction and transportation costs, accruing to the foreign investor and not the indigenous firm, make having some exploitable, firm-specific advantage even more critical.

The specific ownership advantages that propel firms to invest internationally are numerous, the most important one being size. Typically, a firm considering investing internationally is a major player in the home marketplace and has achieved considerable success and size. There are many advantages to being a large firm. First, the firm possesses by definition a large capital base and has access to additional financial capital should it be needed for expansion. Given the firm's success and established track record in borrowing capital, its cost of borrowing will be lower. In addition, given that most foreign investors have originated in the advanced industrialized countries, capital is more accessible because of the higher levels of disposable income and therefore savings, established equity and bond markets, and the country's ability to attract global capital.

Second, although in the early twenty-first and late twentieth century we have witnessed a proliferation of small and medium-sized firms investing internationally, most foreign investors historically have been large established corporations with preexisting multiple investments internationally. Therefore, they already possess the added advantage of experience in manufacturing or marketing products outside their home countries.

Third, it is highly probable that large corporations are industry leaders in their particular product or production process. Sharpened by experience in the intensely competitive markets of the advanced industrialized countries, they most likely possess the latest technology and have achieved some brand recognition. Thus there are many firm-specific competitive advantages inducing firms to invest outside of their home market.

The ownership advantages of size, possession of technology, and access to capital do not necessarily induce a firm to invest internationally. It could still exploit these advantages by continuing to export from the home country and not take the costly and risky step of investing in an overseas manufacturing or service facility. Or the firm could hedge its costs and risks by entering into a joint venture relationship or licensing agreement, as described earlier.

Although these varied relationships have increased in number recently, TNCs generally find these options less attractive than entering the market alone as a wholly foreign-owned enterprise (WFOE). Furthermore, once the TNC has entered a foreign market as a WFOE, evidence suggests that the linkages between it and the WFOE will be stronger than had the subsidiary been a joint venture or a licensee. The subsidiary will be more tightly linked with the parent firm's global strategy, resulting in higher levels of sourcing, increased technology transfer, and additional investment (Moran, 2001: 5).

The reasons for this preference for WFOEs are simple. In joint venture relationships, licensing agreements, and other partnering forms, the firm loses total control over the quality of goods produced and important strategic decisions, such as the timeliness of production, the selling price of its output, the assigned market for that output, and the price at which it is invoiced to the parent in vertically integrated production processes. All of these must now be negotiated with partners whose interests may differ from the home-country firm (Vernon, 1998: 23).

Research confirms the numerous conflicts of interest and disappointing performance that seem to plague these partnering relationships. There is a Chinese expression used to describe the difficulty of sharing management decisions in joint ventures: "Same bed, different dreams." Thus the desire to keep ownership advantages in-house, commonly referred to as internalizing the firm-specific advantages, is a major motivation for entering a market through a WFOE and not through a partnering relationship.

Locational determinants of FDI. Ownership advantages provide an explanation for why firms invest, but they not explain satisfactorily why firms invest in one country and not another. Such advantages provide the push element in push-pull explanations for FDI but not the pull. Specific attractors of FDI, the pull, are found in locational advantages present in the target market.

In the 1950s, 1960s, and into the late 1970s, traditional locational advantages that attracted FDI were the presence of desired natural resources, abundant and low-cost, unskilled or semiskilled labor, and proximity to markets for finished goods. During this time, most of the firms investing outside of Western Europe and the United States were either natural-resource-exploiting firms (petroleum, chemicals, minerals) or those producing low-technology manufactured goods such as textiles and some consumer electronics. The United States and Western Europe, possessing sizeable markets and economies-of-scale advantages, attracted a much wider range of foreign investment to include more advanced technology producers.

Beginning in the later 1970s and continuing to the present, the nature of the locational advantages for foreign investors changed. On the broadest level, world events have had a significant impact on where and why firms invest internationally. As markets in the advanced, industrialized West were becoming saturated with overcapacity, new markets in China, the former Soviet Union, and the formerly centrally planned economies of central Europe became accessible. Simultaneously, advances in technologies of communication, information, and transportation made distance-related transaction costs less consequential (Dunning, 2000: 27).

Regional economic agreements such as the European Union (EU) and the North American Free Trade Agreement (NAFTA) have also impacted locational advantages. They have influenced investment decisions in two respects. First, they have decreased transaction costs among the participating countries by lowering barriers to the flow of goods, services, capital, and labor. The resulting merging of consumer bases provides economies-of-scale and -scope benefits. And second, these agreements have lowered perceptions of risk to foreign investors by incorporating additional protections for both investment and trade, thereby stimulating investment.

Research and development capacity as a locational advantage. Historically, prior to the late 1970s, there was very little research and development (R&D) activity by TNCs outside of their home country. When outside R&D was conducted, it tended to be of a particular kind. Rarely was it fundamental research and development, seeking innovations in products and processes; more often it was simply to adapt and modify home-based R&D and create products and processes more suited to the particular marketplace (Dunning, 2000: 28). It was more modification than innovation. Walter Kuemmerle refers to this as "home base exploiting R and D" (Kuemmerle, 1996: 9).

Since the latter 1970s, the nature of research and development conducted outside the home country has changed. This has contributed to the aggregate flow of FDI. There has been a sharp increase in the amount and kind of R&D, and increasingly, such activity in host states focuses less on adaptation and modification of products and processes and more on truly innovatory activity (Dunning, 2000: 28). Advances in communications technology, rising living standards in the newly industrializing countries of East and Southeast Asia, and the development of a cadre of highly trained, often Western-educated engineers and scientists in countries such as India, China, Taiwan, South Korea, Malaysia, Indonesia, Thailand, Mexico, and Brazil have brought these countries in certain sectors technologically on a par with the United States, Europe, and Japan. This has accelerated foreign investment flows for R&D purposes into these regions.

This does not mean that research-and-development-seeking FDI has not flowed into the United States, Europe, and Japan where specific capabilities were present; these countries have also experienced an increase in R&D investment. It simply highlights that whereas locational advantages were once limited to possession of natural resources or low-cost labor, countries with a highly skilled workforce capable of conducting innovatory research and development can now attract additional foreign investment for that purpose. John Dunning and others refer to this type of FDI as technology- or knowledge-seeking investment.

The increasing prominence of the overseas affiliate in the TNCs' research and development effort reflects larger changes in the competitive environment as a whole. As global competition intensified in the late 1970s through the 1980s and 1990s, the nature of competitive advantage has changed. Prior to the latter 1970s, under less-intense competition than in the 1980s, overseas affiliates operated autonomously, with much duplication of business functions among them. They were generally stand-alone enterprises with little involvement in a globally integrated production process. TNCs could be successful and achieve adequate market share simply by transplanting their operations in kind from the home country to their affiliate subsidiaries.

The hypercompetitive marketplace that appeared in the 1980s changed everything. Competitive pressures caused by the declining dominance of U.S. TNCs and the rise of European and Japanese competitors, coupled with a quickening pace of innovation, have forced firms to become more efficient in all aspects of their production processes. Driven to achieve competitive scale and efficiencies, overseas affiliates have become tightly integrated into the worldwide operations of the parent firm.

Another critical change in the nature of the firm's competitive advantage is the elevation of multinationality as an ownership advantage. According to Dunning, the degree to which a firm is truly multinational, and not the country of origin, has become much more important. Critical for competitiveness are the manner in which the assets and skills of the firm are linked and managed with the capabilities of other allied firms and the way these combined assets interact with the specific endowments of the locations where they are operating. Given the hypercompetitive environment, rapid pace of innovation, and significant scale required to compete successfully, many firms are struggling to go it alone and are driven to establish strategic alliances (Dunning, 2000: 26).

This is particularly true in the rapidly changing technology sectors. Firms are driven to seek out those potential partners and the location-specific attributes that add the most to their value-added activities. Firms that are truly multinational, in the sense that they seek out the best practices and technology on a global basis, are in a better position to innovate, learn, and disseminate knowledge more rapidly among their affiliates than competitors with a more limited geographical reach (Dunning, 2000: 27).

The recent clustering of TNC investment in specific locations is concrete evidence of the competitive desire of companies to wed value-adding alliances with location-specific attributes. Clustering, whether of the information technology industry in Silicon Valley, software providers in Bangalore, or the pharmaceutical industry in New Jersey, provides several location-specific advantages for firms. It allows them to benefit from a common infrastructure. More specifically, clustering enhances learning by placing firms in more immediate contact with innovatory structures such as universities and science centers, competitors, and local producer associations, and it provides a highly trained labor pool and increases contacts between firms and their suppliers (Frost, 2001: 102).

While clustering usually refers to a spontaneous occurrence primarily driven by market forces, governmental entities also have sought to create and nurture location-specific advantages in order to attract investment. The proliferation of export-processing zones, free trade zones, and industrial parks attest to government attempts to attract similar investments and create locationally specific synergies. These various schemes to induce clustering have met with mixed success.

Changing Patterns of Foreign Direct Investment in the Post–World War II Era

Who is investing where and why? How has this changed over time? As previously discussed, the nature of international production has changed dramatically over the post–World War II period. FDI flows immediately following World War II were not driven by the same set of corporate interests and environmental variables that later drove investment flows in the 1980s and 1990s. Moreover, the sectors of the world economy involved in FDI flows were not the same in the earlier and later periods.

In the immediate postwar period, U.S.-headquartered TNCs dominated FDI, but by the latter 1970s, they were increasingly challenged by firms originating in Europe and Japan. These are just a few of the changes that have characterized FDI flows in the postwar era.

Throughout the late 1940s and into the 1960s, FDI flows were limited in several ways. First, most of the firms engaging in FDI originated in the United States. With the decimation of the German, French, and Japanese economies in World War II, these countries' firms were in no position to meet all of their own domestic needs for products and resources, let alone invest and compete internationally. U.S. firms, many of them emboldened by demand for their products in the prosecution of the war effort, dominated FDI flows, reaching a peak in 1967 with 76 percent of global aggregate FDI.

A second respect in which FDI flows were constrained in the immediate post–World War II era was in the investment sectors. Most FDI in the two decades following World War II was concentrated in the extractive and natural resource sector. Firms such as Royal Dutch Shell, Anaconda, British Petroleum, and Exxon had significant investments internationally. During this period, flows in the manufacturing sectors paled in comparison to the natural resource sectors.

In the latter 1960s and 1970s, significant changes occurred in the pattern of FDI flows. Beginning in the late 1960s, U.S. firms placed significant amounts of manufacturing production in Europe. This was largely in response to the rebuilding of Western Europe and the growing competitiveness of firms originating in Europe. Competitive pressures to lower transportation costs and gain a more intimate, insider's knowledge of the growing European market were prime motivators. The shift of production by U.S. manufacturers out of the United States and into other countries, at this time European, was a preview of the nature of investment flows in the 1980s and 1990s.

A century earlier, foreign investment had reached a scale proportionally commensurate with the FDI flows now occurring, but it was portfolio investment and not FDI. For the first time in world history, at the end of the Cold War, firms began to place a significant percentage of their manufacturing outside the geographical confines of their home countries. The end of communism and the embrace of capitalism and protections for private property, opened up many new opportunities for foreign investors that had been previously closed or too risky.

In addition to new opportunities for investment created by liberalization in the former Soviet Union and China, the West was privatizing sectors that in the past had been previously restricted to public ownership. Furthermore, European and Japanese firms began shifting some of their production to the United States due to fear of rising protectionist sentiment. Foreign firms began investing in the United States and establishing production facilities there as a means to preempt anticipated trade restrictions. Simultaneously, U.S. firms expanded into Asia, concentrating their investments in Singapore, Taiwan, Hong Kong, Malaysia, Indonesia, and China.

To date, some countries' firms have in excess of 50 percent of their production outside their home country; the United States and Britain, representing intermediate cases, have an estimated 20 percent or more of their production abroad. While manufacturing since the 1960s accounts for the largest share of FDI flows, the newest and fastest growing wave of FDI flows is in the services sector. Firms such as Nomura Securities, Citibank, and Credit Suisse Boston are but a few of the service-sector enterprises setting up operations internationally (Grunberg, 2001: 348).

Foreign Direct Investment and the Developed Countries

A more focused examination of recent FDI flows reveals significant characteristics and patterns not visible in a broad decade-by-decade analysis. The distribution of international production across countries is highly skewed, with FDI flows from and into the developed countries clearly dominant. Contrary to popular perceptions, a relatively small amount of total global FDI flows into the developing countries. And only a fraction of that is motivated by the desire to exploit inexpensive and unskilled labor.

The United Nations Conference on Trade and Development, the world's foremost monitor of the activities of TNCs, estimates that for much of the post–World War II period developed economies both received most of the FDI flows (over 80 percent) and contributed most of the outflows (over 95 percent). Since 1985, almost 70 percent of total outward FDI and 57 percent of inward FDI came from and was received by only five developed nations: the United States, UK, Germany, France, and Japan. In 1999 alone, ten countries received 74 percent of global FDI flows. Of the total FDI of $636 billion in 1999, approximately 75 percent went to the developed countries. U.S. inflows, driven by large mergers and acquisitions, received a record $276 billion, totaling nearly 33 percent of the world's total. In that same year, developing countries as a whole received approximately 25 percent less FDI than the United States alone, totaling only $208 billion (*World Investment Report,* 2000: xvi).

Within the developed world, foreign investors from the EU nations were particularly active, and within those, TNCs from the UK, France, and Germany accounted for the largest share of the EU's outward flows. In

1999, EU firms invested $510 billion abroad, approximately 65 percent of the world's total outflows. Even though it is a major outward investor, with significant foreign operations in the United States, Europe, and East and Southeast Asia, Japan does not receive significant inward flows from TNCs based in Europe, the United States, or elsewhere. The perceived impenetrability of the Japanese market, reflected in the minimal amount of foreign investment there, is often a source of tension in Japan's economic relations with the outside world. Foreign-owned firms account for less than 1 percent of total sales in Japan. Although FDI flows to Japan quadrupled in 1999, reaching a record $13 billion, most of these inflows came through a small number of mergers and acquisitions (*World Investment Report, 2000:* xvi).

Foreign Direct Investment and the Developing Countries

Of the FDI flowing to the developing world, the concentration in a limited number of countries was equally dramatic. By 2000, ten developing countries received 80 percent of the total FDI in the developing countries. Major recipients include China (including Hong Kong), Malaysia, Indonesia, Singapore, Brazil, and Mexico.

These countries offer two attractions for foreign direct investors. They either possess large and growing internal markets and/or they have developed a sophisticated infrastructure (e.g., banks, port facilities, a highly educated population). Africa, plagued by the AIDS epidemic and political turmoil, has largely been bypassed, attracting less than 1 percent of aggregate FDI.

Within the developing world, recent FDI flows continue to reflect the interest of foreign investors in a limited number of high-potential countries. Mexico continues to receive significant FDI flows following its recovery from the 1994–1995 peso crisis. Its early repayment of funds borrowed from the International Monetary Fund and the United States, its conservative monetary and fiscal policies, and a vibrant U.S. economy have made Mexico the prime destination for FDI flows into Latin America. After a two-year lull following the Asian financial crisis, in which virtually all of the region's countries experienced a significant drop-off in FDI, foreign investment flows into select East and Southeast Asian countries returned to nearly their precrisis levels, reaching $93 billion in 1999, an increase of 11 percent over 1998. This increase in FDI centered on the newly industrializing countries (NICs) of Hong Kong, Singapore, Taiwan, and South Korea (*World Investment Report,* 2000: xvii).

Among the Asian NICs, South Korea, once perceived as nationalistic and hostile to foreign firms and investors, experienced an unprecedented inflow of $10 billion (*World Investment Report,* 2000: xvii). Following the dramatic devaluation of its currency in 1997 and faced with a severe foreign-exchange crisis, South Korea borrowed from the International Monetary Fund to meet its international obligations.

Under IMF tutelage, South Korea was forced to lessen its restrictions on FDI and take other steps to rationalize and interject efficiencies into what had become a highly protected economy. Paving the way for a wave of foreign investment, the stranglehold of the *chaebols* (huge conglomerates) over the Korean economy was weakened as they were forced to divest major business segments. Both the liberalization of laws regarding FDI and the new investment opportunities presented with the divestiture of the chaebols provided many opportunities for foreign firms to expand into Korea.

Conclusion

Much has been written on the role of the TNC within international political economy. The TNC has been the subject of research by scholars from a broad range of disciplines including geography, economics, political science, and management, among others. This chapter was not an attempt to add new knowledge to the literature base on TNCs nor to survey the contributions of each of the relevant disciplines. Its purpose was, by drawing primarily on disciplinary sources in international political economy and management, to correct some of the misinformation and clarify some of the definitional confusion surrounding the TNC.

Defining the TNC poses a challenge. Given the considerable variation along multiple dimensions in the nature of TNCs, it is difficult to speak of them as a single entity. TNCs have significant differences in terms of the degree of multinationality, the nature of their products or services, and the relationships among their subsidiaries.

The desire to increase earnings is a motivation for expanding domestically or internationally common to all firms, but it provides few explanations. Closer analysis of individual investment decisions reveals a range both of ownership variables internal to the firm and locational variables exogenous to the firm, which influence investment flows. Perhaps more interesting is that the relative influence of firm-specific versus locational variables in influencing foreign direct investment decisions has changed over time.

In the analysis of the changing patterns of FDI flows, the post–World War II era provided a rich laboratory for examining the evolving geographical nature of TNCs' international activities. A decade-by-decade account captured the extent to which both the providers and the recipients of FDI flows have changed. It also highlighted the evolving nature of the motivations behind international production. While foreign direct investment in the early postwar era was resource-seeking, market- and knowledge-seeking motivations became more important in the 1970s and beyond.

Definitional clarity is a first and critical step to understanding the TNC; however, it is only the first step. As previously stated, much has already been written on globalization and the TNC, two of the most controversial topics within the international political economy. Further research will certainly inform and deepen the continuing analysis on the role and merits of the TNC in international society.

Notes

1. The literature both supportive and opposed to globalization is vast. Globalization is defined as the process of integration of the financial, currency, and product markets on a worldwide scale. For a succinct overview on recent changes in the nature of international finance, trade, and production that define "economic globalization," see Gilpin (2001: 5–12). Addressing the tension between globalization and domestic social arrangements, see Dani Rodrik, *Has Globalization Gone Too Far?* (Washington, DC: 1997). For a perceptive and entertaining read on these same tensions, see Thomas L. Friedman, *The Lexus and the Olive Tree* (New York: Random House, 2000). A critique of globalization can be found in Richard Falk, *Predatory Globalization* (Oxford: Polity Press, 1999). The notion that the current level of globalization is not unique in history and is not unprecedented is addressed by Cable (1995).

2. See also Vernon (1971).

3. The author would like to recognize the voluminous writings of John Dunning. His contribution to the study of TNCs is unmatched, elucidating the concepts and dynamics that have come to inform most discussions of the TNC and its activities.

References

Balaam, David N. and Michael Veseth. 2001. *Introduction to International Political Economy*. Upper Saddle River, NJ: Prentice-Hall.

Cable, Vincent. 1995. "The Diminished Nation-State: A Study in the Loss of Economic Power." *Daedalus* 124, 2 (Spring).

Caves, Richard E. 1996. *Multinational Enterprise and Economic Analysis*. New York: Cambridge University Press.

Dunning, John. 1993. *The Globalization of Business*. London: Routledge.

————. 2000. "Globalization and the New Geography of Foreign Direct Investment." In Ngaire Woods, ed., *The Political Economy of Globalization*. New York: St. Martin's Press.

Frost, Tony S. 2001. "The Geographic Sources of Foreign Subsidiaries' Innovations." *Strategic Management Journal* 22: 101–123.

Gilpin, Robert. 2001. *Global Political Economy: Understanding the International Economic Order*. Princeton, NJ: Princeton University Press.

Govindarajan, Vijay and Anil K. Gupta. 2001. *The Quest for Global Dominance: Transforming Global Presence into Global Competitive Advantage*. San Francisco: Jossey-Bass.

Grunberg, Leon. 2001. "The IPE of Multinational Corporations." In David N. Balaam and Michael Veseth, eds., *Introduction to International Political Economy*. Upper Saddle River, NJ: Prentice-Hall.

Kuemmerle, W. 1996. "The Drivers of Foreign Direct Investment into Research and Development: An Empirical Investigation." Harvard Business School, Working paper 96:062.

Moran, Theodore H. 2001. *Parental Supervision: The New Paradigm for Foreign Direct Investment and Development*. Washington, DC: Institute for International Economics.

Vernon, Raymond. 1966. "International Investment and International Trade in the Product Cycle." *Quarterly Journal of Economics* 80: 190–207.

———. 1971. *Sovereignty at Bay: The Multinational Spread of U.S. Enterprises.* New York: Basic Books.

———. 1996. "International Investment and International Trade in the Product Cycle." *Quarterly Journal of Economics* 80 (May): 190–207.

———. 1998. *In the Hurricane's Eye: The Troubled Prospects of Multinational Enterprises*. Cambridge: Harvard University Press.

World Investment Report. 2000. New York: United Nations Center on Transnational Corporations.

PART 6

CONCLUSION

26

Coping with Ecological Globalization

Hilary French

In this chapter Hilary French analyzes the impact of the current trade and financial architecture on the global environment and in doing so calls for a strengthening of the international environmental regime. She begins with a detailed listing of the products and natural resources now actively traded in the global economy. True to the title of the book in which this chapter originally appeared, French provides a "state of the world" overview of the environmental health of the planet. Her discussion covers diverse topics such as the depletion of the world's fisheries, declining biodiversity, deforestation, and the depletion of natural resources. According to French, economic growth and increases in global consumption, both accelerated by globalization, have placed the world on a perilous course and have done nothing to reverse the biological damage already unleashed on the planet. French also assesses the policies of the World Trade Organization, International Monetary Fund, and the World Bank. She concludes that despite public statements to the contrary, these organizations pay little heed to the environmental impact of their policies and lending. In a call to action, French argues for a strengthening of the United Nations Environmental Program in the form of a new World Environmental Organization to act both as a counterweight to the economic powerhouse institutions and to insure enforcement of current environmental treaties.

As the twenty-first century dawns, the planet seems to be steadily shrinking. Goods, money, people, ideas, and pollution are traveling around the world at unprecedented speed and scale, overwhelming financial managers, political leaders, and ecological systems. The "global commons," including the atmosphere and the oceans, is under environmental assault. The global-

Reprinted with permission of the Worldwatch Institute, www.worldwatch.org.

ization of commerce is further internationalizing environmental issues, with trade in natural resources such as fish and timber soaring, and with private capital surges giving international investors a growing stake in distant corners of the globe.

Environmental problems are climbing ever higher on the international political agenda, at times preoccupying international diplomats almost as much as arms control negotiations did during the cold war. Industrial countries are increasingly arguing, with the European Union (EU) and the United States now at odds on issues from global climate change to genetically modified organisms (GMOs). Environmental issues have also become acrimonious in North-South relations, with rich and poor countries divided over how to apportion responsibility for reversing the planet's ecological decline.

"Globalization" has become a common buzzword. But it means vastly different things to different people. To some, it is synonymous with the growth of global corporations whose far-flung operations transcend national borders and allegiances. To others, the term is closely linked with the information revolution, and the mobility of money, ideas, and labor that computers and other new technologies have been instrumental in bringing about. In this chapter, globalization is taken to mean a broad process of societal transformation in which numerous interwoven forces are making national borders more permeable than ever before, including growth in trade, investment, travel, and computer networking. "Ecological globalization" is used here to refer to the collective impact that these diverse processes have on the health of the planet's natural systems.[1]

Ecological globalization in its many guises poses enormous challenges to traditional governance structures. National governments are ill suited for managing environmental problems that transcend borders, whether via air and water currents or through global commerce. Yet international environmental governance is still in its infancy, with the treaties and institutions that governments turn to for global management mostly too weak to put a meaningful dent in the problems. Nations are granting significant and growing powers to economic institutions such as the World Trade Organization (WTO) and the International Monetary Fund (IMF), but environmental issues remain mostly an afterthought in these bodies.

Although nation-states are losing ground in the face of globalization, other actors are moving to the fore, particularly international corporations and nongovernmental organizations (NGOs). New information and communications technologies are facilitating international networking, and innovative partnerships are being forged between NGOs, the business community, and international institutions.

Despite these hopeful developments, the world economy and the natural world are both in precarious states as we enter the new millennium, provoking fears that an era of global instability looms on the horizon. Over the course of the twentieth century, the global economy stretched the planet to its limits. The time is now ripe to build the international governance structures needed to ensure that the world economy of the twenty-first century meets peoples' aspirations for a better future without destroying the natural fabric that underpins life itself.[2]

Trading on Nature

International movements of goods, money, and people play a major role in today's unprecedented biological losses. Yet the emerging rules of the global economy pay little heed to the importance of reversing the biological impoverishment of the planet. This mismatch between ecological imperatives and prevailing economic practice will need to be bridged if the world is to halt an unraveling of critical ecological systems in the early decades of this century.

The world's forests are a particularly important reservoir of biological wealth. They harbor more than half of all species on Earth and provide a range of other important natural services, including flood control and climate regulation. But the planet's forest cover is steadily shrinking. Nearly half of the forests that once covered Earth have already been lost, and almost 14 million hectares of tropical forest—an area almost three times the size of Costa Rica—are being sacrificed each year (Myers 1997; overall forest loss from Bryant, Nielsen, and Tangley 1997; 14 million hectares based on estimates in UNFAO 1999a).

The role of international trade in global deforestation has been a subject of controversy over the years. International timber trade is far from the only culprit in forest loss: the clearing of land for agriculture and grazing is also a major cause, as is fuelwood gathering in some regions and the felling of trees for commercial timber for domestic use. Yet the draw of international markets can be an inducement for countries to cut down trees far faster than would be required to meet domestic demand alone. Indonesia and Malaysia, for example, have both pushed plywood exports heavily in recent years, contributing in no small measure to rapid deforestation in both countries. Plywood exports from the two countries combined exploded from just 233,000 cubic meters in 1975 to 12 million cubic meters in 1998. These two countries now account for nearly 60 percent of world plywood exports, up from just 4 percent in 1975 (Abramovitz 1998).[3]

The value of global trade in forest products has risen steadily over the last few decades, climbing from $47 billion in 1970 to $139 billion in 1998. (See Figure 26.1.) Recent years have seen particularly rapid growth in trade in more finished types of forest products such as plywood, pulp, and paper. Exports of industrial roundwood (raw logs), in contrast, have remained relatively constant. For all products other than logs, exports as a share of total

Figure 26.1   World Trade in Forest Products, 1970–1997

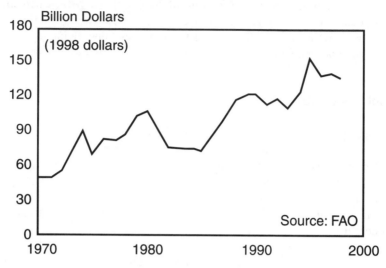

world production increased significantly over this period—an important indication of the growing globalization of the industry.[4]

Mining and energy extraction also imperil the health of forests, as well as mountains, waters, and other sensitive ecosystems. Vast areas are often disturbed for the sake of a relatively small quantity of bounty. For every kilogram of gold produced in the United States, for example, some 3 million kilograms of waste rock are left behind. Prime extraction sites are often located in previously undisturbed forests or wilderness areas. According to the Washington-based World Resources Institute, mining, energy development, and associated activities represent the second biggest threat to frontier forests after logging, affecting nearly 40 percent of threatened forests. Besides disturbing valuable ecosystems, this activity also can be devastating for the indigenous peoples who inhabit them: current exploration targets suggest that an estimated 50 percent of the gold produced in the next 20 years will come from indigenous peoples' lands. Toxic byproducts of mining poison the rivers that local people drink from, and the mining operations themselves destroy the forests and fields that people rely on for sustenance (Young 1992; gold-to-waste ratio based on U.S. Bureau of Mines data provided in Young 1994; frontier forests from Bryant, Nielsen, and Tangley 1997; indigenous peoples figure from Moody 1996).

Industrial countries are large consumers of minerals, accounting for more than 90 percent of bauxite imports, nearly 100 percent of nickel imports, over 80 percent of zinc imports, and roughly 70 percent of copper, iron, lead, and manganese imports. But developing countries are home to much of the world's mineral production, along with the associated environmental damage. Collectively, developing countries account for 76 percent of all exports of bauxite and nickel ore, 67 percent of copper, 54 percent of tin, and 45 percent of iron ore (minerals imports and exports are volume figures from UNCTAD 1995).

Even something as basic as our food supply is now deeply integrated into the global economy. The value of world agricultural trade skyrocketed in recent decades, more than doubling between 1972 and 1997 alone—from $224 billion to $457 billion. (See Figure 26.2.)

Agriculture accounts for 11 percent of the value of all world exports. For some continents, this share is significantly higher—25 percent of Latin America's exports are agricultural, as are 18 percent of Africa's. Trade in basic food grains such as wheat, rice, and corn dominates international agricultural exports in volume terms. Nearly 240 million tons of grain were exported in 1998—some 13 percent of total world production. Global aggregates mask great variations in export and import dependence among countries and regions. Australia, for instance, exports 63 percent of its grain production, and Japan imports 75 percent of its consumption.[5]

The developing world is a net importer of basic foodstuffs such as grain and meat, but it is a major exporter of many cash crops, such as bananas, coffee, cotton, soybeans, sugarcane, and tobacco. As of 1997, developing countries accounted for 97 percent of cocoa exports, 92 percent of palm oil, 88 percent of coffee, and 86 percent of bananas. Although these crops are the mainstays of many national economies, heavy reliance on them can entail substantial social and environmental costs, including the displacement of subsistence farmers from their land and the promotion of

Figure 26.2   World Exports of Agricultural Products, 1970–1997

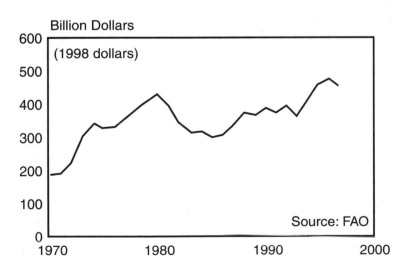

chemical-intensive agriculture. Recent decades have seen particularly rapid growth in so-called nontraditional exports—principally flowers, fruits, and vegetables. These crops tend to command far higher prices than those of traditional agricultural exports, which have been in decline in recent decades. But there are risks associated with these crops as well, one of the most serious of which is exposure to harmful levels of pesticides. A study of nearly 9,000 workers in Colombia's flower plantations indicated exposure to 127 different pesticides, some 20 percent of which are either banned or unregistered in the United Kingdom or the United States (developing countries' share of exports from UNFAO 1999b; nontraditional exports and Colombian flower workers from Thrupp 1995).

The fishing industry is also increasingly linked into the global marketplace. Global fish exports have grown nearly fivefold in value since 1970, reaching $52 billion in 1997. (See Figure 26.3) By volume, nearly half of the fish caught today are traded, up from only 32 percent in 1970. But the steady expansion of the catch, as well as habitat destruction and pollution, are taking a heavy toll on the world's fish stocks: the U.N. Food and Agriculture Organization estimates that 11 of the world's 15 major fishing grounds and 70 percent of major fish species are either fully or overexploited.[6]

Industrial countries dominate global fish consumption, accounting for more than 80 percent of all imports by value. Developing countries, on the other hand, contribute nearly half of all exports. Their share of the total has climbed steadily in recent decades as fleets have turned south in search of fish in response to the overfishing of northern waters. In 1970, developing

Figure 26.3 World Fish Exports, 1970–1997

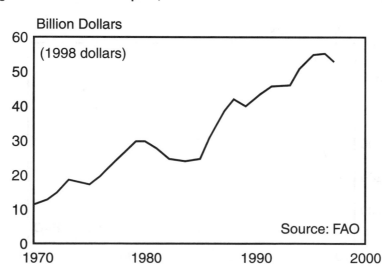

countries accounted for 37 percent of all fish exports, measured by value; by 1997, their share had risen to 49 percent. Thailand, China, Chile, and Indonesia are all now among the world's top 10 fish exporters. Exports from these four countries have nearly quadrupled in value since 1980.[7]

With many Third World fisheries now becoming depleted as well, overfishing for export markets means depriving small-scale fishers of their bounty. It also drives up the price of domestically available fish to the point where it is beyond the means of local people. In Senegal, for instance, species once commonly eaten throughout the country are now either exported or available only to the elite. This trend has serious implications for food security, as nearly 1 billion people worldwide, most of them in Asia, rely on fish as their primary source of protein.[8]

Trade in more exotic forms of wildlife is also a booming business, placing a number of commercially valuable species at growing risk of over-exploitation and even extinction. Each year, some 40,000 monkeys and other primates are shipped across international borders, along with some 2–5 million live birds, 3 million live farmed turtles, 2–3 million other live reptiles, 10–15 million raw reptile skins, 500–600 million ornamental fish, 1,000–2,000 raw tons of corals, 7–8 million cacti, and 9–10 million orchids. The wildlife trade is valued at some $10–20 billion annually, at least a quarter of which is thought to be illegal.[9]

The world community is just now beginning to awaken to a related though far more pervasive threat—the international spread of nonnative "exotic" species, which is known as "bioinvasion." For most of history, natural boundaries such as mountains, deserts, and ocean currents have served to isolate ecosystems and many of the species they contain. But over the centuries these natural barricades have gradually broken down as people and organisms have spread around the globe. This process has accelerated exponentially in recent decades, as trade and travel have skyrocketed. Once exotics establish a beachhead in a given ecosystem, they often proliferate, suppressing native species. Taken as a whole, invasive species now pose the second largest threat to the diversity of life on Earth, after habitat destruction (Bright 1998, 1999).

Besides endangering the health of ecosystems, the spread of microbes around the globe also threatens the health of people. Airplanes carry people to the other side of the world in far less time than the incubation period for many ailments, facilitating the unwitting introduction of foreign microbes into vulnerable populations. More than 30 new infectious diseases have emerged over the past 20 years, including AIDS, Ebola, hantavirus, and hepatitis C and E. According to the World Health Organization, "environmental changes have contributed in one way or another to the appearance of most if not all" of these diseases. Land use changes such as deforestation or the conversion of grasslands to agriculture that alter long-established equilibria between microbes and their hosts are sometimes to blame. In other cases, changes in human behavior are the culprit, such as careless disposal of food and beverage containers or car tires, which can create new breeding sites for disease-carrying organisms such as mosquitoes (role of air travel and new diseases from WHO 1999; quote and environmental changes from WHO 1998).

As world trade continues its steady upward climb, it is placing unprecedented strains on the health of the planet's ecosystems. But today's emerging global governance structures for the most part give short shrift to the urgent need to halt global environmental decline. The World Trade Organization is a case in point.

The WTO Meets the Environment

The WTO came into being in 1994 as an outgrowth of the "Uruguay Round" of global trade talks under the General Agreement on Tariffs and Trade (GATT). Although many people in the business community, government, and academia hailed its creation as an enlightened step toward a new era of global prosperity, critics charged that the new organization elevated corporate rights to a new plane while devastating local communities and the environment. The intervening years have done little to cool the passions on either sides of the debate.

In late November 1999, trade ministers from around the world gathered in Seattle to launch a millennium round of global trade talks. Thousands of NGO activists were also in Seattle, many of them protesting what they see as the WTO's environmental blindness. Critics particularly decry the secrecy that shrouds WTO activities. Many important documents are unavailable to the public, and most WTO committees, as well as all dispute resolution proceedings, are conducted in closed sessions dominated by trade rather than environmental experts.[10]

The text of the agreement that created the WTO ran to an astounding 26,000 pages and covered a bewildering array of issues, including agriculture, intellectual property rights, investment, and services. The organization was charged with overseeing the implementation of the new rules of world trade, including settling any disputes among nations related to their terms. Member-countries granted the WTO unprecedented powers for an international body, including a binding dispute resolution mechanism and provisions for stiff trade penalties to enforce its rulings (Thomas and Meyer 1997).

In a concession to the concerns of environmentalists, the preamble to the WTO agreement includes environmental protection and sustainable development among the organization's goals. The accord also included a commitment to create a Committee on Trade and Environment charged with analyzing the relationship between trade liberalization and environmental protection and with recommending any changes to WTO rules that might be needed to make the two goals "mutually supportive." But more than five years later, the committee has produced much talk but no concrete action.[11]

Widespread public concern about the environmental impact of GATT dates back to September 1991, when a dispute resolution panel shocked U.S. environmentalists by ruling that an embargo against Mexican tuna imposed under the U.S. Marine Mammal Protection Act violated GATT. The United States had imposed the embargo after determining that Mexicans were fishing for tuna with purse-seine nets that often have the unintended effect of ensnaring dolphins as well. In concluding that the tuna embargo contravened GATT rules, the panelists emphasized a key though controversial distinction between import restrictions aimed at the characteristic of products themselves and those keyed to production processes. The panelists decreed that the U.S. law was illegal under GATT because the United States was rejecting the process by which the tuna was harvested rather than the tuna itself (GATT 1991).

Although GATT, and later the WTO, contains a specific provision that ostensibly protects the right of countries to pursue environmental protection policies that might otherwise contradict trade rules, the panelists ruled that this exception pertains only to efforts by countries to protect the environment within their own borders. Because the Mexican tuna fishing took place outside of U.S. waters, the panelists viewed the embargo as tantamount to the United States foisting its environmental laws and values on the rest of the world. This point of view resonated with many people, particularly in the developing world, who looked to the rule-based GATT as a check on the U.S. tendency to wield its economic power unilaterally (GATT 1991).

But the decision exposed some glaring inconsistencies between the rules of the world trading system and emerging international environmental principles and practices. The trading system's aversion to process-related trade restrictions struck many people as particularly arbitrary, as environmental policy is moving increasingly toward focusing on the environmental impacts of products throughout their life cycle—including production, distribution, use, and disposal. Products such as gold or timber may be harmless or beneficial as products, but enormously costly to human or environmental health in the ways they are processed. Reform of extraction and manufacturing processes is essential to making real environmental advances, yet trade rules put up a sizable hurdle to pursuing such efforts in a world economy that is becoming steadily more integrated.[12]

Also worrisome was the ruling's failure to acknowledge the right of countries to take action to protect the atmosphere, the oceans, and other parts of the global commons—a failure that raised questions about the legality under GATT of an array of other environmental policies besides the one aimed at protecting dolphins. What would become of policies aimed at reducing the use of harmful drift nets in fishing, protecting primary forests, or staving off ozone depletion or global warming? By the panel's reasoning, it seemed that even provisions of international environmental agreements designed to protect global resources could be ruled GATT-illegal. This clash between two different spheres of international law presented the world with a major legal challenge, as it is not always clear which agreement trumps the other in cases where two treaties are in conflict.[13]

Despite the furor over the tuna-dolphin decision, the WTO struck against another law in 1998, ruling against a U.S. measure aimed at reducing unintended sea turtle mortality as a byproduct of shrimp trawling. Sea turtles are both extremely endangered and highly mobile, making international action to protect them a high priority. The provisions of the U.S. law in question closed the lucrative U.S. shrimp market to countries that do not require their shrimpers to use turtle excluder devices (TEDs), simple but highly effective pieces of equipment that prevent turtles from getting ensnared in shrimp nets, or that do not have comparable policies in place. Spurred by the threat of U.S. trade restrictions, 16 nations, including 13 in Latin America plus Indonesia, Nigeria, and Thailand, have by now moved to require the use of TEDs. India, Malaysia, and Pakistan chose a different tack, however, deciding to launch a WTO challenge rather than meeting the U.S. requirement. (Thailand joined them in this effort as a matter of principle, even though it had adopted TEDs.)[14]

Although the environmental effectiveness of the U.S. law was clear, both the initial WTO dispute resolution panel and a subsequent appeals panel concluded in 1998 that the measure violated WTO rules. The legal reasoning of the appeals panel was an improvement over earlier rulings, as it acknowledged that countries may in some circumstances be justified in using trade measures to protect global resources. But the panel nonetheless took issue with the way in which the U.S. law had been implemented, arguing that it was applied in an arbitrary manner that failed to treat countries evenhandedly. The bottom line was that the U.S. law would have to be changed in order to comply with WTO rules. This outcome was particularly alarming for environmentalists, as the Uruguay Round had strengthened the rules of dispute resolution proceedings to make rulings binding, and to provide for tougher trade retaliation in cases where countries are unwilling to change offending laws in order to adhere to panel findings (Entous 1998; Swardson 1998; WTO 1998b).[15]

In response to the ruling, the U.S. government altered the way it was implementing the law without seeking any changes to the statute itself. The new guidelines provide for the import of specific shipments of shrimp that have been approved as turtle-safe even if the country as a whole has not met the certification requirements. It remains to be seen whether this response will satisfy the WTO, thus precluding the imposition of trade sanctions against the United States.[16]

In any case, many U.S. environmentalists are unhappy with the government's response. Their primary concern is that the shipment-by-shipment method will be less effective in safeguarding turtles than the earlier blanket restriction, as it will not compel countries to mandate the use of TEDs when fishing for shrimp not destined for the U.S. market. A turtle might thus survive an encounter with a TED-equipped boat only to later fall prey to a TED-free vessel. Environmentalists also worry that the new policy may facilitate the entry of "laundered" shrimp into the United States. Several environmental groups filed suit against the government at the U.S. Court of International Trade, charging that the revised guidelines were inconsistent with provisions of the Endangered Species Act that stipulate adequate protection for sea turtles. In a preliminary ruling in April 1999, the court sided with the environmental groups, placing national law and international trade rules on a possible collision course (*Miami Herald* 1999; Dunne 1999a).

Besides mandating strengthened enforcement, the package that created the WTO also included an Agreement on the Application of Sanitary and Phytosanitary (SPS) Measures that imposes new restrictions on laws designed to protect human, animal, and plant health. Trade specialists had argued that legislators were passing disingenuous laws that lacked a scientific rationale, with the primary goal of keeping foreign products off of their shelves. Although the ostensible reason for the SPS agreement was to prevent countries from using health and safety standards as disguised trade barriers, the worry is that legitimate laws will also run afoul of its rules (WTO undated; Thomas and Meyer 1997).

The European Union argues that this is what is happening in its ongoing dispute with the United States over an EU law that forbids the sale of meat produced using growth hormones. The European Community and the United States have been locking horns over the EU's beef-hormone ban for several years now. Since it went into effect in the late 1980s, the law has always applied equally to domestically raised and imported livestock, and has thus passed the WTO's bedrock test of nondiscrimination. The EU insists the ban is not an intentional trade barrier at all, but only a prudent response to public concern that eating hormone-treated beef might cause cancer and reproductive health problems. But the hormone-hooked U.S. livestock industry was threatened by the law, which blocks hundreds of millions of dollars worth of U.S. beef exports, and it prevailed upon the U.S. government to take up its cause at the WTO.[17]

This effort culminated in February 1998 when a WTO appeals panel ruling upheld an earlier dispute panel ruling that the European law violated WTO rules. In July 1999, the U.S. government imposed WTO-approved retaliatory sanctions on the EU for its refusal to accept U.S. hormone-treated beef, slapping 100-percent tariffs on $116.8 million worth of European imports, including fruit juices, mustard, pork, truffles, and Roquefort cheese. The U.S. sanctions were greeted with widespread consternation in Europe, particularly in France, where a number of McDonald's restaurants were targeted for protests. So far, the EU has refused to back down (WTO 1998c, *New York Times* 1999; on the European response to the ruling, see BRIDGES 1999b, Swardson 1999b).

The panelists' primary argument against the EU law was that it was based on inadequate risk assessment. They explicitly rejected the EU's defense that the import restriction was justified by the precautionary principle—a basic tenet of international environmental law that is steadily gaining ground. The Rio Declaration on Environment and Development, for example, which was agreed to at the June 1992 Earth Summit, declares that: "Where there are threats of serious or irreversible damage, lack of full scientific certainty shall not be used as a reason for postponing cost-effective measures to prevent environmental degradation" (WTO 1998c; on the precautionary principle see Cameron and Abouchar 1996; Rio Declaration from Guruswamy, Palmer, and Weston 1994).

The WTO's provisions, on the other hand, require that health and safety laws be based on scientific principles and not be maintained with insufficient scientific evidence. Although on the face of it these requirements sound reasonable enough, in practice countries often disagree about how much evidence is "sufficient" to justify preventative measures. The WTO shifts the burden of proof to in effect require that chemicals and other food additives be proved harmful before their use can be restricted. The problem with this approach is that extensive testing, sometimes over a period of years, is required to know if a substance has long-term cumulative effects that might cause cancer, damage to the immune system, or other serious ailments (WTO undated, Thomas and Meyer 1997).

The beef hormone dispute is widely viewed as just a warm-up for a more serious trade controversy now brewing over genetically modified organisms. Once again, the European Union and the United States are the primary antagonists. Prompted by public concern over the health and ecological effects of GMOs, the EU passed legislation in 1998 requiring all food products containing genetically modified soybeans or corn to be labeled as such. Several other countries, including Australia, Brazil, Japan, and South Korea, are now following suit. A large share of food products made by U.S. companies—breads, salad oils, and ice cream, among them—now contain GMOs. Many European producers, in contrast, are steering clear of GMOs in the face of public concern. U.S. companies complain that the labeling requirements amount to trade barriers, and the U.S. and Canadian governments are now making this same point at the WTO and in other international forums.[18]

In February 1999, a proposed biosafety protocol to the U.N. Convention on Biological Diversity became the first major victim of the growing international trade war over GMOs. Negotiations under way for a few years had been aimed at putting in place a system of prior consent for the transport of genetically engineered seeds and products. The talks were scheduled to wrap up in Cartagena, Colombia, in February, but six major agricultural exporters—Argentina, Australia, Canada, Chile, the United States, and Uruguay—put a monkey wrench into these plans by blocking adoption of the accord. One of the main U.S. arguments against the protocol was a claim that its provisions ran counter to the rules of the WTO. As of November 1999, negotiators were still hoping to bridge the differences (on the breakdown of the biosafety talks, see Thomson 1999, *Financial Times* 1999a; on continuing negotiations, see *International Environment Reporter* 1999b).

The environmental impact of freeing trade in forest products is another controversial issue looming on the trade horizon. Under a proposed agreement now under consideration, most industrial countries would eliminate tariffs on pulp and paper by 2000, and on wood and other forest products such as furniture by 2002. Developing countries would be given an additional two years to meet these terms. The precise effects of these steps are difficult to predict, but studies suggest that the higher prices paid to producers as a result of tariff reductions will boost production significantly in some countries. A recent U.S. government report concluded that the agreement would likely increased production by nearly 3 percent in Malaysia and over 4 percent in Indonesia, although the report also forecasts production declines in some countries, including Mexico and Russia. With so little of today's timber industry based on sustainable practices, production increases often translate into increased forest destruction.[19]

Although the proposed accord would initially take aim at tariffs alone, its scope might well be expanded in the future to include nontariff barriers to trade. Over the longer term, these provisions might pose a greater threat to the health of the world's forests, and to the diversity of species that inhabit them. What looks to one country or company to be a "nontariff barrier to trade" is often viewed elsewhere as a legitimate environmental law. Even under existing agreements, concern is rising that measures designed to minimize the introduction of harmful exotic species will run afoul of WTO rules. Forest certification initiatives, aimed at creating a market for sustainably harvested timber, could also run head-on into WTO rules in the years ahead (ELDF 1999).

As opposition to the WTO continues to mount, many governments are beginning to acknowledge, rhetorically at least, that reforms are needed to make the world trading system environmentally sound. One idea gaining support is to enlist the WTO in an effort to reduce environmentally harmful subsidies. World trade rules have long discouraged subsidies, as they distort the economic playing field. The United States and six other nations have suggested building on this tradition by making the elimination of fishing subsidies an objective for the upcoming round of trade talks. These subsidies, which add up to some $14–20 billion annually, help propel overcapacity in the world's fishing fleet, which is itself a powerful driving force behind today's depleted fisheries. Other environmentally harmful payouts could also be tackled at the WTO, including multibillion-dollar agricultural, energy, and forestry subsidies.[20]

Taking on environmentally harmful subsidies would be an important step forward, but it does not let governments off the hook for amending existing WTO rules to buffer environmental laws from trade challenges. Among the priorities for reform are clearly incorporating the precautionary principle into WTO rules, protecting consumers' right to know about the health and environmental impact of products they purchase by safeguarding labeling programs, recognizing the legitimacy of distinguishing among products based on how they were produced, providing deference to multinational environmental agreements in cases where they conflict with WTO rules, ensuring the right of countries to use trade measures to protect the global commons, and opening the WTO to meaningful public participation. These changes are imperative if the WTO is to gain the public support it needs to stay in business.[21]

Greening the International Financial Architecture

During the 1990s, money became increasingly mobile in response to a range of factors, including the takeoff in computerized trading as well as the deregulation of international capital markets. International investment surged in response, particularly into the newly established stock markets of the developing world.[22]

Private capital inflows into developing countries and into the former Eastern bloc increased from only $53 billion at the beginning of the 1990s to an all-time high of $302 billion in 1997. (See Figure 26.4.) Large parts of Asia and Latin America were suddenly transformed in the minds of international investors from poor, "developing countries" into glistening "emerging markets." At the same time, new financial instruments such as hedge funds and derivatives created an explosion of foreign exchange trading, with an astounding $1.5 trillion now changing hands every day.[23]

But in 1997 the bubble burst. Thailand was the first economic domino to fall, when it was forced to devalue the country's currency sharply after it came under sustained speculative attack. The crisis soon spread to Indonesia, Malaysia, the Philippines, and South Korea. International investors lost their nerve and raced for the exits. Some $22 billion in 1997 and $30 billion in 1998 flowed out of the Asian countries in crisis. Banks

Figure 26.4   Private Capital Flows to Developing Countries, 1970–1998

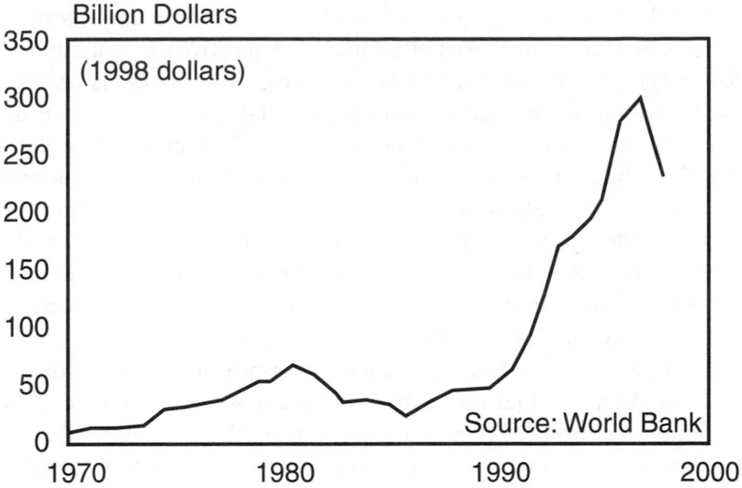

Billion Dollars

failed and stock markets collapsed, sending the economies of the region into a tailspin. And the crisis did not stop at the continent's edge. Shaken by the Asian experience, investors began to pull money out of emerging markets everywhere. Russia's currency and stock market went into a free fall in late August 1998, forcing the country to default on $40 billion in international loans. Brazil appeared to be the next domino waiting to fall, prompting the International Monetary Fund to step in with a $42 billion bailout plan.[24]

The social and environmental fallout from the crisis was severe. In battered Asia, tens of millions of people fell into poverty as jobs were slashed, and as many as a million children were pulled out of school, with some of them pushed into prostitution by their desperate families. Growing poverty tied to the crisis also had environmental costs, such as a surge in Indonesia in the poaching of endangered monkeys, tigers, and other species as destitute people sought quick cash. And environmental spending was slashed to the bare bones by governments and businesses in crisis countries in order to stave off bankruptcy.[25]

The global economic crisis now appears to be in at least temporary remission. International capital has begun to return to most of the countries affected by the crisis, and economic growth rates are again headed upwards, although poverty rates have yet to respond. But many commentators warn against a false sense of complacency. They predict that the next jolt is not far off, as the globalization of international finance has outpaced the ability of governments and international institutions to manage the system effectively.[26]

If there was a silver lining to the crisis, it was the wake-up call it provided about the risks of rapid globalization, and the subsequent launching of a critical international dialogue about how to reform the international financial architecture to meet the demands of the twenty-first century. As Professor Dani Rodrik of Harvard University puts it: "markets are sustainable only insofar as they are embedded in social and political institutions. . . . It is trite but true to say that none of these institutions exists at the global level." As the process of devising international policies for a globalizing world proceeds, the need to protect the natural resource base that underpins the global economy merits a prominent place on the agenda (Rodrik 1998).

The logical place to begin any discussion of a new financial architecture is with existing structures, principally the International Monetary Fund and the World Bank. The IMF came under particularly close scrutiny in the wake of the economic crisis. The Fund's high-profile role as a conduit for multibillion-dollar bailout packages for the crisis-stricken countries was a clear demonstration of the organization's formidable powers. But it also stirred controversy, as prominent economists took issue with the wisdom of the institution's financial advice and the secrecy in which its operations are shrouded (see, for example, Sachs 1997).

Although the World Bank maintained a lower profile during the crisis, it has also been active in channeling funds into the crisis-ridden countries, often in close cooperation with the IMF. Over the last few years, the Bank has substantially boosted both its total lending and the share of its funds that are spent on cash infusions for "structural adjustment." Total Bank lending reached $29 billion in 1999, up from just $19 billion two years earlier. And more than half of the Bank's total lending in 1999 was for structural adjustment, compared with only 27 percent in 1997. Under conventional "structural adjustment" loans as well as the crisis-generated bailout packages, countries receiving funds agree to implement a long and specific list of policy changes intended to restore their to economic health and thus to creditworthiness. Privatization, price and exchange rate stability, and trade liberalization are among the policies commonly recommended.[27]

But the World Bank and the IMF pay insufficient heed to the profound effects of these policies on the ecological health and the social fabric of recipient countries. One important component of most adjustment loans is policies aimed at boosting exports in order to generate foreign exchange with which to pay back debts. Yet the pressure to export can lead countries to liquidate natural assets such as fisheries and forests, thereby undermining longer-term economic prospects. Intensive export-oriented agriculture is also often promoted, sometimes at the expense of small-scale farmers and indigenous peoples. At the same time that structural adjustment loans promote exports of environmentally sensitive commodities, they also often require countries to make Draconian cuts in government spending, causing the budgets of already overburdened environment and natural resource management ministries to plummet (Reed 1996).

All these effects are evident in the recent bailout packages. In Indonesia, the IMF encouraged more palm oil production as part of its broader strategy for pulling the country out of its economic crisis, mandating that the country remove restrictions on foreign investment in this sector. Yet rapid growth in palm oil exports has been a major contributor to the decimation of Indonesia's biologically rich tropical forests in recent years, raising profound questions about the wisdom of pushing such exports further still. Exports of palm oil climbed from 1.4 million to nearly 3 million tons between 1991 and 1997. The devastating Indonesia wildfires of recent years were sparked in part by fires deliberately set to clear land for oil palm and pulpwood plantations.[28]

Environmental spending has declined markedly in the crisis-ridden countries, including Indonesia, the Philippines, South Korea, and Thailand. In Russia, the budget for protected areas was recently cut by 40 percent. And Brazil agreed as part of a recent pact with the IMF to cut its environmental spending by two thirds. A key international program aimed at protecting the Amazonian rainforest from destruction by ranchers, loggers, farmers, and miners is one of the programs to face the chopping block. The timing of these cuts was particularly poor in light of the unusually high rates of deforestation in the Brazilian Amazon over the last few years.[29]

Although structural adjustment programs often lead to environmental harm, they have also been used in a few cases to promote environmentally beneficial policy changes. In 1996 and 1997, the IMF suspended loans to Cambodia after government officials awarded logging concessions to foreign firms that threatened to open up the country's entire remaining forest area to exploitation—while funneling tens of millions of dollars into the bank accounts of the corrupt officials. And despite its worrisome provisions for stepped-up natural resource exports, the recent Indonesian bailout plan also included several provisions intended to benefit forest management in the country (IER 1997, Government of Indonesia 1999, Sunderlin 1998).

As part of an assault on the country's tradition of "crony capitalists," the Indonesian bailout plan required a number of reforms to the country's corruption-laden forestry sector, including tighter control over a government reforestation fund, the revenues of which had more often been used to line the pockets of President Suharto's political allies than to plant trees. The bailout package also included several measures aimed specifically at protecting forests, such as reducing land conversion targets to environmentally sustainable levels, instituting an auctioning system for handing out concessions, and imposing new "resource rent" taxes on timber sales. Although these reforms were a step in the right direction, their ultimate effect on deforestation rates in the country remains to be seen (Government of Indonesia 1999, Sunderlin 1998; abuses in reforestation from World Bank, East Asia Environment and Social Development Unit 1999).

Besides using their influence to discourage unsustainable levels of natural resource exploitation, the IMF and the World Bank are well placed to promote environmentally beneficial fiscal reforms, such as cuts in environmentally harmful subsidies or the imposition of pollution taxes. They could both also help promote improvements in environmental accounting, such as incorporating the depletion of natural resources into national income figures. As things now stand, the destruction of natural assets such as forests, fisheries, and minerals is not typically included in national income figures, which means that policymakers are working from an incomplete set of books. And the IMF could include environmental issues in its mandate to conduct "surveillance" of the economic prospects of its member countries, in part by tracking environmental spending levels and structural adjustment-mandated legislative changes that affect the environment (Durbin and Welch 1998, Gandhi 1998).[30]

Despite the clear links between economic and environmental health, the IMF has long resisted the idea that environmental issues have much to do with its mission. When the organization was first created, its primary role was to help to tide countries over when they faced short-term liquidity problems rather than to help them meet longer-term development goals. But the abandonment of fixed exchange rates in the 1970s deprived the IMF of much of its original mandate. Since then it has become increasingly involved with issues of longer-term development, such as its prominent role in brokering debt restructuring deals in the 1980s. The Fund now accepts that issues such as fighting corruption and alleviating poverty intersect with its mission. It is difficult to see why environmental protection should be any different (evolving role of the IMF from *Economist* 1999 and Welch 1988; see also Gandhi 1998).

On paper, the development-oriented World Bank has been far more open than the IMF to the idea that environmental concerns should be integrated into its structural adjustment lending. The Bank's policy that governs adjustment lending stipulates that the environmental impact of these loans should be fully considered as they are prepared, with a view toward promoting possible synergies and avoiding environmentally harmful results. But an internal review of more than 50 recent loans found few that paid much heed to environmental and social matters. Whereas a 1993 Bank report found that some 60 percent of adjustment loans included environmental goals, the recent study concluded that this share has now plummeted to less than 20 percent. An added problem is the fact that the Bank's policy on environmental impact assessment does not cover broad-based structural adjustment lending, although it is supposed to be applicable to adjustment loans aimed at specific sectors, such as agriculture or energy. IMF loans are also not subject to environmental impact assessment.[31]

Despite the World Bank's growing role in adjustment lending, project lending remains a mainstay of its activities. The Bank has traditionally made loans only to governments, but in the last few years it has increasingly emphasized supporting the private sector. It has done this both by using its own funds to guarantee private-sector projects and by stepping up the operations of two affiliated agencies, the International Finance Corporation (IFC) and the Multilateral Investment Guarantee Agency (MIGA). The IFC lends directly to private enterprises, while MIGA insures against political risks, such as expropriation, civil disturbance, and breach of contract. At last count, in 1998, the World Bank estimated that some 10 percent of all private-sector investment in the developing world was supported at least indirectly by its various private-sector programs.[32]

After more than a decade of pressure from NGOs and determined efforts by committed insiders, the World Bank now has an extensive set of environmental and social policies, which among other things cover environmental impact assessments of projects, forestry lending, involuntary resettlement, protection of wilderness areas, the rights of indigenous peoples, and pest management. The IFC and MIGA both recently issued their own parallel policies, and the World Bank published an updated Pollution Prevention and Abatement Handbook, which provides detailed pollution reduction guidelines for nearly 40 industries. In theory, Bank agencies are bound by their own policies, although the Bank admits that it has a tarnished history in following its own rules. The importance of the World Bank's standards is magnified by the fact that they are often looked to by private investors as the prevailing international norm.[33]

As World Bank environmental and social standards were strengthened over the last decade, private investors turned increasingly to bilateral export credit agencies to find support for projects that no longer pass muster at the Bank. Export credit support climbed from $24 billion in 1988 to $105 billion in 1996. All told, bilateral export promotion in the form of loans and investment insurance now underwrites more than 10 percent of all world trade. Bilateral export promotion often supports environmentally disruptive projects, including mines, pipelines, and hydroelectric dams.[34]

The U.S. government has had environmental policies in place for several years at its main export promotion agencies, the U.S. Overseas Private Investment Corporation and the U.S. Export-Import Bank. But in a global economy, tough national standards can easily be undermined by laggards abroad. The United States learned this lesson the hard way a few years back when its Export-Import Bank refused on environmental grounds to extend credits to companies such as the heavy equipment manufacturer Caterpillar that wanted to participate in China's controversial Three Gorges dam project. The Bank's counterparts in Canada, France, Germany, Japan, and Switzerland stepped into the breach. Stung by the experience, the United States is working to persuade other donor countries to develop environmental guidelines for their export finance agencies. Several countries are now in the process of developing such standards, including Canada, Japan, Norway, and the United Kingdom. Negotiations are also under way to create common environmental standards for the export finance agencies of the major industrial countries. Nongovernmental activists are pushing for these to be set at a high level.[35]

But even if this initiative succeeds, private capital markets can still be tapped for environmentally problematic projects. In the Three Gorges case, a number of prominent investment banks—including Lehman Brothers, Morgan Stanley, and Smith Barney—have sponsored bond offerings over the last few years to help the Chinese government raise funds for the dam. Although convincing private financiers to pay attention to the environment is substantially more difficult than lobbying public institutions such as the World Bank and export credit agencies, several efforts are afoot to encourage a heightened environmental consciousness on the Wall Streets of the world (Houlder 1999, Monroe 1999, NWF and FE-US 1999).

A U.N. Environment Programme (UNEP) initiative launched in 1992 encourages commercial banks to incorporate environmental considerations into their lending programs. So far, 162 banks from 43 countries have signed onto the initiative's Statement by Banks on the Environment and Sustainable Development. The signatories underscore their expectation that borrowers must comply with "all applicable local, national, and. international environmental regulations." They also pledge to update their accounting procedures to reflect environmental risks, such as the potential for chemical accidents or hidden hazardous waste dumps, and to develop banking products and services that promote environmental protection. Although laudable in its goals, the UNEP statement is short on specific commitments. In fact, several signatories were involved with the recent Chinese bond offerings that activists charge are helping to finance the Three Gorges project. In order to minimize gaps between rhetoric and reality, the U.K.-based. Green Alliance suggests strengthening the initiative by transforming the statement into a document whose expected standards of performance are clear enough to be subjected to the scrutiny of an audit (UNEP 1997a; signatories and countries from UNEP 1999a and 1999b, 1997b, Aslam 1999, Hill, Fedrigo and Marshall 1997).

Environmental liabilities could also be better incorporated into the way stock markets are regulated. Companies operating in the United States are required to disclose large environmental risks on the forms they file with the Securities and Exchange Commission. But the information varies widely in quality, with many companies submitting no data at all. Developing countries are particularly well placed to write environmental rules into the regulations governing newly established stock markets. Thailand, for one, requires companies listed on the Stock Exchange of Thailand to undergo an environmental audit that includes an environmental impact assessment as well as a site visit (Schmidheiny and Zorraquín 1996, Benjapolchai 1997).

If financial markets are to reflect environmental risks adequately, transparent information about corporate environmental performance is essential. The last several years have seen an explosion of interest in environmental reporting, but existing efforts have been poorly coordinated, leading to a proliferation of "non-standardized information reported in non-uniform formats," according to the Boston-based Coalition for Environmentally Responsible Economies (CERES). In an effort to address this deficiency, CERES has launched a Global Reporting Initiative in which corporations, NGOs, professional accounting firms, and UNEP are working together to produce a global set of guidelines for corporate sustainability reporting. The goal of the initiative is to elevate environmental reporting to the same plane as financial reporting, making it standard business practice worldwide.[36]

Innovations in Global Environmental Governance

The new rules of the global economy are for the most part being set by institutions such as the World Trade Organization and the International Monetary Fund, where the mindset of traditional economists prevails and where the "rules" are generally aimed at unshackling global commerce rather than harnessing it for the common good. But forging an environmentally sustainable society is about more than economics, and farsighted economics is about more than reducing restrictions on the movement of goods and money. Creating a global society fit for the twenty-first century will thus require not only reform of economic institutions, but also a strengthening of international environmental institutions so that they can act as an ecological counterweight to "today's growing economic powerhouses."[37]

A good place to start is with the hundreds of agreements, declarations, action plans, and international treaties on the environment that now exist. Environmental treaties alone number more than 230; agreement on more than three fourths of them has been reached since the first U.N. conference on the environment was held in Stockholm in 1972. (See Figure 26.5.) These accords cover atmospheric pollution, ocean despoliation, endangered species protection, hazardous waste trade, and the preservation of Antarctica, among other issues.[38]

Judging from the number of treaties, environmental diplomacy over the past few decades appears to have been a spectacular success. And many of these accords have in fact led to important results, such as the facts that chlorofluorocarbon emissions dropped 87 percent from their peak in 1988 as a result of the 1987 Montreal Protocol on ozone depletion, the killing of

Figure 26.5   International Environmental Treaties, 1921–1998

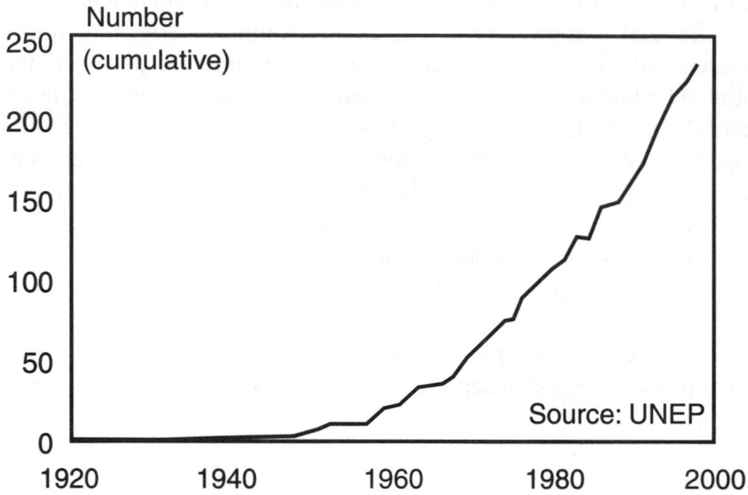

Number
(cumulative)

Source: UNEP

elephants plummeted in Africa following a 1990 ban on commercial trade in ivory, the annual whale take declined from more than 66,000 in 1961 to some 1,100 today as a result of agreements forged by the International Whaling Commission, the volume of oil spilled into the ocean has declined by 60 percent since 1981 even with a near doubling in oil shipments in response to International Maritime Organization regulations, and mining exploration and development have been forbidden in Antarctica for 50 years under a 1991 accord.[39]

Yet even as the number of treaties climbs, the condition of the biosphere continues to deteriorate. Carbon dioxide levels in the atmosphere have reached record highs, scientists are warning that we are in the midst of a period of mass extinction of species, the world's major fisheries are depleted, and water shortages loom worldwide. The notoriously slow pace of international diplomacy needs to be reconciled with the growing urgency of protecting the planet's life-support systems.

The main reason that environmental treaties have so far mostly failed to turn around today's alarming environmental trends is that the governments that created them have generally permitted only vague commitments and lax enforcement. Governments have also for the most part failed to provide sufficient funds to implement treaties, particularly in the developing world. Ironically, environmentalists need to take a page from the WTO and push for international environmental commitments that are as specific and as enforceable as trade accords have become.

One idea now gaining political currency is to upgrade the U.N. Environment Programme into a World Environment Organization (WEO) on a par with the WTO. Although UNEP has had some important successes since it was founded in 1972, it has suffered from meager resources and a limited mandate. Upgrading the status of environmental issues within the U.N. system is long overdue. Still, it is important that debates over form not distract from the ultimately far more important questions of function. A world environment organization could usefully serve as an umbrella organization for the current scattered collection of treaty bodies, just as domestic environment agencies oversee the implementation of national environmental laws. But in order to do so effectively, the treaties themselves would need to stipulate strong enforcement capacities, and the WEO would need to be endowed with sufficient financial resources to catalyze innovative programs.[40]

Tomorrow's international environmental institutions may turn out to be vastly different in character than the bureaucratic bodies that predominate in many quarters today. A nascent system of international environmental governance is now emerging from diverse quarters, proving that governance is no longer just for governments.[41]

In recent years, the private sector has itself become increasingly and often controversially enmeshed in the standard-setting business. One prominent example is the voluntary environmental management guidelines forged by the Geneva-based International Organization for Standardization, a worldwide federation of national standards-setting bodies. Although these guidelines should not to be confused with actual environmental performance standards, they are nonetheless a useful tool. But the credibility of the process has suffered from the fact that it is widely perceived to be industry-dominated (IISD 1996, Krut and Gleckman 1998).

Another type of international standard setting is embodied in the numerous ecolabeling initiatives now beginning to take hold. One strength of these efforts is the diverse range of stakeholders they bring to the table. The organic agriculture community was an early pioneer. As far back as the early 1970s, it came together through the International Federation of Organic Agriculture Movements to stipulate conditions that farmers must meet in order to claim organic credentials. More recently, the Forest Stewardship Council was founded in 1993 to set standards for sustainable forest production through a cooperative process involving timber traders and retailers as well as environmental organizations and forest dwellers. And a Marine Stewardship Council has now been formed to devise criteria for sustainable fish harvesting.[42]

A particularly encouraging development of recent years' has been the steady growth of the international nongovernmental movement. Environmental activists are flourishing at the national and grassroots level in most corners of the globe. Growth has been particularly rapid in the developing world and in Eastern Europe, where democratization over the last decade has opened up political space for NGOs. The number of NGOs working across international borders has also soared over this century, climbing, from just 176 in 1909 to more than 23,000 in 1998. Environmental groups have risen steadily as a share of the total, climbing by one count from just 2 percent of transnational social change NGOs in 1953 to 14 percent in 1993.[43]

Empowered, by e-mail and the Internet, environmental activists have gradually organized themselves into a range of powerful international networks. To name but a few, the Climate Action Network links more than 250 international groups and national organizations active on climate change; the Pesticide Action Network includes at least 500 consumer, environment, health, labor, agriculture, and public interest groups worldwide; the World Forum of Fish Workers & Fish Harvesters brings together people from small-scale fishing communities on six continents; the International POPs Elimination Network coordinates hundreds of NGOs worldwide in their push for an effective treaty to limit persistent organic pollutants; and the Women's Environment and Development Organization links activists from around the world who are committed to increasing female participation in decision-making at the United Nations and in other international forums where issues of concern such as population stabilization are discussed (Longworth 1999; CAN undated; PAN undated; WFFWFH undated; IPOPSEN undated; WEDO undated).

Among their many accomplishments, NGOs have educated millions of people about environmental issues, and then effectively harnessed the power of a knowledgeable citizenry to pierce the veil of secrecy that all too often surrounds both international negotiations and corporate decision-making. Recent NGO successes include exposing the environmental deficiencies of a proposed Multilateral Agreement on Investment and thereby bringing it to a halt, and slowing the introduction of genetically modified organisms worldwide until their effects on both human and ecological health are better understood.[44]

Thirty years ago, photographs of Earth taken from space by the Apollo expeditions indelibly impressed on all who saw them that our planet, while divided by political boundaries, is united by ecological systems. These photos helped inspire the first Earth Day, which in turn motivated numerous countries to pass environmental laws and create environmental ministries. This year, the world will celebrate Earth Day 2000. The time has come for a comparable groundswell in support of the international governance reforms that are needed to safeguard the health of the planet in the new millennium.

Notes

1. For different takes on the meaning of globalization, see, for example, Reinicke (1998), Korten (1995), Soros (1998a), and Friedman (1999).

2. For a warning of instability on the horizon, see Linden (1998).

3. Growth of plywood exports in Indonesia and Malaysia are volume figures from UNFAO (1999b).

4. Trends in forest products trade and Figure 26.1 based on UNFAO 1999b; 1998 figures are preliminary estimates. Figures deflated using the U.S. GNP Implicit Price Deflator, provided in United States Department of Commerce (1999).

5. Figure 26.2 based on UNFAO (1999b) with figures deflated as described in note 4; 11 percent and continental breakdown from WTO (1998a); grain trade statistics from U.S. Department of Agriculture (1999).

6. Figure 26.3 based on UNFAO (1978), and on Montanaro (1999), with figures deflated as described in note 4; share of fish traded today (1997 data) from UNFAO (1999c, 1999d); share traded in 1970 from UNFAO (1978); fishing grounds from Perotti (1997); overexploitation from UNFAO (1997).

7. Share of industrial and developing countries in 1997 based on data supplied by Montanaro (1999); share of developing countries in 1970 from UNFAO (1978); four developing countries from UNFAO (1983, 1999d).

8. Deprivation of small-scale fishers from Kent (1997) and from Ahmed (1997); Buckley (1997); 1 billion and Asian dependence from WRI (1996).

9. Estimate of $10 million does not include timber and fisheries products; this and species trade figures from TRAFFIC North America (1994). Higher estimate of $20 million, illegal trade, and primate numbers from Kakakhel (1999).

10. On expectations for the Seattle meeting, see, for example, Swardson (1999a). On transparency issues, see Wallach and Sforza (1999), Esty (1998), Sampson (1999).

11. "Text of Uruguay Round Ministerial Decision on Trade and Environment," 14 April 1994, provided in NRDC and FIELD (1995); for a useful discussion of the deliberations of the Committee on Trade and Environment, see Torres (1998).

12. For a useful discussion of the clash between the trade and environmental systems on the question of process standards, see the paper by Von Moltke (1998).

13. For a discussion of the tuna-dolphin ruling and its implications, see Christensen and Geffin (1991–1992); on the issue of conflicts between international environmental and trade agreements, see Charnovitz (1996).

14. Urgency and effectiveness of trade measures from Fugazzotto and Steiner (1998); 16 countries from Hogan (1999).

15. For a discussion of the new dispute resolution rules, see Thomas and Meyer (1997).

16. New guidelines from USDOS (1999); on the status of the shrimp-turtle case at the WTO, see BRIDGES (1999a).

17. For the historical backdrop to the beef hormone case, see USOTA (1992); for more recent events, see Jacobs (1999); Suzman (1999); and Balter (1999).

18. De Jonquieres (1999); *Business and the Environment* (1999); *Reuters* (1999a, 1999b); use of GMOs in U.S. food products from Weiss (1999); on the move of European companies away from GMOs, see Willman (1999) and Hargreaves (1999); on the trade conflicts over labeling, see *Nature* (1999), *International Environment Reporter* (1999a).

19. Requirements of proposed agreement from *Reuters* (1999c), USTR and CEQ (1999); for a general discussion on the expected impact of trade liberalization on forests, see Kaimowitz (1999).

20. For acknowledgement of the need for WTO reforms, see Clinton (1999), Group of Eight (1999); proposals to reduce subsidies from *Financial Times* (1999b), WTO (1999); $14–20 billion from Milazzo (1998).

21. For ideas on needed steps to reform the rules of world trade, see USEO (1999), NWF (1999), WWF-International (1999a), Wallach and Sforza (1999).

22. On the reasons for the surge of private capital flows into the developing world in the early 1990s, see World Bank (1997), de Larosiere (1996).

23. Private capital flows and Figure 26.4 from World Bank (1999a), with figures deflated as described in note 4; $1.5 trillion from BIS (1999).

24. History of crisis from World Bank (1998); capital outflows from IMF (1999); $40 billion from Duffy (1998), *U.S. News and World Report* (1998); Brazil from Lozado (1998); $42-billion bailout from *Economist* (1998).

25. Poverty and social fallout from World Bank (1998), Wolfensohn (1998), and Sullivan (1998); Indonesian poaching from Waldman (1998); on the environmental impacts of the crisis, see generally World Bank, East Asia Environment and Social Development Unit (1999) and Dauvergne (1999).

26. Signs of economic recovery from IMF (1999); poverty rates from World Bank (1999b) and Severino (1999); future instability from Garten (1999).

27. Total lending and adjustment lending from World Bank (1999c); policy reforms from Stiglitz (1998).

28. Sunderlin (1998); Indonesian palm exports from UNFAO (1999b); recent fires from *Reuters* (1999d) and *Washington Post* (1997, 1998).

29. Asian cuts in environmental spending from World Bank (1999d); Russia from Friends of the Earth–US (undated); Brazil from Schemo (1999); high rates of deforestation from Nepstad et al. (1999).

30. I am indebted to Frances Seymour of the World Resources Institute for suggesting that the IMF's surveillance function might be expanded to cover environmental issues.

31. World Bank policy on adjustment lending from World Bank (undated); 60 percent from World Bank (1993); less than 20 percent from Dunne (1999b); World Bank environmental assessment policy as it applies to adjustment lending from McPhail (1999); failure of IMF to require environmental impact assessments from Welch (1988).

32. Description of World Bank private-sector operations from World Bank (1999c); 10 percent from World Bank (1995). The World Bank has not updated this estimate in more recent annual reports.

33. For a description of the World Bank Group's environmental policies and guidelines, see World Bank (1999d); IFC (1998); MIGA (undated); on the Bank's shortcomings in implementing policies, see Boulton (1996) and Suzman (1998); on importance of World Bank standards as a point of reference for private investors, see IER(1995) and World Bank (1999d).

34. Knight (1999); Berne Declaration et al. (1999); export credit support in 1988 from Boote (1995); support in 1996 from Boote and Ross (1998); 10 percent is a Berne Union estimate cited in Dunne (1998).

35. USOPIC (1999); US Ex-IM Bank (1998); Three Gorges from Berne Declaration et al. (1999) and *Harvard International Review* (1998); countries working on standards from Foster (1999); international discussions on common standards from Group of Eight (1999).

36. "Global Reporting Initiative," background information available at <www.ceres.org/reporting/globalreporting.html>; *Environmental News Service* (1999).

37. On the need for a global society to complement the global economy, see Soros (1998b) and Rodrik (1998).

38. Treaties and Figure 26.5 are compiled from UNEP (1996), UN (undated), and UNEP (1998a).

39. UNEP (1998b), Taylor (1997); whale takes in 1961 from Kemf and Phillips (1995); current whale takes is a Worldwatch estimate based on WWF-I

(1999b) and on Mulvaney (1999); decline in oil spills from McGinn (1999); The Antarctic Project (1999).

40. For a prominent proposal to create a Global Environmental Organization, see Esty (1993, 1994). Both James Gustave Speth, former Administrator of the U.N. Development Programme, and Renato Ruggiero, former Director-General of the WTO, have voiced support for creating a World Environment Organization over the last few years; see Speth (1996) and Ruggiero (1999).

41. On the distinction between governance and governments, see CGG (1995) and Reinicke (1998).

42. International Federation of Organic Agriculture Movements from Madden and Chaplowe (1997); Forest Stewardship Council (1999); Marine Stewardship Council (1999).

43. For a general discussion of the growing strength of NGOs, see Runyon (1999); on NGO activism in the developing world, see Anheir and Salamon (1998) and Friedland (1997); growth of international NGOs is a Worldwatch Institute estimate based on UIA (1999); environmental NGOs as share of total from Keck and Sikkink (1998), based on data from the Union of International Organizations.

44. On the role of activists in overturning the Multilateral Agreement on Investment, see Drohan (1998); for activists' role in opposing biotechnology, see Lambrecht (1999).

References

Abramovitz, Janet N. 1998. *Taking a Stand: Cultivating a New Relationship with the World's Forests.* Worldwatch Paper 140. Washington, D.C.: Worldwatch Institute. (April).

Ahmed, Mahfuzuddin. 1997. "Fish for the Poor Under a Rising Global Demand and Changing Fishery Regime." *NAGA, The ICLARM Quarterly* (July–December).

Anheier, Helmut K. and Lester M. Salamon, editors. 1998. *The Nonprofit Sector in the Developing World.* New York: Manchester University Press.

The Antarctic Project. 1999. The Protocol on Environmental Protection to the Antarctic Treaty. 14 June. www.asoc.org/currentpress/protocol.htm, viewed 3 November 1999.

Aslam, Abid. 1999. "Finance-Environment: Chinese Dam Tests 'Green' Banking Club." *Inter Press Service*, 13 September.

Balter, Michael. 1999. "Scientific Cross-Claims Fly in Continuing Beef War." *Science*, 28 May.

Bank for International Settlements (BIS). 1999. *Central Bank Survey of Foreign Exchange and Derivatives Market Activity in April 1998.* Basel, Switzerland: BIS. (May).

Benjapolchai, Patareeya. 1997. Stock Exchange Policies for Protecting the Environment. Address by the Senior Vice President, Stock Exchange of Thailand to The Environment and Financial Performance, UNEP's Third International Roundtable Meeting on Finance and the Environment, Columbia University, New York, 22–23 May.

Berne Declaration et al. 1999. *A Race to the Bottom.* Washington, D.C. (March).

Boote, Anthony. 1995. *Official Financing for Developing Countries.* Washington, D.C.: IMF.

Boote, Anthony, and Doris Ross. 1998. *Official Financing for Developing Countries.* Washington, D.C.: IMF.

Boulton, Leyla. 1996. "World Bank Admits to Weakness on Environment." *Financial Times*, 4 October.

BRIDGES. 1999a. "Implementation Status of Shrimp-Turtle Ruling. *BRIDGES: Between Trade and Sustainable Development* (July–August).

———. 1999b. "Big Mac Targeted by French Farmers." *BRIDGES: Weekly Trade News Digest*, 30 August.

Bright, Christopher. 1999. "Invasive Species: Pathogens of Globalization." *Foreign Policy* (Fall).

———. 1998. *Life Out of Bounds*. New York: W.W. Norton.

Bryant, Dirk, Daniel Nielsen, and Laura Tangley. 1997. *The Last Frontier Forests*. Washington, D.C.: World Resources Institute.

Buckley, Stephen. 1997. "Senegalese Fish for a Living in Sea Teeming with Industrial Rivals." *International Herald Tribune*, 4 November.

Business and the Environment. 1998. "EU Finalizes Labeling Rules for Genetically Modified Foods." (July).

Cameron, James, and Julie Abouchar. 1996. "The Status of the Precautionary Principle in International Law." In *The Precautionary Principle and International Law,* edited by David Freestone and Ellen Hey, The Hague: Kluwer Law International.

Charnovitz, Steve. 1996. "Restraining the Use of Trade Measures in Multilateral Agreements: An Outline of the Issues," presentation at the Conference on the Relationship Between the Multilateral Trading System and the Use of Trade Measures in Multilateral Agreements: Synergy or Friction? The Hague, 22–23 January.

Christensen, Eric and Samantha Geffin. 1991–1992. "GATT Sets Its Net on Environmental Regulation: The GATT Panel Ruling on Mexican Yellowfin Tuna Imports and the Need for Reform of the International Trading System." *Inter-American Law Review* (Winter).

Climate Action Network (CAN). Undated. Climate Action Network: A Force for Change. www.climatenetwork.org, viewed 6 July 1999.

Clinton, William Jefferson. 1999. Remarks at the Commemoration of the 50th Anniversary of the World Trade Organization. Geneva, 18 May.

Commission on Global Governance (CGG). 1995. *Our Global Neighborhood*. New York: Oxford University Press.

Dauvergne, Peter. 1999. *The Environment in Times of Crisis*, report commissioned by the Australian Agency for International Development. (April).

Drohan, Madelaine. 1998. "How the Net Killed the MAI." *Toronto Globe and Mail*, 29 April.

Duffy, Brian. 1998. "Market Chaos Goes Global." *U.S. News and World Report*. 14 September.

Dunne, Nancy. 1999a. "Legal Wrangle Engulfs US Shrimp Dispute." *Financial Times*, 14 April.

———. 1999b. "World Bank: Projects 'Fail' the Poor." *Financial Times*, 24 September.

———. 1998. "Environmentalists Damn Export Credit Agencies' Policies." *Financial Times*, 31 July.

Durbin, Andrea, and Carol Welch. 1998. "Greening the Bretton Woods Institutions: Sustainable Development Recommendations for the World Bank and the International Monetary Fund." Washington, D.C.: Friends of the Earth—US. (December).

Earthjustice Legal Defense Fund and Northwest Ecosystem Alliance (ELDF). 1999. *Our Forests at Risk: The World Trade Organization's Threat to Forest Protection*. Seattle, WA: Earthjustice Legal Defense Fund.

The Economist. 1999. "Time For a Redesign?" 30 January.
———. 1998. "The Real 'Thing.'" 21 November.
Entous, Adam. 1998. "WTO Rules Against U.S. on Sea Turtle Protection Law." *Reuters*, 6 April.
Environmental News Service. 1999. "Ceres Green Reporting Guidelines Launched." 3 March.
Esty, Daniel C. 1998. "Non-Governmental Organizations at the World Trade Organization: Cooperation, Competition, or Exclusion." *Journal of International Economic Law* (March).
———. 1994. "The Case for a Global Environmental Organization." In *Managing the World Economy: Fifty Years After Bretton Woods*, Peter B. Kenen, ed., Washington, D.C.: Institute for International Economics.
———. 1993. "GATTing the Greens." *Foreign Affairs* (November/December).
Financial Times. 1999a. "World Trade: Trade Tensions: The Biosafety Protocol Has Been Undermined by a Clash Between the Interests of US Multinationals and European Consumers." 26 February.
———. 1999b. "World News Appeal to End Fishing Subsidies." 2 August.
Forest Stewardship Council. 1999. "Who We Are." information sheet. www.fscoax. org, viewed 29 June 1999.
Foster, Pam. 1999. Discussion with Lisa Mastny, Worldwatch Institute. Halifax Initiative, Ottawa, ON, Canada, 4 November.
Friedland, Jonathan. 1997. "Across Latin America, New Environmentalists Extend Their Reach." *Wall Street Journal*, 26 March.
Friedman, Thomas L. 1999. *The Lexus and the Olive Tree.* New York: Farrar, Strauss and Giroux.
Friends of the Earth—US. Undated. "Environmental Consequences of the IMF's Lending Policies." information sheet, Washington, D.C.: Friends of the Earth.
Fugazzotto, Peter and Todd Steiner. 1998. *Slain by Trade: The Attack of the World Trade Organization on Sea Turtles and the US Endangered Species Act.* San Francisco: Sea Turtle Restoration Project. (July).
Gandhi, Ved P. 1998. *The IMF and the Environment.* Washington, D.C.: IMF.
Garten, Jeffrey E. 1999. "A Crisis Without a Reform." *New York Times*, 18 August.
General Agreement on Trade and Tariffs (GATT). 1991. *United States—Restrictions on Imports of Tuna: Report of the Panel.* Geneva: GATT. 3 September.
Government of Indonesia. 1999. Supplementary Memorandum of Economic and Financial Policies: Fourth Review Under the Extended Agreement. document submitted to Michel Camdessus, Managing Director of the IMF, 16 March. Available www.imf.org/external/np/loi/1999/031699.htm, viewed 19 October 1999.
Group of Eight. 1999. G-8 Communique Koln 1999. press release, Cologne, 20 June.
Guruswamy, Lakshman, Geoffrey Palmer, and Burns Weston. 1994. *International Environmental Law and World Order.* St. Paul, MN: West Publishing.
Hargreaves, Deborah. 1999. "Consumers' Unease Leads to Rethink on Modified Food Supplies." *Financial Times*, 29–30 May.
Harvard International Review. 1998. "Breaking the Wall: China and the Three Gorges Dam." (Summer).
Hill, Julie, Doreen Fedrigo, and Ingrid Marshall. 1997. *Banking on the Future: A Survey of Implementation of the UNEP Statement by Banks on Environment and Sustainable Development.* London: Green Alliance. (March).
Hogan, David. 1999. Letter to author, Office of Marine Conservation, Bureau of Oceans and International Environmental and Scientific Affairs, U.S. Department of State, 24 September.

Houlder, Vanessa. 1999. "Greens Gun for Finance." *Financial Times*, 9 February.

IISD. 1996. *Global Green Standards: ISO 14000 and Sustainable Development.* Winnipeg, Manitoba, Canada: IISD.

International Environment Reporter (IER). 1999a. "U.S., Canada Concerned About Increase in Labeling Measures Affecting GMOs." 23 June.

———. 1999b. "Governments to Discuss Restarting Stalemated Talks on Biosafety Protocol." 23 June.

———. 1997. "IMF Decides Once Again to Halt Disbursement of Loans Because of Illegal Timber Practices." 15 October.

———. 1995. "Attorney Says Environmental 'Trends Will Have Far-Reaching Impact on U.S. Firms.'" 1 November.

International Finance Corporation (IFC). 1998. "Procedure for Environmental and Social Review of Projects." information sheet. Washington, D.C.: IFC. (December).

International Monetary Fund (IMF). 1999. *World Economic Outlook.* Washington, D.C.: IMF. (October).

International POPS Elimination Network (IPOPSEN). Undated. Organizational Structure. www.psr.org/ipen/ipen_structure.htm, viewed 1 July 1999.

Jacobs, Paul. 1999. "U.S., Europe Lock Horns in Beef Hormone Debate." *Los Angeles Times*, 9 April.

de Jonquieres, Guy. 1999. "Genetically Modified 'Trade Wars.'" *Financial Times*, 18 February.

Kaimowitz, David. 1999. "The Potential Environmental Impacts of Trade Liberalisation in Forest Products." *BRIDGES Between Trade and Sustainable Development.* (July–August).

Kakakhel, Shafqat. 1999. Statement made by the Deputy Executive Director, U.N. Environment Programme (UNEP), on behalf of the Executive Director, at UNEP Workshop on Enforcement and Compliance with Multilateral Environmental Agreements, Geneva, 12 July.

Keck, Margaret E. and Kathryn Sikkink. 1998. *Activists Beyond Borders.* Ithaca, N.Y.: Cornell University Press.

Kemf, Elizabeth and Cassandra Phillips. 1995. *Wanted Alive! Whales in the Wild.* Gland, Switzerland: 4VWF-International. (October).

Kent, George. 1997. "Fisheries, Food Security, and the Poor." *Food Policy*, 22, no. 5.

Knight, Danielle. 1999. "Finance-Environment: Increased Lending for Destructive Projects," *Inter Press Service*, 22 February.

Korten, David C. 1995. *When Corporations Rule the World.* West Hartford, CT: Kumarian Press.

Krut, Riva and Harris Gleckman. 1998. *ISO 14001: A Missed Opportunity for Sustainable Global Industrial Development.* London: Earthscan Publications Ltd.

Lambrecht, Bill. 1999. "Biotechnology Companies Face New Foe: The Internet." *St. Louis Post Dispatch*, 20 September.

de Larosiere, Jacques. 1996. Financing Development in a World of Private Capital Flows: The Challenge for Multilateral Development Banks in Working with the Private Sector. The Per Jacobsson Lecture, Washington, DC, 29 September.

Linden, Eugene. 1998. *The Future in Plain Sight: Nine Clues to the Coming Instability.* New York: Simon & Schuster.

Longworth, R.C. 1999. "Activists on Internet Reshaping Rules of Global Economy." *Chicago Tribune*, 5 July.

Lozado, Carlos. 1998. "Brazilian Domino Effect?" *Christian Science Monitor.* 9 November.

Madden, J. Patrick and Scott G. Chaplowe. 1997. *For ALL Generations: Making World Agriculture More Sustainable.* Glendale, CA: OM Publishing.

Marine Stewardship Council. 1999. "Our Empty Seas: A Global Problem, A Global Solution." Information brochure. London: MSC. (April).

McGinn, Anne Platt. 1999. *Safeguarding the Health of Oceans.* Worldwatch Paper 145. Washington, DC: Worldwatch Institute. (March).

McPhail, Kathryn. 1999. Comment at meeting of NGOs with Ian Johnson, Vice President, Environmentally & Socially Sustainable Development, World Bank, 26 May.

Miami Herald. 1999. "Trade Court Backs Protecting Turtles From Shrimpers' Nets," 9 April.

Milazzo, Matteo. 1998. *Subsidies in World Fisheries. A Reexamination*, World Bank Technical Paper No. 406, Fisheries Series. Washington, D.C.: World Bank. (April).

Monroe, Ann. 1999. "The Looming EcoWar." *Investment Dealers' Digest*, 24 May.

Montanaro, Sara. 1999. Statement by Statistical Clerk, Fishery Information, Data, and Statistics Unit, UNFAO Fisheries Department, e-mail to Lisa Mastny, Worldwatch Institute, 6 September.

Moody, Roger. 1996. "The Lure of Gold—How Golden Is the Future?" Panos Media Briefing No. 19. London: Panos Institute. (May).

Multilateral Investment Guarantee Agency (MIGA). Undated. Environmental and Social Review Procedures. <www.miga.org/disclose/soc_rev.htm>, viewed 4 November 1999.

Mulvaney, Kieran. 1999. "The Whaling Effect." news feature. Gland, Switzerland: WWF-International. (October).

Myers, Norman. 1997. "The World's Forests and Their Ecosystem Services." In *Nature's Services*, Gretchen C. Daily, ed., Washington, D.C.: Island Press.

National Resources Defense Council and Foundation for International Environmental Law and Development (NRDC and FIELD). 1995. *Environmental Priorities for the World Trading System.* Washington, D.C.: NRDC. (January).

National Wildlife Federation (NWF). 1999. *What's TRADE Got To Do With It?* Washington, D.C.: NWF.

National Wildlife Federation and Friends of the Earth-US (NWF and FE-US). 1999. "Three Gorges Dam Sneaking Its Way into Capital Markets." *The Bull and Bear Newsletter*, 20 January.

Nature. 1999. "Europe and US in Confrontation Over GM Food Labelling Criteria." 22 April.

New York Times. 1999. "U.S. Imposes Sanctions in Beef Fight." 19 July.

Nepstad, Daniel C. et al. 1999. "Large-scale Impoverishment of Amazonian Forests by Logging and Fire." *Nature*, 8 April.

Perotti, Maurizio. 1997. E-mail statement, from Fishery Information, Data and Statistics Unit, UNFAO, Rome, to Anne Platt McGinn, Worldwatch Institute, 14 October.

Pesticide Action Network North America (PAN). Undated. "What is PANNA?" www.panna.org/panna/whatis.html, viewed 1 July 1999.

Reed, David. ed. 1996. *Structural Adjustment, the Environment, and Sustainable Development.* London: Earthscan Publications.

Reinicke, Wolfgang H. 1998. *Global Public Policy.* Washington, D.C.: Brookings Institution Press.

Reuters. 1999a. "Japan Risks U.S. Ire With GMO Label Plan." 5 August.

———. 1999b. "Australia, NZ Require Mandatory GM Labels on Food." 4 August.

———. 1999c. "U.S. Says Trade Plan Won't Hurt Forests." 4 November.

————. 1999d. "Indonesian Fires Blamed on Plantations." 10 August.

Rodrik, Dani. 1998. "The Global Fix." *New Republic*, 2 November.

Ruggiero, Renato. 1999. Opening Remarks to the High Level Symposium on Trade and the Environment. 15 March. www.wto.org/wto/hlms/dgenv.htm, viewed 14 April 1999.

Runyan, Curtis. 1999. "The Third Force: NGOs." *Worldwatch*. (November/December).

Sachs, Jeffrey. 1997. "IMF Is a Power Unto Itself." *Financial Times*, 11 December.

Sampson, Gary P. 1999. "Trade, Environment, and the WTO: A Framework for Moving Forward." Overseas Development Council Policy Paper. Washington, D.C.: Overseas Development Council. (February).

Saverino, Jean Michel. 1999. East Asia Regional Overview. From Vice President, East Asia and Pacific Region, World Bank. Washington, DC: World Bank. 23 September.

Schemo, Diana Jean. 1999. "Brazil Slashes Money for Project Aimed at Protecting Amazon." *New York Times*, 1 January.

Schmidheiny, Stephan and Federico J. L. Zorraquín [with the World Business Council for Sustainable Development]. 1996. *Financing Change*. Cambridge, MA: MIT Press.

Soros, George. 1998a. *The Crisis of Global Capitalism*. New York: Public Affairs.

————. 1998b. "Toward a Global Open Society." *The Atlantic Monthly*, January.

Speth, James Gustave. 1996. "Note Regarding Questions on UN Reform Proposals." Unpublished document. 4 October.

Stiglitz, Joseph. 1998. More Instruments and Broader Goals: Moving Toward the Post-Washington Consensus. The 1988 WIDER Annual Lecture, Helsinki, Finland, 7 January. <www.worldbank.org/html/extdr/extme/js-010798/wider. htm>, viewed 19 October 1999.

Sullivan, Kevin. 1998. "A Generation's Future Goes Begging: Asia's Children Losing to Destitution." *Washington Post*. 7 September.

Sunderlin, William D. 1998. "Between Danger and Opportunity: Indonesia's Forests in an Era of Economic Crisis and Political Challenge." Consultative Group on International Agricultural Research, 11 September. <www.cgiar.org/cifor/>, viewed 8 October 1998.

Suzman, Mark. 1999. American Farmers Baffled as Europe Steers Clear of Beef Treated By Hormones. *Financial Times*, 22 July.

————. 1998. "World Bank Accuses Itself of 'Serious Violations.'" *Financial Times*, 7 January.

Swardson, Anne. 1999a. "Trade Body Summit Targeted for Protests." *Washington Post*, 2 November.

————. 1999b. "Something is Rotten in Roquefort." *Washington Post*, 21 August.

————. 1998. "Turtle-Protection Law Overturned By WTO." *Washington Post*, 13 October.

Taylor, Caroline. 1997. "The Challenge of African Elephant Conservation." *Conservation Issues*. World Wildlife Fund. (April).

Thomas, Jeffrey S., and Michael A. Meyer. 1997. *The New Rules of Global Trade: A Guide to the World Trade Organization*. Scarborough, Ontario, Canada: Carswell.

Thomson, Adam. 1999. "Efforts to Adopt UN Biosafety Protocol Fail." *Financial Times*, 25 February.

Thrupp, Lori Ann. 1995. *Bittersweet Harvests for Global Supermarkets*. Washington, D.C.: World Resources Institute.

Torres, Hector Rogelio. 1998. *Environmental Rent: Cooperation and Competition in the Multilateral Trading System*. Winnipeg, Manitoba, Canada: International Institute for Sustainable Development.

TRAFFIC North America. 1994. "World Trade in Wildlife." Information sheet, Washington, D.C.: TRAFFIC North America (July).

Union of International Associations (UIA). 1999. *Yearbook of International Organizations 1998–1999*. Munich: K.G. Saur Verlag.

United Nations. Undated. The United Nations Treaty Collection, electronic database, www/un/org/Depts/Treaty, viewed 9 March 1999.

United Nations Conference on Trade and Development (UNCTAD). 1995. *Handbook of World Mineral Trade Statistics 1992–1997*. Geneva: United Nations.

United Nations Environmental Program. 1999a. "19 New Signatories to the Financial Services Initiatives." *The Bottom Line*. (UNEP Financial Services Initiative newsletter), (Spring).

———. 1999b. "New Signatories to the Initiatives." *The Bottom Line*. (UNEP Financial Services Initiative newsletter), (summer).

———. 1998a. International Conventions and Protocols in the Field of the Environment: Report of the Executive Director. prepared for UNEP Governing Council Twentieth Session, 13 November.

———. 1998b. *Data Report on Production and Consumption of Ozone-Depleting Substances, 1986–1996*. Nairobi: UNEP (November).

———. 1997a. "Bankers to Link Environment and Financial Performance." Press release. New York: UNEP, 16 May.

———. 1997b. "UNEP Statement by Financial Institutions on the Environment and Sustainable Development." Revised version, May 1997. www.unep.ch/eteu/finserv/english.html, viewed 3 November 1999.

———. 1996. *Register of International Treaties and Other Agreements in the Field of the Environment 1996*. Nairobi: UNEP.

United Nations Food and Agriculture Organization (UNFAO). 1999a. *State of the World's Forests 1999*. Rome: United Nations.

———. 1999b. *FAOSTAT Statistics Database*, electronic database, <apps.fao.org>, viewed 22 October 1999.

———. 1999c. Y*earbook of Fishery Statistics*, vol. 84. Rome: United Nations.

———. 1999d. *Yearbook of Fishery Statistics*, vol. 85. Rome: United Nations.

———. 1997. *The State of World Fisheries and Aquaculture, 1996*. Rome: United Nations.

———. 1983. *Yearbook of Fishery Statistics*, vol. 53. Rome: United Nations.

———. 1978. *Yearbook of Fishery Statistics*, vol. 45. Rome: United Nations.

United States Department of Agriculture. 1999. *Production, Supply, and Distribution*, electronic database, Washington, DC, updated November 1999.

United States Department of Commerce (USDOC). 1999. *Survey of Current Business*. (July).

United States Department of State (USDOS). 1999. "Revised Guidelines for the Implementation of Section 609 of Public Law 101-162 Relating to the Protection of Sea Turtles in Shrimp Trawl Fishing Operations," Public Notice 3086, *Federal Register*, 8 July.

U.S. Environmental Organizations (USEO). 1999. "The World Trade Organization and the Environment." Technical Statement. 16 July.

United States Export-Import Bank (USEx-Im Bank). 1998. "Ex-Im Bank and the Environment." Information sheet. Washington, DC: Export-Import Bank. (June).

United States Office of Technology Assessment (USOTA). 1992. *Trade and Environment: Conflicts and Opportunities.* Washington, D.C.: U.S. Government Printing Office. (May).

United States Office of the U.S. Trade Representative and Council on Environmental Quality (USTR and CEQ). 1999. *Accelerated Tariff Liberalization in the Forest Products Sector: A Study of the Economic and Environmental Effects.* Washington, D.C.: Government Printing Office. (November).

United States Overseas Private Investment Corporation (USOPIC). 1999. *OPIC Environmental Handbook.* Washington, D.C.: OPIC. (April).

US News & World Report. 1998. "Market Chaos Goes Global." 14 September.

Von Moltke, Konrad. 1998. Untitled paper. In *Policing the Global Economy: Why, How, and For Whom?* Edited by Sadruddin Aga Khan, Proceedings of an International Conference held in Geneva, March 1998. London: Cameron May Ltd.

Waldman, Peter. 1998. "Desperate Indonesians Devour Country's Trove of Endangered Species." *Wall Street Journal.* 26 October.

Wallach, Lori, and Michelle Sforza. 1999. *Whose Trade Organization?* Washington, D.C.: Public Citizen.

Washington Post. 1998. "With Nothing Left to Burn, Fires Mostly Out." 25 April.

———. 1997. "Asian Nations Reach Accord On Fighting Haze." 24 December.

Weiss, Rick. 1999. "In Europe, Cuisine du Gene Gets a Vehement Thumbs Down." *Washington Post.* 24 April.

Welch, Carol. 1988. "In Focus: The IMF and Good Governance." *U.S. Foreign Policy in Focus.* (October).

Willman, John. 1999. 'Consumer Power Forces Food Industry to Modify Approach." *Financial Times.* 10 June.

Wolfensohn, James D. 1998. The Other Crisis. Annual Meetings Address by the President, World Bank Group, Washington, DC, 6 October.

Women's Environment & Development Organization (WEDO). Undated. "About WEDO." www.wedo.org/about/about.htm, viewed 1 July 1999.

World Bank. 1999a. *Global Development Finance 1999.* Washington, D.C.: World Bank.

———. 1999b. "Poverty Trends and Voices of the Poor." Washington, D.C.: World Bank, available at <wb.forumone.com/poverty/data/Tends>.

———. 1999c. *Annual Report 1999.* Washington, D.C.: World Bank.

———. 1999d. *Environment Matters, Annual Review.* Washington, D.C.: World Bank.

———. 1998. *East Asia: The Road to Recovery.* Washington, D.C.: World Bank. (October).

———. 1997. *Private Capital Flows to Developing Countries.* New York: Oxford University Press.

———. 1995. *Annual Report 1995.* Washington, D.C.: Oxford University Press.

———. 1993. *The Evolution of Environmental Concerns in Adjustment Lending: A Review.* prepared for the CIDIE Workshop on Environmental Impacts of Economywide Policies in Developing Countries, Washington, DC, 23–25 February.

———. Undated. "OD 8.60, Adjustment Lending Policy." In *The World Bank Operational Manual.* www.wbln0018.worldbank.org/Institutional/Manuals/OpManuals.nsf

World Bank, East Asia Environment and Social Development Unit. 1999. *Environmental Implications of the Economic Crisis and Adjustment in East Asia.* Washington, D.C.: World Bank (January).

World Forum of Fish Workers & Fish Harvesters (WFFWFH). Undated. www.south-asian-initiative.org/wff/intro.htm, viewed 25 June 1999.

World Health Organization (WHO). 1999. *Report on Infectious Diseases*. Geneva: World Health Organization.

———. 1998. *Health and Environment in Sustainable Development*. Geneva: World Health Organization.

World Resources Institute (WRI). 1996. *World Resources 1996–97*. Washington, D.C.: Oxford University Press.

World Trade Organization (WTO). 1999. Agriculture and the Environment: The Case of Export Subsidies. Submission by Argentina et al. to the WTO's Committee on Trade and Environment. Geneva, 11 February.

———. 1998a. *Annual Report 1998*. Geneva: World Trade Organization.

———. 1998b. *United States—Import Prohibition of Certain Shrimp and Shrimp Products*. Geneva: World Trade Organization. 12 October.

———. 1998c. "EC Measures Concerning Meat and Meat Products (Hormones)." Report of the Appellate Body. Geneva: WTO, 16 January.

———. Undated. "Agreement on the Application of Sanitary and Phytosanitary Measures," in *Final Act: Agreement Establishing the World Trade Organization*, <www.wto.org/wto/eol/e/pdf/15-sps.pdf>, viewed 1 November 1999.

World Wide Fund for Nature (WWF-International). 1999a. *Sustainable Trade for a Living Planet: Reforming the World Trade Organization*. Gland, Switzerland: WWF-International. (September).

———. 1999b. "Japanese Fleet Returns from Whale Sanctuary With 389 Minkes." press release. Gland, Switzerland, 23 April.

Young, John E. 1994. "Gold Production at Record High." In *Vital Signs 1994*, Lester R. Brown, Hal Kane, and David Malin Roodman, eds., New York: W.W. Norton.

———. 1992. *Mining the Earth*. Worldwatch Paper 109. Washington, DC: Worldwatch Institute (July).

27

The Westfailure System

Susan Strange

This work represents one of the last items written by Susan Strange before her untimely death in 1998. As a major contributor to the field of international political economy, Strange offers a penetrating—and pessimistic— look at the future of the state-based international system. At the heart of her analysis are three fundamental failures of the state system: (1) an inability to manage the international financial system, (2) a lack of action to stop environmental destruction, and (3) a failure to stop the growing gap between rich and poor, countries and citizens alike. Not only has the state system failed to deal with these, she argues, but by its very nature is incapable of doing so. Strange offers a brief tantalizing look at the question of "what is to be done." It is unfortunate, then, that her passing makes it impossible for her to elaborate further on this critically important question.

From an international political economy perspective, the international political system of states claiming exclusive authority and the monopoly of legitimate violence within their territorial limits—the so-called Westphalia system—is inseparable from the prevailing capitalist market economy which also first evolved in Europe. Each was a necessary condition for the evolution of the other. To prosper, production and trade required the security provided by the state. To survive, the state required the economic growth, and the credit-creating system of finance, provided by the economic system. But the latter has now created three major problems that the political system, by its very nature, is incapable of solving. First, there is the major failure to manage and control the financial system—witness the Asian turmoil of 1997. Second, there is the failure to act for the protection

Reprinted with permission of the publisher from *Review of International Studies*, volume 2, number 3 (1999), pp. 345–354. New York: Cambridge University Press.

of the environment. Third, there is a failure to preserve a socio-economic balance between the rich and powerful and the poor and weak. The Westfailure system is thus failing Capitalism, the Planet and global (and national) civil society.

From a globalist, humanitarian and true political economy perspective, the system known as Westphalian has been an abject failure. Those of us engaged in international studies ought therefore to bend our future thinking and efforts to the consideration of ways in which it can be changed or superseded. That is the gist of my argument.

The system can be briefly defined as that in which prime political authority is conceded to those institutions, called states, claiming the monopoly of legitimate use of violence within their respective territorial borders. It is a system purporting to rest on mutual restraint (non-intervention); but it is also a system based on mutual recognition of each other's "sovereignty" if that should be challenged from whatever quarter.

But while we constantly refer to the "international political system" or to the "security structure"[1] this Westphalian system cannot realistically be isolated from—indeed is inseparable from—the market economy which the states of Europe, from the mid-17th century onwards, both nurtured and promoted. To the extent that the powers of these states over society and over economy grew through the 18th, 19th and 20th centuries, they did so both in response to the political system in which states competed with other states (for territory at first but later for industrial and financial power) and in response to the growing demands made on political authority as a result of the capitalist system of production and its social consequences. The label "capitalist" applied to the market-driven economy is justified because the accumulation of capital, as the Marxists put it, or the creation and trading in credit as I would describe it, was the necessary condition for continued investment of resources in the new technologies of agriculture, manufacture and services (Germain 1997). As I put it in *States and Markets*, the security structure and the production, financial and knowledge structures constantly interact with each other and cannot therefore be analysed in isolation. The point is "kids stuff" to social and economic historians but is frequently overlooked by writers on international relations.

When I say that the system has failed, I do not mean to say that it is collapsing, only that it has failed to satisfy the long-term conditions of sustainability. Like the empires of old—Persian, Roman, Spanish, British or Tsarist Russian—the signs of decline and ultimate disintegration appear some while before the edifice itself collapses. These signs are to be seen already in the three areas in which the system's sustainability is in jeopardy. One area is ecological: the Westfailure system is unable by its nature to correct and reverse the processes of environmental damage that threaten the survival of not only our own but other species of animals and plants.

Another is financial: the Westfailure system is unable—again, because of its very nature—to govern and control the institutions and markets that create and trade the credit instruments essential to the "real economy." The last area is social: the Westfailure system is unable to hold a sustainable balance between the constantly growing power of what the neo-Gramscians call the transnational capitalist class (TCC) and that of the "have nots," the social underclasses, the discontents that the French call *les exclus*—immigrants, unemployed, refugees, peasants, and all those who already feel that globalisation does nothing for them and are inclined to look to warlords, Mafias or extreme-right fascist politicians for protection. The point here is that until quite recently the state through its control over the national economy, and with the fiscal resources it derived from it, was able to act as an agent of economic and social redistribution, operating welfare systems that gave shelter to the old, the sick, the jobless and the disabled. This made up for the decline in its role—in Europe particularly—as defender of the realm against foreign invasion. Now, however, its ability to act as such a shield and protector of the underprivileged is being rapidly eroded—and for reasons to which I shall return in a while.

In short, the system is failing Nature—the planet Earth—which is being increasingly pillaged, perverted and polluted by economic enterprises which the state-system is unable to control or restrain. It is failing Capitalism in that the national and international institutions that are supposed to manage financial markets are progressively unable—as recent developments in east Asia demonstrate—to keep up with the accelerating pace of technological change in the private sectors, with potentially dire consequences for the whole world market economy. And it is failing world society by allowing a dangerously wide gap to develop between the rich and powerful and the weak and powerless.

The fact that the system survives despite its failures only shows the difficulty of finding and building an alternative. No one is keen to go back to the old colonialist empires. And though Islam and Christian fundamentalism make good sticks with which to beat the western capitalist model, the myriad divisions within both make any kind of theocratic-religious alternative highly improbable. So the old advice, "Keep hold of nurse, for fear of worse" is still widely followed even while faith in her skill and competence is more than a little doubted.

The Symbiosis of Two Systems

To understand how and why the political system based on territorial states and the economic system based on markets and profit came to grow together so closely that they are inseparable the one from the other, a little historical perspective is essential. As I said earlier, this is kids-stuff to historians and sociologists, but perhaps not so much so to many students of international politics.

Recall that the European state in the latter half of the 17th century was almost without exception dynastic, supported by and supporting a land-owning class deriving wealth from agriculture and passing its wealth down by rights of inheritance. The Treaty of 1648 removed one major source of conflict and instability—religion—but did nothing to stop conflicts over the major source of revenue and wealth for the state, which was control of territory and the surplus value created by farming. It would be hard to imagine a political economy further removed from the national economies of the 20th century.

The major difference between the system then and now, in my opinion, concerns the role of money in the state system. In the late 17th century, although states issued coins, they had little control over the choice of the medium of exchange preferred by traders—even within their own national territory, let alone beyond it. The benefits to be derived from seignorage were therefore limited; adding lead to silver coins was common but yielded little extra to state revenues. Thus the opportunities for states to manipulate money for their own advantage were minimal.

Almost coincidentally, the big breakthrough for states came at the turn of the century with the introduction of a new kind of money—state promises-to-pay.[2] Two Scots, John Law and William Patterson, both saw that by this means money could be created with which to replenish the resources of the state by issuing pieces of paper carrying the "guarantee" of the monarch. In France, the venture ended in disaster from overissue of shares and the disgrace of John Law. The Bank of England only just escaped the same fate by passing the management of the state debt to the South Sea Company.[3] But by the end of the 18th century, the idea had caught on. Soldiers could be recruited and wars could be fought on credit; the American War of Independence was funded thus, and Napoleon paid his *Grande Armée* with the issue of assignats—promises to pay said to be guaranteed by the value of French land—but ultimately worthless.

In short, the creation of credit by governments and banks could (and did) boost trade and production in the market economy—but it also allowed the abuse of the system by states. The list of sovereign defaulters on state debt in the 19th century was a long one (Feis 1964). Yet although some economic growth—in the American West especially—was generated by the discovery of new supplies of specie metals, most of it was owed to the creation of credit by banks and by governments (Triffin 1964). Led by Britain and the Bank of England, the developed countries all evolved their own regulatory systems and set up central banks as lenders of last resort to ensure that banks observed prudential rules in creating credit. Britain also passed laws to ensure that the state too behaved prudentially. The Bank

Charter Act of 1844 put strict limits on the right of British governments to expand the money supply—limits only raised when war broke out in 1914. The result was that the value of the pound sterling in terms of gold remained unchanged for a century, thus creating the first stable international money. In the United States, the Federal Reserve System was established belatedly in 1913 only after the shock of the 1907 financial crisis.

These safeguards gave way before the onslaught of a global political system embroiled in the First World War. The Russians on one side and the Germans on the other paid for the war more than most by printing paper. As in Napoleonic times, states in the Westfailure system made desperate by the whip of war practised financial deception on their own and other people. The practice was the Achilles' heel of the market economy. But the history of credit creation clearly showed the symbiosis of the political system of states and the economic system of markets. The entrepreneurs in the market economy needed the security, the law and order, and the state paraphernalia of courts, property rights, contractual rules and so forth to let market forces function with confidence in the other party, whether buyer or seller, creditor or debtor. Equally, the governments of states came to depend on the financial system that private entrepreneurs had developed to create credit. Before the 18th century, heads of state did occasionally borrow from bankers—the Medici were unusual in running their own bank. But it was only after 1700 that the practice took hold of borrowing from society by issuing paper money or government promises-to-pay. By the 20th century, government debt had grown to the point where the financial system had become indispensable for the conduct of state business.

The Three Failures

Let us start with the failure to manage this credit-creating system of finance. Up to summer 1997, the conventional wisdom was that states and their intergovernmental organisations between them were well able to supervise, regulate and control the banks and other institutions that created and traded in credit instruments—from government bonds to securitised corporate paper to derivatives.[4] This was the message of a much-praised study by Ethan Kapstein (1994). While national regulatory systems in each of the major developed economies functioned at the state level, the International Monetary Fund (IMF) and the Bank for International Settlements in Basle (BIS) functioned at the transnational level. This two-level, belt-and-braces system of governance could take care of any problems arising in the markets. But in the course of 1997, events in east Asia cast serious doubt on this comforting conclusion. The turmoil that hit the Malaysian, Indonesian and Thai currencies and stock exchange prices came out of a clear blue sky. Neither of those international regulatory institutions had foreseen or warned against such a contingency. As the turmoil spread and grew, the first rescue packages proved insufficient to restore even minimal confidence and had to be substantially increased. The common factor in all the stricken economies was an influx of mobile short-term capital, too much of which went in ill-considered speculative loans or in unproductive real-estate investments. Prime Minister Mahomed Mahathir of Malaysia blamed George Soros and other foreign speculators who had moved their funds out of the country as quickly as they had taken them in. But it was soon apparent that national regulations over the banks and over short-term capital movements in each of the east Asian countries (Taiwan excepted) had been totally inadequate. The admonitions to embrace financial liberalisation that came from Washington and the IMF had been taken altogether too literally.

But it is not just that the national systems and the international financial organisations were equally unprepared for the shocks of summer and autumn 1997. The case against Epstein's comfortable conclusions concern much more (a) the inadequacy of both the BIS and the IMF as global regulators; and (b) the inadequacy of *all* national systems of financial regulation (Strange 1998: chapters 8, 9). To be fair to Epstein, it only became apparent after he had done his study that the Basle system of capital-adequacy rules devised by the Cooke Committee in the 1980s and subsequently elaborated was not after all really effective. In its 1997 report the BIS more or less admitted as much and, making a virtue out of necessity, announced that in future the supervisory responsibility would rest with the banks themselves. Now, as the Barings story had shown, trusting the poachers to act as gamekeepers was an unconvincing strategy. The bosses at Barings neither knew nor wanted to know what Nick Leeson was up to. Barings' survival under acute international competition made them glad of the profits while discounting the risks he was taking. And even in the most prudent of banks these days, the complexities of derivative trading are often beyond the comprehension of elderly managers.[5]

As for the IMF, its competence to coerce Asian governments into supervising and reforming their banking and financial systems is open to grave doubt. The IMF is used to negotiating with states (especially Latin American ones) over sovereign debts. Its officials—mostly economists—have no experience that helps them catch out wily and secretive bankers when they lie or cover up their business. Moreover, as the record in Kenya, for example, shows, IMF economists have no leverage when it comes to obdurate dictators protecting their corrupt and clientelist power structures. The problem with Suharto is above all political, not technical. The same is true of the African debt problem. Everyone, including the IMF, now agrees that rescheduling old debt in the Highly Indebted Poor Countries (HIPCs) is only making the problem worse, not better. But the IMF and World Bank are unable to force the creditor governments into the necessary agreement on whose debt should be wiped out and by how much (Mistry 1996).

As for the declining effectiveness of national systems of financial regulation and control, this may be less evident to Americans than it is to Europeans and Japanese. The German, French, British and Japanese systems function very differently. But all are currently being undermined by the technological innovations in financial dealing and the almost-instant mobility of capital across borders and currencies (Strange 1998: chapter 8). A dangerous gap is therefore opening up between the international institutions that are unable and unwilling to discipline the banks, the hedge and pension fund managers and the markets, and the national systems of supervision and control whose reach is not long enough nor quick enough to prevent trouble. Eric Helleiner has argued that supervisors now have the technical know-how to trace funds as they move about the global financial system. True, but only far too slowly and with too much painstaking effort; not fast enough nor regularly enough to protect the system (Santiso 1997). So long as tax havens provide a refuge for wrongdoers, from drug dealers to corporate tax-evaders and heads of state who regard their country's aid funds as personal property, the national regulators' hands are tied.

The Environmental Failure

I have put the financial failures of the state-based system first because my recent research has convinced me that it is the most acute and urgent of the current threats-without-enemies. If we do not find ways to safeguard the world economy before a succession of stockmarket collapses and bank failures eventually lands us all in a 20-year economic recession—as the history of the 1930s suggests it might—then no one is going to be in a mood to worry overmuch about the long-term problems of the environment.

On the other hand the environmental danger is much the most serious. The planet—even the market economy—could survive 20 years of slow economic growth. But if nothing is done to stop the deterioration of the environment then the point might come with all these dangers when it was too late. The destructive trend might have become irreversible. Nothing anyone could do then would stop the vicious circle of environmental degradation. And it would be the Westfailure system that brought it about and prevented remedial and preventive action. Why? Because the territorial principle which lies at the heart of it proclaims that the territorial state is responsible for its own land—but not for anyone else's.

There are three distinct kinds of environmental danger. But for each, it is not the lack of technical knowledge, nor of appropriate policy measures that is lacking. It is the ability of the Westfailure system to generate the political will to use them. One is the destruction of the ozone layer. This is mainly attributed to the release of CFC gases from aerosols and other sources. As the "hole" in the ozone layer grows larger, the protection from the sun given by the earth's atmosphere is weakened with serious atmospheric and climatic consequences. Another environmental problem is caused by carbon dioxide and sulphur pollution of the air. Some of this pollution comes from industry. But a lot comes from cars—cars that use petrol or diesel for fuel. Third, there is the depletion of the planet's resources—primarily of water, shrinking the acreage available for cultivation. Secondarily, there is the depletion of forests—not only rainforests—bringing unforeseeable climatic consequences, and also the depletion of species of plants, fish and animals, upsetting ecological balances that have existed for millennia.

With each of these environmental dangers, it is not hard to see that it is the state, with its authority reinforced by the mutual support provided by the Westfailure system, that is the roadblock, stopping remedial action. One consequence of the principle can be seen in the indifference of British governments to the acid rain carried by prevailing westerly winds to Scandinavian forests; or the indifference of US governments to the same kind of damage to Canadian forests. Another can be seen in the impasse reached at the Rio and Kyoto intergovernmental conferences on the environment. European and Japanese concerns left the United States substantially unmoved when it came to stricter controls over CFC gases. Nothing much has changed since. The agreements at the Kyoto conference in 1997 were more cosmetic than substantial. And when it comes to the pollution danger, the biggest *impasse* is between the developed countries and China. Pressure on Beijing from the United States and others to slow down the consumption of fossil fuels for the sake of the environment is met with the question, "If we do, will you pay?" After all, they argue, the environmental dangers you perceive today were the result of your past industrialisation, not ours. Why should you expect us to be more environmentally aware today than you were yesterday? With our growing population, we cannot afford—unless, of course, you are prepared to pay—to slow down our growth to keep the air pure and the water unpolluted. Only rarely, as when Sweden offered to contribute funds to Poland to pay for tougher environmental rules on Polish coal and chemical plants, is the Westphalian territorial principle set aside. But Sweden is rich, was directly damaged by Polish pollution and could justify the transfer on grounds of self-interest. China and the rest of the developing countries are a far bigger nut to crack. So long as the Westfailure system persists, Nature will be its victim.

As Andrew Hurrell commented in a recent review, "the pitfalls outweigh the promise by a very considerable margin" when it comes to transmuting short-term transfers into well-institutionalised long-term commitments on environmental matters (Hurrell 1997: 292). Hurrell also quotes one of the concluding chapters in the book, "The studies of environmental aid in this volume paint a rather dark picture. Constraints on the effectiveness of environmental aid seem more pronounced than windows of opportunity."

The third Westphalian failure is social, or social and economic. The discrepant and divergent figures on infant mortality, on children without enough to eat, on the spread of AIDS in Africa and Asia, and on every other socio-economic indicator tell the story. The gap between rich countries and very poor ones is widening, and so is the gap between the rich and poor in the poor countries and the rich and poor in the rich countries (Kothari 1993). It is not that we do not know the answer to socio-economic inequalities; it is redistributive tax and welfare measures and what Galbraith called countervailing power to make good the tendency of capitalism to private affluence and public penury, and to booms followed by slumps. But applying that answer to world society is frustrated by the Westfailure system, so closely tied in as it is with the "liberalized" market economy. If national Keynesian remedial policies are made difficult by the integrated financial system—as Mitterand found out so painfully in 1983—transnational Keynesian policies are practically inconceivable. We have had one demonstration of this in central Europe in the early 1990s. Here was a case, if ever there was one, for a second Marshall Plan to prime the pump for a rapid transition from state-planning to an open, competitive and therefore productive market economy. But the Reagan and Bush administrations were ideologically unsympathetic and the Germans too self-absorbed in their own unification to bother about the fate of their nearest neighbours. Indifference, whether to central Europe or to Africa, is not just a matter of the selfish, conservative mindsets that Gerald Helleiner recently parodied in verse:

> The poor complain./They always do./But that's just idle chatter./
> Our system brings/Rewards to all/At least to all that matter.(Helleiner1994)

It is actually an inevitable result of the symbiosis between a world market economy and a state-based political system in which those with political authority are inherently unable to see that socio-economic polarisation is not in anyone's long-term interest. It is not just that the underprivileged may riot and loot as in Los Angeles in the 1980s or Jakarta today, or that they may pass their new epidemic diseases to the rich, or wage terrorist campaigns under the guise of religious *jihads*. It is that socio-economic inequality becomes intolerable if people believe it will get worse, not better. They can bear deprivation and hardship if they believe that their children's lot will be better than theirs. Moreover, a flourishing market economy needs new customers, with money to spend, not homeless beggars and starving African farmers. America would not be what it is today without the millions of penniless immigrants that constantly expanded the mass market for its manufactures.

What Is To Be Done?

The two commonest reactions to the three failures of the system I have briefly described are either to deny the failures and to defend the dual capitalism-state system in panglossian fashion as the best of all possible post–Cold War worlds, or else fatalistically to conclude that, despite its shortcomings there is nothing that can be done to change things. Only quite recently has it been possible to detect the first tentative indications of a third response. It is to be heard more from sociologists than from international relations writers, perhaps because sociologists tend to think in terms of social classes and social movements rather than in terms of nation-states. As a recent collection of essays around the theme, "The Direction of Contemporary Capitalism" shows, there is little consensus among them either about current trends or about possible outcomes (RIPE 1997). A good deal of this thinking has been inspired by the rediscovery of Antonio Gramsci and his concepts of hegemony, the historic bloc and social myths that permit effective political action. A common assumption is that the present system is sustained by the power of a transnational capitalist class (TCC).

I have no doubt that such a class exists and does exert its power over the market economy and the rules—such as they are—that govern it. Nearly a decade ago, I referred to it as the dominant "business civilization" (Strange 1990). I think Gill was mistaken in seeing evidence of its power in the Trilateral Commission, which was more a club of well-meaning has-beens than an effective political actor, a mirror rather than a driver. But he was right in spotlighting the emergence of a transnational interest group with powerful levers over national governments including that of the United States and members of the European Union. Recent research in telecommunications, trade negotiations concerning intellectual property rights and a number of other spheres where international organisations have been penetrated and influenced by big-business lobbies all point to the existence of such a TCC. Yet to call it a class suggests far more solidarity and uniformity than in fact exists. The more I look into the politics of international business, the more I am struck by the growing divide between big business—the so-called multinationals—and the people running and employed by small and medium business enterprises. These enjoy few of the perks and privileges of the big corporations yet have to conform to the rules and agencies created by them. For them, globalization is something to be resisted, if only because it so blatantly tramples on the democratic principles of accountability and transparency.

The environmental issue area is a good example of the fissures in the TCC. On the one side are the big oil companies, the giant chemical combines, the vested interests of the car manufacturers and associated businesses. On the other are firms in the vanguard of waste disposal and clean-up technologies and interestingly—the transnational insurance business (Haufler, 1997). Fear of the vast claims that might be made against their clients on environmental grounds is putting insurers increasingly in opposition to the polluters. Their opposition, of course, is predicated on legal systems that are sensitive to public opinion. The power of the latter meanwhile is also evident in the growing sensitivity of some elements in business to shareholders and consumers.

Thus, the notion tentatively posited by some of the neo-Gramscians that while there is some sort of TCC there is also an emerging global civil society is not lightly to be dismissed. To quote Leslie Sklair:

> No social movement appears even remotely likely to overthrow the three fundamental institutional supports of global capitalism . . . namely, the TNCs, the transnational capitalist class and the culture-ideology of consumerism. Nevertheless in each of these spheres there are resistances expressed by social movements. (Sklair 1997: 534)

Similarly, Rodolfo Stavenhagen (1997: 34), writing on "People's movements, the antisystemic challenge" in the collection of essays edited by Bob Cox, finds the growth points of a nascent transnational opposition, or counterforce to Sklair's three institutional supports sustaining the Westfailure system. Not only, he says, are such social movements non-governmental, they are popular in the widest sense of that word; they are alternative to established political systems, and therefore often at odds with national governments and political parties and they seek "to attain objectives that would entail alternative forms of economic development, political control and social organization."

In his introduction to this collection of essays, Cox does not predict the imminent demise of the "fading Westphalian system." The future world, he observes, "will be determined by the relative strength of the bottom-up and top-down pressures." The contest may be a long one and no one should underestimate the power of big business and big government interests behind these top-down pressures. Yet at the same time there is no denying that as Cox says, "people have become alienated from existing regimes, states and political processes." Witness the recent amazing, unforeseen turn-out—a quarter of a million in Paris and the same in London—in anti-government marches by country dwellers of every class and occupation. Everywhere, in fact, politicians are discredited and despised as never before. The state is indeed in retreat from its core competences in security, finance and control over the economy; and this retreat is not inconsistent with its proliferating regulation of many trivial aspects of daily life

(Strange 1996). The new multilateralism Cox predicates "will not be born from constitutional amendments to existing multilateral institutions but rather from a reconstitution of civil societies and political authorities on a global scale building a system of global governance from the bottom up" (Cox 1997: xxvii).

For international studies, and for those of us engaged in them, the implications are far-reaching. We have to escape and resist the state-centrism inherent in the analysis of conventional international relations. The study of globalisation has to embrace the study of the behaviour of firms no less than of other forms of political authority. International political economy has to be recombined with comparative political economy at the sub-state as well as the state level. It is not our job, in short, to defend or excuse the Westphalian system. We should be concerned as much with its significant failures as with its alleged successes.

Notes

1. As used by Cox (1987) and Strange (1988).
2. Michael Veseth (1990) has argued that this was first tried in 14th century Florence. He may be right but it was a political trick not widely copied.
3. The full story is entertainingly told by J. K. Galbraith in Galbraith (1975).
4. Derivatives are contracts to purchase or sell *derived* from some real and variable price. This can be anything from the yen-dollar exchange rate, the price of frozen orange juice or the debt of governments or business enterprises. Derivative trading has grown at a rate of 40 percent a year since 1990 and by 1995 according to the IMF was valued at nearly $50 *trillion* a year, or twice world economic output.
5. A 1997 survey of opinion in the City of London found that most people—bankers included—regarded "bad management at the banks" as the no. 1 threat to the stability of the system (Banana Skins survey by the Centre for the Study of Financial Innovation, 18 Curzon St., London W1).

References

Cox, R., ed. 1997. *The New Realism: Perspectives on Multilateralism and World Order.* New York: St. Martin's Press.
———. 1987. *Production, Power and World Order: Social Forces in the Making of World History.* New York: Columbia University Press.
Feis, H. 1964. *Europe, the World's Banker, 1870–1914.* New York: A. M. Kelly. Published for the Council on Foreign Relations.
Galbraith, J.K. 1975. *Money—Whence It Came and Where It Went.* Boston: Houghton Mifflin.
Germain, R. 1997. *The International Organization of Credit.* Cambridge: Cambridge University Press.
Haufler, V. 1997. *Dangerous Commerce: Insurance and the Management of International Risk.* Ithaca, N.Y.: Cornell University Press.
Helleiner, E. 1994. In *The International Monetary System: Procceedings of a*

Conference Organized by the Banca d'Italia. Peter B. Kenen, Francesco Papadia, and Fabrizio Saccomanni, eds., New York: Cambridge University Press.

Hurrell, A. 1997. "The Politics of Environmental Aid." *Mershon International Studies Review,* 41, no. 2 (November): 291–293.

Kapstein, E. 1994. *Governing the Global Economy: International Finance and the State.* Cambridge: Harvard University Press.

Kothari, R. 1993. "The Yawning Vacuum: A World Without Alternatives." *Alternatives: Social Transformation and Humane Governance* 18, no. 2: 119–139.

Mistry, P. 1996. *Resolving Africa's Multilateral Debt Problem.* The Hague: Fondad.

Review of International Political Economy (RIPE). 1997. Special Issue: The Direction of Contemporary Capitalism. 4, no. 3 (Autumn).

Santiso, J. 1997. "Wall Street face a la cride mexicaine," CEPII working paper. Paris.

Sklair, L. 1997. "Social Movements for Global Capitalism: The Transnational Capitalist Class in Action." *Review of International Political Economy,* 4, no. 3.

Stavenhagen, R. 1997. "People's Movements, the Antisystemic Challenge." In *The New Realism: Perspectives on Multilateralism and World Order,* edited by R. Cox. New York: Columbia University Press.

Strange, S. 1998. *Mad Money.* Manchester, UK: Manchester University Press.

———. 1996. *The Retreat of the State: The Diffusion of Power in the World Economy.* New York: Cambridge University Press.

———. 1990. "The Name of the Game." In *Sea-Changes: American Foreign Policy in a World Transformed,* edited by N. Rizopoulos. New York: Council on Foreign Relations Press.

———. 1988. *States and Markets.* London: Pinter.

Triffin, R. 1964. *The Evolution of the International Monetary System.* Princeton, N.J.: International Finance Section, Department of Economics, Princeton University.

Veseth, M. 1990. *Mountains of Debt: Crisis and Change in Renaissance Florence, Victorian Britain and Postwar America.* Oxford: Oxford University Press.

Index

Association of Southeast Asian Nations (ASEAN), 234
Asian Financial Crisis, 144, 195, 232, 499, 500
    causes of, 270
Asian Monetary Fund
    origins and purposes, 229

balance of payments, 52
balance of power politics, 142
balance of trade, 171
Balladur, Edouard, 60
Bank of International Settlements (BIS), 192, 197, 198, 219, 499
basic force model
    and hegemonic stability theory, 102
Bretton Woods, 63
    collapse of, 106, 111, 112
    origins of, 241, 242
Buchanan, Pat, 60

capital controls, 66
capitalism, 14, 15
    unbridled, 60
central bank system
    origins of, 498, 499
Chile, 125
    and center/periphery polarization, 187
Clinton, William Jefferson,
    and Mexican peso crisis, 197, 198
Coalition for Environmentally Responsible Economics (CERES), 479

collective goods, also public goods, 100
colonialism, 62
commodities
    prices, 74
    production of, 125, 144
comparative advantage, 12, 18, 20, 123, 124, 125
Concert of Europe, 80
core, 18, 19, 30
corporate strategic alliances, 76, 131
cronyism, 272
currency board, 234
currency crises, 60, 65, 66, 195, 196
    benefits of leadership, 226, 227
    benefits of strictly territorial currency, 222
    contagion effect, 197, 272
    and currency competition, 218
    and the extent of cross-border use, 219, 220
    and sovereignty, 223, 226
    Mexican peso crisis and political institutions, 221, 273
currency union, 235

deforestation, 475
Deng, Xiaoping, 64
dependency theory, 30
    definition of dependence, 168
    dependent development, 127, 321, 424, 425
    export sector, 171
    forms of dependence, 169
developmental state, 62

dollarization, 233, 234
downsizing, corporate, 74, 82
dumping, 402

ecological globalization, 460
economic activity, diffusion of, 13
Economic Commission of Latin
    America (ECLA), 169, 171
economic determinism, 17
economic nationalism, 12
education, and national competitive-
    ness, 79, 83
embedded autonomy, 128, 132, 133
Endangered Species Act, 469
Engels, Friedrich, 14
environmental treaties, 479
European Central Bank (ECB), 227,
    228
European Economic Community, 103,
    105, 112, 403
European Monetary Union, 148, 228,
    229, 230, 291
    Basel Agreement, 295
    Delors Report, 296
    European Monetary System, 295,
        296
    European System of Central Banks
        (ECSB), 297, 299
    Maastricht Treaty, 298
    Stabilization and Growth Pact
        (SGP), 300
European Union, 140, 147, 148, 184,
    185
    and agricultural trade, 379, 380,
        381
    enclave economy, 170
    Werner Plan, 294, 295
exchange rates, fixed, 100, 270
export credit agencies, 477, 478

fascism, 61
financial globalization
    and Capital Mobility Hypothesis,
        216
    magnitude of official and private
        flows, 345
    Unholy Trinity, 217
foreign aid, 172
foreign direct investment (FDI), 4
    clustering of, 450
    and the developed countries, 452,
        453

and the developing countries, 453,
    454, 472
Japanese FDI, 271
in Latin America, 173
free rider problem, 101, 254
Free Trade Area of the Americas
    (FTAA), 404, 409

General Agreement on Tariffs and
    Trade, 56, 63, 103
    guiding principles of, 103, 106
Generalized System of Preferences, 393
Germany, and religious tolerance, 142,
    148
global climate change, 460, 502
Global Commons, 459
globalization, 60, 63, 64, 65, 125. *See
    also* financial globalization
    and international capital markets,
        144, 182, 201, 216
    and labor movements, 208
Gorbachev, Mikhail, 64
Great Depression, 144

Heavily Indebted Poor Countries
    (HIPCs), 261, 262
hegemony, 12, 31, 170
    criticisms of, 181
Hobbes, Thomas, 30, 140, 141
human rights, 142, 143
Hume, David, 11

imperialism, 12, 62
    and regionalism, 186
Industrial Revolution, 15, 62
information technology industries, 121,
    127
Interamerican Economic and Social
    Council, 172
interdependence, 12, 16, 21, 22
    complex interdependence, 49, 50,
        51, 52, 53, 54, 55
International Business Machines, 131
international capital movements, 144
international debt crisis, 260, 261
International Development Association,
    348, 355
international division of labor, 122, 123,
    124
    and domestic political and social
        institutions, 125, 132
    and labor mobility, 124

International Energy Agency, 107
International Finance Corporation, 358, 359, 360, 477
International Monetary Fund, 56, 104, 140, 146, 192, 194, 199, 200
  criticisms of, 283, 284
  and the environment, 474, 475, 476
  functions, 242
  lender of last resort, 252, 253
  organizational structure, 242, 243
  tranche system, 253, 254
International Organization for Standardization, 481
international regimes, changes in, 100
International Trade Organization, 372
isolationism, 63

Japan, 61, 140, 228
  and Asian Monetary System, 281
  and regionalism, 228, 229, 230
Jerusalem
  and the Israeli-Palestinian Conflict, 146, 147
just-in-time production, 193, 207

Kautsky, Karl, 12
Kennedy Round, 100, 103
Keynes, John Maynard, 100, 145, 193
  inversion of Keynesian economics, 200
  Keynesian economics and neo-liberalism, 193
Kindleberger, Charles, 100
Krugman, Paul, 78, 123, 231
Kyoto Conference, 502

League of Nations, 143
Lenin, V. I., 12
  imperialism and war, 29
liberalism, 13, 26, 27
  functions of government, 27, 28
  and harmony of interests, 27, 28
List, Friedrich, 30, 123
Lome Convention, 395

market economy
  characteristics of, 11, 16, 17, 18, 19, 20
Marshall, Alfred, 224
Marx, Karl, 14
Marxism, 13, 14, 28, 29, 30

capitalist accumulation and Asia, 187
mercantilism, 26, 85
MERCOSUR, 148, 235
mergers and acquisitions, 79
military power, 10, 52
Mill, John Stuart, 11
Miyazawa, Kiichi, and the New Miyazawa Initiative, 229
monetary blocs, 234, 235
monetary policy, 145
Monthly Review School, 422, 423
Montreal Protocol, 479
Morgenthau, Hans J., 56
Multilateral Agreement on Investments, 202, 477, 482
Multilateral Investment Guarantee Agency, 358, 359

Napoleonic Wars, 142
neoliberalism
  ten commandments of, 200
New International Economic Order, 56
Newly Industrializing Countries, 121, 127
new trade theory, 78
non-aligned movement, 188
nongovernmental organizations
  and the environment, 481, 482
non-tariff barriers, 103, 105, 106
North American Free Trade Agreement (NAFTA), 146, 148, 192
  and the Mexican peso crisis, 198, 396, 403, 404, 409

oil companies
  relationship with host states, 104, 105
oil embargo, 54, 100
Organization of Economic Cooperation and Development (OECD), 192, 342
Organization of Petroleum Exporting Countries (OPEC), 54
  rise of, 106, 107, 111

periphery, 18, 30
planned economies, 17
Plaza Accord, 270
Polanyi, Karl, 14, 60, 61, 62
political economy
  definition of, 10, 11, 49

population bomb, 81
preferential trading arrangements, 402, 403
product cycle theory, 124
Protestant Reformation, 144

rational choice theory, 28
Raytheon Corporation, 72, 73
realism, political, 30, 31, 50
    challenges to, 50, 121
regional economic agreements
    and import substitution, 397
    old and new motivations for, 397, 398, 399, 400
religious tolerance, 142, 143
Ricardo, David, 11, 20, 24, 33, 370
Rio Declaration on Environment and Development, 470
rule of law, 66, 67

Schumpeter, Joseph, 193
seigniorage, 232, 233, 234
    definition of, 222
service sector
    importance of, 77
    as a tradable, 124
Smith, Adam, 18, 24, 112
Smithsonian Agreement, 111
Soros, George, 60, 200
Southern Consensus, 326, 327, 328, 329, 330, 331
special drawing rights, 100, 250
statism
    developmental, 62, 127
    and predatory states, 127
    role of the state in the economy, 122
    transformative role of, 122, 126
    and transnational alliances, 132
Stockholm Environment Conference, 56
Structural Impediments Initiative, 393
sustainable human development, 326, 327, 328
swap arrangements, 229

tariffs, 144
terms of trade, 74, 171
    impact on balance of payments, 172
textiles
    agreements, 105
    as traded goods, 124

Thailand, 270
    New Aspiration Party, 274
    Democratic Party, 274
Thirty Years War, 141
Tokyo Round, 106
totalitarianism, 61, 62
trade retaliation, 43, 44
trade theory, 123
trade unions, 206, 207, 208
trading state, 73, 74
transgovernmental policy networks, 55
transnational corporations
    bargaining and host countries, 421
    internalization theory, 417, 418, 420
    O, L, I framework, 446
    perspectives on, 415, 416
    product life cycle, 420, 444, 445
    transfer pricing, 421, 438, 439, 440
    strategic alliances, 76, 131, 438
transnational non-governmental organizations, 145
Treaty of Munster, 141, 142

unequal development, 179
    and five monopolies, 182, 183
    and polarization, 180
United Auto Workers, 208
United Fruit Company, 146
United Nations Conference on Trade and Development, 171, 326
United Nations Development Program, 363, 364
    sustainable human development approach, 326
United Nations Environmental Program, 478, 480, 481

Vernon, Raymond, 124
virtual corporation, 75

Wapenhaus Report
    and the World Bank, 354
Washington Consensus
    and development thought, 342
    and the Liberal International Economic Order, 322, 323
    as paradigm, 318
    post–Washington Consensus, 332, 333, 334
Weber, Max, 10, 121
Westphalia, Peace of, 141, 495

Wolfensohn, James, 354, 355, 356, 360, 363
World Economic Forum, 197
world systems theory, 123, 321
World Trade Organization, 140, 192
   agriculture, 379, 380, 381
   anti-dumping measures, 379
   beef hormone dispute, 469, 470, 471
   dispute settlement mechanism, 386
   Doha Round, 369

   and the environment, 466, 467, 468, 469, 470
   genetically modified organisms, 470, 471
   investment policy and competition, 381, 382
   labor standards, 382, 383, 384
   non-tariff barriers, 373
   regional trade agreements, 386, 387
   rounds of negotiations, 372

About the Book

Introducing the classic and contemporary ideologies of international political economy—and especially the ways that affect the behavior of states and markets—this anthology has been carefully constructed for classroom use.

Articles representing contending views of IPE are followed by selections on the international monetary system, development assistance, and international trade. With the student reader in mind, each piece is prefaced with an editors' note placing it in context. This new edition thoroughly engages with the past decade of changes in the global political economy.

C. Roe Goddard is associate professor of international studies at the Thunderbird/American Graduate School of International Management (AGSIM). **Patrick Cronin** and **Kishore C. Dash** are assistant professors of international studies at AGSIM.